# THE COLUMBIA
# DICTIONARY OF
# EUROPEAN
# POLITICAL
# HISTORY
## SINCE 1914

**OTHER COLUMBIA UNIVERSITY PRESS REFERENCE BOOKS**

The Columbia Dictionary of Political Biography, *The Economist* (1991)

The Concise Columbia Dictionary of Quotations, *Robert Andrews, ed.* (1989)

The Concise Columbia Encyclopedia, Second Edition (1989)

The Columbia Granger's Index to Poetry, Ninth Edition, *Edith P. Hazen and Deborah J. Fryer, Eds.* (1990)

The Concise Columbia Book of Poetry, *William Harmon, ed.* (1990)

# THE COLUMBIA DICTIONARY OF
# EUROPEAN POLITICAL HISTORY
## SINCE 1914

## JOHN STEVENSON
### GENERAL EDITOR

Columbia University Press · New York

Columbia University Press
New York

**Library of Congress Cataloging-in-Publication Data**

The Columbia dictionary of European political history since 1914/
  John Stevenson, editor.
     p.     cm.
  Originally published: Dictionary of British and European history
since 1914. U.K.: Macmillan.
  Includes bibliographical references.
  ISBN 0-231-07880-3: $69.50
  1. Europe—History—20th century—Dictionaries. I. Stevenson,
John, 1946-  . II. Title: Dictionary of British and European
history since 1914.
D424.C65   1992
940.2′8—dc20                   91-29693
                                  CIP

Clothbound editions of Columbia University Press books are
Smyth-sewn and printed on permanent and durable acid-free
paper.

Typeset and printed in Great Britain.

# Contents

# Preface and Acknowledgements

This book has attempted to bring together in a single volume a wide range of reference material on British and European history since 1914. It has aimed, primarily, to meet the needs of students and teachers and all those with an interest in the history of the 20th century. Inevitably, no single volume reference work can be comprehensive in its coverage; the aim therefore has been to concentrate on those personalities, topics and events which are most commonly encountered in historical writing about 20th-century British and European history. An attempt has been made to provide some pointers to current assessments of some of the issues of the period, including extensive treatment of such topics as the Fischer thesis, the Spanish Civil War and Soviet collectivization. An indication is also given of further reading where these issues can be followed up in more detail. The relationship of Europe with the wider world presents obvious difficulties of coverage; the aim here has been to deal with extra-European events in terms of their significance in European affairs. Also included are the major American figures who impinge directly upon European history.

I have been grateful for the assistance of a team of specialist contributors in particular areas. I would like to express my thanks to Dr C. P. Cook, Dr P. Heywood, Dr D. Kirby, Dr T. Kirk, Mr T. Rees, Dr S. Salter, Dr A. Thorpe and Dr M. Vincent. Mr R. Mirchandani was responsible for engaging my interest in the project in the first instance and I am indebted to Margot Levy at Macmillan for her support and patience while the volume was being compiled. Finally I owe considerable thanks to Linda Hollingsworth for carrying out a large and often difficult typing operation and to Mrs Pat Holland and the secretaries at the Department of History at Sheffield. As editor, I naturally bear responsibility for all errors and omissions. All corrections and suggestions for incorporation into future editions will be most welcome.

*John Stevenson*
Worcester College
Oxford
August 1990

# How to Use the Dictionary

**Alphabetization** of headings is based on the principle that words are read continuously, ignoring spaces, hyphens, accents, bracketed matter etc., up to the first comma; the same principle applies thereafter.

**Bibliographies** are arranged chronologically in order of publication, and alphabetically by author within years.

**Cross-references** are shown in small capitals, with a large capital at the beginning of the first word of the entry referred to. Thus, 'He joined the FRENCH COMMUNIST PARTY' would mean that the entry referred to is not **French Communist Party**, but **Communist Party, French**.

# A

**Abdication Crisis.** British political crisis brought about by the desire of King EDWARD VIII to marry Mrs Wallis Simpson, an American divorcee. Rumours of the liaison were widely circulated in London and in the foreign press, but were not reported in the British press until early December 1936, two weeks after the King declared his intention to the Prime Minister, BALDWIN, of marrying Mrs Simpson and making her his queen. The King's imminent coronation and Mrs Simpson's ending of her second marriage in October brought the issue to a head. Baldwin, the Archbishop of Canterbury and much establishment opinion took the view that the King's marriage to Mrs Simpson was incompatible with his position as titular head of the Church of England. A morganatic marriage with Mrs Simpson not becoming Queen was rejected on several grounds, not least the Cabinet's opposition. Although there was much popular support for the King and attempts to create a 'King's Party' led by WINSTON CHURCHILL, Edward was increasingly faced with a choice between marriage to Mrs Simpson and giving up the throne. On 11 December he broadcast his decision to abdicate in favour of his brother, the Duke of York, who become GEORGE VI. Taking the title Duke of Windsor, he went into exile, where he married Mrs Simpson on 3 June 1937. Although the abdication crisis had the potential to damage the position of the monarchy, popular support for the King's obviously sincere desire not to give up 'the woman I love' and the success of George VI and his consort in fulfilling the role allotted to them, especially during the Second World War, averted any lasting effects. The failure of the 'King's Party' to gather much support in the House of Commons deprived the crisis of serious political repercussions.

C. L. Mowat, *Britain between the Wars, 1918–1940* (1955)
J. Barnes and K. Middlemass, *Baldwin* (1969)
F. Donaldson, *Edward VIII* (1974)

**Abyssinian War.** See ETHIOPIAN CRISIS.

**acid rain.** Form of aerial pollution caused by high acidity in rainfall damaging trees, rivers and lakes. The causes of acid rain are believed to be in the sulphur emissions from power stations and other industrial plant. Damage first became noticeable in Scandinavia in the 1970s and accusations were directed at Britain, from whom westerly air currents deposited acid rain from her industrial areas. By the 1980s the damage was recognized both as more widespread and more complex in origin, affecting Scotland, Germany and Switzerland as well as Scandinavia. The issue helped to promote environmental concern and assisted the rise of Green parties in Europe. Agreements have been reached to limit transnational air pollution and a commitment on general environmental issues formed part of the SINGLE EUROPEAN ACT, agreed by European Community countries in December 1985.

**Acheson, Dean** (1893–1971). US Undersecretary (1945–9), then Secretary of State (1949–53). A major policy-maker in the COLD WAR, he outlined the principles of the TRUMAN DOCTRINE in February 1947, seeking containment of the Soviet Union and military and economic assistance to 'free peoples' threatened by Communist aggression. In May 1947 he advocated the European aid programme, known later as the MARSHALL PLAN and was a major force behind the establishment of NATO. After the Republican victory in 1952, he withdrew from public life, but retained some background influence as an elder-statesman during the KENNEDY era.

D. Acheson. *Present at the Creation* (1970)
M. McCauley. *The Origins of the Cold War* (1983)

**Action Française.** Right-wing political movement founded in France in 1899 by the journalist and poet Charles Maurras (1868–1952). Royalist, monarchist and anti-Semitic, the movement campaigned as an opponent to the decadence of the THIRD REPUBLIC. In 1908 Maurras and Leon Daudet (1867–1942), a novelist, began joint editorship of the movement's newspaper, *Action Française.* Attracting support from intellectuals and right-wing students, it had as its street organization the *camelots du roi* (newsvendors of the King), who were often engaged in street fighting. Although many French clergy supported the organization for its stress upon the Catholic traditions of France, Pius XI condemned the organization from 1926, although the condemnation was largely removed under Pius XII. The movement was heavily implicated in the VICHY GOVERNMENT, Maurras acting as an unofficial philosopher or the reactionary policies of PÉTAIN. The movement was suppressed after the Liberation and Maurras was sentenced to life imprisonment.

E. Weber. *Action Française: Royalism and Reaction in Twentieth Century France* (1962)
R. Remond. *The Right Wing in France from 1815 to de Gaulle* (2nd edn. 1969)
J. S. McClelland. *The French Right from de Maistre to Maurras* (1970)

**Adalen Incident.** Killing of five union demonstrators at a strike at Adalen in Angermanland in 1931. The incident occurred at the height of the depression in Sweden when wage cuts were becoming common. An enquiry punished those responsible. It has been called the 'Peterloo' of Sweden.

**Adenauer, Konrad** (1876–1967). German politician and first Chancellor of the FEDERAL REPUBLIC OF GERMANY. Born in Cologne, Adenauer studied at the universities of Freiburg, Munich and Bonn, and became a lawyer. In 1917 he became Lord Mayor of Cologne. During the WEIMAR REPUBLIC he was a member of the *Reichsrat* (upper house) and was considered for the chancellorship in 1926. In 1933 Adenauer, who was firmly anchored in the German Catholic

political tradition represented by the CENTRE PARTY, was dismissed from office in Cologne by the Nazis. Imprisoned briefly in 1934 and 1944, he spent most of the Nazi dictatorship in retirement. Following the liberation of Cologne by the Americans in March 1945, Adenauer was reinstated in office, only to be dismissed in June in 1945 by the British military government in whose zone Cologne now lay (*see* GERMANY, ALLIED OCCUPATION OF). In the years that followed, Adenauer played a major role in the formation of the CHRISTIAN DEMOCRATIC UNION (CDU) and built up a broad political following in the western occupation zones. In September 1948 he chaired the Parliamentary Council which was charged with drafting the constitution (*Grundgesetz*, 'Basic Law') for a putative West German state made up of the three western occupation zones. Following the approval by the Council of the Basic Law and the establishment of the German Federal Republic in May 1949, he became the first Chancellor of the new state in September 1949. He was re-elected in 1953, 1957 and 1961, and also served as foreign minister from 1951 to 1955. Domestically, his chancellorship was politically low-key and coincided with the 'economic miracle' on the basis of welfare-state capitalism engineered by his appointee to the post of Federal Minister for Economic Affairs, LUDWIG ERHARD. In foreign policy, Adenauer's influence was unchallenged, an influence he used in a pragmatic and level-headed fashion to foster the full acceptance of the Federal Republic by the West European states; acknowledging that the division of Germany after 1949 into two states was likely to be long-lasting. Perhaps less committed to the COLD WAR than some of his domestic critics maintained, he visited Moscow in 1955 and pursued a cautious policy during the crisis surrounding the construction of the BERLIN WALL. From the late 1950s onwards, his conservative style of leadership and tendency towards high-handedness in government faced increasing criticism, criticism which reached a climax following the arrest in October 1962 of the publisher and defence correspondent of the liberal magazine *Der Spiegel* (*see* SPIEGEL AFFAIR). Adenauer promised to relinquish the chancellorship within a year, a promise he fulfilled in October 1963. He continued as chairman of the CDU until his resignation, at the age of 90, in 1966. Adenauer's principal achievements as Chancellor lay in his role in the consolidation of the restored democracy in the Federal Republic and in his cautious and painstaking efforts to promote the integration of the Republic into the West European state system. His personal and political rapport with the French president, CHARLES DE GAULLE, played an important part in the establishment of close Franco–German relations from the late 1950s onwards.

A. Heidenheimer, *Adenauer and the CDU* (1960)
K. Adenauer, *Memoirs* (1966)
R. Hiscocks, *The Adenauer Era* (1966)
T. Prittie, *Adenauer* (1972)

**Afghanistan, Soviet invasion of.** The Soviet invasion of Afghanistan in 1979 followed a lengthy period of instability in an area bordering the Soviet Union and a traditionally neutral 'buffer zone'. Soviet concern was heightened by the rise of Islamic fundamentalism in neighbouring Iran and the fear of growing ethnic and religious unrest amongst its own large Islamic minority. The last King of Afghanistan was deposed in July 1973 and replaced by a republican government headed by General Muhammed Daud, who was elected President for a six-year term in February 1977. In April 1978 Daub was overthrown and killed in a military coup; his government was replaced by the pro-Soviet People's Democratic Party of Afghanistan (PDPA), whose leader, Nur Muhammad Taraki, became President of the Revolutionary Council and Prime Minister. In the ensuing power struggle within the PDPA and with conservative tribal and religious groups, the government looked increasingly to the Soviet Union for aid; in November 1978 a new Afghan–Russian Treaty of Friendship and Co-operation was signed. Following the removal of Taraki in September 1979 and his replacement by Hafizullah Amin, Soviet involvement in Afghanistan became more likely; by December detachments of Soviet forces and pro-Soviet Afghans were positioned to secure vital air bases at Kabul, Bagram and Shendan. The full-scale invasion took place on 26–7 December, when a Soviet airborne division flew into Kabul and seized the major public buildings, including the Duralaman Palace, where Amin was killed in the fighting; at the same time a force of 50,000 Soviet troops with tanks and aircraft crossed the border in a three-pronged blitzkrieg to seize the strategic cities and secure the main routes to Kabul. A new pro-Soviet government was installed under Babrak Karmal, who ordered the Afghan army to co-operate with the Soviet forces.

Although the Soviet Union justified intervention on the grounds that it was at the request of the Afghan government under the terms of the 1978 treaty of friendship to prevent outside interference in Afghan affairs, on 14 January 1980 an emergency session of the United Nations General Assembly called for a Russian withdrawal. Moreover, in spite of control of the cities and major highways, the new government was faced by growing resistance from Mujaheddin guerrillas who refused to accept the Karmal government; a considerable Russian presence had to be maintained to support the Afghan army. A bloody anti-guerilla conflict ensued, with large-scale Soviet forces involved in 'search-and-destroy' missions on Mujaheddin bases. Karmal's Afghan army proved unreliable, with mass desertions and defections, while his attempts to conciliate opposition groups failed to end the guerilla war. By 1986 an estimated 300,000 Afghanis had been killed and 3.5 million forced to become refugees in Pakistan. As well as becoming bogged down in a costly guerilla war, the Soviet Union paid a significant diplomatic cost, including the boycott of the Moscow Olympics and increasing tension in the 'new' COLD WAR. In line with the Reagan administration's support for 'freedom fighters', the Mujaheddin were the recipients of sophisticated military equipment and extensive financial aid, mainly via Pakistan, supporting an estimated 90 guerilla groups of up to 200,000 full- and part-time fighters. In response, the Soviet forces reached over 115,000 in 1985, backed up with considerable armoured and air support.

In June 1982 peace talks began in Geneva but no immediate solution was possible to what by the mid-1980s had become virtually a 'proxy' war between the United States and the Soviet Union. In May 1986 Babrak Karmal resigned and his successor, Major

General Najibollah, announced a six-month cease-fire in January 1987. Although rejected by the Mujaheddin, peace talks resumed in Geneva, and on 14 April 1988 an accord was signed, by which Pakistan and Afghanistan agreed to non-interference in each other's affairs. The Soviet government undertook to begin withdrawal of its troops on 15 May 1988, half to be removed by mid-August and the remainder by mid-February 1989. The United States and the Soviet Union were formal guarantors of the agreements, although both parties reserved the right to continue supplying the Mujaheddin and the Afghan army respectively. The Soviet Union complied with the timetable for the withdrawal of its troops, the last leaving Afghanistan on 15 February 1989. The internal situation remained unresolved, however, as talks to end the fighting failed. Widespread expectations that the Najibullah government would fall quickly to the Mujaheddin forces proved mistaken when guerilla attempts to take the major city of Jalalabad were repulsed in spring 1989 and the Kabul government consolidated its position. A council or *shura* of 400 Mujaheddin leaders convened in Islamabad in February 1989 revealed intense factionalism within the guerilla forces, although Professor Mujadidi was narrowly elected President of the government-in-exile.

The Afghan involvement was the costliest conflict involving Soviet armed forces since the Second World War. Official figures for Soviet casualties during the nine-year intervention were given as 15,000 killed and 37,000 wounded. Soviet intervention took place at a time of weakness for the Carter presidency, distracted by the hostage crisis in Iran, and when the Soviet Union had concluded that the SALT II Treaty (*see* STRATEGIC ARMS LIMITATION TALKS) had no chance of Senate approval. Russian objectives were threefold: immediately, to secure a pro-Soviet regime in an area prey to instability and Islamic fundamentalism which threatened to affect the Soviet populations of Soviet Central Asia; to deter Iranian, Pakistani and American influence in Afghanistan; and to demonstrate Soviet power to Iran, Pakistan, the Gulf States, India and China. It is clear that the extent of the resistance was underestimated; by the time of the accession of GORBACHEV to power the Soviet Union was actively seeking to end a commitment which was causing disproportionate diplomatic, financial and political costs. Gorbachev's agreement to withdraw Soviet troops was portrayed as marking a decisive break with the Brezhnev era, quieted mounting discontent at home, and assisted the rapid thaw in East–West relations. The failure of the Mujaheddin to seize power following Soviet withdrawal has left open the question of whether the Soviet Union had not, in fact, secured the first of its objectives, even if at greater cost than anticipated.

N. P. and R. S. Newell, *The Struggle for Afghanistan* (1981)
H. Bradsher, *Afghanistan and the Soviet Union* (1982)
A. Arnold, *Afghanistan's Two-Party Communism* (1983)

**Agrarian Union, Bulgarian.** An organization founded in 1899 to protect peasant interests and which became the largest party in Bulgaria under its leader STAMBOLISKI. It remained the largest party in the immediate post-war period, obtaining 212 seats in the 1923 elections, but was increasingly subject to harassment and banning under the authoritarian regimes after 1924. Agrarian candidates within the communist-led FATHERLAND FRONT secured 67 seats at the elections of 27 October 1946 and the opposition Agrarian Union 89. On 26 August 1947 the independent Agrarian Union was dissolved and its leader, Nikola Petkov, sentenced to death. A Bulgarian People's Agrarian Union continued to exist as a nominally separate party within the Fatherland Front, but was in effect an appendage of the Communist Party used to call upon peasant support and the traditions of the Agrarian Union.

M. Macdermott, *A History of Bulgaria* (1962)
J. D. Bell, *Peasants in Power: Alexander Stambolisky and the Bulgarian National Union, 1899–1923* (1971)

**Albania.** An independent principality from 1912 with various claimants to the throne. Albania was invaded by Austria in 1916 but its independence was proclaimed on 3 June 1917. By agreement between YUGOSLAVIA, Italy and Greece a provisional government was set up in November 1921, followed by a government under a Council of Regents. On 31 January 1925 Albania was proclaimed a republic with its largest landowner, Ahmed Beg Zogu, as President. On 1 September 1928 he proclaimed himself King Zog I. Italian economic penetration of Albania increased under MUSSOLINI and an Italian invasion in April 1939 forced King Zog to flee, the crown being given to VICTOR EMMANUEL III of Italy on 14 April 1939. Albania formed the base for the Italian invasion of Greece in 1940; this was initially repelled and a Greek counter-offensive carried the war back onto Albanian soil. With the German assault on the Balkans in 1941, Albania fell under AXIS control. Victor Emmanuel relinquished his Albanian title on 30 November 1943 with the withdrawal of Italy from the war. Effective power was wielded by ENVER HOXHA who led the communist-dominated National Liberation movement in a war against the German occupation forces and the rival non-communist resistance groups, the moderate National Front and the pro-monarchist Legality organization. On 24 May 1944 a Congress at Permet repudiated the regime of King Zog and elected an Anti-fascist Council of National Liberation to act as a sovereign body, headed by Hoxha, who also acted as commander-in-chief of the National Liberation Army. On 20 October 1944 a congress at Berat proclaimed the establishment of a Provisional Democratic Republic with Hoxha as Prime Minister; this was recognized by Britain, the United States and Russia on 10 November 1945. Elections on 2 December 1945 produced a communist-controlled assembly, which proclaimed a People's Republic on 12 January 1946, ten days after Zog had been formally deposed *in absentia*. A struggle between pro-Yugoslav and independent elements led by Hoxha was decided in the latter's favour by the Soviet–Yugoslav quarrel in 1948 and Yugoslavia's expulsion from COMINFORM. Albania sided with the Soviets; Hoxha purged his rivals, making Albania one of the most obedient Stalinist satellites in Eastern Europe (*see* STALINISM). The DESTALINIZATION campaign under KHRUSHCHEV left Albania increasingly isolated and its leadership fearful of a Moscow-inspired challenge to its position. As a result Albania in 1961 left both COMECON and the WARSAW PACT, and sided with China in the Sino–Soviet dispute. The withdrawal of Soviet aid and technical support was in part compensated by Chinese loans and food aid. With the development of the increasingly liberal tendencies in China following the death of Mao Tse-tung in 1976, Albania was also cut off from Chinese support when relations were abruptly terminated in July 1977. Hoxha, however, maintained a rigidly Stalinist regime which survived his death in April 1985. Although there were reports of demonstrations in Albania at the end of 1989 it was not until after violent student protests in the autumn of 1990 that free elections were called for March 1991 and opposition parties allowed to form.

J. Amery, *Sons of the Eagle* (1948)
W. E. Griffith, *Albania and the Sino–Soviet Rift* (1963)
S. Skendi, *The Albanian National Awakening* (1967)
S. Pollo and P. Arben, *The History of Albania* (1981)

**Albert I** (1875–1934). King of the Belgians; reigned 1909–34. Heir apparent from 1891, he received a military education and succeeded his uncle Leopold II when the monarchy's prestige was low as a result of Leopold's activities in the Congo. He sought to maintain Belgian neutrality while preparing the army to meet invasion either from Germany or France. He refused German demands for free passage of their troops in their ultimatum of 2 August 1914 and, following their invasion of Belgian territory, appealed to Britain and France for assistance on the 4 August. Appointed commander in chief he directed the Belgian armies personally in defence of Belgian territory. In spite of the occupation of most of Belgium by the Germans, he maintained the independence of the Belgian forces and of Belgian foreign policy, including consideration of a compromise peace. By 1918, however, he was prepared to let Belgian forces co-operate in the final offensives against the Germans, making a triumphal entry into Brussels on 22 November 1918. He proposed sweeping domestic reforms at the conclusion of the war, including equal status for the Flemish language and equal voting rights. In foreign policy he favoured close military collaboration with the French. He was killed in a climbing accident in 1934 and succeeded by his son, Leopold III.

E. Galet, *Albert, King of the Belgians in the Great War* (1931)
J. Helmreich, *Belgium and Europe: A Study in Small Power Diplomacy* (1976)

**Alexander, Harold** (1891–1969). British general. He was educated at Harrow and Sandhurst. He served in the First World War and later in India. In 1939–40 he commanded a division in the BRITISH EXPEDITIONARY FORCE and was evacuated at Dunkirk. He supervised the withdrawal of the British army from Burma to India in 1942. Appointed commander-in-chief in the Middle East in August 1942, he directed the advance which led to the surrender of the AXIS forces in Tunis, and was commander of the Allied armies which landed in Sicily and Italy. Appointed Field Marshal in December 1944, he saw the Italian campaign through to its conclusion. Created a Viscount in 1946 and an Earl in 1942, he served as Governor-General of Canada, 1946–52, then Minister of Defence in the Cabinet, 1952–4

**Alexander I, of Yugoslavia** (1888–1934). King of Yugoslavia 1921–34, ruler of Serbia from June 1914. He was the son of Prince Peter Karadjordjevic (1844–1921), King of Serbia from June 1903. Alexander was educated in Switzerland and St Petersburg. He became Crown Prince of Serbia when his older brother renounced the throne in 1909, and became effective ruler as Prince Regent when his father stepped down following a constitutional crisis in June 1914. At the outbreak of the war he sought Russian support for Serbia and identified himself with the cause of the Slavs within the Austro-–Hungarian empire. He accompanied his army in its retreat to Corfu in 1915 and then toured Allied capitals seeking aid for Serbia. He showed early support for the ideas of a South Slav state. In 1916–17 he purged the BLACK HAND organization, removing its more extreme nationalist elements. He participated in the victorious Salonika offensive in 1918 which recaptured the capital, Belgrade, and set aside the objections of Premier NIKOLA PASIC to become Prince Regent of the Kingdom of Serbs, Croats and Slovenes on 1 December 1918. On his father's death in August 1921 he became King. Under Pasic, who returned as Premier in 1921, the infant state was riven with conflicts between Serbs and Croats. Growing instability led Alexander on 6 January 1929 to suspend Parliament and the constitution, and to institute a royal

dictatorship backed by the army, which aimed to overcome ethnic conflicts, symbolized by the adoption of the new name YUGOSLAVIA. A new Parliament was introduced in 1931 (the *Skupshtina*) but it had little real power. Alexander was favourable to the LITTLE ENTENTE and supported the idea of greater unity in the Balkans, but his career was cut short on 9 October 1934 when he was assassinated at Marseilles by a Croatian terrorist at the start of a state visit to France. He was succeeded by his 11-year-old son, Peter II (1923–70), with Alexander's cousin, Prince Paul (1893–1976) as regent.

A. N. Dragnich, *Serbia, Nikola Pasic and Yugoslavia* (1974).
S. Graham, *Alexander of Yugoslavia* (1974)

**Alexeev, Mikhail** (1857–1918). Commander-in-Chief under Russian Imperial and Provisional governments and a White general. Of a military family, he served in the Russo–Turkish War and the Russo–Japanese War. He held commands on the south-western fronts in the First World War and was promoted to General. In August 1915 he became chief-of-staff to NICHOLAS II and directed Russia's military campaigns until March 1917. He became senior military adviser to the PROVISIONAL GOVERNMENT and chief-of-staff in August 1917. Detained following the October Revolution, he fled south to organize a volunteer army which became the nucleus of the White forces in the south. He died of a heart attack in September 1918, having built up a sizeable military force to challenge the Bolshevik government.

G. Katkov, *Russia 1917: The February Revolution* (1967)

**Alfonso XIII, of Spain** (1886–1941). King of Spain, 17 May 1886 to 14 April 1931. He was the son of Alfonso XII, who died before he was born. Royal power was exercised by his mother, Queen Maria Christina of Habsburg (1858–1929), as regent until he was 16. His rule was unstable, threatened by anarchist violence (*see* ANARCHISM, SPANISH), including several assassination attempts, and by separatist movements, especially amongst the Catalans. He consented to bring in the dictator, PRIMO DE RIVERA, following the humiliation of the Spanish armies in the RIF REVOLT in 1923. His monarchy never recovered from the disaster and the failure of the dictatorship of Primo de Rivera to build up a strong pro-monarchical element. Despised even by many of the military, the attempts by the new Prime Minister, General Berenguer, from January 1930 to maintain the monarchy proved impossible. Catalans who had suffered under the Primo de Rivera dictatorship wanted a republic from which they hoped to obtain autonomy, while the execution, at the King's insistence, of two army officers on 14 December 1930 for a pro-Republican rising alientated much support amongst the governing classes. Failing to obtain the support of political leaders for the return of constitutional government under his monarchy, he held municipal elections in April 1931 to test support. The results showed an avalanche of support for pro-Republican candidates, and when the army generals made it clear they would not assist the King to remain in power he abdicated on 14 April 1931. He went to Italy, where he died ten years later. His grandson, JUAN CARLOS returned to the throne in November 1975.

V. Pilapil, *Alfonso XIII* (1969)

**Algerian War.** Anti-colonial war between Algerian nationalists and the French army, lasting from 1954 until 1962. The rising resulted from France's failure to allow any form of real power and influence to the indigenous population. In November 1954 the war began in the form of a limited armed rebellion. The revolt involved only a small number of isolated groups: there were 359 armed men in the Aures, 200 in Kabylia and 100 in the Algerois. In August 1956 they formed themselves into the Front de Liberation Nationale, the FLN. The rebellion took the form of attacks on the French army and population based in the colony. Violent police raids and countermeasures increased popular sympathy for the rebels, whose numbers swelled accordingly; massacres and atrocities soon became a feature of the war on both sides. From January 1955 to October 1956 the FLN succeeded in building up an army dedicated to the liberation of Algeria. Important battles followed in the east of the country in the departements of Aures-Nememchas,

North-Constantinois and Kabylia. Despite their superiority in numbers, the French army was unable to take the initiative in the fighting. Many of the units were insufficiently trained to deal with guerrilla tactics; only the crack parachute regiments were successful as fighting troops because they had built up guerrilla experience in Indo-China. By May 1956 the war had been responsible for the deaths of 106 European civilians and 1,158 Moslems. The war was intensified as the Arab leaders gave orders that all Europeans between the ages of 18 and 40 were legitimate targets in Algiers. A vicious battle ensued between the FLN and General Massu's 10th Paratroop Division; bombings, counterterrorism, torture and extortion began on a large scale. Eventually the FLN were forced to move their centre of operations to Tunis. Attempts at conciliation by GUY MOLLET in 1956 were spurned, and he abandoned negotiation for further repression. Mollet's fall in spring 1957 was followed by a policy of drift, leaving the war in the hands of the army. International condemnation followed when French planes dropped bombs on the Tunisian town of Sakhiet, bringing the Algerian War to the attention of the UNITED NATIONS. The increasing frustration of the Algerian settlers and the army led to a rising in Algeria on 13 May 1958 led by nationalist and right-wing groups; seizing Algiers and the major towns they established 'Committees of Public Safety'. With most of the French army in Algeria and much of it sympathetic to the French settlers, France was on the brink of a military coup. At this point DE GAULLE let it be known that he was prepared to return to political life. On 1 June 1958 the National Assembly vested him with virtually unconditional powers. He acted to bring the army under control. The commander-in-chief, Salan, was brought to Paris in December 1958 and General Massu, leader of the Algiers 'Committee of Public Safety', was posted away in January 1959. De Gaulle placed general Maurice Challe in charge of the war in Algeria. By extensive use of aircraft and helicopters Challe began seriously to hinder the operations of the FLN. De Gaulle, however, sought a negotiated settlement. As this became apparent he was faced with another attempted insurrection in Algiers in January 1960 – the 'week of the barricades' – which was allowed to peter out. A referendum in January 1961 produced a 75 per cent vote for self-determination. A truce was imposed while negotiations were set up with the FLN. This led to an attempted coup by the underground army of the French settlers, the ORGANISATION DE L'ARMÉE SECRÈTE, led by Generals Salan and Challe on 22 April 1961. It was foiled when de Gaulle appeared on television and called on the army and the French people to support him. Challe's nerve gave way and he surrendered, while Salan fled into hiding. The peace talks began at Évian (see ÉVIAN AGREEMENTS) in May 1961 and a cease-fire was agreed on 18 March 1962, granting Algeria full independence on 3 July.

The Algerian War was one of the bitterest wars of DECOLONIZATION, killing according to some estimates up to 1 million Algerians, although the more accurate figure is probably one-tenth of that. The French lost over 17,000 soldiers; nearly 1,000 European civilians died largely as a result of terrorist attacks. It destroyed the FOURTH REPUBLIC and brought de Gaulle to power. At least three serious assassination attempts by the OAS came close to killing him, and twice France was seriously threatened by a military coup led by its bravest and toughest soldiers. The outcome of the war was decided not in Algeria but within France. Paradoxically, by the time France had sickened of the war in 1960–1, the French forces had broken the strength of the FLN in Algiers and had considerably reduced the number of active guerrillas. The 'Morice Line' along the Tunisian frontier had placed a barrier between the Algerian forces and their 'sanctuary' area while the *regroupment* of villages cut off the FLN from support in the countryside. But the French forces were unable to end the war completely, and Tunisia continued to provide a base for the guerrillas beyond the reach of French operations. Although French losses were under 2,000 a year, there appeared no hope of bringing the war to a successful conclusion without tying up a much larger force or using methods unacceptable either to the French public or to the international community. With the French army being torn apart by the conflict, the FLN was granted a victory it could not obtain on the battlefield. De Gaulle acted to heal the rifts in the army, court-martialling, dismissing or posting away the overtly disloyal, and disbanding the 1st Foreign Legion Parachute Battalion which had supported the coup. But the war largely ended the army's role as a colonial force; it was now increasingly based on metropolitan France, absorbed in conventional training and France's nuclear role.

Indirectly the war had other important effects on France. It brought a flood of *colons* and *pieds noirs* to France, followed soon by a larger wave of Arab immigration which was soon to fuel anti-immigrant feeling and give rise to the extreme right-wing Fronte National led by JEAN-MARIE LE PEN.

D. C. Gordon, *The Passing of French Algeria* (1966)
D. Cook, *Charles de Gaulle* (1984)
A. Horne, *A Savage War of Peace* (rev. edn, 1988)

**Alliance, the.** An alliance of the British LIBERAL PARTY and SOCIAL DEMOCRATIC PARTY was formed in September 1981 following the creation of the Social Democratic Party earlier in the year and the acceptance by both parties of the principle of an alliance at their conferences. The Alliance agreed to an equal share-out of seats for local and parliamentary elections and campaigned under a joint manifesto in both the 1983 and 1987 general elections. In addition, Alliance groups were formed on many local Councils, following local election successes. At one point in 1981 the Alliance had an opinion poll rating of over 40 per cent, but obtained only 26 per cent and 24 per cent respectively in the two general elections of 1983 and 1987 in spite of an impressive string of by-election victories. Calls for a merger of the two parties immediately following the 1987 election and votes in favour of merger by the Liberals and the SDP at special conferences early in 1988 terminated the Alliance and created a new party, the Social and Liberal Democrats (SLD). A group of SDP members led by David Owen remained separate, continuing with the former name. In 1989 the SLD changed its common title to that of Liberal Democrats. The Alliance campaigned for proportional representation, more centrist economic policies, and regionalism. It had some difficulties in reconciling policies on defence and in maintaining cohesion between the two leaders, DAVID OWEN and DAVID STEEL. For a time the Alliance appeared to represent a genuinely effective third force in British politics and a potential rival to the LABOUR PARTY as a major opposition party at a time when the latter was subject to intense internal divisions. The bitterness and confusion of the merger process brought about a slump in the fortunes of the former Alliance partners.

C. P. Cook, *A Short History of the Liberal Party, 1900–88* (3rd edn, 1989)

J. Stevenson, *The Liberal Party and Third Party Politics since 1945* (1992)

**Alliance Party.** Northern Irish political party. The Alliance Party was founded in 1970 as a non-sectarian alternative to the existing Catholic and Protestant parties. Led by Oliver Napier until 1984 and then by John Cushnahan until 1987, the party has failed to return any MPs to Westminster.

**ALÖS.** Auslands-organisation Österreichischer Sozialisten. *See* SOCIAL DEMOCRATIC WORKERS' PARTY, AUSTRIAN.

**Alsace-Lorraine.** Provinces of northern France, annexed by Germany as a result of the Franco–Prussian War of 1870–1. The provinces remained the central feature of French animosity towards Germany and a rallying point for nationalistic sentiment. They were restored to France by the TREATY OF VERSAILLES but declared an integral part of Germany by the armistice agreement with France in June 1940. They became French territory again in 1945.

**'Alternatives'.** *See* GREEN PARTY, AUSTRIAN.

**Alto Adige.** *See* SOUTH TYROL DISPUTE.

**Amnesty International.** International organization founded in 1961 by the British barrister Peter Benenson to campaign for the release of political prisoners, assist their families, and improve the standard of treatment of detainees. Based in London, it is funded by private subscription and has 50,000 members in 57 countries.

**anarchism, Russian.** Anarchism had strong roots in the Russian revolutionary movement, drawing on both populist belief in the MIR as a centre of social and political organization and as a branch of socialist thought which stressed local and small-scale organization. Many of these views were expressed by the two prominent Russian anarchist theorists, Mikhail Bakunin (1814–76) and Peter Kropotkin (1842–1921). Anarchist and anarcho-syndicalist groups participated in the SOVIETS set up during the 1905 revolution and again after March 1917, as well as in the FACTORY COMMITTEES. Anarchist–communist newspapers, *Stormy Petrel* and *The Voice of Labour*, achieved wide circulation in Petrograd and elsewhere. Siding against the PROVISIONAL GOVERNMENT they supported the BOLSHEVIKS in the October revolution (*see* RUSSIAN REVOLUTION). During the RUSSIAN CIVIL WAR, many began to criticize the centralization of Bolshevik power; a number participated in the regime in the Ukraine led by N. I. MAKHNO. Large numbers of anarchists were arrested in April 1918, and their newspapers suppressed. Kropotkin's funeral in February 1921 in Moscow was the last time the anarchists were allowed to appear in public. Following the KRONSTADT MUTINY in March the remaining anarchists were driven into exile or sent to the SOVIET LABOUR CAMPS. The remaining anarchists were weeded out in the later PURGES under Stalin. *See also* MAKHNO, NESTOR.

P. Avrich, *The Russian Anarchists* (1967)

——, *The Anarchists in the Russian Revolution* (1973)

**anarchism, Spanish.** A major force in Spanish politics from the late 19th century, concentrated mainly amongst the peasantry and landless labourers of the south and the industrial workers of the north and Catalonia. It found expression in the CONFEDERACIÓN NACIONAL DEL TRABAJO (CNT), the largest labour organization in pre-Civil War Spain, formed in 1911. The anarchists participated in a general strike in 1917, but were also involved in terrorism, assassinating the Archbishop of Saragossa in 1923 and leading revolts in Barcelona, Saragossa and elsewhere against the SECOND REPUBLIC. The peculiarly violent and anti-clerical tone of Spanish anarchism (*see* ANTI-CLERICALISM, SPANISH) also found expression in attacks on Church property, both before and after the SPANISH CIVIL WAR. As the CNT began to operate more like a conventional labour organization, the more revolutionary anarchists threw their weight behind the Federación Anarquista Iberica (FAI) led by Buenaventura Durruti (1896–1936). The FAI was intended to be an Iberian-wide organization which, it was hoped, would eventually take over the CNT and turn it into a revolutionary rather than a reformist organization. The FAI organized strikes against the Second Republic and mounted a series of insurrections which alienated socialist and other left groupings, but was increasingly forced underground by arrests and repression. When the Civil War broke out, the anarchists played a major part in seizing control of Barcelona and created a militia army to seize Saragossa, the capital of Aragon. They failed to do so; although the anarchist militias and the Army of Aragon continued to provide some of the bravest shock troops of the Republic, they lacked a secure base and regular supplies. Many of the leading anarchists were killed in the fighting, including Durruti, who died in defence of Madrid in November 1936. Only in Barcelona and parts of Aragon did anarchists retain a degree of power as the Republican forces came under greater discipline and communist control. In Barcelona the anarchists mounted a virtual social revolution in the three months after the outbreak of the Civil War but were gradually ousted from power by socialists and Republicans, their local power was broken in the MAY DAYS of 1937. Some anarchists joined LARGO CABALLERO's Cabinet in the autumn of 1936 but resigned the following spring as they found themselves increasingly subject to communist suppression. The anarchist militias were dissolved during 1937 and several anarchist leaders were killed. Although they continued to attempt to contest power within the Republic side, putting up candidates for the Cortes in 1938, and influencing the CNT and FAI through an executive committee, Comite Ejecutivo del Movimento Libertario, composed of Spain's leading anarchists, the movement's power, however, was largely broken. Spain's anarchists were a constant destabilizing force on the left, often uncompromising revolutionaries who continued to practice terrorism – 'propaganda of the deed' – and insurrection right up to eve of the Civil War. Their attempt to mount a social revolution at the outbreak of the Civil War was suppressed in the attempt to concentrate upon winning the war.

G. Brenan, *The Spanish Labyrinth* (1943)
M. Bookchin, *The Spanish Anarchists: The Heroic Years, 1868–1936* (1977)
R. Kern, *Red Years: Black Years: A Political History of the Spanish Anarchists, 1911–1937* (1978)

**Andreotti, Giulio** (1919–). Italian statesman, one of the most prominent leaders of the Christian Democrats (DC) and Prime Minister, 1972–3, 1976–9, and 1989–91. Educated at the University of Rome, he was a member, with ALDO MORO, of the Catholic Graduate Association, joining the Christian Democrats soon after their formation in 1942. He served as a Deputy to the Constituent Assembly in 1945 and sat in Parliament continuously thereafter. He served as under-secretary in the DE GASPERI and Pella governments, 1947–53, as Minister of the Interior in 1954; of Finance, 1955–8; of the Treasury, 1958–9; of Defence, 1959–60, 1960–66 and in 1974; of Industry and Commerce, 1966–8; of Budget and Economic Planning, 1974–76; and as Foreign Minister in 1983. He served as Chairman of the Christian Democratic Party in the Chamber, 1948–72. He helped to resist the 'opening to the left' proposed by Party leadership from the late 1950s and was considered a right-winger in defence of Catholic and capitalist interests, though supporting a cautious centre-left movement towards the Italian Socialists (PSI). In his first premiership he veered to the centre-right, seeking to woo the rising right-wing, neo-fascist vote but was brought down by continuing economic crisis in June 1973. He headed governments of 'National Solidarity' in 1976–9 when Italy faced a major terrorist campaign from Left and Right (*see* TERRORISM, ITALIAN). He refused to compromise with the kidnappers of Moro in 1978, whose killing helped to spread revulsion at the terrorist movement, and secured the tacit co-operation of the Italian Communist Party (PCI). He resigned in January 1979 in the face of growing Communist dissent at further co-operation, but a new coalition failed to win a vote a confidence. He returned to head Italy's 49th post-war government in July 1989 which resigned in March 1991.

P. Ginsborg, *A History of Contemporary Italy: Society and Politics, 1943–88* (1990)

**Andropov, Yuri** (1914–84). Soviet statesman and leader. He joined the Communist Party in 1932 and began his political career as a KOMSOMOL organizer, becoming First Secretary of the Yaroslav committee of the All Union Komsomol in 1936. He served as ambassador to Hungary, 1953–7, and from 1957 to 1967 was head of the Communist Party's Liaison Committee for communist and workers' parties of socialist countries. In 1961 he joined the Central Committee of the Communist Party of the Soviet Union, and between 1967 and 1973 was a full member of the Politburo Central Committee. Promoted to the head of the KGB (*see* KGB) in 1967, he resigned in May 1982 to become Secretary of the Communist Party. On the death of BREZHNEV in November, Andropov was appointed General-Secretary of the Central Committee of the Communist Party of the Soviet Union and, shortly after, a member of the Presidium. In 1983 he was appointed President of the Presidium. He died in February 1984 after a long struggle with kidney disease, his last public appearance having been in August 1983. His tenure of the leadership was thus the shortest in Soviet history. Andropov rose to the highest ranks of the Soviet hierarchy and was preferred as the successor to Brezhnev over CHERNENKO, who eventually succeeded him. Although a hard-liner who assisted in the suppression of the HUNGARIAN UPRISING, he was widely seen as a modernizer after the lack-lustre last years of Brezhnev. His most important lasting achievement was to bring into power a group of younger officials, including his protégé MIKHAIL GORBACHEV, with whom he hoped to inaugurate a greater drive for efficiency in the Soviet Union.

Zh. Medvedev, *Andropov* (1983)
J. Steele and E. Abraham, *Andropov in Power* (1983)

**Anglo–German Naval Agreement.** Signed 18 June 1935, following negotiations begun on 4 June between Sir Samuel Hoare, First Lord of the Admiralty, and RIBBENTROP. By the treaty Germany was permitted to build up to 35 per cent of Britain's naval strength and in submarines up to 45 per cent, or up to 100 per cent in exceptional circumstances. The treaty recognized Germany's breach of the restrictions imposed upon her by the TREATY OF VERSAILLES as she was already building submarines in defiance of the treaty and capital ships greater than the 10,000 ton limit imposed. Seen by some as a condoning of the revision of Versailles and part of the process of APPEASEMENT, it also undermined COLLECTIVE SECURITY as a bilateral arrangement between two powers. The treaty created antagonism between Britain and France, who had not been consulted, subsequently dividing their response over the ETHIOPIAN CRISIS. Germany utilized the agreement to begin the building of a modern fleet of battleships, including the *Bismarck* and *Tirpitz*, which, at 45,000 tons, were the largest and most powerful battleships afloat when commissioned.

W. D. Medlicott, *Britain and Germany: The Search for Agreement, 1930–1937* (1969)
M. Cowling, *The Impact of Hitler: British Politics and British Policy, 1933–1940* (1975)

**Anglo–Irish Agreement.** Signed on 15 November 1985 by British and Irish prime ministers Mrs THATCHER and Dr FITZGERALD at Hillsborough near Belfast. It set up a new Intergovernmental Conference concerned with Northern Ireland and with relations between the two states. The Act enshrined the right of the population of Ulster to decide its own destiny but gave the Irish government a consultative role in the affairs of the North. A joint communiqué stated that the aim of the agreement was to promote peace and stability in the North and to reconcile the two traditions in Ireland. Seen as a major step along the road to a bipartisan Anglo–Irish approach to the ULSTER CONFLICT it was the outcome of regular discussions during 1984–5. It appeared to promise greater Irish co-operation on security and the possibility of reconciling the Catholic population to the situation. The Agreement met fierce Protestant resistance, including massive loyalist demonstrations in Belfast (23 November) and the resignation of all Unionist MPs to fight by-elections as a mini-referendum. This was followed by a Unionist boycott of Westminster which lasted until 1987. Non-co-operation with the Northern Ireland executive was also pursued. The Agreement has remained in force in spite of some misgivings about its real effects on the security situation. It is now seen as a stumbling block on the road to political progress, the Unionists refusing to enter into political dialogue until it is removed or at least suspended.

A. Kenny, *The Road to Hillsborough* (1986)
P. Arthur and K. Jeffery, *Northern Ireland since 1968* (1989)

**Anglo–Irish Treaty.** Treaty signed between Great Britain and Ireland (1921) by which Ireland accepted Dominion status, subject to the right of Northern Ireland to opt out. This right was exercised and the border between the Irish Free State and Ulster was fixed in December 1925 by a tripartite agreement between the Free State, Ulster and Great Britain, and ratified by their respective parliaments. The Treaty was the outcome of the guerrilla war mounted by the IRISH REPUBLICAN ARMY on behalf of SINN FEIN against the British presence in Ireland. It resulted from protracted negotiations between plenipotentiaries from the Irish side with LLOYD GEORGE, and was ultimately signed by MICHAEL COLLINS as Irish leader, and Arthur Griffiths and Erskine Childers on the Irish side, but only narrowly ratified by the Irish parliament on 7 January 1922. Bitterness on the part of extreme Irish nationalists at having surrendered the objective of a united Ireland and having to accept an Oath of Allegiance to the British Crown led to the IRISH CIVIL WAR of 1922–3 between pro- and anti-Treaty forces. *See also* HOME RULE.

Lord Longford (Frances Pakenham), *Peace by Ordeal* (2nd edn, 1972)
C. Younger, *Ireland's Civil War* (1968)

**Anschluss.** The term refers to the union of Austria with Germany. The AUSTRIAN REPUBLIC created by the TREATY OF ST GERMAIN appeared economically and politically impoverished to many Austrians, and union with Germany seemed the only realistic solution. The German Nationalists were most enthusiastic, but both the SOCIAL DEMOCRATIC WORKERS PARTY (SDAP) and the CHRISTIAN SOCIAL PARTY (ÖVP) were also officially in favour of such a union – the latter albeit somewhat reluctantly. However, *Anschluss* was explicitly forbidden at St Germain. The Allies were reluctant to see a defeated Germany enlarged by the post-war settlements. Despite Austria's apparent political and economic stabilization in the 1920s the idea of *Anschluss* was never completely abandoned, and revived during the depression. An abortive attempt to form a customs union in 1931 prompted the withdrawal of French credit from Austria, precipitating the collapse of the CREDITANSTALT, Austria's leading bank. Enthusiasm for *Anschluss* increased after HITLER's appointment as German Chancellor in 1933, not least as a result of the dramatic fall in unemployment in Germany.

A Nazi attempt to seize power in Vienna in July 1934 failed, although the Austrian Chancellor, ENGELBERT DOLLFUSS, was murdered. Direct German intervention was prevented by the opposition of MUSSOLINI at a time when Germany's international position was still relatively weak. By 1936 the balance of power had shifted, although it is now clear that the July Agreement of that year, in which significant concessions were made to Germany, was by no means forced upon Austria, but reflected a certain pro-German sympathy on the part of the new chancellor, KURT VON SCHUSCHNIGG. If Hitler had refrained from greater pressure on Schuschnigg it was for fear of antagonizing Mussolini. However, it was clear from the end of 1937 that neither Italy nor Britain would intervene if Germany occupied Austria. Early in 1938 Schuschnigg requested a meeting with Hitler following the uncovering of Nazi putsch plans in Vienna, and was invited to BERCHTESGADEN in February, where Hitler browbeat him into a series of concessions which would effectively make Austria a German satellite. However, Schuschnigg tried to retrieve something of Austria's independence by announcing a plebiscite on the question. Hitler was surprised by this move, and made plans for a military occupation of Austria, which took place on 12 March 1938, following Schuschnigg's resignation in favour of the Nazi interior minister, ARTHUR VON SEYSS-INQUART (11 March) in response to a German ultimatum.

Until the invasion there had been no firm plans for the integration of Austria into the

Reich. There were several possibilities, including a personal union, with Hitler simply head of state in both countries; the absorption of an integral Austria as a German province; the integration of the Austrian provinces separately as German *Gaue*; and the complete destruction of all Austrian political and administrative structures and the total integration of Austria into the Reich. What took place in 1938 was a combination of the last two. The federal provinces were re-organized as *Gaue* of the Reich, and the name Austria was extinguished not only at national level (where it was replaced by 'Alpine and Danubian *Gaue*') but also at regional level – Lower and Upper Austria became Lower and Upper Danube respectively. On 10 April 1938 a Nazi-controlled plebiscite was held on the 'reunion of Austria with the German Reich', in which a 99.75 per cent vote was recorded in favour of the union.

G. E. R. Gedye. *Fallen Bastions* (1939)
R. Luza, *Austro-German Relations in the Anschluss Era* (1975)

**anti-clericalism.** A major feature of many European states prior to the First World War, where it was often associated with the struggle of liberal and national regimes with churches for supremacy in such matters as education, church property and the conduct of such social affairs as marriage, divorce and, latterly, birth control. The respective spheres of Church and State had been largely arbitrated in Scandinavia, Great Britain, France and Germany prior to 1914, sometimes occasioning bitter clashes, as in the German *Kulturkampf* and the secularization laws in France. In Italy, historic tension between the Catholic Church and the newly-established Italian state was largely resolved by the LATERAN PACTS of 1929, while the government of some new states, such as the Irish Free State, opted to give the Catholic Church a special status within their constitutions. Anti-clericalism of the kind seen in 19th-century Europe had its most potent expression after 1914 in Spain, where SPANISH ANTI-CLERICALISM played a part in the chronic political instability which brought about the SPANISH CIVIL WAR.

A new dimension to anti-clericalism came with the rise of Bolshevism and the establishment of the Soviet Union. Initial toler-

ance of the RUSSIAN ORTHODOX CHURCH and other churches within a framework of the secularization of society gave way to an official campaign of de-Christianization, in which both intellectual criticism of religion and the manipulation of peasant anti-clericalism played a part. The Nazi regime in Germany maintained an uneasy relationship with the churches, although in other countries the Church was frequently seen as an important defence against communism, promoting a violent pro-Christian tendency in movements such as the IRON GUARD and ARROW CROSS.

The victory of the Soviet Union in the Second World War and the establishment of Soviet satellites in Eastern Europe provoked a new period of tension between, mainly, the Catholic Church and the secular authorities. During the Cold War, the chief Catholic representatives of the Eastern European states often found themselves at odds with the communist authorities. Officially secular, most communist regimes placed obstacles in the way of clerical influence on education, the ownership of property and the proselytization of religion outside the churches. These tendencies were at their strongest within the Soviet Union itself, where active participation in religious affairs was discouraged and much church property remained confiscated or secularized. A significant feature of the revival of anti-communist movements in Poland and other parts of Eastern Europe has been their focus upon the churches as a source of legitimacy. The Polish Catholic Church emerged as a strong supporter of SOLIDARITY and the Protestant churches of Eastern Germany as a centre for pro-democratic movements. By 1989 it appeared that virulent, communist-led anti-clericalism had virtually evaporated in Eastern Europe, and within the Soviet Union under GORBACHEV a new spirit of tolerance was officially announced as being a necessary part of GLASNOST.

A fresh dimension was given to anti-clericalism by the rise of fundamentalist Islamic movements, presenting a challenge in those states with large native or immigrant Muslim populations. New tensions have emerged over such matters as the nature of the education of women, the provision of religious schooling, and respect for Islamic traditions. They have in some countries already led to renewed friction between the civil authorities and religious minorities:

**anti-clericalism, Spanish.** The undercurrent of anti-clericalism runs throughout the course of modern Spanish history. Manifest both in party politics and in sporadic outbursts of popular violence, Spanish anti-clericalism was the result of the near complete identification of the national Catholic Church with the old regime of the Restored Monarchy (1875–1931). The decline in religious practice among the working class, a Western European phenomenon, was accentuated in Spain by the fact that this alienation was not confined to the industrial workers of the great cities; it has been estimated that, in rural Andalusia at the turn of the century, less than 3 per cent of male labourers attended church. Here, as in other areas such as Catalonia, anti-clericalism became a feature of the anarchist movement and of socialists and republicans (*see* ANARCHISM, SPANISH).

One of the most dramatic demonstrations of popular anti-clericalism was the Barcelona 'Tragic Week' of 1909 when priests were attacked and church buildings burnt. Both ecclesiastical property and personnel suffered from identification with the political establishment. In a similar incident at the beginning of the SECOND REPUBLIC in May 1931, churches and convents were set alight in large cities all over Spain following provocative displays in Madrid by supporters of ALFONSO XIII. Again, Catholicism suffered from being perceived as the ally of the monarchy and, therefore, the enemy of the Republic. The Church also came under legislative attack in 1931 as the new constitution not only separated Church and State but also expelled the Jesuits and banned religious orders from teaching. In 1933 all orders were forcibly dissolved with a law which, for the first time, did not exempt any congregations involved in welfare work.

All previous attacks on the Church, however, palled in comparison to the orgy of anarchist-inspired anti-clerical violence which took place in the first months of the SPANISH CIVIL WAR. 13 bishops, 4,184 priests, 2,365 monks and 283 nuns were killed in an anti-religious outburst unparalleled in the modern world. With the defeat of the Republic, the Church resumed its old privileges. Its protected position in Francoist Spain was challenged not by external political change but by the dramatic internal upheavals which followed the SECOND VATICAN COUNCIL. With the Church's acceptance of democratic pluralism, anti-clericalism had, by the time of Franco's death, ceased to be a political force in Spain.

J. Connolly Ullman, *The Tragic Week: A Study of Anti-clericalism in Spain, 1875–1912* (1968)
J. M. Sanchez, *Anticlericalism: A Brief History* (1972)
F. Lannon, *Privilege, Persecution, and Prophecy: The Catholic Church in Spain, 1875–1975* (1987)

**anti-Comintern Pact.** Agreement signed between Nazi Germany and Japan on 25 November 1936, declaring their opposition to international communism represented by the Third International or COMINTERN. The Pact was primarily the work of RIBBENTROP, although it predated his appointment as German Foreign Minister by 15 months. Italy joined the Pact on 6 November 1937. It prefigured the alliance of AXIS powers in the Second World War. Initially, the Pact gave Japan recognition for her conquest of Manchuria, giving Germany a potential counterweight to Britain in the Far East.

**anti-Semitism.** Jews had been the subject of attack and discrimination over many centuries, but modern anti-Semitism differed from traditional dislike of minorities in its development of a scientific rationale based on social Darwinism and eugenic ideas. Writers such as Gobineau (1816–82), H. S. Chamberlain (1855–1927) and other philosophers fashioned the idea of racial as opposed to religious anti-Semitism. In the late 19th century a group of German writers began to use the linguistic terms 'Semitic' and 'Aryan' as racial terms and treated the Jews as an inferior species. A virulent anti-Semitism combining both popular and pseudo-scientific anti-Semitism was common in many parts of Europe prior to 1914. In France the Dreyfus affair in 1894 revealed the strength of anti-Semitic feeling amongst the nationalist, Catholic right, represented in groups such as ACTION FRANÇAISE and the right-wing LEAGUES of the inter-war years. In Austria anti-Semitism was common across a broad spectrum of opinion, where poor Jewish immigrants to the cities and their richer brethren found themselves attacked both from the right and by left-wing populists. Pro-nationalist Christian anti-Semitism flourished in Eastern Europe with large-scale pogroms in Tsarist Russia in 1905–9. After the First World War many anti-Semitic movements flourished in the states of Eastern Europe, such as Romania, Hungary, Austria, Poland and the Baltic States.

It was the pseudo-scientific theories of Aryan supremacy and Jewish conspiracy which HITLER fashioned into his own mould in MEIN KAMPF and which found support in the Nazi movement. It was striking, however, that anti-Semitic policies did not need much encouragement amongst some other countries with whom the Nazis came into contact, for example in France, Hungary and Romania. The Nazis' contribution was to provide a systematic policy of discrimination and then of mass extermination (*see* HOLOCAUST) in those areas which they overran or influenced.

Moreover, outside areas of Nazi influence, anti-Semitism also flourished. In the Soviet Union attacks on Jews reappeared in the late 1940s and seemed to lie at the heart of the so-called DOCTORS' PLOT of 1953. Even after Stalin's death, Yiddish theatres, books, newspapers and journals were suppressed and emigration to Israel restricted. Polish and Romanian broadcasts and newspaper articles have attacked the Jews in general and the government of Israel in particular. Russian Jews suffered violence in 1958–9 and in 1962–3; many were executed for 'economic crimes'. Jewish 'DISSIDENTS' were amongst those to feel the weight of Soviet persecution under BREZHNEV. In the turmoil surrounding the Gorbachev era, the voice of extreme right-wing Russian nationalism has again been heard in complaints about excessive Jewish influence in the arts and mass media. *See also* VICHY GOVERNMENT.

K. Schleunes, *The Twisted Road to Auschwitz* (1970)
L. Dawidowicz, *The War against the Jews, 1933–45* (1975)

**Antonescu, Ion** (1882–1946). Romanian soldier and dictator. Born in Pitesti, he served as a Colonel in the First World War, as military attaché in Rome and Berlin, and was made Chief of Staff in 1937. As a supporter of the IRON GUARD he was arrested and imprisoned in 1938, but was released and appointed Minister of War and then Prime Minister on 3 September 1940. With the aid of the Iron Guard he ousted Carol II (abdicated 6 September 1940), ruling in the name of his son, King Michael. Following the dismissal of Iron Guard ministers and officials with whom he had maintained an uneasy coalition, with German backing he put down their insurrection in Bucharest in January 1941 and crushed the movement. Antonescu allied the country with the AXIS powers, and had himself proclaimed 'Conducator' (leader), entering the war against the Soviet Union in June 1941. Defeats for the Axis powers and heavy Romanian losses led King Michael to stage a coup on 23 August 1944. Antonescu was arrested. He was put on trial in May 1946 and executed as a war criminal.

S. Fischer-Galati, *Twentieth Century Rumania* (1970)

**Anotov-Ovseyenko, Vladimir** (1884–1939). Russian revolutionary leader. He joined the RUSSIAN SOCIAL DEMOCRATIC LABOUR PARTY in 1903, and in 1917 was a member of the MILITARY REVOLUTIONARY COMMITTEE of the Petrograd Soviet, which acted as the headquarters for the October Revolution (see RUSSIAN REVOLUTION). He conducted the taking of the Winter Palace and the arrest of the members of the Provisional Government. During the RUSSIAN CIVIL WAR he commanded various army groups but was dismissed from the army in 1925 as a supporter of TROTSKY. Acting in various diplomatic posts abroad he disappeared during the PURGES.

L. Kochan, *Russia in Revolution* (1966)

**Antonov Uprising.** Name given to peasant revolts in the Tambov province in the Black Earth area of Russia in 1920–21. One of a number of large-scale peasant risings in areas such as the Volga Basin, Siberia and the northern Caucasus. Led by a former member of the LEFT SOCIALIST REVOLUTIONARY PARTY, A. S. Antonov, an army made up of peasants, deserters and others displaced by the Russian Revolution attacked Bolshevik requisition squads and party headquarters. Largely a movement of resistance to the exactions of 'WAR COMMUNISM', the Antonov (or 'Green') Army also promulgated through its political wing, the Union of the Toiling Peasantry, demands for the recall of the CONSTITUENT ASSEMBLY, guarantees of civil liberties, and the socialization of the land. At its height in the latter half of 1920, the Antonov Army numbered 20,000 men and controlled a large region of central Russia. The rising was eventually put down during 1921 by troops under the command of ANTONOV-OVSEYENKO and TUKHACHEVSKY with great severity. Some concessions were offered, however, with an end to grain requisitioning and the first trials in the area of the NEW ECONOMIC POLICY.

O. Radkey, *The Unknown Civil War in Soviet Russia: A Study of the Green Movement in the Tambov Region, 1920–21* (1976)

**Appeasement.** A term which has acquired a pejorative meaning for the efforts of Britain and France to placate the dictators, especially HITLER, and avoid war by redressing supposed grievances at the expense of others. The dismemberment of Czechoslovakia under the MUNICH AGREEMENT of 29 September 1938 was the culmination of the policy. It had earlier been evident in the weak reactions to the Japanese aggression in Manchuria in 1931, over Ethiopia (*see* ETHIOPIAN CRISIS) and the HOARE–LAVAL PACT, in the non-intervention policy in the SPANISH CIVIL WAR, acquiescence in the German reoccupation of the RHINELAND, and over the ANSCHLUSS.

Appeasement has been hotly debated. It was seen after the outbreak of the Second World War as a mistaken policy of concessions which served only to make conflict more likely; a policy conducted, moreover, at the expense of weaker powers. Modern research has highlighted the vulnerability of both France and Britain to the threat of renewed war in the 1930s. Widespread agreement that the TREATY OF VERSAILLES required revision, strong anti-war feeling, and economic and political weaknesses encouraged piecemeal attempts to solve particular crises. After 1935 a limited degree of rearmament began in Britain, but it was recognized that Britain faced several potential threats from Japan and Italy, as well as Germany. Attempts were therefore made to appease Italy in Ethiopia and to appease Germany with the ANGLO–GERMAN NAVAL AGREEMENT. Attempts by CHAMBERLAIN at a 'great settlement' in 1937–8 were motivated by the desire to bring the revisionist powers within an orderly framework of negotiated settlements. The aim was to avoid war and possible war situations from arising. The Munich Agreement marked an attempt by Chamberlain to forestall such a conflict. Although a disaster for the Czechs and humiliating to much public opinion in Britain and France, it was seen as a victory for negotiation over armed force. Contrary to belief, Chamberlain had even been prepared to threaten war when Hitler acted unilaterally in the negotiations. The conquest of the rest of Czechoslovakia in early 1939 convinced many appeasers, such as HALIFAX, that the policy was doomed to failure. Chamberlain, however, clung to the belief in negotiated settlements right up to the last days of peace. French policy was dictated as much by a perception of internal divisions and weaknesses. Unwilling to risk war if it could be avoided, the BLUM government went against its instincts in not supporting the Spanish Republic, and willingly attempted to secure an orderly revision of frontiers rather than face another conflict on the scale of the FIRST WORLD WAR.

It has been recognized that appeasement was virtually a consensus policy for much of the 1930s, differences being of emphasis and degree rather than on fundamentals. Almost no one in the early and middle 1930s supported an instant resort to force in the face of aggression. It was only after COLLECTIVE SECURITY and sanctions had obviously failed over Manchuria and Ethiopia that serious divisions became manifest. Even then, the question of whether the dictators were appeasable seemed open, and it was only gradually apparent that it failed to grasp Hitler's mixture of opportunism and long-term aims. The greatest charge against the appeasers is that they encouraged the dictators in their demands, convincing Hitler, in particular, that they would never stand up to him. In fact, they were increasingly prepared to do so after 1938, bringing about the conflict over Poland in September 1939 when Britain stood by the guarantee she had made on 31 March 1939. Appeasement is now seen as a broader policy with roots as far back as the TREATY OF VERSAILLES and in which, by the 1930s, economic and colonial compensations were also being offered to Germany. *See also* MUNICH AGREEMENT.

M. Gilbert, *The Roots of Appeasement* (1966)
W. R. Rock, *British Appeasement in the 1930s* (1976)
A. Adamthwaite, *France and the Coming of the Second World War* (1977)
P. M. Bell, *The Origins of the Second World War in Europe* (1986)
G. Martel (ed.), *The Origins of the Second World War Reconsidered* (1986)
R. Overy and A. Wheatcroft, *The Road to War* (1989)

**April Theses.** Policy statement and programme of action issued by LENIN on his return from Switzerland in April 1917. The programme proposed withdrawal of support by the BOLSHEVIKS from the provisional government, calling for an end to the war, all power to the Soviets, abolition of the existing state apparatus of police, army and bureaucracy, the confiscation of land and its transfer to poor peasants, and the establishment of a Marxist International to promote world revolution. The April Theses demonstrated the growing gap between Lenin's definition of his position and more moderate elements, even the Petrograd and Moscow Bolshevik Committees voting against them. Lenin eventually dropped the demand for an immediate peace and for the complete abolition of the armed forces, but the bulk of the programme was accepted by the Bolsheviks, presenting a radical programme which both undermined the possibility of compromise and offered attractions of its own for the more militant workers, peasants and soldiers. *See also* RUSSIAN REVOLUTION.

A. B. Ulam, *Lenin and the Bolsheviks* (1969)

**Armenia.** The Armenians are a people of north-east Turkey and south-west Russia with an ancient language and culture; mainly Monophysite Christians, they belong to the Armenian Apostolic Church. During most of their history the Armenians have suffered from their minority status within the Ottoman and Russian Empires and were the frequent subject of persecution and ethnic violence. In 1894–6 growing nationalist agitation amongst the Turkish Armenians led to a savage massacre under the Ottoman Sultan, Abdul Hamid II. During the FIRST WORLD WAR the position of sizeable numbers of Armenians living on both sides of the Russo–Turkish border led to a mass deportation of 2 million Turkish Armenians to Syria in 1915–16, during which period an estimated 600,000 died. The SYKES-PICOT AGREEMENT envisaged the population of Turkish Armenia coming under Russian control, but advances by the Russian forces to conquer much of Turkish Armenia by 1917 were nullified by the RUSSIAN REVOLUTION. Under the TREATIES OF BREST-LITOVSK, the province of Kars and a sizeable Russian Armenian population was assigned to Turkish control. With the Turkish defeat in autumn 1918 an independent Armenian Republic, including the province of Kars, came into existence but was crushed by the 'Young Turk' armies under Karabakir Pasha by December 1920, making much of Armenia once again a Turkish province. During the RUSSIAN CIVIL WAR Russian Armenians elected an assembly with separatist intentions but communist reconquest led to the establishment in 1920 of an Armenian Soviet Socialist Republic. This was a party with the Russian Soviet Government of the TREATY OF KARS in 1921, confirming Turkish possession of Kars and the Surmali district of Yerevan, effectively ending hopes of a unified Armenian state. From 1922 Soviet Armenia formed part of the TRANSCAUCASIAN FEDERATED REPUBLIC, but in 1936 Armenia was proclaimed a constituent Republic of the USSR.

Although the expression of Armenian culture and identity was permitted within the Soviet constitution, nationalist and separatist movements were firmly repressed under STALIN. In the more relaxed atmosphere under GORBACHEV the nationalities question in the region was sharpened in February 1988, when large demonstrations took place in Armenia, calling for the redrawing of boundaries with neighbouring AZERBAIJAN, demanding the return to Armenia of NGORNO-KARABAKH, a largely Christian, Armenian region belonging to Armenia prior to 1917 and now part of Moslem Azerbaijan. Gorbachev held out the prospect of discussions to redress Armenian grievances, but serious rioting against Armenians in Ngorno-Karabakh forced the drafting in of large numbers of troops. Armenia planned an independence referendum following the failed Moscow coup of August 1991. *See also* NATIONALITIES QUESTION, SOVIET.

**Arnhem landings.** *See* SECOND WORLD WAR.

**Arrow Cross.** Hungarian fascist party led by Ferenc Szalasi (1897–1946), founded on 9 March 1939 as the successor to his earlier organizations, the Party of the National Will (established March 1935; banned April 1937) and the Hungarian National Socialist Party, (established October 1937; banned February 1938). These groupings were part of a large number of right-wing radical movements set up in Hungary in the 1930s, many of them pursuing nationalist, anti-Semitic, pro-Christian and populist agrarian policies. These included the National Socialist Workers' Party or Scythe Cross (founded 1931), the Hitlerite Hungarian National Socialist Party (founded 1932) and the Hungarian National Socialist Agricultural Labourers' and Workers' Party (founded 1932). Many of these groupings adopted uniforms and emblems of fascist movements elsewhere, though increasingly they adopted the green shirt and arrow cross emblem of Szalasi's organization. Szalasi, an ex-officer of only part Hungarian extraction, pursued the dream of 'Hungarism', the setting up of an advanced agricultural state stretching from the Carpathians to the Adriatic under Magyar 'jurisdiction'. In domestic policy the Party of the National Will was anti-Semitic and pledged to the principles of 'Soil, Blood and Work'.

Imprisoned twice under HORTHY DE NAGYBANYA and his earlier parties dissolved, Szalasi brought under the umbrella of his Arrow Cross Party–Hungarist Movement many of the other right-wing organizations with an ostensibly moderate programme to contest the May 1939 elections. National Socialist Parties won 750,000 of the 2 million votes, returning 48 of the 259 parliamentary seats, 31 of them going to the Arrow Cross. Excluded from power because of distrust of it by Conservatives, the Arrow Cross maintained pressure for land reform and for anti-Semitic legislation, influencing the shift of Horthy's policies to the right. Following his release from prison in 1943, Szalasi purged the party of its more communistic and explicitly pro-German elements in conformity with his dream of the 'Hungarist' state, reducing its membership to about 100,000. The Arrow Cross remained virulently racialist and anti-Semitic, Szalasi proposing a scheme for the reorganization of Europe on a tribal basis.

Following direct German intervention in Hungary in March 1944, the Arrow Cross assisted the round-up of Hungarian Jews for extermination but remained opposed to German domination, insisting on the absorption of their 'Hungarist' ideas as the price of co-operation. With the fall of Horthy in October 1944, Szalasi was made Prime Minister on 16 October following a coup by the Arrow Cross and the army backed by German troops. Szalasi attempted to set up a CORPORATE STATE while directing a terror against his opponents and those Jews still not deported. With the fall of Hungary to the Soviet Army in early 1945 Szalasi gave himself up to the American troops in Austria. He was tried for treason and shot in 1946. *See also* GÖMBÖS DE JAFKA, GYULA.

C. A. Macartney, *History of Modern Hungary, 1929–45* (2 vols, 1956)

E. Weber, 'Hungary', in *Varieties of Fascism* (1964)

M. Lacko, *Arrow Cross Men, National Socialists, 1933–44* (1969)

N. M. Nagy-Ralavera, *The Green Shirts and the Others: A History of Fascism in Hungary and Rumania* (1970)

**Asquith, Herbert** (1852–1928). British politician. He was Liberal MP for East Fife, 1886–1918, and for Paisley 1920–4. In 1925 he was created Earl of Oxford and Asquith. He was Home Secretary, 1892–5, Chancellor of the Exchequer, 1905–8 and Prime Minister, 1908–16. During 1914 he was also Secretary for War. He resigned the premiership in 1916 and became leader of the opposition. In 1926 he resigned the leadership of the LIBERAL PARTY when it failed to endorse his censuring of LLOYD GEORGE for refusing to attend a shadow cabinet. Asquith's term as Premier was a troubled one, embracing the budget, House of Lords and Ulster crises, SUFFRAGETTE militancy and the growing power of the trade unions. He supported Lloyd George's radical reforms of welfare before the war, but often appeared ineffective and indecisive. After the outbreak of the FIRST WORLD WAR he came under considerable pressure to prosecute the war more effectively. In May 1915 he formed a coalition government, but in December 1916 Lloyd George combined with the Conservatives to dislodge Asquith. He continued to oppose Lloyd George, losing his seat, and many of his followers in the 'Coupon' election of 1918, the feud between them doing considerable damage to the Liberal Party. A rapprochement in 1923 and a joint manifesto in the election of that year failed to heal the breach between the two men. His patrician air and relaxed style masked a good grasp of issues.

S. Koss, *Asquith* (1976)
R. Jenkins, *Asquith* (rev. edn, 1978)
M. E. and E. Brock (eds), *Asquith: Letters to Venetia Stanley* (1982)

**Asturias Rising.** Strike and rebellion in the Asturias mining region of northern Spain in October 1934. A socialist call for a general strike on 4 October led to work stoppages in Madrid, Barcelona, the Asturias and other major cities. Two days later in the Asturias the strike developed into an insurrectionary movement as armed miners seized the major towns, including Oviedo. The army was ordered to suppress the rising and under General Ochoa marched on Oviedo and bombed Asturian strongholds. Ochoa's forces were supplemented by Foreign Legion units, including Moroccans, led by General Franco. On 12 October the army recaptured Oviedo using aircraft and artillery and crushed the last centres of resistance at Mieres on the 17th. Approximately 3,000 were killed and 7,000 wounded. 30,000 rebel prisoners were held in Oviedo, some of whom were summarily executed, leading to world-wide protests at the brutality used to suppress the rising. 21 rebels were executed after trial by military courts in February 1935. The Asturias revolt became notorious for the harshness with which it was put down. The area continued to be a strong left-wing centre and overwhelmingly supported the Republic at the outbreak of the Spanish civil war. Groups of miners seized control of the mining operations and ran them by committees largely composed of miners. Communist and anarchist leaders worked together to run local government. The area was overrun by the Nationalists in 1937.

H. Thomas. *The Spanish Civil War* (1977)
A. Schubert. *Road to Revolution in Spain: the coal miners of Asturias, 1860–1936* (1987)

**Atlantic, Battle of the.** Name given to the struggle between German U-boats and Allied convoys in the Second world war. Germany opened the war with a small fleet of submarines (U-boats); some early attacks secured spectacular successes, such as the sinking of the *Royal Oak* at Scapa Flow and the aircraft-carrier *Illustrious* in the Western Approaches. Following diversion to the Norwegian campaign the submarines under the command of Dönitz began to attack convoys from June 1940, achieving rapid success. Dönitz concentrated them in 'wolf packs' to overwhelm escorts and was able to use the bases acquired in France and Norway. British losses began to mount to a third of all ships destined for Britain. As late as February 1941 Dönitz had only 21 U-boats, but from mid-1941 the force was built up with 200 submarines under construction. Allied shipping losses rose from an average of 100,000 tons per month in 1940 to 700,000 tons a month in mid-1941. Although United States entry into the war greatly assisted convoy protection, it opened up new areas of U-boat activities, leading to the loss of over 2.3 million tons of shipping off the US coast between January and July 1942. At the peak of losses, in November 1942, 800,000 tons of shipping were sunk. By the end of 1942 212 U-boats were deployed and had claimed over 6.25 million tons of shipping. Hitler's faith in Dönitz was reflected in his promotion to overall command of the navy in January 1943.

In early 1943 the Battle of the Atlantic reached a new height with a permanent pool of 35–40 U-boats operational in the Atlantic. Heavy losses were being replaced by new boats, but from May 1943 the tide began to turn. Improved radar and the use of long-range aircraft to attack U-boats going to or returning from the Atlantic hunting grounds, the use of specialized destroyer groups, and radio intercepts weighed against the U-boats. On 23 May 1943 Dönitz withdrew his boats from the North Atlantic, seeking targets further afield. They returned in 1944 with new underwater breathing devices, the *Schnor-*

*chel*, and improved torpedoes, but the advantages still lay with the Allies. The loss of French bases from mid-1944 seriously affected the U-boat campaign, and their training areas in the Baltic were under threat from the Soviet advance. Air-raids hit the remaining U-boat bases and disrupted the supply of components from the factories. U-boat losses began to mount alarmingly for little result. In the last three months of 1944 only 14 ships were sunk in the Atlantic for the loss of 55 U-boats. Total U-boat losses for the year were 241, compared with 237 in 1943, and 96 in 1942. Moreover, the Allies were able to devote enormous resources to combat the U-boats, deploying 350 aircraft solely to safeguard the Normandy landings. By 1945 there were 37 escort groups of 426 warships patrolling around the British Isles and another 153 U-boats were destroyed in the last four months of war. At the capitulation 398 U-boats were still on active service.

The most critical point in the Battle of the Atlantic was in 1942–3. In 1942 new construction failed to meet losses of ships. From 1943, not only did losses fall to half the level of the previous year but a major construction effort in the US shipyards poured out four times the total tonnage sunk (1943 losses, 3.6 million tons; US construction, 14.6 million tons). Thereafter a comfortable net balance was maintained. U-boat casualties were amongst the heaviest suffered in the war. 781 of 1,162 U-boats built were lost, and of 40,900 men recruited 28,000 died. On the Allied side 30,132 British merchant seamen were killed as well as thousands of sailors and foreign seamen. Over 15 million tons of allied merchant shipping had been sunk, as well as 175 naval vessels.

D. Macintyre, *The Battle of the Atlantic* (1961)
J. Costello and T. Hughes, *The Battle of the Atlantic* (1977)
P. Padfield, *Dönitz: The Last Führer* (1984)

**Atlantic Charter.** A statement of principles agreed by CHURCHILL and ROOSEVELT on behalf of Britain and the United States in August 1941 on the conduct of international policy in the post-war world. These included no territorial or other expansion; no wish for territorial changes other than those agreed by the peoples concerned; respect for the rights of all peoples to choose their form of government; desire for general economic development and collaboration; the need to disarm aggressor nations and the wish to construct a general system of international security. Although mainly a propaganda exercise, the US refused to acknowledge any future international obligations in spite of British pressure. The charter was endorsed by the Soviet Union and 14 other states at war with the AXIS powers in September 1941.

**atom bomb.** *See* NUCLEAR WEAPONS.

**Attlee, Clement** (1883–1967). British Labour politician and Prime Minister. The son of a solicitor, Attlee went to public school and Oxford before becoming a barrister in 1905. However, he turned his back on the legal profession to become warden of a young men's settlement in London's East End. This led him towards socialism; he joined the INDEPENDENT LABOUR PARTY in 1908. He served in France throughout the First World War, attaining the rank of major. His socialism undimmed, he became Mayor of Stepney in 1919 and an MP in 1922. For a time he served as parliamentary private secretary to RAMSAY MACDONALD, the party leader, and was a junior minister in the 1924 Labour government. From 1927 to 1930 he was a member of a government commission on India, and afterwards became a junior minister in the SECOND LABOUR GOVERNMENT. He had become increasingly disillusioned with the personality of MacDonald and the government's timid approach, however, and when the NATIONAL GOVERNMENT was formed in August 1931 he had no hesitation in following the bulk of the Labour Party into opposition. At the general election which followed, Attlee was one of only three ministers to retain his seat, and so he became, by default, deputy leader of the parliamentary party. At this stage he was seen as a left-winger, but he followed the party back to a more moderate line as the 1930s progressed. The resignation of George Lansbury shortly before the 1935 election left him in charge, but he led the Party to defeat. After the election he was challenged by MORRISON and Arthur Greenwood for the leadership, but through their adverse qualities and the loyalty of members of the 1931 parliament he retained the leadership. Up to the Second World War, however, he was a fairly ineffectual leader: most of the major decisions were taken elsewhere and he was ill for a considerable part of 1939. There were periodic abortive attempts to remove him.

It was in Churchill's wartime coalition that he began to show his real qualities, serving in the small war cabinet and acting as Deputy Prime Minister, overseeing the Cabinet during Churchill's frequent absences and looking after domestic policy in particular. Thus, he showed his competence in a way that, but for the war, would have been very difficult. In 1945 he led Labour to a landslide victory. During the campaign his quiet and reserved manner contrasted favourably with Churchill's bombast in the eyes of an electorate which had had enough of 'great men' for the time being. With the staunch loyalty of BEVIN he routed Morrison's attempt to oust him, and he became Labour's second Prime Minister. The government achieved a great deal, restoring Britain from bankruptcy, creating 'the welfare state', nationalizing many industries and ensuring a lasting alliance with the United States, as well as extricating Britain from the difficult areas of India and Palestine. Attlee was fortunate in being surrounded by able colleagues: he was an effective chairman and co-ordinator of a good team. However, Labour won only a narrow majority at the 1950 election, and the loss of able colleagues like Bevin and CRIPPS, and the resignation of others like BEVAN, signalled new, more difficult times. At the 1951 election Labour was defeated. Attlee remained leader, despite his age and increasing ineffectiveness, largely to thwart his old rival Morrison. The Party was increasingly split and Attlee did little to make things better. After the Party's defeat in 1955, he resigned, now that a clear alternative to Morrison – GAITSKELL – was available. Ennobled, he had a busy retirement, dying in 1967.

Attlee is one of the few leaders of whom the Labour Party has remained proud. His portrait hangs in the foyer of the Party's headquarters. Historians have generally paid tribute to his qualities of quiet efficiency and man-management, and pointed to his sterling work between 1940

and 1951. However, it must be added that outside these dates he was far less effective as Party leader. He was happier in government than in opposition, and, chameleonlike, his performance depended very much on the performance of those around him. He was a good leader of a good team, but lacked the abilities to revive and inspire which are the characteristics of a truly great leader. *See also* LABOUR PARTY.

K. Harris, *Attlee* (1982)
K. O. Morgan, *Labour in Power, 1945–1951* (1984)

**Auslands-organisation    Österreichischer Sozialisten** (ALÖS). *See* SOCIAL DEMOCRATIC WORKERS' PARTY, AUSTRIAN.

**Austria, Allied Occupation of.** The Moscow Declaration of the Allies of November 1943 guaranteed Austria's post-war independence but emphasized that it was dependent on the contribution that Austrians made to their own liberation. But in the event the Allies' plans for Austria resembled more closely those for Germany than for other occupied countries. An Allied Control Commission was set up in July 1945. Austria, like Germany, was divided into four occupation zones, and Vienna, like Berlin, into four sectors. The Soviets, who had liberated much of the country, including Vienna, occupied Lower Austria, BURGENLAND and the part of Upper Austria north of the Danube. Upper Austria south of the Danube and Salzburg were occupied by the United States; Styria and CARINTHIA by Britain, and the Tyrol and Vorarlberg by France. In Vienna the First District, the Inner City inside the *Ringstrasse* was placed under quadripartite control, and the other districts divided between the Allies.

The provisional government set up in April under KARL RENNER had authority only in the area occupied by the Red Army. The Western Allies were reluctant to recognize its authority in their own zones until its reconstruction on a broader political basis in September 1945. Western fears of Soviet influence were further allayed by the results of the first general election (25 November 1945) in which the AUSTRIAN COMMUNIST PARTY (KPÖ) polled much worse than expected, not least as a result of the experience of Soviet occupation in precisely those industrial areas of eastern Austria where the KPÖ had hoped to attract most support. A grand coalition was formed with one communist minister, who left the government in 1947.

The Allied occupation inevitably brought with it economic burdens. Although the Allies agreed to waive reparations payments from Vienna, disagreement continued over the question of German assets in Austria. The Western powers renounced their claim to these assets, while the Soviets, whose own economy had suffered much greater damage during the war, confiscated all German assets in their own zone ('Order No. 17'). The Austrian parliament responded by nationalizing all major industry. A further burden was the maintenance of Allied forces, which was borne partly by the Austrians. On the other hand the occupying powers left the Austrians a measure of political freedom, especially after the new control agreement of 1946 (28 June), which required Allied unanimity to reject Austrian legislation. The occupation was ended by the AUSTRIAN STATE TREATY of 1955.

W. Balder, *Austria between East and West, 1945–1955* (1966)

**Austrian Civil War.** The brief armed conflict between members of the SOCIAL DEMO-CRATIC REPUBLICAN DEFENCE LEAGUE and *Heimwehr* (*see* AUSTROFASCISM) units, which developed into a more general conflict between government security forces and the organized working class. Finding it increasingly difficult to govern with a parliamentary majority of one Chancellor ENGEL-BERT DOLLFUSS suspended parliament in 1933 against a background of economic crisis, political polarization, and street fighting. Government policy towards the labour movement became openly confrontational, and the *Heimwehr*, which was led by Public Security Minister Emil Fey, instituted a series of provocative searches of Social Democratic premises for weapons' caches. In February 1934 Defence League members in Linz informed the hesitant national leadership of the SOCIAL DEMO-CRATIC WORKERS' PARTY (SDAP) that they would respond to the next such provocation with armed resistance. Fighting broke out on 12 February in Linz. Viennese workers immediately demonstrated their support

and labour leaders reluctantly and belatedly called a general strike, which was both incomplete and ineffective. In Vienna police attacked workers' positions, often with military support, but there was not so much a major conflict as a series of isolated armed clashes in working-class suburbs. The fighting was by no means restricted to the capital, and was particularly intense in the heavy industrial districts of Upper Styria. Order was restored within a few days by the overwhelmingly superior government forces. The back of the labour movement had been decisively broken. In Vienna alone 131 civilians, including 25 women and children, had been killed. The SDAP was dissolved and over 2,000 members were arrested. Summary courts were set up and death sentences carried out almost immediately. A fascist constitution was promulgated on 1 May 1934.

**Austrian People's Party** (Österreichische Volkspartei; ÖVP). The major conservative party in Austria, founded in 1945. It took over the political ground and electoral support of the pre-war CHRISTIAN SOCIAL PARTY. In an attempt to distance itself from its tainted historical predecessor the ÖVP emphasized its commitment to democracy, rejected authoritarian solutions in favour of co-operation with the SOCIAL DEMOCRATS, and ruled in coalition with the SPÖ from 1945 to 1965. The party then ruled alone from 1966 to 1970. The core of its support comes from the urban middle classes and farmers. Although not a party member, DR KURT WALDHEIM was sponsored by the ÖVP in his controversial 1986 presidential election campaign. Under the leadership of Alois Mock the party has ruled in a new Grand Coalition with the SPÖ since November 1986.

M. Sully, *Political Parties and Elections in Austria* (1981)

**Austrian Republic.** The First Austrian Republic was declared by the remaining German members of the Austro–Hungarian Imperial Council on 12 November 1918 following the defeat and disintegration of the empire, the secession of the non-German nationalities, and the establishment of the SUCCESSOR STATES. The constitution of the new republic was determined by a constituent assembly which met the following

January. 'Rump' Austria was to become a federal state with nine relatively autonomous provinces (*Länder*), one of which was to be Vienna. The legislature was bicameral, with a lower house or national council (*Nationalrat*) elected on the basis of universal adult suffrage, and an upper house or Federal Council (*Bundesrat*) elected indirectly by the provincial diets. The President was elected by both houses in joint session. The constitution was progressively undermined and flouted by precarious conservative coalition governments from 1930, and replaced by a fascist 'corporate' constitution in 1934. This remained in force until Austria's absorption into the 'Greater German Reich' in 1938. The Second Republic, established in 1945, was based on a similar constitution. The president is now elected directly.

The First Republic was widely perceived by contemporaries as unviable. Where Austria–Hungary had been the third largest state in Europe the new republic was roughly comparable in area and population with Scotland. Grievances arose from the loss of German speakers in the South Tyrol to Italy (*see* SOUTH TYROL DISPUTE), and in the SUDETENLAND to Czechoslovakia. Important manufacturing centres in Bohemia were also lost, as was much of Vienna's agricultural hinterland in Hungary. The other successor states were latently hostile; Yugoslavia claimed and invaded parts of CARINTHIA, the secession of Vorarlberg to Switzerland was only narrowly avoided, and the BURGENLAND secured only with difficulty. The state itself was top-heavy, and dominated by a capital city which accounted for a quarter of the country's total population, and was now redundant as the political, administrative and cultural centre of Eastern Europe. The bold initiatives in municipal socialism developed by Vienna's socialist administration went against the political grain of the new republic and, although successful, generated a resentment among bourgeoisie and peasantry alike which contributed to the political destabilization of the new state.

Most of these problems have been avoided in the Second Republic, which has enjoyed a remarkable degree of political stability and economic prosperity. This domestic stability has been underpinned by

Austria's international position, based on the neutrality provided for in the AUSTRIAN STATE TREATY of 1955.

C. Gulick, *Austria from Habsburg to Hitler* (1948)
K. Stadler, *Austria* (1971)

**Austrian State Treaty.** Allied Foreign Ministers attempting to draw up an Austrian State Treaty repeatedly encountered the same problem: Soviet objections to proposals on the question of German assets in Austria. Although the Soviet Union had agreed with the western Allies to waive reparations demands from Austria itself, it insisted on compensation for the devastation of the Soviet economy by Germany through the confiscation of German assets in Austria. There were other stumbling blocks: the Soviets initially backed Yugoslav territorial claims in Styria and CARINTHIA (until Tito broke away from the Soviet bloc) and protested that former fascists were allowed to hold state office in Austria, and that neo-fascist organizations had been founded, notably the VDU.

It was an initiative of the SPÖ (*see* SOCIAL DEMOCRATIC WORKERS' PARTY, AUSTRIAN), offering Austrian neutrality in return for full independence, which finally overcame Soviet doubts and objections. Initially resisted by Austrian Conservatives, it had become the position of the Austrian government by the early 1950s and was discussed by the Berlin Conference of Allied Foreign Ministers in 1954, where neither the Soviet Union nor the western Allies were entirely happy with the prospect of a 'second Switzerland' as envisaged in Vienna. Allied objections were overcome, however, and the willingness of the ascendant Khrushchev regime to signal an end to Stalinist foreign policy ensured the first unconditional and voluntary Soviet withdrawal from occupied territory since 1945. The treaty was signed in Vienna on 15 May 1955.

**Austrofascism.** In general usage the term 'Austrofascist' has been applied both to the *Heimwehr* movement and to the dictatorship introduced by Chancellor ENGELBERT DOLLFUSS between 1932 and 1934. It was used in the latter sense by contemporary observers of both left and right, including President Miklas. While there has been general agreement about the fascist nature of the *Heimwehr* movement, particularly in the early 1930s, the fascist nature of the CORPORATE STATE (*Ständestaat*) has been disputed and qualified. Disagreements about the term are related to general difficulties of the comparative analysis of fascism.

Native Austrian fascism originated with the *Heimwehren*, paramilitary units formed to defend Austrian territory after the First World War, which quickly aligned themselves with the right. Following their role in the defeat of the general strike of 1927 the *Heimwehren* were increasingly seen by the right and its supporters as allies against the 'Bolshevism' of the SOCIAL DEMOCRATIC WORKERS' PARTY (SDAP). It is also during this period of political and economic crisis that *Heimwehr* ideology became more explicitly fascist. The movement attracted the attention, sympathy and support of both Hungary and Italy, and its fascist intentions were made clear by the KORNEUBURG OATH of 1930 and by an attempted *coup d'état* in 1931.

After the general election of 1930 the federal government itself – which now contained *Heimwehr* ministers – looked increasingly to radical authoritarian solutions to its political problems. It ruled by emergency decree from 1932, and suspended parliamentary government in 1933.

Following the AUSTRIAN CIVIL WAR of February 1934, all political parties were dissolved and replaced by the Fatherland Front, a 'patriotic' organization based on fascist models and founded in the previous year. This was now to form a mass party on the Italian and German models, but was to prove unsuccessful as a vehicle for popular mobilization. Parliamentary democracy was theoretically replaced by a corporative system (constitution promulgated May 1934), but the 'Corporate State' never properly functioned as such. The political system was essentially one of authoritarian rule from above, although the federal nature of the state was preserved for administrative purposes. A single government labour organization, the Unity Union (*Einheitsgewerkschaft*) replaced the trades unions, and in keeping with the radical anti-Marxism of both the *Heimwehr* and the CHRISTIAN SOCIAL PARTY (ÖVP) the organized left was driven underground or into exile.

*Heimwehr* leaders initially played a leading part in the new regime, but their influence waned considerably under Dollfuss's successor as chancellor, KURT VON SCHUSCHNIGG. The regime's propaganda referred frequently to Christianity, and the clerical conservativism of the ÖVP was as important an element as the influence of Italian and German fascism. But if the system was openly fascist in ideology and intention it did not live up to expectations, failing in particular in its belated attempt to create a nationalistic enthusiasm for Austria in a country with a weak sense of its own separate national identity which was persistently undermined by strong undercurrents of pan-German nationalism.

F. L. Carsten, *The Rise of Fascism* (1967)
——, *Fascist Movements in Austria from Schonerer to Hitler* (1977)
G. Earl Edmondson, *The Heimwehr and Austrian Politics, 1918–1936* (1978)
S. Larsen, J. P. Mykleburst and B. Hatvet, (eds), *Who Were the Fascists?* (1979)

**Aventine secession.** *See* MATTEOTI CRISIS.

**Axis.** A term first used by MUSSOLINI in Milan on 1 November 1936 to describe the relationship between Nazi Germany and Fascist Italy established by the October Protocols of 1936. Mussolini said of the 'Berlin–Rome Line' that it was 'not a diaphragm but rather an axis'. Italy acceded to the German–Japanese ANTI-COMINTERN PACT on 25 November 1936; in May 1939 Germany and Italy entered into a formal alliance, the PACT OF STEEL. On 27 September 1940 Germany, Italy and Japan signed a TRIPARTITE PACT. During the SECOND WORLD WAR the term 'Axis Powers' was applied to the three countries and their East European allies: Bulgaria, Hungary, Romania and Slovakia.

E. Wiskemann, *The Rome–Berlin Axis* (1949)
F. W. Deakin, *The Brutal Friendship* (1966)

**Azaña, Manuel** (1881–1940). Spanish politician. He studied law at Madrid and Paris and entered the civil service, as well as becoming a journalist. He founded a Republican Party in 1924 but it was suppressed and he was briefly imprisoned. He became Minister of War in 1931 and then Prime Minister in October as the head of a broad coalition of forces that ranged from the socialists to moderate Republicans. Azaña's ambitious programme of political, social and economic reforms, at first apparently successful, ultimately proved too unsettling, both to his own coalition and to outside forces. He resigned in September 1933; while in opposition he was accused of fomenting an insurrection in Barcelona in 1934, but exonerated. The major figure in inspiring the new leftist coalition that came to be called the Popular Front, he again became Prime Minister after its electoral victory of 16 February 1936. In office, he speeded up the pace of reform in a desperate bid to satisfy the increasingly revolutionary working class movements. Becoming President of the Republic on 10 May 1936, he remained head of state during the SPANISH CIVIL WAR but could not satisfy the divergent groupings which fell increasingly under communist control. He made attempts to seek a negotiated peace in 1938, retaining the presidency only in the hope of salvaging a compromise with FRANCO, dying a year later. The basically irrelevant role he played during the war contrasted sharply with his place in the peacetime Republic.

More than any other figure, he shaped the aspirations of the progressive periods (1931–3 and February to July 1936) of that regime. *See also* SECOND REPUBLIC, SPANISH.

F. Sedwick, *The Tragedy of Manuel Azaña* (1963)

**Azerbaijan.** Largely Moslem region of south-west Russia, it declared independence in 1918 but in 1920 was proclaimed a Soviet Socialist Republic. In 1922 it became with Georgia and Armenia part of the TRANSCAUCASIAN FEDERATED REPUBLIC. In 1936 it became a separate Union republic of the USSR. Its boundaries include the disputed Christian enclave of NGORNO-KARABAKH, the scene of serious ethnic rioting in 1988–9. Demands from ARMENIA to redraw the boundaries of Azerbaijan and return Ngorno-Karabakh to its pre-1917 status as part of Armenia remain unfulfilled. As a result, Azerbaijan remained pro-Moscow under its hardline President Ayaz Mutalibov with no clear plans for independence. His identification with the leaders of the August coup in Moscow threatened an internal power struggle in autumn 1991. *See also* NATIONALITIES QUESTION, SOVIET.

# B

**Babi Yar.** Ravine near Kiev where SS EIN-SATZGRUPPEN were responsible for the massacre, in September 1941, of over 30,000 Jews from the Kiev area, including many of the leading figures of the Ukrainian intelligentsia. One of the largest mass slaughters of the Second World War, it formed part of a policy of systematic liquidation of Jews and others carried out by Nazi forces in the wake of the advancing German armies. After the Second World War the massacre of Babi Yar was used as a symbol of the need to speak out against anti-Semitism, celebrated in a famous poem by the Soviet poet Yevgeny Yevtushenko. *See also* HOLOCAUST.

**Bad Godesberg programme.** *See* SOCIAL DEMOCRATIC PARTY, GERMAN.

**Badoglio, Pietro** (1871–1956). Italian soldier and politician. Born in Piedmont, he was commissioned in the artillery and fought in Ethopia in 1896, in Libya in 1911–12, and in the First World War as a General on the Isonzo front, helping to stabilize the front after the defeat at Caporetto in 1917. He was Chief of Staff, 1919–21, Ambassador to Brazil, 1924–5, and was promoted Field Marshal in 1925. He served as Chief of the General Staff until 1928 when he became Governor-General of Libya, conducting through RODOLFO GRAZIANI a fierce campaign against rebel forces led by Omar el Muktar, in which an estimated 60,000 died. He left Libya in December 1933. Initially opposed to the Ethiopian war (*see* ETHIOPIAN CRISIS), he was appointed to succeed Emilio de Bono when the campaign bogged down in November 1935. After initial reverses, by extensive use of artillery, airpower and poison gas he defeated the Ethiopians at Mai Chew in March 1936 and

entered Addis Ababa on 5 May. He served briefly as Viceroy of Ethiopia before returning to Italy. Appointed Chief of Staff in June 1940, he resigned following the failures in the campaign in Greece on 4 December 1940. From mid-1942 he began to make soundings as a possible replacement to MUSSOLINI, and upon Mussolini's arrest on 25 July 1943 he was appointed Chief of Government by the King. He attempted to assure the Germans that the war would be continued while treating with the Western Allies. An armistice was concluded on 8 September and he fled with the King to the Allied lines, but gave no opportunity for the Italian armies to resist being disarmed by the Germans. As a result the Germans maintained a hold over the bulk of the Italian peninsula and were able to deny the Allies entry to Rome until June 1944. He retired into private life shortly thereafter.

**Balbo, Italo** (1896–1940). Italian politician and aviator. One of the major fascist leaders, Balbo was brought up in a Republican background, serving as a lieutenant in the First World War and took a degree in political science at the University of Florence in the immediate post-war period. He accepted appointment as the political secretary of the FASCI DI COMBATTIMENTO in Ferrara, organizing them on military lines and suppressing the local socialist groups with his fascist squads. He was one of the four-man *quadrumvir* charged with organizing the MARCH ON ROME, with special responsibility for the Fascist Militia. After MUSSOLINI's accession to power he remained head of the Militia, but was forced to resign in 1923 after fascist thugs killed a priest. He founded a newspaper, *Il Corriere Padano*, before rejoining the government first as under-secretary (1926–9) then minister (1929–33) of aviation. He led aviators in spectacular transatlantic flights which earned him international celebrity and helped to raise the prestige of Italian aviation. His plans for strengthening the air force and the navy in 1933 were rebuffed by Mussolini, who instead appointed him governor of Libya where he energetically developed Italian colonization, road construction and infrastructure. In January 1939, the four coastal provinces were declared part of Italy, but his plans to integrate the whole of the Libyan population into the Italian state was blocked in Rome. He openly opposed close links with Germany, anti-semitic legislation, and entry into the war, but in June 1940 loyally accepted command of the Italian forces in North Africa. He was killed in error by Italian batteries when flying over Tobruk.

P. Corner, *Fascism in Ferrara* (1975)

**Baldwin, Stanley** (1867–1947). British politician. Conservative MP for his father's old constituency of Bewdley, Worcs. from 1908 to 1937. In 1917 he became joint financial secretary to the Treasury and held that post until 1921. He was President of the Board of Trade, 1921–2, and Chancellor of the Exchequer, 1922–3. He served as prime minister, 1923–4 and 1924–9. From 1931 to 1935 he sat in the NATIONAL GOVERNMENT as Lord President of the Council, and in 1932–3 was also Lord Privy Seal. His final term as Prime Minister ran from June 1935 to 1937, when he resigned. In 1937 he was created an earl. In many ways Baldwin's achievements as Premier were considerable. He succeeded in uniting a divided party and in pursuing a successful electoral course in the inter-war years. Some controversy surrounds his role in the GENERAL STRIKE, where it is not clear to what extent he deliberately allowed the TUC to manoeuvre themselves into an impossible position in which they had to call a strike and were then defeated. His moderation after the strike was important, but his handling of foreign policy has been heavily criticized, primarily for failing to warn the public early enough of the need for rearmament and for a policy of drift and APPEASEMENT to the aggression of MUSSOLINI and HITLER. He had considerable ill-will directed against him in the early years of the war as one of those who had left Britain unarmed. In fact, some rearmament did take place, especially in the air force and navy. In economic matters he concentrated on orthodox policies, designed to ensure 'natural recovery'. These did bring recovery by the mid-1930s, but with a legacy of bitterness that nothing more urgent had been done. Beneath the image he cultivated of an avuncular, pipe-smoking man of the people, Baldwin was a tough-minded Conservative, determined to destroy the LIBERAL PARTY and defeat socialism. *See also* CONSERVATIVE AND UNIONIST PARTY; NATIONAL GOVERNMENT.

J. Barnes and K. Middlemass, *Baldwin* (1969)
J. Ramsden, *The Age of Balfour and Baldwin, 1902–40* (1978)

**Balfour, Arthur James** (1848–1930). British politician. Balfour was Conservative MP for Hertford, 1874–85, for Manchester East, 1885–1906, and for the City of London, 1906–22. He was created an earl in 1922. Balfour served as Parliamentary Private Secretary to his uncle, Lord Salisbury, 1878–80. In 1885 he was President of the Local Government Board and in 1886 was Secretary for Scotland. He was Chief Secretary for Ireland, 1887–91, and leader of the Commons and First Lord of the Treasury, 1891–2 and 1895–1902. He became Prime Minister in 1902, resigning in 1905. He resigned the leadership of the Conservative Party in 1911. In 1914 he was made a member of the Committee of Imperial Defence and attended meetings of the War Cabinet, 1914–15. He served as First Lord of the Admiralty, 1915–16 and as Foreign Secretary, 1916–19. He was Lord President of the Council, 1919–22 and 1925–9. A well-connected Conservative, Balfour proved a highly intelligent and able administrator in most offices. After the Liberal government's reform of the House of Lords, accusations of ineffectuality and nepotism helped persuade Balfour to resign the leadership. Best known in international circles for the BALFOUR DECLARATION, giving assurances of a Jewish homeland in Palestine.

J. Ramsden, *The Age of Balfour and Baldwin, 1902–40* (1978)

**Balfour Declaration.** Document crucial to the Jewish claims to Palestine. In a letter of 2 November 1917 to the British Zionist leader Lord Rothschild, ARTHUR BALFOUR, the Foreign Secretary, stated Great Britain's support for the establishment of a Jewish national home in Palestine. It included the provision that nothing should be done to prejudice the civil and religious rights of the non-Jewish communities in the area. The letter's terms were incorporated into Britain's LEAGUE OF NATIONS mandate for Palestine (*see* MANDATES). *See also* WEIZMANN, CHAIM; ZIONISM.

L. Stein, *The Balfour Declaration* (1961)
H. W. Sachar, *History of Israel: From the Rise of Zionism to Our Own Time* (1985)

**Balkan Pacts.** Attempts to bring the Balkan countries into a mutual agreement occurred in 1933, sponsored by King ALEXANDER I of Yugoslavia, who proposed a Pact involving Yugoslavia, Romania, Greece, Turkey and Bulgaria. The Bulgarians refused to join when the Pact was formed in February 1934. The Pact evolved into a Balkan Entente with a permanent council and arrangements for regular conferences, but was broken up by aggressive actions of the AXIS powers, Italy and Germany. Following the Second War War, TITO showed an interest in reviving the idea, but was limited in scope by the COLD WAR and the non-participation of the Eastern bloc countries. A second Balkan Pact was formed at Bled in August 1954 between Yugoslavia, Greece and Turkey. The Pact became defunct with the growing hostility between Greece and Turkey over CYPRUS.

**Baltic States.** Estonia, Latvia and Lithuania. Part of the Russian empire prior to 1917, each territory supported separatist movements following the February revolution, but rivalries between Bolshevik and non-Bolshevik groupings had not been resolved when the German forces advanced into the area following the breakdown of the negotiations at Brest-Litovsk (*see* BREST-LITOVSK, TREATIES OF). Following the conclusion of the treaty Lithuania and Latvia were formally removed from Russian control. An Estonian Republic was proclaimed in February 1918, a Latvian Republic in November, and a Lithuanian Republic in the same year, but they were challenged by pro-Bolshevik elements backed by the RED ARMY. The Baltic States were the scene of confused fighting between anti-Bolshevik forces, backed by German troops up to and beyond the armistice of November 1918, and the Red Army. The Soviet Union recognized the independence of the Estonian Republic on 2 February 1920; of Latvia at the Treaty of Riga in August 1920, and of Lithuania at the Treaty of Moscow in July 1920. Recognized by the great powers as independent states, the Baltic Republics pursued their independent courses between the world wars. Primarily agricultural, Estonia saw the break-up of its large estates after independence and the development of a prosperous peasant agriculture. A centre for White Russian emigrés, it was subject to a dictatorial regime under Konstantin Paets, from 1934 to 1940. Latvia became a virtual dictatorship in May 1934 under Prime Minister Karlis Ulmanis, President from 1936. Lithuania was in a particularly vulnerable position, with disputes over Vilna with Poland (*see* VILNA DISPUTE) and over MEMEL with Germany.

The future of the Baltic States was determined by the secret protocol of the NAZI–SOVIET PACT in August 1939 which placed them in the Russian sphere of influence and allowed the Soviet Union a free hand with them. Following the German invasion of Poland in September 1939 and the occupation of eastern Poland by Soviet troops two weeks later, the Baltic States were forced to accept Soviet occupation by a series of mutual assistance treaties signed with Estonia on 5 October and with Latvia and Lithuania on 10 October. High-ranking Soviet officials were despatched to supervise the destruction of the independence of the Baltic States and the election of puppet pro-Soviet governments who 'requested' incorporation into the Soviet Union in June–July 1940; in August 1940 they became constituent republics of the USSR. During the course of the ensuing year a full programme of Sovietization was introduced, including the nationalization of land, industry and finance, the purging of cultural institutions and education of national influences, and the forced deportation in June 1941 of over 100,000 of the most prominent Estonians, Latvians and Lithuanians to exile and forced labour in the Soviet Union. The German invasion of the Soviet Union led to anti-Soviet risings in the Baltic States, but the advancing German forces did not seek to re-establish their separate identity. Following their re-occupation in 1944, the Soviet Union continued the Sovietization campaign begun in 1940–41. Agriculture was collectivized in 1949 and further deportations of KULAKS, collaborators and nationalists occurred. Groups of anti-Soviet partisans remained active until the early 1950s.

Since the upheaval of the war years, the Baltic States have undergone considerable change. Industrialization and an influx of Russian-speakers have significantly altered their character. But RUSSIFICATION was balanced in the post-Stalin period by the reawakening of national cultures under the protection of local party secretaries. In 1971 an Estonian National Front was set up with an underground journal and in 1980 there were demonstrations against Russian influence. A Lithuanian National Popular Front emerged in 1974, also demanding greater cultural and political autonomy and a 'maximum programme' calling for a plebiscite on independence. Following the accession of GORBACHEV to power nationalist movements were accelerated. In August 1987 there were mass demonstrations in the capitals of Lithuania, Latvia and Estonia protesting against 'Russification' and demanding greater autonomy and the right of separation. A key demand in Latvia was the publication of the secret protocol of the Nazi–Soviet Pact, implicitly reopening the question of the nature of the incorporation of the independent states into the USSR. By 1988 all three republics had popular front movements expressing with various degrees of strength the desire for greater autonomy. Although Gorbachev had indicated that full independence might ultimately be granted, the Baltic States opened the question of the right to secession, and in December 1989 the Lithuanian Soviet voted to end the 'leading role' of the Communist Party, the first Soviet Republic to do so. Its nationalist Sajudis Movement, founded in 1988, ran 150 candidates in the elections in early 1990, obtaining an overall majority for substantial change. On 11 March 1990 the Lithuanian Supreme Council voted in favour of a declaration of indepenedence and elected a non-communist, Vytautas Landsbergis, as the Republic's first President. The Soviet Union reacted by declaring an economic blockade, forcing negotiations over a more orderly progress to autonomy. Estonia and Latvia proceeded more cautiously, but both installed nationalist majorities in elections in March 1990. In the autumn and winter of 1990–91, relations with the Soviet government were hardened by armed clashes between Soviet forces and pro-nationalist elements leading to several deaths. The failed coup in Moscow of August 1991 ended Soviet resistance to independence. Estonia, Latvia and Lithuania becoming fully independent states by early September. *See also* NATIONALITIES QUESTION, SOVIET.

G. von Rauch, *The Baltic States: The Years of Independence, 1917–40* (1974)

R. Misiunas and R. Taageera, *The Baltic States: The Years of Dependence, 1940–80* (1983)

**Basic Treaty.** Signed on 21 December 1972 as a treaty of friendship and mutual recognition between the FEDERAL REPUBLIC OF GERMANY and the GERMAN DEMOCRATIC REPUBLIC. The outcome of West German Chancellor BRANDT's OSTPOLITIK, it was followed by the entry of both states into the UNITED NATIONS in the following year.

**Basques.** A people of northern Spain and south-western France with a distinct language and culture. Their ancient 'capital' is the city of GUERNICA, but the largest centres of population are on the Biscay coast, notably the city of Bilbao. Frequently in conflict with the central government of Spain, the Spanish Basques developed a strong sense of national identity and growing self-confidence with the industrial development of northern Spain at the end of the 19th century and formed the Partide Nationalista Vasco (PNV). Under its leader José Antonio Aquirre (1904–60), the PNV developed into a mass movement in the 1930s, drawing support from the million-strong Basque community and demanding almost complete autonomy for the three Basque provinces of Vizcaya, Guipuzcoa, and Alava and Navarre. Reflecting the strong Catholic traditions of the area, the party's programme was Christian democratic in other spheres. The Nationalists, however, had to share support in the region with left-wing groupings and the Carlists (*see* CARLISM): in 1936 obtaining under a third of the votes over the four provinces. The party supported the Republic as attempts were made to draw up a plan for autonomy. Three proposals failed and the fourth was in discussion when the SPANISH CIVIL WAR broke out, it was finally brought into effect in October 1936 when Aquirre was elected President of the Basque Republic of Euzkadi.

Although considerable sections of the Basque population, particularly in Navarre, supported the Carlists and the anti-Republican revolt, the Left and Basque nationalists supported the Republic. Aquirre's Republic had barely time to organize itself before being overwhelmed by the Nationalist forces. Apart from Vizcaya, most of the three provinces allotted to the new Republic had been overrun by October 1936. Poorly armed and equipped, the Basques prepared to defend Vizcaya and the port and industrial hinterland of Bilbao by a defensive line, the *cinturon de hierro*. On 31 March 1937 General MOLA launched the Army of the North against the Basques, aided by Italian artillery and the CONDOR LEGION. The latter carried out the bombing attack which destroyed Guernica on 27 April. Seven weeks of fighting saw the breach of the Basque defences on 11 June and the fall of Bilbao a week later. Although the Euzkadi Republic was extinguished, Aquirre attempted to keep alive a Basque government-in-exile in Catalonia and later in France.

FRANCO suppressed all nationalist organizations and stripped all autonomy from the Basque heartland of Vizcaya and Guipuzcoa. Under the dictatorship Basque nationalism was forced underground, developing a terrorist wing, the Euzkadi Ta Askatasuna (ETA), which operated from the early 1960s. By the early 1970s Basque terrorism was a major destabilizing force with several hundred people killed in over a decade of incidents, culminating on 20 December 1973 with the assassination of Admiral Luis Carrero Blanco, Franco's Prime Minister, in Madrid.

The death of Franco and the accession of King JUAN CARLOS in November 1975 allowed demands for Basque autonomy to re-emerge publicly but progress in satisfying them was accompanied by continuing terrorism by an ETA movement which drew upon links with international terrorist groups. In December 1977 the Spanish government introduced 'pre-autonomy' systems in anticipation of setting up a more federal system of government. Discontent with the extent of autonomy being allowed led to a fresh wave of ETA murders and severe police counter-measures. Although the main Basque parties eventually announced their willingness to accept autonomy within the Spanish state and denounced terror, ETA and its political wing, the Koordinatora Abertzale Sozialista, still insisted on complete independence. Negotiations by Premier Suarez with the Basque Nationalist Party in July 1979 led to an autonomy statute which provided the Basques with their own legislature and judiciary and control over the police, judiciary and taxation. The Basque parliament was opened in March 1980, but ETA has remained unreconciled, continuing a campaign of terror against the Spanish army and police through its three sub-organizations, ETA-Militar, ETA-Politico-Militar and the Comandos Autonomos. Its strategy of provoking a right-wing backlash by the Spanish authorities, thereby destabilizing the state, has failed to materialize. Greater prosperity, Spanish membership of the EEC and NATO, plus the granting of virtually complete autonomy has left the extremists with less discontent upon which to work. The current political front organization for ETA, the Herri Batasuna, won five seats in the 1986 Spanish elections,

S. G. Payne, *Basque Nationalism* (1975)
R. Clark, *The Basques* (1979)
M. Heilburg, *The Making of the Baroque Nation* (1990)

**Bauer, Otto** (1881–1938). Austrian politician. Born in Vienna, Bauer studied law, philosophy and politics at the university and was an early contributor to Marxist theoretical debate. He published his first major work, on the Habsburg nationalities and Social Democracy, at the age of 26. In the same year (1907) he became parliamentary secretary of the AUSTRIAN SOCIAL DEMOCRATIC WORKERS' PARTY (SDAP) and co-founded the party journal *Der Kampf*. Although on the left of the party, he was an opponent of Bolshevik revolution on the Russian model, and served briefly as Foreign Minister in the Grand Coalition government which took power in Austria after the First World War. Bauer led the SDAP during its long period of opposition in the 1920s. He fled to Brno in 1934, and later to Paris, where he died in 1938.

**BBC.** *See* BRITISH BROADCASTING CORPORATION

**BEF.** *See* BRITISH EXPEDITIONARY FORCE

**Belgian language question.** A conflictive issue during the interwar and immediate postwar period, the language question moved towards resolution in the 1970s. Tension between French-speaking Walloons and Dutch-speaking Flemings which had led to rioting, brought about a revision of the Belgian Constitution by laws of 24 December 1970 and 28 July 1971, establishing three regions and two cultural councils. Laws for preparatory regionalization were enacted in July 1974. The Regionalization Law in 1980 made provision for three regional parliaments with executive councils, becoming effective in January 1982. The executives are autonomous from the central government, preparing legislation for their respective regions. Brussels was defined as a region of its own, but has no executive council. Dutch is the official language of the Flemish Region and French of the Walloon area. Most political parties have subsequently divided on linguistic lines.
S. Clough, *History of the Flemish Movement in Belgium* (1930)

**Belorussia.** Area of western Russia and eastern Poland inhabited by East Slavic peoples with their own language and literature. Prior to 1914 they were subject to a particularly harsh process of RUSSIFICATION, their language suppressed, their distinctive Uniate Church merged with the Russian Orthodox, and name changed to 'West Russia'. Only slight relaxation had taken place by 1914 before Belorussia was swept into the turmoil of war and revolution. In 1918 Belorussia was occupied by the Germans and a puppet Belorussian Republic created. By the terms of the Treaty of Riga in 1921 Belorussia was divided into a Soviet Belorussian Republic with 80 per cent of the population (about 4 million people) and Polish Western Belorussia. Generous treatment by the early Soviet government sought to encourage Belorussian loyalty to the Soviet Union, of which it became a constituent republic in 1924. From 1929, however, under STALIN, virtually the whole Belorussian national leadership was purged and executed as 'bourgeois nationalists' or 'Polish spies', the culture suppressed, and agriculture collectivized. Former Polish Belorussia formed part of the Soviet sphere of influence agreed between the Nazis and the Soviet Union in the secret clauses of the NAZI–SOVIET PACT of 1939. With the German invasion of Poland the Soviet armies occupied western Belorussia, forcibly deporting up to a million people before the Nazi invasion in 1941. As in the UKRAINE many Belorussians welcomed the German invaders as liberators, but were quickly alienated by harsh Nazi rule, including forced labour in Germany. The redrawing of the Polish–Soviet frontier in 1945 brought all former Polish Belorussia within the boundaries of the Soviet Union. *See also* POLAND; SECOND WORLD WAR.
N. P. Vakar, *Belorussia: The Making of a Nation* (1956)
R. Pearson, *National Minorities in Eastern Europe, 1848–1945* (1983)

**Benedict XV, Pope** (1854–1922). Pope, 1914–22. Born Giacomo Della Chiesa in Genoa, he studied at the University of Genoa, then in Rome. He was ordained in 1878 and became a Vatican diplomat. In 1907 he became Archbishop of Bologna and was made a Cardinal in May 1914. He was chosen Pope on 3 September 1914. Concerned about the fate of the Catholic powers in Europe during the First World War, he attempted to restrain Italy from intervening, using his position to encourage negotiations between Italy and Austro–Hungary. A peace appeal was made on 1 August 1917 after background diplomacy had indicated some hopes of progress, but the intensification of the war prevented it from having any success. He was not invited to send a representative to the PARIS PEACE CONFERENCE, but turned his attention to bolstering anti-communist forces in Italy. He stimulated the formation of the Catholic lay movement, Catholic Action, and agreed to the formation of a Christian Democratic party, the PARTITO POPOLARE ITALIANO (PPI) in January 1919, the first mass political party in Italy backed by the Church. After the party had enjoyed initial success, the Vatican undermined its independence, creating divisions within it as early as 1920. Nonetheless, by lifting the ban on Catholic participation in national politics, Benedict had opened the way to the creation of a powerful electoral force in Italian politics. He also · encouraged the formation of Christian 'White' unions to combat left-wing trade union influence. He died on 22 January 1922.

C. Seton-Watson, *Italy from Liberalism to Fascism, 1870–1925* (1967)

**Benelux.** Belgium, the Netherlands and Luxembourg. Specifically, the economic union between these three countries, begun by the Benelux Customs Convention, signed by the governments-in-exile in 1944, which from 1948 abolished all customs duties between the three countries and instituted a common external tariff. In 1958 a treaty establishing the Benelux economic union was signed in the Hague; this provided for free movement of persons, goods, capital and services, and for co-ordination of economic and social policies. A number of institutions, including an Inter-Parliamentary Consultative Council and a College of Arbitration were established by this treaty. The union has lessened in importance with the development of policies common to the whole EUROPEAN ECONOMIC COMMUNITY.

**Benes, Eduard** (1884–1948). Czechoslovak statesmen. Born into peasant family in Bohemia, he was educated at Prague and in France, where he obtained a law doctorate at Dijon in 1908. In 1912 he took a post in the sociology department at Prague University. Already prominent in Czech national politics, he joined with TOMAS MASARYCK in opposing Austrian rule. In 1915 he went to Paris and helped to raise support for the Czech cause. Appointed general secretary to the Czech national council the same year, he saw it recognized as the pro-visional government of Czechoslovakia in 1918. He served as principal Czech representative at the PARIS PEACE CONFERENCE and was Foreign Minister, 1918–35, in which his major efforts were in building up the LITTLE ENTENTE and developing close ties with France and the Soviet Union. Prime Minister, 1921–2, he returned to the office on the death of Masaryk. He felt bitterly betrayed by the MUNICH AGREEMENT, resigning office and going into exile. In 1940 he became head of a Czechoslovakian provisional government in London, only receiving recognition in July 1941. He agreed to Soviet backing for the new Czech government in order to rid the country of the Sudeten Germans after the war. He returned to Czechoslovakia via Moscow with the Soviet-backed Czech forces under General Svoboda. He was re-elected President in June 1946 and attempted to maintain his independence as the communists under GOTTWALD seized power in February 1948. He resigned on 7 June 1948, recognizing a Communist *fait accompli*. He died three months later.

E. Benes, *My War Memoirs* (1928)
C. D. Mackenzie, *Dr Benes* (1946)
J. W. Bruegel, *Czechoslovakia before Munich* (1973)

**Berchtesgaden.** Town in southern Bavaria where Hitler built his show-piece retreat, the 'Eagles' Nest', where he entertained foreign visitors and held a number of pre-war and wartime conferences. Visited by Chancellor SCHUSCHNIGG prior to the ANSCHLUSS and by Chamberlain during the MUNICH CRISIS on 15 September 1938, the retreat was increasingly forsaken for the military headquarters in East Prussia, the 'Wolf's Lair', and the command bunker in Berlin. Berchtesgaden was considered as the centre for a 'National Redoubt' held by fanatical Nazis as Germany collapsed in 1945, but the plans never materialized. The area was captured by General LECLERC. The complex was destroyed to prevent it becoming a site for neo-Nazi revival.

**Beria, Lavrenti** (1899–1953). Georgian communist and head of the Soviet security services under Stalin. He joined the Bolshevik Party in 1917, organizing a Bolshevik group in Baku, then worked for the CHEKA and GPU (*see* GPU) in Transcaucasia against anti-Bolshevik forces, eventually becoming first secretary of the Georgian Communist Party. As a fellow Georgian he gained the support of STALIN, and at the height of the PURGES in December 1938 he was appointed head of NKVD (*see* NKVD) as Commissar for Internal Affairs, a position he retained until after Stalin's death. He also served as Deputy Prime Minister, 1941–53, and was created a Marshal of the Soviet Union in 1945. After Stalin's death in March 1953 he became First Deputy Premier, but was viewed with widespread suspicion because of his part in Stalin's terror and his apparent attempt to succeed Stalin by building up his own power base through the security apparatus. In July 1953 it was announced that he had been dismissed from office and in December that he had been tried and executed as an 'imperialist agent'. Beria played a sinister part in abetting Stalin's obsessive search for new enemies. As a veteran hunter of anti-Bolshevik and nationalist opponents in Transcaucasia, he turned his attention to the deportation of people from the Baltic States and eastern Poland from 1940–1 and supervised the security police in the satellite states of Eastern Europe after 1945. Although some of the stories about his behaviour were exaggerated (for example, he was accused of hastening Stalin's death), he undoubtedly shared the vindictive and suspicious qualities which helped to maintain Stalin's terror. In the immediate aftermath of Stalin's death he proved a convenient scapegoat to account for Stalin's 'excesses'. A more realistic assessment is that the purges were under way when he was appointed to head the NKVD, and that he was seen as a willing and compliant lieutenant to Stalin, who showed little scruple or ideological concern in his pursuit of personal aggrandizement. He does appear to have called a halt to the great purge of 1937–8 which had reached increasingly destructive levels. *See also* KGB.

R. Conquest, *The Great Terror* (1968)

**Berlin, Battle of.** See SECOND WORLD WAR.

**Berlin Airlift.** Air supply operation to the blockaded Western sectors of Berlin from June 1948 to May 1949, one of the first major confrontations of the COLD WAR.

Growing tension between the former wartime allies over the future of Germany became focused on Berlin, 100 miles within the Soviet zone, jointly administered by Britain, France, the United States and the Soviet Union, and divided into four zones mirroring the division of Germany. An election held in the city in autumn 1946 had already decided against the fusion of the socialist and communist parties as had happened throughout the Soviet zone, with the effect that Berlin remained a non-communist outpost and an important symbol for the Western powers of the survival of a 'free' Germany. Access to Berlin from the Western zone was guaranteed along specified road, rail and air routes upon which it was easy for the Soviet Union to put pressure, threatening a decisive defeat for the Western powers if they were unable to maintain their presence and the surrender of the whole of Berlin to Soviet control, possibly precipitating the loss of Germany as a whole to the Eastern bloc.

The demarcation of Germany into two spheres was, however, increasingly evident, emphasized by the American offer in 1947 of economic aid through the MARSHALL PLAN to the whole of Europe, including the Western zones of Germany, and Stalin's refusal to allow the Eastern European countries, including the Soviet zone of Germany, to participate. Plans for the economic recovery of Germany provided the immediate cause of the crisis when disputes arose with the Soviets over currency reform. Soviet refusal to agree to proposals in the winter of 1947–8 led Britain, France and the United States agreeing to go it alone in the Western sectors, leading in March 1948 to the walk-out of the Soviet delegation from the Allied Control Council, the military government of Germany (*see* GERMANY, ALLIED OCCUPATION OF), and a Soviet declaration two days later that the Council had ceased to function. A few days later the first Western trains on their way to Berlin were stopped and turned back.

As access was further restricted the situation escalated into a full-blown crisis over the ability of the West to sustain West Berlin. In June the restrictions had turned into an almost complete blockade of land routes to Berlin across the Soviet zone of East Germany. The decision was taken to organize a massive airlift to supply the city. The USAF began 'Operation Vittles' followed shortly by the RAF's 'Operation Plainfare' to provide a constant shuttle of planes via the three air corridors across East Germany to the Berlin airfields of Tegel, Gatow and Tempelhof. By mid-July 1,500 tons were being carried every day under the united command of Major-General William Turner, who had directed the airlift 'over the Hump' from India to China in 1944. Within Berlin the West Berliners had to prepare to withstand a possible Soviet putsch, organizing mass demonstrations of Social Democrats, and their mayor and deputy mayor resisting Soviet harassment designed to permit the third deputy mayor, a Soviet supporter, to take office.

By September it was clear that the airlift could keep Berlin adequately supplied. The Soviets responded by effectively cutting the city in two. The Soviets had withdrawn from the quadripartite government of Berlin on 1 July 1948 and thereafter systematically obstructed access to the municipal offices in the Soviet Sector of Berlin. On 30 November 1948 a separate Municipal Government was set up in East Berlin which was later declared the capital of East Germany when the GERMAN DEMOCRATIC REPUBLIC came into existence on 7 October 1949.

The airlift was continued throughout the winter of 1948–9. In all 2.3 million tons of supplies were brought in, the record being set on 16 April 1949 when 1,400 aircraft landed in West Berlin with 12,940 tons. Eventually, in May 1949, the Soviets called off the blockade, the first road convoys arriving on 12 May, although the airlift continued through into September. Although talks were resumed over the future of Germany, the unification of the Western zones into a single, federal state, the FEDERAL REPUBLIC OF GERMANY was ratified on 21 September 1949. The Soviet response was the promulgation of a constitution for the German Democratic Republic with East Berlin as its capital.

In practice the blockade and airlift to Berlin marked the effective end to attempts by either the West or the Soviet Union to reunify Germany as part of the post-war settlement. It consolidated the line of division between the Soviet zone of occupation and the rest of Germany, and demonstrated the willingness of the West and the Berliners themselves to sustain West Berlin as a 'free' enclave. The Soviet response to divide the city was an acceptance that any further restriction of the blockade or interference with West Berlin would lead to war. The blockade therefore brought a settlement of the German question on the basis of a divided Germany. In Cold War propaganda the blockade and airlift was to elevate Berlin into the symbol of resistance to communist advance in Europe, and the scene of further, if lesser, confrontations over access.

W. Phillips Davison, *The Berlin Blockade* (1974)

**Berlin    Uprising.**    *See*    EAST    GERMAN WORKERS' UPRISING.

**Berlin Wall.** A set of fortified barriers dividing the former German capital, erected in 1961 and breached in 1989. The background to the construction of the Wall lay in the division of Germany after 1945 into two separate states and the status of Berlin as a city whose government was deemed ultimately to be the responsibility of the four powers which had occupied Germany in 1945. During the occupation, Berlin acted as a route for those seeking to leave the Soviet zone of occupation and, later, the GERMAN DEMOCRATIC REPUBLIC for the zones occupied by the Western allies and, subsequently, the FEDERAL REPUBLIC OF GERMANY. Isolated within the German Democratic Republic, Berlin was a potential flashpoint for tension between the superpowers and their associated allies during the COLD WAR.

The steady exodus through Berlin to the Federal Republic after the failure of the Soviet blockade of the city and the BERLIN AIRLIFT of 1948 imposed a serious strain on the economy of the German Democratic Republic. In November 1958 KRUSHCHEV demanded a rapid solution to the problematic status of Berlin, a demand which was repeated with growing intensity in the succeeding two years. The combination of mounting Soviet threats to the continued independence of the Western sectors of the city and the introduction of radical collectivization policies in the German Democratic Republic from 1959 onwards led to a dramatic upsurge in the number of those fleeing to the Federal Republic via Berlin. Between January and August 1961 155,000 East Germans registered as West German citizens in Berlin, bringing to over 3 million the number who had fled from the area of Germany which had been occupied by the Soviet Union in 1945.

Early on 13 August 1961 the East German government acted to stem the mounting population loss, blocking many of the street crossings between the two areas of the city, cutting telephone links and closing down public transport connections with the exception of one tightly-policed transit point. Whilst the East German authorities made no attempt to interfere with the road and rail links between West Berlin and the Federal Republic, in the following months the initial barriers dividing the city and isolating West Berlin from the German Democratic Republic were elaborated and extended. The construction of the Wall led to important changes in the status of East Berlin, control of which the Soviet Union now handed over to the East German government. The Wall also facilitated stabilization of the East German regime, which was now able to pursue markedly more repressive policies in the knowledge that the principal escape route hitherto open to its citizens had been blocked. Throughout the period from 1961 to 1989, however, East Germans continued to attempt to flee the German Democratic Republic via Berlin, hundreds being killed in the attempt. The Wall came to assume ideological importance as a symbol of the divided state of Europe in the post-war period, a symbolic importance which was confirmed by US President KENNEDY's visit to Berlin and to the Wall in June 1963.

The liberalization of the Polish and Hungarian regimes in 1989, and their willingness to allow East Germans to travel direct to the Federal Republic, effectively negated the function of the Wall as a barrier to emigration from the German Democratic Republic. By early November 1989 1.3 million East Germans had applied to emigrate. Faced by the refusal of their WARSAW PACT allies to stand in the way of emigration through their territories, the East German government opened a number of transit points in the Berlin Wall on 9 November, in the hope that a voluntary concession of freedom to travel would curtail emigration through other Warsaw Pact states. By early January 1990 the East German government agreed to the demolition of the remainder of the Wall, an action soon overtaken by the reunification of East and West Germany. *See also* GERMANY, ALLIED OCCUPATION OF; HONECKER, ERICH; OSTPOLITIK.

D. Childs, *The GDR: Moscow's German Ally* (1983)
H. A. Turner, *The Two Germanies since 1945* (1987)

**Bernadotte, Count** (1895–1948). President of Swedish Red Cross and a UNITED NATIONS mediator. As a Swedish soldier he was involved with Red Cross in the First World War. In the Second World War he arranged for the exchanges of sick and disabled prisoners at Gothenburg in 1943 and 1944. He was used by HIMMLER in 1945 as intermediary to seek the surrender of German forces to the British and Americans, but the proposal was rejected in London and Washington. After the war he was invited by the UN Secretary General to serve as UN Mediator in Palestine, where he was assassinated by Jewish terrorists in 1948.

**Bessarabia.** Area on the Soviet–Romanian border bounded on the north and east by the River Dniester and to the south and west by the Danube and the Prut. Of mixed Romanian and Ukranian population, it was disputed between the two states but remained part of the Russian Empire until 1918, when it threw off Russian (now Soviet) rule and proclaimed union with Romania. Romania's acquisition was confirmed at the PARIS PEACE CONFERENCE in 1919 but never recognized by the Soviet Union. A Soviet ultimatum on 28 June 1940 forced Romania to cede the territory. It was administered by Romania for much of the Second World War but became part of the Moldavian Soviet Socialist Republic in 1944. *See also* MOLDAVIA.

S. Fischer-Galati, *Twentieth Century Rumania* (1970)

**Bethmann-Hollweg, Theobald von** (1856–1921). Reich Chancellor of the German Empire, July 1909 to July 1917. Born in Hohenfinlow, Brandenburg, East Prussia, Bethmann-Hollweg studied law and became a Prussian civil servant. Beginning his career as a provincial administrator in Brandenburg, he became Prussian Minister of the Interior in 1905, and State Secretary at the Reich Office for Internal Affairs in 1907. In the latter capacity he was responsible for piloting through the REICHSTAG the Reich Association Law of 1908, which contributed to the partial liberalization of the laws governing right of assembly in the individual federal states. He succeeded Bülow as Reich Chancellor in 1909 after the collapse of the former's draft tax reform proposals. A typical product of the senior Prussian civil service, Bethmann-Hollweg was a conscientious and competent administrator, though with little experience of foreign affairs. Politically a moderate conservative, he accepted the need for some reform of the Prusso–German political system; though his commitment to gradual reform stopped short of the introduction of executive accountability to the *Reichstag*, or of reform of the Prussian three-class franchise system.

Bethmann's chancellorship was increasingly dominated by the deterioration of Germany's international situation against the background of growing domestic political deadlock. From the 1912 *Reichstag* elections, in which the SPD made major gains, it proved difficult to construct a stable bloc of support for the government in the lower house, and government was increasingly carried on by means of imperial decrees: Bethmann-Hollweg became ever-more dependent on the ministerial bureaucracy, the military and the camarillas which exercised influence over the Kaiser. The second Moroccan Crisis (1911) and the deterioration of relations with France and Russia in 1913, led to a growing influence of the military, which Bethmann was powerless to prevent. The apparent failure of his policy of seeking a rapprochement with Britain signalled by the Anglo–Russian naval agreement of July 1914, undermined Bethmann's position *vis-à-vis* the military even further; and his support of Austria–Hungary against Serbia in the July 1914 crisis may have been dictated less by a desire to unleash a 'drive for world power' than by a final, desperate attempt to regain the political initiative.

Once the July crisis had escalated into a

European war, Bethmann sought to suppress the debate over war aims which soon broke out in Germany; both in order to retain the maximum degree of flexibility for the Imperial government in any peace negotiations and in order to keep the support of the Social Democrats and the labour movement, whose support for the war effort was conditional upon its defensive nature. Gradually, however, Bethmann lost control of the war aims debate, his position undermined by pro-annexationists both within and outside of the *Reichstag*. Military stalemate on the WESTERN FRONT from the end of 1914 onwards resulted in pressure on Bethmann to sanction the use of unrestricted submarine warfare in order to starve Britain into defeat. He resisted this pressure – forcing Tirpitz's resignation in March 1916 over this issue – rightly fearing that it would lead to American entry into the war on the side of the Allies. In August 1916 he approved the appointment of HINDENBURG and LUDENDORFF to head the Army High Command, hoping that their appointment would strengthen his hand against his annexationist domestic political opponents. The new High Command, however, rapidly came to play a dominant role in domestic politics, forcing Bethmann to agree to the introduction of unrestricted submarine warfare in January 1917. His position was further undermined by the gradual radicalization of the working class as a consequence of the material privations of war; and by growing demands for both constitutional reform and a negotiated end to the war. Bethmann sought to assuage the former demand by persuading the Kaiser to commit himself to reform of the Prussian three-class franchise. This the Kaiser did in his 'Easter message' of 1917. The postponement of such reform until after the end of the war, however, led to growing opposition to Bethmann in the *Reichstag*. When a majority in the *Reichstag* indicated its intention of passing a resolution calling on the government to press for a negotiated peace without annexations, he desperately sought to avoid this by accelerating the timetable for reform of the Prussian franchise. Hindenburg and Ludendorff sought to exploit this situation to force Bethmann's dismissal, which they achieved by mid-July 1917.

Recent historical scholarship on Bethmann's chancellorship has focused on his role in the unleashing of war in 1914 and on the extent to which he was committed to extensive annexations in the event of a German victory. Whilst Bethmann cannot escape a major share of responsibility for the outbreak of war in 1914, his role thereafter seems best understood as that of an increasingly embattled moderate in the war aims debate, vainly seeking a peace settlement and desperately concerned to maintain the 'civic truce' of 1914 which was threatened by any clear statement of war aims. *See also* FIRST WORLD WAR; FISCHER CONTROVERSY

K. Epstein, *Matthias Erzberger and the Dilemma of German Democracy* (1959)
J. H. Jarausch, *The Enigmatic Chancellor: Bethmann Hollweg and the Hubris of Imperial Germany* (1973)
W. J. Mommsen, *Max Weber and German Politics, 1890–1920* (1985)

**Bevan, Aneurin** (1897–1960). British politician. He was Labour MP for Ebbw Vale, 1929–60; Minister of Health, 1945–51; Minister of Labour, 1951; and deputy leader of the LABOUR PARTY 1959–60. He emerged from a Welsh coal-mining background to become spokesman for the South Wales miners in the GENERAL STRIKE of 1926. He pioneered the NATIONAL HEALTH SERVICE, resigning in protest at GAITSKELL's proposals to introduce Health Service charges to meet defence expenditure. He led the unilateral wing of the Party (*see* UNILATERALISM) and was a much loved leader of the left of the Party. He is still regarded as one of its most impressive post-war figures.

M. Foot, *Aneurin Bevan, 1945–60* (1973)
J. Campbell, *Nye Bevan* (1987)

**Beveridge, William** (1879–1963). British economist and author of the Beveridge Report on Social Insurance and Allied Services (1942), which became the blueprint for Britain's WELFARE STATE policies and institutions. He was particularly interested in unemployment in his early career, and was Director of Labour Exchanges, 1909–16. He became Director of the London School of Economics, 1919–37; Master of University College, Oxford from 1937; and Liberal MP for Berwick-on-Tweed, 1944–5. He transformed a technical enquiry into the rationalization of Britain's

existing social welfare provision into a comprehensive scheme to provide support 'from the cradle to the grave'. He co-operated with JOHN MAYNARD KEYNES to persuade the Treasury that the costs were supportable and extensively publicized the results of his report. The radical gloss he gave to the report masked its foundation on the insurance principle of contributions from employee, employer and the State, and an assumption that full employment would be possible after the war. His proposals were broadly accepted in a government White Paper in 1944 and implemented in the National Insurance Act of 1946.

P. Addison, *The Road to 1945: British Politics and the Second World War* (1975)
J. Harris, *William Beveridge* (1977)

**Bevin, Ernest** (1881–1951). British trade union leader, Labour politician and cabinet minister. The illegitimate son of a Somerset midwife, Bevin had only an elementary education before moving to Bristol. There he worked as a carter and was an active socialist and trade unionist, becoming a full-time official of the dockers' union in 1911. By 1918 he was a leading figure in the National Transport Workers' Federation (NTWF). In 1920 he shot to national prominence as 'the Dockers' KC' (King's Counsel) in his successful presentation of their case on wages and conditions before the Shaw Inquiry. He played a leading role in the decision not to support the miners over their lockout in 1921, 'BLACK FRIDAY', but the weakness of the NTWF convinced him of the need for a more integrated transport union, and in 1922 he formed the Transport and General Workers' Union (TGWU), which was to become Britain's largest union, and of which he was General Secretary, 1922–40. The defeat of the GENERAL STRIKE in 1926 confirmed his view that unions should collaborate with government and employers, and with Walter Citrine, the TUC General Secretary, he was the leading figure in the 'corporatist' tendencies of British trades unionism between the wars. In the 1931 crisis he played a leading role in ensuring that RAMSAY MACDONALD was abandoned by the LABOUR PARTY, and after the election defeat of that year set about making Labour more union-orientated. Throughout the inter-war years he was a fierce anti-communist in both the TGWU and the wider Labour movement. In CHURCHILL's wartime coalition (1940–5) he was Minister of Labour and National Service (being elected to parliament for the first time in 1940), and used his massive influence with the unions to ensure that labour co-operated fully in maximizing war production. Following Labour's victory at the 1945 election he became Foreign Secretary, and continued his fierce anti-communism in that field, playing a leading role in the British decision to build its own atomic bomb, taken by only a handful of ministers (*see* NUCLEAR WEAPONS), and the formation of the NORTH ATLANTIC TREATY ORGANISATION in 1949. The onset of the COLD WAR had left Britain with little alternative, although there was criticism, which as always was greatly resented, from the Left. He gave steady support to the Prime Minister, Clement Attlee, and blocked moves to replace him in 1945 and 1947. In poor health, he resigned from the Foreign Office to become Lord Privy Seal in 1951, but died within a few weeks of taking up his new post.

Bevin was undoubtedly one of the greatest products of the Labour movement. A huge, tough and often brutal man, whose intelligence and ability belied his lack of formal education, he formed what became Britain's largest union, helped reorientate the Labour movement in the later 1920s and the 1930s, and played a key role in the wartime and post-war governments.

A. Bullock, *The Life and Times of Ernest Bevin* (3 vols, 1960–85)

**Biennio Rosso.** 'Red biennium'; a term applied to the period of intense strikes, factory occupations, land seizures and food riots in Italy in 1919–20. The hardships of the war and the growth of left-wing militancy produced the largest wave of industrial unrest seen in Italy. The stability of governments was threatened and the way was paved for the growth of MUSSOLINI's fascist movement. In 1919 there were 1,663 strikes, mainly concentrated in April–June, followed the next year by over 1,800 strikes involving over 1 million workers. From August 1920 there began factory occupations which threatened an armed conflict between workers and the army. The Prem-

ier, GIOLITTI, waited out the occupations, granting concessions on food prices and wages which gradually brought the movement to an end.

**BKP.** Bulgarska Komunisticheska Partiya. *See* COMMUNIST PARTY, BULGARIAN.

**Black and Tans.** Special additional recruits of the Royal Irish Constabulary, first introduced in March 1920, whose popular name was derived from their uniform of dark green, almost black, caps and khaki tunics and trousers. Between March 1920 and January 1922 the Black and Tans were responsible for excessively severe reprisals against terrorist activity in suppressing Irish nationalist unrest and combating the IRISH REPUBLICAN ARMY. Their destruction of Balbriggan, near Dublin, and the killing of two Irishmen in September 1920, followed three months later by the firing of the library and county hall in Cork served to fuel republican resentment at British rule. *See also* HOME RULE.

R. Bennett, *The Black and Tans* (1959)
C. Townshend, *The British Campaign in Ireland, 1919–1921* (1979)

**'Black Friday'.** Label given to the date of 15 April 1921 by British trade unionists when the TRIPLE ALLIANCE broke down over the refusal of transport workers and railwaymen to support the miners in a strike. Railwaymen and transport workers were due to join the miners in a sympathetic strike on Saturday, 16 April, but following the withdrawal of the miners from negotiations and their refusal to re-enter them, the two other unions cancelled their sympathetic strike. The miners struck alone and remained on strike until June, but were forced to give way and accept heavy wage cuts. As well as contributing to the bitterness in industrial relations in the mining industry which was to lead to the BRITISH GENERAL STRIKE of 1926, 'Black Friday' marked the watershed in post-war industrial militancy in Great Britain, ending the immediate threat of co-ordinated action by the most powerful unions.

H. Pelling, *A History of British Trade Unionism* (4th edn, 1987)

**Black Hand.** Popular name of the Serbian terrorist group (*Ujedinjenje ili Smrt*; 'Unity or Death') formed in Belgrade in May 1911. Led by Colonel Dragutin Dimitrievic and consisting mainly of young army officers, the society's main aim was the unifying of Slav minorities in Austria–Hungary and the Ottoman Empire with the independent state of SERBIA. They were responsible for the plot in which GAVRILO PRINCIP assassinated the Austrian Archduke FRANCIS FERDINAND at Sarajevo on 28 June 1914. Although it was widely believed that the Serbian government was involved in the assassination, no direct link has ever been proved, and the Serbian Premier, PASIC, kept the organization at arms' length because of its maverick role in Balkan politics. The Black Hand remained at odds with the Serbian government after the outbreak of the FIRST WORLD WAR. In December 1916 Dimitrievic and his colleagues were arrested for an alleged plot against Prince Regent Alexander (*see* ALEXANDER I) of Serbia. He and two others were shot in June 1917 and the society suppressed. The Black Hand was one of the most powerful of several groups attempting to unite the Slavs with considerable influence in Serbian ruling circles up to 1914.

V. Dedijes, *The Road to Sarajevo* (1966)
Z. A. B. Zeman, 'The Balkans and the Coming of the War', in R. J. W. Evans and H. Pogge von Strandmann (eds.), *The Coming of the First World War* (1988)

**Blitz, the.** Name given to the sustained bombing of British cities and towns in the SECOND WORLD WAR, primarily from early September 1940 to May 1941. London bore the heaviest brunt of the raids, which destroyed one-third of the area of the old City of London and caused particularly extensive damage in the East End and Dockland areas. Almost all the major ports and industrial centres suffered attack, with especially concentrated raids on Exeter, Plymouth, Manchester, Liverpool and Sheffield among others. The most concentrated raid was on Coventry on the night of 14 November 1940, when 503 tons of high explosive and 30,000 incendiaries destroyed the centre of the city and a total of 60,000 buildings, including the cathedral. Raids slackened after 1941 as German air power was diverted to other theatres and increasingly to the defence of Germany itself from the ALLIED BOMBING OFFENSIVE. Night-time 'tip-and-run' raids continued during the rest of the war, and in spring 1942 a series of so-called Baedecker Raids were launched on cultural targets, such as Bath and York, in retaliation for the bombing of the historic port of Lübeck on the night of 28 March 1942. These were the last concentrated raids before the V-WEAPONS offensive of 1944–5. Total casualties in Britain from aerial bombardment, excluding V-weapons, were 51,209 dead and 61,423 wounded, mostly concentrated in the period up to the summer of 1941. Almost 0.5 million private homes were destroyed and over 4 million damaged. The strategy of diverting German air strength from the 'Battle of Britain' to the bombing of civilian targets has been seen as a major cause of the German failure to defeat Britain in late 1940. Raids against RAF airfields were just proving critical when the first raids on London were ordered by HITLER in retaliation for the RAF bombing raids of Berlin on the night of 25–6 August. The switch to the destruction of civilian targets denied the Germans the opportunity to wear down British air strength. Though considerable damage and heavy casualties were inflicted on Britain, Germany did not possess the heavy bombers necessary to carry out the degree of destruction necessary to disrupt war production or break resistance. The Blitz developed its own mythology of stoic endurance, which played an important part in winning over American opinion to entry to the war and in sustaining morale in Britain itself. Subsequent studies showed that demoralization and war-weariness did affect towns suffering from the most concentrated raids and that there was much criticism of inadequate shelters and precautions. Morale, however, was generally sustained.

A. Calder, *The People's War* (1969)
T. Harrison, *Living through the Blitz* (1976)

**Blitzkrieg.** German for 'lightning war', used to describe a rapid attack on a narrow front to achieve penetration in depth, characterized by the use of fast-moving mechanized warfare by armoured forces and aircraft in combination. A technique which attempted to overcome the static, attritional warfare seen on the Western Front in the FIRST WORLD WAR, it was promoted by a number of military thinkers and writers between the wars, including Sir Basil Liddell Hart (1895–1970), J. F. C. Fuller (1878–1966), and J. B. Estienne and taken up with some enthusiasm by serving soldiers such as Marshal TUKHACHEVSKY, CHARLES DE GAULLE and General HEINZ GUDERIAN. Only in the German armed forces, however, was the doctrine fully realized, being used to devastating effect in the German conquest of Poland in September 1939 and giving the term general currency. The German attack on France in May 1940 utilized the same technique with even mure stunning results. By concentrating seven armoured divisions amongst the 44 allotted to the offensive through the Ardennes, supported by 3,000 aircraft, including 400 dive-bombers, the German armies achieved a breakthrough and swift advance to the Channel coast which knocked France out of the war after only 46 days' fighting. Similar campaigns were mounted in the Balkans with the assaults on Yugoslavia, Greece and Crete in 1941, followed by the massive offensive against the Soviet Union in June 1941. Here the use of armoured columns, tactical air support, and the bypassing of areas of strong resistance failed to achieve the desired knock-out blow to the Soviet government of capturing Moscow before the onset of winter, committing Germany to a protracted struggle. Although as a technique of warfare, Blitzkrieg was utilized in further offensives in Russia and elsewhere, occasionally, as in the Ardennes offensive of 1944–5, achieving limited gains, there was no more swift victories of the type seen in 1939 and 1940. As well as gaining HITLER's support as a novel and aggressive form of warfare, Blitzkrieg complemented Hitler's policy of 'armament in width', allowing him to build up a predominance in armed forces for a limited war which would not arouse domestic opposition or commit Germany to a protracted TOTAL WAR which she might lose. After 1942 Hitler was forced to adapt the German war effort to a lengthy struggle, though it is doubtful if he ever gave up the belief in a repetition of his earlier swift successes. The shortened form 'BLITZ' is used to describe the bombing of British towns and cities in the SECOND WORLD WAR.

B. Liddell Hart, *Strategy: The Indirect Approach* (1929)
H. Guderian, *Panzer Leader* (1952)
B. H. Klein, *Germany's Economic Preparations for War* (1959)

**Blum, Léon** (1872–1950). French politician. Born in Paris of Jewish parentage, he worked as a journalist and joined the socialists in 1899. He became a socialist deputy in 1919 and leader of the SOCIALIST PARTY (SFIO) in 1925. He led the electoral coalition of the Socialist Party, the RADICAL PARTY and the FRENCH COMMUNIST PARTY which agreed a common programme for the elections of 1936. The programme included measures to ban the right-wing LEAGUES, reform the press and guarantee secular education, as well as support the LEAGUE OF NATIONS, the nationalization of war industries, a reduced working week, public works, agriculture and economic expansion. In spite of uneven commitment to the programme by its constituents, the coalition triumphed in the May elections and Blum became Prime Minister of the POPULAR FRONT government on 5 June 1936 as France's first socialist Prime Minister. He took office in the midst of a huge wave of strikes and factory occupations, and on 7 June oversaw an agreement between employers and the CONFÉDÉRATION GÉNÉRALE DU TRAVAIL (CGT), at which the employers agreed to respect trade union rights, grant wage increases, allow factory delegates to be elected, and introduce collective bargaining in return for the strikers' respecting the law and ending occupations. This 'Matignon Agreement' (after the Prime Minister's office in the Hotel Matignon) was backed by Blum's promise to introduce laws to give collective bargaining a legal framework and to legislate for a 40-hour week. These reforms were enacted and Blum also introduced social welfare reforms, including holidays with pay, unemployment relief and old-age pensions.

The outbreak of the SPANISH CIVIL WAR in July created immense difficulties for Blum. Although keen to support the Spanish Republic, he feared provoking a new European war and yielded to British pressure to maintain a policy of non-intervention. Opposed now by the Left and Radicals, the early optimism of Blum's government was tarnished by the splits the war provoked in the Popular Front, signalled by the abstention of communist deputies in a vote on Spanish policy on 5 December. Further industrial unrest led to attempts by the employers to recover ground lost in the Matignon Agreement. A growing financial crisis forced Blum to renege on a promise not to devalue the currency, devaluing the franc by 25–35 per cent in mid-September 1936. Increasingly forced to slow down the pace of reform, Blum called for a 'pause' in February 1937 so that the government could stabilize the economy. In March he announced moves to balance the budget, cutting back or cancelling the programme of public works, indexed wage increases and social welfare reforms. On 16 May the suppression of violent demonstrations at Clichy against a right-wing meeting leaving five dead and 200 injured isolated Blum still further and provoked a run on the franc. By June the Radicals were openly seeking to break free of the Popular Front, their President and Deputy Prime Minister DAL-ADIER making a veiled attack on Blum's record on 6 June. On 22 June Radical defections led the Senate to refuse Blum powers to deal with the financial crisis, and when Blum appealed to Radical colleagues in the Cabinet, they resigned. Having lost his majority in the Chamber he resigned on 22 June 1937 and was replaced by his former minister, the Radical Camille Chautemps. He returned to office for a few weeks in spring 1938 but with little effect, being replaced by Daladier on 10 April 1938.

In 1940 Blum was imprisoned by the VICHY GOVERNMENT and tried at Riom in 1942 (*see RIOM TRIAL*) as one of those responsible for the French defeat. Blum, like the other defendants, was able to show that some rearmament had begun and placed the blame on the military for the defeat in 1940. He was put in a German concentration camp until 1945 but survived. He re-entered politics, serving as Prime Minister of an all-socialist government for five weeks in December 1946 to January 1947. Although popular, it resigned on formal grounds following the election of a President of the Republic.

Blum's reputation is bound up with that of the Popular Front. He was attacked at the time from the Left for failing to harness the strike wave and turn it into a more thoroughgoing transformation of French society and for betraying the Spanish Republic. To the more conservative his policies were a danger to both social order and the economic well-being of the country. With no majority of his own and dependent on Radical and Communist support, Blum attempted to keep to the programme of the Popular Front. Unfortunately his partners took different views about what was most important in it, especially as many Radicals were suspicious of the economic consequences of the programme after the June strikes polarized opinion. On the Left, the Communists refused to join the Cabinet, remaining influential enough to arouse conservative suspicions, but without committing themselves to Blum's government. Instead the PCF aimed to develop its own mass movement further, seeing the Popular Front more as a means than an end.

J. Colton, *Leon Blum: humanist in politics* (1966)
D. Brower, *The New Jacobins: The French Communist Party and the Popular Front* (1968)
P. Warwick, *The French Popular Front: A Legislative Analysis* (1977)
D. A. Levy, 'The French Popular Front, 1936–37', in J. Graham and P. Preston (eds.), *The Popular Front in Europe* (1987)
J. Jackson, *The Popular Front in France, 1934–38* (1988)

**Bolsheviks.** Name from Russian *bolsheviki*, 'the majority', as opposed to the *mensheviki*, 'the minority', for LENIN's radical faction of the RUSSIAN SOCIAL DEMOCRATIC LABOUR PARTY, when they obtained a majority in one vote at the party's second congress in London in 1903. The characteristic of the Bolsheviks was their aim, given theoretical and practical expression by Lenin, of forming a highly-centralized 'vanguard' party of professional revolutionaries to bring about a revolution. The Bolsheviks remained a radical but distinct group within the Russian Social Democratic Labour Party until 1912, when they set up a separate Central Committee. During the RUSSIAN REVOLUTION the Bolsheviks were given a decisive programme in Lenin's APRIL THESES and spearheaded the October Revolution, becoming the sole political party of the Soviet Union. The name Bolshevik formed part of the official title of the Com-

munist Party from 1918 to 1952. *See also*
COMMUNIST PARTY OF THE SOVIET UNION;
MARXIST-LENINISM.

L. H. Harrison, *The Russian Marxists and the Origins
of Bolshevism* (1955)
A. B. Ulam, *The Bolsheviks* (1965)
L. Shapiro, *The Government and Politics of the Soviet
Union* (rev. edn, 1967)

**bombing offensive, Allied.** During the 1930s
it was widely believed that airpower could
decide the outcome of future wars. The use
of airpower against civilians in Ethiopia, in
the SPANISH CIVIL WAR, and by the Japanese
in China, appeared to confirm this view. In
retaliation for THE BLITZ on British cities
from 1940, the RAF began daylight raids
against Germany. These proved very costly,
and from May 1940 to the end of 1941 the
British mounted 44,000 night sorties, dropping 45,000 tons of bombs. Early surveys
showed these were largely ineffective. The
decision was taken by Air Chief Marshal
Harris (1892–1984), leader of Bomber
Command from 1942, to concentrate on
area bombing to demoralize the enemy.
Using four-engined bombers, attacks were
made in February 1942 on the historic
Baltic ports of Lübeck and Rostock to demonstrate the effect of area bombing. In May
he launched a '1,000 bomber' raid on Cologne and began the systematic night-time
bombing of German cities. In August 1942
the RAF was joined by the United States
Air Force who conducted daylight raids
with heavily-armed Flying Fortresses. In
August 1943 successive waves of bombers
struck Hamburg, creating a firestorm which
killed 45,000 people. The bombing offensive grew in intensity from 1943. From January 1943 to March 1944 301,000 tons of
bombs were dropped by the RAF and
USAF, over half against area targets. From
April 1944 to April 1945 1,457,000 tons
were dropped, but with greater concentration on transport and specialized targets,
such as oil, rocket and aircraft plants. The
weight of RAF night attacks, however, continued to fall on cities. In spite of great
efforts by the German air force, which
inflicted heavy losses throughout the campaign, by 1944 the Allied air forces were
able to wreck the German cities and
increasingly pinpoint critical targets. By
July 1944 every major oil plant in Germany

had been attacked, the vital rocket research
station at Peenemunde hit, and widespread
disruption caused to the German transport
system. Even so, Harris stubbornly maintained over a half of his tonnage for area
targets. Most controversial was the raid on
Dresden on 13–14 February 1945 when the
RAF and USAF created a firestorm which
killed at least 60,000 civilians in a largely
non-industrial city.

The Allied bombing offensive has
aroused considerable controversy, particularly over the area bombing of cities. Until
long-range escort fighters became available
from December 1943, sustained precision
bombing of key targets was virtually
impossible because of the losses likely to be
sustained. For example, the raids on the
ball-bearing plants at Schweinfurt on 14
October 1942 cost the USAF 60 planes lost
and 138 damaged out of a force of 291. But
the resort to area bombing was inconclusive
as a means of winning the war. Surveys
conducted after the war showed that though
sustained bombing demoralized people, it
did not stop them working and did not
affect the Nazi grip on power. More seriously, it was found that Nazi war production had risen rapidly in spite of the
bombing. Dispersal of factories, underground plants and the lack of sustained targeting on vital sectors until mid-1944 rendered much of the effort indecisive. On the
other side, it has been argued that the huge
deployment of German airpower, anti-aircraft weapons, and labour to combat and
repair bombing must have played a part in
the German defeat. Bomber command lost
50,000 dead in raids on Europe, while an
estimated 500,000 German civilians were
killed by the Allied air attacks.

N. Frankland, *The Bombing Offensive against Germany*
(1965)
A. S. Milward, *The German Economy at War* (1965)
D. Irving, *The Rise and Fall of the Luftwaffe* (1973)
M. Hastings, *Bomber Command* (1979)

**Boris III, of Bulgaria** (1894–1943). King of
Bulgaria, 1918–43. The eldest son of FERDI-
NAND I, he served on the Macedonian front
in the First World War and succeeded on
the abdication of his father on 4 October
1918, thwarting an incipient Republican
movement with the peasant leader STAM-
BOLISKY as its head. Boris benefited from

the right-wing coup of June 1923 which murdered Stambolisky, freeing him from a major threat. From 1936 he ruled virtually as dictator of Bulgaria, seeking to preserve Bulgarian interests in the Second World War by allying with Germany in 1941 to obtain territorial concessions from Greece and Yugoslavia, but keeping Bulgaria out of the war against Russia. He died suddenly on 28 August 1943, three days after a flight to visit HITLER in East Prussia. He was succeeded by the six-year-old King Simeon II with Boris's brother, Prince Syril (1895–1945), as Regent.

S. Groueff, *Crown of Thorns: The Reign of King Boris III of Bulgaria* (1987)

**Bormann, Martin** (1900–1945). Senior Nazi Party figure and secretary to HITLER. A member of a right-wing paramilitary FREI-KORPS unit in the early 1920s, Bormann was imprisoned for a year as an accomplice to a politically-motivated murder. On his release in 1925, he joined the NAZI PARTY (NSDAP) in Thuringia, becoming regional press officer and, in 1928, regional business manager of the party. Between 1928 and 1930, he was attached to the SA Supreme Command and, before the Nazi seizure of power, gained access to the NSDAP's Reich directorate as director of the NSDAP Relief Fund. In 1933 he became Staff Chief to Hitler's deputy, HESS, a position which he held until 1941 and which brought him into frequent contact with Hitler: during the 1930s he advised Hitler on the management of funds made available to the dictator as an individual from industry and other sources, and also took charge of the development of Hitler's summer residence. On the outbreak of war in 1939, he became attached to Hitler's central headquarters. Bormann's combination of control of the NSDAP's political co-ordinating central office and constant access to Hitler made him an increasingly powerful figure in the Nazi regime after 1939. Following Hess's flight to Britain in 1941 Bormann was appointed head of the Party Chancellery, which replaced Hess' office, a position which was accorded ministerial rank. In August 1942 Hitler ordered that all communications from leading party figures concerning party matters should be channelled through Bormann, and in April 1943

granted him the additional office of 'Secretary to the Führer'. Now in a powerful position to influence Hitler's decisions on party personnel matters, Bormann also extended his influence to the government of the state through an agreement in June 1943 with the head of the Reich (i.e. governmental) Chancellery, Lammers, governing access to Hitler. Through this agreement, which largely worked to Bormann's advantage, he became the most important figure in governmental as well as party matters by the later war years. Unprepossessing and self-effacing, Bormann cultivated his influence through assiduous attention to the minutiae of administration and direct influence on Hitler. An ideological fanatic on racial issues and on the conflict between the NSDAP and the Christian churches, Bormann's ascendancy after 1942–3 may serve as an index of the steady radicalization of the Nazi regime. Pandering to Hitler's increasing detachment from reality, Bormann cultivated the growing isolation of the Führer after 1943 – an isolation which even SPEER found difficult to breach. A bureaucratic intriguer to the end, Bormann undermined the position of GÖRING and HIMMLER in April 1945, was present as a witness at Hitler's marriage and was charged as executor of Hitler's will. Reports of Bormann's death in Berlin in May 1945 have often been challenged. Condemned to death *in absentia* by the tribunal at the NUREMBERG TRIALS in October 1946, he was officially pronounced dead by a West German court in April 1973.

H. R. Trevor-Roper, *The Last Days of Hitler* (3rd edn, 1966)
M. Broszat, *The Hitler State* (1981)

**Bosnia-Herzegovina.** Balkan province under nominal Turkish sovereignty until 1908. Formally annexed by Austria–Hungary in October 1908, provoking the 'Bosnian Crisis' with Russia, which was forced to back down by German suppport for Austria–Hungary. Austrian occupation was resented by many of the occupants of the region, who felt fellow-feeling with other Slav groups in the Balkans, notably Serbia. Secret societies such as the BLACK HAND attracted the support of young Bosnians such as GAVRILO PRINCIP in attempting to throw off the 'Austrian slavery', leading to the assassination of Archduke FRANCIS FERDINAND at Sarajevo on 28 June 1914. Following the First World War Bosnia-Herzegovina was absorbed in the Kingdom of Serbs, Croats and Slovenes (Yugoslavia after 1929). The rugged countryside of Bosnia-Herzegovina was one of the principal strongholds of TITO's partisans and the scene of bitter fighting with German counter-partisan forces. Bosnia-Herzegovina became one of the six federal republics under the Yugoslav constitution of 1946.

**Brandt, Willy** (1913–). German politician and Chancellor of the FEDERAL REPUBLIC OF GERMANY. Born Herbert Frahm in Lübeck, Brandt devoted much of his youth to social-democratic politics, before fleeing to Norway in 1933. There he changed his name, assumed Norwegian citizenship and studied at Oslo University. In 1940 he fled from Norway to Sweden. He returned to Germany in 1945 and worked as a foreign correspondent for Scandinavian newspapers, becoming a West German national in 1948. He entered the *Bundestag* in 1949 and became Mayor of West Berlin in 1957. In his tenure of this office, which lasted until 1966, he showed himself to be capable of resisting Soviet pressure during the crisis surrounding the construction of the BERLIN WALL. As leader of the SOCIAL DEMOCRATIC PARTY (SPD), he challenged ADENAUER for the chancellorship in 1961, entering government in 1966 as Vice-Chancellor and Foreign Minister in the 'Grand Coalition' formed between the CHRISTIAN DEMOCRATIC UNION (CDU), CHRISTIAN SOCIAL UNION (CSU) and SPD and headed by Chancellor Kiesinger. In September 1969 he led the SPD to victory in the *Bundestag* elections and became Chancellor of a government based on a coalition between the SPD and the FREE DEMOCRATIC PARTY (FDP). The principal achievement of his chancellorship was the normalization of relations with the communist states of Central and Eastern Europe, which Brandt achieved through a number of treaties signed between 1970 and 1972. Brandt's dynamic OSTPOLITIK was initially opposed by the CDU–CSU, and he was obliged to force an election on this issue in November 1972, an election in which the SPD made substantial gains and which led to the confirmation of his position

as Chancellor. In domestic affairs, Brandt's government expanded the welfare state by increasing substantially pensions for the disabled and retired, broadened the scope of the works councils established to promote worker participation, and began reform of often antiquated criminal and civil laws. More generally, the Brandt era witnessed a liberalization of German society and the dissipation of the stifling conformism and conservatism which had characterized the Adenauer 'restoration' period, a process of liberalization which was only marginally checked by the extension of police powers and the introduction of political vetting of prospective employees by the governments of the federal states in 1972 in response to the terrorist outrages of the Red Army Faction (*see* ROTE ARMEE FAKTION). The onset of economic recession in the wake of the oil crisis of 1973–4 undermined the reforming thrust of Brandt's government in domestic matters. The exposure of one of his senior aides as an East German spy led to his resignation as Chancellor in May 1974. Brandt's contribution to the improvement in relations between the two Germanies and between the Federal Republic and the other Central and East European states, for which he was awarded the Nobel Peace Prize in 1971, has led many historians to regard him as one of the outstanding West European statesmen of the post-war period.
T. Prittie, *Willie Brandt* (1974)

**Bratianu, Ion** [Iond] (1864–1927). Romanian Premier and the dominant political figure of the first part of the 20th century in his country. Born of a prominent political family on their estates north-east of Bucharest, he was educated at Paris, elected a deputy to the Romanian parliament and a cabinet minister in 1897. He served as foreign minister and minister of the interior before becoming Premier in 1909, thereafter serving either as Prime Minister or a principal adviser until his death. He guided Romanian policy in the FIRST WORLD WAR, helping to restrain the pro-German Carol I and his successor FERDINAND I from entry to the war on the side of the CENTRAL POWERS. He skilfully exploited Romania's position to bargain for territorial concessions as the price of continued neutrality and for entering the war, aiming primarily to enlarge Romania by the acquisition of Austro–Hungarian territory, but also maintaining negotiations with the Central Powers. The successful Russian offensive by BRUSILOV in the summer of 1916 and French pressure precipitated Romania's entry to the war on 27 August 1916 with a pledge of substantial territorial gains. Following the defeat of the Romanian forces in 1917 Bratianu accepted an armistice with the Germans on 9 December, but delayed the conclusion of a peace settlement until he could resign, escaping the charge of having betrayed his former allies. Working behind the scenes he delayed full ratification of the Peace of Bucharest on 7 May 1918, encouraging Romania's re-entry into the war on the side of the Entente when it was clear the Central Powers were close to collapse, a day before the armistice in the West. Resuming office as Premier in December 1918 he represented Romania at the Versailles Peace Conference. In spite of the evidence to the contrary, he maintained Romania's claim as a loyal ally of the Entente, demanding the honouring of the earlier pledges to Romania. He was assisted by Romanian occupation of much of the territory, the support that the doctrine of self-determination gave to his claims over largely Romanian peoples in the former Austro–Hungarian Empire, and the position of the Romanian monarchy as a bulwark against Bolshevism. Resigning in September 1919, he conducted affairs from the sidelines, supervising the doubling of Romania in size as a result of the TREATY OF ST GERMAIN and the TREATY OF TRIANON. He returned to office in January 1922, and was Prime Minister until March 1926. He died a year later.

D. S. Spector, *Romania at the Paris Peace Conference:
    A Study of the Diplomacy of Ioan Bratianu* (1962)
S. Fischer-Galati, *Twentieth Century Rumania* (1970)

**Brazzaville Declaration.** An agreement between the FREE FRENCH leader CHARLES DE GAULLE and representatives of the French colonies upon a post-war 'French Union' in which the colonies would be directly represented in the French Assembly and be given local assemblies and economic powers. *See also* DECOLONIZATION.

**BRD.** Bundesrepublik Deutschland. *See* GERMANY, FEDERAL REPUBLIC OF.

**Brest-Litovsk, Treaties of.** Treaties of the CENTRAL POWERS with Soviet Russia and the Ukraine signed on 3 March 1918. By the Russian treaty the Soviets lost control of large sections of the former Russian empire, including Estonia, Latvia, Lithuania and Finland; Poland was to become independent, while the provinces of Kars and Batoum were lost to Turkey. The Soviets also agreed to recognize the independence of the Ukraine; in addition they agreed to pay 3,000 million gold roubles to Germany as war reparations. The harsh terms of Brest-Litovsk followed the cease-fire agreed by the Soviets early in December 1917 following the RUSSIAN REVOLUTION and protracted negotiations by representatives of the Central Powers, the Soviets and the Ukraine at the town of Brest-Litovsk. The Germans and Austro–Hungarians sought to maximize their political and economic gains from the collapse of the Russian war effort, but the expansionist aims entertained by the General Staff and sections of the court were initially tempered by the desire to release as many troops as possible from the Eastern Front for use in the west and by fear of inflaming anti-war sentiment in their own countries by being seen to pursue annexationist policies. Initially the Soviet government entered peace negotiations from the standpoint of a conviction that communist revolution would soon sweep through the other countries of Europe. Accordingly TROTSKY, who headed the Soviet delegation from January, sought to delay signing an agreement for as long as possible. A German ultimatum in February for Soviet evacuation of the Baltic territories led to the withdrawal of the Soviet delegation and the resumption of the advance of the Central Powers deep into Soviet territory. On 24 February a decision of the Central Executive Committee of the Congress of Soviets to approve an earlier decision of the Bolshevik Party's Central Committee ordered the Soviet peace delegation to accept German terms immediately.

The treaty represented a huge loss of territory and population for the Soviet Union, amounting to some 1 million square miles and 46 million people. Although opposed by some Bolshevik leaders, such as BUKHARIN, on the grounds that it betrayed the revolutionary hopes of communist movements elsewhere in Europe, LENIN saw it as a justifiable prelude to world-wide revolution. Its immediate impact on the FIRST WORLD WAR was to permit the transfer of German divisions from the east to participate in the western spring offensive of 1918. The Central Powers also sought access to the agricultural and mineral resources of the Ukraine, but although publicized to the domestic population as a *Brotfrieden* (Bread Peace) the results proved disappointing because of the inadequate transport and administrative structure in the area. Even the acquisition of part of the Russian gold reserve by a supplementary protocol of 27 August 1918 proved of little assistance as the Central Powers crumbled to defeat.

The terms of the Soviet Treaty of Brest-Litovsk were paralleled by a treaty between the Central Powers and the Ukrainian Central Council guaranteeing the Ukraine's independent status. The Council, however, had little real authority and its leader Hetman Skoropadsky was little more than a German puppet, soon overthrown by the Ukrainian peasant leader, PETLYURA.

The Treaty of Brest-Litovsk was formally invalidated by the German armistice of November 1918, although several aspects of its provisions, such as the loss of former Russian territories in Finland, the Baltic and Poland were carried forward to the TREATY OF VERSAILLES. Lenin's acceptance of a punitive peace bought the Soviet Union time to organize itself sufficiently to pursue the RUSSIAN CIVIL WAR successfully, although his hopes of an early spread of revolution throughout Europe proved false. In practice, the Bolsheviks had little alternative but to sign the peace, although their deliberate decision to procrastinate may have proved ultimately more costly than an immediate peace following the ceasefire.

Although superseded by the defeat of the Central Powers, the Versailles Treaty and the effects of the Russian Civil War, the Treaty of Brest-Litovsk has attracted wider interest merely than as an interim settlement of the conflict on the Eastern Front. German attempts to acquire influence over a broad swathe of the Ukraine and the Baltic States have been seen as a vindication of the 'Fischer thesis' (*see* FISCHER CONTROVERSY) about long-term expansionist German war aims. Moreover, the development of annexionist ambitions amongst the German High Command and court circles *after* Brest-Litovsk – which included abrogating the boundaries fixed in March, sending troops into Voronezh, Kursk and the Crimea, and plans to set up a puppet 'South-Eastern league' covering the area from the Don to the Caucasus – have been seen as marking a forerunner of the policies of LEBENSRAUM later associated with Nazi foreign policy objectives in the east.

J. Wheeler-Bennett, *The Forgotten Peace: Brest-Litovsk, March 1918* (1938)

**Bretton Woods Conference.** Financial conference at Bretton Woods, New Hampshire, in the United States attended by representatives of 28 nations in July 1944. Called by President ROOSEVELT to organize a system of international monetary co-operation in order to avoid financial crises and upheavals such as that which triggered the great DEPRESSION of 1929. It was agreed that participants would establish a World Bank to provide credit for countries that required finance for major projects. An International Monetary Fund (IMF) was also set up to utilize cash reserves in order to meet crises facing individual states. The World Bank was formed on 27 December 1945 and came into operation in June 1946. All members had to be members of the International Monetary Fund. By 1985 the World Bank had made over 2,500 loans, totalling $114,656 billion to 105 countries. By 1989 the World Bank and IMF had 149 members.

**Brezhnev, Leonid** (1906–82). Soviet statesman; First Secretary of the COMMUNIST PARTY OF THE SOVIET UNION, 1964–82, and Chairman of the Presidium of Supreme Soviet of the USSR, 1972–82. Born in Dneprodzerzhinsk in the Ukraine where he studied engineering, he became a Communist Party official in 1928 and served as a political commissar on the Ukrainian front, 1941–5. A protégé of KHRUSHCHEV, he was elected to the Supreme Soviet in 1950, to the Party Central Committee in 1952, and to the Politburo in 1957. As President of the Presidium of the Supreme Soviet from May 1960 to July 1964 he obtained considerable power within the party machine, succeeding Khrushchev as First Secretary on 15 October 1964, and emerging as the leading figure in a nominally collective leadership and eclipsing the Prime Minister KOSYGIN. Revision of the constitution in 1977 allowed him to become President, head of state as well as head of party. He died on 10 November 1982 and was succeeded by YURI ANDROPOV.

Brezhnev's early period of power was notable for his decision to invade Czechoslovakia in 1968 to crush the 'PRAGUE SPRING', an act which decisively checked the spread of liberal communism in Eastern Europe and for the enunciation of the BREZHNEV DOCTRINE, justifying interference in the affairs of other socialist states. Thereafter, there was a period of DÉTENTE which saw the SALT I arms agreements (*see* STRATEGIC ARMS LIMITATION TALKS), US withdrawal from Vietnam and progress in the solution of conflicts in the Middle East. The late 1970s, however, saw a period of renewed COLD WAR, with an extensive arms build-up, widespread support for overseas conflicts, the SOVIET INVASION OF AFGHANISTAN and the imposition of martial law on Poland. Internally, Brezhnev had emerged as a consensual leader, reversing the most unsettling aspects of Khrushchev's policies and adopting the slogan 'stability of cadres'. After more than a decade, however, Brezhnev's 'stability' had hardened into a conservative gerontocracy in which the average age of the leadership had risen substantially and proved resistant to change in either political or economic directions. By the time of Brezhnev's death the acquisition of further distinctions, including Marshal of the Soviet Union and the Lenin Prize for Literature (for his memoirs) were seen as evidence of a corrupt *ancien régime*. Accordingly, under GORBACHEV the Brezhnev era has been subjected to harsh criticism as a period of stagnation, corruption and 'mistakes'. Through the increasingly strident tone of recent anti-Brezhnev propaganda, it might be discerned that while it did little to achieve economic or political reform, the Brezhnev era had witnessed a vast extension of Soviet power overseas via the growth of the Soviet navy, the Soviet rise to at least nuclear parity with the United States, and the frustration of political liberalization in Eastern Europe for almost two decades.

A. Brown and M. Kaser (eds.), *The Soviet Union since the Fall of Khrushchev* (2nd edn, 1978)
H. Bradsher, *Afghanistan and the Soviet Union* (1982)
M. McCauley (ed.), *The Soviet Union under Brezhnev* (1983)

**Brezhnev Doctrine.** Announced in an article in *Pravda* on 28 September 1968, following the Soviet invasion of Czechoslovakia six weeks earlier, to suppress the 'PRAGUE SPRING'. The article recognized the right of each nation to follow its own 'separate road to socialism' but required that such a course should not damage 'socialism' within the country nor impair the 'fundamental interests' of other socialist countries or the world-wide socialist movement. Dubbed the Brezhnev Doctrine by Western commentators after the current Soviet leader, LEONID BREZHNEV, it implied the right of the Soviet Union and its Warsaw Pact allies to intervene in the affairs of other socialist countries in Eastern Europe should they deviate from the essential characteristics of Soviet-style communism, principally the leading role of the Communist Party and a centrally-planned economy. The 'doctrine' represented both a justification and a warning to satellite countries about the potential for future intervention. In the Polish crisis of 1981 brought about by the rise of SOLIDARITY it was anticipated that the Brezhnev Doctrine might have been invoked again; in the event it was not, partly because a compliant Polish leader, General JARUZELSKI could be found to act to carry out Soviet wishes. The doctrine was officially repudiated by MIKHAIL GORBACHEV in the autumn of 1989 when he stated that the Soviet Union would allow each Eastern bloc country to determine its own form of socialism without risk of Soviet intervention. By 1990 it appeared that this freedom also extended to departure from the WARSAW PACT and COMECON.

J. Valenta, *Soviet Intervention in Czechoslovakia, 1968: Anatomy of a Decision* (1979)
M. McCauley (ed.), *The Soviet Union under Brezhnev* (1983)

**Briand, Aristide** (1862–1932). French statesman. Born at Nantes, he began his political life as a socialist, but was expelled from the SOCIALIST PARTY for taking office as Minister of Public Instruction and Worship under CLEMENCEAU, 1906–7, where he supervised the final separation of church and state in France. As Minister of Justice from 1907 he acted strongly against strikers, a policy he continued during his first premiership from July 1909 to November 1910. Moving increasingly to the patriotic right he allied with POINCARÉ, supporting his bid for the presidency and replacing him as Premier in January 1913. In office for less than two months (18 January–24 March 1913), i.e then played a leading part in promoting the law which extended the period of military service to three years. He rejoined the cabinet in August 1914 as Minister of Justice, serving also as Vice-President of the Council of Ministers. He supported the strategy of opening up other fronts to defeat the CENTRAL POWERS, especially the idea of a landing in Salonika to assist SERBIA and bring the Balkan states into the war on the side of the Entente powers. As a supporter of the 'Eastern' strategy and with growing disillusion about the failures on the WESTERN FRONT, Briand was appointed Prime Minister again on 29 October 1915, serving as his own Foreign Minister. Although well equipped by his knowledge of domestic and foreign policy, Briand found the constraints and factions within French politics limited his sphere of action. His former ally and now President, Poincaré, was himself determined to play an active role, while a truculent National Assembly and increasingly independent High Command made decisive action difficult. In December 1915 he promoted JOFFRE to Commander-in-Chief of the French armies and survived pressure to withdraw from the Salonika front following the defeat of Serbia. He backed the decision to defend Verdun following the German attack in February 1916, but in spite of its successful defence, the failures elsewhere, on the Somme and in Romania, brought increased pressure on Briand's conduct of the war. His backing of Nivelle as a more successful commander proved a false hope, but he had already fallen in March 1917 before he too proved a failure. His resignation resulted from his refusal to share military secrets with some of the left-wing deputies.

He played no further part in war-time politics but returned as Premier in January 1921, once again serving as his own Foreign Minister, until January 1922. He was Premier again from November 1925 until August 1926, and from July to November 1929, serving as Foreign Minister for most of the period from November 1925 to January 1932. He proved a strong supporter of the LEAGUE OF NATIONS and collective security, becoming the major influence on French foreign policy in the post-war decade. Although initially he insisted on full German REPARATIONS, his first post-war ministry fell when he began to modify his position. He supported the LOCARNO TREATIES of 1925 and the withdrawal of French troops from Germany. Awarded the Nobel Peace Prize in 1926 with STRESEMANN, he was one of the proponents of the KELLOGG PACT in August 1927 renouncing war as a means of settling disputes and signed by most of the major powers. Briand also built up closer ties with the SUCCESSOR STATES of Eastern Europe, notably Poland and Czechoslovakia. He died in Paris in March 1932.

Briand headed ten governments in all, although as many were short, his total period as Premier was just under five years, dominated by his war-time ministry which was not successful in giving France determined leadership. His greatest importance lay in his role as Foreign Minister after the war. His attempts to promote reconciliation with Germany have, with hindsight, been criticized in surrendering French security. His work, however, was widely recognized as part of an era of some optimism in foreign affairs before the onset of the worst phase of the DEPRESSION and the rise of the NAZI PARTY.

J. C. King, *Generals and Politicians: Conflict between France's High Command, Parliament and Government, 1914–18* (1951)

H. Gatzke, *European Diplomacy between the Two World Wars* (1972)

**Britain, Battle of.** Decisive aerial conflict between the German LUFTWAFFE and the British RAF in July–September 1940. Following the fall of France and the evacuation from Dunkirk, the Germans sought to establish air supremacy over the English Channel preparatory to an invasion of Britain: 'Operation Sealion'. The Luftwaffe entered the battle with approximately 2,800 aircraft, many of them fighter-bombers and ground-support aircraft, while the RAF front-line strength was approximately 550 aircraft, almost entirely Hurricane and Spitfire fighters in a ratio of about 2:1. German attacks on merchant shipping in July forced the RAF into heavier engagements, but in August attacks switched to radar stations and RAF airfields. Major assaults by German airpower on 13 August, dubbed 'Eagle Day' by GOERING, the Luftwaffe head, and two days later, failed to destroy British air power. DOWDING, the head of RAF Fighter Command, carefully husbanded his resources, using the radar network and a well-organized fighter-control structure to meet attacks only when they crossed the coast, thus maximizing his effort. The Luftwaffe was hampered by having only a brief endurance over southeast England for its best fighter, the Me–109, and by the decision to protect the bomber fleets rather than allow the fighters to roam freely. The Germans also failed to appreciate the significance of the radar network, not pressing home their assault on the eyes and ears of Fighter Command, and showed some confusion of objective in the later stages of the battle when highly damaging attacks upon airfields were given up for raids upon London. Although it was on 20 August that WINSTON CHURCHILL made his famous speech in praise of 'the few', some of the heaviest air battles had still to be fought, several of which had the RAF at full stretch. But insupportable Luftwaffe losses and the evident failure to destroy the RAF led to a switch in German tactics to an assault on British cities from 7 September. Although the raids proved damaging and losses were high, they gave some respite to the badly damaged fighter airfields. As it became apparent that the RAF was not broken and that air supremacy had not been obtained, Hitler made successive postponements of his invasion plans, finally halting them for the year on 12 October, although the BLITZ of British cities was maintained. Aircraft losses were widely exaggerated by both sides, but it is clear the German losses were higher at 1,733 aircraft against 915

British. *See also*: DOWDING, LUFTWAFFE, SECOND WORLD WAR.

D. Richards, *The Royal Air Force, 1939–1945, Volume I* (1953)
B. Collier, *The Battle of Britain* (1962)

**British Broadcasting Corporation** (BBC). British radio and later, television, broadcasting organization, formed initially as the British Broadcasting Company in October 1922. The first 'public service' broadcasting organization in Europe set up as a monopoly under the auspices of the Postmaster-General, a British Minister of the Crown, and run by an independent Director-General and Board of Governors. Under its first Director-General, from 1922 to 1938 Sir John Reith, the organization established a reputation for independence of direct government control and high quality of service. Reformed as the British Broadcasting Corporation on 1 January 1927, it was novel amongst broadcasting organizations being set up elsewhere in being non-commercial, paid for by an annual 'licence fee' on receiving equipment. Reith's interpretation of 'public service' broadcasting involved a somewhat highbrow approach, but the medium soon developed to cover major sporting and national events, as well as providing a wide range of entertainment. The BBC moved to purpose-built headquarters at Broadcasting House in Portland Place, London in 1932. By the Second World War it had established a reputation for impartiality, though this was often interpreted largely as being uncontroversial on pressing matters of direct political and social concern. Its monopoly role served to standardize public taste in culture and entertainment, popularizing a calendar of national events such as the Oxford and Cambridge Boat Race, the Grand National and the Football Cup Final. Royal Christmas broadcasts were begun under GEORGE V and important announcements such as the abdication speech of EDWARD VIII (10 December 1936) and Neville Chamberlain's declaration of war against Germany (3 September 1939) were carried by radio to a mass audience. Broadcasts to the Empire began in 1932 and a foreign-language World Service in 1933. During the Second World War the BBC provided a major source of information not only in Britain but abroad, greatly increasing its reputation and audience. Experiments with television broadcasting began in 1929 and the first regular television broadcasts started in 1936. Interrupted by the war, they resumed in 1946, soon becoming the dominant branch of the BBC with the growth of television ownership, though continuing to be based upon the 'public service' and 'licence fee' principle. The BBC's monopoly of television broadcasting was broken by the introduction of commercial channels under the Independent Broadcasting Authority (IBA) in 1954 and in radio by the licensing of commercial radio stations in 1972. Recurrent enquiries into the future of broadcasting (Pilkington Committee, 1962; Peacock Committee, 1986) have so far left the non-commercial, public-service principles intact, although the Broadcasting Act of 1990 under Mrs THATCHER has committed the BBC to operating in a more competitive climate, encouraging the introduction of satellite and cable television, greater access for independent television productions in the BBC, and the licensing of 'community radio'.

A. Briggs, *History of Broadcasting in the United Kingdom* (1961–79)

**British Commonwealth of Nations.** The British Commonwealth is a free association of member nations and their dependencies. From the late 19th century, the term 'British Commonwealth' was used to denote the British Empire, and came into increasing currency after 1918 to refer to the relationship between Britain and her self-governing dominions. At the Imperial Conference in 1926 the dominions were referred to as 'autonomous communities within the British Empire, equal in status, in no way subordinate one to another in any respect of their domestic or foreign affairs, though united by a common allegiance to the Crown, and freely associated as members of the British Commonwealth of Nations'. The political position of the Dominions was given legal status in the Statute of Westminster of 1931, which established the basis of the Commonwealth of independent nations owing allegiance to the British Crown and with legislatures on an equal footing with that of Britain. The term 'British Commonwealth and Empire' remained in use until 1947, when India and Pakistan obtained independence and the term 'Empire' was relinquished. India's intention of becoming a Republic while remaining a member of the Commonwealth led to a redefinition of the statutory basis of 1931. From 1947 the Dominions Office established in 1925 was replaced by the Commonwealth Relations Office, which merged in 1966 with the Colonial Office to form the Commonwealth Office. In 1968 the Commonwealth Office combined with the Foreign Office to form the Foreign and Commonwealth Office dealing with all Britain's external relations. In 1965 a Commonwealth Secretariat was established to serve all member states. It has observer status at the UNITED NATIONS and acts to promote political, economic and cultural co-operation; it is headed by a Secretary-General. The Commonwealth acts collectively through its biennial Heads of Government meetings, since 1971 attended by what are known as 'delegations', but which are usually led by the executive presidents concerned.

The Commonwealth has been widely interpreted as a means by which Britain made the transition from formal Empire to a looser association with former colonies and territories. Almost all former Dominions and Colonies chose to remain within the Commonwealth, although Burma did not join on independence, Ireland left in 1949, South Africa left in 1972, Pakistan left in 1972 (though applied to rejoin in 1989) and Fiji left in 1987. The Queen is titular Head of the Commonwealth, the revision of the legal basis of the Commonwealth in 1949 refers to her as 'the symbol of the free association of independent member nations and as such the Head of the Commonwealth'. Membership in 1989 stood at 48 (Pakistan pending) and included recently independent states such as Zimbabwe (1980) and Vanuatu (1980). Of these states 26 are officially republics and four are indigenous monarchies. The looseness of the association is such that the Commonwealth acts primarily as a means of mutual consultation and assistance, the only formal sanction over its members being that of expulsion. In spite of that, the Commonwealth has achieved some success as an association of states at widely differing stages of development but with a common heritage as former members of the British Empire. This has given it an almost unique position as a meeting place for a number of influential states. Although usually amicable, relations within the Commonwealth have been put under strain by the attitude to be taken towards the South African regime. Pressure for greater economic sanctions to be applied in the 1980s were resisted by the THATCHER government, leading to talk of Britain's expulsion from the Commonwealth. Britain has chosen to maintain a minority position on this issue in spite of virtual unanimity amongst Commonwealth countries about action to be taken against South Africa. The issue of sporting links with South Africa has also served to disrupt sporting events within the Commonwealth, including boycotts of the Commonwealth Games by African members of the Commonwealth. In spite of these difficulties, the Commonwealth has been judged an example of relatively successful management of DECOLONIZATION, and in Britain governments of both parties and the monarch, ELIZABETH II, have invested considerable importance in the Commonwealth as a link with Britain's former imperial past and part of a continuing world role. The latter has occasionally involved Britain in military action in support of member states, as in the case of 'Confrontation' with Indonesia over Malaysia in 1963–6 and a garrison in Belize (former British Honduras).

J. Bowle, *The Imperial Achievement: The Rise and Transformation of the British Empire* (1977)
D. Judd, *The Evolution of the Modern Commonwealth* (1982)
N. Mansergh, *The Commonwealth Experience* (1982)

**British Expeditionary Force** (BEF). The contingents of British troops sent to France in 1914 and in 1939 at the onset of the First and Second World Wars. The BEF of 1914 consisted of six infantry and one cavalry division, which saw service in countering the initial German attack through Belgium and northern France in accordance with the SCHLIEFFEN PLAN. Small, but extremely well-trained, it played an important part in slowing the German advance and in halting the German attacks at the First Battle of the Marne. Its paper fighting strength of 84,000 men had been overtaken by

the official number of casualties by 30 November 1914. The BEF of 1939–40 consisted of ten divisions plus a tank brigade which took up position in Belgium alongside French and Belgian forces to meet an anticipated German thrust along the lines of 1914. In the event it was forced into headlong retreat by the German breakthrough in the Ardennes, forcing its retreat to the Channel. The bulk of the BEF was evacuated at Dunkirk between 26 May and 4 June 1940.

C. Falls, *The First World War* (1960)
B. Liddell Hart, *The Second World War* (1970)
M. Howard, *The Continental Commitment* (1972)

**British Union of Fascists** (BUF). Founded by Sir OSWALD MOSLEY after the failure of his NEW PARTY in the 1931 general election. In 1932, after Mosley's visit to Italy, the New Party changed its name to the British Union of Fascists (BUF), adopting uniforms and mass rallies on the model of continental fascist parties. The BUF urged a radical economic programme to solve the problem of unemployment, and envisaged itself taking power in the event of a breakdown of conventional politics. By 1934 the BUF had obtained as many as 40,000 members and the backing of influential people, including Lord Rothermere, the proprietor of the *Daily Mail*. The violence of Mosley's supporters towards their opponents at the Olympia Meeting of June 1934, however, alienated public opinion, and improving economic circumstances limited the movement's appeal. The BUF did not contest the 1935 election and advised its members not to vote. In 1936 it changed its name to the British Union of Fascists and National Socialists (BUFNS) and adopted a distinctly anti-Semitic tone. A series of provocative marches through Jewish districts in London led to clashes between the police and anti-fascist demonstrators, notably at Cable Street in October 1936, leading to the Public Order Act, which banned the wearing of uniforms and provided for the prohibition of marches. The BUFNS gained some support in the London County Council elections of 1937 in the East End of London, but failed to secure any seats. In May 1940 Mosley and other leading members were detained under the Emergency Powers Defence Regulations and in July the British Union was banned. In 1948 Mosley re-entered active politics by forming the Union Movement, which adopted a neo-fascist stance and called for a ban on immigration. *See also* DEPRESSION; SECOND LABOUR GOVERNMENT.

R. Skidelsky, *Oswald Mosley* (1975)
R. Thurlow, *Fascism in Britain, 1918–1985* (1986)
D. S. Lewis, *Illusions of Grandeur: Fascism and British Society, 1931–81* (1987)

**Brownshirts.** *See* SA.

**Brüning, Heinrich** (1885–1970). German politician and Chancellor of the WEIMAR REPUBLIC, 1930–32. Born in Münster, the son of an industrialist, Brüning studied at the University of Bonn and was commissioned during the First World War. He was employed as the business manager of the League of German Trade Unions (Christian Unions) from 1920 to 1930. A Catholic, he entered the REICHSTAG in 1924 as a CENTRE PARTY deputy representing Breslau in Silesia. He was a monarchist at heart and stood on the right wing of the Centre Party. He became chairman of the parliamentary fraction of the Centre Party in late 1928, after the election of the reactionary Monsignor Kaas as party chairman. With the collapse of the centre-left coalition of Chancellor Müller in March 1930, Brüning was appointed Reich Chancellor by President HINDENBURG. Lacking a coalition of support, Brüning secured new elections in September 1930 after the *Reichstag* had rejected economic measures which he sought to implement using presidential emergency powers. The 1930 elections brought major gains for the NAZI PARTY, and from September 1930 until his fall in May 1932 Brüning was to rule through emergency powers, dependent on the 'toleration' of the SOCIAL DEMOCRATIC PARTY (SPD) in the *Reichstag* for the implementation of his policies and on the goodwill of the President for his continued tenure of office. At home, Brüning pursued a rigidly deflationary policy in an attempt to cope with the impact of the DEPRESSION on Germany. But this policy was intimately linked with his prime political concern – to free Germany of the burden of REPARATIONS. He hoped to persuade the Allies to abandon reparations by demonstrating Ger-

many's incapacity to pay these. Brüning's policy met with some success: in June 1931 US President Hoover proposed a one-year moratorium on reparations payments, a moratorium which was extended by the Lausanne Conference of June–July 1932 into a shelving of reparations. In domestic-political terms, however, Brüning's economic policy led to a rapid erosion of support for the government, the mounting hostility of the German National People's Party (*see* DNVP), and may have boosted support for the NAZI PARTY. Hindenburg, alarmed by Brüning's antagonism of the nationalist Right in German politics and his dependence on the toleration of the SPD in the *Reichstag* to secure the acceptance of his policies, began gradually to withdraw his support for Brüning. When, in spring 1932, the DNVP ran a candidate against Hindenburg in the presidential elections and Hindenburg's re-election was secured only with the support of the SPD and the Centre Party, Brüning's days were numbered. His plans for the break-up of some of the more bankrupt *Junker* estates in the east antagonized the agrarian élite, which was well-represented in the camarilla around Hindenburg; and his imposition of a ban on the Nazi paramilitary SA (*see* SA) in April 1932 sealed his fate by alienating General VON SCHLEICHER, who spoke for the army in politics and sought the replacement of the Brüning government by an authoritarian presidential regime further to the right and tolerated by the Nazis. Hindenburg dismissed Brüning as Chancellor at the end of May 1932.

Brüning's chancellorship remains the subject of some controversy amongst historians. In the 1950s and 1960s, the significance of his appointment as Chancellor was hotly contested: did this represent merely an attempt to overcome the party-political stalemate which had arisen by spring 1930? Or did Brüning's appointment inaugurate the move towards an increasingly authoritarian 'presidential regime' by-passing both *Reichstag* and political parties? The publication of Brüning's memoirs in 1970 cast new light on this debate by revealing Brüning's fundamental anti-republicanism, his desire to see a restoration of the Hohenzollern monarchy and his plans to align the Centre Party firmly with the anti-republican forces in German politics. Whilst he may have sought to secure parliamentary support for his policies, he was more than willing to act as Hindenburg's tool, and was clearly aware of the anti-democratic plans being hatched by the camarilla around the President. Whilst the cogency and farsightedness of Brüning's political objectives as revealed by his memoirs may be the product of hindsight on his part, there can be no doubting their fundamentally authoritarian and anti-democratic thrust. Until recently there existed among historians a much greater agreement about palpable failures of Brüning's deflationary economic policies. This consensus has now been called into question by the suggestion that, given the deflationary economic wisdom of the period, the burden of reparations and the political necessity of avoiding inflation, Brüning's room for manoeuvre in economic policy may have been much more limited than was assumed by his Keynsian critics in the post-war period. Whilst the most recent research tends to confirm that Brüning did not deliberately exacerbate the impact of the DEPRESSION in order to secure Germany's release from reparations burdens, it is clear that he did exploit the Depression to this end, to the exclusion of less severe economic policy options, hoping thereby to remove a major obstacle to his co-operation with the nationalist right to extend the presidential regime.

A. J. Nicholls, *Weimar and the Rise of Hitler* (2nd edn, 1979)
H. James, *The German Slump. Politics and Economics, 1924–1936* (1986)
E. Kolb, *The Weimar Republic* (1988)

**Brusilov, Alexei** (1853–1926). Russian general. He served in the Russo–Turkish War of 1877 and Russo–Japanese War of 1904–5. During the FIRST WORLD WAR he commanded the army in Galicia in 1914–15 and appointed to command the south-west Russian front in spring 1916. In June 1916 he launched the most successful Russian offensive of the war against the Austrians, forcing a wholesale retreat in which the Austrians lost over 1 million men. The offensive, however, ground to a halt in August ending Russia's last major chance of victory against the CENTRAL POWERS and seriously depleting the last reserves of man-

power. Brusilov became supreme commander under the PROVISIONAL GOVERNMENT and organized the unsuccessful offensives by the Russian forces against the Central Powers in June-July 1917. Following the October Revolution Brusilov served as a military adviser to the RED ARMY, becoming Chairman of the Special Committee commanding all-Russian armed forces in May 1920 and inspector of cavalry, 1923–4. He was one of the few ex-Tsarist generals to assist the BOLSHEVIKS.

A. A. Brusilov, *A Soldier's Notebook* (1930)
G. Jukes, *Carpathian Disaster: Death of an Army* (1971)
N. Stone, *The Eastern Front, 1914–17* (1975)

**Brusilov offensive.** *See* BRUSILOV, ALEXEI; FIRST WORLD WAR.

**Brussels, Treaty of.** A 50-year mutual guarantee signed on 17 March 1948 between Belgium, Great Britain, France, Luxembourg and the Netherlands of military and other assistance in the event of attack. Joined by West Germany and Italy in May 1955, it became the WESTERN EUROPEAN UNION.

J. W. Young, *Britain, France and the Unity of Europe, 1945–51* (1984)

**Bucharest, Treaty of.** A treaty between Romania and Germany, ending Romania's involvement in the First World War. Romania had entered the war on the side of the Entente powers on 27 August 1916, but by the end of 1917 an invasion by German, Austrian, Bulgarian and Turkish forces and the collapse of Russian resistance had forced the Romanian government to evacuate Bucharest and sue for peace. An armistice was agreed with the Germans at Focsani on 9 December 1917, but the veteran Romanian politician BRATIANU claimed it was merely an agreement with the occupying forces, fearing the loss of Romania's chance to make gains in the event of an eventual Entente victory. When Germany pressed for a conclusion to peace talks, Bratianu resigned as Prime Minister, placing the pro-German conservative, Alexandru Marghiloman (1854–1925), in power on 18 March. Marghiloman, it was hoped, would obtain more favourable terms for Romania, but although he obtained German permission to annex BESSARABIA, the terms of the treaty of Bucharest on 7 May 1918 were punitive. Romania was reduced to a position of dependence upon Germany and occupied indefinitely by German forces. Romania had to pay all occupation costs, demobilize part of her army, accept German control of her oil fields and hand over agricultural surpluses. The treaty was ratified by Germany in June, but King FERDINAND I of Romania avoided signing it. The failure of Romania to implement the treaty allowed Bratianu to claim that Romania had not reneged on its pledges to the Entente powers and press her claims after the eventual victory over the German and Austro–Hungarian forces.

S. Spector, *Rumania at the Paris Peace Conference: A Study of the Diplomacy of Ioan Bratianu* (1962)

**BUF.** See BRITISH UNION OF FASCISTS.

**Bukharin, Nikolai** (1888–1938). Russian communist leader and Marxist theoretician. He joined the BOLSHEVIK faction of the SOCIAL DEMOCRATIC LABOUR PARTY in 1906. He was imprisoned and deported, but returned to Russia in 1917, becoming a member of the party's central committee, editor of PRAVDA (1917–29), and in 1919 was elected to the executive committee of the COMINTERN. He became identified with the LEFT COMMUNISTS and opposed the TREATIES OF BREST-LITOVSK, proposing instead revolutionary war and the spread of communist revolution worldwide. At first a supporter of Workers' Control, he swung behind LENIN to support enthusiastically the NEW ECONOMIC POLICY, easing controls on the peasants and lowering industrial prices. A member of the Politburo from 1924, he supported STALIN in the power struggles with ZINOVIEV and KAMENEV, eventually succeeding Zinoviev as President of the Comintern. He joined RYKOV and TOMSKY in the so-called RIGHT OPPOSITION to Stalin's economic policy and was dismissed from his party positions in 1929. In 1937 he was arrested and put on trial, charged with treason in March 1938 with other prominent Bolshevik veterans; he admitted to 'counter-revolutionary' activities, was found guilty and shot. One of the most prominent victims of Stalin's PURGES, Bukharin has been rehabilitated in the GORBACHEV era with growing interest in his ideas and writings, principally as offering an alternative route to the centralized state control exercised by Stalin. See also COLLECTIVIZATION, SOVIET; INDUSTRIALIZATION DEBATE, SOVIET.

N. Bukharin and E. Preobrazhensky, *The ABC of Communism* (1969)
S. F. Cohen, *Bukharin and the Bolshevk Revolution* (1974)

**Bukovina.** A small region of south-eastern Europe centred on Czernowitz (Cernauti, Chernovtsy) inhabited mainly by Ruthenes, the most westerly sub-group of the Ukrainian peoples. Part of the Austro–Hungarian Empire up to 1919, by the TREATY OF ST GERMAIN the Bukovina was incorporated in Romania as part of Romanian enlargement following its involvement in the war against the Central Powers. On 28 June 1940 the Romanians were forced to cede Bukovina with BESSARABIA to the Soviet Union as part of the assignment of territories agreed in the NAZI–SOVIET PACT of 1939. The Bukovina was incorporated in the Ukrainian Soviet Socialist Republic on 2 August 1940.

P. R. Magosci, *The Shaping of a National Identity: Sub-Carpathian Rus, 1848–1949* (1978)

**Bulganin, Nikolai** (1895–1975). Russian statesman and Prime Minister of the USSR, 1935–58. He joined the COMMUNIST PARTY in 1917, played a prominent role in the CHEKA and rose to become Chairman of the Moscow Soviet and in 1947 Deputy Prime Minister. In 1934 he had become a member of the Central Committee, and in 1948 of its Presidium. In 1955 he was appointed Prime Minister as part of the collective leadership with KHRUSHCHEV but was ousted from the Presidium in 1958 when Khrushchev assumed the premiership himself and dismissed his opponents, termed the 'anti-party group', who had attempted to remove him from power.

**Bulgarska Komunisticheska Partiya** (BKP). See COMMUNIST PARTY, BULGARIAN.

**Bulge, Battle of the.** See SECOND WORLD WAR.

**Bundesrepublik Deutschland** (BRD). See GERMANY, FEDERAL REPUBLIC OF.

**Burgenland.** A narrow strip of territory east of the River Leitha which in 1867 was designated the administrative frontier between Austria (Cisleithania) and Hungary (Transleithania). The Burgenland – its name taken from the four districts of Pressburg, Wieselburg, Ödenburg and Eisenburg – was predominantly German-speaking and the subject of a protracted struggle between Austria and Hungary after the First World War. It was eventually incorporated into Austria.

S. Wambaugh, *Plebiscites since the World War* (1933)

**Butler, Richard ('Rab')** (1902–82). British Conservative politician. He is most noted for his work as President of the Board of Education (1941–5), when he was the inspirational force behind the Education Act of 1944. Frequently termed the 'Butler' Act, the 1944 legislation established a tripartite educational system of modern, technical and grammar schools which remained intact until the 1960s, when comprehensive schooling was enforced under the Labour government of HAROLD WILSON. Butler, during his political career, epitomized the centrist, consensus politics which developed in Britain during the 1950s. ANEURIN BEVAN coined the term 'Butskellism' to denote the similarity in financial policy between Labour's leader HUGH GAITSKELL and Butler, both of whom were successive Chancellors of the Exchequer. The term was henceforth used to describe the convergence in political thinking of the liberal wing of the CONSERVATIVE PARTY and right wing of the LABOUR PARTY. Butler, whom many consider to have been the rightful successor to HAROLD MACMILLAN as Conservative leader in 1963, held virtually all the major governmental posts during his career. Minister of Education, 1941–5; Chancellor of the Exchequer, 1951–5; Leader of the Commons, 1955–61; Home Secretary, 1957–62; Deputy Prime Minister, 1962–3; Foreign Secretary, 1963. He was passed over at the critical moment during Harold Macmillan's illness in October 1963, leaving ALEC DOUGLAS-HOME to become Prime Minister, an episode which was attributed to his failure to mount a sufficiently determined bid for power. He accepted a peerage in 1965 and subsequently became Master of Trinity College, Cambridge.

R. A. Butler, *The Art of the Possible* (1971)
R. Blake, *The Conservative Party from Peel to Thatcher* (1985)

# C

**Caetano, Marcello** (1906–). Portuguese politician and professor. A former close collaborator of SALAZAR, he held a number of posts including Minister for the Colonies, 1944–7 and Deputy Prime Minister, 1955–8. He succeeded Salazar as Prime Minister in September 1963. Although he attempted social and economic reforms, he preserved the form of the Salazar dictatorship and continued the increasingly burdensome colonial conflicts which led to his overthrow in a military coup on 25 April 1974 and his replacement by a Junta of National Salvation.

L. A. Sobel (ed.), *Portuguese Revolution, 1974–6* (1976)
T. Gallagher, *Portugal: A Twentieth Century Interpretation* (1983)

**Caillaux, Joseph** (1863–1944). French politician. Born in Le Mans of a wealthy provincial family, he trained in law and economics, and entered the Ministry of Finance in 1886 as a treasury official. He was elected to the Chamber of Deputies in 1898 and allied with Alexander Ribot and RAYMOND POINCARÉ. He served as Minister of Finance from 1899 in numerous Cabinets, earning himself left-wing support for his proposal of a progressive income tax in 1907. His actions to defuse the Moroccan Crisis in 1911 when he was Premier earned him the reputation of being pro-German in nationalist circles. He did little to detract from this reputation by criticizing his former colleague Poincaré of being overeager to bring about a conflict with Germany. Support for him as a Prime Minister was blocked in 1914 by a scandal surrounding the case of his wife, who had shot and killed the editor of *Le Figaro* for publishing letters between Caillaux and a mistress. Although his wife was acquitted after a famous trial at the end of July, he had missed the chance of the premiership. Debarred by his alleged pro-German tendencies from a useful job, he served in various minor capacities but was increasingly seen as the potential Premier should France need to negotiate her exit from the war. Caillaux avoided any treasonable contacts, but was the target of hostility from the more nationalistic press. In late November 1917 Poincaré chose CLEMENCEAU rather than Caillaux as Premier, choosing to fight on with the promise of American reinforcement in 1918. Clemenceau's determination to fight 'defeatism' made Caillaux a natural scapegoat in this campaign. Caillaux shed his immunity and asked for trial by the Senate. Refusing to go into exile, he was arrested in January 1918, but was not charged until October and not tried until 1920. Convicted on a minor charge, he was rehabilitated as disenchantment grew in the 1920s. Granted an amnesty in 1924, he returned as Finance Minister in 1925 and again in 1935–6, when he was engaged in unsuccessful attempts to form a government. He died in November 1944. A great political survivor, Caillaux was typical of the 'hardy perennial' ministers who staffed the frequent Cabinets of the THIRD REPUBLIC, but one who might have found himself negotiating a French peace with Germany in 1917.

J. Caillaux, *Mes Memoires* (3 vols., 1942–7)
E. Franzins, *Caillaux: Statesman of Peace* (1952)

**Callaghan, James** (1912–). British Prime Minister. He became Prime Minister in 1976, after defeating MICHAEL FOOT for the LABOUR PARTY leadership on the resignation of HAROLD WILSON, who had led the party since 1963. Callaghan first entered the House of Commons as Labour MP for Cardiff South in 1945 and became Labour member for Cardiff South East in 1950. Before assuming the premiership, he held the following governmental posts: Parliamentary Secretary to the Ministry of Transport, 1947–50; Parliamentary Secretary to the Admiralty, 1950–51; Chancellor of the Exchequer 1964–7; Home Secretary, 1967–70; Foreign Secretary, 1974–6. Callaghan had risen to prominence through the trade union movement and the Labour Party ranks; unlike his three predecessors as party leader, who all went to Oxford, Callaghan received no university education. Throughout his political career he was associated with the centre-right of the Labour Party. His early career was blighted by being the Chancellor of the Exchequer at the time of devaluation in 1967 and by his opposition to membership of the EUROPEAN ECONOMIC COMMUNITY. Callaghan inherited a difficult position in 1976 with serious economic difficulties of strikes and inflation. He accepted restrictions on government policy in return for support from the International Monetary Fund in 1976, beginning a period of severe restraint on wage increases, government spending and local authority finance which in some ways prefigured the early THATCHER years. Forced to seek support from the minority LIBERAL PARTY in the LIB–LAB PACT of 1977–8, many believed Callaghan had done sufficiently well to risk an election in the autumn of 1978. He delayed and the subsequent industrial strife of 1978–9, the 'WINTER OF DISCONTENT', when he attempted to force a pay norm on the trade unions, fatally compromised his party's standing, leaving an impression of apparently 'ungovernable' trade unions and high inflation. In March 1979 his government fell on a vote of 'no confidence' as a result of the defection of Welsh and Scottish nationalist support, and was defeated in the subsequent general election by the Conservatives led by Mrs Thatcher. Callaghan retired as leader of the party in 1980, making way for Michael Foot. Seen by some on the Left of the party as continuing the abandonment of socialism begun by Wilson, his departure paved the way for bitter inter-party conflict which led to the breakaway of the SOCIAL DEMOCRATIC PARTY in 1981, led by four prominent ex-Labour ministers, and Labour's crushing defeat in

the 1983 general election. He was created Earl Callaghan in 1987.

K. O. Morgan. *Labour People* (1986)
P. Hennessy and A. Seldon (eds.). *Ruling Performance: British Governments from Attlee to Thatcher* (1987)

**Campaign for Nuclear Disarmament** (CND). British anti-nuclear movement, founded on 17 February 1958 by Bertrand Russell and Canon L. John Collins, to demand the abandonment of NUCLEAR WEAPONS and a large reduction in British defence expenditure. It grew out of protest demonstrations at Aldermaston Atomic Weapons Research Establishment during Easter 1956. The annual Easter 'Aldermaston' March, culminating in a demonstration in Trafalgar Square, London, drew large support between 1958 and 1964. At its peak in 1960–61 CND had thousands of active supporters, and in 1960 the LABOUR PARTY conference passed a resolution in favour of unilateral disarmament (*see* UNILATERALISM). But from 1961 to 1979 CND's fortunes were on the wane. In 1961 the Labour Party reversed its position: the Labour government which took office in 1964 had no great sympathy towards CND, while the partial TEST BAN TREATY of 1963 appeared to have made the movement obsolescent.

The revival of CND in recent years dates from 1979 and was echoed in the peace movements developing in Germany and the Netherlands. In that year NATO ministers agreed on a DUAL-TRACK POLICY involving the siting of a new generation of nuclear missiles in Europe. From 1980 the membership of CND rose from a floor of 9,000 members to almost 100,000 at the height of the campaign against the siting of CRUISE MISSILES at bases at Greenham Common and Molesworth. The former became the scene of major demonstrations by CND and peace movement activists in April 1983. CND had influential support in the Labour Party via its long-time member, MICHAEL FOOT, leader of the Labour Party from 1980 to 1983, and 120 Labour MPs in the Commons CND group. By the 1983 general election the Party stood on a unilateralist platform on defence issues.

Although CND captured a mass following in the early 1980s, there was evidence that unilateralism, with which the movement was associated, remained electorally unpopular, apparently confirmed in the defeats of the Labour Party in 1983 and again in 1987. By 1988 CND membership had fallen back to under 70,000. CND's political effect has been difficult to gauge. Conservatives argued that it was a tough stance including the deployment of cruise missiles that brought about major breakthroughs in arms control from 1987; CND and other supporters claimed that their campaigns for disarmament had played a crucial role in influencing political decisions in East and West.

F. Parkin. *Middle Class Radicalism: The Social Bases of the British Campaign for Nuclear Disarmament* (1968)

**CAP.** *See* COMMON AGRICULTURAL POLICY.

**Caporetto, Battle of.** Major Italian defeat in the FIRST WORLD WAR, following an attack on 24 October 1917 by Austro-Hungarian forces reinforced by six German divisions across the Julian Alps. A short artillery bombardment by 2,000 guns and a brief gas attack routed superior Italian forces, advancing a hundred miles to the River Piave and inflicting 600,000 casualties by 9 November. Attempts to follow up the rapid advance were hampered by difficulties of lateral communications, and reinforcements of British and French troops were rushed to the Piave to shore up the front. The defeat destroyed the Premiership of Paolo Boselli, already under pressure from the Right for an absence of strong leadership and from the neutralist block in the Chamber. Voted from office the day after the attack when the scale of the route was already becoming clear, he was replaced by ORLANDO on 30 October. Assuming office in a crisis which threatened to knock Italy out of the war, he undertook a complete mobilization of the Italian war effort, revamped the high command, replacing General Cadorna with the more vigorous, younger General Diaz, obtained Anglo-French assistance, and proclaimed his determination to prosecute the war at all costs. His institution of a small, permanent War Cabinet of military and civil men and vigorous war policy made Caporetto a turning point in the Italian war effort.

**Carinthia.** The most south-eastern province of Austria, Carinthia was claimed by the new state of Yugoslavia after the First World War. This claim was disputed by Austria and rejected in a plebiscite of 10 October 1920, when the southernmost district of Carinthia (Zone A), with its overwhelming majority of Slovene speakers, voted to remain Austrian. Similar claims were made by TITO in 1945, again unsuccessfully.

S. Wambaugh. *Plebiscites since the World War* (1933)
T. M. Barker. *The Slovene Minority of Carinthia* (1972)

**Carlism.** The Spanish Carlists were the inheritors of a dynastic tradition which originated in 1833 with the pretender Don Carlos's claim to Isabella II's throne. Despite the near-disastrous effects of three unsuccessful civil wars (1833–40, 1846–49, 1872–76), Carlism survived into the 20th century, although until the SECOND REPUBLIC popular support for the cause was confined to its Navarrese heartland in the Spanish Pyrenees. Bitterly opposed to all forms of liberalism, secularism and even modernity, Carlism became increasingly anachronistic as the 20th century progressed. A belief in the divine right of kings, for example, was retained into the 1930s. The coming of the Second Republic in effect saved Carlism from dwindling into an increasingly insignificant regional curiosity. From the inauguration of the Second Republic in 1931, Carlism served as a focus for right-wing discontent with the new democratic, pluralist and secularizing regime. With the passing of the anti-clerical constitution in 1931 (*see* ANTI-CLERICALISM, SPANISH), the Carlists' uncompromising hostility to the Republic and their convinced belief in the need to overthrow the regime by violent means led to something of a revival with centres of support emerging in the Basque country (*see* BASQUES), CATALONIA and, for the first time, Andalusia. This new, regional strength remained important even after the rise of the CONFEDERACIÓN ESPAÑOLA DE DERECHAS AUTÓNOMAS (CEDA), which drew some support away from the Carlists.

In Navarre, the new constitution had been the signal for preparations for revolt to begin in earnest. The Carlist militia of *Requetés* began training in the mountains and, from 1934, arms-smuggling across the Pyrenees became a regular operation. In the spring of 1936 Pamplona, the Navarrese capital, became a centre for the generals' conspiracy, and after the rising of 18 July 1936 the *Requetés* became some of FRANCO's most valued troops. Paradoxically, however, the rebellion for which the Carlists had been preparing for so long rang the death-knell of their movement. In his creation of a unitary state, and eradication of potential opposition, Franco decreed that the Carlists should merge with the FALANGE to create a single 'Movement'. The red berets of the Carlists thus joined with the blue shirts of the Falangists in an unwieldy state party which denied autonomy to them both. *See also* SPANISH CIVIL WAR.

G. Brenan, *The Spanish Labyrinth* (1943)
M. Blinkhorn, *Carlism and Crisis in Spain, 1931–1939* (1975)

**Carol II, of Romania** (1893–1953). King of Romania, 8 June 1930 to 6 September 1940. The eldest son of FERDINAND I and Queen Marie, he was disinherited in 1925 because of his scandalous liaisons and chose to live in exile with his mistress. As a result, it was Carol's six-year-old son Michael who succeeded to the throne at the death of Ferdinand in July 1927, ruling through a Council of Regency. In June 1930 Carol was persuaded to return to the country by the Prime Minister, Juliu Maniu; an Act of Parliament confirmed his accession to the throne. Initially he offered support to right-wing and anti-Semitic governments in a country increasingly prey to the terrorism of the neo-fascist IRON GUARD and strikes organized by the underground BULGARIAN COMMUNIST PARTY. Influenced by Mussolini's example of the CORPORATE STATE he began to establish a royal dictatorship in 1937 when the governing party failed to gain the 40 per cent of votes which under the Romanian constitution guaranteed it a majority of seats; Parliament was dissolved in December 1937 and Carol first ruled through the minority right-wing Christian League of National Defence. They were dismissed on 10 February 1938 and a Government of National Concentration formed. On 20 February a new constitution dissolved all political parties except the roy-

alist National Renaissance Front, reduced the electorate from 4.5 million to 2.0 million, and established royal nominees to the Senate of an equal number to those elected. The new constitution was confirmed by plebiscite on 24 February 1938 by an overwhelming majority (4,283,395 votes to 5,413). A corporatist Parliament was elected on 2 June 1939, representing the major national interest groups. Other corporatist institutions were introduced in 1939, including an executive Principal Council and advisory Grand Council, reflecting the three groups of agriculturalists, the professions and workers. Beyond the constitutional forms Carol acted with great brutality; Corneliu Codreanu, the leader of the 'Iron Guard', which had been permitted to reform after the dissolution in December 1933, was arrested in 1938 and murdered while serving a sentence for treason; this was followed by the execution of hundreds of his followers and the public exhibition of the corpses. Carol's dictatorship proved short-lived. His attempt to play off the great powers to Romania's advantage in the diplomatic prelude to the SECOND WORLD WAR was undermined by his failure to secure German support, and by the NAZI–SOVIET PACT which left BESSARABIA in the Soviet sphere of influence. Pressure from the Soviets, Hungary and Bulgaria forced Romania to accept the loss of part of TRANSYLVANIA to Hungary by the second VIENNA AWARD, BUKOVINA and Bessarabia to the Soviet Union and part of DOBRUDJA to Bulgaria. Carol's abject diplomatic failure led to a brief rising by the Iron Guard, supported by the army, which forced his abdication on 6 September 1940.

S. Fischer-Galati, *Twentieth Century Rumania* (1970)

**Carrillo, Santiago** (1915–). Spanish journalist and communist leader. Secretary-General of *Juventud Socialista Unificada* in 1936. Secretary-General of the SPANISH COMMUNIST PARTY, 1960–82, playing a major part in the transition to democracy after FRANCO's death and bringing the Party into the Congress of Deputies after its legalization in 1977. Sat in the Congress of Deputies from July 1977. Expelled from the hardline Communist Party in 1985, he became President of the *Unidad Com-*

*munista*, October 1985, then President of the Workers-Communist Unity Party from February 1987. *See also*: COMMUNIST PARTY, SPANISH.

R. Carr and J. P. Fusi, *Spain: Dictatorship to Democracy* (1979)

D. Gilmour, *The Transformation of Spain* (1985)

**Casablanca Conference.**Meeting between President ROOSEVELT and Prime Minister CHURCHILL on 14–24 January 1943 which reaffirmed insistence on the unconditional surrender of the AXIS powers. The decision was also taken to invade Italy through Sicily and to intensify the ALLIED BOMBING OFFENSIVE against Germany before mounting an attack on occupied France.

**Casement, Roger** (1864–1916).Irish nationalist. Born in Kingstown (now Dun Laoghaire), near Dublin, he served in the British consular service from 1892 and knighted in 1911. He became an active Irish nationalist after his retirement from the consular service, and in 1914 travelled to Berlin to secure German assistance for an Irish insurrection. As well as attempting to gain Irish recruits to fight for Germany from amongst prisoners of war, he arranged for an arms shipment to arrive on a German ship, the *Aud*, on the eve of the Easter Rising (23 April 1916). Due to confusion, the *Aud* was seized by the British and scuttled. Casement, put ashore from a German submarine near Tralee, was arrested. Tried for treason at the Old Bailey, he was found guilty and executed on 3 August. Attempts at a reprieve were destroyed by the circulation of his diaries, which contained homosexual passages.

B. Inglis, *Roger Casement* (1973)

**Catalonia.**Region of north-eastern Spain with its own language and culture. During the 19th century it became the major industrial centre of Spain and developed strong nationalist tendencies. Perhaps the most dynamic area in the 20th-century Spain, due to movements for Catalan regional autonomy and the presence of a strong working-class movement, *as well as great cultural and economoic vitality*. Its first period of great turbulence, from 1905 to 1923, witnessed the appearance of bitter tensions between Catalanists and the army in 1905, the fierce anti-clerical riots of 1909 (*see* ANTI-CLERICALISM, SPANISH), the achieve-

ment of a very limited form of home rule (the Mancommunidad) in 1913, a period of savage class warfare and urban terrorism in Barcelona between 1919 and 1923. The chief actors were: among the working classes, the anarchosyndicalist CNT (*see* ANARCHISM, SPANISH); among the Catalanists, the Lliga, a moderate party, ready to compromise with Madrid because it feared the workers. Catalan autonomy was stifled under the PRIMO DE RIVERA dictatorship, but reemerged after its fall in 1930, with the dominant party now becoming the Esquerra Republicana, led by Francesc Macia and Luis Companys. In 1932, the SECOND REPUBLIC, during its progressive AZANA phase, granted a high degree of self-government to the Catalan Generalitat. Relations with Madrid soured once more after November 1933, when a new central government threatened to cut back Catalan gains. An attempted insurrection by separatists in October 1934 was defeated, but only after Companys had gone so far as to declare Catalonia a separate state within a Spanish Federal Republic. Companys was arrested and the Generalitat suspended, but both actions were reversed in February 1936, when the POPULAR FRONT government came to power. Catalonia was enthusiastically on the Republican side when the SPANISH CIVIL WAR broke out, the local Civil Guard' militias to forestall army units seizing control. Because of CNT strength, the Generalitat was obliged to accept political and economic structures in which left-wing influence was predominant. In August 1936 an Economic Council of Catalonia was created to control all aspects of Catalan industry and commerce, putting forward a Plan for the Socialist Transformation of the Nation, which included the introduction of co-operatives, union control over private enterprise, and collectivization of agriculture as well as industry and services. Growing rivalries between the various factions, especially between the CNT and the 'Trotskyite' PARTIDO OBRERO DE UNIFICATION MARXISTA (POUM) on the one hand, and the Esquerra and a new party, the PSUC, which combined Communists and Socialists, on the other, culminated in the May Days of 1937 when the two sides openly fought against each other for control. The

CNT and POUM were defeated, but the Catalan regionalists also found themselves displaced as the central Republican government moved its headquarters to Barcelona in the autumn of 1937. The various militias were brought under more regular army discipline, industry was taken out of workers' control and the Generalitat reduced to powerlessness. Catalonia's social and political revolution was largely over when the region fell to FRANCO's forces in early 1939. His regime immediately suppressed all manifestations of Catalan regional feelings, and restricted sharply even the use of the Catalan language. With the gradual liberalization of the Franco regime in the 1960s and early 1970s, left-wing and regionalist movements began to appear again. When Franco died, Catalan regionalism was generally regarded as one of the larger problems facing the stability of the new democratic state. But in late 1977, under ADOLFO SUAREZ, 'pre-autonomy' statutes were introduced which committed the country to a federal path. After considerable negotiations, arrangements for local self-government were finalized in July 1979. The new Generalitat, first under the presidency of Josep Tarradellas, then under that of Jordi Pujol, has consolidated itself very successfully, and by the late 1980s it was evident that Catalonia was experiencing a renaissance, politically, culturally and economically.

G. Orwell. *Homage to Catalonia* (1937)

**Catholic Church, Spanish.** The considerable influence, both political and social, of the Catholic Church has made an indelible impression upon modern Spanish history. Since the mid-19th century, patterns of Catholic allegiance within Spain have varied greatly, breaking down along both regional and class lines. In broad terms, the Catholic north has stood in marked contrast to the anti-clerical south (*see* ANTI-CLERI-CALISM, SPANISH). Industrial and urban workers were, however, unlikely to be practising Catholics, regardless of where they lived. Although the increasing disaffection of the working class was by no means a uniquely Iberian phenomenom, the trend was exaggerated in Spain by the Church's identification with the corrupt oligarchic politics which characterized the ostensibly liberal parliamentary regime of the Restored Monarchy (1875–1931). As this system disintegrated into the violent upheaval of 1917–23, an acute fear of social revolution gripped Spain's old élites. The Church's horror of incipient Bolshevism seemed confirmed by the assassination of the Archbishop of Zaragoza in June 1923 and, three months later, the hierarchy demonstrated its preference for authoritarian solutions to social problems with its rapturous welcome for the King's chosen dictator, MIGUEL PRIMO DE RIVERA. Such a preference was shown again in 1931 by the bishops' unenthusiastic and trepidatious reaction to the declaration of a Republic.

The Spanish Church's inability to accept cultural and religious pluralism underlay its antipathy to Republican democracy. Cardinal Pedro Segura (1880–1957) refused to accommodate the new government on any religious issue, not even freedom of worship. The anti-clerical clauses of the 1931 Constitution served to mobilize Catholics against the Republic, and by the time of FRANCO's rising in July 1936 the Church's support for the generals was inevitable. After the massacres of religious personnel in the first months of the war, Catholics worldwide rallied to the Nationalist cause and Franco's civil war was baptized a 'crusade'.

In return for the ideological legitimation of National-Catholicism, the Church resumed its entrenched position in Francoist Spain under the protection of the government. This new alliance of throne and altar continued for two decades, until the SECOND VATICAN COUNCIL introduced a new kind of Catholicism into Spain and, from the late 1960s, 'worker-priests' became increasingly involved in the anti-Franco opposition movement. After this rejection of Francoism, the Spanish Church withdrew from party politics and left the process of democratic transition to laymen. There is no significant Christian Democrat party in Spain and the 1978 Constitution simply recognizes Catholicism as being 'the religion of the majority of Spaniards'. *See also* CONFEDERACIÓN ESPAÑOLA DE DERE-CHAS AUTÓNOMAS.

F. Lannon. *Privilege, Persecution, and Prophecy. The Catholic Church in Spain, 1875–1975* (1987)
J. M. Sánchez. *The Spanish Civil War as a Religious Tragedy* (1987)

**CBI.** *See* CONFEDERATION OF BRITISH INDUSTRY.

**CDU.** Christlich Demokratische Union. *See* CHRISTIAN DEMOCRATIC UNION, GERMAN.

**Ceauşescu, Nicolai** (1918–89). Romanian President and dictator. He was born 26 January 1918 at Scornicesti, near Bucharest, the son of poor peasants. He left school at 14 and joined the Union of Communist Youth the next year, becoming a youth leader and organizer. A full member of the underground Communist Party in 1936, he was imprisoned under CAROL II, serving two and a half years for agitation; in prison he met GHEORGHIU-DEJ, later General Secretary of the ROMANIAN COMMUNIST PARTY. On his release he returned to organizing young communists. Following the Soviet invasion of Romania, he became Secretary of the Union of Communist Youth and its delegate to the First Central Committee Conference in October 1945. A protégé of Gheorghiu-Dej, who backed him as a 'native' Romanian like himself (as opposed to those who had returned from exile in Moscow), he was elected to the Grand National Assembly and in 1948 to the Central Committee. Serving first as Deputy Minister for Agriculture, then Deputy Minister for the Armed Forces, he escaped the purges of the 'Moscovites' and 'revisionists' to become a member of the party secretariat in April 1954, and from 1957 he was second only to Gheorghiu-Dej. In March 1965 he succeeded him as General Secretary of the Romanian Communist Party, becoming President of the Presidium in December 1967. Like his predecessor he pursued an independent line in foreign policy, showing support for DUBČEK's liberalization in Czechoslovakia and refusing to support the Soviet invasion in 1968. He cultivated friendships with the West and sought close links with China to provide a counterweight to Soviet influence. Courted by the West in the 1970s as one of the most independent of the Eastern bloc leaders, Ceauşescu's power at home became increasingly corrupt. In 1981 he began a crash programme to pay off Romania's foreign debts, imposing severe shortages and rationing on the population, and carrying out extensive purges of government and party leaders in 1982. He also placed as many as 40 members of his family in major offices and lucrative sinecures; his brother, Ilie, was in charge of the military, his son a member of the Permanent Bureau of the Communist Party, and his wife, Elena, First Deputy Prime Minister. Ceauşescu's grandiose schemes for rebuilding Bucharest and his demolition of thousands of villages to make way for agro-industrial complexes attracted adverse comment in the West. Party opposition was expressed in an open letter criticizing his policies in March 1989, but was met with firm repression and the arrest and harassment of the signatories. The fall of other Eastern bloc countries to popular governments in November and early December led to demonstrations in the city of Timisoara, savagely put down by the Security Police on 19 December. Three days later a popular uprising in Bucharest, joined by the army, forced Ceauşescu to flee. Following bitter fighting between his security forces and the army, Ceauşescu and his wife were seized, tried by military tribunal, and shot on 25 December.

S. Fischer-Galati. *Twentieth Century Rumania* (1970)
F. Fetjo. *A History of the People's Democracies: Eastern Europe since Stalin* (2nd edn. 1974)

**CEDA.** *See* CONFEDERACIÓN ESPAÑOLA DE DERECHAS AUTÓNOMAS.

**Central Powers.** Members of the Triple Alliance concluded by Bismarck in 1882: Germany, Austria–Hungary and Italy. On the outbreak of war in 1914 Italy remained neutral; the term was then applied to Germany, Austria–Hungary, their ally Turkey, and later Bulgaria.

**Centre of Social Democrats, French.** French Christian Democrat party favouring a mixed economy. It superseded the Centre Democratie et Progres, founded by followers of POMPIDOU in 1973, and the Centre Democrate. Both supported GISCARD D'ESTAING before merging in 1976.

**Centre Party, German.** German political party committed to the defence of the interests of Roman Catholics, who formed one-third of the population of the German Empire founded in 1871. The party was established in 1870 and rapidly mobilized the Catholic electorate of the new state against the anti-clerical measures introduced by the government during the early 1870s (see ANTI-CLERICALISM). From the mid-1870s until 1912 it regularly won around a quarter of the seats in the REICHSTAG; and, from the 1890s onwards, its support was essential for the passage of most legislation. During the First World War, the party changed its position from enthusiastic support of extensive annexations in the event of a German victory to advocacy of a non-annexationist negotiated peace settlement; one of its leaders, Matthias Erzberger, was the moving force behind the REICHSTAG PEACE RESOLUTION of July 1917. During the WEIMAR REPUBLIC the Centre, together with its Bavarian sister party, the Bavarian People's Party, continued to attract a steady 15–16 per cent of the popular vote; and participated in almost all of the coalition governments formed between 1919 and 1930. Aside from its confessional basis, the Centre's political nature was formed by its class base, which comprised both the Catholic lower-middle class and a significant portion of the Catholic working class. Stigmatized as the political representative of an 'outsider' group in Imperial Germany, the Centre was, until 1930, committed to the maintenance of Weimar democracy. A significant shift to the right took place within the Centre Party after 1928–9, however, and by mid-1932 it had entered into negotiations with the NAZI PARTY about the formation of a coalition government. Following HITLER's appointment as Chancellor in January 1933 and the Nazi seizure of power, the Centre's main concern was to protect Catholic institutions and state employees; it voted for the Enabling Act of March 1933 which consolidated Hitler's power. Despite its accommodating attitude, however, the Centre came under increasing pressure during the early months of 1933 from grass-roots Nazi activists: the conclusion of a Concordat between the Vatican and the Nazi regime in July 1933 sealed its fate, and it dissolved itself. The political tradition of moderate conservatism and confessional representation embodied in the Centre Party was to provide a major inspiration for the formation of the CHRISTIAN DEMOCRATIC UNION and the CHRISTIAN SOCIAL UNION in West Germany after 1945.

E. L. Evans, *The German Center Party, 1870–1933* (1981)
E. Kolb, *The Weimar Republic* (1988)

**Cernik, Oldrich** (1921–). Prime Minister of Czechoslovakia, April 1968 to January 1969, and of the central, federal government from 1 January 1969 until 3 January 1971. Held various posts in the CZECH COMMUNIST PARTY and associated with DUBČEK, who as First Secretary of the Party led the reform movement of the 'PRAGUE SPRING'. Following the Soviet invasion of Czechoslovakia Cernik continued in office until he was forced to resign and was suspended from the Communist Party.

**CFTC.** See CONFÉDÉRATION GÉNÉRALE DU TRAVAIL.

**CGT.** See CONFÉDÉRATION GÉNÉRALE DU TRAVAIL.

**CGTU.** See CONFÉDÉRATION GÉNÉRALE DU TRAVAIL.

**Chamberlain, Austen** (1863–1937). British Conservative politician. He was the son of Joseph Chamberlain, whose parliamentary seat he took over in 1914. Unionist MP for Worcestershire East, 1892–1914; MP for Birmingham West from 1914; Chancellor of the Exchequer, 1903–5, 1919–21; Secretary of State for India, 1915–17; Lord Privy Seal, 1921–2, when he was also Conservative leader; Foreign Secretary, 1925–9; First Lord of the Admiralty, 1931. He won the 1925 Nobel Peace Prize for his prominence in the discussions leading to LOCARNO TREATIES.

W. N. Medlicott, *British Foreign Policy since Versailles, 1919–1963* (rev. ed. 1968)

**Chamberlain, (Arthur) Neville** (1868–1940). British Conservative politician. He was Lord Mayor of Birmingham, 1915–16, and Director-General of National Service, 1916–17. He entered parliament as MP for Birmingham Ladywood in 1918, a seat he held until 1929. From 1929 he was MP for Birmingham Edgbaston. Chamberlain held office as Postmaster-General, 1922–3; Paymaster-General, 1923; Minister of Health,

1923; Chancellor of the Exchequer, 1923–4; Minister of Health, 1924–9, 1931. From 1931 to 1937 he was again Chancellor of the Exchequer, and was Prime Minister from 1937 to 1940. In 1940 he resigned the premiership and became Lord President of the Council in CHURCHILL's war cabinet. That same year he retired from politics completely on health grounds. Chamberlain proved a dynamic and efficient administrator at the Ministry of Health and the Exchequer, but as Prime Minister his reputation is bound up with the debate on APPEASEMENT. He attempted to pursue a 'general settlement' of foreign policy issues in 1937, but was forced increasingly to meet the crises brought about by HITLER's aggressive intent towards his neighbours. He took the initiative in trying to avert war over the SUDETENLAND, flying to Germany to bargain with Hitler and eventually secure the MUNICH AGREEMENT. He promoted gradual rearmament and defence planning, believing Britain could not sustain a war until further preparations had taken place. Often accused of craven concession to Hitler, he was prepared to threaten war if Hitler broke the framework of international agreements and attached considerable importance to the 'piece of paper' he induced Hitler to sign in Munich renouncing war between the two states and accepting consultation and negotiation as the basis for solving problems in the future. Unable to restrain Hitler, he was forced to declare war on 3 September 1939, an outcome which he saw as a failure of his policy. He proved an uninspiring war leader, and the debacle of the Norwegian campaign in May 1940 led to a fall in his majority, which prompted his resignation. See also APPEASEMENT, NATIONAL GOVERNMENT.

M. Gilbert. *The Roots of Appeasement* (1966)
K. Robbins. *Munich* (1968)
D. Dilks. *Neville Chamberlain* (1985)
R. Overy and A. Wheatcroft. *The Road to War* (1989)

**Champagne offensive.** *See* FIRST WORLD WAR.

**Chanak Crisis.** Crisis in Anglo–Turkish relations in autumn 1922 arising out of the resurgence of Turkish power under Kemal Ataturk. Having defeated the Greek forces in western Anatolia and captured İzmir (Smyrna) on 11 September 1922, Ataturk stood ready to carry the war to Constantinople, garrisoned by international forces, and into the area of eastern Thrace allotted to Greece by the unratified TREATY OF SÈVRES. Although the French and Italian forces withdrew, recognizing the *fait accompli* of revived Turkish power, the British Prime Minister, LLOYD GEORGE, supported the Greek cause and ordered the British garrison at Chanak, on the Asiatic shore of the Dardanelles, to stand firm. The crisis was defused when the local British commander, General Harrington, concluded an agreement with the advancing Turkish forces at Mudania on 11 October 1922. The agreement pledged the return of eastern Thrace to Turkey, repudiating the Treaty of Sèvres and the neutralization of the Dardanelles and Bosphorus seaways. The agreement formed the basis for the TREATY OF LAUSANNE signed the following year and brought a settlement to the Turkish frontiers. The crisis had important repercussions in British domestic politics, contributing to the break-up of the coalition led by Lloyd George, who was felt to have brought the country to the brink of war with Turkey. On 19 October a vote of the Conservative Parliamentary Party at the Carlton Club decided that the coalition should end. Lloyd George resigned the same day. *See also* GRAECO–TURKISH WAR.

Lord Kinross, *Ataturk: A Biography of Mustafa Kemal, Father of Modern Turkey* (1965)
M. Kinnear. *The Fall of Lloyd George: The Political Crisis of 1922* (1973)
K. Morgan. *Consensus and Disunity: The Lloyd George Coalition Government* (1979)

**Charles [Karl], of Austria** (1887–1922). Austrian Emperor, 21 November 1916 to 11 November 1918. Charles succeeded FRANCIS JOSEPH as Emperor. Although keen to reform the monarchy and secure a separate peace with the Entente powers, he was unable to achieve either aim and left Austria in 1918 during the revolutionary upheavals which followed the end of the war without formally abdicating. He made two unsuccessful attemots to return to the Hungarian throne in 1921 which were resisted by the HORTHY regime. He died in exile.

G. B Sheperd. *The Last Habsburg* (1968)

**Charter 77.** Declaration signed by Czech human-rights activists supporting the rights to individual liberties guaranteed by the Soviet Union at the 1975 HELSINKI AGREEMENT. 1977 was a Human Rights Year, but the group became subject to persecution and imprisonment by the Czech authorities in spite of protests by the west. One of the original signatories was VACLAV HAVEL, subsequently President of post-communist Czechoslovakia.

**Cheka.** A security organization established in December 1917 by the BOLSHEVIKS as the Extraordinary Commission for Struggle with Counter-revolution and Sabotage. Headed by Felix Dzerzhinsky (1877–1926), a Polish veteran of opposition against the Tsars, the Cheka was originally instituted to combat looting and black market trading, and to search out opponents of the Bolsheviks. Able to operate virtually without supervision, the Cheka soon began to undertake arbitrary arrests, trials and executions. Following the LEFT SOCIALIST REVOLUTIONARY PARTY rising in July 1918 and the attempt on Lenin's life in August it became the means of carrying out the RED TERROR in which the number of those killed ran into tens of thousands. The Cheka carried to a new and increasingly arbitrary degree the role of the old Tsarist secret police, the OKHRANA, although now acting in the name of the defence of the revolution. During 1918 the Cheka was installed in a headquarters on Lubyanka Square, Moscow, from which was conducted an increasingly systematic campaign against groups deemed to be 'enemies of the people'. Members of the old ruling class, priests and rich peasants or 'KULAKS' were executed and thousands more sent to LABOUR CAMPS. The Cheka operated behind the lines of the RED ARMY to deal with 'White' collaborators, and began to make habitual use of terror and arbitrary violence, resisting most attempts to restrain its powers. In spite of opposition from within the Bolsheviks, the Cheka did much to establish extra-legal forms and authoritarian tendencies in the new Soviet state. In 1922, with the Civil War over, the Cheka's functions were passed over to the People's Commissariat for Internal Affairs. A new organization, the State Political Adminis-

tration, the GPU (*see* GPU) was set up to exercise its functions.

G. Leggett, *The Cheka: Lenin's Political Police* (1981)

**Chernenko, Konstantin** (1911–85). Soviet leader. A Siberian, Chernenko emerged into prominence as a close supporter of BREZHNEV, joining the Central Committee of the Communist Party in 1971 and becoming its General Secretary; he was a candidate member of the Politburo in 1977, and in 1978 became a full member and, subsequently, Secretary. He was passed over in favour of ANDROPOV on the death of Brezhnev in 1982 because of the opposition of other senior politicians, but succeeded after Andropov himself died on 13 February 1984. At 72 Chernenko was the oldest man ever to take office as Soviet leader, and his succession was widely regarded as a victory for the 'old guard' against the newer, modernizing forces promoted by Andropov. Widely known to suffer from ill-health, Chernenko was also seen as a stop-gap Premier; this was proved quickly when he too died after 13 months in office on 10 March 1985. MIKHAIL GORBACHEV was named as party General Secretary four hours after the announcement of Chernenko's death.

**Chernobyl.** A major accident at a Soviet nuclear reactor complex at Chernobyl in the Ukraine on 26 April 1986. Following a safety experiment which went wrong, a fire and explosion in the Number 4 reactor spread nuclear contamination over a wide area of Russia and northern Europe. Although the immediate death toll was low, the permanent evacuation of the neighbouring town of Pripyat was necessary, and it was estimated that 'excess' deaths in the affected areas would number at least several hundred. Some areas of agricultural land have been permanently affected and restrictions on certain highland areas as far away as the British Isles were still in force three years later. The largest nuclear accident in Europe since that at Windscale (Sellafield) in the United Kingdom in 1957, the Chernobyl incident did much to highlight concern about the environment and promote Green parties in Europe. In spite of much scepticism at the time about its effects upon the Soviet nuclear programme, the damaged reactor was sealed off and the other three in the complex returned to full activity by 1988.

**Chetniks.** Originally the name for Serbian guerrillas fighting to liberate their homeland from the Turks, Chetnik groups were active in MACEDONIA prior to the outbreak of the Balkan Wars of 1912–13, fighting on behalf of Serbian expansion and continued to operate behind German lines in the First World War when the country was overrun. The Chetniks remained in being as a symbol of Serbian nationalism even after the formation of the new Kingdom of Serbs, Croats and Slovenes in 1918, renamed Yugoslavia in 1929. Following the fall of Yugoslavia to the Germans in 1941 the Chetniks were organized by General Drazha Mihailovic (1893–1946), a Yugoslav royalist officer, trained in guerrilla warfare during the 1930s. Operating from the rugged country of western Serbia against the occupying forces and the Croatian USTASE, the Chetniks received support from the British as the recognized non-communist partisan group operating in Yugoslavia and Mihailovic was formally appointed Minister of War by the Yugoslav government-in-exile based in London in January 1942. The Chetniks became increasingly absorbed in rivalry with the communist partisans led by TITO and some of their commanders co-operated with the AXIS occupying forces. British support for the Chetniks was withdrawn early in 1944 after reports that the Chetniks had acted against Tito's partisans and with growing evidence that it was the latter who was mounting the most determined opposition to the Axis occupation. The recognition given in 1944 to a provisional government headed by Tito sealed the fate of Mihailovic and the Chetniks, Mihailovic being dismissed by the London government-in-exile in May 1944. Although his forces remained in being they took little active part in the later stages of the fighting in Yugoslavia, although rescuing a number of Allied airmen who fell into their hands. Mihailovic was captured in March 1946 and tried for war crimes in Belgrade in June. After a five-week trial he was sentenced to death and shot on 17 July 1946.

Much confusion was caused during the Yugoslav conflict by the use of the term 'Chetnik' both by Mihailovic's pro-monarchist organization and some of the genuinely collaborationist groups working for the German puppet government based in Belgrade. But Mihailovic's Chetniks did, on occasion, attack Tito's partisans and were prepared to co-exist with the Italian occupying forces. The growth of Tito's communist-led partisan movement to an army half a million strong and its growing recognition as the only force tying down significant German forces, deprived the Chetniks of support and left them as the losers in the struggle to control the post-war Yugoslav state.

M. R. D. Foot, *Resistance* (1976)

**Chirac, Jacques** (1932–). French politician; Prime Minister of France 1974–6, 1986–8. Elected to the National Assembly in 1967, held various government posts under DE GAULLE and POMPIDOU, becoming Prime Minister under President GISCARD D'ESTAING in 1974. Increasing tension between Chirac as leader of the neo-Gaullist Rassamblement pour la République (RPR) and Giscard led to his emergence as a political rival to the President. Chirac was elected Mayor of Paris in 1977, giving him a highly prominent power base which he used to challenge Giscard and MITTERRAND, unsuccessfully, in the 1981 presidential election. Following the Gaullist victory in the March 1986 parliamentary elections, he began a period of unprecedented 'cohabitation' as Prime Minister with the socialist President Mitterrand. Student protest, labour unrest, terrorism and a currency crisis undermined Chirac's standing in the polls by 1987, losing support both to the Right and the Left. The government's PRIVATIZATION programme ran into problems in October 1987 as a result of the Stock Exchange crash, and there were unresolved difficulties with Kanak separatists in New Caledonia. The presidential elections of May 1988 ended two years of 'cohabitation'. Of the nine candidates who stood in the first round on 24 April only Chirac and Mitterrand went through to the second round two weeks later. In the second round Chirac was defeated gaining only 46 per cent of the vote to Mitterrand's 54 per cent. Mitterrand appointed Michel Rocard, leader of the social democratic wing of the Socialist Party, as his Prime Minister, asking him to form a centre-left administration in May 1988; Rocard remained in post following the inconclusive legislative elections in June. Chirac stayed confined to the sidelines as Mayor of Paris, where he displayed his continued independence by promoting his own Parisian celebrations for the bicentenary celebrations of the French Revolution in 1989.

**Christian Democratic Party, Italian.** Founded in 1943 as the successor to the prefascist PARTITO POPOLARE ITALIANO, the party has participated in all Italian governments since 1945, and has been the dominant force in Italian politics, especially since its greatest electoral victory in 1948 when it was led by ALCIDE DE GASPERI. In its early stages the party decisively rejected TRIPARTISM when it expelled its communist members from a coalition cabinet in May 1947, along with the more left-wing socialists. Thereafter the Christian Democrats ruled with Liberals, Social Democrats and Republicans in a bewildering variety of coalitions. The party firmly allied Italy to the West, accepting the MARSHALL PLAN, joining the NORTH ATLANTIC TREATY ORGANISATION and the EUROPEAN ECONOMIC COMMUNITY. The party enjoyed socialist support for a time in the 1960s and in the 1970s was in *de facto* coalition with the ITALIAN COMMUNIST PARTY after the 'Historic Compromise' was arranged to deal with the growing crises of inflation and terrorism (*see* TERRORISM, ITALIAN). The party is broadly conservative, though it has pursued agrarian reform, the mixed economy, and an extension of social welfare. In 1983 the party's vote slipped below 38 per cent for the first time since 1946 (to 33 per cent), just three per cent ahead of the communists. In 1983 the socialist leader BETTINO CRAXI formed a five-party coalition in which the Christian Democrats, as ever, formed the largest element. The Christian Democrats reversed their declining share of the vote winning 234 seats in the 1987 elections, providing once again the basis for a multiparty coalition.

R. A. Webster, *Christian Democracy in Italy* (1961)
P. Ginsbourg, *History of Contemporary Italy, 1943–1988* (1990)

**Christian Democratic Union, German.** (Christlich Demokratische Union; CDU). Moderate conservative party in the FEDERAL REPUBLIC OF GERMANY. Emerging from the remnants of the CENTRE PARTY of the WEIMAR REPUBLIC, the CDU was established at regional level in 1945–6 in the Western zones of occupied Germany. Committed to transcending the confessional divisions which had long plagued German politics, the CDU initially advocated 'Christian socialism' in opposition to both free-market conservatism and communism and social democracy, a philosophy which found expression in the party's Ahlen programme of February 1947. Yet, under the influence of Protestant groups within the party, especially those from North Germany which had been associated with the DNVP and DVP (*see* DNVP; DVP) during the Weimar period, the party increasingly moved towards advocacy of a neo-liberal market economy, a political shift enshrined in its 'Düsseldorf guidelines' of April 1949. In regional (*Land*) elections permitted by the Western occupying powers during 1946–7, the CDU gained on average 37.6 per cent of the popular vote, emerging as the largest party. Following the promulgation of the Basic Law of May 1949, elections were held to the Federal Parliament (*Bundestag*) of the new West German state in August 1949: the CDU, in alliance with its Bavarian wing, the CSU (*see* CHRISTIAN SOCIAL UNION) emerged as the largest grouping and provided the first Federal Chancellor, KONRAD ADENAUER. Since 1949 the CDU has played a very prominent role in West German politics at all levels. It was continuously in government from 1949 to 1969, usually in alliance with the FREE DEMOCRATIC PARTY (FDP); and formed the basis of the coalition supporting the KOHL government after October 1982. Committed to a moderate conservativism domestically, the CDU remained opposed to recognition of the East German state in the late 1960s and early 1970s: a keen supporter of West German membership of NATO, the CDU finally accepted the normalization of West Germany's relations with its communist neighbours achieved by Brandt's OSTPOLITIK prior to reunification in 1990.

G. Pridham, *Christian Democracy in Western Germany* (1977)

H. A. Turner. *The Two Germanies since 1945* (1987)

**Christian Social Party, Austrian** (CSP). The Christian Social Party was founded in 1889. The dominant personality of its early years was Dr Karl Lueger, whose pragmatic anti-Semitism ('I'll determine who is a Jew') appealed to the burgeoning lower middle classes of Vienna, where he was elected Lord Mayor. Conservative and strongly pro-Catholic, the party emerged as the principal party of the right after the First World War and the dominant partner in the 'bourgeois block' coalitions of the First Republic, when its leading figure was Mgr Ignaz Seipel. Following the suspension of parliament by Chancellor ENGELBERT DOLLFUSS in 1933 and the brief AUSTRIAN CIVIL WAR of February 1934, the party was dissolved, along with all other political parties and subsumed within the Fascist Fatherland Front. After the Second World War the political ground and electoral support of the CSP was taken over by the AUSTRIAN PEOPLE'S PARTY (ÖVP).

J. Boyer. *Political Radicalism in Late Imperial Vienna* (1981)

**Christian Social Union, German** (Christlich Soziale Union; CSU). Conservative political party of the FEDERAL REPUBLIC OF GERMANY. Essentially the Bavarian wing of the CHRISTIAN DEMOCRATIC UNION (CDU), the CSU has almost always acted at the national political level in conjunction with the CDU, whilst retaining a more conservative approach to both domestic politics and relations between the Federal Republic and its communist neighbours. Under its chairman, FRANZ-JOSEF STRAUSS, it was an intransigent opponent of the normalization of relations between the Federal Republic and the German Democratic Republic proposed by the BRANDT government in the early 1970s.

H. A. Turner. *The Two Germanies since 1945* (1987)

**Christlich Demokratische Union** (CDU). *See* CHRISTIAN DEMOCRATIC UNION, GERMAN.

**Christlich Soziale Union** (CSU). *See* CHRISTIAN SOCIAL UNION, GERMAN.

**Churchill, Winston Leonard Spencer** (1874–1965). British statesman. Churchill entered parliament as Conservative MP for Oldham in 1900. In 1904 he became a Liberal in protest at the Conservative policy on Tariff Reform, but remained member for Oldham until 1906. He was Liberal MP for Manchester North West, 1906–8, and for Dundee, 1908–22. He represented Epping, 1924–45, originally as a Constitutionalist, but later as a Conservative. He was Conservative MP for Woodford, 1945–64. Churchill held office as Under-Secretary for the Colonial Office, 1906–8; President of the Board of Trade, 1908–10; Home Secretary, 1910–11; First Lord of the Admiralty, 1911–15; Chancellor of the Duchy of Lancaster, 1915; Minister of Munitions, 1917–19; Secretary for War and Air 1919–21; Secretary for Air and Colonies, 1921; Colonial Secretary, 1921–2; Chancellor of the Exchequer, 1924–9; First Lord of the Admiralty, 1939–40; Minister of Defence and Prime Minister, 1940–45. He was then Leader of the Opposition, 1945–51; Prime Minister, 1951–5 and Minister of Defence, 1951–2. In 1953 Churchill was appointed Knight of the Garter. Churchill's career was long and varied. After leaving the CONSERVATIVE PARTY he became a radical and reforming minister. In the First World War disputes at the Admiralty and the failure of the Gallipoli Expedition led to a temporary fall from grace, but he returned to office and served in the post-war coalition. He returned to the Conservative Party as Chancellor of the Exchequer and presided over Britain's return to the GOLD STANDARD. During the inter-war period suspicions that he was at heart a reactionary appeared confirmed by his militant attitude against the GENERAL STRIKE and his opposition to the movement for Indian independence. But India and the question of rearmament also distanced him from his leaders in the 1930s, and allowed his return as an alternative to NEVILLE CHAMBERLAIN. His natural dynamism inspired the country during the SECOND WORLD WAR, but he was less in tune with the electorate's desire for post-war reform, and led his party to defeat in 1945. By 1951 he had come to terms with the post-war situation of Britain and returned to lead a Conservative government which pursued social reform, including important housing programmes under MACMILLAN, and removed restrictions from the economy. His last years were marred by his growing debility, and it was widely held he remained in power too long. He was a man of immense talents and energy. His supreme achievement lay in encouraging Britain's will to resist during the Second World War and harnessing its resources to eventual victory. His Anglo-American background assisted him in forging a strong personal relationship with ROOSEVELT which played a critical part in securing American LEND-LEASE and eventual American entry into the war against Germany. His role in the war-time conferences was restricted by Britain's dependence on America, but he sought to preserve British influence and the British Empire as a counter-weight to the United States and the Soviet Union. Recognising from an early stage the extent of Soviet ambitions in Europe, he negotiated spheres of influence with STALIN which formed the basis for the post-war division of eastern Europe and the Balkans. Although proved right on APPEASEMENT he was less sure-footed in domestics affairs, considered a maverick for much of the inter-war years, his rejection by the electorate in 1945 represented a distrust in his ability to adjust to the demands of peace. One of few British twentieth century politicians to count as a world statesman, he is regarded as one of the greatest of the country's Prime Ministers. *See also* APPEASEMENT.

M. Gilbert, *Winston S. Churchill* (1966-)
M. Cowling, *The Impact of Hitler* (1976)
H. Pelling, *Winston Churchill* (1987)

**Ciano, Galeazzo** (1903–44). Italian politician. Born in Leghorn, the son of an admiral, he entered the Foreign Service in 1925 and became MUSSOLINI's son-in-law in April 1930. He served in diplomatic posts in China for two years before becoming chief of the Press Office in 1933 and eventually Minister of Press and Propaganda in 1935. He served in the Ethiopian War as a bomber pilot, but was a surprise appointment as Foreign Minister in June 1936. He concentrated power on himself, but followed Mussolini's policies of pursuing intervention in the SPANISH CIVIL WAR, penetration of the Balkans and the signing of the AXIS agreements with Germany. Fearful of German dominance, he person-

ally insisted on the invasion of Albania in 1939, but urged Mussolini to remain outside the war and fashioned the policy of non-belligerency followed by Italy from 1 September 1939 until June 1940. He returned to active service following Italian entry into the war, but backed intervention in Greece, where the Italian defeats damaged his reputation. His return to the Foreign Ministry in April 1941 left him with little independent role and he was replaced in February 1943, becoming Ambassador to the Holy See. He voted for the resolution to overthrow Mussolini in late July 1943, but, placed under house arrest and threatened with investigation, he fled to Germany, where he was arrested. He was returned to the Italian Social Republic, Mussolini's puppet state in the north, where he was tried and executed in January 1944. His *Diaries* have become an important source for historians of the period, often revealing his antagonism to the Germans.

G. Ciano, *Ciano's Diplomatic Papers* (1948)
——, *Ciano's Hidden Diaries, 1937–1938* (1952)

**Civic Forum.** Pro-democracy movement founded on 19 November 1989 by VACLAV HAVEL and other Czech DISSIDENTS. It led the mass demonstrations which toppled the Czechoslovak Communist regime in early December 1989, followed by leading members of Civic Forum taking ministerial posts and Havel becoming President on 29 December. With its less dominant Slovak counterpart Public Against Violence, it obtained a majority in the first free elections held in Czechoslovakia for over forty years in June 1990, obtaining 169 of the 300 seats. Unlike the East German civil rights group, New Forum, which failed to make the transition from protest movement to an effective political force, Civic Forum traded heavily upon the prestige of Havel and the support of the former Communist leader DUBCEK to become the majority party and form a government.

**Civil Guard, Spanish.** Originally formed in 1844 to protect property and persons from widespread banditry, this paramilitary police force rapidly acquired a reputation as a staunch defender of the established order and a fierce, often repressive, opponent of dissent and protest in Spain.

Posted away from their native regions and isolated in fortified barracks, the Guards were often the only force of law and order. Involvement in the social and political conflicts of the RESTORATION, seen in bloody clashes with strikers and demonstrators, earned the force an equal measure of opprobrium and admiration. Subsequent attempts during the SECOND REPUBLIC by the Republican-Socialist government to replace the Guard with a new force, the Assault Guard, were successfully resisted by the army and political Right. Despite the continued prominence of the Guard in politics and against the labour movement – seen most dramatically in the ASTURIAS RISING of 1934 – the outbreak of the SPANISH CIVIL WAR produced a split in the ranks some 15,000 of 42,000 remained loyal to the Republic and were essential in defeating the military insurrection in Barcelona. Under FRANCO the Civil Guard became a key component of the repressive apparatus of the regime, in the guerrilla war of the late 1940s, in supervision of the populace and in the suppression of strikes and demonstrations. Even so, the Guard survived the transition to democracy and retains a variety of roles from local policing and highway patrol, to anti-terrorist activities in the Basque country (*see* BASQUES). A reminder of its chequered past came during the failed *coup d'état* of February 1982 when Civil Guard Lieutenant-Colonel Tejero invaded parliament at gunpoint.

S. G. Payne. *Politics and the Military in Modern Spain* (1967)

**Clause Four.** Clause Four of the BRITISH LABOUR PARTY's constitution of 1918 included the following statement of the party's objectives: 'To secure for the workers by hand or by brain the full fruits of their industry and the most equitable distribution thereof that may be possible upon the basis of the common ownership of the means of production, distribution, and exchange, and the best obtainable system of popular administration and control of each industry or service.'

The clause became seen by many on the left of the party as the touchstone of loyalty to socialist principles. Reference to 'Clause Four socialism' was usually taken to imply a commitment to the NATIONALIZATION of major industries, banks and other commercial enterprises. It formed the basis for the programme of nationalization carried on by the Labour Government under ATTLEE from 1945 and again under HAROLD WILSON from 1964. Attempts to dilute Clause Four caused bitter disputes between the Labour leader HUGH GAITSKELL and the left of the party in the 1950s and continued to act as an irritant to party unity in subsequent decades. Attempts to remove Clause Four or substantially alter it have so far failed, but since defeat in the 1987 general election the British Labour Party under NEIL KINNOCK has reviewed the nature of its commitment to Clause Four, abandoning a policy of nationalization in favour of what is termed 'social ownership'.

H. Pelling, *A Short History of the Labour Party* (8th edn, 1985)

**Clemenceau, Georges** (1841–1929). French politician. Born in La Vendée, he studied medicine at Nantes, then Paris. He settled in Monmartre where he became Mayor in 1870. A Radical member of the Chamber of Deputies, 1876–93, and Senator for Var, 1902–20. Strongly Republican and anticlerical, he was seen as a destructive and fearsome enemy, earning the nickname 'The Tiger', but was himself defeated in 1893 after implication in the Panama Scandal. Returning as a Senator, he first held office in March 1906 as Minister for Home Affairs, becoming Prime Minister in October. His period of office saw a strengthening of relations with Great Britain and attempts to deal with industrial unrest, but the government fell in 1909 as a result of outspoken criticism of the French navy. A 73-year-old elder statesman in 1914, he offered to serve in government only if one of the major government posts were made available. Passed over, he devoted himself to criticizing the incompetence of the French war effort and any evidence of defeatism. By 1917 his vehement criticisms and evident determination to see the war through to the bitter end made him the only viable alternative to a Premier who would seek a negotiated peace, for which CAILLAUX was the obvious candidate. POINCARÉ chose Clemenceau, who took up his post on 17 November 1917. He rallied France through the last year of the war, arresting 'defeatists' such as Caillaux, reforming the Cabinet and filling it with technicians, and retaining the key post of Minister of War for himself. He reasserted control over the military and was fortunate in having in PÉTAIN and FOCH, two of the more able French commanders to emerge in the war. Crucially, he remained loyal to his commanders as the German offensive of 1918 neared Paris, allowing them the opportunity to regroup and launch the counter-attacks which finally defeated the German armies. Clemenceau presided over the PARIS PEACE CONFERENCE. Although he earned a reputation as the architect of a punitive peace with Germany and was subsequently blamed in the interwar period for an almost neurotic concern for French security which only served to make a renewed war more likely, Clemenceau's determination to achieve security was balanced by a pragmatic notion of what his allies would accept. As a result he found himself having to fend off pressure from Marshal Foch, backed by Poincaré, for French annexations in the Rhineland or the setting up of a puppet French state. As a result he found himself attacked by the Right for having betrayed French security in the Versailles settlement and by the Left for having behaved high-handedly towards defeatists and pacifists. Failing in his attempt to succeed Poincaré as President, he retired from public life in January 1920. He remained an intransigent opponent of Germany and fearful of her resurgence, views he set out in his memoirs. He died in Paris in November 1929. *See also* VERSAILLES, TREATY OF.

G. Clemenceau, *The Grandeur and Misery of Victory* (1930)

J. C. King, *Generals and Politicians: Conflict between France's High Command, Parliament and Government, 1914–18* (1951)

D. R. Watson, *Georges Clemenceau: A Political Biography* (1974)

**CND.** *See* CAMPAIGN FOR NUCLEAR DISARMAMENT.

**CNT.** *See* CONFEDERACIÓN NACIONAL DEL TRABAJO.

**Cold War.** In general terms, a protracted state of tension between countries, fought with propaganda and economic weapons, as opposed to the 'hot war' of actual military engagement. The phrase was first used in a US Congress debate on 12 March 1947 and became the term used to describe the state of relations between the USA and the USSR in the aftermath of the SECOND WORLD WAR, developing into a global struggle between the two, each supported by their European allies organized into the NORTH ATLANTIC TREATY ORGANISATION (NATO) and the WARSAW PACT, as well as their supporters and allies in the rest of the world.

The Cold War began in Europe with disagreement over the division and future of Germany, as well as of the Eastern European states which had fallen under Soviet control following the defeat of Hitler's Germany. Misunderstanding and suspicion between Russia and the Western Allies had its origins in the Second World War when the Soviet Union suspected delays in the launching of a 'second front' against Germany as a deliberate attempt to weaken Russia and reduce her bargaining power following Hitler's defeat, while the West, particularly WINSTON CHURCHILL, suspected Russian intentions towards Eastern Europe. Although at the wartime conference at Yalta and Potsdam (*see* YALTA CONFERENCE, POTSDAM CONFERENCE) the Allies agreed that the ODER–NEISSE LINE would mark the new boundary between Germany and Poland and to a division of Germany into zones of occupation, co-operation between the Allies soon turned into animosity and recrimination after the surrender of Germany. While some Russia reparations from Germany had been agreed, the victorious powers were supposed to supervise the reconstruction of Germany as a single economic unit in order to avoid a repetition of the European-wide dislocation which had been caused by the destruction of the German economy and the REPARATIONS demanded from Germany after the FIRST WORLD WAR (*see also* DEPRESSION). Disagreements quickly arose over the scale of Russian reparations exacted from their occupation zone as well as those demanded from the other zones and which appeared to threaten the economic ruin of Western Europe by bringing about the total collapse of the German economy and prevent its revival. With each side accusing each other of bad faith the

Council of Foreign Ministers charged with working out the details of the peace settlement reached deadlock on the question of Germany's political and economic unification.

Ideological differences came increasingly to the fore as a result of Soviet control of Eastern Europe and the fostering of communist regimes in the countries which they occupied, a process completed in February 1948, when the Communist Party seized control of Czechoslovakia. From the West it appeared increasingly that the Soviet Union was turning Eastern Europe into a Russian-dominated communist bloc and was poised for further advance into Western Europe and the Balkans. As early as March 1946 Churchill had dramatically emphasized the division of Europe in his 'IRON CURTAIN' speech and fears of the expansion of communist influence were heightened by the GREEK CIVIL WAR. President Truman's enunciation of the 'TRUMAN DOCTRINE' led to direct American military aid to the anti-communist forces in Greece and to the MARSHALL PLAN intended to revitalize the European economies and to help forestall the rise of communism in Europe. Initially the United States had hoped to include Eastern as well as Western European countries in a vast programme of European recovery, but Marshall Aid was rejected by the Soviet Union for itself and its satellites, who instead founded COMECON. Marshall Aid for Western Germany also led to adoption of a new West German currency in June 1948, to which the Russians replied with an East German mark for their zone. This total lack of co-operation hardened into further mutual antagonism with the Berlin blockade and airlift (see BERLIN AIRLIFT) beginning on 30 March when the Russians imposed traffic restrictions on access to Berlin. Lasting for almost a year, the Berlin blockade marked the first major confrontation of the Cold War. Against this background the decision was taken to form NATO in 1949, by which the United States became pledged to the defence of Western Europe. With the admission of Greece and Turkey to the alliance in 1951 and the continuing Soviet hegemony over Eastern Europe the division of Europe and the rigidity of the Cold War was intensified. The incorporation of West Germany into the NATO alliance in 1955 meant that the reunification of Germany had become virtually impossible and the Cold War battlelines in Europe were drawn up between the forces of NATO and the Warsaw Pact, formed in the same year.

Already, however, the Cold War had taken on a global dimension, with the outbreak of the Korean War in 1950 and the intervention of the United Nations and American troops to resist the invasion of South Korea by the communist North Korean forces, backed by Communist China and the Soviet Union, as well as American support for non-communist regimes and alliances all over the world in line with the Truman Doctrine. Nonetheless, although tension was to flare up on the boundaries of the superpowers' spheres of influence, there was no direct American–Russian confrontation in Europe. Moreover, although at its height the Cold War was marked by intense propaganda efforts by both sides, an underlying basis for coexistence lay in the mutual understanding that any attempt to alter the *status quo* in Europe would lead to war. In part, this situation was strengthened by the possession by both powers after 1950 of NUCLEAR WEAPONS and their deployment for use in the event of conflict in Europe. As early as July 1955 a summit meeting in Geneva of US, USSR, British and French leaders promised some relaxation of tension, but the outbreak of the HUNGARIAN UPRISING in autumn 1956 and the SUEZ CRISIS of the same year led to an end to these hopes. A renewed hardening of attitudes was seen in 1961 with the building of the BERLIN WALL, symbolizing not only the division of the city but also the permanence of the division between communist and non-communist Europe. In 1962 the discovery of Russian missiles in Cuba – the 'Cuban missile crisis' – was widely recognized as marking the high point of tension between the superpowers when war seemed imminent. Cold War tensions were somewhat relaxed in the aftermath and during the 1960s in spite of conflicts in Vietnam, the Middle East, Africa and the Russian invasion of Czechoslovakia to end the 'PRAGUE SPRING' in 1968.

The post-Stalin era and fear of nuclear war bred greater interest in DÉTENTE. The

TEST BAN TREATY and the SALT I treaty (*see* STRATEGIC ARMS LIMITATION TALKS) provided the tangible evidence of greater East–West co-operation for the pursuit of peaceful relations, but subject to clashes of interest in the world at large. Thus the 1979 SALT II treaty, agreed in principle between the United States and the Soviet Union, was not ratified by the US Senate as a result of the SOVIET INVASION OF AFGHANISTAN. In addition, Western alarm at the growth of the Soviet nuclear armoury and concern about Russian treatment of DISSIDENTS was met by Russian criticism of an American arms build-up in Europe (*see* CRUISE MISSILE) and doubts about the good faith of the Reagan administration in its negotiations. These disagreements together with Western support for the Polish SOLIDARITY movement served to heighten tension again.

With the death of BREZHNEV and the eventual emergence of MIKHAIL GORBACHEV as Soviet leader, a new process of negotiations began towards further arms talks and the easing of East–West tensions. During 1985–9 progress was rapid. A series of summit meetings between Presidents Reagan and Gorbachev began the resumption of arms talks and cuts in nuclear forces. Soviet withdrawal from Afghanistan and the operation of GLASNOST in the Soviet Union greatly eased tension. In 1988 Gorbachev effectively abandoned the BREZHNEV DOCTRINE, followed by the formation of non-communist governments in Poland in 1989 and the end of the communist monopoly in Hungary. In the autumn of 1989, the opening of the Berlin Wall, followed by the collapse of communist regimes in East Germany, Czechoslovakia and Bulgaria, led Presidents Bush and Gorbachev at the Malta summit on 4 December 1989 to declare the Cold War 'at an end'. By the end of the year, Gorbachev had made it known he would allow the Eastern European countries to seek their own paths, even by early 1990 accepting the unification of East and West Germany and the dissolution of the Warsaw Pact as a military alliance.

The Cold War is normally considered to have reached its maximum intensity between the end of the Second World War and the Cuban Missile Crisis, lending its name to a period – the Cold War era – of tense, suspicious and antagonistic relations between the capitalist and communist worlds. Its interpretation has been influenced by its history and to some extent by the ideological commitments of the parties concerned. The traditional interpretation (often represented in the writings of Western statesmen involved in the events of the period) viewed the Cold War as the result of the Soviet Union's self-interested determination to turn the countries of Eastern Europe into satellite states, to prevent the reunification of Germany, and to spread communism and communist influence within and without Europe. This view emphasizes the Soviet failure to participate genuinely in the plans to reunify Germany, its destruction of democracy in Eastern Europe and its continued repression of any movements there which threatened its hegemony, and the threat posed by Soviet and Warsaw Pact forces to the security of Western Europe. The 'revisionist' view stresses the long-term antagonism of the capitalist world to communism and the Soviet Union from its inception in the Bolshevik Revolution (*see* RUSSIAN REVOLUTION), symbolized by the Allied intervention in the RUSSIAN CIVIL WAR, the APPEASEMENT of fascism prior to the Second World War, and Western allies' conduct in the Second World War. In this view, a Russia devastated by invasion, the loss of 20 million dead, and having borne the brunt of the war against the German land forces was afraid of her economically more powerful former allies, backed, initially, by their sole possession of nuclear weapons. In this context, the Stalinist takeover of Eastern Europe was a defensive reaction to the threat from the West, and the Cold War was the result of mutual misunderstanding, exacerbated by the anti-communist rhetoric of Western leaders in the immediate post-war period. These views of the Cold War remain in contention and are likely to remain so, but have led to fresh and more detached assessments of the origins of Cold War and of the immediate post-war years.

W. Lafeber (ed.), *The Origins of the Cold War* (1977) and M. McCanley, *Origins of the Cold War* (1983) have documents.

H. S. Truman, *Year of Decisions, 1945* (1955) and *Years of Trial and Hope, 1946–53* (1956) and D. Acheson,

*Present at the Creation* (1970) are memoirs of western participants. L. J. Halle, *The Cold War as History* (1967) W. Lafebar, *America, Russia and the Cold War* (1982) and S. E. Ambrose, *Rise to Globalism* (1983) give the Western viewpoint. A. B. Ulam, *Expansion or Coexistence* (1968) speaks for the Soviet side. T. M. Wolfe, *Soviet Power and Europe, 1945–70* (1970); V. Rothwell, *Britain and the Cold War, 1941–7* (1983) presents the British perspective

**collective security.** Term widely used in international diplomacy between the two world wars, first coined at the 1924 Geneva Conference, denoting a policy whereby the security of individual countries was guaranteed jointly by others. It was the basic principle of the LEAGUE OF NATIONS and required acceptance by individual members of collective decisions backed up, if necessary, by military action. The term was also applied to attempts to establish a system of multilateral alliances for defence against Germany in the 1930s. Collective security was widely seen to have failed following the Japanese invasion of Manchuria in 1931 and the Italian invasion of Ethiopia in 1935.

**collectivization, Soviet.** General term for the amalgamation of individual peasant holdings into collective farms (*kolkhozy*). The Decree on Land of 8 November 1917 had socialized all land ownership but left it to be divided up by the rural authorities for peasant use on an egalitarian basis. The resulting development of small peasant holdings, some 23 million by 1924, was, in fact, contrary to Bolshevik policy, which envisaged the creation of model collectives which would encourage the peasantry to join them. A small number of these were begun in the RUSSIAN CIVIL WAR, including *kommuna* where all property was held in common, the cartel in which households maintained their own houses and plots but shared the rest of the land and the equipment to cultivate it, the TOZ or 'association for common cultivation' in which part or all of the land was farmed collectively, and state farms (*sovhozy*) where labourers were paid a regular wage. By 1927 these made up only 2 per cent of the total landholding in the Soviet Union. In contrast, the NEW ECONOMIC POLICY had increased the number of individual smallholdings by over a third in the ten years since the revolution, the average size of which was actually less in 1927 than at the time of the revolution.

Grain supply to the towns and to the industrial workers remained precarious both because of the chronic inefficiency of peasant agriculture and a tendency for peasants to consume a larger portion of their own produce or cut back on production if they found industrial and consumer goods too expensive or unavailable, provoking a 'SCISSORS CRISIS' and falling agricultural output. Even the best harvest under the New Economic Policy, in 1926, although a significant increase on the disastrous levels of 1920–21, was below the level of 1914 and one-fifth less per head than pre-war. The failure of agriculture to supply sufficient grain to feed the towns and provide a basis for industrialization was the major motive for a return to requisitioning and the attack on the KULAKS in 1928. The adoption of collectivization aimed not only to eliminate small landholdings and group them into larger, more efficient units, but also to resolve the endemic problem of procuring sufficient food from the peasants to sustain industrial growth. In effect, the capital required for industrial development was to be supplied by depressing the living standards of the peasants.

The first FIVE YEAR PLAN envisaged the collectivization of approximately a fifth of the land by 1933, and during 1929 a campaign to create collective farms merged into the process of forced food procurement. The new collective farms now became the focus of a massive propaganda campaign and a much more rapid process than envisaged. A Central Committee resolution in January 1930 called for 'total collectivization' by early 1932 and in some regions a year earlier. STALIN urged party volunteers to go out into the country and speed the process of creating the new collectives. Using a mixture of inducements, such as new machinery, and threats of heavy taxes and punishments, collectivization turned into a frenzied and almost chaotic process. Many peasants reacted by slaughtering their livestock, consuming their stores of grain, and even burning their homes rather than hand them over to the collectives. Stalin tried to slow the process down with an article in *Pravda* at the end of March 1930, 'Dizzy with Success'. The programme was revived later in the year, although more carefully managed and designed to allow each household a private plot. By the summer of 1931 a half of all peasant households were collectivized, by 1932 more than three-quarters. In less than four years over 18 million peasant households, over 90 million people had been collectivized.

Undoubtedly the most rapid period of activity in the early months of 1930 had been greater than was possible to achieve without massive disruption to output. The number of peasant households collectivized rose from just 17 per cent in January 1930 to almost 58 per cent three months later. As a consequence, the immediate economic results of collectivization were disappointing. Grain output did not reach 1928 levels again until 1938, and losses in livestock reduced the number of cattle and pigs by 50 per cent and of sheep and goats by two-thirds. As a result of de-Kulakization and collectivization many of the most efficient peasant farmers were now dead, deported or submerged in the new collectives. The human cost has been variously estimated, at least 2 million people died, the effects of reorganization being compounded by a devastating famine in the Ukraine and elsewhere. The cost to the peasantry and the effects of the famine were intensified by the increase of state procurements, both in absolute figures and as a percentage of the total crop, rising from 14 per cent of grain in 1928 to almost 40 per cent by 1935, providing the food supplies necessary to sustain Stalin's programme of industrialization.

Collectivization altered the whole structure of Soviet agriculture and was to have profound effects. The great majority of farms were organized as *kolkhozy* working to delivery plans dictated by the Commissariat for Agriculture. Its delivery targets were enforced through Machine Tractor Stations (MTS) who provided machinery and equipment to groups of *kolkhozy* in return for deliveries. The MTS had direct access to the state security apparatus to deal with any recalcitrants. *Kolkhoz* members were organized into brigades and paid for each day's work from the surplus left to the collective after meeting their procurement targets and deliveries to the MTS. As passports were required for a change of residence from 1932 and these were refused

to *kolkhoz* members, the ex-peasants were depressed to the level of brigade members, with little incentive to work. The Model Kolkhoz Statute of 1935 did, however, permit members to cultivate a small plot of land and keep a limited number of animals, from which surpluses could be sold at licensed markets. These soon began to provide a significant supply of food to the towns, and after 1938 the collectives began to achieve output higher than before collectivization. When the Soviet Union occupied the BALTIC STATES in 1940 it extended collectivization to those areas.

During the Second World War, with the loss of huge areas of agricultural land to the Germans, the *kolkhoz* structure was loosened, permitting peasants to operate the *zveno* ('link') system in which small family groups took over responsibility for land hitherto farmed collectively and were free to dispose of any surplus after meeting the procurement targets; some were even allowed to farm privately sections of collective land. These modifications were a reflection of what was recognized as the inefficiency of the collective system and the greater productivity of the private plots. These relaxations also had some support at upper Party levels, but a decree in September 1946 returned all private land to the collectives, increased taxes on private plots, and reimposed the full rigours of the procurement system. To improve efficiency the *kolkhozy* were amalgamated, more than halving their number. Collectivization was 'exported' to satellite states, such as Poland. Stalin's death, however, prompted the admission that agriculture remained a weak point in the Soviet economy. Production in 1953 remained below pre-war levels. Under KHRUSHCHEV there were deliberate attempts to increase productivity on the collectives by reducing taxes on private plots and raising prices for goods procured by the state. Under BREZHNEV there were further relaxations, procurement targets were to be set over a longer period and higher prices paid; investment, already increased heavily under Khrushchev, was raised again, encouragement given to private animal-rearing, and experiments with the 'link' system revived.

Collectivized agriculture is recognized as the source of some of the most pressing problems facing the Soviet economy. Almost from their inception, the produce of the private plots, a tiny percentage of the total acreage, have played a disproportionate part in feeding the towns with scarce and good quality produce. In spite of massive investment under both Khrushchev and Brezhnev, the collectives remain inefficient by Western European or American standards. GORBACHEV's campaign to revitalize the Soviet economy has still to find a decisive solution to the legacy bequeathed by Stalin. See also INDUSTRIALIZATION DEBATE, SOVIET.

M. Fainsod, Smolensk under Soviet Rule (1958)
L. Volin, A Century of Russian Agriculture: from Alexander II to Khrushchev (1970)
R. W. Davies, The Socialist Offensive: The Collectivisation of Soviet Agriculture, 1929–30 (1976)
G. A. Hosking, A History of the Soviet Union (1985)

**Collins, Michael** (1890–1922). Irish soldier and politician. Born at Sam's Cross, West Cork, he was the son of a farmer. He worked in London but returned to Ireland to take part in the EASTER RISING of 1916. He was imprisoned in Frongoch internment camp, where he emerged as a leader. After his release in December 1916 he became Secretary to the reformed IRISH REPUBLICAN BROTHERHOOD. He was a member of the Provisional Dail Eireann and Minister of Finance in the Provisional Government, but also organized and led attacks on the British forces from 1919, including the killing of 11 British intelligence officers in Dublin on 21 November 1920. Collins proved a ruthless and energetic guerrilla commander, but also a skilful negotiator in the Dail's delegation to the London Conference of October 1921, which sought to achieve a settlement. He was a party to the agreement of December 1921 which proposed the setting up of an Irish Free State of 26 counties with Dominion status. He used his prestige to support the pro-treaty proposals in the Dail and became Ireland's first Prime Minister in January 1922. During the Civil War which followed between pro- and anti-treaty forces Collins was killed in an ambush by Republican forces at Beal na Blath in Cork on 21 August 1922. Widely admired as a courageous and romantic leader of the Irish revolution – known universally as 'the Big Fellow' – Collins proved a highly successful guerrilla leader, but also a political pragmatist.

F. O'Connor, The Big Fellow: Michael Collins and the Irish Revolution (1965)
C. Younger, Ireland's Civil War (1968)

**Comecon** (Council for Mutual Economic Assistance). An organization established in Moscow in January 1949 with the aim of improving trade between the USSR and other Eastern European socialist states. It was used by STALIN as an instrument for enforcing a commercial boycott of Yugoslavia between 1948 and 1955, but also served as a Soviet response to the growing economic interdependence of Western European nations. Original members were Albania (expelled in 1961), Bulgaria, Czechoslovakia, Hungary, Poland, Romania and the USSR. East Germany joined in 1950, Mongolia in 1962 and Cuba in 1972. The organization came under increasing strain during the late 1980s as several Eastern bloc countries adapted to more democratic regimes and free-market policies. In early 1990 Comecon decided that it would in future trade in hard currencies rather than the artificially rated rouble, a move seen as a crucial opening up of the organization to world-wide economic influences. German reunification and the independence of the former communist states of eastern Europe had virtually destroyed Comecon by the summer of 1991.

Z. Brzezinski, The Soviet Bloc (1974)

**Cominform** (Communist Information Bureau). Established in October 1947 following a secret conference near Warsaw attended by communist leaders from the Soviet Union, France, Italy, Bulgaria, Czechoslovakia, Hungary, Poland, Romania and Yugoslavia. The timing of the meeting indicated the desire of the Soviet Union to co-ordinate the activities of communist parties throughout Europe in light of the introduction of the MARSHALL PLAN and ensure that communist countries such as Poland and Czechoslovakia did not participate. The Soviet delegation was headed by ANDREI ZHDANOV, who helped to shape the organization, which remained a much looser and solely European body in contrast with the old COMINTERN, dissolved in 1943. None the less, it represented an attempt to orchestrate communist policy and opinion as the battle-lines of the COLD WAR were hardening. Accordingly its second meeting in January 1948 was concerned primarily with attacking the United States. Soon after, it was disrupted by the quarrel between STALIN and TITO, leading to the expulsion of Yugoslavia from Cominform in June 1948. As a result of the quarrel, the headquarters of Cominform was moved from Belgrade to Bucharest, where Cominform held its last meeting in November 1949 confined largely to attacks upon Tito. Stalin's decision to set up COMECON in 1949 largely rendered the need for Cominform superfluous, a point reinforced by the creation of the military alliance of the WARSAW PACT in 1955. By that time, KHRUSHCHEV's attempts at a *rapprochement* with Tito also made it expedient to dispense with the organization which symbolized former disagreements. On 17 April 1956 Cominform announced its own dissolution on the grounds that its composition and activities no longer were in accord with the 'new situation'.

A. B. Ulam, *Titoism and Cominform* (1952)
W. S. Sworakowski, 'The Communist Information Bureau', in W. S. Sworakowski (ed.), *World Communism: A Handbook, 1918–1965* (1973)

**Comintern** (Communist International). The Russian Bolshevik International or 'Third International' founded on 2 March 1919 at a Congress in Moscow. During 1918 the Bolshevik government in Russia established links with Bolshevik parties and republics abroad, mostly in the immediate vicinity of the Soviet State, and a preliminary 'international meeting' was convened in Petrograd on 19 December 1918. A spur to action was a call to revive the second SOCIALIST INTERNATIONAL, from whose reformism the Bolsheviks wished to disassociate themselves, intending to supplant it by a body committed to promoting revolutionary Marxism and world revolution. The first Congress was attended by 51 delegates from 30 countries, heavily dominated by Soviet representatives and those of neighbouring communist parties. Initially the Comintern was limited both by the existence of relatively few communist parties and the condemnation of socialists who denounced the Bolshevik International as an attempt to

split the international working class and place them under Bolshevik domination. Moreover, both LENIN and TROTSKY envisaged the rapid success of revolutionary movements elsewhere in Europe. When these failed to materialize, the Comintern became both the focus of discussions about the proper response of communist parties and the increasingly well-organized means of disseminating programmes of action to national parties. In 1921 the third Congress acknowledged that world revolution was several years away and called on communists to apply 'flexible tactics'. By the fourth Congress in November–December 1922 the Comintern had developed a secretariat, executive and 'regional bureaus', largely funded by the Soviet Union. Increasingly it became absorbed in transmitting a clear 'line' on policy to national parties and front organizations, and in resolving organizational and ideological disputes. As many communist parties found themselves banned or driven underground, the Soviet Union became not only the spiritual home but the actual base of their operations. In the mid-1920s, especially after the death of Lenin and the eclipse of Trotsky, the character of the Comintern became increasingly that of an arm of Soviet policy. The Fifth Plenum of the Comintern Executive in 1925 confirmed the end of the period of 'revolutionary upsurge', carrying with it the implication that the furtherance of socialism in the Soviet Union was the principal task of the International. The triumph of STALIN's doctrine of 'SOCIALISM IN ONE COUNTRY' saw Comintern increasingly reflect the changing emphases of Soviet foreign policy. As a result, the Sixth Congress in July–September 1928 heard BUKHARIN inaugurate the 'third period' of new conflicts and internal tensions within the capitalist world in which communists should adopt a 'class against class' policy. This called on communist parties to sever links with other reformist socialist parties and, indeed, to concentrate their attacks upon them as 'social fascists'. While Stalin appears to have taken little interest in the affairs of Comintern while engaged in the COLLECTIVIZATION campaign and the first FIVE YEAR PLAN, this policy of sectarian exclusiveness seriously reduced the membership of some national parties and weakened the opposition to the rise of fascism in Germany and elsewhere. Internal evidence suggests that Comintern was itself confused about how to react to the consequences of the DEPRESSION and the rise of the Nazis (*see* NAZI PARTY). After HITLER's accession to power, Comintern policy gradually shifted, from 1934 playing an important role by backing the POPULAR FRONT movement in which co-operation between communist parties and other 'anti-fascist' groupings was now encouraged. The seventh Congress, meeting in 1935, deleted all references to world revolution in favour of 'anti-fascism'. Although of limited success because of the antagonisms created by earlier communist attitudes, the changed tone of Comintern contributed to the formation of Popular Front governments in France and Spain and attempts to do so elsewhere. In many countries, however, the changed 'Moscow line' came too late to prevent the consolidation of fascist or dictatorial regimes. After 1936 Comintern was active in organizing aid to the Spanish Republic, including the INTERNATIONAL BRIGADES and a major propaganda offensive on behalf of the Republican side in the SPANISH CIVIL WAR. The extent to which Comintern had become bound up with Soviet objectives was demonstrated by the widespread purges of its officials carried out in Stalin's terror, virtually destroying the personnel of some national bureaus. A further demonstration came when national parties were required to follow the volte-face in Soviet foreign policy resulting from the NAZI–SOVIET PACT of 1939, then switch again when the Nazis invaded the Soviet Union in the summer of 1941. Once engaged in the grand alliance with Britain and the United States against the Nazis, Stalin was prepared to close down Comintern as a gesture to his allies that he did not seek interference in the affairs of other states. It was formally dissolved on 22 May 1943.

L. Trotsky, *The First Five Years of the Communist International* (1973)

F. Claudin, *The Communist Movement: From Comintern to Cominform* (1975)

**commissar.** Soviet term for a high-ranking official, such as a minister, but extended to 'political commissars' who took over a supervisory role in the RED ARMY. They were introduced by Trotsky in 1918 when the Red Army was forced to reintroduce hierarchical organization and recruit extensively from ex-Tsarist officers and unreliable elements in the peasantry. The 'political commissars' were Party-approved appointees who were placed on an equal footing with the military commanders to ensure ideological conformity among both officers and men. Subsequently their powers fluctuated according to the perceived military and political priorities of the Soviet Union. The system was abolished for a short time in 1940 following weaknesses shown up in the RUSSO–FINNISH WAR of 1939–40; they were reinstated again in every unit in 1941 following the German invasion, then reduced in power again in 1943, remaining in existence to the present.

M. McKintosh, *Juggernaut: A History of the Soviet Armed Forces* (1967)

T. J. Colton, *Commissars, Commanders and Civilian Authority: The Structure of Soviet Military Politics* (1979)

**Commission of the European Community.** An independent body with a central place in the formulation and execution of European Community policy. Until 1967 the EUROPEAN ECONOMIC COMMUNITY (EEC) EUROPEAN COAL AND STEEL COMMUNITY (ECSC) and EURATOM each had separate Commissions (in the ECSC called the High Authority). The MERGER TREATY of 1965 replaced these with a single body. The members are appointed by agreement between the governments of the member states for four-year terms. One of them is appointed president (chairman) for a two-year, renewable, term. They are required to be completely independent and do not represent the countries from which they come. They can only be removed as a body, and only by a vote of the European Parliament. Each Commissioner is responsible for one or more of the main areas of Community policy, for example, regional policy, but they act as a collegiate body and take collective responsibility for their proposals and actions. The Commission's functions are laid down by the treaties. Under the TREATY OF PARIS the High Authority (Commission) was assigned the major role in applying the rules laid down in the treaty. The EEC and Euratom treaties lay more stress upon the action of the Council of Ministers, although the Commission maintains a vital role. The Commission drafts Community laws, submitting its proposals to the COUNCIL OF MINISTERS, the EUROPEAN PARLIAMENT and the ECONOMIC AND SOCIAL COMMITTEE. It implements decisions reached by the Council of Ministers and draws up the budget. Formally it is responsible for ensuring that the treaty obligations are fulfilled by all the member states, and it may refer infringements to the Court of Justice. *See also* COUNCIL OF MINISTERS OF THE EUROPEAN COMMUNITY; COURT OF JUSTICE OF THE EUROPEAN COMMUNITY.

**Committee of National Liberation, Polish.** *See* LUBLIN COMMITTEE.

**Committee of Permanent Representatives of the European Community** (Coreper). A committee composed of representatives of the member states of the EUROPEAN ECONOMIC COMMUNITY, who have the task of ambassador; the committee is frequently known, from the French version of its title, as Coreper. Although such a body, consisting of senior national officials, existed from the early days of the EUROPEAN COAL AND STEEL COMMUNITY (ECSC) it was given a formal place amongst the European Community's institution by Article 4 of the 1965 MERGER TREATY. Its functions are there defined as being to prepare the work of the Council of Ministers and to carry out tasks which the Council assigns to it. Coreper meets as two groups, a meeting of the Permanent Representatives and a meeting of their deputies. Business is divided between the two groups according to its subject matter. Coreper forms the apex of the COUNCIL OF MINISTERS machinery, which examines proposals for Community legislation produced by the COMMISSION OF THE EUROPEAN COMMUNITY. Coreper is not concerned with agricultural policy, which is handled by a Special Committee on Agriculture. It negotiates the major issues which remain unsolved during the technical discussions in working groups. If agreement can be reached between the member states in Coreper, the proposed legislation is passed to the Council of Ministers and is formally endorsed, without discussion, at the next Council of Ministers meeting whatever the nature of the main business being considered. If agreement cannot be reached, the issues are then negotiated at the next meeting of the Council concerned with the appropriate topic. Coreper's activities are not confined to legislation but may also cover the Community's position in being essentially inter-governmental negotiations, which, although a representative of the Commission is present, are confidential.

R. Pryce, *The Politics of the European Community* (1973)
H. Wallace, *National Governments and the European Communities* (1973)

**Common Agricultural Policy** (CAP). Developed under Articles 38 to 47 of the TREATY OF ROME as an essential part of the achievement of a common market in agricultural products among members of the EUROPEAN ECONOMIC COMMUNITY, this policy was designed to replace the wide variety of different measures used by THE SIX to protect and support their agricultural producers with a single, Community-wide system. Its objectives, set out in Article 39 of the Treaty of Rome, were to increase agricultural productivity; to ensure a fair standard of living for the agricultural population; to stabilize markets; to guarantee supplies; and to ensure reasonable prices to consumers. The Community, from the beginning, based its policy on supporting agricultural producers by fixing a price for their products which would ensure that they received a reasonable income. It protected them against competition from cheaper imports by taxing imports so as to bring the price of the imported products up to the level of the price fixed for Community products. Essentially, then, the farmer is supported directly by the consumer (instead, for example, of support from subsidies paid for indirectly by general taxation). If, however, the agricultural producer is unable to sell his products at the fixed price, perhaps because of over-production, the Community, through the mechanism of national intervention agencies, itself buys the products.

A common policy for marketing many agricultural products was agreed by 1964, and the first uniform prices, for cereals, were implemented in 1967. These prices, usually linked together in a package, in the hope that some parts will prove sufficiently attractive to each member state to enable all to accept the whole package, are the subject of intensive, sometimes all-night, bargaining in the annual meetings of the Agriculture Council of the Council of Ministers. The negotiations are subject to pressures from agricultural producers in their own countries, from COPA, which represents agricultural producers throughout the Community, and increasingly from consumers.

Successive treaties of accession have provided for gradual application of the CAP to the new members of the Community. In addition to the achievement of common prices for agricultural products, the Common Agricultural Policy is intended to encourage the 'structural' improvement of farming, for example by encouraging the amalgamation of small and inefficient farms, and the provision of modern buildings and machinery. In 1968 proposals, known as the Mansholt Plan, were produced to further this policy, and a number of measures to this end were adopted by the Council of Ministers in 1972. This aspect of the policy has, however, had much less impact than the pricing and marketing policies, and national measures continue to be important in the field. By the late 1970s there was growing concern about the effects of agricultural subsidies under the CAP in creating huge surpluses of produce: wine 'lakes', butter and grain 'mountains' and large stockpiles of meat and meat products. Temporary solutions were found in the distribution of food to foreign countries as aid, subsidized exports to Eastern Europe, and hand-outs to the elderly and disadvantaged in Community countries. With the CAP taking up to two-thirds of the Community budget and new leaders such as Mrs Thatcher arguing for a policy more in accordance with market realities, the Community began from 1983 an attempt to cut back on agricultural subsidies and reduce surpluses. In 1988 a package of farm reforms was agreed which further attempted to cut back on food production with the aim of eliminating the stockpiles. Systems of quotas for dairy produce, incentives to diversify agriculture, and for taking land out of production have become features of agricultural policy in most Community countries.

D. Swann, *The Economics of the Common Market* (1964)

L. Tsoukalis (ed.), *The European Community: Past, Present and Future* (1983)

**Commonwealth.** *See* BRITISH COMMONWEALTH OF NATIONS.

**Communist Party, Austrian** (Kommunistische Partei Österreichs; KPÖ). Formed during the revolutionary upheavals of November 1918, the KPÖ has failed throughout its history to attract significant electoral support. In the First Republic it was thwarted by the radicalism and relative success of the AUSTRIAN SOCIAL DEMOCRATIC WORKER'S PARTY (SDAP), particularly in Vienna. Its popularity increased during the Austrofascist dictatorship and during the Second World War, when it was disproportionately over-represented in the resistance to Nazism. It participated in the Provisional Government of 1945, but its popularity receded rapidly. Its remaining strength lies in the trade unions. A pro-Soviet rather than a Euro-Communist party, it was last represented in parliament in 1959, and on the Vienna City Council in 1969.

**Communist Party, British.** The Communist Party of Great Britain was founded at a Unity Convention held in London in July–August 1920. Most of the delegates at the conference were representatives of the British Socialist Party which had previously agreed to merge into the new party. Attempts in the early years to affiliate to the LABOUR PARTY were rebuffed. J. T. W. Newbold became the first Communist MP (for Motherwell) in 1922. In 1924 S. Saklatvala was elected for Battersea North (he had won the seat for Labour in 1923, even though he was CP member). That same year the Labour Party declared that Communists could not become individual members of the Labour Party, and turned down Communist requests for affiliation in 1935, 1943 and 1946. The Party has enjoyed little electoral success: Willie Gallagher was elected Communist MP for West Fife in 1935 and again in 1945, when he was joined by P. Piratin (Stepney, Mile End). Since the 1945 general election the CP has failed to return an MP, and there has been a steady decline in the total votes cast for it. In the October 1974 general election all 29 Communist candidates lost their deposits. This may well explain the reappraisal of the party's position in 1977–8. The party was rent by internal division over the revision of its programme, 'The British Road to Socialism', and proposals to adopt a strategy based on building a 'Broad Democratic Alliance', laying emphasis on parliamentary methods and 'Euro-Communist' (*see* EURO-COMMUNISM) in tone. In 1979 the party's candidates polled 16,858 votes, but only 11,606 in 1983 with 35 candidates. Continuing divisions of the Euro-Communist wing controlling the party machine and hardliners of the *Morning Star* newspaper were reflected in a split candidature in 1987 of 19 Communist candidates, 13 Red Front candidates and 10 Workers' Revolutionary Party candidates. Further splits in the party have occurred in the late 1980s, resulting in the formation of a grouping which has considered dropping the word 'communist' from its title, following the example of Euro-Communist parties elsewhere in Europe.

The failure of the Communist Party to flourish in Britain has been variously interpreted, but most historiography points to the early growth and strength of a moderate socialist Labour Party, closely allied to the trade union movement, leaving little room for communist influence to gain a foothold. Although communist influence on some trade unions and in some areas has been strong at times, there has been little scope under the British 'first past the post' electoral system for substantial communist representation. Memories of communist attacks on Labour and moderate trade unionists under the party's 'class against class' policy from 1928 to 1933 have always aroused suspicions of Soviet domination, hardened by the COLD WAR after 1945. Labour leaders such as ATTLEE, GAITSKELL and WILSON have preferred to operate in the centre ground eschewing any approaches from or co-operation with the Communist Party. As a result, the Party has remained a sectarian, minority organization. Its peak membership in the Depression was only 18,000 (1937), rising to 43,000 in the Second World War at the height of Anglo–Soviet co-operation. In the post-war period it fell back, heavily hit by the Soviet suppression of the HUNGARIAN UPRISING in 1956 and the Soviet action to suppress the 'PRAGUE SPRING' in 1968. As a result, younger left-wingers tended to join TROTSKYITE and more dynamic, less authoritarian left-wing groupings. The advent of Euro-Communism from the 1970s has seen serious splits within the party with the formation of a New Communist Party of Great Britain (NCPB) in 1977 and in 1987 a Communist Part of Britain (CPB). In early 1991 the 6,300 members of the old CPGB renamed themselves the Democratic Left, committed to a democratic structure and a pluralistic, radical stance.

H. Pelling, *The British Communist Party* (1958)
R. Martin, *Communism and the British Trade Unions, 1924–33* (1969)

**Communist Party, Bulgarian** (Bulgarska Komunisticheska Partiya; BKP). Founded from a splinter group of the Bulgarian Social Democratic Party in 1903 which was renamed the Bulgarian Communist Party (Narrow Socialists) in 1919. By 1920 it claimed a membership of 38,000, and in the elections of March 1920 it obtained 50 of the 229 seats in the National Assembly, second only to the Bulgarian National Agrarian Union, with 184,616 votes. Following participation in an armed uprising in September 1923 the party was dissolved by legal decree and its leaders, including GEORGI DIMITROV and Vulko Chervenkov fled abroad. Reorganized as the legal Workers' Party (*Rabotnicheska Partiya*, RP) in 1927, it rose again to a membership of 30,000, obtaining 31 of the 274 deputies in the 1931 elections. When all political parties were dissolved in 1934 it continued an illegal existence as the Bulgarian Workers' Party (Communist) or BRP(K). In August 1943 under Dimitrov's direction it formed the FATHERLAND FRONT in alliance with socialists, agrarians and independents to press for Bulgaria's departure from the war. In 1944 it collaborated with the Soviet Union's invasion in September, and under the protection of the Red Army and the umbrella of the Fatherland Front seized control of the government on 9 September 1944. During the course of the next two years the communists liquidated and purged opponents. On 15 September a People's Republic was proclaimed and in the general election in the following month (27 October) the communists and their allies in the Fatherland Front obtained 364 sets (277 communist) out of 467. In 1947 the Communist Party absorbed the Socialists, and dissolved other parties. In 1948 the party became the Communist Party of Bulgaria (BKP) operating under the umbrella of the Fatherland Front as the dominant partner with the Bulgarian People's Agrarian Union. Under the leadership of Dimitrov, Premier from 1947, it initially showed some support for TITO, but on Stalin's orders swung back into hard-line opposition to 'revisionism', culminating in a series of purges in 1949–53 which included as a casualty the execution in 1949 of Traycho Kostov, the expected successor to Dimitrov. Under Chervenkov the Party was one of the most subservient of Soviet satellites, and it was Khrushchev's opposition to Chervenkov that led to his gradual demotion and eventual purge in 1962, accumulating further power in the hands of the Party General Secretary since 1954, TODOR ZHIVKOV. Party membership rose rapidly in the post-war era to 495,000 in 1948, fell back in the purges and expulsions after 1949, but reached 528,000 members in 1962 and 892,000 in 1984. Its leading role via the Fatherland Front has been ended following the removal of Zhivkov on 10 November 1989 and the call for free elections to be held in 1990. Reformed as the Bulgarian Socialist Party (BSP) it obtained a majority of seats in the elections held in June 1990, with 47 per cent of the vote against the opposition Union of Democratic Forces with 36 per cent.

J. Rothschild, *The Communist Party of Bulgaria: Origins and Development, 1883–1936* (1959)

——, *East Central Europe Between Two World Wars* (1974)

F. Fetjo, *A History of the People's Democracies: Eastern Europe Since Stalin* (2nd edn, 1974)

**Communist Party, Czechoslovak** (Komunisticka Strana Československa; KSC). Founded in 1921, the party claimed 300,000 members in its first months, but was reduced by purges and expulsions to about 100,000 by 1925. In that year it became the second largest party in the country, with 41 seats. Weakened in 1929 to 30 seats, the party was purged by STALIN's authority. It increased its membership amongst trade unionists during the DEPRESSION, mounting strikes and demonstrations, but came out in favour of a Popular Front in 1935–6. Following the Nazi seizure of Czechoslovakia in 1939, the party was banned. In the spring of 1945 there were only about 25,000 members of the KSC left in the country, but in 1946 it became the largest party in the industrial provinces of Bohemia and Moravia, and the second largest in Slovakia. It formed a major constituent of the National Front Government in 1946 under KLEMENT GOTTWALD as Premier. Following a coup in February 1948, the KSC obtained 214 of the 300 parliamentary seats on a National Front list in the May elections, proclaiming Czechoslovakia a People's Democracy with Gottwald as President. Attempts under DUBČEK to liberalize the communist regime in the 'PRAGUE SPRING' were crushed, and under HUSAK the regime was considerably more repressive. Growing internal opposition from DISSIDENT groups such as CHARTER 77, the liberal communist movements in Hungary and Poland, and the fall of the East German communist regime led to the breakdown of Communist Party control in a wave of mass demonstrations in December 1989. The Party contested the first free elections held in June 1990 for over forty years, obtaining the second largest number of seats, 48, in the 300 seat federal parliament against the CIVIC FORUM/Public Against Violence total of 169.

**Communist Party, French** (Parti Communiste Français; PCF). Founded in December 1920 as a result of a split in the SOCIALIST PARTY (SFIO) by those members who wished to affiliate to COMINTERN. The PCF retained control of the majority of the membership (109,000) the newspaper *L'Humanité*, and the party headquarters. Shortly afterwards it adopted the name of the Communist Party, French Section of the Communist International. During its early years it remained loyal to Comintern, but electorally weak retaining only 13 of the 68 socialist deputies in 1920. The leaders of the party were arrested in January 1923 for agitation against French occupation of the

Ruhr (*see* RUHR OCCUPATION), by which time expulsions and defections had reduced it to 45,000 members. In the 1924 elections it won 26 seats and then began a process of 'Bolshevization' in compliance with Comintern, creating a more centralized party structure with greater emphasis on creating distinct communist sections in factories and trade unions. During the Comintern's third phase of 'class against class' from 1928, the PCF mounted mass demonstrations in August 1929 which resulted in the arrest of leaders and restrictions upon its activities. Party membership fell from 58,000 in 1928 to 28,000 in 1933, while the PCF deputies were reduced from 14 in 1928 to 12 in 1932.

Following HITLER's rise to power in 1933 the PCF became engaged in serious clashes with right-wing organizations on the streets of Paris on 6 and 9 February 1934. Initially it sought to promote a 'United Front from below', bypassing co-operation with socialist leaders or non-communist trade unions. On 12 February 1934 the PCF for the first time agreed to join a demonstration organized by the socialists at Vincennes, followed on 27 July 1934 by a pact between the PCF and SFIO to unify their action against fascism and to campaign for a 'popular front'. The PCF in October 1934 extended co-operation to the Radicals, and on 14 July 1935 a rally inaugurating the Popular Front of PCF, SFIO and the RADICAL PARTY was held. Under MAURICE THOREZ the PCF joined the electoral alliance which won the general election of May 1936, returning 72 deputies, with 15 per cent of the total vote. Although remaining outside the government formed by LÉON BLUM, the PCF refused to capitalize on the industrial unrest which swept the country in June 1936, concentrating their efforts on attempting to influence French foreign policy in opposition to fascism. From 1936 to 1939 the party pursued a 'French Front' policy, urging rearmament and the strengthening of the FRANCO–SOVIET PACT of February 1936. As a result of the Popular Front campaign and the unification of the wings of the trade union movement in 1935, PCF membership rose to 341,000 by the end of 1937.

The NAZI–SOVIET PACT in August 1939 led to a volte-face by the PCF, who, following the outbreak of the Second World War in

September, adopted a policy of 'revolutionary defeatism'. The PCF was made illegal on 29 September; communist deputies were arrested and tried in spring 1940; and sabotage by communist activists led to the execution of several militants in May 1940. After France's defeat, the PCF attacked the VICHY GOVERNMENT but was also opposed to DE GAULLE, calling for a government with communist participation. These led to large-scale arrests of French communists, and it was only after the German invasion of the Soviet Union in June 1941 that the party emerged actively in resistance. The PCF formed one of the strongest resistance movements in France and in January 1943 pledged its allegiance to the FREE FRENCH headed by de Gaulle; PCF representatives were included in his provisional government in London in April 1944 and the PCF emerged from the war both well-organized and with greatly enhanced prestige and membership.

Attempts to unite the PCF and the socialists proved abortive in June–August 1945, but in the elections of 21 October the PCF emerged as the largest single party with over 5 million votes (26 per cent) and 152 deputies. But although five Communists entered government, de Gaulle excluded them from the key ministries. In the elections of November 1946 the PCF obtained 166 seats and joined the government formed in January 1947 by the socialist Paul Ramadier. But following communist support for strikes in April 1947 and growing disagreements about the INDO-CHINESE WAR, the communists were excluded from Ramadier's cabinet. The years 1945–7 marked the nearest the PCF came to taking power constitutionally; the refusal of the socialists to form a united French Labour Party, fearing communist domination, meant that the party did not have the overwhelming support it required to take power against the opposition of other non-communist groupings. Moreover, from 1947 the battle lines of the COLD WAR were hardening. Stalin's refusal to participate in the MARSHALL PLAN and the creation of a rival bloc in COMINFORM in September 1947, joined by the PCF, increasingly prevented it from participation in government. Cominform upbraided the PCF for its constitutionalism, leading it to back a wave of strikes in late 1947 and to increasingly strong opposition to the United States, the war in Indo-China and NATO. As a result the PCF lost both seats and membership. From a peak of over 800,000 members in 1946, it was reduced to under 300,000 by 1953, with only 97 deputies in the 1951 elections. It continued to influence political developments, however, supporting MEN-DÉS-FRANCE's premiership in 1954 and voting against a European Army.

The party lost further support over the HUNGARIAN UPRISING and found itself increasingly outflanked by younger TROTS-KYITE groups and beset by rifts over DE-STALINIZATION and the Sino–Soviet conflict. Although able to command consistently over one-fifth of the vote up to the 1970s, the PCF was notable during the student protests of 1968 for its refusal to back revolutionary action. It had been prepared to back the socialist presidential candidate MITTERRAND in the 1965 presidential elections, but appeared ambivalent in its attitude, neither fully of the system nor opposed to it. During the 1970s it had a common programme with the socialists from 1972 but was increasingly overshadowed by the Parti Socialiste (PS; see SOCIALIST PARTY, FRENCH). In 1977 the socialists gained more seats than the PCF, who took under 20 per cent of the vote for the first time since 1945. With growing strain between reformists and hardliners the common programme with the PS collapsed in 1978, and in 1981 the socialists under Mitterrand won an outright victory, with the PCF reduced to only 44 seats. Although the PCF was given four cabinet posts, in July 1984 the PCF withdrew from the government over its austerity programme. In the 1986 election its vote fell below 10 per cent, returning only 35 deputies. In growing disarray, the PCF was thought to have done well to retain 27 seats in the elections of May 1988, partly secured through local electoral deals with the PS. Increasingly the latter has become the dominant force on the left of French politics, with Mitterrand's establishment of a more centrist position, leaving the PCF marginalized. Following its rapid decline the PCF has been exposed to a continuous debate about its programme and the adop-

tion of a Euro-Communist (see EURO-COM-MUNISM) stance to rescue its fortunes.

One of the most Stalinist (see STALINISM) parties between the wars, the PCF has enjoyed two peaks of support, under the Popular Front, from 1936–9, and following the Second World War. Following the end of post-war TRIPARTISM in May 1947 and until 1981, it has been handicapped by its Soviet links and, latterly, by the creation of an effective Socialist Party under Mitterrand. Its main strength continues to be in the trade unions and industrial centres. See also CONFÉDÉRATION GÉNÉRALE DU TRAVAIL.

R. Tiersky, *The French Communist Party, 1920–1970* (1974)
E. Mortimer, *The Rise of the French Communist Party, 1920–1947* (1984)
R. McGraw, 'France', in S. Salter and J. Stevenson (eds.), *The Working Class and Politics in Europe and North America, 1929–45* (1990)

**Communist Party, German** (Kommunistische Partei Deutschlands; KPD). Established in late December 1918, the KPD emerged from the SPARTACIST LEAGUE, a group of dissenters within the Independent Social Democratic Party (see USPD), led by ROSA LUXEMBURG and KARL LIEBKNECHT. Following an uprising in Berlin in early January 1919, in the aftermath of which both Luxemburg and Liebknecht were murdered by right-wing paramilitary FREIKORPS units, the KPD boycotted the elections to the National Assembly, the constituent assembly of the WEIMAR REPUBLIC.

Affiliated to the COMINTERN from 1919, the KPD initially lacked a significant base in the working class, gaining only 2.1 per cent of the popular vote in the June 1920 REICHSTAG elections. Only when the left wing of the USPD joined it after October 1920 did the party achieve political significance. Following an insurrectionary strategy, the party organized abortive uprisings against the Weimar Republic in March 1921 and October 1923. During the period 1924–30, the KPD continued to attract about 10 per cent of the popular vote in elections to the *Reichstag* but played little role in the mainstream labour movement, the energies of its leaders being largely absorbed by internal dissension. The real significance of this period in the history of the party lay in its transformation under

Ernst Thälmann into a 'Stalinist' bureaucratic machine.

With the onset of the world DEPRESSION, the KPD was to benefit from the growing disenchantment with the SOCIAL DEMOCRATIC PARTY (SPD) and radicalization of sections of the working class: in the September 1930 *Reichstag* elections it gained 13.1 per cent of the vote, a figure which was to rise to 16.9 per cent in the November 1932 elections. The membership of the party during the Depression years, which rose to 330,000 in November 1932, was largely drawn from the unemployed, especially the young unemployed, and displayed a marked volatility. Directed by the Comintern, the KPD's strategy during the later Weimar years was dictated by the 'social fascism' thesis, which identified the SPD as the main obstacle to a successful communist revolution in Germany and weakened possible working-class resistance to the rise of the NAZI PARTY.

Whilst the KPD was bitterly opposed to Nazism, and often confronted the Nazis in street brawls, it underestimated the radical dynamic of the Nazi Party as well as their strength of support. Despite apparently elaborate plans for underground activity, the KPD was essentially unprepared for the systematic onslaught directed against it by the Nazi government after the REICHSTAG FIRE of February 1933: the leadership of the party was captured as early as March 1933, and in the succeeding two years the GESTAPO was to destroy the KPD's underground resistance organization. Directed by leaders in exile in Moscow, the KPD abandoned its hierarchical clandestine organization from 1936 onwards in favour of more loosely organized underground cells which were more difficult to detect. Yet the 'Trojan horse' strategy of penetration of Nazi organizations which it pursued in the later 1930s brought it equally little success. Largely insignificant after 1935, communist resistance in Nazi Germany virtually disappeared following the NAZI–SOVIET PACT of August 1939: only in the later stages of the war were communists to resume any noteworthy resistance activity, concentrating their efforts on foreign and slave workers within the German economy. The sacrifices made by those participating in communist-directed resistance in Nazi Germany were quite disproportionate to its effectiveness and were, in the longer term, politically significant in only one respect – that of providing a cloak of legitimacy for the KPD's successor, the Socialist Unity Party (*see* SED) and the East Grman state it was to dominate for 40 years.

W. Angress, *The Stillborn Revolution: The Communist Bid for Power in Germany, 1921–1923* (1963)
B. Fowkes, *Communism in Germany under the Weimar Republic* (1984)

**Communist Party, Greek** (Kommunistikon Komma Ellados, KKE). Formed in 1920 when the Socialist Workers' Party of Greece affiliated to COMINTERN, adopting the Communist name in 1924. It obtained ten seats in the elections of 1926, but was riven by divisions between different factions, some of whom opposed Moscow's attempt to dictate its foreign policy. In the 1930s it recovered, rising to 8,000 members by 1935 and fifteen deputies in the 1936 elections, holding the balance of power. Co-operating in a Popular Front Government with the Liberals, a period of unrest and general strikes led to the METAXAS dictatorship from August 1936 until April 1941. Banned by Metaxas, the KKE at first opposed Greek support for Britain but, following the German invasion of the Soviet Union, formed the People's Liberation Front (*Ellenikon Laikon Apeleutherikon Straton* – ELAS). As well as resisting German occupation, ELAS became involved in a bloody civil war with anti-communist elements and, eventually with the British forces which returned to Greece in late 1944 (see GREEK CIVIL WAR). Prior to its defeat in the civil war, the KKE was banned, in 1947, but maintained an existence abroad following the final defeat of its forces in 1949. A legal organization within Greece was maintained from 1951 as the United Democratic Left (EDA), but the KKE was not allowed to return to legal existence until 1974. EDA had as many as 100,000 members by 1965 and obtained nearly a million votes in 1958 and a peak strength of 79 seats. It fell back in the 1960s, to only 21 seats in 1965, prior to the Colonels' coup. The Communist 'bogey' played an important part in the Colonels' dictatorship. During it a new split appeared with the formation of a Marxist movement independent of Moscow in 1968, the KKE-interior. After the return to democracy in 1974, the KKE participated in elections, obtaining approximately ten per cent of the vote, the KKE-interior obtaining a much smaller share. As an Alliance of the Left, the Communists have played a significant part in weak coalitions formed during the stalemate of Greek politics in 1989–90, taking a share in power for the first time since 1944. See also: GREEK CIVIL WAR.

G. Kousoulas, *Revolution and Defeat* (1965)

**Communist Party, Hungarian** (Magyar Kommunista Part; MKP). The ruling party in Hungary from 1945 to 1989. It was founded on 24 November 1918 by a group of left-wing activists, including former prisoners-of-war in Russia, such as BÉLA KUN. It established a Soviet-style regime under Kun in March–August 1919, but this was dispersed by the intervention of the Romanian army. Fugitives fled to various places, leading to feuds between the Moscow-based Kun and members of the party Committee abroad. COMINTERN suppressed the party in 1922 as a result of factionalism, but a reformed congress met in Vienna in August 1925 and a legal left socialist party, the Hungarian Socialist Workers' Party (MSZMP), was formed, earlier in the year. The arrest of its leader in 1927 largely eroded its influence. A small, clandestine organization during the inter-war years, the party's leading figures were either in prison or working for Comintern from Moscow. The party in Hungary refused to co-operate with the POPULAR FRONT policy in 1935, and Comintern disbanded the top levels of clandestine organization in Hungary and transferred the headquarters to Prague. An attempt was made in 1939 to reinvigorate the party with the help of foreign cadres, but several hundred communist activists were killed or imprisoned in Stalin's PURGES including Kun himself, leaving amongst the survivors IMRE NAGY, Erno Gero, György Lukács, Ieno Varga and RÁKOSI. The domestic party was virtually in dissolution after the end of Comintern in May 1943, although communists joined in the National Independence Front which formed the basis for the ruling coalition in post-war Hungary.

The party was refounded as the Hungarian Communist Party (MKP) by Rakosi and former Moscow associates with 'native' groups led by Janos Kadar and Laszlo Rajk. Rakosi purged the Party of dissidents and expanded the membership from its small base of just over 1,000 members in 1944. The Party obtained 17 per cent of the vote in the elections of November 1945 and took part in the post-war coalition government, gradually incorporating other opposition parties to oppose the dominant Smallholders' Party. Backed by Soviet forces and having obtained control of the police, the Premier, Ferenc Nagy, was ousted from power, and in the August 1947 elections the communist-led opposition bloc took 45 per cent of the votes and forced the dissolution of the Smallholders' Party.

In June 1948 the Social Democratic Party merged with the communists to form the Hungarian Workers' Party (MDP) which ruled the country as a stern Stalinist regime under Rakosi. He executed Laszlo Rajk after a show trial in late 1948 and purged 'Titoists' and non-communist party leaders during the next five years. His replacement as Premier by Nagy in July 1954 marked an attempted 'new course', limited by Rakosi's continued influence as General Secretary and control of the police apparatus, eventually securing Nagy's expulsion from the Central Committee in April 1955. In late 1955 and 1956 the pressure for liberalization grew and led to the removal of Rakosi as General Secretary and his replacement by Gero. Rajik was rehabilitated and Nagy readmitted to the Central Committee. The HUNGARIAN UPRISING of October 1956 directed against the secret police and then against the Communist Party led to the Central Committee's supporting Nagy's acquisition of power. The MDP dissolved itself and reformed itself as the new Hungarian Socialist Workers' Party.

Following the suppression of the uprising by Soviet troops Janos Kadar oversaw the widespread arrest and imprisonment of those involved in the uprising, including the execution of Nagy and his chief associates. Readmissions to the party, however, raised its membership to over 340,000, and in 1958–9 Hungary embarked on a forced collectivization. Gradually, however, Kadar relaxed the regime and pursued a policy of DE-STALINIZATION, expelling former leading figures Rakosi and Gero and others from the party in 1961–2. He fostered a move towards a mixed economy, partly financed by foreign loans, building up party membership to 511,000 in 1965 and to 852,000 by 1983.

By the 1980s the Hungarian Socialist Workers' Party was running one of the more relaxed communist regimes in Eastern Europe. A law of January 1982 recognized small business concerns as protected in law. The accession of Karoly Grosz as Prime Minister in June 1987 began a dismantling of most of the subsidies to basic foods and fresh tax increases, pushing the party further along the road to a Western-style economy than almost any other Eastern bloc country. In May 1988 Kadar was relegated to the role of Party President while Grosz was promoted to replace him as Party General Secretary. At the same time the Politburo and Central Committee were purged of the old guard and replaced by reform-minded technocrats. The relaxation of censorship permitted attempts to reinterpret the events of 1956, culminating in the rehabilitation of Imre Nagy and his reinterment with full honours.

In January 1989 the Communist Party effectively abandoned its monopoly status, permitting the formation of other political parties. In March 1989 the new draft constitution omitted any reference to the party's leading role and at the end of 1989 the Communist Party declared itself a socialist party to contest the elections due in March 1990. By that time a rapid loss of support and the formation of new political groupings had completely transformed its position to that of one party amongst many seeking political power within a pluralistic political system. In the March 1990 elections it performed poorly with only 11 per cent of the vote behind the conservative Hungarian Democratic Forum and the liberal Alliance of Free Democrats.

**Communist Party, Italian** (Partito Communista Italiano; PCI). Founded in January 1921 from the various factions which split off from the SOCIALIST PARTY Congress at Livorno (Leghorn) when the majority refused to expel reformists. The new party was organized by Amadeo Bordiga (1889–1970), but he fell into conflict with COMINTERN who favoured his rivals ANTONIO

GRAMSCI and PALMIRO TOGLIATTI. During the fascist seizure of power the party lost several thousand members imprisoned or driven into flight, but retained 19 seats in the Chamber and withdrew in protest at the MATTEOTI CRISIS. In January 1926 Bordiga was expelled from the party's Central Committee, but internal quarrels were overtaken by the repression of MUSSOLINI's exceptional decrees of November 1926. Most of the leadership was arrested and imprisoned, including Bordiga and Gramsci. Only Togliatti, who was in Moscow, escaped; when Gramsci died in prison in April 1937 Togliatti became its leader.

The party continued to exist as a clandestine organization and was 'Bolshevized' from 1928 into a sectarian grouping which reflected Comintern influence. From July 1934 it adopted the prevailing POPULAR FRONT stance, announcing a pact with the Socialist Party. The Italian Popular Front based on Paris had some 45,000 members by the late 1930s and formed a focus for anti-fascist activity; Togliatti and other Italian communists proved active in the SPANISH CIVIL WAR. The fall of France in 1940 led to the arrest of many Italian communists in France, but Togliatti fled to Moscow. The clandestine Communist Party provided the strongest force in the resistance, organizing strikes in the northern industrial areas in March 1943, and after Mussolini's fall developing rapidly within the Italian labour movement. When the Germans took control of northern Italy after the armistice of 8 September 1943 the party mobilized committees of national liberation which conducted partisan warfare against the Nazis and fascist groups.

Togliatti returned in April 1944 to Allied-held southern Italy and urged support for a constituent assembly to prepare for a referendum on the monarchy. The PCI emerged with great prestige and support from the struggle against fascism and the Nazi occupation. It had almost 2.5 million members in 1948 and obtained more than one-fifth of the vote. The party shared power under TRIPARTISM until 31 May 1947, when the centrist government of DE GASPERI eliminated it from office. A member of COMINFORM, it launched a strike wave and campaigned against the NORTH ATLANTIC TREATY ORGANISATION and the MARSHALL

PLAN. It remained one of the largest communist parties in Western Europe, with 23 per cent of the vote in 1953 and 140 deputies, though it was excluded from government.

The party lost members over the HUNGARIAN UPRISING in 1956 but increased support in elections. Togliatti also developed the party's appeal to a broad electorate, taking advantage of DE-STALINIZATION to pursue the 'Italian road to Socialism'. In 1965, the year after Togliatti's death, it had 1,600,000 members and in 1968 took 28 per cent of the vote, electing 177 deputies.

Under Enrico Berlinguer (1922–84) its general secretary from 1972, the party asserted its independence from Moscow and embraced what became known as EURO-COMMUNISM. Following a generation of exclusion from political power, it made the 'historic compromise' of offering support for the Christian Democrats and saw its support rise to over 30 per cent in the elections of 1976 and 1979, obtaining over 200 deputies. From 1978, through the mediation of ALDO MORO, the communists became almost unofficial partners of the governing coalition. This was interrupted by Moro's death, and in spite of Berlinguer's breach with Moscow over the imposition of martial law in Poland, there was growing concern that the party had 'peaked' and might be going into 'inevitable decline'. Berlinguer was widely mourned, but under Alessandro Natta, party leader from 1985 to 1988, the party lost seats in 1987, being reduced to 177 deputies again.

Achille Occhetto from 1988 sought a 'new course'; this led to a full-scale reappraisal of the PCI's position, leading at the end of 1989 to the proposal to give up the name 'communist' and relaunch itself as a mass social democratic party on West European lines. After a special congress in March 1990 gave support, the PCI was relaunched as the Democratic Party of the Left (*Partito Democratico di Sinistra* – PDS) in January 1991.

D. L. M. Blackmer, *Unity in Diversity: Italian Communism and the Communist World* (1968)

**Communist Party, Portuguese** (Partido Communists Portuguěs, PCP). Founded in 1921 as a splinter group of the Portuguese Socialist Party, but was declared illegal in 1926 and its leaders imprisoned or exiled. It maintained a clandestine existence and was involved in sporadic industrial and student activity, supporting the opposition candidate for the Presidency in 1958, General Delgado, and stimulating unrest with the SALAZAR regime. It participated in the broad-based opposition Patriotic National Liberation Front founded in Algiers in 1962 and remained the best-organized opposition group in Portugal at the time of Salazar's death. The Party was legalized in 1974 following the military coup of April 1974 playing a leading part in the PORTUGUESE REVOLUTION. Led from 1965 by a former prisoner of the Salazar regime, Alvaro Cunhal, the Party rose from a few thousand activists to a membership of 165,000 in the mid-1970s. In 1979 it formed an electoral alliance with the People's Democratic Movement, the United Peoples Alliance (APU). In elections since 1975 it has obtained between twelve and nineteen per cent of the vote with a peak of 47 deputies in 1979. Its strength has declined during the 1980s, falling to 38 seats in 1985. It remains one of the most dogmatically Stalinist of the Communist Parties of Europe.

**Communist Party, Romanian** (Partidul Comunist Roman; PCR). Originally a splinter group of the Romanian Social Democratic Party, founded as a separate party on 13 May 1921. In 1923 the party was banned and its leaders either went underground or fled to Moscow, where some perished in the PURGES. Two of the exiles, Ana Pauker and Peter Borila, returned to Romania backed by the RED ARMY in 1944, joining with surviving domestic communists such as GHEORGHIU-DEJ, who became General Secretary in 1945. Contesting elections under the umbrella of the National Democratic Front, the Communist Party secured an overwhelming majority in the elections of 19 November 1946, forcing the abdication of King Michael in December 1947 and proclaiming a People's Republic on the 30th. Renamed the Workers' Party, they absorbed the Social Democrats and secured an overwhelming victory in alliance with peasant parties as the National Democratic Front at elections for the National Assembly on 28 March 1948. A new Soviet-style constitution was promulgated on 13 April 1948 and the Workers' Party consolidated control, purging the leadership and the rank and file between 1948 and 1950, including the ex-Moscow exile, Ana Pauker. Promoting 'national Stalinism' in opposition to revisionism and 'Khrushchevism' in the 1950s, the Workers' Party laid the basis for the semi-independent role played by the Romanian Party in relation to Moscow. Fearful of a repetition of the HUNGARIAN UPRISING, the Romanian communists were tolerated by the USSR in pursuing friendship with China and an 'anti-revisionist' line in policy. The Romanian Workers' Party was renamed the Romanian Communist Party in 1965 and under the leadership of NICOLAI CEAUŞESCU pursued a policy of loosening ties with the Soviet Union, even to the point of opposing the WARSAW PACT invasion of Czechoslovakia in 1968. Increasingly, however, the party was dominated by the corrupt and despotic regime of Ceauşescu. He promoted a determined drive to industrialize the country with a series of ambitious Five Year Plans, in 1981 calling for a paying off of all foreign debts and the conversion of thousands of villages into agro-industrial complexes. Austerity and food rationing were introduced alongside the placing of members of the Ceauşescu clan in prominent positions and increasingly grandiose building projects in Bucharest. Dissent was stifled by a large security force and frequent purges of opposition. Formally, the party operated still under an umbrella organization, the renamed Socialist Democracy and Unity Front, which was the sole organization to put up candidates in elections. Some dissent with the Ceauşescu regime from within the party was signalled by extensive purges in 1982 and the arrest of signatories of an open letter criticizing policy in March 1989. The popular uprising of 22 December 1989 appeared to have broken the party's power, but many of its elements remained as members of the National Salvation Front which secured an overwhelming victory in the May 1990 elections.

S. Fischer-Galati, *Twentieth Century Rumania* (1970)
F. Fetjo, *A History of the People's Democracies: Eastern Europe since Stalin* (2nd edn, 1974)

**Communist Party, Spanish** (Partido Comunista Española; PCE). Founded in 1921, the PCE remained a minor element in Spanish politics before the SPANISH CIVIL WAR, with only 35,000 members in February 1936 and 16 seats in the Cortez. Suppressed under PRIMO DE RIVERA from 1923 to 1930, it was marginalized until it joined a Popular Front pact with left-wing socialists in January 1936. It rapidly gained influence in the Unified Socialist Youth Movement founded in April 1936 and the Catalan Unified Socialist Party (PSUC). After the outbreak of the war it grew rapidly to almost 300,000 by March 1937. With the backing of COMINTERN and Soviet aid, it began to assert itself against other left-wing groups, such as the PARTIDO OBRERO DE UNIFICACIÓN MARXISTA (POUM), and sought to oust LARGO CABALLERO from the permiership. By mid-1937 it had become the major political force in Republican Spain and increasingly distrusted or even hated by other groups. The communist mixture of great effectiveness in the war effort and of considerable opportunism and brutality against opponents made their role in the war very controversial. The party was a mainstay of the NEGRIN government until March 1939, but did not control it, as is often asserted. Banned and persecuted under Franco, the PCE maintained a clandestine existence in Spain, participating in labour unrest in Madrid in 1947, Barcelona in 1951 and in the Asturias in 1958–9. Further strikes in Asturias in 1962 led to the execution of a communist leader. The Party was legalized in 1977, taking 20 seats in the Lower House, 23 in 1979, 4 in 1982 and 7 in 1986. It has become increasingly Euro-Communist in inclination (*See* EURO-COMMUNISM) but has lost support to the SOCIALIST WORKERS' PARTY (PSOE). This change was reflected in a change of name to the United Left (*Izquierda Unida*) in late 1990. It continues to dominate the *Comisiones Obreras*, the successors to the illegal trade unions under Franco, and now the second largest union grouping in Spain.

B. Bolloten, *The Spanish Revolution: The Left and the Struggle for Power during the Civil War* (1979)

**Communist Party, Yugoslavian** (Savez Komunista Jugoslavije; SKJ). The ruling party of Yugoslavia since 1944. The first organized groups of communists were formed into the Socialist Workers' Party of Yugoslavia in April 1919, changed to the Communist Party of Yugoslavia (KPJ) following the second party congress in June 1920. The KPJ had about 60,000 members by 1920 and won 58 seats in the Yugoslav elections of November 1920. The party was banned from propaganda activities at the end of December 1920 and then declared illegal in August 1921 following assassination attempts on the Prince Regent and the murder of the Minister of the Interior. The party remained illegal between the wars and was beset with factional and ethnic rivalries which saw membership dwindle as low as 200 in 1932. The party recovered somewhat in the POPULAR FRONT era but most of the exiled leadership perished in Stalin's PURGES before Josip Broz, 'TITO', was appointed general secretary in 1937 to rebuild the party on Stalinist lines (see STALINISM). By the outbreak of the partisan war against the Nazi occupation in June 1941 (see PARTISANS), the party had reached 12,000 members. Although most of those were killed in the war, Tito's successful struggle against the Nazis and his elimination of rivals saw membership rise to 141,000 by 1945. Under Tito's control the party initially pursued a faithful Stalinist line, introducing collectivization, a Five Year Plan, and complete communist control of the state and army apparatus. The quarrel with Moscow, however, and Yugoslavia's expulsion from COMINFORM on 28 June 1948 began a process of readjustment. The rigid economic controls were relaxed, setting up workers' councils with devolved planning powers in July 1950 followed by the legalization of private agriculture from March 1953. Considerably greater decentralization was also introduced into the constitution. Its federal features were emphasized in a new constitution in 1963 which gave considerable autonomy to popularly elected People's Councils or Communes and allowed the national minorites within Yugoslavia complete freedom within their own republics in economic and cultural affairs. Further decentralizing measures followed in 1974, when a new constitution set up work-place assemblies as the principal form of government within the framework of the individual republics. The Communist Party changed its name in 1952 to the League of Communists, declaring itself to have an educative rather than an administrative role. Its chief organ, the Pol-

itburo, likewise changed its title to the Executive Committee and was reorganized to represent the national republics within Yugoslavia. In 1984 the League of Communists claimed 2.2 million members; it formed one of the most decentralized communist regimes in existence, for long seen as a model for liberal communists in other countries. From 1989, however, the party came under increasing pressure from nationalist and economic problems. Following a walk-out by Slovenian communists from the Yugoslav Party, free elections in SLOVENIA and CROATIA gave non-communists groups majorities in the Republics in April 1990. As the existing state dissolved in 1991, the Party's rule disintegrated. See also DJILAS, MILOVAN; YUGOSLAVIA.

G. W. Hoffman, *Yugoslavia and the New Communism* (1962)
I. Avakumovic, *History of the Communist Party of Yugoslavia*, vol. 1 (1964)

**Communist Party of the Soviet Union** (CPSU). The party which has exercised power in the Soviet Union since the 1917 RUSSIAN REVOLUTION. In 1918 the Bolshevik Party which had seized power in November 1917 changed its name to the All-Russian Communist Party (Bolsheviks), then in 1925 to the All-Union Communist Party (Bolsheviks) and in 1952 to the Communist Party of the Soviet Union. The party is territorial and functional, the territorial organization being parallel to the administrative sub-division of the country. At the All-Union level the organization comprises the All-Union Congress and the principal organs of party administration; the next tier consists of the party organizations of the Union republics (except the Russian Soviet Federated Soviet Republic) the autonomous republics and the autonomous regions; the final tier is composed of city, urban and rural district organizations. The functional organization of the party consists of primary party organizations in factories, state and collective farms, and government educational, cultural, military and scientific establishments, of which there were nearly 400,000 in 1985. The party is organized in such a way that the largest Union Republic, the Russian Soviet Federated Soviet Republic, has no party organization distinct from the All-Union Communist Party, while the party organizations in the Union Republics are branches of the All-Union party, providing a centralized party structure for the whole of the USSR (*See* UNION OF SOVIET SOCIALIST REPUBLICS.)

According to its rules, the supreme body of the party is the All-Union Congress. The Congress elects a Central Committee and a Central Revision Commission. The Central Committee elects a Political Bureau (Politburo) and a Secretariat; the Central Committee also 'sets up' a Committee for Party Control. These bodies are reproduced with modifications in the lower tiers of the organization.

The All-Union Congress meets every four years and the degree of representation is decided by the Central Committee. It is usually attended by several thousand delegates and is a formal occasion where the Central Committee makes a report and approves the party programme and rules. The Central Committee is charged with the conduct of business between Congresses and has usually consisted of up to 200 members and a smaller number of 'candidate members' who replace full members. It is made up of the leading party and government officials as well as representatives of the military, police, education, arts and sciences. The supreme policy-making body is the Political Bureau (Politburo), renamed the Presidium in 1952, but reverting to its earlier name in 1966. Although nominally elected and responsible to the Central Committee, it has normally been the effective seat of power, consisting of eleven members and eight 'candidate' members. The Secretariat of the Central Committee, responsible for the selection of officials and with checking on the carrying out of party decisions, has also become one of the most powerful organs of the party, particularly as it developed under STALIN, controlling appointments within the party and in national life and exercising general supervisory control over the party network in the country. The Secretariat is headed by the General Secretary (known as the First Secretary from 1953 to 1966) who usually presides over the meetings of the Politburo. Other members of the secretariat are each responsible for a group of subjects or a single department, depending on seniority;

each department is administered by its own permanent staff.

An important element is the party's control by the system of *Nomenklatura* ('list of names'). These are a set of documents which set out the appointments to be filled and the officials at different levels, both party and state, who are to be consulted and decide on the filling of appointments. The lists cover appointments at every tier from the lowest level of town and rural organization right up to the Central Committee of the CPSU, and embrace virtually all positions of responsibility in the country. Effectively, posts can only be filled with the approval of the equivalent level of the Communist Party and only those whose names are on the list can be appointed. The system ensures an overwhelming degree of party influence upon appointments and party members have the sole right to put up in elections. In addition, the party organizes all aspects of social life, controls the trade unions, is represented in the armed forces by the political COMMISSARS, and, through the KOMSOMOL is the largest youth organization.

The CPSU was conceived as the dominant political, economic and social force in the Soviet Union. According to the rules adopted at the 22nd congress in 1961 it 'unites, on a voluntary basis, the more advanced, politically more conscious section of the working class, collective farm peasantry, and intelligentsia of the USSR' and whose principal objects are to build a communist society by means of the gradual transition from socialism to communism, to raise the material and cultural level of the people, to organize the defence of the country, and to strengthen ties with the workers of other countries.

Party membership had grown substantially. Before the Bolshevik seizure of power in August 1917, it numbered about 200,000 members. In March 1920 it had over 600,000, most of whom had joined since 1919, but numbered less than 500,000 by January 1923, following a considerable turnover of membership, including many expulsions. By 1928 the party's strength had reached 1,304,000 and rose steadily to over 3,500,000 in 1933. The effects of the PURGES, however, reduced membership to just over 2,000,000 by 1 January 1937.

Rapid recruitment raised the total by February 1941 to 3,877,000, when over two-thirds of the party had joined since 1929. Recruitment was increased during the Second World War to reach 5,760,000, but only resumed its rapid rise again in 1957, reaching 12,471,000 in 1966 and 17,500,000 in 1981. Under GORBACHEV, however, major changes began to occur in the role of the CPSU. In February 1990 the Central Committee voted unanimously to end the leading role of the Party under Articles 6 and 7 of the Consitution. This was ratified by the Congress of People's Deputies in March which also saw the creation of an executive Presidency. As a result the Soviet Union had opened the way to a multi-party system and detached the executive office from direct dependence on the party. Free elections to local government and to the Supreme Soviets of the Republics from December 1989 had already seen the Communist Party deposed in many parts of the country. Gorbachev's attempt to reform the CPSU from within was shattered by the hardline coup attempt of August 1991. Massive resentment at Party involvement forced him to agree to its dissolution and the end of its 84-year rule.

L. Shapiro, *The Government and Politics of the Soviet Union* (2nd edn. 1967)
M. McCauley, *Politics and the Soviet Union* (1977)
R. Little, *Governing the Soviet Union* (1989)

**Condor Legion.** The Condor Legion formed the nucleus of German forces aiding the Nationalist side in the SPANISH CIVIL WAR, following the decision of HITLER to supply aid in July 1936. In contrast to the piecemeal deployment of ground and naval forces, the Legion was constituted in November 1936 to provide organized air support and technical advice. It eventually developed to contain three bomber, three fighter, one reconnaisance and one seaplane squadrons, plus anti-aircraft batteries and support units – some 6,000 men and 100 aircraft at any one time – led successively by generals Hugo von Sperrle, Volkmann and Von Richtofen. The Legion participated in all of the important battles of the war, except Guadalajara, often providing decisive close support to Nationalist infantry and artillery, using tactics that were to become familiar in the Second World War. It was

also responsible for the bombardments of defenceless towns and civilian population, most infamously at GUERNICA in April 1937.

A. Vinas, *La Alemania Nazi y el 18 de Julio* (1974)
R. H. Whealey, *Hitler and Spain: The Nazi role in the Spanish Civil War, 1936–39* (1989)

**Confederación Española de Derechas Autónomas** (CEDA; Spanish Confederation of Autonomous Right-Wing Groups). The CEDA was Spain's first mass political party of the Right. Founded in February 1933, it grew out of the circles around the national Catholic newspaper *El Debate*. The coming of the SECOND REPUBLIC, which had taken the Right very much by surprise, had nevertheless been met by an initial mobilization, led by the paper's editor Angel Herrera Oria (1886–1968), into an umbrella grouping of the Right known as Acción Popular, which was to become the CEDA in 1933. Acción Popular's acceptance of the legality of the newly-constituted Republic and its refusal to categorize itself as either Monarchist or Republican, ensured that the *El Debate* grouping soon emerged as the spearhead of the 'accidentalist' Right which followed Vatican theory in proclaiming forms of government to be unimportant. Unlike the 'catastrophist' Monarchists, both Alfonist and Carlist (*see* CARLISM), the CEDA accidentalists were not dedicated to the violent overthrow of the Republic, but rather adopted an alternative 'legalist' tactic. They participated in the electoral process in an attempt to gain outright political power and then legislate against the pluralist Republic, in order to replace it with a more authoritarian, corporatist regime.

Popular support for the CEDA's anti-Republican position was demonstrated in the 1933 elections, when the Left lost control of the government following a large swing to the Right in the November poll. The CEDA, the largest single party in the Cortes, participated in a coalition with the Radicals from October 1934 and was extensively implicated in the bloody reprisals for the ASTURIAS RISING, precipitated by the entry of Gil Robles into government. The aftermath of Asturias contributed towards the Right's defeat in the February 1936 elections, when it was successfully challenged by the POPULAR FRONT. The accidentalist tactic had failed and, as entire youth sections of the CEDA went over to the FALANGE and party funds were made available to the army conspirators, the hollowness of the CEDA's loyalty to the Republic was clearly revealed. Nor was there any place for the CEDA in Nationalist Spain; in April 1937, it was officially dissolved. Gil Robles spent the Civil War in Portugal although he returned to Franco's Spain, emerging in the 1960s as a leading proponent of Christian Democracy, a label which, despite the claims of some historians, was clearly unsuitable for the CEDA.

R. Robinson, *The Origins of Franco's Spain: The Right, the Republic and Revolution, 1931–1936* (1970)
R. Preston, *The Coming of the Spanish Civil War: Reform, Reaction and Revolution in the Second Republic, 1931–1936* (1978)

**Confederación Nacional del Trabajo** (CNT; National Confederation of Labour). Formed in 1911, this anarcho-syndicalist organization was the largest labour movement in Spain until 1939, playing a complicated role in all of the major developments of the period. Much of the apparent internal confusion that characterized the evolution of the CNT stemmed from its origins in Barcelona in the aftermath of the 'Tragic Week' disturbances of 1909. It combined new theories of industrial unionism and the use of the general strike with existing ideas of revolutionary anarchism. The resulting uneasy collaboration of anarchist individualist and trades unionists, personified in its early years by the leading figures of Manuel Buenacasa and Salvador Segui, kept the movement in constant tension.

The resulting ideological mixture of an uncompromising rejection of the existing order and a commitment to syndical activity proved highly popular among landless labourers of the south and industrial workers in Catalonia. Organization spread rapidly among these groups, transforming the CNT into a much larger union federation than the rival socialist UNIÓN GENERAL DE TRABAJADORES (UGT). Against a background of post-war wage cuts and unemployment, the loose structure of CNT unions proved inadequate for collective bargaining but very effective in mounting strikes. Employers responded to this revol-

utionary threat with repression that led to terrorist actions from small anarchist factions within CNT like Buenaventura Durruti's *solidarios*. In Barcelona the situation degenerated into a virtual local civil war that was brought to an end by the PRIMO DE RIVERA coup of 1923.

Though suppression under the dictatorship inhibited all public activity, fierce internal debates continued. In 1927 these became formalized with the creation of the Federación Anarquista Iberica (FAI). This secretive anarchistic group was determined to prevent any drift in the wider organization towards purely union rather than revolutionary ends. Syndical leaders were pressing for changes towards a more orthodox union structure, concentration on winning immediate improvements for workers and abandonment of terrorism. The rapid organizational expansion that occurred under the SECOND REPUBLIC was accompanied by further internal battles over strategy and tactics. *Faistas* viewed with alarm the tighter internal structure and control of the unions, and suggestions by conservatives within the CNT ledership to separate from the FAI and develop into a political force able to benefit from the Republic. In response the FAI moved to gain control over the CNT, ousting union moderates like Angel Pestaña and Juan Peiro. This internal struggle contributed enormously to the uncertain position of CNT under the Republican regime. During 1931–3, periods of conventional union activity were interspersed with insurrectionary general strikes. CNT was pushed into internecine disputes with a collaborationist socialist movement, forced to take some responsibility for the repression of uprisings. This divided working class support, played into the hands of the Right and threatened the reforming efforts of the Republican regime. The culmination was a massacre of anarchist militants at Casas Viejas, that brought down the government and contributed to the electoral victory of a resurgent Right in November 1933. Repression during the next two years merely strengthened the hands of the FAI and pushed CNT moderates further to the left. Nevertheless, members of the CNT supported the POPULAR FRONT in February 1936, in contrast to their previous abstention from voting, helping to ensure victory. In the chaos that preceded the outbreak of the SPANISH CIVIL WAR, the CNT again grew rapidly in support and engaged in activities ranging from strikes to street-fighting with fascist groups.

CNT support was vital in frustrating the army rising of July 1936. In its heartlands in Catalonia, Aragon and, briefly, Andalusia, the movement was the only effective force in a political vacuum. The revolution that was unleashed transformed these regions into anarchist experiments in collectivization and communal living. Formal government was replaced by committees of Anti-Fascist Militias, which organized a war effort based upon revolutionary anarchism. This brought the movement into direct conflict with Republican forces, particularly the growing COMMUNIST PARTY, which favoured a centralized war effort. CNT dilemmas over participating in political leadership, resisted by the FAI but broadly favoured by many union leaders, contributed to a growing crisis. This came to a head in the MAY DAYS of 1937 in Barcelona, when communist-led attempts by government forces to reassert control of the city gave rise to direct confrontation. The defeat of the CNT, made possible in part by its internal confusions, led to the forced dissolution of all revolutionary gains and the incorporation of the militias into a centralized Popular Army. CNT leaders, such as Federica Montseny, eventually joined the Republican government, but popular enthusiasm for the war was severely shaken. Following defeat, the CNT operated in exile in France and Mexico, playing little effective part in opposition to the dictatorship. Though legalized in the post-Franco era, CNT has failed to regain anything approaching the primacy it once had in the labour movement. See also ANARCHISM, SPANISH.

M. Bookchin, The Spanish Anarchists: The Heroic Years (1978)
R. R. Kern, Red Years: Black Years: A Political History of Spanish Anarchism, 1911–37 (1978)
B. Bolloten, The Spanish Revolution (1979)
J. Gomez Casas, Anarchist Organisation: The History of the FAI (1986)

**Confédération Générale du Travail** (CGT; General Confederation of Labour). An organization of French trade unions founded in 1895. It was heavily influenced by syndicalism in its early years, rejecting parliamentary socialism. It failed to achieve a general strike prior to 1914, when trade union militancy was harshly suppressed by CLEMENCEAU and BRIAND. Following the split in the FRENCH SOCIALIST PARTY in 1921, which led to the creation of the FRENCH COMMUNIST PARTY, a militant minority formed the Confédération Générale du Travil Unitaire (CGTU). The CGTU contained various shades of opinion, revolutionary socialists, anarcho-syndicalists and communists, but it was the communists who dominated in swinging the organization behind COMINTERN policy, for example forming a joint action committee to oppose the RUHR OCCUPATION in 1922–3. The two organizations were almost evenly matched in terms of numbers, by 1926 the CGT had 524,000 members, the CGTU 431,000, but this reflected a combined membership less than half that of the unified CGT of 1920 with almost 2 million members. They drew from different strata: the CGT's strength lay in the public sector amongst the civil service, teachers and postal workers, its members increasingly reformist; the CGTU had more manual workers and retained something of the syndicalist fervour deriving from the pre-war and post-war strike wave. By 1934 the effects of the DEPRESSION had driven combined union membership down to a third of the 1920 level.

The mass demonstrations and rallies which occurred in early 1934 in opposition to a threatened right-wing coup was followed by the unification of the two wings of the trade union movement in late 1935. The huge strike wave of May–June 1936 which ushered in LÉON BLUM's POPULAR FRONT government pushed CGT membership up rapidly to a record 4.5 million members. The fall of the Popular Front and the attempts by the Government and employers to claw back the concessions made by the Popular Front, particularly the 40-hour week, provoked an unsuccessful general strike of 2 million workers on 30 November 1938. From 4 million members at the beginning of 1938 the CGT fell to 2.5 million members in September 1939, then 1 million in May 1940. By then, however, the policy of 'revolutionary defeatism' pursued by the Communist Party in relation to the war had led to its dissolution and the removal of communists from leading positions in the CGT. The communists were amnestied in 1944, following the leading part played by communist trade unionists and resistance groups in opposition to the Nazis. They took up important positions in the CGT, but the quasi-insurrectionary strike wave in 1947 led once again to a split in French trade unionism. The moderates broke off to form the Confédération Générale du Travail–Force Ouvrière (CGT–FO) leaving the communists in control of the CGT. Once again there was a decline in membership, from 6 million members in 1946 to a little over 1 million in 1965, the CGT–FO remained even smaller. The recurrent splits in the French trade union movement were compounded by the existence from 1919 of a separate organization of Catholic trade unionists, the Confédération Française des Travailleurs Chrétiens (CFTC) set up on 3 November 1919. By 1920 it had 156,000 members, rising to 400,000 in 1934 and to 500,000 by 1939. This divided in 1964, with a breakaway group retaining the old name and the main body continuing under the new name Confédération Française Démocratique du Travail (CFDT). A managerial and staff confederation was formed in 1944, the Confédération Générale des Cadres (CGC). As a result the trade union movement was often divided in its political impact and in its ability to speak with a single voice with government or employers. The vitality of the French Communist Party meant that for much of the post-war period the French Socialist Party was unable to bank upon the close alliance with organized labour enjoyed by, for example, the British Labour Party or the Swedish Social Democrats. Only with decline in communist political support in the 1970s and the emergence of the reformed Parti Socialiste (PS) as the majority party of the left have the trade union leaders begun to work with a political socialist party. Nonetheless the traditionally communist-led CGT was in 1982 the strongest body, supported by 2.8 million members, the CGT–FO had 1.4 million, the CFTC 650,000 and the CGC 740,000.

V. Lorwin, *The French Labour Movement* (1955)
R. Tierky, *French Communism, 1920–72* (1974)
R. McGraw, 'France', in S. Salter and J. Stevenson (eds), *The Working Class and Politics in Europe and America, 1929–1945* (1990)

**Confederation of British Industry** (CBI). The Confederation of British Industry was formed in 1965 to represent the employers and management in British industry. It is often involved in consultation with government and the trade unions and is part of the National Economic Development Council. It was formed as a result of a merger between the British Employers' Federation (concerned with industrial relations), the Federation of British Industry (responsible for promotion abroad and negotiation with government) and the National Association of British Manufacturers.

**conscientious objectors.** Persons who refuse to enlist for military service on religious or moral grounds. The position of such persons became a matter of controversy in Britain with the introduction of compulsory CONSCRIPTION in 1916. Conscientious objectors were screened by local tribunals and some 16,500 conscientious objectors obtained exemptions in this way, the majority taking up non-combatant duties and others being drafted into labour camps run by the Home Office. Others were unable to convince the tribunals and were sent to France, where a number refused to accept military discipline and 41 were sentenced to death. After a considerable outcry, they were brought back from France and joined a total of 1,298 imprisoned for their views, of whom 70 died. Conscientious objectors were generally unpopular and were disfranchised by the 1918 Representation of the People Act, although later regarded as heroes with the growth of pacifist feeling between the wars. Conscription Acts from 1939 made provision for conscientious objectors on somewhat more generous grounds.

D. Boulton, *Objection Overruled* (1967)
J. Rae, *Conscience and Politics: The British Government and the Conscientious Objector to Military Service, 1916–1919* (1970)
M. Ceadel, *Pacifism in Britain, 1914–45* (1980)

**conscription** Compulsory recruitment of citizens of a country for service, usually in the armed forces. After considerable controversy, it was first introduced in Britain by ASQUITH's government in January 1916 by the Military Service Act, which conscripted unmarried men between the ages of 18 and 41. It lapsed in 1919. Conscription was reintroduced for the first time in peace in April 1939. The National Service Act in 1947 provided for the continuation of conscription, which was initially for a period of 12 months, but was increased to 18 months in December 1948 and to two years in September 1950. In a White Paper published in April 1957 the government announced the phasing out of national service, and no men were called up after 1960.

**Conservative and Unionist Party, British**
One of the two major governing parties in Britain since the First World War and one of the most successful political parties in Europe in electoral terms. The modern party was established under Benjamin Disraeli (1805–81) as successor to the Tory Party. Disraeli highlighted the need for the Conservative Party to develop a national appeal to all social classes by adopting a more reformist approach to social issues; the notion that the Conservative Party is a national and not a class-based party has pervaded its 20th-century ideology.

The Conservative Party held power from 1900–5, but was divided over tariff reform and was heavily defeated by the LIBERAL PARTY in the 1906 general election. The party remained out of office until it joined the First World War Coalition Government in May 1915. The Coalition continued until 1922, when the Conservative Party was returned to power. It failed to obtain an overall majority in the 1923 general election but was returned to power in 1924 and remained in office until 1929. The party was stronger during the mid to-late 1920s under the leadership of STANLEY BALDWIN than had previously been the case. It adhered to the GOLD STANDARD, free trade and a balanced budget. In 1931 the party joined Ramsay MacDonald's coalition NATIONAL GOVERNMENT which convincingly won the general elections of 1931 and 1935. During the 1930s the party became more interventionist in its social, economic and industrial policies and moved away from the free-trade doctrine. The Conservatives shared power with Labour and the Liberals in Sir WINSTON CHURCHILL's Second World War Coalition Government (1940–45).

The party's defeat in the general election of 1945 led to its adoption of a more modern, collectivist approach to policy formation. 'The Industrial Charter' (1947) presented it with a new formula for planning in a mixed economy. The party was returned to power in 1951 and remained in office until 1964, winning the 1955 and 1959 general elections. Under Churchill, ANTHONY EDEN, and HAROLD MACMILLAN it adopted policies which reflected its acceptance of the welfare state and a mixed economy. The party was out of office from 1964 to 1970, having been defeated in the general elections of 1964 and 1966 under the leadership of Sir ALEC DOUGLAS-HOME and EDWARD HEATH, but won the 1970 general election. During their term in power the Conservatives maintained public expenditure on the social services and secured British membership of the EUROPEAN ECONOMIC COMMUNITY in 1973. The party's industrial relations policy and resulting THREE-DAY WEEK was largely responsible for its downfall in the February 1974 general election.

After the defeat in the general election of October 1974 MARGARET THATCHER replaced Edward Heath as leader in 1975. Under Thatcher, the party put forward more right-wing, less consensus-orientated policies. Following the 'WINTER OF DISCONTENT' and the collapse of the Labour Government under CALLAGHAN, Mrs Thatcher won the 1979 general election. In spite of great unpopularity as a result of the world depression and heavy unemployment, victory in the FALKLANDS WAR and the division of the opposition permitted a crushing election victory in June 1983. In the 1987 general election the Conservative Party was returned to office for the third successive time under Mrs Thatcher's leadership. However, her growing unpopularity especially over European policy and the Poll Tax saw her replaced by JOHN MAJOR in November 1990.

R. Blake, *The Conservative Party from Peel to Thatcher* (1985)
A. Sked and C. Cook, *Post-War Britain: A Political History* (3rd edn, 1988)

**Constantine I, of Greece** (1868–1923). King of Greece, 18 March 1913 to 11 June 1917 and 5 December 1920 to 27 September 1922. The eldest son of George I (1845–1913), he married Sophie, sister of Kaiser WILHELM II. As Crown Prince he led the Greek armies in the Balkan Wars, coming to the throne following the assassination of his father. Pro-German in sympathies, he found himself in direct conflict with his pro-Entente premier ELEUTHERIOS VENIZELOS. He frustrated Venizelos's attempt to bring Greece into the war on the side of the Entente in early 1915, forcing his resignation, and opening close ties with the CENTRAL POWERS. The return of Venizelos following an election victory in June 1915 led to renewed conflict. Although the Greek army was mobilized and he could not prevent the landing of a large Anglo–French force at Salonika, he sacked Venizelos in October and kept open his contacts with the Central Powers. Forced to concede port facilities and logistic support to the Allied armies in Salonika Constantine made no secret of his opposition to them. When in 1916 he made similar concessions to the advance of the Bulgarians, now in alliance with the Central Powers, Venizelos in September set up a pro-Entente government in Crete (later moved to Salonika) which received recognition in London and Paris. An unsuccessful attack by French and British forces on Athens in December 1916 led pro-royalist Greek forces to carry out widespread persecutions against supporters of Venizelos. A low-level civil war now came into being between royalists and Venizelists, which was temporarily settled in favour of the latter when the French and British, in June 1917, forced Constantine's abdication in favour of his son, Alexander. The death of Alexander on 25 October 1920 and the defeat of Venizelos in the elections of November 1920 allowed Constantine's return to the throne in December, following a plebiscite. His attempt to extend Greek power in Asia Minor in the aftermath of the Turkish defeat in the FIRST WORLD WAR was undermined by his purging of Venizelist officers from the army. A disastrous defeat in Anatolia, which produced millions of refugees as the ancient Greek settlement then crumbled, forced him into a second and final abdication in September 1922. He died in exile the following year but the 'Schism' he helped to foster between royalists and Venizelists continued to plague Greek political life for decades.

A. Palmer, *The Gardeners of Salonika* (1965)

C. Theodoulou, *Greece and the Entente, August 1, 1914–September 25, 1916* (1971)
G. B. Leon, *Greece and the Great Powers, 1914–1917* (1974)

**Constantine II, of Greece** (1940– ). King of Greece, 6 March 1964 to 1 June 1973. He succeeded his father, Paul I (1901–64). His favourable reception was marred by the CYPRIOT CIVIL WAR, which had begun the previous year, and a growing conflict with his prime minister GEORGE PAPANDREOU. This intensified when he ousted Papandreou in July 1965 and tried to govern with minority cabinets. The consequent disorder and loss of democratic legitimacy made possible a coup by the GREEK COLONELS on 21 April 1967, which suspended parliamentary government, claiming to be acting in the name of the King. Constantine remained in the country, but on 13 December attempted a counter-coup when he flew to the northern headquarters of the Third Army Corps in the mistaken belief it would rally to him. A radio broadcast calling on all democrats to assist him in removing the military government brought no response and pro-Royalist officers were arrested. Constantine fled to Italy. The Colonels formally abolished the monarchy on 1 June 1973 on the grounds that Constantine was continuing to plot against their regime. Their fall the next year was followed (8 December 1974) by a referendum on the position of the monarchy which decided by 69 per cent to 31 per cent against Constantine's return.

**Constituent Assembly, Russian.** The PROVISIONAL GOVERNMENT set up in Russia in March 1917 was intended only to exercise power until an elected Constituent Assembly could be convened. Progressively delayed because of the difficult situation of the country, the Assembly elections were not held, in fact, until after the Bolshevik seizure of power in the October Revolution. In theory, the Constituent Assembly was to be the body to draw up a constitution and exercise power backed by the first elections since the outbreak of the war. In the event, of the 41 million votes cast, the SOCIALIST REVOLUTIONARY PARTY obtained 15.8 million, compared with 9.8 million for the BOLSHEVIKS and 2 million for the Kadets (*see* CONSTITUTIONAL DEMOCRATIC PARTY, RUSSIAN), 7.5 million for national minority parties, and the rest unclassified. Of the 707 delegates, 175 were Bolsheviks, 370 Socialist Revolutionaries, 40 Left Socialist Revoltionaries (*see* LEFT SOCIALIST REVOLUTIONARY PARTY, RUSSIAN) 16 MENSHEVIKS, 17 Kadets, and the rest national minority representatives. Although Bolshevik support had increased amongst workers, peasants and soldiers, especially in Moscow and Petrograd, three-quarters of the votes had been anti-Bolshevik. LENIN determined to suppress the Assembly once it met, arguing in PRAVDA that it was a 'bourgeois institution' and attachment to its legalistic forms 'a betrayal of the cause of the revolution'. When the Assembly opened on 18 January the Bolsheviks put before it a 'Declaration of the Rights of the Toiling and Exploited Peoples', calling for recognition of the decrees of the All-Russian Congress of Soviets on Land, Industry and Peace, and explicitly limiting the powers of the Assembly. When the declaration was rejected by 237 votes to 136, the Bolshevik and Left Socialist Revolutionary delegates withdrew and the Assembly session was adjourned. The Bolsheviks then voted for dispersing the Assembly the next day. On the 19th, RED GUARDS refused to admit delegates to the locked building. Half-hearted attempts organized by the Socialist Revolutionary majority to protest against the dissolution were dispersed. The dissolution of the Constituent Assembly effectively ended any possibility of a rallying of the non-Bolshevik forces, short of full-scale armed conflict. Lenin's ruthless appreciation of the weakness of his opponents in Petrograd and Moscow, his contempt for parliamentary forms, and the support of the Red Guards ended the possibility of a moderate constitutionalist regime appearing.

L. Shapiro, *The Origin of the Communist Autocracy* (1965)

**Constitutional Democratic Party, Russian** (Kadets). Formed in 1905 as heirs to the liberal tradition of the 19th-century intelligentsia. Unlike the Socialist Revolutionaries (*see* SOCIALIST REVOLUTIONARY PARTY, RUSSIAN) they did not reject private property. They sought a liberal constitution based on universal suffrage, freedom of expression, representative institutions and an independent judiciary; their programme also included autonomy for Finland and Poland, greater freedom for the national minorities, progressive labour legislation, a secular non-state education system, and social welfare for the old and sick. Drawing support from the professions and intelligentsia they formed the major party in the first DUMA but had their representation cut to 58 in the fourth Duma following revision of the electoral law. They made up most of the members of the PROVISIONAL GOVERNMENT established in March 1917, but found themselves increasingly squeezed by the mass support of the Socialist Revolutionaries and the determined tactics of the BOLSHEVIKS. In the elections to the CONSTITUENT ASSEMBLY of January 1918 they obtained only 2 million votes (out of 41 million) and only 17 delegates. Even before the Assembly met, however, the Bolsheviks had issued a decree outlawing the leading Kadets as 'enemies of the people', closed down their newspapers, and arrested some of their members. Following the dispersal of the Assembly and in the ensuing development of the RUSSIAN CIVIL WAR the Kadets participated in short-lived regional governments in the Urals and elsewhere, but were effectively extinguished with the Bolshevik victory. Lack of mass support and the broad middle class that existed in other countries seriously weakened the position of a party of constitutional liberalism in Russia even before revolutionary events overtook them in 1917. Closely identified with the leadership of the Provisional Government they suffered the same fate of being overtaken by other larger or more determined groupings. *See also* RUSSIAN REVOLUTION.

G. A. Hosking, *The Constitutional Experiment: Government and Duma, 1907–1914* (1973)

W. G. Rosenberg, *Liberals in the Russian Revolution* (1974)

**Continuation War.** Name given to Finnish intervention against the Soviet Union following the German invasion of Russia in June 1941. Finnish troops reoccupied territory lost in the RUSSO–FINNISH WAR of 1939–40, but Field Marshal MANNERHEIM would not overstep the 1939 boundaries. No formal alliance with Nazi Germany was concluded, although German supplies were critical in maintaining the war effort. In effect the Finns held the north-western sector during the siege of Leningrad but a Russian attack in June 1944 and the increasing signs of German defeat led the Finns to conclude an armistice in September. Finland was forced to make further territorial concessions in the Arctic, losing the port of Petsamo, lease the naval base at Porkkala, 10 miles from Helsinki, to the Soviet Union for 50 years, and pay an indemnity. Finland entered the war on the Allied side on 9 March 1945.

D. Kirby, *Finland in the Twentieth Century* (1979)

**Conventional Armed Forces in Europe Treaty (CFE).** Agreed at CSCE Summit in Paris on '19 November 1990 between 22 heads of state to reduce substantially levels of conventional forces held in Europe. The Treaty will remove 100,000 pieces of heavy equipment from the armouries of NATO and the WARSAW PACT countries, to eliminate the prospect of a surprise attack by either side. Verification procedures have been agreed for the implementation of the Treaty, seen as a major act in the ending of the COLD WAR.

**Cook, Arthur** (1885–1931). British trade unionist. A former boy preacher in Somerset, he became active in the South Wales Miners' Federation after 1905 as a syndicalist. Imprisoned briefly for his opposition to the First World War, he became a leader of the South Wales miners and Secretary of the Miners' Federation of Great Britain in 1924. He led the miners into the conflict which provoked the GENERAL STRIKE of 1926. He is best known for his slogan 'not a penny off the pay, not a second on the day'. His public intransigence concealed attempts to negotiate an end to the seven-month lock-out of miners which followed the defeat of the General Strike. Only briefly a member of the BRITISH COMMUNIST PARTY, until 1921, he turned to support the LABOUR PARTY in response to the defeat of its militant syndicalism. Remembered as a brilliant orator, he died from overwork, aged 47.

P. Davies, *A. J. Cook* (1987)

**Coreper.** *See* COMMITTEE OF PERMANENT REPRESENTATIVES OF THE EUROPEAN COMMUNITY.

**Corfu incident.** The shooting of an Italian general and four members of his staff on Greek soil while mapping the Greek–Albanian frontier on 27 August 1923 prompted MUSSOLINI to lodge a claim to' compensation and bombard and occupy the Greek island of Corfu four days later. The Greeks appealed to the LEAGUE OF NATIONS for assistance in what was a flagrant breach of the Covenant of the League. Under pressure from Britain and France, Mussolini withdrew his force from Corfu on 27 September. The dispute was referred by the League to the Council of Ambassadors, who persuaded the Greeks to apologize and pay compensation. The incident provides an early example of Mussolini's bullying tactics in foreign policy towards his weaker neighbours and the difficulties of the League in obtaining adherence to the principles of the Covenant. *See also* ALBANIA.

D. Mack Smith, *Mussolini's Roman Empire* (1977)

**corporate state.** Term used to describe a form of social organization in which corporations act as the major organizing forces within society and act as intermediaries between citizens and the state. Fascist states have frequently been cited as examples of corporatism in practice, often attempting to set up institutions which combine interest groups across class lines, placing them at the service of the state, and imposing social discipline upon potentially disruptive groups. As such, the corporate state drew upon a rejection of the inevitability of class conflict along Marxist lines and sought to introduce vertically integrated institutions. Its fullest development was seen in MUSSOLINI's Italy, where the Pact of Palazzo Vidoni in 1925 between employers and the regime imposed fascist unions on the factories to negotiate with employers' organizations. All other bargaining groups were banned, strikes outlawed and labour courts were to impose arbitration, confirmed by the Rocco Law of April 1926. In July of the same year a Ministry of Corporations was set up to oversee the legally recognized associations. From March 1930 a National Council of Corporations was established as an economic parliament, representing worker and employer organizations for agriculture, industry, commerce, the professions and the arts. By 1934 there were 22 corporations governing different areas of Italian economic life. Echoes of the corporate ideal could be found in the Spain of PRIMO DE

RIVERA and later in the ideas of the FALANGE. Similar elements were present, though less well-developed in Nazism (*see* NAZI PARTY). The corporate state has frequently been seen as marking a 'third way' between communism and capitalism. It has had some support from Catholic social thinking as a means of representing legitimate interests and encouraging harmonious social relationships.

A. J. Gregor, *The Ideology of Fascism* (1969)
C. S. Maier, *Recasting Bourgeois Europe* (1969)

**Cossacks.** People of south and southwestern Russia with a tradition of military service to the state in return for land and economic privileges. Organized in 11 communities (*voiskos*), there were some 4 million Cossacks in 1914, the male population of which was subject to four years' military service and eight years in the reserve. Although 300,000 Cossacks served in the First World War their most important political role was as a peace-keeping force in the major cities. In spite of their reputation for conservatism, the Cossacks had grievances over the administration of their communities by non-Cossack officers and civil servants, and retained a desire to see some revival of traditional Cossack 'liberties'. Following the February Revolution, when Cossack regiments had shown little enthusiasm for suppressing the crowds in Petrograd, the Cossacks formed an All-Cossack Congress in April to represent their interests, representing the 11 *voiskos* and chaired by a Cossack general. A congress in June was attended by 600 Cossack delegates and a Cossack newspaper published. Amongst the largest Cossack community, the Don Cossacks, a 'Union of the Don Cossacks' was set up and called for a *krug* or traditional assembly and an elected headman, or *ataman*. Accordingly in May a 'Great Krug' was established and General Kaledin elected *ataman*. Similar developments occurred in the other Cossack communities, with assemblies electing their own leaders. As beneficiaries of the more liberal climate under the PROVISIONAL GOVERNMENT, the Cossacks assisted in putting down the Bolshevik rising in July, but were themselves divided by the anti-war propaganda of the Bolsheviks and the formation of a minority 'Soviet of Cossacks'.

These divisions persisted following the Bolshevik seizure of power in November 1917, when some Cossacks tried to retake Petrograd but others refused to leave their barracks. Short-lived Cossack administrations were set up in several areas, notably the Don and the Kuban areas, and attempts by the Bolshevik government to win over the Cossacks were often undermined by the actions of the RED ARMIES in carrying out forcible requisitioning. By 1919 Cossack forces were widely engaged in 'White' armies in the RUSSIAN CIVIL WAR, especially those in the south commanded by DENIKIN and WRANGEL. Although promises were made by Lenin in the summer of 1919 to respect the separate status of the Cossacks, victory in the Civil War was followed by a decree in March 1920 abolishing the separate Cossack institutions. In the event, hundreds of thousands of Cossacks were to join the White forces in exile, many of them evacuating with Wrangel's forces from the Crimea.

The Cossack emigrés were to play a significant part after 1941, when sections of them were organized in Yugoslavia under General Krasnov to fight TITO's partisans. There they were joined by prisoners-of-war captured from the Soviets and who volunteered to fight on the German side. Many of these were handed back ('repatriated') in controversial circumstances to the Yugoslav and Soviet governments in 1945 to fulfil agreements made between Stalin, Roosevelt and Churchill at the YALTA CONFERENCE. Most of them were executed or sent to labour camps. *See also* UKRAINE.

P. Longworth, *The Cossacks: Five Centuries of Turbulent Life on the Russian Steppe* (1969)
P. Kenez, *Civil War in South Russia, 1918–20* (2 vols., 1971–7)

**Council of Europe.** Founded on 5 May 1949, by the signing of the Statute of the Council of Europe, with the aim of achieving greater unity between members through co-operation over economic, social, cultural, scientific, legal and administrative matters and over human rights. The original members were Belgium, Denmark, France, Ireland, Italy, Luxembourg, the Netherlands, Norway, Sweden and the United Kingdom. They have since been joined by Austria, Greece, Turkey, Iceland, West Germany,

Cyprus and Malta. The institutions of the Council are a Committee of Ministers meeting about twice a year, which may make recommendations to member governments, if it decides unanimously to do so, and a Consultative Assembly, composed of members either appointed by their national governments or elected by their national parliament which meets in Strasbourg for about one month a year. Transnational political groups have been organized within the Assembly. The Consultative Assembly acts either through recommendations to the Committee of Ministers, or through resolutions expressing an opinion, and serves as a general forum for the expression of parliamentary opinion on European matters. The actual powers of the Council of Europe are thus very limited in effect, being confined to the expression of opinions. Its activities have been nonetheless of great importance, since under its aegis over 70 conventions and agreements have been drawn up. These have, of course, entered into force in the member states only in so far as they have been ratified by them. The first and most important of these was the EUROPEAN CONVENTION ON HUMAN RIGHTS.

**Council of Ministers of the European Community.** Composed of one ministerial representative of each of the member states of the European Community, it is the central decision-making body of the Community. Following the MERGER TREATY of 1965 it replaced the separate Councils of Ministers of the EUROPEAN ECONOMIC COMMUNITY, EURATOM and the EUROPEAN COAL AND STEEL COMMISSION (ECSC). Its composition varies according to the nature of the subjects under discussion, thus a Transport Council will be attended by Ministers of Transport. The Council of Foreign Ministers is regarded as the senior body. The chairmanship (presidency) of the Council is held by each member state in turn for six months, in alphabetical order. A minister of the country holding the presidency for the time being thus takes the chair at every Council meeting and the Foreign Minister of that country is regarded as being the President of the Council of Ministers. The Council of Ministers takes its decisions upon the basis of proposals made by the COMMISSION OF THE EUROPEAN COMMUNITY,

members of which are present at all meetings. It may ask the Commission to submit proposals, but is not entitled to take the initiative in formulating them itself. On the whole, ministers accept that the decisions which the Council of Ministers reaches should be good for the Community as a whole, but each minister represents his own national government and seeks to further its particular interests. According to the treaties, many decisions may be made by a system of weighted majority voting. In practice such voting is rare, both because wherever possible agreement is reached through negotiations, packages and compromises, often achieved after lengthy 'marathon' sessions, and because some members have insisted upon their right of veto where vital national interests are concerned. The Council of Ministers is supported in its work by a secretariat of about 1,500 staff. All the proposals which reach the Council from the Commission are subjected to detailed discussion and negotiation in confidential meetings of working groups and *ad hoc* committees composed of national officials, with Coreper at their apex (*see* COMMITTEE OF PERMANENT REPRESENTATIVES). The chair is taken by officials of the country holding the presidency of the Council of Ministers at that time; representatives of the Commission attend. The Council of Ministers takes into account the views expressed by the EUROPEAN PARLIAMENT but is not responsible to it. The opinions of the ECONOMIC AND SOCIAL COMMITTEE are also considered. The Council of Ministers is involved in making law. It may issue regulations, directives or decisions which are directed only at specified people. Legislation issued under the ECSC treaty has a slightly different nomenclature. The operation of the European Community can be regarded as a dialogue between the Commission and the Council; the Council however, retains the paramount position, and is likely to continue to ensure that the wishes and interests of the member states' national governments dominate Community affairs. See also EUROPEAN COUNCIL.

R. Pryce, *The Politics of the European Community* (1973)

**'Coupon' Election.** Name given to the British general election of 1918 from the letter of approval or 'coupon', signed by LLOYD GEORGE, leader of the section of the LIBERAL PARTY in coalition with the Conservatives, and BONAR LAW, the Conservative Party (*see* CONSERVATIVE AND UNIONIST PARTY, BRITISH) leader, which was distributed to candidates in the general election. The letters or 'coupons' were, in effect, endorsements of the candidates as Coalition candidates. 531 coupons were issued, 150 of them to Liberals, ensuring that they would not be opposed by candidates of the other party in the Coalition. 362 'coupon' candidates were returned, a majority of them Conservatives. In all 478 Coalition members were returned, 133 of them Coalition Liberals, dwarfing the 28 Liberals who preferred to stand outside. The election both strengthened the hand of the Conservatives within the Coalition and contributed to the divisions within the Liberal Party.

T. Wilson, *The Downfall of the Liberal Party, 1914–35* (1966)

K. O. Morgan, *Consensus and Disunity: The Lloyd George Coalition Government 1918–22* (1979)

**Court of Justice of the European Community.** The final arbiter of all legal questions arising under the treaties establishing the EUROPEAN COAL AND STEEL COMMUNITY, the EUROPEAN ECONOMIC COMMUNITY and EURATOM. It deals with disputes between member states or between member states and European Community institutions and may hear appeals from a member state, the COMMISSION OF THE EUROPEAN COMMUNITY, the COUNCIL OF MINISTERS OF THE EUROPEAN COMMUNITY or an individual on European Community matters. It also hears cases where individuals or firms directly affected wish to challenge the legality of Community legislation. The work of enforcing European Community law is undertaken by the national courts of the member states, for European Community law operates, once it has been made by the Community institutions, within each member state without any further process, as if it were national legislation, and is enforced in the same way. However, national courts may refer questions of the interpretation of European Community law to the Court of Justice for a preliminary ruling; the final settlement of the case in which such questions arise will be made by the national court. The Court consists of nine judges, who decide cases by majority vote; dissenting judgments are not published. The Court is assisted by four advocates-general, whose role is to give a' summing-up and expert legal opinion on each case before the judges reach a decision.

**CPSU.** *See* COMMUNIST PARTY OF THE SOVIET UNION.

**Craxi, Bettino** (1934–). Italian Socialist politician. Born in Milan and active in the Socialist Youth Movement, becoming a member of the Central Committee of the ITALIAN SOCIALIST PARTY (PSI) in 1957. He became a member of its National Executive in 1963; Deputy General Secretary, 1970–76 and has been General Secretary since 1976. He helped to revive the fortunes of the Party by bringing it into coalition with the CHRISTIAN DEMOCRATS and becoming Italy's first Socialist prime minister in July 1983 with Christian Democrat support. However he resigned the Premiership early, in February 1987, to put him in a position to force an election at a time of his own choosing by withdrawing socialist support. In the June 1987 election, Craxi's Socialists improved their support to 94 seats, providing the basis for a continued coalition with the Christian Democrats. In May 1989 Craxi's socialists brought down Mr. De Mita's government, forcing the return of the veteran ANDREOTTI. Craxi has been seen as reviving the position of the Socialist party to one in which it determined the future of the Centre-Left coalition and increased its support. He has also taken advantage of the disarray of the COMMUNIST PARTY, winning support at its expense in 1987. *See also*: SOCIALIST PARTY, ITALIAN.

P. Ginsborg, *A History of Contemporary Italy: Society and Politics, 1943–1988* (1990)

**Creditanstalt.** Following a series of bank mergers in the 1920s the Creditanstalt had become Austria's leading financial institution by 1931. Its collapse in May of that year precipitated a whole chain of economic and political crisis in Austria. Its repercussions were also felt abroad, particularly in Germany.

**Cripps, Richard Stafford** (1889–1952). British Labour politician. He was Labour MP for Bristol East, later South East, 1931–50; Solicitor-General, 1930–31; Lord Privy Seal and Leader of House of Commons, 1942; President of the Board of Trade, 1945–7; Chancellor of the Exchequer, 1947–50. He is best known as the public face of 'austerity' in the ATTLEE governments after 1945. His earlier career had been marked by left-wing views which led to his expulsion from the Labour Party in 1939. He was readmitted to the party in 1945 and proved an able, if rather severe Chancellor of the Exchequer. He was unable to prevent devaluation of the pound in September 1949, but had an important role in staving off bankruptcy and organizing a reduction of home consumption to permit exports to rise.

M. Sissons and P. French (eds.), *The Age of Austerity* (1963)
K. O. Morgan, *Labour in Power, 1945–1951* (1983)
H. Pelling, *The Labour Governments, 1945–51* (1984)

**Croatia.** Part of the Kingdom of Hungary and the Austro–Hungarian empire prior to 1914. Political leaders such as ANTE TRUMBIC increasingly supported the idea of a South Slav (Yugoslav) union. Trumbic was instrumental in the formation of a Yugoslav Committee in London during the First World War and obtained the Corfu Pact in 1917 with the Serbian government-in-exile led by NIKOLA PASIC and Prince Regent Alexander (*see* ALEXANDER I) which agreed to the setting up of a Kingdom of Serbs, Croats and Slovenes under the Serbian royal house. Cultural differences between Serbs and Croats, the former being largely Orthodox in religion and the Croats being Roman Catholic, as well as fears of Serbian domination of the new state produced tensions and unrest which led to the assumption of a royal dictatorship by Alexander in 1929. Croatian resentments crystallized in the formation of a terrorist organization, the USTASE, in 1929 led by Ante Pavelic (1889–1959), which conducted terrorist activities against the Yugoslav state, including the assassination of King Alexander at Marseilles in 1934. The German conquest of Yugoslavia in 1941 led the *Ustase* to set up an independent Kingdom of Croatia, with an Italian duke as titular King of Croatia. Collaborating with the Germans and Italians, the *Ustase* fought against TITO's partisans and other opponents of the AXIS occupation, committing many massacres and atrocities against Jews and rival nationalities. With the German withdrawal from Yugoslavia and the victory of Tito's forces, the *Ustase* were largely imprisoned, killed or forced into exile, Pavelic fleeing to Spain and ultimately to Argentina. Croatia became one of the federal republics in the Yugoslavian constitution promulgated in 1946. Exiled Croatian groups have conducted terrorist acts in several European states since the 1960s. In spring 1990 the first free elections in Croatia for fifty years led to a victory for the pro-nationalist Democratic Union over the Communists and steps to seek autonomy. An independence declaration in spring 1991 was met by armed resistance from Serbian irregulars and federal army units, leading to heavy fighting.

F. Singleton, *Twentieth Century Yugoslavia* (1976)
L. J. Cohen, *Political Cohesion in a Fragile Mosaic; the Yugoslav Experience* (1983)

**cruise missile.** An intermediate-range, ground- or air-launched nuclear missile, using highly sophisticated terrain-mapping radar to achieve pin-point accuracy. United States deployment of land-based cruise missiles in Western Europe in 1983 in response to the Soviet Union's deployment of SS-20 intermediate-range nuclear missiles sparked off widespread anti-nuclear protests in Britain, West Germany and the Netherlands. In December 1987 President REAGAN and General Secretary GORBACHEV signed the INTERMEDIATE NUCLEAR FORCES TREATY which provided for the withdrawal and destruction of all land-based nuclear missiles in Europe with ranges of between 500 and 5,500 kilometres; included in the Treaty were American cruise missiles and Soviet SS-20s. Removal of cruise missiles under strict verification procedures had begun by the end of 1989.

**CSCE.** Conference on Security and Co-operation in Europe. *See* HELSINKI AGREEMENT.

**CSP.** *See* CHRISTIAN SOCIAL PARTY, AUSTRIAN.

**CSU.** Christlich Soziale Union. *See* CHRISTIAN SOCIAL UNION, GERMAN.

**Cuban Missile Crisis.** On 22 October 1962 President KENNEDY announced on television that United States surveillance had established the presence of Soviet missile sites in Cuba and that he was imposing a naval blockade or 'quarantine' of Cuba to prevent the shipment of further offensive weapons. The following day a Soviet broadcast denounced the blockade and the United Nations Security Council met to attempt to resolve the crisis. Several days of tense negotiations followed between the American President and KHRUSHCHEV, in which the threat of all-out nuclear war seemed imminent. On 26 October Khrushchev offered to withdraw the missiles under United Nations supervision in return for a lifting of the American blockade on Cuba. A further letter from Khrushchev on the 27th linked the initial offer to the removal of American missiles from Turkey. President Kennedy replied on the basis of the first proposal. The following day, the 28th, firm undertakings were given by the Soviet government on the removal of the missiles from Cuba under United Nations supervision. Soviet vessels headed for Cuba turned back, and the United States lifted its naval blockade. One of the most tense crises of the COLD WAR, the Cuban Missile Crisis was interpreted in the West as an attempt by the Soviet Union to take advantage of the new American President. The strong line taken by the American government forced what was seen as a climb-down by Khrushchev. The Soviet Union was also seen not to have the global naval power which could contest naval superiority around Cuba. The crisis was the nearest the United States and the Soviet Union came to nuclear war in the post-war era, with America's strategic nuclear forces on full alert. One result of the crisis was the attempt to improve communications be-tween the superpowers through the installation of a 'hot line', agreed on 5 April 1963. As compensation for the loss of the missiles, Cuba was reinforced with up-to-date conventional weapons, including supersonic aircraft, anti-aircraft missiles, and missile-equipped patrol boats. In this way the Soviet Union ensured that Cuba remained a strong, pro-Soviet force in the Americas. America was forced to guarantee that Cuba would not be invaded, and to accept the presence of an unwelcome regime only a few miles off the American mainland.

E. Able, *The Missiles of October: The Story of the Cuban Missile Crisis* (1966)

G. Allison, *Essence of Decision: Explaining the Cuban Missile Crisis* (1971)

**Cult of Personality.** The development of servile adulation of individual leaders, most usually associated with STALIN, but also seen in other dictatorial regimes including those of MUSSOLINI, HITLER and Eastern bloc countries such as Albania under HOXHA and Romania under CEAUŞESCU. The personality cult of Stalin emerged following his defeat of the opposition and the celebration on his 50th birthday in December 1929, when all Soviet newspapers carried flattering eulogies of Stalin and extensive reports of birthday tributes to him. Orchestrated adulation gave way to the fabrication of the historical record to elevate Stalin's role in the RUSSIAN REVOLUTION and the elimination in documents and photographs of rivals and opponents. Stalin contributed to the rewriting of history via the *Short Course* of 1938, which became an obligatory text for all schoolchildren and students. The cult of personality increased as a result of victory in the SECOND WORLD WAR, culminating in Stalin's entombment alongside Lenin after his death in March 1953. KHRUSHCHEV's campaign of DE-STALINIZATION, beginning with his secret speech at the twentieth Party Congress in 1956, concentrated on the excesses of Stalin's cult of personality. In practice the cult of personality has been a tool of both communist and fascist regimes in the 20th century, elevating the role of the leader as the source, guardian and embodiment of the ruling ideology within a totalitarian system where propaganda and the power of the state offer unprecedented opportunities for its promotion. Even after Stalin's death and partial denunciation, later Soviet leaders, such as BREZHNEV, have accorded themselves honours and awards far removed from their actual accomplishments. The 'cult of Lenin' is still widely prevalent, though it differs from that of other Soviet leaders in being an entirely posthumous phenomenon.

**Cumann na nGaedheal.** Irish organization founded in 1900 to advance the cause of

Irish independence by developing a fraternal spirit amongst Irishmen, and supporting cultural, economic and recreational movements. It acted as a loose co-ordinating body to which other societies could affiliate, but amalgamated with other societies to form the Sinn Fein League in 1907. In 1923 Cumann na nGaedhael was reformed as a political party to rally the pro-treaty forces in the IRISH CIVIL WAR and to bring together those willing to co-operate in building the new state. It formed the largest grouping in the Irish parliament (Dail) elected in August 1923, with 63 members and provided the head of the government, W. T. Cosgrave. The Party saw Ireland through ten years of reconstruction and the establishment of a parliamentary system, including the admission of the anti-treaty forces led by DE VALERA and FIANNA FAIL to constitutional politics. Losing power in the elections of 1932 to its opponents, Cumann na nGaedael merged in 1933 into a new Party, FINE GAEL, comprising its old adherents, the Farmer's Party, and members of the right-wing, neo-fascist National Guard led by General Eoin O'Duffy.

F. S. L. Lyons, *Ireland since the Famine* (rev. edn, 1973)

**Curragh Incident.** Also known as the Curragh 'mutiny'. In June 1914 57 officers of the Third Cavalry Brigade stationed at the Curragh, Dublin, said they would resign rather than impose HOME RULE on Ireland. The War Office gave them written assurances that they would not be asked to coerce fellow Irish citizens. The incident was taken to show the difficulties the British government would have in coercing Ulster to accept Home Rule.

**Curzon Line.** A proposed armistice line in the RUSSO–POLISH WAR, named after the British Foreign Secretary, Lord Curzon (1859–1925). It was proposed with Polish consent to the Russians by LLOYD GEORGE in July 1920. The Soviet government turned down the proposal but subsequently agreed to a frontier much more in Poland's favour at the Treaty of Riga of 18 March 1921. The 'Curzon Line' re-emerged as the suggested Polish–Soviet frontier in the Second World War, forming the basis for the boundary between the German and Russian spheres of occupied Poland. In 1945 it became the basis for the frontier between Poland and the Soviet Union.

**Cypriot Civil War.** Conflict between Greek and Turkish Cypriot communities developed into fighting in December 1963 following President MAKARIOS's proposals for constitutional reform. A cease-fire was declared on 25 December 1963 and a UNITED NATIONS peace-keeping force established in March 1964. On 6 August Turkish planes attacked Greek positions in northern Cyprus in retaliation for attacks on Turkish Cypriots. Renewed fighting between Greek and Turkish communities took place in 1967, when mediation by the United Nations led to the withdrawal of Greek regular troops and the stand-down of Turkish forces preparing to invade the island. The development of serious fighting on Cyprus overshadowed Greek politics in the mid-1960s, fuelling the conflict with Turkey and the strains within the NATO alliance (*see* NORTH ATLANTIC TREATY ORGANISATION) of which both Greece and Turkey were members. The continuing possibility of 'enosis' offered a prospect of reunion of Cyprus with Greece which was eventually to lead to the TURKISH INVASION OF CYPRUS in 1974. *See also* CONSTANTINE II.

**Cyprus crises.** A period of protracted civil strife in Cyprus from April 1955 between sections of the Greek population and British colonial forces. Agitation for union with Greece, 'enosis', was resisted by the British government. A campaign of terrorism was carried on by the militant wing of the Enosis movement, EOKA, led by Colonel George Grivas (1898–1974), and appeared to receive tacit support from Archbishop MAKARIOS. A state of emergency was declared on 27 November 1955, and in ensuing terrorist and guerrilla attacks British military and civilian losses amounted to 142 dead and 684 wounded, with nearly 1,000 Greek and Turkish Cypriots killed or wounded. Archbishop Makarios was deported to the Seychelles in 1956 and a cease-fire came into effect on 13 March 1959, prior to the establishment of an independent republic of Cyprus on 16 August 1960, with Makarios as its first President. The agreement not to pursue 'enosis' caused deep divisions in the Greek community and exposed Makarios to assassination and coup attempts by the surviving members of EOKA. Grivas was able to return to Cyprus in 1967 and was given command in the Greek National Guard, where his actions against Turkish Cypriots forced his recall to Athens. He continued to plot against Makarios until his death early in 1974. While the Cyprus emergency was for Britain only one of a number of small wars on the road of imperial retreat, for Greece Cyprus remained one of the most sensitive and divisive issues, souring relations with Britain and Turkey. Cyprus itself was only to find peace after two periods of renewed fighting and partition. *See also* CYPRIOT CIVIL WAR.

C. M. Woodhouse, *British Foreign Policy since the Second World War* (1961)

K. Markides, *The Rise and Fall of the Cyprus Republic* (1977)

**Cyprus, Turkish invasion of.** The GREEK COLONELS' regime in Greece was involved in encouraging the deposition of President Makarios on 15 July 1974 in a coup organized by the Cypriot National Guard. Makarios was replaced by Nikos Sampson, a former EOKA fighter, signalling to Turkey that 'enosis' (union) with Greece was about to take place. Fighting broke out between Greek and Turkish Cypriots and on 20 July regular Turkish forces invaded northern Cyprus, forcing Sampson's resignation three days later. A cease-fire on 30 July was followed by a renewed Turkish advance in mid-August which left them in control of a third of the island. The Turkish invasion produced a permanent partition of the island, which involved the flight of most of the Turkish and Greek populations of the island to the sectors controlled by their countrymen. The involvement of the Greek Colonels in an episode which proved a disaster for the Greek Cypriot community and ended finally any lingering hopes of union with Greece brought about the downfall of their regime on 23 July, when KARAMANLIS was invited to form a caretaker administration in Athens.

**Czech Legion.** In July 1917 permission was given by the RUSSIAN PROVISIONAL GOVERNMENT to establish a Czechoslovak Legion from prisoners-of-war taken by the Russians who wished to fight for a Czechoslovak

state against the CENTRAL POWERS. By the end of 1917 a disciplined body of some 45,000 men, under French command, were stationed in Siberia. In February 1918 MASARYK obtained permission for the Legion to leave Russia via Vladivostock in return for giving up its arms, but relations between the local BOLSHEVIKS and the Czechs deteriorated. Following quarrels when a group took over the town of Chelyabinsk in May 1918 TROTSKY ordered them disarmed. In reaction the Czechs summoned a 'National Congress' at Chelyabinsk, refusing to disarm unless guaranteed unhindered departure from the country. Trotsky's attempt to suppress them by ordering any armed Czech to be shot led to their lightning advance by early June to control most of the central Volga and Siberia; by the end of the month virtually the whole eastern end of the Trans-Siberian Railway was in their hands. The Czech defiance of the Bolsheviks and the presence of a large disciplined army astride the major east–west artery encouraged Allied intervention and the open opposition of anti-Bolshevik forces within Russia. Peasant and SOCIALIST REVOLUTIONARY PARTY risings took place in several areas and Czech control of the Samara region allowed the convening of a Socialist Revolutionary regional government, led by a Czech. The Czechs, however, were mainly concerned to return home and became increasingly demoralized when Allied shipping was not made available to them when the war ended in November 1918. Forced to co-operate with the 'White' forces of Admiral KOLCHAK they remained in Russia until early 1920, when they finally handed Kolchak over to the Bolsheviks and were allowed, in February, to leave Russia. Although the Czech Legion was a potent symbol of the Czechoslovak nation emerging from the destruction of the Austro–Hungarian empire, it became, in effect, a pawn in international politics, being used to shore up the anti-Bolshevik forces; it only escaped disaster because of its own military qualities and continued Japanese and American control of Vladivostock as a port of embarkation. *See also* RUSSIAN CIVIL WAR.

D. Footman, *Civil War in Russia* (1961)

R. H. Ullman, *Intervention and the War* (1961)

**Czechoslovakia, Soviet Invasion of.** *See* 'PRAGUE SPRING'.

# D

**Daladier, Edouard** (1884–1970). French politician. Born near Avignon, he became a teacher before representing his area as a Radical deputy, 1919–40, 1946–58. He was Minister of Colonies in 1924, and served two short terms as Prime Minister, January–October 1933 and January–February 1934. He served as Minister of War and Defence, December 1932–January 1934, June 1936–18 May 1940. His second term as Minister of Defence was as part of LÉON BLUM's POPULAR FRONT government. He succeeded Blum as Prime Minister on 10 April 1938. He pursued a policy of APPEASEMENT and was one of the signatories of the MUNICH AGREEMENT in 1938, but launched a crash programme of rearmament in order to prepare France for war. The outbreak of the Second World War led him to act against the 'revolutionary defeatism' of the communists; he arrested their deputies and dealt harshly with communist-organized strikes. On 21 March 1940 he was replaced by PAUL REYNAUD, but remained in the government, serving as Foreign Minister in late May and early June 1940. His attempts to set up a government in North Africa following the fall of France led to his arrest and trial at Riom by the VICHY GOVERNMENT in February 1942. He was deported to a German concentration camp in 1943 and kept in custody until 1945. He returned as a deputy under the FOURTH REPUBLIC, although he never held ministerial office again.
A. Adamthwaite, *France and the Coming of the Second World War* (1977)

**D'Annunzio, Gabriele** (1863–1938). Italian poet and adventurer. A well-known novelist, he used his literary talents to encourage nationalism after 1914, promoting Italian entry into the war. He served in the Italian Air Force, 1915–18, and was decorated for valour. Feeling that Italy had been betrayed by the PARIS PEACE CONFERENCE, on 12 September 1919 he seized FIUME, which was under dispute between Italy and YUGOSLAVIA. He administered the city as a part of Italy, even though Italy and Yugoslavia agreed on 12 November to its independence. In a show of nationalist bravado, d'Annunzio declared war on Italy, and was finally ejected by a naval task force on 4 January 1921. He acted to stimulate nationalist feeling against the Liberal government of GIOLITTI, whose search for an amicable settlement he saw as shameful. He welcomed MUSSOLINI's accession to power but spent the rest of his life in retirement.
Gerald Griffin, *Gabriele d'Annunzio* (1935)
A. Rhodes, *The Poet as Superman* (1959)

**Danube Commission.** Set up by a meeting of Danube countries who signed the Belgrade Convention on 18 August 1948. This reaffirmed that navigation of the Danube from Ulm to the Black Sea should be free and open to the nationals, shipping, and merchandise of the signatories. The Convention came into force in 1949, governed by a Commission containing a representative from each Danube country. Its headquarters since 1954 has been Budapest. The Commission has legal status and its own seal and flag; its officers have diplomatic immunity.

**Danzig** (Gdansk). Port on the mouth of the Vistula river. It was part of Prussia and Germany until 1919, when the TREATY OF VERSAILLES made it a Free City administered by the LEAGUE OF NATIONS to give Poland an outlet to the sea. The city was run by a League of Nations commissioner

107

with an elected Senate. From 1933 Danzig passed under the control of the local NAZI PARTY. A series of incidents were provoked by the Nazis in order to demonstrate the oppression of the German population by the Poles. Following the SUDETENLAND Germans, they were the next group of ethnic Germans whom HITLER sought to bring within the Reich. On 1 September 1939 the Nazi GAULEITER of Danzig proclaimed the union of Danzig with Germany as German forces moved into Poland, so starting the SECOND WORLD WAR. Danzig was absorbed into Hitler's Germany but was captured by the Soviet Army on 30 March 1945. In the revision of frontiers which followed two months later, Danzig became a Polish city, Gdansk. Most of the Germans had either fled or were expelled. As a major industrial city, Gdansk and the neighbouring port of Gdynia with which it was administratively linked became the scene of violent worker opposition to communist policies over price rises in 1970–1 and the birthplace of SOLIDARITY in 1981.

**Dardanelles campaign.** FIRST WORLD WAR campaign to seize control of the narrow channel between European and Asiatic Turkey, linking the Aegean Sea and the Sea of Marmora and forming with the Bosphorus further north the sole sea route between the Mediterranean and the Black Sea. Turkey's declaration of war in 1914 on the side of the Central Powers, Germany and Austria-Hungary, blocked the strategic waterway and British and French access to southern Russia. In January 1915 concern about Russia's position and the desire to rally Bulgaria and Greece to the Entente powers led to a plan by FISHER, the First Sea Lord, and CHURCHILL, First Lord of the Admiralty, to force the Dardanelles with warships and to seize the Gallipoli peninsula on the southernmost European shore of the Dardanelles with Constantinople, on the Bosphorus, as the ultimate objective. In initial disagreements about whether troops should be employed alongside naval vessels, Fisher threatened to resign, but on 28 January a purely naval plan was adopted. Naval bombardment of Turkish forts opened on 19 February, followed by an attempt to force the straits with a large Anglo-French fleet. When several of the vessels were disabled by mines, the naval assault was abandoned and a force of 78,000 men directed to seize the Gallipoli peninsula. The landings began on 25 April 1915, by the British at Cape Hellas on the tip of the peninsula, by a French force on the mainland of Asia Minor, and by Australian and New Zealand Army Corps (ANZAC) at Ari Burun, twenty-five miles further north up the peninsula. The Turks under the command of the German general, von Sanders, were prepared for the landings and inflicted very heavy casualties on the British and Anzac forces. Turkish command of the strategic high points prevented the attacking forces moving inland and achieving their objective. A further landing at Suvla Bay on 6 August failed to break the stalemate and the British commander, Sir Ian Hamilton, was relieved of his command on 15 October. The new commander, Sir Charles Monroe, recommended evacuation, confirmed by KITCHENER in November. Between 10 December 1915 and 9 January 1916 all troops were withdrawn after suffering 250,000 casualties. The failure of the campaign cost Fisher's resignation as early as 15 May 1915 and contributed to the political crisis which forced ASQUITH to form a Coalition Government on 25 May 1915. Churchill was forced out of the Admiralty and eventually out of the Government in November. Seen by one group of politicians and military men, the 'Easterners', as an attempt to break the deadlock on the Western Front, its failure reinforced the arguments of the 'Westerners' that the decisive theatre lay in Europe.

**Darlan, Jean** (1881–1942). French admiral and politician. Born in Aquitaine, he had a distinguished career in the First World War, becoming executive head of the French Navy, 1933–9, then commander-in-chief. Like many French naval men he was outraged by the British attack on the French fleet at Mers-el-Kebir in the Gulf of Oran on 3 July 1940, especially after he had given assurances that the French fleet would not be allowed to fall into German hands. He served as Minister of Marine under the VICHY GOVERNMENT, and was appointed as Deputy Prime Minister, Foreign Minister and successor to PÉTAIN in February 1941.

After negotiating with the Germans on behalf of the Vichy government, he was demoted by Pétain for collaborating too closely with the Germans; his protocols of May 1941 offering them extensive facilities in the Middle East and protection from the French fleet. Darlan was High Commissioner in Algiers when the Anglo–French landings took place in November 1942. The German reaction of occupying the FREE ZONE of southern France in direct contravention of the armistice agreement of 1940 freed Darlan from his allegiance and he ordered the French troops to lay down their arms. Under an agreement struck with EISENHOWER he was then given overall civil command of the French colonies in North Africa, an act which antagonized DE GAULLE's FREE FRENCH in London as an apparent condoning of Vichy collaborators. The potential rift was resolved when Darlan was assassinated by a young royalist on 24 December 1942. *See also* GIRAUD, HENRI.

P. Aron, *The Vichy Regime, 1940–4* (1958)
R. Paxton, *Vichy France* (1972)

**Dawes Plan.** Plan drawn up and submitted to the Allied Reparations Committee in April 1924 by the American banker Charles G. Dawes (1865–1951) to modify German REPARATIONS payments which had fallen into default. The plan involved annual payments according to a fixed scale of 2,500 million marks per annum. A key part of the plan was the reorganization of the German State Bank and the provision of foreign loans to Germany in order to meet the payments. An initial loan of 800 million marks was agreed, beginning a series of loans, mainly from the United States, which allowed Germany to stabilize her economy and meet the payments on schedule until the Great Crash of 1929. The Plan has been criticized for enticing Germany into paying her reparations with borrowed money, making her prosperity in the middle and late 1920s particularly vulnerable to any decline in business confidence. In the short term, however, the plan permitted a revival of the German economy and inaugurated a more optimistic phase in the domestic and international politics of the WEIMAR REPUBLIC.

**D-Day.** Code name for the first day of Operation Overlord, 6 June 1944, which saw Allied troops land on the coast of Normandy between the River Orne and the Cotentin peninsula, in the largest ever seaborne invasion. Three divisions from the Canadian and British army landed on 'Gold', 'Juno', and 'Sword' beaches west of the Orne and two divisions of the American First Army at 'Omaha' and 'Utah' beaches one on either side of the Vire estuary. After a fierce battle on 'Omaha' a substantial beach-head – 24 miles long and 4 miles deep – was established by nightfall, at a cost of 10,000 casualties.

**DDP** (Deutsche Demokratische Partei; German Democratic Party). German left-liberal party during the WEIMAR REPUBLIC. Established in November 1918 in the aftermath of the GERMAN REVOLUTION, the DDP represented a fusion of the Progressive Party of the Imperial era and the left-wing of the National Liberal Party. Aiming to unite the liberal middle class politically, the DDP gained 18.5 per cent of the popular vote in the January 1919 elections to the constituent assembly of the Weimar Republic. Its spokesmen played a leading role in the formulation of the Weimar constitution, and it was to participate in almost all of the coalition governments of the republic between 1920 and 1930. Damaged, however, by the formation of the right-wing liberal DVP, it rapidly declined in influence after 1920, attracting less than 4 per cent of the vote in the 1930 election. Renamed the German State Party in 1930, its electorate abandoned it for the Nazi party thereafter. It dissolved itself in spring 1933.

L. E. Jones, *German Liberalism and the Dissolution of the Weimar Party System, 1918–1933* (1989)

**DDR.** Deutsche Demokratische Republik. *See* GERMAN DEMOCRATIC REPUBLIC.

**decolonization.** Decolonization has been one of the major transforming forces in the world since 1945, transferring political control from imperial powers to independent states. At the end of the First World War the largest European empires, those of Britain and France, reached their greatest extent by including German colonies and parts of the Turkish empire as MANDATES. In 1926 there were 80 colonies and dependencies of the European states and the

USA, comprising one-third of the population and land area of the world. The seven West European countries Britain, France, Spain, Holland, Portugal, Belgium and Italy controlled colonies with populations of approximately 700 million people.

The process of decolonization began when the British white colonies were given virtual self-government as Dominions. In 1931 the Statute of Westminster established the basis of the BRITISH COMMONWEALTH OF NATIONS, consisting of independent countries owing allegiance to the British crown, with legislatures on an equal footing to Britain. Colonial rule in Africa and Asia was expected to continue, however. Colonial revolts in Morocco, Libya, Syria and elsewhere were suppressed, while aggressive powers such as Italy and Japan were actively engaged in enlarging their colonial possessions, seen in Italy's conquest of Ethiopia and the creation of an enlarged East African empire. But the inter-war years also witnessed the rise of nationalist agitation in India led by Mahatma Gandhi (1869–1948) and Mohammed Jinnah (1876–1948) for complete independence from Britain.

With the Second World War the pace of decolonization quickened. The over-running of the European empires in the Far East by Japan and the new strains placed upon the imperial countries transformed the situation. Britain had accepted eventual self-government for India by the India Act of 1935, but the Second World War made it an imminent reality. Britain's post-war weakness could not sustain opposition to a growing tide of Indian and Pakistani nationalism which culminated in Indian independence on 15 August 1947. In the Far East, the Dutch attempted to retain hold of their colonies in the Dutch East Indies, but in December 1949 accepted their independence. France sought to maintain her colonies by policies of integration and assimilation. At the Brazzaville Conference in 1944 they were offered incorporation into a French Union with representatives elected to the French National Assembly. Taken up by some African states, the policy was overtaken by the communist insurrection in Vietnam which brought about the INDO-CHINESE WAR of 1946–54. After France's shattering defeat at Dien Bien Phu in 1954, the French presence in south-east Asia was ended by the GENEVA AGREEMENTS. Elsewhere France, like Britain, vacated the Middle East. France left Syria and Lebanon by 1945, Britain left Palestine in 1947 and the Suez Canal in 1956. North Africa proved a more stubborn problem. Tunisian independence was granted in 1956, but the ALGERIAN WAR proved a protracted nightmare for France and Algeria alike, not settled until 1962. Britain, too, fought campaigns to slow down the pace of decolonization. The Mau Mau Rebellion in Africa from 1952 to 1960 cost 11,000 lives and the communist insurgency in Malaya was only officially defeated in 1960. Meanwhile, the first wave of black African colonies obtained independence in the 1950s. The Gold Coast (Ghana) became independent in 1957, followed by Nigeria in 1960. When British Premier Macmillan gave his 'Wind of Change' speech in South Africa in February 1960 he was speaking amidst the rapid dismantling of the European empires. More than 15 states achieved independence from Britain and France in that one year alone. By the 1960s decolonization had become an avalanche. Belgium vacated the Congo in June 1960, plunging it into temporary chaos and requiring UNITED NATIONS intervention. Of the larger European empires, only those of Portugal held out fighting protracted guerrilla wars in Angola, Mozambique and Guinea-Bissau until an army coup in Portugal in April 1974 ended Portuguese resistance to independence. The white Rhodesian government resisted black majority rule by declaring UDI (*see* UDI), but eventually was forced to a settlement in 1980 at Lancaster House, London, after a protracted guerrilla war.

The decolonizing process has attracted various interpretations. An initial tendency to focus on the nationalist movements and their leaders has given way to studies of the pressures on decision-makers in the European countries. Economic and military weaknesses, the inability to sustain colonial rule in the face of opposition, and an ideological climate which was unsympathetic to imperialism have all been put forward. Attention has shifted towards 'neo-colonialism', forms of economic control and dependency, such as debt relationships and aid, which have survived independence and even increased as the new states sought to modernize. Politically, the most important effects of decolonization was its potential to upset domestic politics in the home countries. In fact, decolonization was often hastened to prevent burdens of colonial defence becoming insupportable. The SUEZ CRISIS was the most visible occasion when Britain was faced with the reality of its powerlessness to engage in colonial actions. For France, Dien Bien Phu and the Algerian War marked the end of colonial ambitions and caused great political turmoil, bringing DE GAULLE to power. Portugal was brought to revolution in 1974 by the strain of continuing colonial wars.

R. Betts, *France and Decolonization* (1982)

D. Judd, *The Evolution of the Modern Commonwealth* (1982)

M. E. Chamberlain, *Decolonization: The Fall of the European Empires* (1985)

**De Gasperi, Alcide** (1881–1954). Italian statesman. Born in Trentino he was active in the movement for the separation of the province of Trentino from Austria, and from 1921 he was a PARTITO POPULARE ITALIAN member of the Italian Parliament. He was imprisoned from 1926 to 1929, working thereafter in the Vatican. He was active in the Italian Resistance during the Second World War, and was a founder of the ITALIAN CHRISTIAN DEMOCRATIC PARTY. He was the major figure in post war Italy, playing the leading role in shaping its future than any other politician. He served as Prime Minister, 1945–53, and Foreign Minister, 1944–8, 1951–3. He aligned Italy with the West, expelling the Communists from the government in 1947, favoured a mixed economy and land reform, and joined NATO. He was active in the movement for European Unity, and an important supporter of the SCHUMAN PLAN.

E. Carrillo *Alcide De Gasperi, The Long Apprenticeship* (1965)

**de Gaulle, Charles.** *See* GAULLE, CHARLES DE.

**Delcassé, Théophile** (1852–1923). French statesman. Born at Pamiers in the Pyrenees, he was the son of a legal officer. He studied at Toulouse, became a schoolteacher, then took up a career as a journalist. In 1889 he entered the Chamber of Deputies and supported overseas expansion, becoming Minister of Colonies, 1893–5. As Foreign Minister from June 1898 to June 1905 he worked to achieve the Entente Cordiale with Britain in 1904, but was sacrificed to German pressure in 1905 when his views on Morocco were seen as an obstacle to satisfactory relations. His attack on the weakness of the French navy in 1909 precipitated the fall of CLEMENCEAU's government; he returned as Navy Minister in 1911–13 in which post he worked to improve Anglo–French co-operation. By the time he left office in January 1913 the French government had signed naval conventions with both Russia (July 1912) and Great Britain (October 1912). The implicit allocation of French naval responsibility to the Mediterranean and of British to the North Sea and the Channel formed part of the network of moral obligations which helped to bring Britain into the war on the side of France in August 1914. Serving as ambassador to Russia from February 1913 to January 1914, he encouraged plans to improve the facilities for Russian mobilization with the promise of loans for railway construction. On his return home to France, he led a successful campaign to increase the term of military service for recruits to three years. Returning as Foreign Minister on the outbreak of war, he proved willing to make highly controversial bids in order to maintain allies in the field or attract new ones, promising Russia control over the Straits, and bringing Italy into the war in May 1915 with the promise of territorial gains. He was less successful in the Balkans, where Bulgaria sided with the CENTRAL POWERS in spite of the offence he caused to Greece and Serbia in asking them to make territorial concessions to her. His opposition to sending an expeditionary force to Salonika led to his resignation in October 1915. Following the defeat of Germany, Delcassé was one of those who demanded that France be given the Rhine as a frontier and was bitter at the final terms of the TREATY OF VERSAILLES, refusing to vote for it. He retired from politics in 1919, dying at Nice in February 1923. *See also* FIRST WORLD WAR.

C. W. Parker, *The Career of Theophile Delcassé* (1936)

S. R. Williamson, *The Politics of Grand Strategy: Britain and France Prepare for War, 1904–1914* (1969)

**Delors, Jacques** (1925– ). French and European civil servant. He was the son of a peasant farmer, later a bank guard. He attended lycée but left university to escape the Nazis. He worked as a banker and in French financial planning, and was adviser to Premier Chaban-Delmas, 1969–72. He joined the FRENCH SOCIALIST PARTY in 1974 and served as a member of the European Parliament and as French Finance Minister from May 1981 to July 1984, overseeing the austerity package which MITTERRAND was forced to introduce from 1983. Delors became President of the European Commission in January 1985 and was responsible for plans for greater economic and political integration within the EUROPEAN ECONOMIC COMMUNITY, starting with moves to institute a single market, agreed in the SINGLE EUROPEAN ACT of December 1985. Further progress along the lines favoured by Delors include the setting up of a European Central Bank and Monetary Union, to be followed by greater political integration. *See also* DELORS PLAN.

**Delors Plan.** Plan drawn up by the Delors Committee headed by the President of the COMMISSION OF THE EUROPEAN COMMUNITY, JACQUES DELORS set up in 1988. The Plan consists of three phases to create greater monetary and political unity in the EUROPEAN ECONOMIC COMMUNITY. The first phase will consist of the EUROPEAN MONETARY SYSTEM in which all countries will participate and also permit co-ordination of economic policies throughout the Community. Phase two will set up a European system of central banks which will gradually assume greater control upon national monetary policy, while the Council of Ministers acts to do the same for fiscal policies. The European Community would thus move towards phase three, of interlocked exchange rates, central monetary control and binding central control over budget deficits. At the Madrid Summit of European Community ministers in 1989, the governments agreed to accept the report as a basis for future planning of European Monetary Union (EMU). Some resistance has been shown, notably by Mrs THATCHER to the proposals for central control of national budgets. Phase one of the Plan was due for implementation in July 1990.

**Democratic Forum.** Leading Hungarian party to emerge from the return of multi-party politics in Hungary since 1989. Founded as a pro-democracy pressure group in 1987 it was legalised with other parties in January 1989 and led the discussions with the ruling Communist Party to devise an electoral system for free elections in March 1990. Led by Jozsef Antall (1932– ) from October 1989 Democratic Forum obtained 43 per cent of the votes cast and 165 of 386 seats. It has formed a coalition government with Christian Democrat and Smallholder groups to govern the country. The Party is pledged to seek rapid access for Hungary to the European Community and a speedy adoption of western economic models.

**Democratic Progressive Party, Austrian** (DFP). A splinter party formed by the leader of the Austrian Trades Union League, Franz Olah, after his expulsion from the Socialist Party (SPÖ) in 1965. Campaigning on an anti-communist, pro-Christian platform, it won 150,000 votes in the 1966 elections, but only 17,000 in 1970. Its appeal was undermined by the electoral success of the SPÖ under Bruno Kreisky.

**Democratic Unionist Party** (DUP). Northern Irish Political Party. Led by the Rev. Ian Paisley, the DUP was formed in 1971 out of the earlier Protestant ULSTER UNIONIST PARTY. It represents the more militant and populist wing of the loyalist community and has usually returned three MPs to Westminster. Initially a vehicle for Paisley's distinctive, fundamentalist views, its deputy leader, Peter Robinson, has increasingly come to prominence. It strongly opposed the ANGLO–IRISH AGREEMENT, boycotting Parliament for two years in 1985–7. It remains an essential element of any likely compromise political solution to the Northern Irish question, maintaining a powerful hold on popular Unionist opinion. *See also* ULSTER CONFLICT.

P. Arthur, *The Government and Politics of Northern Ireland* (2nd edn, 1987)
P. Arthur and K. Jeffrey, *Northern Ireland since 1968* (1988)

**De-Nazification.** *See* GERMANY, ALLIED OCCUPATION OF.

**Denikin, Anton** (1872–1947). White general in RUSSIAN CIVIL WAR. The son of a former serf, he rose to command a corps in the FIRST WORLD WAR. He supported the February Revolution, becoming chief-of-staff under the PROVISIONAL GOVERNMENT. Imprisoned for his support of KORNILOV in the attempted coup of September 1917, he escaped to raise an anti-Bolshevik army in the Don area. In March 1918, following Kornilov's death, he assumed command of the White armies in southern Russia. With Allied support he launched an offensive in July 1919 which took him within 250 miles of Moscow, but the unpopularity of the White government of the reconquered territories and poor relations with minority populations, such as the COSSACKS, halted his advance. By January 1920 his forces had been forced to retreat to the south; they were evacuated to the Crimea in March, before their ultimate defeat in November, when the BOLSHEVIK armies reached the Crimea. By that time Denikin had handed over command to WRANGEL and gone into exile in France.

D. Foorman, *Civil War in Russia* (1961)
D. V. Lehovich, *Denikin* (1974)

**depression.** A period of decline in economic activity. The term 'Great Depression' is used by economic historians to refer to the slump in agricultural prices and deceleration in the British economy in the last quarter of the 19th century. 'The Depression' usually refers to the inter-war years and in particular the period of severe downturn in economic activity which followed the slump in share prices on the United States Stock Exchange in October 1929, known as the Wall Street Crash, and which precipitated economic crises in Britain and Europe. This period from 1929 until recovery began in 1933–4 is sometimes known as the 'Great Depression' or the 'Great Slump'. In some countries the deeper crisis of 1929–34 was difficult to distinguish from a more generalized depression which followed the First World War. A hectic post-war boom in France, Britain and elsewhere was followed by a serious downturn in activity in the early 1920s. The dislocation of the German and central European economies caused by the war, the burden of reparations payments, and the loss of British export markets to overseas competitors reduced economic activity to below pre-war levels. In Britain mass unemployment reached almost 2 million in 1921–2 and was to remain stubbornly over 1 million throughout the inter-war years as a result of overcapacity in the major pre-war export industries of coal, shipbuilding, iron and steel, and textiles. Low world agricultural prices also affected the less industrialized economies of Europe and indirectly reduced exports of manufactured goods because of low prices for primary products amongst non-European producers. Britain's attempt to return to her pre-war position by returning to the GOLD STANDARD in 1925 saddled her with an overvalued currency and left many of the old industrial areas suffering from heavy unemployment. A measure of economic revival occurred in the late 1920s, particularly in Germany, where an easing of the REPARATIONS burden and American loans re-stimulated the economy. The Wall Street Crash of 1929, however, shattered confidence and reduced economic activity worldwide. In May 1931 the major Austrian bank, the CREDITANSTALT failed and a wave of bankruptcies and failures spread through Europe. German banks defaulted on reparations payments and by the summer of 1931 the British Government was faced with a major financial crisis which led to the fall of the SECOND LABOUR GOVERNMENT, the formation of a NATIONAL GOVERNMENT and the abandonment of the Gold Standard by the end of the year. The most important manifestation of the depression was mass unemployment, which rose rapidly in almost every country from 1929. By 1932 unemployment in Britain had reached almost 3 million, about a quarter of the insured workforce, over 5.5 million in Germany, and almost 14 million in the United States. The less industrialized countries suffered severely from reductions in demand for primary products; unemployment in Poland, for example, by 1933 stood at 0.75 million, two-fifths of the total industrial workforce.

Recovery began from 1933–4, primarily as a result of the revival of world trade stimulated by recovery in America, at least partially caused by the New Deal of President ROOSEVELT, and by counter-cyclical investment in countries such as Germany and Sweden which laid foundations for recovery in the mid-1930s. France experienced the depression relatively late, forcing devaluation of the franc in 1936. In Britain the National Government pursued orthodox economic policies from 1931, a degree of protection was introduced following the OTTAWA CONFERENCE in 1932 and low interest rates helped to stimulate sectors such as house-building and consumer goods. Unemployment fell from 1933 but remained over 2 million up to 1935 and over 1 million into the first year of the Second World War. From the mid-1930s several countries began significant degrees of rearmament, injecting state spending into the economies and reviving some of the harder-hit heavy industries. The levels of spending were sufficient in Britain and Germany to overcome a temporary downturn in world trade in 1937–8 which saw unemployment threaten to rise once again.

The effects of the inter-war depression on politics have been seen as stimulating the growth of right-wing authoritarian movements which seized power in many states between the wars. In many cases the depression served to heighten the fears of established interests and the middle classes of a swing to the left. As a result the classic scenario of inter-war politics was the overturning of left-liberal regimes by right-wing movements. Only in France, Britain and the Low Countries, Scandinavia, and Czechoslovakia did recognizably democratic politics survive the depression. Workers' responses were undermined by the debilitating effects of unemployment and unfavourable economic conditions for trade union militancy, witnessed in the collapse of strike movements in 1920–21 as the depression began to affect Europe and declining levels of strike activity and union membership during the trough of the depression after 1929. Divisions between communists, socialists, and other left-wing groups hampered a common response, and the era of POPULAR FRONT co-operation occurred after the worst phase of the depression was over and the NAZI PARTY had taken power in Germany.

A common feature of the depression was the breakdown of the international trading system. Britain partly abandoned free trade for protection from 1932, bilateral trade

arrangements became common and economic autarky were responses in Italy and Germany. In part these reflected the aims of foreign policy and rearmament, but were also symptomatic of the breakdown of the old order of world trade that had existed prior to 1914. One consequence was the attempts during the Second World War to ensure that greater economic co-operation through international agreements would take place and the creation of new international financial and banking institutions, seen for example in the BRETTON WOODS CONFERENCE.

The depression also stimulated consideration of new economic systems. The work of JOHN MAYNARD KEYNES gave theoretical support for *ad hoc* policies pursued in countries such as Sweden. Increased state intervention in the economy and the abandonment of earlier orthodoxies of the self-regulating market were to become features of post-war economic policies in Western Europe. The development of the Soviet Union and its experiment with planning, confirmed by the apparent success of the American 'New Deal' and subsequently of war-time organization, were to make economic planning a prominent feature in post-war economic thinking and the reconstruction of the European economies.

G. Rees, *The Great Slump* (1970)
D. H. Aldcroft, *From Versailles to Wall Street, 1919–1929* (1977)
C. P. Kindleberger, *The World in Depression, 1929–1939* (1977)
S. Salter and J. Stevenson (eds.), *The Working Class and Politics in Europe and America, 1929–1945* (1990)

**de-Stalinization.** Term used to refer to the relaxation of the rigours of STALINISM in the Soviet Union and elsewhere. The process began with the 20th Party Congress, the first following Stalin's death, held in 1956. A closed session was convened after the formal end to the Congress at which KHRUSHCHEV made a speech denouncing STALIN's crimes and reading out LENIN's Testament which voiced suspicions about Stalin's character and intentions, and which had been suppressed since 1924. Khrushchev blamed the CULT OF PERSONALITY for 'serious and grave' perversions of party principles, party democracy and revolutionary legality. Although the 'Secret Speech' was not published, it became the focus of discussion within the CPSU (*see* COMMUNIST PARTY OF THE SOVIET UNION) and foreign parties. Khrushchev's comments were notable for limiting criticism to the era of the PURGES of the party after 1934 and for concentration of blame upon Stalin and the higher echelons of the security apparatus. There was no condemnation of COLLECTIVIZATION or the pace of the industrialization, but criticism concerning the fate of the prominent leading figures destroyed by Stalin's terror. Such criticism, even confined within party ranks, marked a major break with the unswerving and inflexible adherence to the inevitable 'correctness' of the course taken by the Soviet Union under Stalin. It permitted a greater questioning, not only of past actions, but also of future directions, seen most directly in Khrushchev's espousal of 'separate roads to socialism'. It triggered off strikes and protest movements in Poland which culminated in the coming to power of WLADYSLAW GOMULKA and the HUNGARIAN UPRISING. Fears of the spread of unrest to the Soviet Union led to an attempt to unseat Khrushchev by the 'anti-party group', which was defeated by 1958 when its leaders BULGANIN, MOLOTOV and MALENKOV were demoted. In 1961 Khrushchev's denunciations of Stalin were made public at the 22nd Party Congress and symbolized by the removal of Stalin's body from the Lenin Mausoleum. This was followed by a loosening of ideological constraints and a reform of the party's structure to enforce rotation of offices and greater involvement of party members. At the economic and social level, Khrushchev introduced greater emphasis on consumer goods, housing and education, as well as major legal reforms and a new criminal code to eliminate arbitrary procedures.

Although Khrushchev's period of de-Stalinization did little to alter the fundamental political and economic basis of the Soviet state, he transformed the climate from the terror and suspicion associated with the Stalin era to one of greater normality. The process of de-Stalinization also had its effects on the attempt to liberalize the communist regime in Czechoslovakia in 1968 in the 'PRAGUE SPRING'. Although crushed, the legacy of Stalin has again been called into question in the reform movements under

GORBACHEV and subsequent upheavals in Eastern Europe. The demands for a pluralistic political and economic system carried into government by SOLIDARITY in Poland and in the rest of Eastern Europe in 1988-9, combined with the encouragement for PERESTROIKA, have implicitly sought to reassess some of the more fundamental aspects of the Stalinist system, notably collectivization and central planning.

F. Fejto, *A History of the People's Democracies: Eastern Europe since Stalin* (2nd edn, 1974)
R. and Zh. Medvedev, *Khrushchev: The Years in Power* (1977)
R. W. Davies, *Soviet History in the Gorbachev Revolution* (1989)

**Détente.** Term applied to the improved relations, beginning November 1969, between the WARSAW PACT countries (led by the USSR) and the West (headed by the USA), which were inaugurated by the STRATEGIC ARMS LIMITATION TALKS (SALT). These ended in agreement on arms reductions in May 1973. Further SALT talks began in November 1974 and an agreement was reached in May 1978, but the continued build-up of Soviet arms and the SOVIET INVASION OF AFGHANISTAN in December 1979 called into question the validity of détente. As a result SALT II remained unratified and the détente period was perceived as ended, followed by a period of renewed COLD WAR under President REAGAN and Premier BREZHNEV.

C. Bell, *The Diplomacy of Détente* (1977)

**Deutsche Demokratische Partei.** See DDP.

**Deutsche Demokratische Republik** (DDR). *See* GERMAN DEMOCRATIC REPUBLIC.

**Deutsche Volkspartei.** See DVP.

**Deutschnationale Volkspartei.** See DNVP.

**De Valera, Eamonn** (1882–1975). Irish statesman. He was born in New York, but was educated in Ireland. He joined SINN FEIN and took part in EASTER RISING. He was saved from execution by his American passport. After his return to Ireland he became President of Sinn Fein, 1917–26. Imprisoned at Lincoln in 1918–19, he escaped and fled to the United States where he raised money for the IRISH REPUBLICAN

ARMY. He opposed the treaty signed by COL-LINS refusing to accept the Oath of Allegiance to the British Crown, and gave his support to the anti-treaty forces in the IRISH CIVIL WAR; he accepted a cease-fire in 1923. He split from the militant Sinn Fein to found his own party, FIANNA FAIL in 1926, entering the Dail. He formed a government in February 1932 and remained Premier for 16 years. He set out to reduce the links with Britain, conducting a tariff war and creating the sovereign state of Eire in 1937 with a new constitution. He maintained Irish neutrality in the Second World War but lost office in 1948. He returned as Premier 1951–4 and 1957–9. He stood successfully for President in 1959 and again in 1966, he retired from politics at the age of 90 in May 1973. An inveterate opponent of Britain and a staunch nationalist, he remained a link with Ireland's struggle for independence.

M. Moynihan (ed.), *Speeches and Statements by Eamon de Valera, 1917–73* (1980)

J. Bowman, *De Valera and the Ulster Question, 1917–73* (1982)

**devolution.** Term used in Britain to describe proposals for the establishment of local assemblies in the constituent nations of the United Kingdom with considerable powers over local matters, in effect a new word for HOME RULE. Northern Ireland had devolved powers via the Stormont parliament from 1921, although these were suspended in 1972 as a result of the deepening crisis there. The word became current in the 1970s to describe the moves to give Scotland and Wales greater self-government. The Kilbrandon Report was published in November 1973 following the successes of the SCOTTISH NATIONALIST PARTY and PLAID CYMRU (Welsh Nationalist Party) in British parliamentary elections. The report recommended the setting up of elected assemblies in Wales and Scotland and formed the basis of referendums carried out in March 1979 in Scotland and Wales. A high threshold of 40 per cent of eligible voters was required to support devolution, which was narrowly missed in Scotland, but overwhelmingly lost in Wales. The devolution issue was laid to rest for some years, but further successes by the Scottish Nationalists in 1988 and the acceptance by two of the major parties, the LABOUR PARTY and the Liberal–SDP ALLIANCE of devolution policies have led to its return to the political agenda; only the Conservative Party (*see* CONSERVATIVE AND UNIONIST PARTY, BRITISH) is now openly opposed to devolution for Scotland and Wales. Informal agreements have been reached on a cross-party basis in Scotland, which led to the meeting of a Scottish Convention in 1989 (boycotted by the Scottish Nationalists) which urged devolution as a matter of urgency. In Northern Ireland, successive attempts have been made to introduce devolved forms of government, including a Northern Ireland Assembly which met briefly in 1974 and from 1982 to 1986. A successful formula for devolution in Northern Ireland has remained elusive.

A. Butt-Phillips, *The Welsh Question: Nationalism in Welsh Politics, 1945–70* (1975)

C. Harvie, *Scotland and Nationalism: Scottish Society and Politics, 1707–1977* (1977)

T. Nairn, *The Break-up of Britain* (1977)

P. Arthur and K. Jeffrey, *Northern Ireland since 1968* (1988)

**DFP.** *See* DEMOCRATIC PROGRESSIVE PARTY, AUSTRIAN.

**Dilution.** *See* SHOP STEWARD'S MOVEMENT.

**Dimitrov, Georgi** (1882–1949). Bulgarian communist leader. Born at Pernik, he rose through the trade union movement and was one of the founder members of the BULGARIAN COMMUNIST PARTY in 1919. Forced to flee to Moscow following an attempted armed rising in September 1923, he directed the party's affairs from abroad with Vasil Kolarov through COMINTERN. In March 1933 he was arrested and put on trial by the Nazis for complicity in the REICHSTAG FIRE. His stirring defence attracted international attention and he was acquitted and deported to the Soviet Union. Dimitrov became Secretary-General of Comintern in 1934, and at the seventh Congress in 1935 he proclaimed the anti-fascist POPULAR FRONT policy as the new official line, although veering once again in 1939–40 in support of the NAZI–SOVIET PACT. In 1942 he called for a BULGARIAN FATHERLAND FRONT, and was instrumental in creating a coalition of communists and non-communists to support Bulgarian withdrawal from the war. In

1944 the Fatherland Front supported by the Soviet army, which had invaded Bulgaria on 5 September, seized power. Dimitrov returned to Bulgaria in November 1945, where he helped to organize the Fatherland Front's elimination of opposition and election victory in October 1946. As the first Premier of communist Bulgaria, he initially showed some independence, signing an agreement with TITO at Bled in August 1947 and speaking in favour of a Balkan Federation to include Romania. Summoned by STALIN to Moscow, he returned to Bulgaria to initiate a purge of the Bulgarian Communist Party, which was continued by his successor Chervenko following the expulsion of Yugoslavia from COMINFORM in June 1948. Already in ill-health, Dimitrov died in Moscow in July 1949.

J. Rothschild, *The Communist Party of Bulgaria: Origins and Development, 1883–1936* (1959)

**Disarmament Conference.** Conference held at Geneva from 1932–4 of 60 nations under the LEAGUE OF NATIONS, but with non-League members, the United States and the Soviet Union. The conference met for session in 1932, 1933 and 1934 but failed to achieve any tangible results. A central difficulty was French suspicions of Germany and of disarmament without a scheme of general security. Germany withdrew from the conference in October 1933.

Lord Noel-Baker, *The First World Disarmament Conference 1932–3 and Why it Failed* (1979)

**dissidents.** Term used to describe individuals and groups who oppose Eastern bloc regimes, increasingly used from the 1950s. The treatment of dissidents became a major issue in the West with the trial and imprisonment of the writers Yu Daniel and Abram Sinyavsky in February 1966. Earlier concern about the restrictions on the publication of major writers like Boris Pasternak found new focus in the suppression of the work of ALEXANDER SOLZHENITSYN and his deportation in 1974. The issue of the treatment of dissidents achieved international recognition with the HELSINKI AGREEMENT of 1975, at which the USSR agreed to respect 'human rights and fundamental freedoms'. As a result a HELSINKI HUMAN RIGHTS GROUP was set up in the Soviet Union in May 1976 to monitor human rights viola-

tions, but itself became the target of persecution with the arrest and imprisonment of its leaders. In 1980 the most prominent Soviet dissident, ANDREI SAKHAROV, was sentenced to internal exile in Gorky. The treatment of dissidents and human rights violations became a major issue of diplomatic exchanges between the Soviet Union and the West in the later years of BREZHNEV and his two short-lived successors. There was increasing concern expressed about the denial of rights of emigration for Jews who wished to leave the Soviet Union, the imprisonment of writers and artists who criticized the regime, and the use of psychiatric hospitals to incarcerate dissidents. The advent of MIKHAIL GORBACHEV to the Soviet leadership produced rapid concessions on the treatment of dissidents, including the release of Sakharov and his public rehabilitation, the easing of emigration restrictions and the release of prisoners from labour camps and mental hospitals, as part of a general thaw in East–West relations. Notable dissidents in other Eastern bloc countries have included members of the CHARTER 77 group in Czechoslovakia, including the playwright and politician VACLAV HAVEL.

L. Labedz and M. Hayward (eds.), *On Trial: The Case of Siriyasky and Daniel* (1967)
P. Reddaway, *Uncensored Russia: The Human Rights Movement in the Soviet Union* (1972)
M. S. Shatz, *Soviet Dissent in Perspective* (1980)

**Djilas, Milovan** (1911– ). Yugoslavian communist and writer. Born in Montenegro, he joined the illegal YUGOSLAVIAN COMMUNIST PARTY while at Belgrade University. Imprisoned under the dictatorship of King ALEXANDER I 1933–6, he was one of the young, professional revolutionaries with whom TITO sought to rebuild the party when he became General Secretary in 1937. Djilas served with distinction as a partisan commander against the German occupation after 1941. As a close friend of Tito he played a leading part in the early Yugoslavian state after 1945, serving for a time as Vice-President. Initially, like Tito, a committed Stalinist (*see* STALINISM) he moved beyond Tito's objections to Stalin's tutelage to become an outspoken critic of what he saw as the potentially corrupting influences of Stalinism within the Yugoslavian Communist Party. In his articles for the newspaper *Borba*, and the journal he edited, *Nova Miseo* (New Thought) and in his books and essays, he argued for a more widely diffused power structure. His criticisms proved too radical for Tito, and he was demoted from his state and party posts by 1954. Although he resigned from the party, he was given a suspended prison sentence in 1955, the year his book, *The New Class*, which had to be published abroad, argued that a monopoly of power inevitably created a self-perpetuating oligarchy of corrupt officials. He was imprisoned, 1956–61, and rearrested in 1962, not being freed until 1966. The radical voice of the Yugoslavian experiment, he remained a committed socialist, one whose views did much to encourage debates about the future of socialist and communist regimes elsewhere in Eastern and Western Europe. *See also* EURO-COMMUNISM.

M. Djilas, *The New Class* (1956)
M. Djilas, *Anatomy of a Moral: The Political Essays of Milovan Djilas* (1959)

**DNVP** (Deutschnationale Volkspartei; German National People's Party). German nationalist and conservative political party during the WEIMAR REPUBLIC. Founded in November 1918, the DNVP united supporters of the conservative and anti-Semitic parties of the Imperial period with the right wing of the former National Liberal party. It was also supported by sections of heavy industry and large-scale agrarian interests. An explicitly monarchist party, the DNVP was hostile to the Weimar Republic and opposed fulfilment of the TREATY OF VERSAILLES. Its electoral support grew from 10 per cent of the popular vote in the 1919 constituent assembly elections to a peak of over 20 per cent in the December 1924 REICHSTAG elections. It briefly entered coalition government in 1925 and again in 1927–8, but its extremism on foreign policy issues isolated it from most other Weimar parties. Under its leader, Hugenberg, it co-operated in 1929 with the NAZI PARTY in the campaign against the reparations YOUNG PLAN and reverted to radical anti-republicanism after 1930. Many of its supporters abandoned it for the Nazi Party after 1930 and in the *Reichstag* elections of July 1932 it gained less than 6 per cent of the vote. It

entered government as the junior coalition partner of the Nazi Party with HITLER's appointment as Chancellor in January 1933, yet was rapidly outflanked during the Nazi seizure of power. It dissolved itself in June 1933.

E. Kolb, *The Weimar Republic* (1988)

**Dobrudja.** An ethnically mixed part of the Black Sea littoral bounded by the northward loop of the River Danube. It has been a disputed area between Romania and Bulgaria. Recognized by the Treaty of Berlin in 1878 as Romanian, the southern Dobrudja was awarded to Bulgaria following the Treaty of Bucharest in 1913. It formed one of the demands of the Bulgarians as a price for entry on the side of the CENTRAL POWERS during the FIRST WORLD WAR and was occupied in May 1918 following the collapse of the Romanian armies in 1917–18. It was returned to Romania as one of the victorious powers by the TREATY OF NEUILLY in 1919, but surrendered again to Bulgaria in September 1940 as part of the forced dismemberment of Romania dictated by the Nazis. The PARIS PEACE CONFERENCE in 1947 left the southern Dobrudja as part of Bulgaria.

**Doctors' Plot.** Alleged plot announced by STALIN in the newspapers in January 1953 in which a group of Moscow doctors, many of them Jewish, were accused of planning the deaths of high Soviet officials and of responsibility for the death of the Leningrad Party boss, ANDREI ZHDANOV. The accusations appear to have heralded a new round of PURGES with strong overtones of ANTI-SEMITISM. Accusations of 'cosmopolitanism' and 'Zionism' had already been deployed since the creation of the state of Israel in 1948, with the arrest, trial and petty persecution of Jews in the Soviet Union and Eastern Europe. The charges against the 'doctors' of spying, terrorism and conspiracy, as well as the alleged murder of Zhdanov, bore an uncanny resemblance to the wave of purges following the assassination of KIROV in 1934. Stalin's death on 5 March prevented the purge developing, although the arrest of two of Stalin's own close attendants, his chief bodyguard and his personal physician, have prompted unconfirmed suspicions that those most vulnerable to a fresh purge, notably BERIA, may have murdered Stalin or at least hastened his death.

J. Whitney, *Khrushchev Speaks* (1963)
A. Werth, *Russia: The Post-war Years* (1971)

**Dollfuss, Engelbert** (1892–1934). Austrian Chancellor and dictator. He was born in Texing, near Mank, Lower Austria, the illegitimate son of Josepha Dollfuss, who married his stepfather, Leopold Schmutz, the following year. From 1904 to 1913 Dollfuss attended a seminary, and then went on to study theology at Vienna university. Before volunteering for military service in 1914 he had transferred to the law school, and returned there to finish his degree in 1918, after active service as an officer on the German front. His political career began in his student days, when he became involved in a student 'corporation' with a Pan-German political outlook.

Dollfuss became chancellor and foreign minister in May 1932 at a difficult time for the CHRISTIAN SOCIAL PARTY (CSP), which he had joined after the First World War. Its electoral support had been eroded by the Nazis and other right-wing extremists during the depression, and the Chancellor suspended parliament in 1933 rather than face defeat in the next national elections. Provocative actions by the *Heimwehr* (*see* AUSTROFASCISM) in February 1934 prompted armed conflict between the labour movement and the government. The resistance of the labour movement was crushed within a few days, during which time workers' housing blocks were shelled by government troops. The 'uprising' provided Dollfuss with an excuse to promulgate a fascist constitution (1 May 1934) and dissolve all the republican political parties. His aim was to create a 'clerical-fascist' Austria based on vague notions of a neo-medieval corporate state which would incorporate some elements of Mussolini's Italian fascism. He co-operated closely with Italy and Hungary in foreign relations. Dollfuss was assassinated in July 1934 by Nazis unsuccessfully attempting to stage a *coup d'état*. KURT VON SCHUSCHNIGG succeeded him as chancellor.

G. E. R. Gedye, *The Fallen Bastions* (1939)
G. Brooke-Shepherd, *Dollfuss* (1961)

**Dönitz, Karl** (1891–1980). German admiral. He entered naval academy and joined the submarine service in 1916, seeing service until his capture in 1918. He was given the task of building up the submarine fleet after the ANGLO–GERMAN NAVAL AGREEMENT. He published theories of submarine tactics, including the 'Wolf Pack', and commanded German submarines from the outset of he war but had only a limited number of vessels. He conducted U-boat operations in the BATTLE OF THE ATLANTIC, eventually persuading HITLER to expand the fleet. On 30 January 1943 he was appointed Commander-in-Chief of the German navy and pressed home the U-boat war in the Atlantic, but was forced to withdraw in mid-1943 in the face of new Allied tactics, especially the use of radar and long-range aircraft. He encouraged new technologies and deployed a large submarine fleet right up to the last days of the war. Hitler nominated Dönitz as his successor on 29 April 1945, and on 4 May Dönitz surrendered German forces in the north and north-west to MONTGOMERY, hoping to continue to fight the Soviets. He was arrested on 23 May and sentenced to ten years' imprisonment at the NUREMBERG TRIALS.

J. Costello and T. Hughes, *The Battle of the Atlantic* (1977)
P. Padfield, *Dönitz: The Last Führer* (1984)

**Dorpat, Treaty of.** *See* TARTU, TREATY OF.

**Dowding, Hugh** (1882–1970). British air force leader. He joined the army in 1900 but served in the Royal Flying Corps during the First World War and stayed in the Royal Air Force when that was founded in 1918. From 1930 to 1936 he was air member for research and development on the Air Council, where he encouraged development of Spitfire and Hurricane planes and authorized expenditure for experiments on building up a radar chain. He was appointed head of Fighter Command in 1936. He opposed the sending of fighter squadrons from England to France in 1940, carefully husbanding his forces for what he rightly saw as a coming trial of strength with the German air force. He directed the British victory in the Battle of Britain, once again carefully managing his limited resources. He retired in 1942. ·*See also* SECOND WORLD WAR.

R. Hough and D. Richards, *The Battle of Britain* (1990)

**Dresden, bombing of.** *See* BOMBING OFFENSIVE, ALLIED.

**Dual-track Policy.** Also known as 'twin-track'; a policy adopted by NATO ministers in December 1979 to deploy 572 medium-range missiles under United States control in Western Europe, while at the same time seeking bilateral negotiations between the USA and USSR with a view to fixing an overall ceiling on the number of such missiles deployed by both sides in Europe. There were thus to be two tracks to NATO policy in responding to the targeting of Soviet SS-20 missiles on Western Europe. Deployment of the US missiles was scheduled for December 1983. Although arms talks were opened in Geneva on 30 November 1981, failure to reach agreement led to the deployment of CRUISE MISSILES in Europe in 1984. Subsequent discussions, however, brought about an INTERMEDIATE NUCLEAR FORCES TREATY in December 1987 which led to the withdrawal of such missiles from Europe, claimed as a victory for the dual-track approach. *See also* CAMPAIGN FOR NUCLEAR DISARMAMENT.

L. Freedman, *The Evolution of Nuclear Strategy* (1981)
J. Newhouse, *The Nuclear Age: A History of the Arms Race from Hiroshima to Star Wars* (1989)

**Dubček, Alexander** (1921–). Czechoslovak politician. Born in Uhrovek, Slovakia, he moved with his family to the Soviet Union in 1925, returning to Slovakia in 1938. He joined the COMMUNIST PARTY in 1938 and fought with Slovak partisans during the Second World War. A party official in 1949, he spent three years in Moscow from 1955–8, being influenced by the DE-STALINIZATION campaign of KHRUSHCHEV, before becoming head of the Slovak Communist Party. He was nominated the successor to NOVOTNY as First Secretary of the CZECHOSLOVAK COMMUNIST PARTY on 5 January 1968, and was the key figure in the 'PRAGUE SPRING'. He supported moves from within the party to adopt a more liberal form of communism sometimes known as 'socialism with a human face'. He called for Parliament 'to adopt laws which will ensure free-dom of speech and criticism, freedom of press and of assembly, together with socialism and the inviolability of Czechoslovak socialist statehood and socialist achievements'. As increasingly radical proposals were put forward, including the prospect of opening up the party to democratic elections, Dubček came under increasing pressure from the Soviet leadership. Discussions with the Soviet leadership from 29 July–1 August on the Slovakian–Ukrainian border and at Bratislava on 3 August with WARSAW PACT allies failed to allay their suspicions, in spite of Dubček's assurances that Czechoslovakia would remain within the Warsaw Pact and that the Communist Party would retain a major role. An invasion by Soviet forces accompanied by other Warsaw Pact detachments on 20–21 August 1968 led to the crushing of the reform process. Dubček was arrested and taken to Moscow on 12 September, and returned visibly shaken and broken. Under the terms of an agreement with them he was forced to renounce continuing offers of support from dissident student and factory groups, accept the return of press censorship, and the reduction of the powers of workers' councils set up during the summer and autumn to decentralize economic control. Having conducted on behalf of the Soviets a complete reversal of the reform programme, Dubček was replaced as First Secretary in April 1969 by GUSTAV HUSAK, becoming Speaker of the Federal Assembly until September 1969. He served for a period as Ambassador to Turkey (December 1969–June 1970), before being expelled from the Communist Party and demoted to a series of minor administrative posts, ending up as a forestry inspector in Slovakia. His almost total obscurity from public view lasted until 1988, when he went to Italy to receive an honorary degree. With the fall of the hard-line regime in Czechoslovakia in late November 1989, he re-emerged on the public stage making common cause with the Civic Forum opposition group led by VACLAV HAVEL. On 26 December Dubček was elected Speaker of the Czechoslovak Parliament. He was one of the most prominent communists who attempted to follow in the wake of the Yugoslav experiment and de-Stalinization by Khrushchev with a more open form of communism, while remaining a committed party member. It was never clear how Dubček envisaged the combination of a free press and a more pluralistic political system with a leading role for the Communist Party. His genuine charm and warmth did little to allay the Soviet suspicions which led to his downfall. His re-emergence to play a part in the new reform movement in 1989 has explicitly linked the new reform movement with the earlier, failed attempt to liberalize the system, though Dubček is still viewed with some suspicion as a life-long communist, albeit a liberal one. *See also* BREZHNEV DOCTRINE.

G. Golan, *Reform Rule in Czechoslovakia: The Dubček era, 1968–9* (1973)
H. Gordon Skilling, *Czechoslovakia's Interrupted Revolution* (1976)

**Dulles, John Foster** (1888–1959). US Secretary of State, 1953–9. A lawyer with deep and long understanding of international affairs, he was appointed by EISENHOWER as Secretary of State, 1953. Dulles built up the NORTH ATLANTIC TREATY ORGANISATION as part of his belief in opposing Soviet threats with the deterrent of MASSIVE RETALIATION. His inability to collaborate with EDEN led to tension in Anglo–American relations over the SUEZ CRISIS, during which Dulles strongly opposed the Anglo–French invasion of Egypt.

**Duma.** Tsarist legislature instituted by NICHOLAS II following the revolutionary uprisings of 1905. The electoral franchise was narrowed after the second Duma (1907) was dissolved for its radicalism and the fourth Duma, which sat from October 1912 to 1917, was elected on the same basis. It completed a series of educational reforms begun by the third Duma, but met briefly only twice in August 1914 and February 1915 for routine business before it was suspended following a session in August–September 1915 for proposing modest domestic reforms. The Duma met again in February 1916, replacing the Prime Minister I. L. Goremykin with B. V. Stürmer, and forcing the retirement of the foreign and war ministers. As the crisis deepened early in 1917, the Duma again met on 27th February. Blamed by the Tsar for contributing to the increasing disorder in the capital from 8

March, Nicholas attempted to dissolve the Duma three days later. It remained in informal session, however, and on the 12th elected a 'Provisional Committee' of 12 members to take up the reins of government. With the abdication of the Tsar on 15 March, the Provisional Committee asked Prince LVOV to form a PROVISIONAL GOVERNMENT, thereby completing the first phase of the RUSSIAN REVOLUTION.

G. Katkov, *Russia 1917: The February Revolution* (1967)
G. A. Hosking, *The Russian Constitutional Experiment* (1973)
R. B. McKean, *The Russian Constitutional Monarchy, 1907–1917* (1977)

**Dunkirk, evacuation of.** *See* SECOND WORLD WAR.

**Dunkirk, Treaty of.** Anglo–French agreement signed on 4 March 1947 to provide mutual assistance against German aggression. The treaty also contained provisions for joint consultation over matters of mutual concern. The status of the treaty belongs largely to the post-war era and the re-emergence of France as the major European power, prior to the revival of West Germany, and the development of plans for European unity.

W. Lipgens, *A History of European Integration, 1945–7* (1982)
J. W. Young, *Britain, France and the Unity of Europe, 1945–51* (1984)

**DUP.** *See* DEMOCRATIC UNIONIST PARTY.

**DVP** (Deutsche Volkspartei; German People's Party). German right-wing liberal party during the WEIMAR REPUBLIC. Established in December 1918 as a right-wing alternative to the left-liberal DDP (*see* DDP), the DVP was initially revisionist in foreign policy and hostile to the Weimar Republic. The crisis of 1922–3 over the RUHR OCCUPATION and hyper-inflation, however, led it to modify its stance and to enter a coalition government. Under its leader, GUSTAV STRESEMANN, it played an important part in the coalition governments of the middle years (1924–30) of the Weimar Republic; representing the interests of the upper-middle classes and some sections of German industry. Its ambivalence towards the Republic was shared by its supporters at the polls, who increasingly abandoned it after 1928 for economic-interest splinter parties and, later, the NAZI PARTY.

L. E. Jones, *German Liberalism and the Dissolution of the Weimar Party System, 1918–1933* (1989)

# E

**Easter Rising.** An armed insurrection in central Dublin and isolated points elsewhere in Ireland between 24–29 April 1916 with the aim of asserting Ireland's claim for independence. From 1914 groups in SINN FEIN and the IRISH REPUBLICAN BROTHERHOOD (IRB) considered staging an uprising. Talks with German leaders by Sir ROGER CASEMENT led to the promise of German arms. In April Casement left Germany in a submarine to rendezvous with the German arms ship the *Aud*. The plan failed, Casement was seized on 22 April and the *Aud* was scuttled. The leader of the IRB attempted to stop the Volunteer parade which was to act as the signal for the rising, but a group decided to go ahead. PATRICK PEARSE led five battalions of the IRB and James Connolly 200 of the Sinn Fein CITIZENS ARMY. They seized the General Post Office in Sackville Street (which became their headquarters), the Four Courts, St Stephen's Green and Boland's Flour Mill. A south Dublin workhouse was captured but attempts on the castle and the arsenal in Phoenix Park failed. Pearse proclaimed an Irish Republic with himself president of its provisional government. Heavy street fighting began on the first day (Easter Monday), and after five days the British army forced the rebels into unconditional surrender. Connolly, Pearse and 12 other leaders were executed in Kilmainham Gaol; Casement was hanged for treason and 3,000 more were interned but were granted an amnesty in June 1917. Though many Irish people regarded the uprising as a treacherous attack because Britain was heavily engaged at the time in the First World War and many Irish troops were serving in the British army, the courage of the rebels made a deep impression and the subsequent executions increased sympathy for their cause. The rising marked the beginning of a major swing in Irish opinion away from the moderate Home Rulers to the nationalists of Sinn Fein. The subsequent attempts to introduce conscription in Ireland and the delay in implementing the Home Rule Act created a situation which the nationalists were able to exploit to hasten the end of British rule. *See also* HOME RULE.

M. Caulfield, *The Easter Rebellion* (1964)
T. M. Coffey, *Agony at Easter: The 1916 Irish Uprising* (1969)

**East German Workers' Uprising.** Following the death of Stalin in March 1953 it seemed that some of the austerities of the regimes in Eastern Europe might be lifted; by June 1953 WALTER ULBRICHT and Oscar Grotewohl (1894–1964) were making concessions in East Germany. However, an upward revision of production targets led to a group of building workers' downing tools on 16 June 1953. Demonstrations occurred in which the crowds refused to listen to Communist Party officials. A general strike was called for 11 June and a crowd estimated at over 1 million marched on government buildings in Berlin. By then the authorities were prepared, and the demonstrators were met by armed police and Soviet tanks. More than 300 other places were affected, including several major towns, such as Magdeburg, Halle, Jena, Gorlitz and Brandenburg. Curfew and martial law restrictions remained in force until 12 July 1953. In all 21 civilians were killed and 187 injured in dealing with the protests. The uprising did not prevent further economic liberalization.

**East Germany.** *See* GERMAN DEMOCRATIC REPUBLIC.

**Ebert, Friedrich** (1871–1925). · German Social Democratic politician, Reich Chancellor and first President of the WEIMAR REPUBLIC. By training a saddler, Ebert worked as SOCIAL DEMOCRATIC PARTY (SPD) journalist before becoming a party functionary, first in Bremen, later in Berlin. Elected to the REICHSTAG in 1912, he became co-chairman (with Haase) of the SPD's executive in 1913. An advocate of the party's support for the war effort after 1914, Ebert was co-leader of the parliamentary SPD (with Scheidemann) from 1916, and in 1918 became chairman of the *Reichstag* 'Main Committee'. With the outbreak of the GERMAN REVOLUTION, Ebert succeeded Prince MAX OF BADEN as Reich Chancellor on 10 November 1918. As chairman of the provisional government (Council of People's Deputies), made up of representatives from the Majority Social Democratic Party and the Independent Social Democratic Party (*see* USPD), Ebert had as his principal objectives the negotiation of an armistice with the Western Allies and the maintenance of public order until elections to a constituent assembly could take place. To achieve the second of these aims he concluded a secret agreement with the Army High Command whereby the Army pledged its loyalty to the new government in return for an undertaking by the Council of People's Deputies to support the attempts of the Army to maintain discipline in the ranks and preserve the authority of the officer corps. Following elections in January 1919 Ebert was elected President of the new Republic by the National Assembly on 11 February 1919; in October 1922 his period of office was extended by the *Reichstag* until June 1925. As President, Ebert proved himself to be even-handed, appointing and supporting Chancellors from both the Left and the Right, and using the emergency powers he possessed under Article 48 of the constitution to defend the Republic during the Franco–Belgian RUHR OCCUPATION and the MUNICH PUTSCH of November 1923. Ebert died on 28 February 1925, a few months before his term of office as President was due to expire.

**Economic and Monetary Union of the European Community** (EMU). The TREATY OF ROME committed the member states of the EUROPEAN ECONOMIC COMMUNITY (EEC) to regarding their short-term economic policy as a matter of general interest and to co-ordinate their economic policies so as to provide for greater economic stability. The devaluation of the French franc in 1969 emphasized the problems which changes in economic conditions and rates of exchange could cause to common policies. In February 1969 the Barre Plan urged co-ordination or economic policies and monetary co-operation. This was agreed at the Hague summit, a meeting of the heads of government of the then six members of the EEC (*see* THE SIX), in December 1969. In 1970 a second Barre Plan was proposed by the COMMISSION OF THE EUROPEAN COMMUNITY, setting out three stages by which economic and monetary union could be achieved by 1978. Another plan, the Werner Report, suggested 1980 as a terminal date, but differences of emphasis about the staging of economic and monetary union and concerns about national sovereignty prevented implementation. Although the Paris summit meeting of heads of state in October 1972 accepted 1980 as the date for the achievement of EMU, the project remained unrealized. The shocks to the world monetary system caused by the oil-price rise and the temporary threat of world-wide recession led to a concentration on short-term objectives. In 1970 and 1971 arrangements were made for members of the EEC to provide short- and medium-term aid to member states with balance of payments difficulties and in April 1973 a European Monetary Co-operation Fund was set up to oversee the regulation of currencies operating within the framework of the European 'snake', a system whereby currencies could fluctuate within fixed limits. The TINDEMANS REPORT of 1975 offered further support for EMU, but was unable to overcome the reluctance of states to surrender their individual discretion over economic policy at a time of greater economic uncertainty, fears which were revitalized by the depression of the late 1970s and early 1980s. EMU returned to the agenda at the Hanover summit of June 1988 when the SINGLE EUROPEAN ACT and plans for completing an internal market by 1992 revived initiatives largely dormant. JACQUES DELORS was given chairmanship of a committee to prepare plans for monetary union. This produced the DELORS PLAN, proposing a three-stage movement towards a full currency union and a European Bank, debated at the Madrid summit in June 1989. It was agreed that the first stage, the adherence of the 12 EEC members to the EUROPEAN MONETARY SYSTEM (EMS) would begin from 1 July 1990, while an inter-governmental conference would consider the two subsequent stages. The United Kingdom, after some hesitation, joined the EMS in October 1990. It was broadly accepted that the completion of the internal market in 1992 and the adherence of member states to the EMS were the first steps, with full economic and monetary union to be considered more fully in due course. Plans for a European Central Bank were nonetheless being pursued actively by Delors and members of the EEC, in spite of some reluctance on the part of the United Kingdom and other states to commit themselves prematurely.

J. Palmer, *Trading Places: The Future of the European Community* (1988)
R. Owen and M. Dynes, *The Times Guide to 1992* (1989)

**Economic and Social Committee of the European Community** (ESC). An advisory body set up to deal with a wide range of matters including: agriculture, transport, energy and nuclear power, industry and commerce, social questions, regional development and the protection of the environment, public health, and consumer affairs. Under the TREATY OF ROME a number of areas are specified where consultation is mandatory before directives and regulations may be approved, but consultation also takes place on a wide range of other issues. Membership of the ESC is intended to reflect three groups: employers; workers; and other interest groups, such as the self-employed, consumers and academic and similar interests. Members are appointed by the COUNCIL OF MINISTERS following nomination by governments. Current membership is 189, members being appointed for renewable terms of four years. The committee has its headquarters in Brussels and has nine specialist sections which produce advisory documents.

S. A. Budd and A. Jones, *The European Community: A Guide to the Maze* (rev. edn, 1989)

A. J. C. Kerr, *The Common Market and How it Works* (rev. edn, 1990)

**ECSC.** *See* EUROPEAN COAL AND STEEL COMMUNITY.

**EDC.** *See* EUROPEAN DEFENCE COMMUNITY.

**Eden, Anthony** (1897–1977). British politician and Prime Minister, 1955–7. He entered Parliament in 1923, serving as Foreign Secretary three times in 1935–8, 1940–45 and 1951–5. His first term as Foreign Secretary was ended by his resignation after disagreement over the extent of APPEASEMENT towards MUSSOLINI. As virtual understudy to CHURCHILL and Deputy Prime Minister, 1951–5, he obtained virtually unparalleled experience in the world of international diplomacy before, during and after the Second World War. His premiership was considered by many too long delayed, by which time he was suffering from recurrent illness as a result of an operation in 1953. He attempted to meet the growing tension in the Middle East during the SUEZ CRISIS with a firm hand which may have resulted from his earlier experiences of dealing with the pre-war dictators. He was persuaded to join in a French plan to collude with Israel in an invasion of the Suez Canal Zone following the nationalization of the canal by Nasser on 26 July 1956. The Anglo–French invasion on 5 November divided the country and provoked an outcry both in Britain and abroad; Eden's decision to halt the advance of the troops the next day and his subsequent decision at the end of the month to withdraw the troops altogether under United States pressure created the impression of an inept and vacillating leadership. The Suez débâcle contributed to a collapse in Eden's health and his resignation in January 1957. He was created Earl Avon in 1961. Eden's reputation has always been judged in relation to the Suez Crisis which destroyed his career. His earlier record as an opponent of the dictators was perhaps not as straightforward as is sometimes made out, being more finely nuanced than a mere rejection of appeasement. His conduct of the Suez Crisis is principally open to criticism for his abandonment of negotiations with Nasser in favour of force and the accompanying subterfuge of appearing not to know of the Israeli attack on Egypt which was in fact, pre-planned. His failure then to ride out the hostility that the invasion incurred, halting it when most of the military objectives were in sight and the humiliating withdrawal under obvious US pressure left him with few allies. *See also* NON-INTERVENTION COMMITTEE.

D. Carlton, *Anthony Eden: A Biography* (1981)
A. R. Peters, *Anthony Eden at the Foreign Office, 1931–1938* (1986)
R. Rhodes James, *Anthony Eden* (1986)

**Edward VIII, of Great Britain** (1894–1972). King and Emperor; reigned 20 January to 11 December 1936. The eldest son of GEORGE V and Queen Mary, he was formally invested as Prince of Wales at Caernarvon, 13 July 1911. He served with the Grenadier Guards on the Western Front during the First World War and later in Italy and Egypt; thereafter he represented George V on visits to the Empire and the United States. Edward earned much popular support for his concern about social conditions, especially amongst the unemployed. On a visit to South Wales in 1936 his comment 'Something must be done' was regarded as a dangerous intervention in political affairs, though his major role was in sponsoring philanthropic activity. His liaison from 1931 with Mrs Wallis Simpson, an American divorcée, and his desire to marry her and make her his Queen provoked the ABDICATION CRISIS in November–December 1936, leading to his relinquishing the throne on 11 December in favour of his younger brother, the Duke of York, who became GEORGE VI. Taking the title Duke of Windsor, he went into exile in France, where he married Mrs Simpson in June 1937. Concern about the ex-King's pro-German sympathies and the danger that he might become a ploy in HITLER's designs on Britain led to his being offered the Governorship of the Bahamas, 1940–45. Never returning to Britain, he died in Paris in May 1972, but was buried at Windsor. He was survived by Mrs Simpson, who died on 24 April 1986.

F. Donaldson, *Edward VIII* (1974)
M. Bloch, *The Duke of Windsor's War* (1982)

**EEC.** *See* EUROPEAN ECONOMIC COMMUNITY.

**EFTA.** *See* EUROPEAN FREE TRADE ASSOCIATION.

**Eichmann, Adolf** (1906–62). Nazi German functionary engaged in the implementation of the murderous 'Final Solution' (*see* HOLOCAUST). Born in Solingen, but growing up in Linz, Austria, Eichmann joined the Austrian Nazi Party in 1932. Having joined the Nazi security service (SD) in 1935, he was appointed to head the 'Office for Jewish Emigration' established in Vienna after the ANSCHLUSS. From March 1939 he held a similar position in Prague. During October 1939 he organized the deportation to German-occupied Poland of Jews from Vienna, Upper Silesia and occupied Czechoslovakia. In December 1939 he was transferred to head the bureau within the Reich Security Head Office concerned with 'Jewish Affairs–Evacuation Affairs', and from summer 1940 was charged with developing plans for the establishment of a settlement in Madagascar to which European Jews were to be deported after the end of the war. His office also played a central role in the implementation of the mass murder of the European Jewish population from 1942 onwards, co-ordinating the deportation of Jews in German-occupied Europe to the extermination camps in Poland. Between March and July 1944, he supervised the deportation of the Jewish population of Hungary. Interned by the Americans in 1945, he escaped to Argentina in 1946. In May 1960 he was tracked down by Israeli secret agents and was kidnapped and smuggled to Israel. At his trial, which lasted from April to August 1961, he was convicted of crimes against humanity and the Jewish people. He was hanged in May 1962.

H. Arendt, *Eichmann in Jerusalem* (1963)
J. Noakes and G. Pridham (eds.), *Nazism 1919–1945*, vol. 3: *Foreign Policy War and Racial Extermination* (1988)

*Einsatzgruppen.* Units of special Nazi police who were responsible for carrying out systematic massacres of Jews in occupied Russia and the Ukraine from 1941. Operating in detachments approximately 3,000 strong, they carried out by shooting the first phase of the mass liquidation of the Jews under Nazi policy, before systematized slaughter by gassing became the major method of mass extermination. Amongst the largest massacres carried out was the killing of Ukrainian Jews at BABI YAR. By the end of 1941 it is estimated that *Einsatzgruppen* had been involved in the killing of almost 1.5 million Jews. *See also* HOLOCAUST.

**Eisenhower, Dwight** (1890–1969). American general and politician; President of the United States 1953–61; Supreme Allied Commander for the invasion of Europe in 1944. Eisenhower's direct role in European affairs dates from his appointment to conduct the Allied forces during the Anglo–American invasion of North Africa in November 1942, bringing both MONTGOMERY and ALEXANDER under his command in the North African theatre by the time the campaign was concluded in May 1943. He then planned and executed the invasion of Sicily on 10 July 1943, followed by the landing in mainland Italy in September. Given supreme command for the invasion of Normandy in June 1944, he had to face serious difficulties in dealing with his subordinate commanders, notably Montgomery and Patton. Taking a more cautious line than either of them, he nonetheless supervised the destruction of the German forces in France by the autumn of 1944. Although there was disappointment that Eisenhower had not managed to win the war by the end of 1944, his slow, cautious advance was not thrown off course by HITLER's final offensive through the Ardennes in December 1944 – 'the battle of the Bulge'. Showing great decisiveness and no little daring, he placed Montgomery in command of all forces in the area, allowing a German breakthrough to be prevented and the Germans driven back in defeat. In the final campaigns in Germany in early 1945 he continued to favour a 'broad front' advance, resisting Montgomery's strategy for a narrow armoured thrust to the heart of the Ruhr. Eisenhower preferred to retain his more methodical strategy. One fateful decision was to halt the advance of his armies on the Elbe, leaving the capture of Berlin to the Soviets; instead he diverted his leading forces to the

mythic 'Alpine Redoubt' said to have been prepared by the Nazis for a final stand. Following the German surrender Eisenhower commanded the armies of occupation, becoming the first commander of the NORTH ATLANTIC TREATY ORGANISATION. He subsequently entered politics, serving two terms as President. As a military commander in the Second World War Eisenhower's greatest strength lay in his organizational ability, shown in the detailed and elaborate planning which lay behind the invasions of Sicily in 1943 and Normandy in 1944. He could act decisively when required and showed great diplomacy as a supreme commander in his dealing with often difficult subordinates and with his political masters in London and Washington.

H. C. Butcher, *My Three Years with Eisenhower* (1946)
J. Keegan, *Six Armies in Normandy* (1982)
R. F. Burk, *Dwight D. Eisenhower: Hero and Politician* (1987)

**Elizabeth II, of Great Britain** (1926–). Queen of the United Kingdom and Head of the British Commonwealth. She came to the throne on the death of her father, GEORGE VI, on 6 February 1952. She was privately educated and served in the Auxiliary Transport Service at the end of the Second World War. In November 1947 she married Lieutenant Philip Mountbatten, later Prince Philip. Her coronation in June 1953 was the first to be televised, and was marked by popular celebrations throughout the country. As Queen for over 35 years, she has acquired vast experience of international and national affairs. She has paid particular attention to maintaining links with the BRITISH COMMONWEALTH OF NATIONS, and has undertaken extensive foreign tours, visiting almost every country in the world apart from the Soviet Union. Her reign has seen the development of the monarchy into an age of more intense and intrusive media coverage, which has been accommodated by greater openness about the workings of the Royal household. The investiture of the heir to the throne, Prince Charles (1948–) as Prince of Wales, in 1969, has led to his playing a larger role in public affairs with sometimes outspoken comments on social and cultural matters. The Queen, nonetheless, has continued to fulfil all the major duties of a constitutional monarch through successive changes of administration. She has continued the tradition of Christmas broadcasts to the country and the Commonwealth which are now televised.

R. Lacey, *Majesty: Elizabeth II and the House of Windsor* (1977)

A. Morrow, *The Queen* (1983)

**EMS.** *See* EUROPEAN MONETARY SYSTEM.

**EMU.** *See* ECONOMIC AND MONETARY UNION OF THE EUROPEAN COMMUNITY.

**END.** *See* EUROPEAN NUCLEAR DISARMAMENT.

**EOKA.** *See* CYPRUS EMERGENCY.

**Erhard, Ludwig** (1897–1977). West German economics minister and Chancellor. Born at Fürth, Erhard studied economics at university and became professor of economics at Munich University in 1945. An adherent of the Freiburg School of neo-liberal economics, he served as head of the Bavarian industrial reconstruction organization established after 1945, and promoted the idea of the 'social market economy', in which a free-market economy is combined with state responsibility for promotion of economic development and a welfare state. He was appointed director of economic administration within the British and American 'Bizone' of occupation in March 1948, his social market philosophy exercising an increasing influence on the CHRISTIAN DEMOCRATIC UNION (CDU). Entering the Federal Parliament (*Bundestag*) of the new FEDERAL REPUBLIC OF GERMANY as a CDU deputy in 1949, he was immediately appointed Minister for Economic Affairs by Chancellor ADENAUER. Erhard initiated a number of policies which are often held to have been responsible for the West German post-war *Wirtschaftswunder* ('economic miracle'): government intervention in the economy was kept to a minimum, businesses were relieved of many of the restrictions imposed by the occupying powers, a vigorous anti-cartel policy was introduced, and tax laws and other legislation affecting businesses were reframed so as to encourage investment and enterprise. Domestic capital formation was supplemented by American aid under the MARSHALL PLAN

and the economic recovery received another stimulus from the upsurge in demand associated with the Korean War. Gross domestic product grew at an average annual rate of 8.2 per cent between 1950 and 1954, at 7.1 per cent between 1955 and 1958. On the back of the 'economic miracle' an extensive welfare state apparatus was constructed. The achievement of full employment by the late 1950s and the introduction of limited worker participation in management reduced industrial disputes: by the early 1960s, West German industrial relations were being held up as a model by many foreign observers. Appointed Deputy Chancellor in 1957, he succeeded Adenauer as the second Chancellor of the Federal Republic in October 1963. As Chancellor, Erhard maintained the HALLSTEIN DOCTRINE whilst seeking to improve trade relations with West Germany's communist neighbours. In the interest of improved relations with the United States, his government moved away slightly from the close Franco–German alignment promoted by Adenauer. Having led the CDU–CSU successfully into the 1965 *Bundestag* elections, Erhard fell from office in October 1966 as a consequence of the refusal of his coalition partners, the FREE DEMOCRATIC PARTY, to sanction tax increases to fund the state's welfare commitments during a short-lived recession. He lived in retirement until his death in 1977.

G. Hallett, *The Social Economy of West Germany* (1973)

**Erzberger, Matthias** (1875–1921). German politician. He trained as a teacher; as deputy for the CENTRE PARTY from 1903, he became an expert on fiscal policy and was critical of colonial policy. Matthias organized German propaganda abroad during FIRST WORLD WAR and initially endorsed annexionist war aims in the west. Later, he denounced unrestricted U-boat warfare and introduced a resolution in July 1917 for peace without annexations or indemnities. Although instrumental in bringing about the fall of the Chancellor, BETHMANN HOLLWEG, he failed to achieve the appointment of BULOW and was forced to acquiece in LUDENDORFF's rise to dominance. His pessimistic views of the war earned him opposition, but he entered the government in October 1918, serving as a member of the armistice commission and signing the agreement at Compiégne. He supported the socialist's use of force against the Left in 1919 and supported acceptance of the TREATY OF VERSAILLES. He served as deputy Chancellor and Finance Minister from June 1919, radically reforming the tax system. Accused and tried for financial irregularity, he resigned in March 1920. Re-elected to the Reichstag in June 1920, his close association with the Versailles Treaty made him a target for the extreme right. He was murdered by two former naval officers in August 1921. See VERSAILLES, TREATY OF; WEIMAR REPUBLIC

K. Epstein, *Matthias Erzberger and the Dilemma of German Democracy* (1959)

**ETA.** See BASQUES.

**Ethiopian Crisis.** Tension between Italy and Ethiopia (Abyssinia) mounted with MUSSOLINI's attempts to extend the Italian empire in East Africa and to avenge the humiliation of the Italian defeat at Adowa in 1896 at the hands of the Ethiopian Emperor. Disputes arose over the control of the Walwal oasis on the border of Italian Somaliland, leading to a clash of Italian and Ethiopian forces on 5 December 1934 in which Italian troops were killed. Mussolini demanded the oasis and compensation for the deaths (Ethiopian losses were, in fact, higher). The Emperor Haile Selassie appealed to the LEAGUE OF NATIONS, whose mediations were rejected by Mussolini. A build-up of Italian reinforcements was followed by a full-scale invasion of Ethiopia on 2 October 1935. The League of Nations swiftly declared Italy the aggressor and applied economic sanctions, but they were applied haphazardly, initially excluding oil, coal and steel, while other powers who had either withdrawn from the League or were favourable to Italy refused to apply them. Attempts to appease Mussolini by the HOARE–LAVAL PACT, which would have left some independence to Ethiopia at the price of major territorial concessions, caused an outcry when they were made public. The rejection of the plan led to the replacement of Hoare by Sir ANTHONY EDEN as British Foreign Secretary. Eden sought to tighten sanctions, but still excluded oil from the embargo. Although Ethiopian forces put up stiffer resistance than expected, the Italian use of aircraft, poison gas and tanks broke resistance at the battle of Mai Chew by April 1936 and allowed the Italian forces under Marshal BADOGLIO to enter Addis Ababa on 5 May. Haile Selassie was forced into exile and VICTOR EMMANUEL III of Italy proclaimed Emperor of Ethiopia, which became part of a united Italian East Africa with the territories of Eritrea and Somalia. The outcome was a public humiliation for the League of Nations and a further demonstration of its inability to defend states from aggression. The weak resolve of France and Britain to stand up to the dictators was shown, encouraging further aggression, while the attempt dating from 1935 to build up an alliance with Mussolini in the STRESA FRONT lay in ruins.

G. Baer, *The Coming of the Italian–Ethiopian War* (1967)
D. Mack Smith, *Mussolini's Roman Empire* (1979)

**ETUC.** See EUROPEAN TRADE UNION CONFEDERATION.

**Euratom.** The European Atomic Energy Community. Set up by a treaty signed at the same time as the TREATY OF ROME establishing the EUROPEAN ECONOMIC COMMUNITY (EEC) in March 1957, it came into being on January 1958. The institutions provided for by the treaty were similar to those for the EEC, although its Commission had only six members. In 1965 the MERGER TREATY established a single Council of Ministers and a single Commission for the EEC, the EUROPEAN COAL AND STEEL COMMUNITY (ECSC) and Euratom. The European Parliament, Court of Justice and the Economic and Social Committee have always served both Communities. Its aim, stated in Article 1 of its treaty, was to create the conditions required for the rapid establishment and growth of nuclear industries. It was provided with powers to promote research, disseminate information, lay down health and safety standards, co-ordinate investment and establish a common supply policy of a common market on nuclear material. Euratom has not achieved the important role for which it was planned; member states have been reluctant to provide it with funds and have been anxious to maintain their separate national nuclear industries. Its main activity has been to establish a joint Research Centre and to participate in nuclear and allied research elsewhere.

**Euro-Communism.** Term used to describe the policies adopted by post-1945 communist parties in Western Europe, notably the ITALIAN COMMUNIST PARTY and the SPANISH COMMUNIST PARTY. The desire of these parties to compete effectively within the electoral systems of their respective countries led to their abandonment of the Soviet model of communism associated with MARXIST–LENINISM and STALINISM. The lead was taken by the Italian Communist Party under TOGLIATTI in accepting parliamentary democracy and the mixed economy as necessary steps in the long-term transformation towards a communist society. The policy used new theoretical positions derived from the work of ANTONIO GRAMSCI to follow the route taken earlier by 'revisionists' in the GERMAN SOCIAL DEMOCRATIC PARTY (SPD) and in the moderate 'gradualism' of the BRITISH LABOUR PARTY. In policy terms it led to an acceptance of the NORTH ATLANTIC TREATY ORGANISATION (NATO) and the EUROPEAN ECONOMIC COMMUNITY by the Italian Communist Party, growing electoral success and a brief period of support for the ITALIAN CHRISTIAN DEMOCRATIC PARTY, the majority party in 1976, the so-called 'Historic Compromise'. The Spanish Communist Party, which re-emerged into legal existence after the death of Franco in 1975, followed similar policies, abandoning its hard-line stance associated with the SPANISH CIVIL WAR era. The 'Communist' label has been so diluted that pressures for changes in name became real, and in late 1989 the Italian Party abandoned the name 'Communist', as did the British party. In Eastern Europe the rapid development of pluralistic democratic politics during 1989 also saw similar adjustments, the Polish Communist Party changing its name to the Polish Social Democratic Party in February 1990. The rise of Euro-Communism is seen as marking the abandonment of the rigidities of democratic centralism and centralized planning for an acceptance of liberal democracy and the mixed economy as an at least temporary staging post on the road to communism. In practice it is difficult to distinguish Euro-Communist parties from the traditional moderate socialist parties of Britain, Germany and Scandinavia.

D. Robertson, *The Penguin Dictionary of Politics* (1985)

**European Coal and Steel Community** (ECSC). Founded on the basis outlined by the SCHUMAN PLAN and brought into being in August 1952, the ECSC organized a common market in coal and steel and the development and control of the coal and steel production industries on a supranational basis. The institutions of the ECSC are a Council of Ministers and the High Authority, now merged with those of the European Community, and the Common Assembly, now merged with the EUROPEAN PARLIAMENT. The ECSC was the earliest organization of what was to become the EUROPEAN ECONOMIC COMMUNITY (EEC). Its initial purpose went beyond economic co-operation, with the intention that by joining together the European coal and steel industries it would prevent the member states from ever going to war with each other. As a result the preamble to the ECSC Treaty referred to the need 'to substitute for age-old rivalries the merging of essential interests', to create 'the basis for a broader and deeper community among peoples' and 'to lay the foundations for institutions which will give direction to a destiny henceforward shared'. Its institutions became the prototype for the EEC, which extended the principles and practices of the ECSC to the setting up of a Common Market and the development of greater economic and political union within Europe. Although the ECSC's institutions became merged with other Community institutions, the COMMISSION OF THE EUROPEAN COMMUNITY, as the successor to the High Authority, retains considerable power over the steel and coal industries. Under the TREATY OF PARIS it can adopt even wider powers and has been responsible for regulatory steps to deal with the crisis in European steel production by enforcing restrictions on production, monitoring imports and establishing fair competition within Europe. A voluntary cartel, Eurofer, was established in 1977 under the 'Davignon Plan', named after the EEC Commissioner responsible for industry, Viscount Etienne Davignon. In 1980 a state of 'manifest crisis' in steel was declared and the cartel was tightened to control four-fifths of steel output. From 1985 a phased deregulation took place, following the loss of 152,000 jobs in steel and the shedding of 32 million tons of capacity. The 'crisis' was declared over in June 1988 and the quota system ended. The coal industry has been less rigidly monitored, but steps were taken from the rise in oil prices in the 1970s to increase the market share of coal within Europe as part of a policy of reducing dependence on imported oil and the diversification of supply.

L. Tsoukalis, *The European Community: Past, Present and Future* (1983)

**European Convention of Human Rights.** Drawn up under the aegis of the COUNCIL OF EUROPE, signed in Rome on 4 November 1950, entered into force in September 1953. It now binds Austria, Belgium, Cyprus, Denmark, West Germany, Iceland, Ireland, Italy, Luxembourg, Malta, the Netherlands, Norway, Sweden, Turkey and the United Kingdom. Greece withdrew from these obligations in 1970, and France and Switzerland, although members of the Council of Europe, have not accepted the Convention. It consists of 18 articles, largely based on the Universal Declaration of Human Rights, with institutions to facilitate their enforcement. Those who are bound by it undertake to secure to all persons under their jurisdiction, without discrimination, a number of civil and political rights: freedom from torture and inhuman treatment, freedom from slavery and compulsory labour, the right to liberty and security of person, the right to a fair trial, the right to respect the family, the home, and correspondence, freedom of thought, religion, expression, association and assembly, and the right to marry and found a family. The institutions established under the Convention include the Europe Commission of Human Rights. The Commission has as many members as the number of states who are party to the Convention; in fact, one member of each nationality. Any party to the Convention, or any individual, may refer an alleged breach of the Convention to the Commission, which must then establish the facts and attempt to arrive at a solution agreed between all those con-

cerned. The case is reported to the Council of Ministers of the Council of Europe, and if a solution has not been reached it may go before the European Court on Human Rights, which consists of independent judges, one for each Member of the Council of Europe, who sit in chambers of seven judges. A case can be referred to the Court only by the Commission or by a member state government concerned. Alternatively a decision on the case is taken by the Council of Ministers of the Council of Europe. Most of the complaints which come before the European Commission on Human Rights are complaints of individuals or groups against their governments. Cases of complaints between governments are rare, although one such case arose in 1971, when Ireland complained of the United Kingdom's actions over the introduction of internment in Northern Ireland.

**European Council, the**. Name given from 1974 to regular 'summits' of EEC Heads of State to decide community policy. Technically it has only the same status as other meetings of the COUNCIL OF MINISTERS, but has latterly been the driving force behind major initiatives such as the Single European Act and Monetary Union.

**European Defence Community** (EDC). A plan proposed in 1952, intended to be supranational, embracing states with common institutions, which was to have an international army and budget, be more coherent than NATO (*see* NORTH ATLANTIC TREATY ORGANISATION) and mutually guarantee the security of its members. Membership was open firstly to members of the EUROPEAN COAL AND STEEL COMMUNITY (France, Italy, West Germany and Benelux), but it was hoped that other European states including Britain would join. A draft treaty was produced after negotiations in Paris between February 1951 and 8 May 1952; it was initialled by the members of the Coal and Steel Community and signed by the respective foreign ministers on 27 May 1952. However, it had to be ratified by the national parliaments before taking effect; the French parliament refused and the idea was abandoned.

E. Furson, *The European Defence Community* (1981)

**European Economic Community** (EEC). The European Economic Community, also known as the Common Market, was first envisaged in June 1955 when the foreign ministers of the members of the EUROPEAN COAL AND STEEL COMMUNITY (France, Italy, West Germany and Benelux) met at Messina. The Belgian minister PAUL-HENRI SPAAK was instructed to make proposals for an expansion of the existing community to one based on free trade, free movement of labour and capital, common social and economic policies and the removal of restrictive trade practices. On 25 March 1957 'the Six' signed the TREATY OF ROME and the EEC came into being on 11 January 1958. Under the agreement any member could veto the admission of a future applicant. In fact DE GAULLE of France used it to veto applications made by Britain on 10 August 1961 (vetoed January 1963) and again in May 1967 (vetoed 19 December), when negotiations on British entry were stopped but the application was not withdrawn. Following de Gaulle's resignation in April 1969 an invitation to join the EEC was extended to Britain, Eire, Denmark and Norway in June 1970. These four countries signed a treaty of accession in Brussels on 22 January 1972, but in September Norway withdrew after a referendum had shown that most Norwegians opposed entry. The other three became members and joined from 1 January 1973. On 5 June 1975 a referendum in Britain (called as a result of left-wing LABOUR PARTY opposition to the EEC) showed more than 67 per cent of the public to be in favour of membership. In January 1981 Greece joined. On 24 February 1982 Greenland, part of the Kingdom of Denmark, voted to leave. Spain and Portugal joined in 1986.

In 1973 the EEC agreed to free trade in manufactured goods between its members and those of the EUROPEAN FREE TRADE ASSOCIATION (EFTA), and on 28 February 1975 it signed the first LOMÉ CONVENTION, giving 46 developing countries access to the EEC market. In December 1985 the SINGLE EUROPEAN ACT was agreed at the Luxembourg summit, allowing a wide range of issues to be decided by majority decision. Earlier in the year, 1992 was set as the date for the completion of an internal market within the EEC. In June 1988 the DELORS Committee on Economic and Monetary Union was set up, and 1992 declared 'irreversible'. The Delors Committee put forward proposals for a European Central Bank and Monetary Union which would form the first steps towards 'European Government'. The DELORS PLAN was attacked by Mrs Thatcher in a speech at Bruges on 20 September 1988 expressing opposition to the creation of 'a European super-state'. Disputes over the implications of 1992 and further progress towards fuller monetary and political unification have become a major issue. In July 1989 Britain agreed to participate in Stage One of the Delors Plan for joining the EUROPEAN MONETARY SYSTEM (EMS) but without stating a deadline. Stages Two and Three for further economic and political union remain under discussion. *See also* COMMISSION OF THE EUROPEAN COMMUNITY; COUNCIL OF MINISTERS OF THE EUROPEAN COMMUNITY; COURT OF JUSTICE OF THE EUROPEAN COMMUNITY; COMMON AGRICULTURAL POLICY.

R. Pryce, *The Politics of the European Community* (1973)
L. Tsoukalis, *The European Community, Past, Present and Future* (1983)
E. Wistrich, *After 1992: the United States of Europe* (1989)

**European Free Trade Association** (EFTA). Founded in January 1960 on the basis of the Stockholm Convention of 1959, with eight member countries, Austria, Denmark, Norway, Portugal, Sweden, Switzerland and the United Kingdom. Finland became an associate member in June 1961 and Iceland joined in 1970. Denmark and the United Kingdom left EFTA on joining the EUROPEAN ECONOMIC COMMUNITY (EEC) on 31 December 1972. EFTA is administered by a council of representatives of the governments of member states meeting in Geneva; usually the governments are represented by ambassadors, but twice a year ministers meet. All important decisions must be taken unanimously. The aim of EFTA was to establish free trade in industrial products and promote trade in agricultural products between the member countries. By the end of 1966 all customs duties and quotas on industrial trade between EFTA members had been abolished; a number of non-tariff barriers had also been removed. When Denmark and the United

Kingdom left EFTA to join the EEC the remaining EFTA members negotiated free trade agreements with the EEC, so that after a transitional period ending in 1977 there would be free trade in most industrial goods between all the former EFTA countries and all EEC members. EFTA was founded in part in response to a British Government initiative, following their decision not to participate in the creation of the EEC, with the intention of allowing its members to benefit from the increase in trade which might result from the abolition of duties and quotas without a commitment to procedures other than inter-governmental negotiations.

**European Monetary System** (EMS). System originating in 1979 by which the exchange rates of the EUROPEAN ECONOMIC COMMUNITY (EEC) countries are calibrated by the Exchange Rate Mechanism (ERM) with rates fixed in relation to the European Currency Unit (ECU). The ECU itself is based upon a 'basket' of currencies, mainly those participating in the EMS. The participating states have their relationship to the ECU fixed at sessions of finance ministers from the member countries. Between realignments members of the EMS support member currencies above its 'floor' level on the foreign exchanges, drawing upon a European Monetary Co-operation Fund, based on members' gold and currency reserves. The aim of the EMS is to stabilize currency fluctuations after the partial collapse of the Bretton Woods system (*see* BRETTON WOODS CONFERENCE) and the 'Snake', by which currency fluctuations occurred within set limits. The Council-Commission of the EEC declared in June 1988 that all currencies should join the EMS by 1992. Membership of the EMS by all states is envisaged as Stage One of the DELORS PLAN for ECONOMIC AND MONETARY UNION. After considerable hesitation Britain joined the EMS in October 1990.

**European Nuclear Disarmament** (END). British-based movement formed in 1980 and headed by E. P. Thompson, who is also a leading figure on the national council of the CAMPAIGN FOR NUCLEAR DISARMAMENT. The initial objective of END was to secure the removal of all nuclear weapons from

Europe, but it has since developed into a pressure-group fighting for a reunited Europe free from domination by either the USSR or the USA. In this capacity END has established links with peace groups behind the IRON CURTAIN, such as the Moscow-based Group to Establish Trust, which suffered greatly from official persecution. END has argued that the new circumstances of the ending of the COLD WAR and the incipient reductions or removal of American and Soviet troops from Europe have vindicated its pan-European approach to security. The INTERMEDIATE NUCLEAR FORCES TREATY of December 1987 represents part-fulfilment of its aims.

**European Parliament.** A body instituted by the TREATY OF ROME as the Assembly of the EUROPEAN ECONOMIC COMMUNITY (EEC). A similar Assembly was provided for the EUROPEAN COAL AND STEEL COMMUNITY (ECSC) as a purely advisory body, at Strasbourg in September 1952: this had 78 members, deputed by their national parliaments. It was expanded to 142 members in 1958 when its competence was extended to cover the EEC and EURATOM. It soon took the title of the European Parliament and its members were increased to 198 in 1973 and eventually to 518 with the enlargements of the EEC to include a total of 12 states. Its powers were increased over budgetary matters in 1970 and 1975, but it remained a nominated body until 1979, when the first direct elections took place to elect the then 410 members. Elections have subsequently taken place at five-yearly intervals to elect full-time representatives or Members of the European Parliament (MEPs). France, West Germany, Italy and the United Kingdom elect 81 MEPs each, Spain 60, the Netherlands and Portugal 25, Belgium and Greece 24, Denmark 16, Ireland 15, and Luxembourg 6. All states apart from Great Britain use a system of proportional representation to elect their MEPs on the basis of large Euro-constituencies, representing a total of 100 million voters. The European Parliament has supervisory powers under the Treaty of Rome to question and discuss the work of the COMMISSION OF THE EUROPEAN COMMUNITY and the COUNCIL OF MINISTERS OF THE EUROPEAN COMMUNITY. It has the theoretical right through a motion of censure passed by two-thirds of the votes cast to dismiss the Commission, but this remains a remote possibility in current circumstances. The European Parliament has a wide consultative role in all EEC legislation, consultation being mandatory; it can propose amendments and its power to co-operate with the Council of Ministers in legislation has been strengthened by the SINGLE EUROPEAN ACT. The Parliament is also the joint budgetary authority with the Council of Ministers and the budget must be approved by it. In practice the budgetary powers of the Parliament are more limited, with little control over a large portion of the budget, the so-called 'compulsory' element being written into EEC treaties and covering almost three-quarters of the total, and limits to the increase it can make to the non-compulsory part.

There is no single meeting place for the European Parliament, although one is envisaged. Sessions of the Parliament are held for one week each month in Strasbourg, most of the committees operate in Brussels and the Secretariat is based in Luxembourg. MEPs sit in cross-national groupings, reflecting broad political allegiances. In 1989 the largest group was the Socialist Group (about 180 MEPs), followed by the European People's Party or Christian Democrats (about 121 MEPs), the Liberal and Democratic Group (about 49 MEPs), the European Democrats or Conservatives (about 34 MEPs), Greens (about 30 MEPs), two Communist groups (about 43 MEPs), and smaller Gaullist, European Right, and Rainbow (Regionalist) groups.

D. Marquand, *Parliament for Europe* (1979)
S. A. Budd and A. Jones, *The European Community: A Guide to the Maze* (rev. edn, 1989)

**European Trade Union Confederation** (ETUC). Formed in February 1973 by 15 members of the International Confederation of Free Trade Unions within Europe, later accepting members from the World Confederation of Labour. Its original members were Austria, Belgium, Denmark, Finland, France, the Federal Republic of Germany, Iceland, Italy, Luxembourg, the Netherlands, Norway, Sweden, Switzerland, the United Kingdom and the Spanish trade union movement. It later included the Irish Congress of Trade Unions and the Italian Communist Trade Union Centre. Its aims are to deal with matters of interest to European working people both inside and outside the EURO-PEAN ECONOMIC COMMUNITY. It represents (1989) 43 million workers from 34 organizations in 20 countries.

**Événements de Mai.** Events beginning on 2–3 May 1968, when French students demonstrating against education cuts in Paris clashed with the police. The brutality of the French riot police, the CRS, triggered a general reaction with mass demonstrations, the occupation of universities, and strikes involving over 10 million workers. The movement became a protest against the authoritarianism of General DE GAULLE's government, continuing until June. Although de Gaulle considered using force to suppress what verged on a revolutionary situation, he made timely concessions on educational reform, promising greater student participation and granting wage increases to the workers. De Gaulle called an election in June 1968 which produced a landslide victory for the Gaullists, giving the regime a continued mandate to rule. De Gaulle's prestige, however, had been seriously damaged and provoked a major currency crisis for France. Both Gaullists and de Gaulle himself began to prepare for an end to his presidency. He resigned on 28 April 1969. The demonstration by students and radical activists were also part of an inchoate development of left-wing activism drawing its inspiration from Mao Tse-Tung, Che Guevara and other revolutionary Third World leaders. The Left, represented by the FRENCH SOCIALIST PARTY and the FRENCH COMMUNIST PARTY, were taken by surprise by the strength of the movement and found themselves unable to channel it. As a result the student movement developed a momentum of its own, generating a variety of ideas of an anti-materialistic, anti-establishment kind often loosely dubbed 'Maoist' or 'TROTSKYITE'.

The events of May–June 1968 in Paris have been seen as marking the high point of a wave of unrest which swept Europe and North America in the late 1960s dominated by student and left-wing activists. In fact the events in Paris and elsewhere in France occurred after a spate of student sit-ins, anti-Vietnam demonstrations, and Civil Rights protests as far afield as North America, Italy, Germany, London and Northern Ireland. The events in France contributed to a further wave of mass protests seen in renewed anti-Vietnam war demonstrations in London in October 1968, Civil Rights marches in Northern Ireland in October 1968 and January 1969, and further student protests in the United States. The events of 1968 generated widespread demands for political change and liberation from economic, institutional and social oppression. As well as swelling the ranks of left-wing groups all over Europe, usually outside the existing communist parties, they also contributed to the rise of grass-roots activism on a variety of fronts – political, feminist and ecological.

B. E. Brown, *Protest in Paris* (1974)
D. Caute, *'68: The Year of the Barricades* (1988)

**Évian Agreements.** Agreements which ended the ALGERIAN WAR following talks at Évian in France in March 1962. Prime Minister POMPIDOU was the principal spokesman for the French Government, with Ben Bella, the Algerian leader released from internment, speaking for the Front de Liberation Nationale (FLN). An immediate cease-fire was agreed prior to the granting of Algerian independence and the withdrawal of all French forces by the end of 1962. The Agreements were put to referendums in France on 8 April and in Algeria on 1 July, receiving overwhelming ratification in spite of the opposition of Algerian settlers and army officers in the ORGANISATION DE L'ARMÉE SECRÈTE (OAS).

# F

**Fabian Society.** British political society founded in London in January 1884 with the aim of reorganizing society 'by the emancipation of land and capital from individual and class ownership, and the vesting of them in the community for the general benefit'. The name is taken from the Roman general Quintus Fabius Maximus who sought to weaken Hannibal during the second Punic War by harassing operations while avoiding pitched battle. The name is meant to imply the rejection of revolutionary methods and the belief that universal suffrage will eventually result in socialism after a process of educational and legislative advance. The Fabian Society was one of the constituent elements responsible for the foundation of the Labour Representation Committee (later the LABOUR PARTY) in 1900. For most of the 20th century the society has acted as a specialized research agency for the Labour Party. Notable Fabians have included SYNDEY and BEATRICE WEBB, George Bernard Shaw and Graham Wallas.

M. Cole, *The Story of Fabian Socialism* (1961)
N. and J. Mackenzie, *The First Fabians* (1977)

**factory committees.** Factory or 'shop' (workshop) committees which sprang into existence in Russia during the strike wave of February to March 1917 in individual factories or workshops. Operating at a lower tier than the SOVIETS they provided direct representation for the grievances of the factory workers. While the BOLSHEVIKS and anarchists (*see* ANARCHISM, RUSSIAN) saw them as the precursors of a new system of running industry, others saw them as essentially informal trade union organizations representing workers' interests. With the development of the RUSSIAN REVOLUTION from March 1917 they often took charge of their factories and began to press for direct workers' control of their concerns. LENIN'S early pronouncements supported worker's control of their enterprises, and the Bolshevik decree of 14 November 1917 gave elected factory representatives the power of supervision over industrial and commercial enterprises, but only within the centralized norms of the Supreme Council of the National Economy. In January 1918 the factory committees were converted into local branches of the trade unions and the whole structure was subordinated to centralized regulation under the Supreme Council. During 1917 factory committees provided the armed guards which defeated the KORNILOV putsch, and under the MILITARY REVOLUTIONARY COMMITTEES undertook the seizure of power in November 1917.

S. A. Smith, *Red Petrograd: Revolution in the Factories, 1917–18* (1983)

**Falaise Pocket.** *See* SECOND WORLD WAR.

**Falange.** Founded in October 1933, the Falange Española followed an ideological path already mapped out by the fascist-inspired Juntas de Ofensiva Nacional-Sindicalista (JONS), established two years earlier in 1931. Indeed, the similarities between the two groups were so great that they merged in February 1934 to form the Falange Española de las JONS. Despite the merger, however, the Falange remained little more than a splinter group on the far right of Spanish politics under the SECOND REPUBLIC. The small number of members (a suggested figure is under 10,000 in February 1936) meant that the Falange's national impact was largely confined to the career of the charismatic José Antonio Primo de Rivera (1903–1936), son of the former dictator and founder of the original Falange

Española. In the elections of November 1933, José Antonio was one of the two Falangists returned to the Cortes. A noted orator, he used his parliamentary position to develop Falange doctrine, although the often contradictory nature of his thought and the mystifying rhetoric which he frequently employed cannot have helped the course of 'intellectual' fascism in Spain. 'Militant' fascism, on the other hand, was becoming increasingly prominent. Falangist gunmen and street fighters, conspicuous in their blue shirts, were involved in numerous violent incidents in the capital, usually directed against rival socialists and communists. After the victory of the POPULAR FRONT in February 1936, this street violence became increasingly common as the Falange's ranks were swelled by mass defections from the CONFEDERACIÓN ESPAÑOLA DE DERECHAS AUTÓNOMAS (CEDA) youth movement. The Right had failed to wrest power from the Left by legal means and, in that 'ominous spring' of 1936, the Falange attracted a degree of popular support it had never before experienced.

On 14 March 1936, the Falange was outlawed by the Popular Front government and José Antonio was arrested and imprisoned. The movement's expansion continued, however, and the Falange seemed capable of developing into a mass movement. Its numbers were boosted still further by the Nationalist uprising of July 1936, but the generals' revolt was not a political success for the Falange. Although Falangist leaders, including José Antonio, had been involved in plotting the revolt, the party failed to win any concessions or guarantees from the army conspirators. Despite the substantial contribution made by the Falangist militias to his war effort, General FRANCISCO FRANCO seized control of the party in April 1937, and forced it to merge with the Carlists (*see* CARLISM) to become the Falange Española Tradicionalista y de las JONS, the state party or 'Movement' of the new Francoist regime.

Franco's castration of the Falange was made simpler by the fact that José Antonio had met his death in front of a Republican firing squad in November 1936. Other Falangist leaders who resisted Franco's plans, including Manuel Hedilla (1902–1970) the last independent leader of the party, were imprisoned. However, José Antonio's execution turned him into the Nationalists' official martyr. After the war his body was brought back from the Alicante gaol in which he died to be buried in state in the Valley of the Fallen, Franco's mausoleum and monument to the Nationalist dead of the Civil War. José Antonio's writings were prescribed reading for all schoolchildren and his name headed the lists of the dead put up on the outside walls of churches throughout Spain. The family connection with the Falange was continued by his sister Pilar, head of the Women's Section. With an estimated 580,000 members by 1939, the Women's Section was extremely successful in mobilizing women during the Civil War and it continued its work after 1939, particularly in the fields of welfare and education.

However, in spite of the continuing institutional existence of the Falange under Franco, it was a movement devoid of content. The new dictator had borrowed the Falangist trappings of blue shirt, fascist salute, and yoked arrows emblem but these could not disguise the fact that the only role for Falangists in the new state was that of Francoist bureaucrats, servants of the regime they had helped to create. After the defeat of the AXIS powers in the Second World War, the Falange became ever more marginal within Spanish politics as Franco sought to distance himself from his erstwhile fascist allies. *See also* FRANCO; SPANISH CIVIL WAR.

S. Payne, *Falange: A History of Spanish Fascism* (1961)
S. Ellwood, *Spanish Fascism in the Franco Era* (1987)

**Falkenhayn, Erich von** (1861–1922). German General. He trained as a professional soldier; served in China and achieved rapid promotion. Falkenhayn defended the officer corps prior to 1914 against criticism in the Reichstag and was Prussian war minister, 1913–15. He replaced the younger Moltke as Chief of Staff on 14 September 1914 following the failure of the SCHLIEFFEN PLAN, and it was he who ordered the drive to the sea in September-October 1914 and mounted costly offensives at Ypres in October-November. He believed that the decisive struggle must take place on the WESTERN FRONT, but was forced to remain on the defensive in 1915 because of successes in the East. He planned the VERDUN offensive of February 1916 as part of a deliberate policy of attrition, but his plan was frustrated by the BRUSILOV OFFENSIVE in the East and the opening of the SOMME offensive in the West, as well as by stubborn French resistance. His critics secured his replacement by HINDENBURG on 29 August 1916. From September he commanded the German forces against Romania, securing a complete victory and occupying Bucharest by December. He later served in Palestine, but was replaced in February 1918. He ended the war on the Eastern front in Lithuania, serving until February 1919. He retired from the army in June 1919. *See also* FIRST WORLD WAR.

**Falklands War.** The Falkland Islands in the South Atlantic have been a cause of dispute between Britain and Argentina for a number of years, Argentina maintaining a long-standing claim to the islands, which it calls the Malvinas. On 2 April 1982 the Argentine dictatorship led by General Galtieri launched a successful invasion of the islands, forcing the small garrison to surrender. Argentine forces also seized the island of South Georgia. On 5 April a British Task Force set sail to recapture the Falklands and on 7 April Britain declared an exclusion zone of 200 miles around the islands. Attempts to resolve the conflict by diplomatic means proved unavailing and on 25 April South Georgia was recaptured and air attacks began on the Argentine garrison on the Falklands a week later. On 2 May the Argentine cruiser *Belgrano* was sunk by a British nuclear submarine with heavy loss of life, followed two days later by the crippling of the British cruiser *Sheffield* (and its eventual sinking) by an Argentine air-launched Exocet missile. These actions ended whatever hopes of a negotiated settlement remained, although subsequent investigation suggested that the hopes for peace were already faint. On 21 May British troops went ashore at San Carlos Bay on East Falkland and took Darwin and Goose Green by the end of May after some sharp military engagements. In air attacks by the Argentine two British frigates, *Ardent* and *Antelope*, were lost in San Carlos Bay, and a major blow was delivered to military operations by the sinking of the supply ship

*Atlantic Conveyor* by an Exocet missile, delaying the assault on the major Argentine garrison at Port Stanley. An attack delivered on 11–14 June forced the surrender of the Argentine forces and the return of the islands to British control. The conflict cost 255 British lives and 720 Argentinian. Initially the seizure of the islands threatened considerable embarrassment to Mrs THATCHER's government, it being widely interpreted that cost-cutting and the withdrawal of a survey ship, the *Endurance*, from the area had transmitted the wrong signal to the Argentine government. It prompted a display of unanimous feeling in the House of Commons that the islands and their 1,800 settlers should be defended from aggression, and obliged the resignation of the Foreign Secretary, Lord Carrington. But Mrs Thatcher's conduct of the war enormously enhanced her status, transforming a weak position in the opinion polls to one of great strength once victory was obtained. The return of the Task Force produced scenes of popular rejoicing and patriotic sentiment unknown since the end of the Second World War. Britain's victory, while undoubtedly owing much to the professionalism of the British armed forces against largely conscript opponents (apart, that is, from the Argentine airforce), was also dependent on the strong diplomatic and logistical support of the United States. The Argentine dictatorship had few friends and quickly collapsed after defeat, but Britain's success was only narrowly achieved. One further consequence was the decision to build a large modern airstrip on the Falklands and to maintain a permanent garrison capable of reinforcement in time of emergency. No concessions to talks about the sovereignty of the islands was countenanced after 1982 and diplomatic relations between Britain and Argentina were only re-established in 1989. The legacy of heavy defence costs in maintaining the islands – the 'Falklands factor' – remains.

S. Jenkins and M. Hastings. *The Battle for the Falklands* (1983)
L. Freedman and V. Gamba-Stonehouse. *Signals of War: The Falklands Conflict of 1982* (1990)

**Fasci di Combattimento.** The earliest organization of the Italian fascist movement. The first *fascio* was formed in Milan on 23

March 1919 by MUSSOLINI, composed of various socialists, nationalists and war veterans. The original movement soon spread to 70 other towns and cities, providing a focus for those who felt that some form of action was necessary to express their discontent at the *status quo*. They attacked the headquarters of the socialist daily *Avanti!* and harassed socialists, but had no precise programme. Their support fell back by the end of 1919 but expanded dramatically in 1920–21, acting as opponents of socialists and trade unionists in the great strike wave which swept Italy. By December 1921 there were 830 *fasci* with almost 250,000 members. Expanding into the countryside they countered the socialist leagues backed by landowners and the more prosperous peasants. They developed into more structured organizations with armed squads – *squadristi* – for raids on opponents and street fighting. Local *fasci* developed their own emphases out of particular regional and municipal issues. When the movement was transformed into a political party in autumn 1921 with an organization and programme, Mussolini as *Duce* of the fascist movement attempted to curtail their independence. They provided the backbone of his provincial control in the run-up to the MARCH ON ROME in October 1922 but after his assumption of power he was concerned to bring them under full control. As the fascist dictatorship was established they were increasingly brought into the state administration and bureaucratized, playing little role thereafter.

A. Lyttleton, *The Seizure of Power* (1973)

**Fascist Party, Italian** (Partito Nazionale Fascista; PNF). The development of the FASCI DI COMBATTIMENTO in 1920–21 into a mass movement almost 250,000 strong and MUSSOLINI's desire to harness its energies in the political arena led him to consider forming a more organized structure which he could control more effectively. The party was approved at the Rome National Congress in November 1921, organized with a Central Committee and *Direzione* elected by the national congress. Local federations and *fasci* were directed to follow the political and administrative policies laid down by the central party organs, with locally elected officials. The creation of a Fascist Grand Council in December 1922 supplanted the elected party *Direzione*, which was finally abolished in May 1923 and replaced by an executive committee. Tensions between central organization and provincial independence continued to elude resolution. In October 1923 the executive was replaced by a new National Directorate, increasingly under Mussolini's control. Reliance on provincial support in the MATTEOTI CRISIS set back attempts to control local bosses, but from 1925 the party was increasingly centralized and disciplined by the general secretary Roberto Farinacci. Local *fasci* were dissolved and reconstituted, local secretaries replaced, and many members purged. Under Augusto Turati from March 1926, the party was increasingly centralized and integrated into the fascist state. A new party statute in October 1926 placed the *Duce* as the head of the party hierarchy and established the Fascist Grand Council as the supreme organ of fascism. The Grand Council held the appointment of party secretary and of the National Directorate, the party secretary appointed provincial secretaries and they, in turn, the local secretaries of the *fasci*. Local fascist newspapers were purged and an official press established as well as a party newsheet carrying official directives. A high turnover of membership saw extremists and dissidents removed and an influx of those who wished to demonstrate loyalty to the regime. Under Giovanni Giurati as secretary from September 1930 further large-scale expulsions followed, though many were reinstated when Giurati was replaced in December 1931 by Achille Starace. The party rolls were closed from 1927, membership being only through fascist youth organizations. Under Starace, however, a mass membership was sought and its rolls reopened in 1932. Membership rose from just over 1 million in October 1932 to over 2.5 million in 1939. Membership was made virtually obligatory for anyone seeking public employment after 1932–3. By the outbreak of war the party had become an increasingly depoliticized and dependent part of a centralized state bureaucracy, losing most of the provincial radicalism which had made it a force in the rise of Mussolini to power.

D. Germino, *The Italian Fascist Party in Power: A Study in Totalitarian Rule* (1959)

A. Lyttleton, *The Seizure of Power* (1973)

**Fatherland Front, Bulgarian.** An organization originally formed by the communist leader, GEORGI DIMITROV in 1942 as an antifascist coalition of communists, socialists and agrarians. It collaborated with the Soviet Union following its declaration of war on Bulgaria on 5 September 1944, staging a bloodless coup and forming a Fatherland Front government on 9 September. With the backing of the Soviet forces, the COMMUNIST PARTY filled the most important posts in government, established Fatherland Front local committees and a People's Militia, and began a wholesale purge of opponents. A People's Republic was proclaimed on 15 September 1946. At a general election on 27 October 1946 the Fatherland Front composed of Communist, Agrarian, Socialist and Sveno Parties obtained 364 seats, 277 of which went to the Communists, and 101 to the opposition. On 26 August 1947 the oppositionist Agrarian Union was dissolved and its leader Nikola Petrov hanged on 23 September. The Socialist Party merged into the Communist Party in August 1948 and the Sveno Party dissolved itself. The Fatherland Front became in 1948 a non-political mass organization containing two political parties, the BULGARIAN COMMUNIST PARTY and the Bulgarian People's Agrarian Union, in which the Communist Party is the dominant partner. The Front had nearly 3,770,000 individual members in 1984. It provided the sole list of candidates for elections drawn from the Communist Party and the People's Agrarian Union until 1989.

**Fatherland Party.** See VATERLANDSPARTEI.

**FDP.** Freie Demokratische Partei. See FREE DEMOCRATIC PARTY, GERMAN.

**Ferdinand I, of Bulgaria** (1861–1948). Ruler of Bulgaria, 7 July 1887 to 4 October 1918. A son of the German house of Saxe-Coburg, he was chosen by the Bulgarian National Assembly following the overthrow of the previous ruler, Prince Alexander of Battenberg. Following the removal of the leading politician Stambulov in 1895 he dominated Bulgarian politics, playing off rival political groups and pursuing an expansionist policy. In 1908 he shed the last vestiges of Turkish rule and substituted the

title 'Tsar' for that of 'Prince'. Leading the country into the Balkan Wars of 1912–13 with the aim of acquiring the Turkish province of MACEDONIA, he was forced to accept an inconclusive peace at Bucharest in August 1913. In September 1915 he agreed to bring Bulgaria into the FIRST WORLD WAR on the side of the CENTRAL POWERS in return for extensive territorial concessions, including Macedonia, in spite of the fierce opposition of the Agrarian Party leader, STAMBOLISKI. Facing a deteriorating military situation and growing domestic unrest, he attempted to reshuffle the political leadership by replacing the pro-Austrian VASIL RADOSLAVOV with Alexander Malinov in June 1918, but would not permit armistice negotiations. Following the collapse of the Macedonian front in September he faced a mutiny in the army and was forced to call on Stamboliski for assistance; he eventually had to use German troops to save his throne. A few days later he was forced to abdicate and go into exile as a condition of the victorious Entente powers. He was known as the 'Richelieu of the Balkans', but was less successful.

R. J. Crampton, *A History of Modern Bulgaria* (1987)

**Ferdinand I, of Romania** (1865–1927). King of Romania, 11 October 1914 to 21 July 1927. Born 24 August 1865, a member of the Swabian branch of the HOHENZOLLERN family and a cousin of WILHELM II. The nephew of the childless King Carol of Romania (1839–1914), he was adopted by him and declared heir presumptive. Thoroughly Germanized through his education at Tübingen and Leipzig and his service in the German army, he was married to a granddaughter of Queen Victoria, the Princess Marie. With the pro-French sympathies of the Romanian élite, she provided a countervailing force to the king's pro-German leanings when he ascended the throne in October 1914. Under the guidance of the experienced Minister BRATIANU he pursued a policy of neutrality until August 1916, when he entered the war on the side of the Entente powers with the offer of substantial gains of territory from the Austro–Hungarian Empire. The initial campaigns proved a disaster, however, and by the winter of 1916–17 he was forced back to the north-east corner of his country, basing himself at Jassy. In order to rally the populace behind the war he pledged radical land reform and an extension of the franchise in April 1917, but the collapse of his Russian allies forced him to accept an armistice with the CENTRAL POWERS and a pro-German Premier. He avoided signing a treaty with them, however, and renewed hostilities the day before the armistice in the west on 10 November 1918. As a result, Ferdinand and Bratianu were able to lay claim to the territories promised in 1916. By the TREATY OF ST GERMAIN and the TREATY OF TRIANON Romania was more than doubled in size, Ferdinand and his wife being crowned monarchs of Greater Romania in October 1922. Increasingly conservative, Ferdinand granted only a limited land reform in 1922, but universal franchise for the Chamber of Deputies was introduced, and by the 1923 constitution the King's powers were defined as those of a constitutional monarch, sharing legislative power with the Chamber and Senate. In 1926 an electoral law awarded a party which obtained 40 per cent of the vote 50 per cent of the seats plus a proportionate share of the seats remaining, assuring the ruling party a majority. Ferdinand's eldest son, Carol (*see* CAROL II), a notorious playboy, was disinherited in 1925 and went to live in exile. As a result, Ferdinand was succeeded on his death in July 1927 by his grandson, the six-year old Michael, ruling through a Council of Regency. *See also* FIRST WORLD WAR.

D. S. Spector, *Romania at the Paris Peace Conference: A Study of the Diplomacy of Ioan Bratianu* (1962)
S. Fischer-Galati, *Twentieth Century Romania* (1976)

**Fianna Fail.** Irish political party founded by EAMONN DE VALERA in 1926. Largest Irish party which but for infrequent breaks (such as 1973–7; 1982–7) has been the party in government since 1932. It has a wide populist appeal, involving a mix of republicanism, welfare statism and deference to big business. Unity of the party was severely strained during the ULSTER CONFLICT from 1968 and the implication of members of the Fianna Fail government in 'gun-running' activities supporting the IRISH REPUBLICAN ARMY. However, with the expulsion of Neil Blayney and the temporary disgrace of CHARLES HAUGHEY, unity, and the prestige of the then leader JACK LYNCH, was restored. In 1977 it was surprisingly returned to office with a large majority, following a campaign mainly concerned with the credibility of Fianna Fail's expansive economic promises. The party returned to power with Charles Haughey as leader and Prime Minister from December 1979 until June 1981; he was again Prime Minister of Fianna Fail governments in 1982 (for nine months) and from 1987. With its Republican background there was some concern whether a Fianna Fail goverment would abide by the terms and conditions of the ANGLO–IRISH AGREEMENT reached with the British Government in November 1985 by the FINE GAEL Premier, GARRET FITZGERALD. In spite of somewhat tense relations with the British Government, particularly over the failure to achieve significant progress in the solution to the Northern Irish question, Fianna Fail has continued to support the agreement and its workings.

**Fifth Republic, French.** Created on 5 October 1958 following the call on DE GAULLE to assume power. De Gaulle's constitution gave the President far wider executive powers than had been the case under the THIRD REPUBLIC and FOURTH REPUBLIC. Under the Fifth Republic the President is head of the government as well as head of state: He can dissolve parliament, negotiate treaties and deal with emergencies without counter-signature; he appoints (rather than formally nominates) the Prime Minister; and he is indirectly elected for a seven-year term, but there is no bar to re-election. He may submit matters to the Constitutional Council for opinion, ask Parliament to reconsider bills, and give ruling on proposals to submit bills to referendum. Before acting outright in an emergency he must consult both executive and legislature, but he is not bound to follow their advice. Nor is he bound to accept the resignation of the government if the National Assembly has caused it to resign. The Constitutional Council is appointed for nine years, one-third of its members retiring every three years. The National Assembly now has 491 members directly elected for five years (474 from Metropolitan France) and neither the Prime Minister nor any of the cabinet is allowed to hold seats in it. The Council of the Republic continues as the Senate, and all bills go to it. The Senate has 305 members (287 from Metropolitan France), indirectly elected for nine years, one-third retiring every three years. The programme of the National Assembly is determined by the government, not by the house itself.

Having been elected President of the Republic in December 1958 and taking office on 8 January 1959, de Gaulle implemented his policies through prime ministers Debré (1959–62), Pompidou ('1962–68) and Couve de Murville (1968–9). His most decisive early acts were to grant independence to Algeria and suppressing the attempted coup by the ORGANISATION DE L'ARMÉE SECRÈTE (OAS). De Gaulle gave a distinctive stamp to French politics, aiming to assert French prestige in Europe and the world at large. He withdrew France from the NATO (see NORTH ATLANTIC TREATY ORGANISATION joint military command and built up France's independent nuclear forces, the *Force de Frappe*. His determination to preserve Franco–German dominance led to his twice blocking Britain's entry into the EUROPEAN ECONOMIC COMMUNITY (EEC).

In 1968 de Gaulle's government and the Fifth Republic itself was rocked by student riots and strikes. Although de Gaulle survived, he took the opportunity of defeat in a referendum on minor constitutional reforms of the Senate to resign on 28 April 1969. He was succeeded, after an interim presidency, by GEORGES POMPIDOU on 20 June 1969. Pompidou's presidency was marked by the consolidation of the Fifth Republic and successful negotiations for Britain's entry into the EEC. Following his death in April 1974 he was succeeded on 27 May by VALÉRY GISCARD D'ESTAING who defeated the socialist FRANÇOIS MITTERRAND. Seven years later with Giscard d'Estaing beset by scandals and growing economic problems, François Mitterrand was elected to the presidency, also securing an outright socialist majority government, although electoral reverses forced him to work for two years, 1986–8, with the conservative JACQUES CHIRAC in what was known as 'cohabitation'. In May 1988 Mitterrand was decisively re-elected President, defeating Chirac, followed by the election of a socialist government under Michel Rocard.

The Fifth Republic has proved a successful constitutional balance between a strong executive and a democratic Assembly. What was initially a system designed to suit de Gaulle's autocratic style of rule has proved capable of outlasting him under his successors.

P. M. Williams and M. Harrison, *Politics and Compromise: Politics and Society in de Gaulle's Republic* (1971)
J. Ardagh, *The New France* (1978)
D. Cook, *Charles de Gaulle* (1984)

**Final Solution.** *See* HOLOCAUST.

**Fine Gael.** Irish political party which succeeded CUMANN NA NGAEDHEAL in 1933. It was the party which supported the Anglo–Irish Treaty of December 1921 which brought to an end the revolutionary war at the price of a partitioned Ireland. As such, it was the party of the more conservative forces in society, the party of the bishops, farmers and businessmen. It has tended to maintain this self-image of itself and hence suffered by failing to create a base among the lower socio-economic groups. Nor has it gained compensation by achieving the support of the newer industrial élites. Suggestions of a more liberal outlook within the party occurred periodically, and its new leader, Dr GARRET FITZGERALD from 1977 suggested a widespread review of policy. Between 1973 and 1977 Fine Gael formed a coalition government with Labour but suffered disastrously in the 1977 election. It returned to power in June 1981 with Dr Fitzgerald as Prime Minister, and following a short interruption in 1982 (March–December) remained in power until 1987. During that period it attempted to tackle the serious economic problems facing the Irish government without outstanding success. A major achievement, however, was the signing of the ANGLO–IRISH AGREEMENT with Mrs Thatcher in November 1985. This was seen at the time as a far-sighted attempt to resolve the Northern Ireland crisis by simultaneously affirming the status of Northern Ireland as part of the United Kingdom until a majority of its population agreed otherwise and giving the southern Irish government a consultative role in Northern Irish affairs. Fine Gael lost power in the general election of 1987 largely on account of continuing economic difficulties. Shortly afterwards, on 11 March, Dr Fitzgerald resigned as leader of Fine Gael.

**First World War.** The immediate causes of the First World War arose from the assassination of the heir to the Austro–Hungarian throne, Archduke FRANCIS FERDINAND at Sarajevo in Bosnia on 28 June 1914 by GAVRILO PRINCIP, a pro-Slav terrorist enlisted by the BLACK HAND. The reaction of the Austro–Hungarian Empire in delivering an ultimatum to Serbia on 23 July and Serbia's rejection of one part of it on 25 July led Austria–Hungary to declare war on Serbia on 28 July. On 30 July Russia, which had pledged to support Serbia, ordered a general mobilization. On 31 July Germany demanded that Russia cease mobilization and when she did not do so declared war on Russia on 1 August. On 2 August Germany sent an ultimatum to Belgium demanding passage for her troops. The next day Germany declared war on France and began the invasion of Belgium. The same day Britain delivered an ultimatum to Germany to withdraw from Belgium, and when she did not do so Great Britain declared war on Germany on 4 August. On 5 August Austria–Hungary declared war on Russia; France declared war on Austria–Hungary on 10 August, and Britain declared war on Austria–Hungary two days later.

Operating according to a modified SCHLIEFFEN PLAN the German forces seized the Belgian forts and advanced into northern France to the Marne. This marked the furtherest point of German penetration of France, and between 5–11 September the first BATTLE OF THE MARNE halted the German advance with a successful counter-attack by General JOFFRE. The two opposing forces then executed outflanking manoeuvres known as the 'race to the sea' which left them facing each other from November in a trench line which stretched from the Channel coast to the Swiss frontier. Attempts by the French forces to take the offensive on the fronts in Lorraine, on the Sambre and the Aisne in August–September were decisively rebuffed. In the east, Russian troops entered East Prussia and

Galicia during August but were heavily defeated by the Germans at Tannenberg (26–29 August), losing 125,000 men. Just over a week later, HINDENBURG and LUDENDORFF attacked the Russians at the first battle of the Masurian Lakes (9–14 September), causing a Russian retreat and the loss of 145,000 men. Austria's attempts to crush Serbia were halted at the battle of Jadar (10–20 August) and again in early September and November until 2 December when Austrian forces occupied Belgrade. In early 1915 French assaults in the battle of Soissons (8–15 January) were halted, but in the east the Germans encircled another Russian army at the second battle of the Masurian Lakes.

As a result of Turkey having entered the war on the side of Germany in October 1914, there were attempts to force the DARDANELLES by a naval force which was recognized as a failure by mid-March. On 25 April 75,000 Australian, New Zealand, French and British troops were landed at Gallipoli in an attempt to knock Turkey out of the war and open up the supply route to Russia via the Straits and the Black Sea. The expedition met dogged Turkish resistance and suffered heavy casualties. British and French attacks on the WESTERN FRONT in 1915 achieved little success. At Neuve Chapelle (10–13 March) a British advance was halted with heavy casualties. A major German offensive, the Second Battle of Ypres (22 April–25 May 1915) was marked by the first use of poison gas, and cost both British and German armies almost 100,000 men before it was halted.

In the east, a joint Austro–Hungarian and German advance in May broke the Russian lines at Gorlice-Tarnow, taking 150,000 prisoners. A rapid follow-up took the advance deep into Russian territory by early September. Russia's losses included 151,000 killed, 683,000 wounded and 895,000 prisoners.

The war was widened in 1915. As well as the unsuccessful assault on Turkey via the Dardanelles, Germany commenced a submarine offensive on 18 February. The sinking of the liner *Lusitania* on 7 May 1915 off the coast of Ireland came close to bringing America into the war, leading to a limitation of the submarine campaign. In May Italy was induced to enter the war on the side of the Entente powers by the TREATY OF LONDON; she declared war on Austria–Hungary on 23 May and on Germany in 1916. In September Bulgaria came into the war on the side of the CENTRAL POWERS. Attention was focused on the Balkans at the latter part of 1915. An Anglo–French force landed in Salonika on 5 October in an attempt to open up an alternative front and shore up the resistance of the Serbian forces. A joint German, Austro–Hungarian and Bulgarian offensive on 6 October, however, began the final defeat of Serbia. Belgrade was taken on 9 October and the country overrun, losing 150,000 prisoners, only the Serbian army and King Peter escaping to regroup on the island of Corfu.

Late in 1915 the high commands were reshuffled amongst the Western Allies. General Joffre became French commander-in-chief on 3 December and HAIG took over the British forces on 19 December. 1916 opened with one of the largest offensives of the war. GENERAL ERICH VON FALKENHAYN (1861–1922) planned an offensive against the French armies at VERDUN in the deliberate attempt to wear down French manpower. The offensive opened on 21 February and in an epic struggle which lasted until July the French under PÉTAIN managed to hold on, with terrible casualties on both sides. Approximately 600,000 men were killed in the battle, and by the time French troops had moved onto the offensive in the autumn to regain ground lost, the French losses in dead and wounded had reached half a million and German losses were only a little less. The German Verdun offensive had to be slowed because of the opening of an Anglo–French offensive on the SOMME. The Somme battle began on 1 July 1916 with the largest artillery bombardment seen so far in the war. The result was a disaster: 57,000 British casualties were lost on the first day, none of the expected objectives was taken, and the hoped-for breakthrough of the German lines was not achieved. The battle dragged on into the autumn, claiming over 1 million casualties. In the east, the Somme was matched by the offensive led by BRUSILOV. For a few weeks from 4 June, the Russian forces smashed through the Austro–Hungarian lines south of the Pripet Marshes, causing huge losses. The momentum, however, could not be sus-

tained, and by September the Russian forces were in retreat, virtually drained of their last reserves of manpower.

The war also continued to draw in new combatants. Italy extended its earlier declarations of war to Germany on 26 August and the next day Romania entered the war. 1916 also saw the long anticipated clash of the British and German battlefleets at Jutland on 31 May 1916. The result was inconclusive. Although the material losses of the British fleet were the greater – three capital ships and three cruisers to the German losses of one old battleship and four light cruisers – the German Navy had come close to destruction at the hands of the main British fleet. The German surface fleet never again challenged British control of the North Sea. Moreover, an extensive blockade maintained against Germany began to have serious consequences by 1917. Raw materials and food supplies began to become a factor in German calculations of how long the war could be allowed to continue. On 31 January 1917 Germany decided that she had to use every means to end the war and sought to inflict maximum damage on Britain by going over to a campaign of unrestricted submarine warfare. Although it was known that this would bring America into the war, it was believed that victory could be won before America would be able to affect the outcome.

America's declaration of war on 6 April offered the potential of a genuine superpower to assist the Entente powers with a population of 100,000 million and huge agricultural and industrial output. Her regular army, however, was tiny – smaller than Portugal's – and it was believed she could not put armies in the field for 15 months, by which time it was hoped that Germany would have forced Britain to her knees through starvation and fresh offensives with forces released from the east, where Russia was on the brink of revolution. The RUSSIAN REVOLUTION of March 1917 did not immediately bring Russia out of the war as her PROVISIONAL GOVERNMENT decided to fight on. Moreover, the U-boat offensive against shipping led to the adoption of effective counter-measures, the convoy system, which allowed the Allies to sustain the war effort in spite of heavy losses and the imposition of rationing.

Militarily, however, the immediate outlook for the Entente powers remained bleak. The French under a new commander-in-chief, Nivelle (1850–1925), launched an offensive in Champagne on 16 April 1917. The attacks failed, with over 150,000 casualties. Most seriously of all, the morale of the troops gave way and by May almost half of the French army regiments were affected by mutiny. Nivelle was replaced by Pétain on 15 May, who acted to restore discipline and improve conditions, the French army requiring a period of convalescence before it could take the offensive again on a large scale. Undaunted by the Somme disaster, Haig placed his faith in a new offensive in Flanders, known as the Third Battle of Ypres. Preceded by another huge barrage the offensive moved off in the Ypres salient on 1 July. Torrential rain and strong German resistance blunted the attack. The battle, popularly called Passchendaele from the name of one of the villages cited as an objective was nonetheless persisted in. By the time it was called off in November the British had lost 324,000 casualties, 50 per cent more than the defenders. Autumn also brought the BOLSHEVIK Revolution in Russia, LENIN's propaganda had already bred considerable disaffection by mid-summer, leading to a failed Russian offensive in July. By November Russia was effectively out of the war. Finally, to end a year of near-disasters the Italian armies were overrun by a joint German–Austrio–Hungarian offensive at CAPORETTO (24 October–12 November), losing 600,000 men, a half of them prisoners. Only reinforcements from the Western Front managed to hold the line from further defeat.

1918 opened with German preparations for a final offensive utilizing divisions from the Eastern Front, where Russia had made an armistice to achieve a knockout block. The German offensive launched on 21 March 1918 ripped a 50-mile-wide breach at the junction of the English and French armies. A follow-up attack on 9 April appeared to threaten Paris, but the Anglo–French lines just held. American troops were rushed into the line, a hastily arranged agreement gave FOCH overall control of the Western Front, and Haig issued his famous 'Backs to the Wall' order. Further German

attacks on 27 May and 15 July were contained, and by the latter month half a million Americans had arrived in France. On 18 July Foch counter-attacked in what became known as the second BATTLE OF THE MARNE, pushing the Germans back. On 8 August, the British attacked at Amiens with 456 of the new 'tanks', breaking the German line. The 8th was referred to by Ludendorff as 'the black day of the German army' as units crumbled without resistance. The Allies were now able to mount a series of offensives which, although costly, broke through the SIEGFRIED line in November. One by one the allies of the Germans and Austro–Hungarian forces were capitulating. A determined offensive in Palestine had forced Turkey to capitulate on 30 October, Austria–Hungary sought peace on 3 November and on 5 November Germany itself sought peace on the basis of the FOURTEEN POINTS. An armistice was signed on 11 November 1918.

The manpower losses were on a vast scale. Britain and her empire lost almost 1 million dead, 2 million wounded and 0.5 million prisoners; France lost almost 1.5 million dead, 4.25 million wounded and 0.5 million prisoners; Germany lost nearly 2 million dead, 4 million wounded, and over 1 million prisoners; Austria–Hungary lost 1 million dead, 2 million wounded and 1.75 millions prisoner; Russia has lost at least 2 million dead, 5 million wounded, and 2.5 million prisoners; Italy lost 0.5 million dead, almost 1 million wounded, and 0.5 million prisoners of war.

Various interpretations have been given the origins of war. Initial blame upon Germany as the aggressor, enshrined in the 'war guilt' clause in the TREATY OF VERSAILLES was supplanted by the view that the alliance system and the interlocking military plans of the great powers created an environment in which general war became almost certain. Tension between the alliance systems grew with repeated diplomatic crises and naval rivalry between Britain and Germany; in 1914 another Balkan crisis brought the two sets of alliances into conflict. From concentration on the alliance systems and the war plans of the great powers the Fischer thesis (*see* FISCHER CONTROVERSY) revived interest in Germany's role in destabilizing the European order for her own expansionist interests. Most recently of all, historians have sought in the wider climate and culture of Europe in 1914 reasons for the readiness with which the various countries went to war in 1914. It has always to be borne in mind that explanations for the outbreak of war in 1914 need to operate on more than one level, explaining how a conflict between Serbia and Austria–Hungary developed into a general European conflict in which each power had a different rationale for its participation.

Militarily, the generals of 1914 had been trained to think of mobile, offensive warfare. Instead, on the Western Front at least, the situation soon became one of stalemate in which barbed wire, machine guns and heavy artillery dominated the battlefield and produced casualties on an unprecedented scale. Only gradually did the generals find solutions to this situation in the West, developing new tactics and new mobile weapons of warfare such as tanks and aircraft to break the deadlock. As a result, earlier criticism of the military men has been somewhat modified in the light of the difficulties they faced in developing new forms of warfare by trial and error. It was seen too, that warfare became as industrialized conflict between mass armies of millions with the full mobilization of the 'home fronts' behind them: whole economies were geared to war production; the young, elderly and women were recruited to the factories and farms; and propaganda and the intellectual elites were drawn upon to bolster morale and vilify the enemy. The strain on the societies involved was immense, destroying three established empires, changing governments and precipitating the first communist revolution in the world. The map of Europe was permanently reshaped, bringing more new nations into existence than at any time before the period of decolonization.

Domestically, the effects of war were immensely varied, but have often been interpreted in terms which call upon the concept of the effects of 'total war' in encouraging the growth of liberal democratic institutions, including the extension of the franchise, women's suffrage, the growth of trade unions and socialist movements, and schemes of greater social wel-

fare and reconstruction. The immediate aftermath of war was a wave of revolutionary ferment seen in the GERMAN REVOLUTION, the rise of fascism in Italy, the BÉLA KUN regime in Hungary, and labour unrest in Italy, Britain and France. Increasing interest has also been shown in the permanent legacy in many states of government intervention in daily life, seen in the introduction of CONSCRIPTION in Britain, the use of rationing and regulations of every kind, and the development of greater homogeneity and conformity in many aspects of popular culture. Finally, the cultural legacy of the war was seen in the accentuation of the crisis of liberal rationalism already evident before 1914 and the rise of new ideologies, of which Marxist–Leninism and fascism were the most significant for the immediate future.

C. Falls, *The First World War* (1960)
J. Terraine, *The Western Front* (1964)
A. Marwick, *The Deluge: British Society and the First World War* (1965)
A. J. May, *The Passing of the Habsburg Monarchy* (2 vols, 1966)
N. Stone, *The Eastern Front* (1978)
J. J. Becker, *The Great War and the French People* (1983)
J. Joll, *The Origins of the First World War* (1985)
J. Kocka, *Facing Total War: German Society, 1914–18* (1985)
R. J. W. Evans and H. Pogge von Strandmann (eds), *The Coming of the First World War* (1988)

**Fischer Controversy.** A major historiographical debate which took place during the 1960s and 1970s concerning the origins and nature of German participation in the FIRST WORLD WAR. Its name derives from that of its instigator, the Hamburg historian Fritz Fischer (born 1908).

Until the early 1960s the outbreak of the First World War was usually seen by western non-Marxist historians as a consequence of the mismanagement of the July 1914 diplomatic crisis by statesmen overtaken by events and by the logic of the alliance systems and mobilization plans to which the European great powers adhered. Germany was seen as one great power among many, with clearly defined national interests which she was compelled to defend; and as bearing no specific responsibility for the outbreak of war. The publication of Fischer's *Griff nach der Weltmacht* in 1961 (Eng. trans: *Germany's Aims in the*

*First World War*, London, 1967) posed a fundamental challenge to this traditional interpretation.

Based on intensive study of a vast range of documents, Fischer's thesis highlighted the wide-ranging nature of German war aims as these developed after 1914. He argued that not only had the elites within German society and the German government supported massively annexationist war aims, but also that German policy during the July 1914 crisis had been informed by a determination to go to war in order to realize such goals, and thus bore primary responsibility for the outbreak of war in 1914. In the ensuing bitter debate, new documents came to light which seemed to demonstrate beyond all reasonable doubt the large measure of responsibility borne by German policy in the development of a regional conflict between the Austro–Hungarian Empire and Serbia into a general European war.

Fischer adopted a more radical position in his *Krieg der Illusionen*, published in 1967 (Eng. trans.: *War of Illusions*, London, 1975), in which he argued that the German government had deliberately sought war before 1914, possibly from 1911, and certainly from late 1912. War, Fischer argued, was intended to break the deadlock to which Germany's previous attempts to achieve world-power status (through the acquisition of colonies and greater overseas influence) had led: such a war might also overcome Germany's worsening economic situation, deteriorating military situation and domestic political impasse. This argument has found much less acceptance amongst historians than Fischer's initial thesis about German policy in July 1914 and the development of German war aims thereafter.

It is by no means clear that Germany's overseas imperialist policies had reached the dead-end suggested by Fischer. Nor is it clear that Fischer's assembly of aggressive imperialist and nationalist statements by leading industrialists, army officers, figures within the government and the Kaiser is beyond methodological reproach: Fischer barely asked *which* of these groups or individuals were forceful advocates of war as a solution to Germany's problems, or how far such views actually shaped German policy

before 1914. Finally, Fischer's exclusive concentration on developments within Germany seems to leave little room for the developing policies of the other great powers as dynamic factors in pre-war international relations. Whilst there is a consensus among historians that German policy was the principal factor contributing to the escalation of a local conflict into a general European war, Fischer's more radical theses that such policy was the logical furtherance of the German government's determination to bring about a general war, and that such a general war was intended to permit the realization of war aims which became clear after 1914, have now been generally rejected.

Fischer's work was a major stimulus to reach into the domestic political and social history of pre-war Wilhelmine Germany and, perhaps inevitably, the fruits of this research have largely undermined his more extravagant claims. Most historians are now inclined to seek the origins of the fateful policy pursued by the German government in July 1914 less in any carefully elaborated plan for the establishment of German hegemony in Europe, than in the fragmented decision-making processes characteristic of Imperial Germany and in a political structure in which the military and elite groups around the Kaiser possessed an influence which could not be countered by a Reich Chancellor with very limited constitutional authority. In this system, perceptions mattered as much as realities; and it was the belief that Germany's military and strategic situation could only deteriorate after 1914 that led the military elites to press for a preventative war, pressure that a politically weakened Reich Chancellor proved unable to resist. *See also* BETHMANN-HOLLWEG, THEOBALD VON.

J. A. Moses, *The Politics of Illusion: The Fischer Controversy in German Historiography* (1975)
W. J. Mommsen, 'Domestic Factors in German Foreign Policy before 1914', in J. J. Sheehan (ed.) *Imperial Germany* (1976)
F. Fischer, *From Kaiserreich to Third Reich* (1986)

**Fisher, John** (1841–1920). British naval leader. Fisher joined the navy in 1854 and served in the Crimean War. He had great energy and enthusiasm for new developments in naval warfare. As commander-in-chief in the Mediterranean 1899–1902, he introduced new techniques in training and tactics, and as First Sea Lord, 1904–10, he pushed through the creation of a British battlefleet of big-gun ships. The first, the *Dreadnought*, with ten 12-inch guns, was launched in 1906. He retired in 1910, but returned as First Sea Lord in October 1914. He resigned in 1915 after clashes with Churchill, the First Lord of the Admiralty, over the wisdom of the Dardanelles Expedition. The architect of the British navy which fought at Jutland, he was past his prime when the First World War broke out and was not as effective as many expected.

A. J. Marder, *From the Dreadnought to Scapa Flow*, vol. 1: *The Road to War, 1904–14* (1961)
R. F. Mackay, *Fisher of Kilverstone* (1973)
P. Kennedy, *The Rise of the Anglo–German Antagonism, 1980–1914* (1980)

**Fitzgerald, Garret** (1926–). Irish politician. Taoiseach (Prime Minister) of the Irish Republic, June 1981–March 1982 and December 1982–March 1987. Leader of the FINE GAEL party, 1977–87; served as Foreign Minister, 1973–77. Dr Fitzgerald attempted to modernize the appeal of his party, while tackling some of the serious economic problems facing the Irish state. His attempts to reform the law relating to divorce failed, at the cost of alienating much conservative support. A major achievement was the signing of the ANGLO–IRISH AGREEMENT with the British government in November 1985, but continuing economic difficulties contributed to Fitzgerald's defeat in the general election of early 1987. He resigned as leader of Fine Gael on 11 March 1987. He strove hard to improve Anglo–Irish relations from his election as Prime Minister in December 1982. He organized a summit meeting with Mrs THATCHER in November 1983, setting up an intergovernmental council which met 30 times before the conclusion of the Anglo–Irish Agreement. His efforts at improving this key element in Ireland's foreign relations were his major contribution, the problems of the Irish economy and a finely balanced political situation proving less tractable.

**Fiume** (Rijeka). Hungarian port on the Adriatic with predominantly Croatian and part Italian population. Claimed by both Italy and Yugoslavia in 1919. The port was seized on 12 September 1919 by the Italian adventurer D'ANNUNZIO. On 12 November 1920 the GIOLITTI government signed an agreement at Rapallo settling disputes with Yugoslavia and creating an independent state of Fiume. Following clashes between Fiuman troops and Italian troops, D'Annunzio was forced out of Fiume on 5 January 1921. In January 1924 most of Fiume was incorporated into Italy, with Yugoslavia retaining the small port of Susak. Following the Second World War it was ceded to Yugoslavia by the TREATIES OF PARIS.

**Five Year Plans, Soviet.** The formulation of a plan for economic development formed one of the distinctive features of the development of the Soviet economy and agriculture from the 1920s. The setting up of GOSPLAN in 1921, initially for the co-ordination of economic activities and the provision of national statistics, provided a mechanism for state planning which was shared with *Vesenka*, the state Council of National Economy. The SOVIET INDUSTRIALIZATION DEBATE permitted a consensus on the formulation of a long-term plan which began in 1927. On 8 June 1927 the Council of People's Commissars called for the creation of 'a united all-union plan' for the maximum utilization of resources for the purpose of industrializing, the country. Various planners and bodies were involved, but increasingly the 'teleological school', as it was called, which favoured heavy industry, gained the upper hand over the more scientific and cautious planners largely based in Gosplan. The triumph of the heavy industry side of the debate and the increasing pressures from Stalin to modernize the country quickly led to more and more ambitious targets being projected. In fact large-scale investment in heavy industry began even before the formal beginning of the first Five Year Plan in October 1928. Expansion of mining, railway construction and the Dnieper Dam project all began before 1928, with a doubling of investment in construction, mainly large industrial projects. The actual plan itself was only submitted to the 16th Party Congress in April 1929, six months after its start date. The planners had been persuaded and pressured into agreeing highly optimistic targets; these were then revised upwards twice, as well as the decision to achieve the Five Year Plan in four years, with official termination in December 1932. Stalin's almost manic pressure on the planners which included the arrest and trial of those failing to conform to his desire for more ambitious targets – produced in its finally amended form impossibly high target figures. Coal output was to be trebled, oil production quadrupled, and iron ore and pig iron output raised by even higher amounts.

Accompanied by the increasingly rapid pace of SOVIET COLLECTIVIZATION, Stalin made the crash industrialization of the Soviet Union the urgent priority, arguing in 1931 that Russia must catch up with the West or 'go under'. The effects were to produce ever more urgent demands for plans to be fulfilled and an almost warlike atmosphere of 'campaigns', 'fronts' and 'victories'. Gosplan produced the plans, but they were carried out by centralized ministries, the People's Commissariats, responsible for each branch of industry. Exemplary 'overfulfillment' of the target was the only sure way to escape punishment, and an increasingly reckless note entered the plan in its final stages. In spite of the distortions produced by frantic competition between different sectors to fulfil their targets and the sheer rate of the increases attempted, the first Five Year Plan did witness an increase in the output of major industrial goods of something of the order of 100 per cent, including the completion of the Dnieper Dam project and the development of new industrial centres in the Urals and Siberia. It was achieved, however, at the cost of huge suffering for many industrial workers and the effects of collectivization in agriculture. By the end of the first plan the number of industrial workers (including transport and construction) had doubled to 10 million. The first Five Year Plan was followed by a second (1933–7) with more modest but still high growth targets, but leaving a little more space for the recovery of some of the consumer sector almost reduced beyond endurance by 1932. A third plan was begun in 1938, but interrupted by the Second World War. In 1946 a fourth plan was begun which aimed to restore pre-war output by 1950. Five Year Plans, often with overenthusias-tic targets also figured prominently under Khrushchev and Brezhnev.

The adoption of Five Year Plans and the apparent success of the showpiece projects such as the Dnieper Dam had considerable effects in raising the prestige of Soviet-style 'planning', especially in the POPULAR FRONT era. It left a legacy of interest in central direction and state intervention which affected a wide range of democratic, socialist and even conservative economists, writers and politicians, and which was to have a powerful influence on the reconstructionist movements in Europe after 1945 when modified to suit more democratic societies. The Five Year Plan remained central to Soviet and Eastern European economic life after 1945, the 'command structure' and planned economy distinguishing Eastern European countries from the free market societies of the West. In recent years, the rigidity and inefficiences of central planning have been widely blamed for poorer levels of growth and chronic shortages apparently inseparable from the centrally planned economies, and a movement towards greater economic liberalism was a keynote of changes affecting much of eastern Europe by 1989.

A. Nove, *An Economic History of the USSR* (1969)
R. W. Davies, *The Industrialisation of the Soviet Union* (1980)

**Flexible Response.** A military doctrine adopted by the NORTH ATLANTIC TREATY ORGANISATION (NATO) from 1967 to replace MASSIVE RETALIATION as the response to a Soviet threat in Europe. The lack of credibility of massive retaliation and the fears of Europeans about the effects of using tactical nuclear weapons in the heart of Europe as weapons of first resort brought about a rethink of policy. Flexible response sought to extend the conventional phase of dealing with Soviet aggression in Europe by strengthening conventional forces, followed by a controlled escalation of force to be devised by NATO's Nuclear Planning Group, set up in 1965. The Nuclear Planning Group allowed for the first time the sharing of details about the US nuclear arsenal in Europe and introduced such ideas as the selective use of tactical nuclear weapons as a demonstration of intent, to be followed by a controlled nuclear escalation.

Planning also included consideration of the use of the so-called 'neutron bomb', primarily an anti-personnel nuclear device, but this concept was withdrawn after consideration in 1977–8, following a strong lobby by anti-nuclear groups. Flexible response still lies at the centre of NATO strategy to respond to a Soviet threat.

H. Schmidt. *Defence or Retaliation* (1957)
S. T. Cohen and W. R. Cleave, *Tactical Nuclear Weapons: An Examination of the Issues* (1978)

**Foch, Ferdinand** (1851–1929). French Marshal. Born at Tarbes in the Department of Hautes-Pyrenees, the son of a civil servant and devout Catholic, he served as a private soldier in 1870 and was commissioned into the artillery in 1873. He served mainly as a teacher and professor of strategy and tactics at the École de Guerre, 1895–1900, then commandant, 1907–11. His book *Principes de la guerre* (1903) stressed the importance of the need to establish psychological superiority over the opponent, 'the will to conquer', helping to reinforce the faith in the offensive which characterized French military thinking up to 1914 and into the early campaigns. He commanded a corps in the Battle of the Frontiers in 1914, and as JOFFRE's protégé led the French Ninth Army at the Marne. His signal 'My centre is giving way, my right is falling back, situation excellent, I am attacking' became famous, but after serving in Flanders and in command of the French armies on the Somme, he fell from favour with Joffre and was given an advisory post in December 1916. Returning as Chief of Staff to the Commander-in-Chief PÉTAIN in May 1917 he helped to shore up Italian resistance after the defeat at CAPARETTO in October 1917. As a result he was appointed Generalissimo of the Allied armies on the Western Front to deal with the German offensive of spring 1918, eventually extending his authority over the Allied armies in every theatre. He co-ordinated the defence which halted the German assault and then mounted the counter-offensive known as the Second Battle of the Marne in July 1918; this was continued in August–September with the offensives which brought about the end of the war. Created a Marshal of France in August 1918 and later, an honorary British Field Marshal, he exerted his enormous prestige at the PARIS PEACE CONFERENCE at Versailles to seek to impose harsh terms on Germany. Foch was France's most able soldier of the Great War, showing an ability to modify his offensive temperament with the lessons of the new style of warfare and diplomatic talents as co-ordinator of the Allied armies. His post-war forays into diplomacy earned him the opposition of CLEMENCEAU but he declined the opportunity to seek a political career, and went into honoured retirement.

J. C. King, *Foch versus Clemenceau: France and German Dismemberment, 1918–1919* (1960)
T. M. Hunter, *Marshal Foch: A Study in Leadership* (1961)
J. Marshall-Cornwall, *Foch as Military Commander* (1972)

**Foot, Michael** (1913–). British Labour politician and journalist. A follower and supporter of BEVAN, a member of the CAMPAIGN FOR NUCLEAR DISARMAMENT and a leading TRIBUNITE, he was elected leader of the LABOUR PARTY in succession to James Callaghan in November 1980. He saw the party split, with the defection of the SOCIAL DEMOCRATIC PARTY, and presided over a period of left-wing advance in the constituencies and in the party programme. Defeated by a crushing majority by Mrs THATCHER in June 1983, he stood down as leader shortly afterwards. A cultivated man of the Left, he was felt by many to lack the necessary qualities to revitalize the party after its defeat in 1979 but managed to limit the right-wing breakaway to a small minority of MPs.

P. Seyd, *The Rise and Fall of the Labour Left* (1987)
H. Pelling, *A Short History of the Labour Pa.ty* (8th edn, 1988)

**Force de Frappe.** Name for French nuclear forces, subsequently changed to '*force de dissuassion*', originating in the early 1950s when France sought to assert its independence from the US 'nuclear umbrella'. Greatly encouraged by DE GAULLE, France exploded her first nuclear device in 1960, and developed a force of Mirage 1VA bombers, land-based missiles, and missile carrying submarines. As a political statement of France's determination to retain her great power status, the force has been retained and upgraded under leaders of different political persuasions, notably by MIT-

TERAND. The effective part of the force now rests on the missile carrying submarines, although plans to replace the obsolete land-based missiles with a new mobile missile have been shelved as a result of the ending of the COLD WAR and the dissolution of the WARSAW PACT. *See also* NUCLEAR WEAPONS.

C. Chant and I. Hogg, *The Nuclear War File* (1983)

**Forces Françaises Libre.** *See* FREE FRENCH.

**Fourteen Points.** A peace programme put forward by President Woodrow Wilson to the US Congress on 8 January 1918 and accepted as a basis for an armistice by Germany and Austria–Hungary. The original points were: the renunciation of secret diplomacy; freedom of the seas; the removal of economic barriers between states; arms reductions; impartial settlement of colonial disputes; evacuation of Russia by Germany and her allies; restoration of Belgium; German withdrawal from France and the return of Alsace-Lorraine; readjustment of the Italian frontiers; autonomous development of nationalities in Austria–Hungary; evacuation of Romania, Serbia and Montenegro and guarantees of Serbian access to the sea; free passage through the Dardanelles and the self-determination of minorities in the Ottoman Empire; creation of an independent Poland with access to the sea; and the creation of a general association of states. With the amendment of the tenth point to read 'complete independence for the people of Austria–Hungary', Germany and Austria–Hungary accepted the fourteen points as the basis for the request for an armistice. Later many Germans argued that the PARIS PEACE CONFERENCE violated the principle of self-determination by preventing ANSCHLUSS between Germany and Austria. *See also* VERSAILLES, TREATY OF.

R. H. Ferrell, *Woodrow Wilson and World War I, 1917–1921* (1985)

**Fourth Republic, French.** On 21 October 1945 the provisional government led by DE GAULLE and the Committee of National Liberation was replaced by an elected Constituent Assembly with de Gaulle as Head of State and a Government of National Unity. The Assembly was to draft a new constitution which had to be submitted to a referendum within seven months. On 20

January 1946 de Gaulle resigned, claiming that the work of reconstruction was over, but exasperated at the petty squabbling of the parties over the new constitution. When the draft was rejected in May 1946 by 1 million votes, de Gaulle came out openly in favour of a strong presidential system, but growing concern about the prolongation of uncertainty led to the acceptance of the constitution on 13 October by a similar margin to its earlier defeat, but with one-third of the voters abstaining. The new constitution came into force on 24 December 1946. It was closely modelled on that of the THIRD REPUBLIC. The Senate was replaced by the Council of the Republic as a purely advisory body, with the Chamber of the National Assembly as the legislative body. The executive had limited power to dissolve parliament, and popular sovereignty was invested in the referendum. The position of the President was similar to that under the Third Republic, except that the President of the Council of Ministers (Prime Minister) had taken over some of his powers, principally the power to propose legislation to parliament and to issue edicts to supplement the law. The programme of the cabinet had to be approved by public vote by an absolute majority of the National Assembly before the Council of Ministers could be appointed. Once appointed they were responsible to the Assembly but not to the Council of the Republic. The Prime Minister in theory had considerable powers: he assured the execution of all national laws, directed the armed forces and appointed most civil and military officials. In practice, however, he spent much of his time trying to maintain a cohesive executive when no one party was ever strong enough to govern alone.

The Fourth Republic had more than 20 administrations in its 11-year existence. New alignments of political forces meant that the Gaullists (*see* GAULLISM), the SOCIALIST PARTY and the COMMUNIST PARTY were the strongest forces, with the Catholic MOUVEMENT REPUBLICAIN POPULAIRE (MRP) and the RADICAL PARTY as smaller groupings. Internally the Republic saw considerable strides in the economic sphere, with the assistance of the MARSHALL PLAN and strong centralized planning, France also embarked on the European economic co-operation which led to the formation of the EUROPEAN ECONOMIC COMMUNITY (EEC). The political climate, however, was dominated by the INDO-CHINESE WAR, terminated in 1954, and the ALGERIAN WAR. Major political figures such as MENDÉS-FRANCE and MOLLET were unable to negotiate the treacherous cross-currents of unstable party alliances and the running sore of the Algerian conflict. It was the revolt of the Algerian settlers in May 1958 which led the President, René Coty (1882–1962), to call upon General de Gaulle to lead the Government and institute a new constitution for what became the FIFTH REPUBLIC.

P. M. Williams, *Crisis and Compromise: Politics in the Fourth Republic* (1964)
J. F. McMillan, *Dreyfus to de Gaulle: Politics and Society in France, 1898–1969* (1985)
J.-P. Rioux, *The Fourth Republic* (1987)

**Four Year Plan.** Nazi economic plan aiming to make the German economy as self-sufficient as possible, especially in raw materials essential for the rearmament programme. The background to the plan, which was introduced in September 1936, was the growing shortage of strategic raw materials which had developed by the spring of 1936. From 1933 onwards, Germany's balance of payments position had deteriorated sharply: export prices had fallen whilst the price of imports had risen; and demand for imports had risen dramatically as a consequence of the job-creation and rearmament programmes introduced by the regime at a time when exporting had become more difficult in a protectionist world market. Moreover, imports of strategic raw materials and foodstuffs were in competition with one another for scarce foreign exchange credits – a conflict between 'guns' and 'butter'. Raising exports would have been one solution, but this could only be a medium- to long-term solution to a pressing problem which, in the short term, would inevitably have meant a curtailment of the rearmament programme. Increased self-sufficiency – especially in crucial areas such as oil, rubber and metals – was more attractive to the Nazi leadership. Prime movers behind the shift to a greater degree of industrial autarky were GÖRING, commander-in-chief of the *Luftwaffe* and (from April 1936) Reich Commissioner for

Raw Materials and the giant I. G. Farben chemicals combine, which sought a guaranteed market for the synthetic manufacture of oil and rubber which it had been developing since the 1920s. The Reich Minister of Economics and President of the *Reichsbank*, SCHACHT and the Reich Commissioner for Prices, Goerdeler, opposed the shift to autarky in state economic policy and were supported in this opposition by commerce and the more export-orientated sections of industry.

In August 1936 HITLER drafted a lengthy memorandum on Germany's economic and strategic situation, supporting a shift to greater autarky in strategic raw materials and declaring as his objective the readiness of the German armed forces and economy for war within four years. Göring presented the memorandum to the cabinet in early September and was charged with its implementation in mid-October 1936. Göring established a specific Four Year Plan Organization to oversee the realization of the plan, an organization which rapidly outflanked and subordinated the Ministries of Labour, Agriculture and Economics in the formulation and implementation of state economic policy. The plan witnessed the introduction of new – and tighter – controls on prices, wages, labour mobility and the financial markets. Yet, despite the fact that the plan absorbed about 50 per cent of total German industrial investment between 1936 and 1942, its achievements were modest. By 1939 the German economy was still dependent on imports for one-third of its raw materials requirements; and, although the synthetic production of fuel was a priority investment area within the plan, by 1939 synthetically produced fuel still covered only 18 per cent of demand.

W. Carr, *Arms, Autarky and Aggression: A Study in German Foreign Policy, 1933–1939* (2nd edn, 1979)
J. Noakes and G. Pridham (eds), *Nazism 1919–1945: A Documentary Reader*, vol.2 (1984)

**FPÖ.** *See* FREEDOM PARTY OF AUSTRIA.

**Francis Ferdinand** [Franz Ferdinand], **of Austria** (1863–1914). Archduke of Austria. He was the nephew of FRANCIS JOSEPH and from 1889 to 1914 heir to the Austro–Hungarian throne. Though thought to have favoured political concessions to the Slav minorities he was assassinated by GAVRILO PRINCIP at Sarajevo on 28 June 1914. Princip was supplied with weapons by the Serbian BLACK HAND organization and the assassination led to an Austrian ultimatum to Serbia on 23 July. Serbia's refusal to accept all the points in the ultimatum brought about an Austrian declaration of war on Serbia on 28 July which provoked a general European war by early August (*see* FIRST WORLD WAR).

J. Remak, *Sarajevo: The Story of a Political Murder* (1959)

**Francis Joseph** [Franz Joseph], **of Austria** (1830–1916). Austrian Emperor, who came to the throne in the revolutionary year 1848, and reigned until his death in 1916. The centralized, autocratic and conservative nature of the monarchy was established by Prime Minister Prince Felix von Schwarzenberg (1848–52). Yet the multinational Habsburg monarchy was becoming increasingly anachronistic in an age of industrial nation states, and the reign of Francis Joseph witnessed Austria's relative decline and incipient disintegration. After the defeat at Sadowa/Königgrätz (1866) Austria was excluded from Germany, and forced to compromise with Hungary over a new state structure. Francis Joseph was crowned King of Hungary in 1867, when that country gained a degree of autonomy in internal affairs. After Schwarzenberg's death in 1852 the Emperor attempted to rule Austria as a neo-absolutist monarch, and at the same time to change the nature of the monarchy as an institution, investing it with the disinterested authority of the neutral state. He was admired more for his devotion to his official duties than for his statesmanship. His death in 1916 deprived the Empire of an important symbol of unity.

O. Jászi, *The Dissolution of the Habsburg Monarchy* (1929)
A. J. May, *The Habsburg Monarchy, 1867–1914* (1960)

**Franco, Francisco** (1892–1975). Spanish general and dictator. Born at El Ferrol in Galicia to a naval family, he was educated at the Toledo Military Academy, 1907–10, and served in the army, 1910–27, seeing distinguished service in suppressing the 'RIF REVOLT' of Abd-el-Krim. In 1927 he became a full General and Principal of the Sara-

gossa Military Academy. Keeping clear of politics, he was nonetheless demoted in 1931 to a minor post in Corunna and then sent to the Balearic Islands in 1933. He then commanded forces which suppressed the ASTURIAS RISING in October 1934, using Moroccan troops and arousing bitter criticism for his severity. Appointed Chief of Staff by the CONFEDERACIÓN ESPAÑOLA DE DERECHAS AUTÓNOMAS (CEDA) Minister of War, Gil Robles, in May 1935, he was again demoted following the POPULAR FRONT victory in February 1936 and sent as Governor to the Canary Islands. At first he remained in the background amidst the growing number of plots being generated by the army and right-wing forces, but he gradually incorporated himself into the conspiracy which launched the revolt against the Republic on 18 July 1936 which began the SPANISH CIVIL WAR. Commanding the Army of Africa he began the conquest of southern Spain, and on 29 September was proclaimed Generalissimo and Head of State by a junta of officers at Salamanca. His position as head of the 'Nationalist' forces was aided by the deaths of potential rivals, such as General Sanjuro in July, one of the earlier plotters, and José Antonio, the leader of the FALANGE in November. The Carlist leader was exiled and in 1937 the other major military leader, General MOLA was killed in an air crash. Franco acted to unify his somewhat disparate forces, forcing a union of the Falange and the Carlists in April 1937 into the National Movement or Falange with himself as Caudillo. Franco portrayed himself as the champion of the traditional, Catholic Spain against the forces of communism. Once a swift victory had eluded him, he was able to mobilize greater and, ultimately, more unified support than his opponents. Although Franco had fascist supporters and his rhetoric reflected corporatist ideas, Franco emerged as the defender of the Church, big business and the landowners, as well as of a centralized Spanish state. He also skilfully manipulated foreign assistance which provided him with important technical assistance, $569 million worth of arms and over 10,000 German and Italian troops, while avoiding making major diplomatic or economic concessions either during the war or after it. Franco proved a cautious and methodical general during the war itself. Only after almost two years of fighting did he finally divide the great bloc of Republican territory with his 'drive to the sea' in March–April 1938 and Madrid held out until the final surrender. Franco's policy of unconditional surrender from 1937 left little room for compromise, and the final victory was accompanied by a toll of executions and killings which added at least 50,000 to the toll of deaths from the war. A fierce repression was maintained until 1942–3, when the first amnesties and pardons were granted, but still leaving thousands of former Republicans in Francoist gaols and thousands more in exile.

Franco proved remarkably successful in avoiding further entanglements with his Italian and German partners. He refused to enter any formal commitments, remaining neutral when the Second World War broke out. At his meeting with HITLER at Hendaye on the Franco–Spanish border on 23 October 1940, he refused to join an alliance in spite of the offer of Gibraltar. Franco pleaded Spain's war-ravaged economy and was also conscious of the threat of British seapower and Spain's dependence on access to the Anglo–American market for vital raw materials, such as oil, virtually unobtainable from the AXIS powers. He did, however, abandon neutrality for non-belligerency on 12 June 1940, endorsing the Axis, and two days later seized Tangier. Following the German invasion of Russia in June 1941, he also sent a division, the Blue Division, to fight for the Nazis on the Eastern Front. As a result Spain was subject to a partial Anglo–American blockade for most of the war, and having rejected the lure of loans from either Germany or Britain in 1939 was left to grapple with serious shortages and war damage unaided. Responding to the successes of the Allies, Franco pledged neutrality again in October 1943, gradually withdrawing his forces from Russia. Nonetheless, as the last major surviving Western dictator, Franco remained in diplomatic isolation in the immediate postwar years, only a commercial treaty with Argentina permitting some relief from the economic autarky pursued since the end of the Civil War.

Domestically Franco balanced the traditionalist and fascist elements of his supporters, refusing to countenance the return of the monarchy in his lifetime, and resisting the radicals on the right who sought a more thoroughgoing social revolution. A nationwide referendum in July 1947 confirmed him as life regent, the future King JUAN CARLOS beginning his education in 1948 under Franco's supervision. A Concordat with the papacy was signed in 1953, but the most important new dimension to Franco's regime was given by the COLD WAR and Franco's role as a staunch anti-communist. In 1950 the United States opened diplomatic relations, and in 1953 an agreement was signed for four US air and naval bases. Visits by JOHN FOSTER DULLES in 1955 and President EISENHOWER in 1959 brought the regime out of the cold, and in the latter year Franco opened the door to foreign investment. Increasingly Franco allowed himself to be influenced by younger technocrats who began the transformation of Spain's economy aided by the rise of a large tourist industry. Franco's regime remained at odds with clandestine left-wing groups, the regionalist movements of the BASQUES, and the Catalans (see CATALONIA) as well as with progressive sections of the clergy and the intelligentsia. His primary concern in his later years was to ensure a succession, leading on 22 July 1969 to his nomination of Prince Juan Carlos to succeed him. Juan Carlos assumed sovereign powers on 30 October 1975 during Franco's last illness; Franco died three weeks later on 20 November 1975.

Franco has remained a controversial figure with the legacy of bitterness engendered by his victory in the Civil War obscuring his assessment. Primarily a right-wing authoritarian in a Spanish tradition he stressed his desire for the unity of Spain; his regime, particularly in its early years, employed some of the elements of the CORPORATE STATE. He emphasized a disciplined, centralized state, suppressing regionalism, liberal democratic ideas, and any form of dissent whether from the Right or the Left. In social matters Franco did not move far beyond the conservative paternalism associated with Catholic social thinking. In the economic sphere there was no attempt to redistribute wealth or, initially, to resolve the chronic poverty of much of Spain's population. Significantly, however, Franco seems to have offered little ideological objection to the wave of foreign investment which began to revitalize Spain from the 1960s. Politically, he was prepared to subordinate ideology to the necessities of the situation, providing social order and the unity of Spain was guaranteed, his true priorities. Discussion of whether Franco was, in fact, a fascist remains a lively source of debate. Concentration upon Franco's rise to power has tended to obscure the most marked feature of the latter years of his rule, the transformation of Spain from one of the poorest and most rural countries in Europe in the 1930s to a relatively affluent, increasingly urban society by the time of Franco's death. A central issue remains whether Spain could have begun the process of modernization earlier under more democratic leadership, as seen in Italy. Also of interest is the linked question of the transition to democracy and the extent to which the peacefulness of the process was due to changes in Spanish politics and society in the latter years of Franco's rule.

R. Carr and J. P. Fusi, *Spain: Dictatorship to Democracy* (1979)

R. Carr, *Spain, 1808–1975* (rev. edn, 1982)

S. Payne, *The Franco Regime* (1987)

J. Fusi, *Franco: A Biography* (1987)


**Franco–Soviet Pact.** A non-aggression pact was signed between the Soviet Union and France in November 1933 as part of a wave of Soviet non-aggression pacts arranged by LITVINOV to bolster Soviet security. Further arrangements with France awaited Soviet entry into the LEAGUE OF NATIONS in 1934, and was followed by a mutual assistance pact signed on 2 May 1935. Both powers pledged to defend each other against unprovoked aggression. The French Foreign Minister from 7 June, PIERRE LAVAL, was not enthusiastic about the arrangement and its ratification was delayed until 1936. It was largely rendered ineffective by the absence of any military talks between the powers.

W. E. Scott, *Alliance against Hitler: The Origins of the Franco–Soviet Pact* (1962)

A. Adamthwaite, *France and the Coming of the Second World War* (1977)

R. Overy and A. Wheatcroft, *The Road to War* (1989)


**Free Corps.** *See* FREIKORPS.

**Free Democratic Party, German** (Freie Demokratische Partei; FDP). West German liberal party. Established in December 1948, the FDP emerged from liberal groupings which had formed in the three western zones of occupied Germany. Initially standing on the right of the political spectrum and containing strongly nationalistic elements, the FDP gained almost 12 per cent of the popular vote in the elections to the Federal Parliament (*Bundestag*) held in August 1949. Advocating classical liberal *laissez-faire* economic principles, championing the rights of the individual against the state in almost all spheres and opposing religious involvement in education, the FDP drew its support during the 1950s largely from middle-class Protestants, especially businessmen and professionals. A coalition partner of the CDU–CSU (*see* CHRISTIAN DEMOCRATIC UNION, GERMAN; CHRISTIAN SOCIAL UNION, GERMAN) from 1949 to 1956 and 1961 to 1966, it was only in the 1960s that the FDP came to occupy a more centrist position within West German politics. Entering a tentative coalition with the SDP (*see* SOCIAL DEMOCRATIC PARTY, GERMAN) under Chancellor BRANDT in 1969, the party remained the coalition partner of the SDP until 1982. The right wing of the FDP nevertheless, remained sceptical about Brandt's OSTPOLITIK, and its advocacy of government expenditure cuts after the 1973–4 oil shock often strained the party's coalition with the SDP supporting Chancellor SCHMIDT's government. Its switch of coalition partners to the CDU–CSU brought down Schmidt's government in October 1982: thereafter it supported the government of Chancellor KOHL. Uncertain electoral support has often threatened the extinction of FDP representation in the *Bundestag*: despite its precarious position, however, it has wielded considerable influence on the policies pursued by successive West German governments. *See also* GENSCHER, HANS-DIETRICH.

H. A. Turner, *The Two Germanies since 1945* (1987)


**Freedom Party of Austria** (FPÖ). The Austrian FPÖ is in part the successor to prewar German Nationalist parties, and more immediately to the League of Independents (VdU), which drew on the support of former Nazis, and was formed to contest the elections of 1949 despite a post-war ban on German National parties. The FPÖ itself was established in 1956 by the merger of the VdU with the extreme right Free Party, and was led by former Nazis until 1975. The party is structured on a federal basis, and regional parties enjoy a great deal of autonomy. There is particular tension between a more liberal Viennese wing, and a more nationalist wing based largely in Carinthia. The party first came to power in 1983 as the junior coalition partner of the SPÖ. In 1986 the leader of the extreme right-wing Carinthian party was elected national leader, precipitating the break-up of the ruling SPÖ–FPÖ coalition and fresh elections in November of that year. Following the general election, in which the party doubled its share of the popular vote the party was again excluded from power by the formation of an SPÖ–ÖVP grand coalition. Nevertheless, it went on to win considerable gains in regional elections of 1989.

E. Riedlsperger. *The Lingering Shadow of Nazism: The Austrian Independent Party Movement since 1945* (1978)

**Free French.** The Forces Françaises Libre, made up of French troops, air and naval personnel who continued the fight against Nazi Germany after the fall of France in June 1940. In opposition to the VICHY GOVERNMENT established in France, DE GAULLE on 18 June 1940 called on the French to rally to him forming a Council for the Defence of the Empire, later the Comité National Français. Initially the Free French forces were small in numbers, only some 7,000 troops choosing to stay with de Gaulle in England after the armistice between Germany and France, many of them from the former French colonies. Small detachments of Free French forces fought with distinction in North Africa, Syria and elsewhere, and operated a small independent air force of two squadrons by early 1942. All these were dwarfed in size by the forces under the control of the Vichy regime and under the command overseas of Admiral DARLAN in North Africa and General Deutz in Syria. On 19 July 1942 the Free French forces were renamed the Forces Françaises Combatantes (Fighting French Forces, FFC) under the control of

the Free French Committee of Liberation. With the Anglo–American landings in North Africa on 8 November 1942, 'Operation Torch', and the German occupation of the FREE ZONE of southern France on 17 November in breach of the armistice agreement of June 1940, there was an increasing flow of recruits to the Free French forces, while Admiral Darlan put the French forces in North Africa at the disposal of the Allies. Following the assassination of Darlan on 24 December, General GIRAUD was made commander-in-chief of the military forces, but was forced by de Gaulle to accept his subordination to the Free French Committee of National Liberation. In the forces now commanded by Giraud, those who had originally rallied to de Gaulle formed only a minority. Supplied and re-equipped by the Americans, the Free French forces took part in the final battle of Tunis which defeated the AXIS forces in North Africa. The First French Army was then transferred to Italy to fight under the command of General Alphonse Juin (1888–1967), fighting at Monte Cassino and spearheading the drive on Rome in May 1944. Meanwhile, French forces in North Africa prepared for 'Operation Dragoon', the invasion of southern France, the landings taking place on 15 August under the command of General JEAN DE LATTRE DE TASSIGNY with units drawn from Juin's forces in Italy. Once engaged on French territory, the Free French forces were joined by over 100,000 French resistance fighters of the Forces Françaises de l'Interieur (FFI). For de Gaulle, the most important task was to ensure that the French forces under the command of the Committee of National Liberation were recognized as the legitimate government of France. General LECLERC's entry into Paris at the head of the Second French Armoured division on 25 August went some way to ensure this, but de Gaulle had still to fight to assert independence of the Allied command, threatening to remove de Lattre's forces from Eisenhower's control in January 1945 when he was ordered to withdraw from Strasbourg. The FFC continued to represent de Gaulle's claim to be the true representative of French liberation, and he ensured that it was engaged in the final campaigns against Germany in order to guarantee France's claims at the eventual settlement. Although not entirely successful, de Gaulle was able to ensure that it was the authority of his Committee, rather than the generals who had initially served Vichy, who determined France's post-war destiny.

M. R. D. Foot. *Resistance* (1978)
D. Cook. *Charles de Gaulle* (1984)

**Free Zone.** Unoccupied area south of the Loire allowed to France by the armistice of 22 June 1940 and the seat of the VICHY GOVERNMENT. France was permitted to keep 100,000 lightly armed troops in the zone for internal order. The area provided a refuge for millions of French citizens who wished to escape German occupation, but was policed by the Vichy regime to prevent resistance or clandestine arming. Nonetheless, the Free Zone provided the basis for resistance groups and contacts with the Allies in the build-up to the Anglo–American invasion of North Africa on 8 November 1942. On 17 November the German forces invaded the Free Zone in spite of protests from PÉTAIN that it was contrary to the armistice. The occupation of the Free Zone convinced many hitherto loyal to Vichy that France had little shred of real independence while the Nazis remained masters of Europe.

**Freie Demokratische Partei** (FDP). *See* FREE DEMOCRATIC PARTY, GERMAN.

*Freikorps* (Free Corps). German paramilitary units active during the early years of the WEIMAR REPUBLIC. The *Freikorps* were volunteer units composed of right-wing ex-army officers and NCOs, were often financed by industry and formed initially to quell left-wing challenges to the authority of the EBERT government during the winter of 1918–19. They participated in the bloody suppression of the uprising carried out in January 1919 by the SPARTACIST LEAGUE and one such unit was responsible for the murders of ROSA LUXEMBURG and KARL LIEBKNECHT. Under the terms of the TREATY OF VERSAILLES they were to be disbanded. Government attempts to implement this policy led to the abortive right-wing KAPP PUTSCH of March 1920. Other *Freikorps* units participated in the suppression of

workers' militias set up in the Ruhr in spring 1920; and in the fighting in May 1921 which preceded the partition of Upper Silesia. Disbanded in 1921–2, many of their former members joined illegal anti-republican successor organizations which were responsible for a number of political murders including that, in June 1922, of the Foreign Minister WALTER RATHENAU. *See also* GERMAN REVOLUTION; SA.

R. G. L. Waite, *Vanguard of Nazism: The Free Corps Movement* (1952)

**French, John** (1852–1925). British Field Marshal. He served in Egypt in 1884–5 and in the Boer War, where he demonstrated his skill as a cavalry commander. Promoted as a result of distinguished actions in South Africa, he was made Inspector-General then Chief of the General Staff. He resigned as a result of the CURRAGH INCIDENT, but was recalled to command the BRITISH EXPEDITIONARY FORCE (BEF) at the outbreak of the FIRST WORLD WAR. He commanded the British forces during the opening campaigns of the war on the WESTERN FRONT, including the battles at Mons and Le Cateau, which helped to stabilize the front and in the first battle of the Marne. His forces were almost destroyed in the first battle of Ypres in October–November 1914, the original BEF suffering almost 80 per cent casualties by early November. His attacks on Neuve Chapelle in March 1915 failed to defeat the enemy, and at the battle of Loos in October–November 1915 his forces lost 65,000 in an attempt to recapture territory lost to the Germans the previous autumn. Criticisms of these offensives and of his failures to co-operate effectively with the French commander JOFFRE led to his replacement on 17 December 1915 by HAIG. French was posted back to the United Kingdom as Commander-in-Chief of Home Forces. A difficult individual who was suspicious of the French, he was unable to utilize his skills as a cavalry commander in the conditions dominating warfare on the Western Front.

R. Holmes, *The Little Field Marshal: Sir John French* (1981)

**Front, National, French.** *See* LE PEN, JEAN MARIE.

# G

**Gaitskell, Hugh** (1906–63). British politician. He was Labour MP for Leeds, 1945–63; Chancellor of the Exchequer, 1950–51; the LABOUR PARTY leader, 1955–63. He is considered by some to be the outstanding representative of the social democratic tradition within the Labour Party. He clashed with Bevanites over Health Service charges, but later united with BEVAN to denounce EDEN's Suez policy; he sought unsuccessfully after the 1959 election defeat to persuade his party to drop socialist commitments to CLAUSE FOUR and waged bitter battle against the unilateralists in the party (*see* UNILATERALISM). Defeated at the 1960 Party Conference on the issue, he made a famous commitment to 'fight and fight again' to reverse the decision, which he achieved in 1961. His unexpected death in 1963 deprived him of the expected victory in the forthcoming general election. He was succeeded by HAROLD WILSON as leader. The followers of Gaitskell's policies were known as 'Gaitskellites'.

S. Haseler. *The Gaitskellites* (1969)
P. Williams. *Hugh Gaitskell* (1979)
H. Pelling. *A Short History of the Labour Party* (8th edn. 1985)

**Gallipoli.** *See* FIRST WORLD WAR.

**Gamelin, Maurice** (1872–1958). French general. He graduated from Saint-Cyr in 1893 and commissioned in the Algerian Tirailleurs. A colonel on General JOFFRE's staff in 1914, he was promoted Major-General in 1915 and by 1918 commanded a division. He suppressed the Druze rebellion in Syria, 1925–7. He became a full General in 1931 and Chief of the General Staff in 1938. On the outbreak of war he was simultaneously Allied Commander-In-Chief,

French Commander-in-Chief and Chief of Staff. Committed to the strategy of an advance into Belgium, the Dyle Plan or Plan 'D', to counter an anticipated German attack along the lines of the SCHLIEFFEN PLAN of 1914, while relying on the defences of the MAGINOT LINE elsewhere, Gamelin was completely outmanoeuvred by the German armoured thrust through the Ardennes. Gamelin was already distrusted by the Premier REYNAUD, who had tried to remove him on the eve of the German assault for his poor performance in the Norwegian campaign. He was finally replaced by General WEYGAND on 19 May. Gamelin has been criticized for being remote from the battle in the fortress of Vincennes, out of radio contact with his forces and inattentive to the crisis engulfing his armies.

G. P. M. Benoist-Mechin, *Sixty Days that Shook the West: The Fall of France* (trans., 1974)
A. Horne. *To Lose a Battle: France, 1940* (1979)

**Gauleiter.** Regional leaders of the NAZI PARTY during the WEIMAR REPUBLIC and THIRD REICH. With the refoundation of the Nazi Party after the abortive MUNICH PUTSCH, Germany was divided into regions (*Gaue*) led by prominent party activists with the support of the Munich leadership of the party. In 1928 a restructuring of the party organization resulted in the establishment of 35 *Gaue* corresponding to the electoral districts of the Weimar Republic. The main function of the *Gau* organization was propaganda and recruitment of party members. Following HITLER's appointment as Chancellor and the Nazi seizure of power in 1933, the role of the GAULEITER changed, many of them being appointed head of the administration in the individual federal states and Prussian provinces, thus promoting a fusion of Party and State office in practice if not in theory. Drawing largely from the veteran 'old fighters' of the Nazi Party, the *Gauleiter* jealously guarded their regional political and administrative power bases, often appealing to Hitler (to whom they enjoyed direct access) in an attempt to frustrate central government measures they deemed damaging to their authority or to the interests of their regions. Given the overlapping lines of authority characteristic of the Nazi political system, their capacity for asserting themselves, even at the expense, for example, of rational manpower allocation policies during the Second World War, proved considerable. Several *Gauleiter* were appointed as 'Reich Commissioners' in command of areas occupied by Germany after 1939.

M. Broszat. *The Hitler State* (1981)

**Gaulle, Charles de** (1890–1970). French soldier and statesman. Born at Lille, the son of a teacher, he was educated at Paris. He served as a Captain under PÉTAIN in the First World War, was wounded three times and cited for bravery, and spent the last two and a half years as a prisoner-of-war in Germany. He served as a member of the French military mission to Poland, 1919–20, then lectured at Saint-Cyr military academy. Appointed secretary to the National Defence Council, he published several military studies, including *Vers l'armée de metier* (Towards a Professional Army, 1934), arguing that France needed a highly specialized army using tanks and mechanized weapons to overcome her geographical and manpower weaknesses. His emphasis on a highly professionalized army earned him disfavour with the Minister of War, DALADIER, and he was moved from Paris to a tank command at Metz. After the outbreak of the war, he saw action leading a tank attack in May against the German advance. Following the appointment of REYNAUD as Prime Minister, de Gaulle was appointed Under-Secretary for War and made a Brigadier-General. As France crumbled he sought to organize resistance in the French colonies or the west of France, flying to London and proposing plans for an Anglo–French Union, but this was rejected by the French cabinet. He fled to London, and on 18 June broadcast a call

for Frenchmen to rally to him and carry on resistance. Though ordered to reappear before a military tribunal in France, he established a FREE FRENCH movement in London which was recognized by Britain as the French National Committee on 23 June. CHURCHILL guaranteed the restoration of French independence in return for the Free French forces continuing the war against Germany. Initially de Gaulle had only 7,000 troops and few supporters of any consequence as most Frenchmen accepted the authority of the VICHY GOVERNMENT. He rallied support in the remaining French colonies, but an attempt to retake Dakar in September 1940 failed when the Vichy forces refused to join him. The Anglo–American invasion of North Africa in November 1942 placed the largest body of French troops under his control, but only after he had circumvented an attempt to place them under the command of General GIRAUD. De Gaulle also established contacts with the resistance groups in France, eventually securing their allegiance to him as head of the French Committee of National Liberation. De Gaulle returned to Paris in August 1944, having landed a week after D-DAY and insisting that French troops under General LECLERC should liberate Paris.

After Liberation, de Gaulle asserted his authority as *de facto* head of an all-party provisional government, bringing collaborators to trial, nationalizing major public services, and giving French forces a share in the final defeat of Germany. During the arrangements for the creation of a new constitution, de Gaulle proposed setting up a constituent assembly which would have to seek a further mandate on its constitutional proposals. Once the constituent assembly was approved, de Gaulle resigned on 20 January 1946, dissillusioned by the quarrels between the parties. After the constitutional proposals were rejected at the referendum held on 5 May 1946, de Gaulle spoke out at Bayeux on 18 June in favour of a constitution with strong presidential powers – 'the Bayeux constitution'. Although a Gaullist Union was founded to support the Bayeux proposals, de Gaulle refused to re-enter politics until after the original constitution was passed, founding on 7 April 1947 the Rassemblement du

Peuple Français (RPF), a new, non-party movement designed to reform the constitution, combat communism and regenerate national life. In the autumn his movement set up an 'inter group' which all deputies except communists were invited to join, but both the SOCIALIST PARTY and the MOUVE-MENT REPUBLICAN POPULAIRE (MRP) forbade their members from adhering. Although the RPF soon had a large block of seats, it refused to form alliances, and de Gaulle remained aloof from politics, retiring from its leadership in 1953 to Colombey-les-deux-Eglises, and awaiting a call to power.

De Gaulle re-entered politics in May 1958 when the FOURTH REPUBLIC had reached a crisis in the ALGERIAN WAR and faced the threat of a military coup. He headed a government of national unity on 29 May with powers to frame a new constitution. The constitution for the FIFTH REPUBLIC was approved by referendum four months later and de Gaulle was elected President on 21 December 1958 with 78 per cent of the vote. Under the constitution he had strong executive powers and was backed by a strong Gaullist Party in the Assembly. He suppressed attempted coups by the soldiers and settlers in Algeria and survived several assassination attempts by the ORGANIZATION DE L'ARMÉE SECRÈTE (OAS). He initially maintained the war against the Algerian nationalists but authorized the peace negotiations at Évian (*see* ÉVIAN AGREEMENTS) which brought about Algerian independence in 1962. He pursued a vigorously independent line in foreign policy, developing a French nuclear deterrent, twice vetoing British applications to join the EUROPEAN ECONOMIC COMMUNITY (EEC) in 1963 and 1967, and exercising his veto against his EEC partners in 1965 following disagreements over the COMMON AGRICULTURAL POLICY. In July 1966 he withdrew French military forces from the NORTH ATLANTIC TREATY ORGANISATION (NATO) and had NATO installations removed from France by the following year. A consistent theme was his opposition to American influence, and he accordingly sought bilateral agreements with West Germany and the Soviet Union, enunciating the creation of a Europe 'from the Atlantic to the Urals'. De Gaulle's government pressed ahead with military and infrastructure

investment but was increasingly seen as autocratic and conservative. The worker and student protests of May–June 1968 shook the regime to its foundations, de Gaulle having to seek assurance that the army would support him if necessary in dealing with the situation. In the event, concessions quelled the protests, but de Gaulle chose a technical matter of defeat on constitutional reforms in April 1969 to resign. He retired to Colombey, where he died on 9 November 1970.

De Gaulle is the outstanding figure of recent French history, with enduring stature as France's wartime leader and for the economic and political transformation of France. A Catholic conservative by background, de Gaulle sought to regenerate France and to establish her prestige in the world. Unlike Pétain and the older generation of conservatives, he was a modernizer, prepared to work with anyone who shared his patriotic objectives. He recognized the need for concessions to the Left, securing communist support for the Free French in 1943 and bringing communists into the provisional government in 1944. Later, however, he was to denounce them as 'separatists' and see them as enemies of French national integrity. He pursued a vision of France as a strong, independent power, backed by nuclear weapons and a strong economy. His apparent anti-Americanism stemmed from his view of the erosion of European independence by the American superpower, which led to his suspicions of Britain as an 'Atlanticist' rather than European power. He also, however, resisted plans for European integration which would dilute French independence. He extricated France from the Algerian War with relatively little damage to his prestige and he was able to fashion a constitutional system in the Fifth Republic which has provided France with more stable government than either of its two predecessors. Under his leadership France grew to become one of the strongest economies in Europe and a major independent force in international affairs. Frequently arrogant and aloof, he became something of an anachronism in his last years. His political movements, however, did not easily outlive him. GAULLISM was too specifically his own creation, although several have taken on the mantle of being his successors, notably POMPIDOU and CHIRAC.

P. M. Williams and M. Harrison, *Politics and Compromise: Politics and Society in de Gaulle's Republic* (1971)
D. Cook, *Charles de Gaulle* (1984)
J. Lacoutre, *De Gaulle the Rebel, 1890–1944* (1990)

**Gaullism.** Conservative and nationalistic political movement in post-war France named after CHARLES DE GAULLE. The Gaullists have represented the major force of the Right in post-war French politics under a number of political labels. The earliest was the Gaullist Union of 1946 followed by de Gaulle's Rassemblement du Peuple Français (RPF), established as an anti-communist group in April 1947, and which obtained the largest number of seats in the 1951 elections, although de Gaulle refused to intervene directly in government. Following his return to power in May 1958 the Gaullists were grouped under the Union for the New Republic (UNR) and formed the largest single bloc of seats in the elections of 1958, 1962, 1967 and 1973. A successor body, the Union of Democrats for the Republic (UDR), was founded in 1967 in the hope of forming a vehicle for Gaullist policies which would outlive de Gaulle. It was succeeded in 1976 by the Rassemblement pour la Republique (RPR), following the split between the Gaullists, led by JACQUES CHIRAC and GISCARD D'ESTAING. The RPR, headed by Chirac, is now the major vehicle for Gaullist policies, although it no longer enjoys the electoral dominance it had under de Gaulle's leadership. The conservative forces since the 1970s have been split between a number of groupings, of which the RPR and the Union pour la Démocratie Française (UDF) have obtained the largest number of seats. Although prepared to co-operate as a non-socialist bloc, the parties of the right have shown differing emphases. Gaullist policies were identified with a centralized state, a powerful executive and an independent foreign policy with strong defences, reflecting the views of de Gaulle in the immediate aftermath of the Second World War and in the creation of the FIFTH REPUBLIC in 1958. They supported the strong central planning which characterized economic life and the somewhat authoritarian and autocratic style of

de Gaulle's presidency; in defence policy the creation of independent French nuclear forces, the Force de Frappe, and partial French withdrawal from NATO (*see* NORTH ATLANTIC TREATY ORGANISATION). In foreign policy it involved an independent line, especially in relation to the United States and resistance to the entry of Britain into the EUROPEAN ECONOMIC COMMUNITY as too committed to an 'Atlanticist' outlook. De Gaulle, in particular, combined these specific policies with a belief in the pursuit of the national interest over and above the petty squabblings of political parties. Following the resignation of de Gaulle, Gaullism became more identified with a broad, nationalistic conservatism. It has also seen the rise of competitors on the right, from JEAN-MARIE LE PEN's neo-fascist Front National (FN), founded in 1972, with strong anti-immigrant views and a strong defence policy, and from the moderate non-Gaullist conservative parties such as the UDF. In recent years one of the distinguishing features between the Gaullists and other conservatives has been the issue of European integration. Traditional Gaullist concern at preserving French independence has led them to be less enthusiastic about European union than Barre's UDF. Under Chirac, Gaullism also became associated with policies of 'privatization' and bowed to right-wing pressure to take a tougher stand on immigration. Rapid policy changes and the willingness of MITTERRAND to maintain France's nuclear forces have emptied the label 'Gaullism' of much distinct meaning.

P. M. Williams and M. Harrison, *Politics and Compromise: Politics and Society in de Gaulle's Republic* (1971)
M. Anderson, *Conservative Politics in France* (1974)
D. Cook, *Charles de Gaulle* (1984)

**Gdansk.** *See* DANZIG.

**GdVP.** Grossdeutsche Volkspartei. *See* GREATER GERMAN PEOPLE'S PARTY.

**Geddes Axe.** Economics in government expenditure, recommended by a committee appointed by LLOYD GEORGE in August 1921 and chaired by Sir Eric Geddes in response to pressure from right-wing members of the Liberal–Unionist coalition. They were charged with investigating the scale and nature of government spending. They reported in February 1922, proposing economies of £86 million, few of which were actually made, although the climate of economy did much to end the strong tide of spending on reconstructionist social welfare legislation on housing and education.

**General Strike, British.** The origins of the General Strike lay in a miners' strike. In 1924 the mine-owners agreed to pay rises, but could not give them after the return to the GOLD STANDARD and the fall of exports. BALDWIN set up a Royal Commission under Herbert Samuel, but its report was unfavourable to the miners, who, led by ARTHUR COOK, coined the Slogan 'Not a penny off the pay, not a second on the day'. A temporary government subsidy ran out on 1 May 1926, and all sides prepared for a trial of strength. The TRADES UNION CONGRESS (TUC) agreed to support the miners. When negotiations were broken off on 3 May because compositors stopped production of the *Daily Mail*, the General Strike began. The government, using the time gained by the Samuel Commission and the subsidy, was prepared, and troops, police and volunteers maintained essential services. Moderate union leaders became worried about the direction of the strike; led by J. H. Thomas they set up a Negotiating Committee to meet with Samuel and seek a solution. They accepted the cabinet offer, though many saw this as a surrender, and work was resumed on 12 May. The miners continued their strike for almost six months, but were eventually forced to accept wage cuts and longer hours. The General Strike occupies a central place in the record of defeats and setbacks to organized labour in the inter-war depression. Union membership and strike levels had already fallen from a peak in the years 1919–21, and the defeat of the General Strike accelerated the decline – strike figures and union membership falling to a low point in the early 1930s. The immediate result of the strike was a tightening of labour legislation in the Trades Disputes and Trades Union Act, outlawing general strikes and sympathetic strikes. The moderate TUC leaders such as BEVIN and Citrine increasingly turned their attention to support for the LABOUR PARTY to obtain their objectives.

P. Renshaw, *The General Strike* (1975)
G. A. Phillips, *The General Strike: The Politics of Industrial Conflict* (1976)
A. Clegg, *A History of British Trade Unions since 1889*, vol. 2: *1911–33* (1985)

**Geneva Agreements.** Agreements signed on 20–21 July 1954 which ended the first INDO-CHINESE WAR. They were negotiated at a meeting of the foreign ministers of the United States, Britain, France and the People's Republic of China, and followed the French defeat at Dien Bien Phu and the decision to abandon her colonial empire in Indo-China. Laos and Cambodia became independent states and Vietnam was divided between a communist North Vietnam and the Republic of South Vietnam along the 17th parallel. The agreements provided for an International Control Commission to supervise compliance with agreements and for all-Vietnam elections to take place to unify the country. South Vietnamese suspicions of communist intentions led them in July 1955 to refuse to participate in the elections, leading to the *de facto* separation of the two states and the beginnings of a communist guerrilla campaign from the North.

J. Cable, *The Geneva Conference of 1954 on Indochina* (1986)
A. Short, *The Origins of the Vietnam War* (1989)

**Genscher, Hans-Dietrich** (1927–). West German politician and Foreign Minister since 1974. Trained as a lawyer, Genscher was politically active in the Liberal Party (LPDP) in the Soviet occupation zone after 1945. Leaving East Germany for the FEDERAL REPUBLIC OF GERMANY in 1952, he joined the FREE DEMOCRATIC PARTY (FDP) and entered the West German parliament in 1965. In 1968 he became deputy chairman of the FDP. With the formation of the SPD–FDP coalition government under BRANDT in 1969, Genscher became Minister of the Interior. When SCHMIDT replaced Brandt, he appointed Genscher foreign minister. He was chairman of the FDP from 1974 to 1984. He survived severe criticism from within his own party after the FDP's withdrawal from the Schmidt government in September 1982 and has been Foreign Minister in the CDU/CSU–FDP coalition government of Chancellor KOHL since October 1982.

**George V, of Great Britain** (1865–1936). King-Emperor, reigned 1910 to January 1936. The second son of Edward VII and Queen Alexandra, he served in the navy, 1877–92. George married Princess May of Teck (1867–1953), later Queen Mary. Following the reign of Edward VII, he proved a dutiful and conscientious monarch, attempting to assist in the reconciliation of the HOME RULE crisis at a conference at Buckingham Palace in July 1914 and leading the nation during the First World War. He began the tradition of Christmas broadcasts on the BRITISH BROADCASTING CORPORATION to the country and the empire, bringing the monarchy into more direct contact with both than ever before. His involvement in politics was sometimes important: for example, in calling on BALDWIN to form a government in 1923 and persuading RAMSAY MACDONALD to remain as Prime Minister of a NATIONAL GOVERNMENT in August 1931. His Silver Jubilee in May 1935 was genuinely popular; he died on his Sandringham Estate in January 1936. He was succeeded by his eldest son, EDWARD VIII.

H. Nicholson. *King George V: His Life and Reign* (1952)
K. Rose. *George V* (1983)

**George VI, of Great Britain** (1895–1952). King-Emperor, reigned 11 December 1936 to 6 February 1952. The second son of GEORGE V and Queen Mary, he served in the Royal Navy, 1909–17, as Prince Albert, and later in the Royal Air Force. In 1923 he married Lady Elizabeth Bowes-Lyon, later Queen Elizabeth. Duke of York from 1920, he came to the throne as a result of the ABDICATION CRISIS of 1936 in which he took no personal part himself. Unlike his elder brother, EDWARD VIII, George had not been groomed for the throne and suffered from both a difficult stammer and shyness. During the Second World War his maintenance of a residence at Buckingham Palace during THE BLITZ, and visits to bombed areas earned him and his Queen great affection. Although conservative in temperament and outlook, he co-operated with the sweeping reforms of the post-war Labour governments under Attlee. He was succeeded by his daughter, ELIZABETH II. His widow, the Queen Mother, has continued

to provide a link with an older, war-time generation.

J. W. Wheeler-Bennett. *King George VI* (1958)
S. Bradford. *King George VI* (1989)

**George, David Lloyd** (1863–1945). British Liberal politician. From poor Welsh background, Lloyd George was Liberal MP for Caernarvon Boroughs, 1890–1945. He served as President of the Board of Trade, 1905–8; Chancellor of the Exchequer, 1908–15; Minister of Munitions, 1915–16; Secretary for War, 1916; and Prime Minister, 1916–22. He led the LIBERAL PARTY from 1926 to 1931. In 1945 he was created Earl Lloyd George. As Chancellor he proved a radical social reformer, and as Minister of Munitions and wartime Prime Minister was an efficient and dynamic administrator and leader. His decision to oust ASQUITH from the premiership in 1916, and then to continue the wartime coalition after the 1918 'COUPON' ELECTION did irreparable harm to the Liberal Party and damaged his reputation permanently. He pursued a vindictive policy towards Germany in the run-up to the 1918 election, but at the PARIS PEACE CONFERENCE he was concerned to moderate French demands in order to return to normal conditions as soon as possible. Having secured the surrender of the German fleet and the distribution of German colonies as MANDATES he felt he had secured most of Britain's interests. Even before the end of the war Lloyd George opened a reconstruction campaign to appease working-class discontent and fulfil his radical aspirations. Housing Acts were passed in 1919 (known as the Addison Acts after the Minister of Health, Dr Christopher Addison), education reform introduced and social insurance extended. These programmes were cut short by a round of economies in 1921, the GEDDES AXE. He brought the Irish situation to a conclusion by the ANGLO–IRISH TREATY of 1921, setting up the Irish Free State. The Conservatives who made up the majority of the coalition grew restive at his leadership, and he was forced to resign over the CHANAK CRISIS in 1922. Although he made a temporary truce with Asquith to fight the 1923 election, he retained his own organization and funds. In 1926 he assumed the leadership of a Liberal Party reduced to a mere 40 seats in the 1924 election. He showed considerate interest in policies to solve the problem of mass unemployment between the wars, producing the ORANGE BOOK in 1929, offering a programme of public works and government spending, which drew upon the ideas of JOHN MAYNARD KEYNES. He was still considered a possible contender for office in 1931, but was ill at the time of the crisis of the SECOND LABOUR GOVERNMENT. He continued to promote ideas for economic regeneration and expressed admiration for what HITLER had done in Germany. After 1939 he was considered for office in the War Cabinet, but felt himself too old to carry responsibilities. A remarkably energetic and dynamic politician, Lloyd George proved a very successful war leader. His dynamism and ambition, however, left him untrusted and in the political wilderness after 1922.

K. O. Morgan, *The Age of Lloyd George* (1971)
D. Grigg, *Lloyd George* (1973)
J. Campbell, *Lloyd George: The Goat in the Wilderness, 1922–1931* (1977)

**Georgia.** Area of the Russian empire prior to 1917 between the Black and Caspian Seas, latterly a constituent republic of the USSR. Although largely Orthodox Christians and of mixed ethnic origin, the Georgians have a strong sense of national identity. Following the RUSSIAN REVOLUTION a Georgian assembly was elected, and following the TREATY OF BREST-LITOVSK, Germany sought to stimulate national aspirations in the region and a short-lived independent Georgian Republic came into existence in 1918. With the defeat of Germany and the collapse of the southern White Russian forces in the RUSSIAN CIVIL WAR Georgia became part of the Transcaucasian Federated Republic with Armenia and Azerbaijan. With BERIA as general secretary of the Georgian Communist Party and head of the security apparatus, nationalist sentiment was fiercely suppressed. Georgia became a Union Republic in 1936, but in common with the BALTIC STATES demands for greater autonomy and even national independence emerged in the GORBACHEV era. Mass demonstrations in Tibilisi in early 1989 were brutally repressed, leaving several dead, amidst widespread accusations of the use of poison gas by Soviet troops. The dismissal

of local communist party bosses followed. The election of the nationalistic Zviad Gamsakhurdia as President in spring 1991 promoted virtual independence, confirmed after the failed Moscow coup in August when Georgia refused to join even the loosest association within the old Soviet Union. *See also* TRANSCAUCASIAN FEDERATED REPUBLIC; NATIONALITIES QUESTION, SOVIET.

A. Yarmohinski, *The Jews and Other Minor Nationalities under the Soviets* (1928)
K. D. Antadze, *Soviet Georgia* (1972)
Z. Avalishuili, *The Independence of Georgia in International Politics, 1918–1921* (1974)

**German Democratic Party.** *See* DDP.

**German Democratic Republic** (Deutsche Demokratische Republik; DDR). East German State formed in October 1949 from the Soviet post-1945 occupation zone (*see* GERMANY, ALLIED OCCUPATION OF) with its capital in East Berlin, the DDR's governmental structure is in theory governed by the constitution approved in May 1949 by a People's Council appointed by the People's Congress elected in the same month. The constitution closely paralleled that of the FEDERAL REPUBLIC OF GERMANY, guaranteeing fundamental civil liberties, the right to emigrate and the right to property. Embodying limited federalism, the constitution established a Chamber of States with restricted powers of veto. The centre-piece of the constitution, however, was the People's Chamber (*Volkskammer*), which had much greater powers than the West German *Bundestag* and was to be elected through a system of proportional representation at least every four years by all citizens aged 18 or over. The head of government was designated the Minister-President, to be elected by the People's Chamber and requiring a majority in that body. The head of state was a president elected every four years by a joint session of the People's Chamber and the Chamber of States. Only political parties which accepted democracy were to be allowed to function. With the establishment of the new state in 1949, it rapidly became apparent that real power was to lie not with the elected bodies set up by the constitution but rather with the communist-dominated SED (*see* SED), which, with Soviet support, had coerced the non-communist political parties into a coalition known as the National Front. Strengthened by the mass organizations under its control which were also represented in the National Front, the SED was able to determine the 'unity lists' of candidates placed before the electorate for approval or rejection. In all elections held after 1950 the electorate, which was discouraged from making use of the right to a secret ballot guaranteed by the 1949 constitution, endorsed such 'unity lists' with massive majorities. In 1952 a federal reorganization replacing the five states with 14 administrative districts subject to the control of the central government effectively eliminated the federal elements from the constitution. In 1954 the Council of Ministers (cabinet) was given powers to enact legislation when the People's Chamber was not sitting; and power was further concentrated by the creation of a small Presidium which assumed the powers of the Council of Ministers between its infrequent meetings. In 1963 the composition of the People's Chamber was frozen, with the SED and its mass organizations controlling 292 of the 500 seats. SED domination of government at all levels and of all spheres of public life outside the harrassed churches was consolidated during the 1950s. State control of all sectors of the economy was extended during the 1950s and 1960s. Throughout the period from 1949 to 1989 the DDR was to be the Soviet Union's staunchest ally in central and east–central Europe, joining COMECON in 1950 and the WARSAW PACT in 1955. Under WALTER ULBRICHT and ERICH HONECKER, civil liberties guaranteed by the 1949 constitution were widely disregarded as the state repressed all criticism of the dominant role of the SED in the DDR. In 1953 the armed forces were used to suppress a workers' uprising in Berlin (see EAST GERMAN WORKERS' UPRISING). The regime's attempts to prevent emigration from the DDR led to the erection of the BERLIN WALL in 1961, closing the last gap in the IRON CURTAIN. The population of the DDR was partly compensated for its loss of civil and political liberties by a steady rise in the standard of living, which, together with the omnipresence of agents of the state repressive apparatus, served to reduce popular protest against the regime. The dismantling of its

section of the Iron Curtain by the Hungarian government in May 1989, and the increased opportunity provided for illegal emigration, led to a general crisis of the regime, a crisis which became more acute with the development of the 'New Forum' opposition group and peaceful mass demonstrations in Leipzig and other major cities. The clear reluctance of the USSR under President GORBACHEV to support the ailing Honecker government opened the way for more confident expression of demands for fundamental democratic reform. Honecker's successor, Egon Krenz, rapidly gave way to the reformist former Lord Mayor of Leipzig, Hans Modrow, who, late in 1989, promised the holding of free elections in spring 1990. The elections on 18 March 1990 were a victory for the Alliance for Germany, a coalition of conservative parties, backed by the West German CDU and Helmut Kohl. Their landslide victory on a programme of rapid reunification, immediate unification of the economies of east and west on the basis of the western currency, and the introduction of a social market economy, efffectively marked the end of the German Democratic Republic as an independent state. Currency unification, achieved on 1 July 1990, was then followed by full reunification on 3 October 1990.

M. McCauley, *The German Democratic Republic since 1945* (1983)
H. A. Turner, *The Two Germanies since 1945* (1987)

**German National People's Party.** *See* DNVP.

**German People's Party.** *See* DVP.

**German Revolution.** The political upheaval of 1918–19 which led to the collapse of the Imperial German state, the abdication of WILHELM II and the end of the HOHENZOLLERN dynasty, and the establishment of the WEIMAR REPUBLIC. The origins of the revolution lie in the impact of the FIRST WORLD WAR on German society, leading to the alienation of large sections of the population from the Imperial state, and in the polarization of politics which took place around the issues of war aims and domestic political reform. In its attempts to harness all of Germany's human and material resources for the war of attrition which had emerged by late 1914, the Imperial state increasingly came to intervene in most sectors of the economy. Yet, given the class structure of Wilhelmine Germany and the influential position occupied by the *Junker* nobility, there were clear constraints on the ability of the state to distribute the burdens of total war equitably. Whilst the hardships of war led to a polarization of society along class lines, most Germans seem to have responded to such hardship with growing antagonism towards the bureaucratic state apparatus whose intervention in the economy they deemed to be either ineffective or discriminatory. Thus, whilst urban consumers demanded greater state intervention in order to regulate the food supply, peasant farmers resented state attempts at price-setting and requisitioning of agricultural produce, and responded by diverting a greater proportion of their produce on to the black market. Similarly, white collar workers resented the relative decline in their earnings as their market power diminished and the erosion of their salaries by inflation – itself a consequence of the way in which the government financed the war effort. The trade unions demanded greater state intervention in the economy to regulate wages and working conditions in return for their co-operation; yet industrialists resented the limited intervention which did take place. By 1918, largely as a consequence of mismanaged intervention in the war economy, the Imperial state had lost legitimacy in the eyes of wide sections of the population.

The war also led to a polarization of politics around the related issues of war aims and domestic political reform. The *Burgfrieden* ('truce of the citadel') of August 1914, under which all parties supported the war effort, was seen by the SDP (*see* SOCIAL DEMOCRATIC PARTY, GERMAN) and the trade unions as entailing their support for a defensive war against Tsarist autocracy in return for reform of the most objectionable features of the Imperial political system (such as the plutocratic three-class franchise in Prussia). The conservative parties and the right-wing liberal National Liberal party, by contrast, understood the *Burgfrieden* as an unconditional undertaking by the SDP and the labour movement to support the war effort and to shelve the question of domestic political and social reform;

a war effort, moreover, whose objective was not purely defensive but rather entailed extensive annexations and the establishment of German hegemony on the Continent following victory. The Chancellor, BETHMANN-HOLLWEG, realized that a debate around war aims, in which the government would eventually be obliged to assume a clear position, could only result in the loss of support of either the elites or of the working class and its political organizations: he therefore sought to suppress any such debate.

The government's position, however, was steadily undermined by pro-annexationists within the *Reichstag*, annexationists outside it and the growing influence of the military in politics: Bethmann-Hollweg's 'policy of the diagonal' on the war aims issue finally collapsed after the assumption of leadership of the Army High Command by HINDENBURG and LUDENDORFF. The passage by the *Reichstag* of a 'peace resolution' in July 1917 had been preceded by Bethmann-Hollweg's resignation; and his successors, Michaelis and Hertling, were effectively puppets of the High Command which, supported by the extra-parliamentary VATERLANDSPARTEI, pursued nakedly annexationist policies. These policies found their expression in the TREATY OF BUCHAREST and the TREATY OF BREST-LITOVSK.

Despite apparent victory on the Eastern front by 1918, the High Command's acknowledgement in late September that the war in the West was lost, demoralized and paralysed those groups which had set everything on a German victory, an annexationist peace and the maintenance of the pre-war domestic status quo.

Against the background of imminent defeat, Ludendorff, Hindenburg and von Hintze, the State Secretary in the Foreign Ministry, persuaded the Kaiser to appoint a new Chancellor to introduce constitutional reform, gain the involvement of the majority parties of the *Reichstag* in government and the negotiation of an armistice, and prevent the overthrow of the monarchy by a 'revolution from below'. In the course of October 1918, the new Chancellor, Prince MAX of Baden, secured the passage through the *Bundesrat* (Federal Council) of constitutional changes which removed the most important monarchical privileges over the army and navy, introduced the principle of ministerial accountability to the *Reichstag*, and cleared the way for reform of the Prussian three-class franchise. Yet the decision taken by the Admiralty to embark on a sortie against the British navy, a decision of which the government was ignorant, led to a mutiny by sailors in Kiel and Wilhelmshaven in early November 1918 which soon spread to army units stationed throughout Germany. Ludendorff's successor, General Groener, sought to enlist the support of the SPD leadership for the maintenance of order in a rapidly deteriorating situation. Yet, the price demanded by the SPD chairman, EBERT – the abdication of the Kaiser and the establishment of a regency under one of his sons – was deemed unacceptable by the High Command. The overthrow of the Wittelsbach dynasty and the outbreak of revolution in Bavaria on 7 November forced the pace of events, however; and on 9 November, Prince Max announced not only his own resignation but also the abdication of the Kaiser, and handed over his office to Ebert. The following day, the Workers' and Soldiers' Councils of Berlin, claiming to represent the council movement which had developed in Germany as a whole, confirmed in office the 'Council of People's Deputies', a coalition of leaders of the SPD and USPD (*see* USPD).

During the 1950s the council movement was often seen as consisting of radical socialist bodies committed to the introduction of a Soviet-style 'dictatorship of the proletariat'. Research during the 1960s and 1970s altered this picture fundamentally, and most historians are now agreed that the councils were essentially *ad hoc* organs of local democratic administration which sprang up to fill the power vacuum created by the collapse of the Imperial state. Dominated by delegates whose political allegiance was to the SPD and USPD rather than to the marginal proto-communist SPARTACIST LEAGUE (*see also* LIEBKNECHT, KARL; LUXEMBURG, ROSA), the councils' principal concern was with the maintenance of a semblance of orderly administration at the local level: they were more than content to leave national political control, pending elections to a constituent National Assembly, in the hands of the Council of People's

Deputies, which they expected to initiate democratic reform of the army officer corps and civil service and to move towards greater public control of heavy industry. The fundamentally moderate orientation of the bulk of the council movement was confirmed by the decision of the first national congress of the Workers' and Soldiers' councils (held in Berlin 16–20 December 1918) to hold elections to a constituent assembly in January 1919; and by the congress's rejection of the proposal that the councils should be vested with supreme legislative and executive power in the new Republic.

The moderation of the council movement, however, does not seem to have been fully apparent to Ebert and the SPD leadership, which saw the councils as potential rivals for power. Mounting frustration with the Ebert government's failure to initiate fundamental reform of the economy and bureaucracy led to growing radicalization within some of the councils, a process which was accelerated by the withdrawal of many moderate SPD delegates from the councils following the calling of elections to the National Assembly. The withdrawal of the USPD ministers from the Council of People's Deputies at the end of December 1918, following the decision by the SPD ministers to use troops against demonstrators in Berlin, left the government solely in the hands of the SPD ministers supported by the Imperial civil service and the army, which had pledged its loyalty to the new government (in a secret agreement concluded between Ebert and the most influential figure within the General Staff) in return for an undertaking by the government not to undermine the authority of the officer corps.

The elections to the National Assembly, which took place on 19 January 1919 following an abortive coup in Berlin by the Spartacist League seemed an endorsement of Ebert's strategy since November 1918 and of his scepticism about the extent of support for radical restructuring of German society: together with its putative coalition partners, the CENTRE PARTY and the German Democratic Party (*see* DDP), the SPD gained over three-quarters of all votes cast. The National Assembly convened in Weimar on 6 February 1919 to begin drafting a constitution for the new Republic. A law for the provisional exercise of political power was passed by the Assembly on 10 February: it contained provisions for the exercise of supreme executive authority by a president, to be elected by the Assembly, who would in turn appoint a cabinet which was to possess the confidence of the Assembly. Ebert was elected president by the Assembly on 11 February; and charged Scheidemann, a former SPD member of the Council of People's Deputies, with the task of forming a government.

Throughout the period February–May 1919, radical elements within the surviving councils launched a series of major strikes and, in some parts of Germany, established a short-lived council-based republic. These radical experiments were brutally suppressed by the widespread deployment of FREIKORPS units acting with the support of the government. Increasingly disillusioned by the apparently cautious and conservative course being pursued by the SPD, many industrial workers and grass-roots party members either withdrew into political inactivity or transferred their allegiance to the USPD, which made major gains in local and regional elections during the spring of 1919.

The loss of support suffered by the SPD after the January 1919 elections, and its consequent weakness vis-à-vis its coalition partners in government, helps to explain why it was liberal rather than socialist ideas which informed the draft constitution. The adoption of the Weimar constitution by the National Assembly on 31 July, and its ratification by the president on 11 August 1919, signalled the inauguration of the WEIMAR REPUBLIC and an end to the revolutionary upheaval – though not of political instability – that had followed upon German military defeat during the First World War.

Whilst the overwhelming majority of historians now reject the idea that the council movement aimed at the establishment of a Soviet-style regime in Germany in the months after November 1918, debate continues about the inevitability of the thorough-going compromise made by the SPD leadership with the leading elements of the old Imperial order. It nevertheless seems clear that, whilst some co-operation between the SPD leadership and elements of the old regime was essential, such co-operation went much further than the political and economic situation demanded: had the SPD shown greater political will, more fundamental democratization of the army and civil service might have proved possible, democratization which would have enhanced the long-term prospects of the new Republic's survival.

A. J. Ryder, *The German Revolution of 1918* (1967)
J. Kocka, *Facing Total War: German Society, 1914–1918* (1984)
E. Kolb, *The Weimar Republic* (1988)

**Germany, Allied occupation of.** Following the German unconditional surrender in early May 1945 which brought the SECOND WORLD WAR in Europe to an end, the Allies (France, the UK, USA and USSR) implemented the agreement reached at the YALTA CONFERENCE in February 1945 whereby Germany was to be divided into occupation zones pending the meeting of a peace conference to draw up a peace treaty and determine the territory of any German successor state. The United States was responsible for Bavaria, Baden-Württemberg, Hesse and an enclave around Bremen and Bremerhaven; the United Kingdom for the Rhineland and northern Germany; France for the south-west and the Palatinate; and the Soviet Union for the area between the rivers Elbe and Werra in the west and Oder and Neisse in the east. Berlin was divided into four occupation zones and administered by an Inter-Allied authority under the military commanders of the occupying forces. In the process of the invasion of Germany in 1945, the Soviet Union had transferred pre-war German territory as far west as the ODER–NEISSE LINE to the new Polish government and had divided former East Prussia, itself absorbing the area around Königsberg (renamed Kaliningrad). The German population of the areas absorbed by Poland and the USSR, some 9.5 million people, were expelled. The joint Allied declaration of 5 June 1945 stated that, whilst the occupying powers intended to implement no annexations, they would assume governmental authority in their occupation zones. Within each zone the military commander was to head the administration, following instructions from his national government. In order to deal with issues concerning Germany as a whole (such as economic affairs, prisoners of war and reparations) an Inter-Allied Control Commission was established with its own administrative apparatus. At the POTSDAM CONFERENCE of July–August 1945, the UK, USA and USSR agreed that de-Nazification and de-militarization policies should be implemented, as should the break-up of major industrial concerns. Local government was to be established and political parties might be set up with the agreement of the occupying powers. Reparations were to be extracted in kind, with the USSR receiving 25 per cent of the reparations extracted from the industrial zones occupied by the British and Americans in return for shipments of foodstuffs and raw materials from its largely agricultural occupation zone. In the medium term, the German population was, however, to be left with sufficient resources to survive economically without requiring assistance from the Allies. All of these arrangements were deemed by the participants at Potsdam to be provisional, pending the meeting of a peace conference.

In the event, no peace conference ever met and, with the onset of the COLD WAR in 1945–6, the policies pursued in the British, French and American zones and those pursued in the Soviet zone began to diverge. Once the initial and fundamental problem of feeding the German population had been mastered, the occupying authorities in the Western zones encouraged the re-establishment of economic activity essentially along free-enterprise lines; the Soviet occupation authorities meanwhile embarked on a wide-ranging programme of land reform (breaking up large estates) and nationalization of industry. Similarly, apart from the trial of the major war criminals at Nuremberg presided over by judges from the four occupying powers (see NUREMBERG TRIALS), de-Nazification policies agreed at Potsdam were implemented differently in the different zones: in the Western zones, especially in the American zone, the authorities attempted an ideological and political screening of millions of Germans, a process which was to peter out in the late 1940s in the face of the massive bureaucratic complexities it generated; whereas in the Soviet zone, a much more limited ideological

screening was carried out, the authorities concentrating on ousting the economic and social elites which had sustained the Nazi regime. Finally, the formation of political parties for the German population differed markedly: in the Western zones free political parties were formed from 1945–6 onwards, whilst in the Soviet zone the communist-dominated SED (see SED) assumed effective control of German politics. An important step towards the formation of a bloc made up of the western occupation zones was taken in January 1947 with the formation of the Anglo–American Bi-Zone, which integrated the economies of the two zones: the administrative institutions established to control the Bi-Zone were made up of representatives from the democratically-elected state parliaments and came to form a proto-government for the future West German state. In April 1949 the French occupation zone was integrated with the Bi-Zone to form the Tri-Zone.

The future division of Germany into two separate states was probably inevitable from February 1948, when the UK and USA decided that they could no longer postpone decisions on the future of Germany. In the absence of any progress towards a peace settlement by the council of foreign ministers of the occupying powers, the UK and USA invited France and the Benelux states to a conference to consider the future of Germany. The London Conference, which met in February–March and April–June 1948 agreed to the extension of the MARSHALL PLAN to the Western occupation zones and called for the formation of a German government in these zones. In June 1948 the occupying powers in the Western zones approved a major currency reform which established the basis for economic revival. The Soviet response to the June 1948 currency reform, the Berlin blockade and BERLIN AIRLIFT of 1948–9 merely served to harden the division between the Western and Soviet occupation zones. In September 1948 a Parliamentary Council, made up of representatives from the state parliaments in the Western occupation zones, had met to draft a constitution for a West German state. The provisional 'Basic Law' which emerged in early May 1949 was accepted by the Western occupying powers and the individual states and the FEDERAL REPUBLIC OF GERMANY officially came into being on 24 May 1949. Whilst the Federal Republic was initially not a sovereign state, accepting the Occupation Statute drafted by the occupying Western powers and the right of these powers to control foreign relations, foreign trade and militarily-sensitive areas of industry, as well as to veto legislation which conflicted with the policies of the occupying powers, its capacity to pursue independent policies was to grow steadily, culminating in the recognition of full West German sovereignty in 1955. In the Soviet occupation zone, the moves towards the formation of a West German Government undertaken by the western Allies in 1948–9 led to election of an SED-dominated People's Congress in May 1949: this in turn appointed a People's Council which approved a draft constitution drawn up beforehand. The GERMAN DEMOCRATIC REPUBLIC came into being in early October 1949.

Responsibility for the division of Germany into two separate states by October 1949 has been much debated. The origins of the division of the country are perhaps ultimately to be sought in the deep divisions between the victors of 1945. Although the USSR undoubtedly had a good claim to substantial reparations following a ruinous war unleashed by the Nazi regime, the Western powers saw no reason why they should fund such reparations by pouring scarce resources into their occupation zones to feed the German population whilst the USSR extracted goods and foodstuffs not only from its occupation zones but also from the Western zones under the agreement reached at Potsdam. Confronted by the need to relieve themselves of the massive cost of provisioning the defeated Germans, and fearing the political consequences of allowing the Western occupation zones to degenerate into destitution, the British and American governments constantly encountered Soviet objections to attempts to revive the German economy, objections which stemmed from anxiety about restored German industrial strength. They were thus forced to side-step the requirement of four-power unanimity agreed at Potsdam if they were to make any

progress. This breach of the agreements reached at Potsdam enabled the USSR to claim that the Western powers were responsible for the division of Germany.

T. Sharp, *The Wartime Alliance and the Zonal Division of Germany* (1975)

H. A. Turner, *The Two Germanies since 1945* (1987)

**Germany, Federal Republic of** (Bundesrepublik Deutschland; BRD). West German state established in May 1949, formed from the American, British and French post-1945 occupation zones (*see* GERMANY, ALLIED OCCUPATION OF). Only reunited with East Germany on 3 October 1990, the Federal Republic's constitutional structure is determined by the 'Basic Law' (*Grundgesetz*) agreed by representatives from the Western occupation zones and accepted by the Western Allies in May 1949. The *Grundgesetz* follows quite closely the constitution of the WEIMAR REPUBLIC. The key institutions are: the Federal Parliament (*Bundestag*), whose approval is required for all legislation, elected at least every four years by all citizens aged 18 or over on a proportional representation basis, excluding parties which receive less than 5 per cent of the vote; the Federal Council (*Bundesrat*), which contains delegates from the ten provinces (*Länder*) comprising the Federal Republic and has absolute powers of veto over legislation affecting the rights and jurisdiction of the individual provincial states and a 'suspensive veto' over other legislation; and the Constitutional Court, which is elected by the *Bundestag* and *Bundesrat* jointly and, independent of both the executive and legislature, adjudicates on fundamental constitutional issues such as disagreements between the provincial state governments or between these and the federal government. The head of state of the Federal Republic is a president, much less powerful than his predecessors during the Weimar Republic, who is indirectly elected every five years by an assembly drawn from the *Bundestag* and the provincial states: his duties are largely ceremonial, and only in the most exceptional circumstances may he intervene to dissolve the *Bundestag*. All incumbents of the office have striven to make it essentially non-partisan. The head of government, the Federal Chancellor, is elected by the *Bundestag* and must possess its confidence. He may be forced to resign by a no-confidence vote in the *Bundestag*, but only if this vote also nominates a successor: tenure of the chancellorship has thus been for longer periods than was the case in the Weimar Republic. There have been six Chancellors of the Federal Republic since 1949: ADENAUER, ERHARD, Kiesinger, BRANDT, SCHMIDT and KOHL. The Federal Republic has been a member of NATO (*see* NORTH ATLANTIC TREATY ORGANISATION) since 1955, of the EUROPEAN ECONOMIC COMMUNITY since 1957 and of the UNITED NATIONS since 1973. *See also* CHRISTIAN DEMOCRATIC UNION, GERMAN; CHRISTIAN SOCIAL UNION, GERMAN; GERMAN DEMOCRATIC REPUBLIC; HALLSTEIN DOCTRINE; OSTPOLITIK; SOCIAL DEMOCRATIC PARTY, GERMAN.

H. A. Turner, *The Two Germanies since 1945* (1987)

**Gestapo** (Geheime Staatspolizei; secret state police). Nazi German secret police. Established by GÖRING in his capacity as Minister-President of Prussia in November 1933, after the seizure of power by HITLER and the NAZI PARTY, the Gestapo became an independent branch of the internal administration charged with monitoring political activity hostile to the state. With the appointment of HIMMLER as 'Inspector of the Gestapo' in April 1934, the organization increasingly came under the control of the SS (*see* SS), a process which was accelerated after Himmler's appointment as 'Chief of the German Police' in June 1936. Himmler immediately combined the Gestapo and the criminal police to form separate sections of a new 'Security Police' placed under the command of HEYDRICH. This organizational structure remained in place until the reorganization of the entire security apparatus and the formation of the Reich Security Head Office in September 1939. Although in theory a state, rather than a party, organization the Gestapo gradually became permeated with the values and ethos of the SS and its intelligence service, the SD. With an elaborate network of regional and local offices, which used modern police methods, the Gestapo was remarkably successful in rooting out organized opposition to the Nazi regime. Its surveillance activities embraced the churches, freemasons and even Jehovah's Witnesses, in addition to social democrats and communists. After the outbreak of war in 1939, the Gestapo was to become increasingly involved in the maintenance of work-discipline in German factories and policing of the large foreign labour force employed in German industry, as well as the detection and arrest of critics of the Nazi regime.

H. Krausnick *et al.*, *Anatomy of the SS State* (1968)

**Gheorghiu-Dej, Gheorghe** (1901–65). Romanian communist leader. He started life as a tramway worker, joining the illegal ROMANIAN COMMUNIST PARTY in 1929. Initially viewed with some suspicion by the exiled Moscow leadership, who disavowed the railway strike he led at Grivita in 1933. Subsequently imprisoned, he remained captive until his escape in 1944, adding the suffix 'Dej' to his name to mark his imprisonment there. He became General Secretary of the Communist Party in 1945 and served in the coalition government as Minister of National Economy. He made himself totally subservient to STALIN in order to outmanoeuvre the Romanian Communists who had returned from Moscow in 1944, and when a People's Republic was proclaimed in 1948 he was re-elected General Secretary. Extensive purges of the leadership and rank and file culminated in the removal from power of the 'Moscovite group', Ana Pauker, Vasile Luca and Teohari Georgescu in 1952, leaving him in complete control of the party. He exploited the opportunities of KHRUSHCHEV's policy of peaceful co-existence to open up economic contacts with the West, while the HUNGARIAN UPRISING left him with sufficient room to manoeuvre to pursue a policy of national communism and the furtherance of Romanian interests. The Sino–Soviet conflict also permitted the cultivation of an alternative source of economic and military aid and justification for national varieties of socialism. He remained on sufficiently good terms with Khrushchev to secure the removal of Soviet troops from Romania in 1958. In March 1961 he became President of the Presidium, the post he held until his death in March 1965. His legacy to Romania included a greatly expanded industrial base under a series of Five Year Plans begun in 1950, and a significant degree of independence in foreign policy while remaining within the WARSAW PACT. These policies were taken up by his successor, CEAUŞESCU.

G. Ionescu, *Communism in Rumania, 1944–1962* (1964)
S. Fischer-Galati, *The New Romania: From People's Democracy to Socialist Republic* (1967)

**Gibraltar.** British crown colony and base in southern Spain commanding the entrance to the Mediterranean. Captured by Britain in 1704 it was ceded to Britain at the Treaty of Utrecht in 1713 and defended against Spanish attacks on several occasions in the 18th century, notably in 1779–80. Spain renounced its claim to Gibraltar in 1783. Gibraltar was claimed again by FRANCO in 1939 and was offered by HITLER as a bribe for his entry into the war on the side of the AXIS in 1940: this Franco declined to do. The naval base was of immense strategic importance to Britain, especially in the Second World War, when it formed a crucial staging post for operations in the Atlantic, Mediterranean and North Africa. Franco persisted in his claims in the post-war period and these were taken to the UNITED NATIONS. A referendum in September 1967 produced an overwhelming majority in favour of maintaining British rule, and was accompanied by greater moves towards self-government in 1964 and in 1969. The latter led to Franco imposing a blockade of Gibraltar by closing the land frontier with southern Spain in June 1969. The declining strategic importance of Gibraltar, Spain's desire for support for its entry into the EUROPEAN ECONOMIC COMMUNITY and the death of Franco brought about new talks on Gibraltar's future in Madrid in 1977. Agreement was reached in April 1980 to ease restrictions, and in January 1982 Spain agreed to lift the siege of the colony in return for talks on Gibraltar's future. Although interrupted by the FALKLANDS WAR, the border was re-opened on 15 December 1982 and the final restrictions lifted in February 1985.

**Gierek, Edward** (1913–). Polish communist leader. Before the Second World War he worked as a miner in France and Belgium, where he joined the Communist Party. He returned to Poland in 1948 and rose in the party hierarchy. He replaced GOMULKA as First Secretary of the Polish United Workers' Party in December 1970, following widespread unrest on the Baltic coast as a result of price rises. The price rises were rescinded and Gierek visited the centres of unrest, including the Gdansk shipyards, where he admitted the errors of the previous leadership and promised a new economic regime. Gierek borrowed heavily abroad to modernize Polish industry and provide consumer goods, but the 1973 oil crisis produced inflation and a falling off in exports. By 1976 a new round of price rises was necessary, sparking off riots in Radom and Ursus. Although the price rises were withdrawn, the disturbances were put down with large-scale arrests, and some strikers were beaten up. These disturbances saw the formation by a small group of intellectuals of a Workers' Defence Committee (KOR) to provide legal and financial support to the arrested workers. By the late 1970s Gierek's regime was in serious difficulties; mounting foreign debts, the failure of Polish agriculture to provide sufficient food to satisfy urban needs, and an unbalanced industrial structure overdependent on heavy industry forced Gierek to attempt a new round of economic reforms. Price rises in the summer of 1980 sparked off strikes and demonstrations in Gdansk and elsewhere which gave birth to the SOLIDARITY movement. Gierek was forced on 31 August 1980 to sign the Gdansk Agreement permitting free trade unions and strikes. Shortly afterwards he was replaced as First Secretary by Stanislaw Kania. Gierek's attempt to gamble on growth, paid for by foreign borrowings, proved a failure. While for a time in the early 1970s Poland had one of the fastest growing economies in the world, his policy was wrecked by the consequences of the 1973 Oil Crisis and the renewed depressionary cycle after 1979. Moreover, Polish agriculture remained highly inefficient, with prices to consumers kept artificially low through vast subsidies. Gierek's attempts to break out of the cycle in 1976 and 1980 by a more realistic pricing strategy brought about his fall and the rise of a new political movement.

T. Garton Ash, *The Polish Revolution: Solidarity, 1980–1982* (1982)
N. Ascherson, *The Polish August* (1987)

**Giolitti, Giovanni** (1842–1928). Italian statesman. He entered parliament as a liberal in 1882, and became Minister of Finance in 1889. He was Prime Minister five times between 1892 and 1921 dominating almost completely the years 1903 to 1914, generally known as the 'Giolittian Era'. His first ministry, 1892–3, was ended by a scandal involving irregularities at the Bank of Rome. His fourth ministry, March 1911 to March 1914, witnessed war with Turkey and the acquisition of Libya and the Dodecanese. Out of office when the European war broke out, he became a strong opponent of intervention; he was subjected to a hostile press campaign but retained a powerful bloc of supporters in the Chamber. At the peak of the interventionist crisis, in May 1915, Giolitti declined to use his parliamentary strength to form a neutralist government, probably fearing civil war. He remained out of political life until mid-1917, and took office again as Prime Minister in June 1920. His fifth and final ministry, to June 1921, fully exemplified the complex policies that make Giolitti perhaps Italy's most controversial modern politician. He ousted D'ANNUNZIO from FIUME, concluded the Treaty of Rapallo with Yugoslavia and ended the worst phase of industrial unrest. But he helped legitimize Mussolini by admitting fascist candidates to his electoral coalition as a counterweight to socialist power, hoping he could tame and constitutionalize them. Giolitti continued to hold these illusions until well after Mussolini took office in October 1922. Gradually alienated by fascist violence, he finally withdrew his support from the government in November 1924. He spoke out against the new fascist electoral law just before his death in 1928.

A. William Salomone, *Italy in the Giolittian Era* (1960)
C. Seton Watson, *Italy from Liberalism to Fascism, 1870–1925* (1967)

**Giraud, Henri** (1879–1949). French soldier. He served in the First World War and rose to prominence as lecturer at the French École de Guerre and Governor of the Fortress of Metz. Commander of the Seventh, then the Ninth Army during the fall of France, he was captured on 19 May 1940 and imprisoned in Konigstein Castle. He escaped in 1942 and went to live in the French FREE ZONE. He was contacted by the Americans as a potential commander of the French forces in North Africa following the Anglo–American landings in November 1942, and was taken to Gibraltar. Agreement was reached on 13 November between EISENHOWER and DARLAN that Giraud would take military command of the French forces in North Africa with Darlan as civil authority. Following Darlan's assassination, he became civil and military commander on 24 December, much to DE GAULLE's displeasure. He became co-President of the National Committee for Liberation and commanded the FREE FRENCH forces under the control of the National Committee. He superintended the liberation of Corsica in September 1943, but resigned the co-presidency in October 1943, yielding to de Gaulle the position of overall head of the Free French. Further pressure from de Gaulle led to his resigning his command of the armed forces in April 1944. Potentially a major rival to de Gaulle's control of the French forces, he was outmanoeuvred by him and eventually forced out of an active role.

**Giscard d'Estaing, Valéry** (1926–). French statesman and President of France, 1974–81. A member of the National Assembly, 1956–74, he led the Independent Republican Party which supported DE GAULLE after the creation of the FIFTH REPUBLIC but retained its independence. Giscard served as Minister of Finance from 1962 under de Gaulle and introduced policies to reduce inflation, but was dismissed in 1966. He was recalled to the post by POMPIDOU in 1969 and remained in post until 1974. He successfully contested the presidential elections in 1974, drawing support from the Gaullists in the National Assembly. His term of office was marked by continued economic growth and a continuation of the loosening of the more authoritarian legacy of de Gaulle. His aristocratic demeanour earned some unpopularity, but his downfall was contributed to by friction with those who saw themselves as true heirs of de Gaulle, such as CHIRAC. Financial scandals plagued his presidency, the most serious being that he had accepted diamonds from the corrupt and brutal Emperor Bokassa of the Central

African Empire. These allegations hindered his campaign in the presidential elections of 1981. Contested in two stages, Giscard was faced by a challenge on the Right from Chirac and a much strengthened Socialist challenge under MITTERRAND. Mitterrand emerged ahead of Giscard on the first round and the relatively poor performance of the communists made a nonsense of Giscard's claim that any Socialist president would be a puppet of the far left. Chirac's vote at 18 per cent showed the disunity of the Right and left the way open to a convincing victory for Mitterrand at the second round, leading to his assumption of the presidency on 21 May 1981. Giscard and his followers continued to act as a fraction of the Right in France, but he was increasingly overshadowed as a spokesman for the antisocialist forces by Chirac. He did not enter the first ballot for the presidential election in 1988. See also GAULLISM.

**Glasnost.** Russian term meaning 'openness'. Widely promoted by MIKHAIL GORBACHEV following his election to leadership of the Soviet Union. Gorbachev called for more openness about public affairs in order to further progress with the process of PERESTROIKA or 'restructuring'. Glasnost implied a candidness about current problems and also about those of the past. From 1985 there was displayed an unprecedented willingness to examine some of the darkest corners of the history of the Soviet Union, including recognition of some of the excesses of the PURGES, and crimes committed in the Second World War, such as the KATYN MASSACRE. To Western observers the most visible sign of *glasnost* was the greater access of Soviet statesmen to the media and greater freedom of contact between the Soviet Union and the West.

M. Gorbachev, *Perestroika* (1988)
R. W. Davis, *Soviet History in the Gorbachev Revolution* (1989)

**Goebbels, Josef** (1897–1945). Nazi activist and propagandist. Born in the Rhineland, Goebbels studied at the University of Heidelberg where he gained his doctorate in 1920. Crippled from childhood as a consequence of having contracted polio, Goebbels was declared unfit for military service during the First World War. He joined the

NAZI PARTY (NSDAP) in 1922 and initially associated himself with the populist wing of the party around GREGOR STRASSER. Business manager of the NSDAP in the region (*Gau*) Rhineland-North, Goebbels abandoned his attempts with Strasser and others to alter the Nazi Party programme in a 'socialist' direction in 1926, when HITLER insisted on the immutability of, the programme. In November 1926 he became GAULEITER in Berlin. Establishing his own newspaper, *Der Angriff* (The Attack), Goebbels devoted his efforts to building up the Berlin party; he developed street violence as a form of propaganda for the party, alongside broadsheets, posters and rallies. He was elected to the REICHSTAG in May 1928. Goebbels's success in galvanizing the Berlin NSDAP led to his appointment by Hitler as Reich Propaganda Leader in April 1930. He co-ordinated the NSDAP's propaganda campaigns for the 1930 and 1932 elections, establishing an intricate chain of command for the dissemination of propaganda themes, stretching from the Reich Propaganda Department down to the branch party organizations within the individual regions. He was also responsible for the increasing sophistication of NSDAP propaganda, both in the techniques used (co-ordinated press campaigns, film shows, airborne tours by leading Nazi party figures, etc.), and in the development of specific propaganda themes to attract the support of individual social groups.

With the Nazi seizure of power, Hitler – whose propaganda image as a *Führer* (leader) endowed with super-human qualities Goebbels had done so much to establish – appointed him Minister for Propaganda and Popular Enlightenment in March 1933. In this position, Goebbels had total control of the media – radio, press, publishing, the cinema and other arts – which he rapidly 'co-ordinated' and transformed into pliable instruments for the dissemination of the regime's propaganda. In May 1933, he staged the public burning of books deemed by the regime to be subversive.

An intelligent and entirely unscrupulous master of invective and abuse, Goebbels played a major role in maintaining the dynamism of grass-roots Nazi anti-Semitism, and was the chief instigator of the November 1938 pogrom against German and Austrian Jews. To the extent that his propaganda machine did much to set the vicious anti-Semitic tone of public life in the Third Reich, he must be considered a major contributor to the cumulative radicalization of Nazi anti-Semitic policies (*see* HOLOCAUST).

During the SECOND WORLD WAR Goebbels's influence increased as the military situation turned to Germany's disadvantage. With the onset of the Allied air offensive against German cities, Goebbels sought to promote a spirit of defiant solidarity amongst the German people, and was the only Nazi leader to visit heavily bombed cities. Following the Allied demand for unconditional surrender by Germany, Goebbels was the chief architect of the propaganda of 'total war', whipping up wild emotion in his February 1943 'total war' speech in the Berlin *Sportpalast*. Having played a major role in defeating the JULY BOMB PLOT, Goebbels was appointed Plenipotentiary for Total War on 25 July 1944 and given full powers to direct both the civilian population and redistribute manpower within the armed forces. In the final stages of the war Goebbels's basic nihilism became clear as he sought to stage-manage the inevitable defeat along heroic lines. Remaining loyal to Hitler to the end, he had his children poisoned before shooting his wife and committing suicide on 1 May 1945.

E. K. Bramsted, *Goebbels and National Socialist Propaganda, 1925–1945* (1965)
D. Welch (ed.), *Nazi Propaganda: The Power and the Limitations* (1983)

**Gold Standard.** Currency system in which all money is convertible into gold on demand. The system was general in Europe and the USA before 1914 and involved keeping a gold reserve large enough to meet all likely demands to back the issue of notes. Britain went off the Standard, in effect, during the First World War but returned to it in 1925, although at a level which overvalued sterling and proved insupportable during the period of the Great Crash in 1929–31. British politicians and financiers regarded the maintenance of the Gold Standard as essential to Britain's national prestige and place as a centre of international finance, placing serious restraints upon the economic policies they could pursue in the face of the DEPRESSION. Defence of the Gold Standard led indirectly to the fall of the SECOND LABOUR GOVERNMENT in August 1931, but the succeeding NATIONAL GOVERNMENT was forced finally to abandon it in September 1931. Although direct convertibility with gold has been abandoned, the level of gold reserves still has a part to play in underpinning international credit arrangements and individual currencies.

**Gömbös de Jafka, Gyula** (1886–1936). Hungarian politician. Born in Swabia, he was a Captain in the Austro–Hungarian army during the First World War. He was Minister of War in the anti-Bolshevik government based on Szeged in 1918–19. He became proponent of radical right-wing ideas and resigned from the army to further a political career. Influenced by MUSSOLINI towards a CORPORATE STATE, he was anti-Semitic, but was also opposed to inherited wealth and aristocratic privilege, favouring radical land reform and describing himself as a 'Hungarian National Socialist'. In foreign policy he was suspicious of Germany but was pledged to the recapture of Hungary's former territories. Prime Minister from October 1932, he sought to build an 'axis of fascist states' with Germany and Italy to break the 'encirclement' of Hungary by the LITTLE ENTENTE and France's influence in south-eastern Europe. In domestic policy he launched a 'National Work Plan' in response to the depression, also proposing land and tax reforms, but these were increasingly overshadowed by his attempt to create a fascistic 'Greater Hungary' backed by his own organization of 60,000 'vanguard fighters' and the renamed government party, the Party of National Unity. Attracting support from right-wing groupings by his attacks on the aristocracy, the Jews and the Left, he came under increasing pressure from moderate elements. He reacted with a sudden dissolution of the Lower House on 5 March 1935 to prevent an opposition attack on his position. A rigged election on 11 April 1946 gave Gömbös's supporters 44 per cent of the vote and a majority of the deputies. On a visit to Berlin in September 1935 he openly promised to make Hungary a one-party system within two years, modelled on Germany. His plans were nullified by his unexpected death at Munich on 6 October 1936. Although he responded to the DEPRESSION with some vigour, Gömbös secured only limited success in the economic sphere. His proposals for radical land reform led to an Act in 1934 which redistributed some of the larger estates, but involved only an estimated 37,000 families and 8 per cent of the land area. He forged strong links with Mussolini, and, although suspicious of HITLER, faced an increase in German influence. He signed the Rome Protocol on 17 March 1934 with Italy, but opposed German activity in Austria. Before his death in October 1936 he obtained a 100 million mark loan from Germany and was negotiating with Hitler about territorial acquisitions, part of the growing entanglement of Hungary with the AXIS powers in spite of Gömbös's distinctive Hungarian nationalism. By his death his right-wing, populist views were increasingly overtaken by the more extreme views of groups such as the ARROW CROSS. See also HORTHY DE NAGYBANYA, MIKLOS.

J. K. Hoensch, *A History of Modern Hungary, 1867–1986* (trans., 1988)

**Gomulka, Wladyslaw** (1905–82). First Secretary of Polish Communist Party, 1956–70. Born in Austrian Galicia, he was a trade unionist before 1939. In 1943 he became Secretary-General of the clandestine Polish Workers' Party, which played a major role in the resistance movement. From 1945 he was Minister responsible for territories annexed from Germany but was dismissed and imprisoned in 1948 for a nationalistic speech. Released in 1954, he was re-admitted to the party in 1956 and elected First Secretary after anti-Soviet riots in Poznan. Gomulka retained defence links with the Soviet Union, but stopped agricultural collectivization and made limited political reforms, although these were abandoned in 1962–3 for fear of internal unrest. Following bloodily suppressed food riots in 1970, he was replaced as First Secretary by GIEREK. One of the most important communist leaders of the postwar era, leading his country for 13 years. He was representative of a new tendency of more liberal communism, but one which stopped short of

the direction attempted by DUBCECK in Czechoslovakia.

M. K. Dziewanowski, *The Communist Party of Poland: An Outline History* (1959)
N. Bethel, *Gomulka, his Poland and his Communism* (1972)

**Gonzales, Felipe** (1942– ). Spanish Socialist and Prime Minister. Born in Seville and trained as a lawyer, he joined the Socialist Youth Movement and, in 1964, the SOCIALIST WORKERS' PARTY. One of the youngest of Spain's leaders in the post-FRANCO era, he modelled the Party on moderate, democratic lines, securing an overall victory in the 1982 elections and becoming Prime Minister and President of the Council of Ministers. He pursued free market economic policies and educational reform, as well as presiding over Spain's entry into the EEC and confirmation of membership of NATO. In June 1986 he secured a further majority and weathered serious economic difficulties and worker opposition to high unemployment and cuts in welfare to secure a narrow overall majority once again in October 1989.

D. Gilmour, *The Transformation of Spain* (1985)
R. Gilespie, *The Spanish Socialist Party: A History of Factionalism* (1989)

**Gorbachev, Mikhail** (1931–). Soviet statesman. General Secretary of the COMMUNIST PARTY OF THE SOVIET UNION since 1985; member of its Central Committee since 1971, its Secretariat (with responsibility for agriculture) from 1978, and the Politburo from 1980. Born into a peasant family in the agrarian district of Stauropol, he studied law at Moscow University, returning to his home area to begin his political career. He became head of Komsomoc and First Secretary of the Party in Stauropol in 1970, specializing in agricultural development where he introduced a contract system of payment by results for work teams on collective farms. Seen as an effective technocrat, he moved to Moscow in 1978 to become agriculture secretary of the Central Committee. Joining the Politburo as ANDROPOV's protégé, he assumed a wider range of responsibilities, including the KGB and foreign affairs, visiting London in 1984. His emergence as a forceful leading member of the Politburo was temporarily stalled with the death of Andropov and the stop-gap leadership of CHERNENKO. However, on Chernenko's death he was chosen as General Secretary, despite being the youngest member of Politburo; following over a decade of rule by old men, he brought a new dynamism to both domestic and foreign policy. His more open style won him international support and contributed to improved relations with President REAGAN, whom he met in Geneva in 1985, in Iceland in 1986, and in Moscow in 1988. Gorbachev ended the SOVIET INVASION OF AFGHANISTAN, achieving withdrawal by 1989 without major humiliation to the Soviet forces. Its effect was to speed the process of thaw in the COLD WAR, confirmed in the resumption of arms talks between the superpowers and a successful meeting at Malta in December 1989 with President Bush, where the Cold War was declared to be ended. Gorbachev also encouraged the political transformation of Eastern Europe from a monolithic bloc dominated by Soviet-style communist parties to varying degrees of pluralism. Gorbachev implicitly sanctioned the creation of a SOLIDARITY government in Poland, the ending of the communist monopoly in Hungary, Czechoslovakia and East Germany, and the opening of the BERLIN WALL. Domestically his policies of GLASNOST and PERESTROIKA have been seen as attempts to breathe new life into Soviet society. Much greater freedom of expression and criticism was encouraged, many political prisoners freed, DISSIDENTS released from restrictions, emigration permitted, and distinguished refugees in the arts field allowed to return. Gorbachev's campaign of *perestroika* had however, yet to achieve decisive effects in the economic field, where attempts to reform inefficiencies in agriculture and industry were not yet showing sufficient results to placate criticism. Most difficult of all, however, Gorbachev's more liberal policies produced an explosion of ethnic and national unrest in ARMENIA, GEORGIA, the UKRAINE, MOLDAVIA and the BALTIC STATES. The ability to contain these developments while reforming a sluggish economy formed pressing questions with continued speculation about Gorbachev's survival. Some permanent effects, however, had been obtained in the retirement of the BREZHNEV old guard, the promotion of younger, pro-Gorbachev sup-

porters, the introduction of greater democracy. Of most significance was the creation of a popularly elected Congress of People's Deputies in spring 1989, effectively opening up the Soviet Union to non-Party forces. Its lively debates, votes and televised proceedings transformed the climate of political dialogue and opened the way to a multiparty system. In March 1990 the Congress ratified the end of the 'leading role' of the Communist Party, enshrined in Articles 6 and 7 of the Consitution. In the same session Gorbachev was elected to a new post of executive President by a vote of the Congress deputies; subsequent elections to be by popular vote. Although the powers assumed antagonized radicals, the post distanced the Government of the Soviet Union further from Party control. The constitutional changes, however, were met by hostility from remaining hardliners in the CPSU and Gorbachev remained dogged by problems with ethnic groups, especially in Lithuania, and by a failure to deliver significant economic progress. During 1990 and early 1991 the reform process seemed stalled. Leading Gorbachev supporters were forced to resign and in January 1991 Soviet forces killed protesters in Lithuania. Further reform initiatives, however, were brought forward to change the ideology of the Communist Party to one of social democracy and acceptance of the market and private property. Reform included a new All-Union Treaty to reshape the Soviet Union. This provoked, in late August 1991, an anti-Gorbachev coup by hard-liners in Moscow, temporarily detaining him at his Crimean holiday retreat. Its failure rapidly accelerated change with greater authority now wielded by the radical Russian President, Yeltsin. Gorbachev resigned as General Secretary and dissolved the Communist Party, granted the Baltic states independence and sought a much looser union with the Republics. These events finally produced fundamental political change in the former Soviet Union, ending decades of Communist rule. Internationally, the freeing of eastern Europe and the end of the Cold War have produced the greatest upheaval in Soviet international politics since 1945.

M. Gorbachev, *Perestroika* (1987)

T. Hasegawa and A. Pravda (eds.), *Perestrioka: Soviet Domestic and Foreign Policies* (1990)

**Göring, Hermann** (1893–1946). German Nazi politician and commander of German Air Force (*Luftwaffe*), 1935–1945. Born in Rosenheim, Bavaria, the son of a colonial official, Göring joined an infantry regiment in 1914 before transferring to the air force. He received the highest award for bravery and was the last commander of the famous Richthofen fighter squadron. Joining the NAZI PARTY (NSDAP) in 1922, he was appointed by HITLER as first commander of the paramilitary SA (*see* SA). He participated in the abortive MUNICH PUTSCH of November 1923, was wounded and forced to flee abroad. He returned to Germany in 1927 under a general amnesty and was elected a member of the *Reichstag* in 1928. Following the July 1932 elections, Göring was elected President of the *Reichstag* with the support of deputies from the NSDAP and CENTRE PARTY. On Hitler's appointment as Chancellor in January 1933, Göring joined the cabinet as Reich Minister without Portfolio, Reich Air Commissioner and acting Prussian Minister of the Interior.

As President of the *Reichstag*, Göring played a major role in securing the passage of the Enabling Act of March 1933, a major legislative step in the Nazi seizure of power. As Prussian Interior Minister, he used his powers to purge the Prussian administration of elements unsympathetic to the Nazi government and ordered the arrest of thousands of communists in the run-up to the March 1933 elections. In April 1933 he created the GESTAPO (*Geheime Staatspolizei*, Secret State Police) as an instrument of state coercion; and was appointed its head by a law of November 1933. In June 1934, he was charged with organizing the operations in Berlin of the purge of ERNST RÖHM and other leaders of the SA. He succeeded PAPEN as Minister-President of Prussia, following the former's appointment as German ambassador to Vienna in July 1934. In March 1935 he was appointed Commander-in-Chief of the LUFTWAFFE and was responsible for the rapid build-up of German air power in the pre-war period. In October 1936, he was appointed Plenipotentiary for the FOUR YEAR PLAN, and in 1937 was responsible for the creation of a massive state-controlled steel agglomeration, the Hermann–Göring Werke.

In the autumn of 1937, when SCHACHT was forced to resign as Minister of Economics, Göring incorporated his Ministry into the Four Year Plan Office. In the course of 1937 Göring began to evolve his own strategy for the absorption of Austria through a combination of German economic penetration and political pressure; and in the events which formed the background to the ANSCHLUSS of March 1938, Göring was responsible for forcing the pace. Created a Field Marshal in February 1938, Göring also saw his influence and power stretch into the sphere of Nazi anti-Semitic policy: from the end of 1937 he was the main driving force behind the attempt to 'Aryanize' the German economy, by forcing Jewish businessmen to sell their businesses to 'Aryan' German firms at prices well below the market level; and was responsible for levying a massive fine on the German Jewish population after the *Reichskristallnacht* pogrom of November 1938, complementing this with a decree designed to drive German Jews out of economic life entirely. Indeed, by the end of 1938, Göring seemed to have asserted his total control over Nazi anti-Semitic policy; yet this was gradually to be lost to the SS (*see* SS) in the following months.

On the outbreak of war in September 1939 Göring was appointed chairman of the Reich Defence Council and officially designated as Hitler's successor. Whilst he remained a powerful figure in the internal politics of the Nazi regime after the outbreak of war, Göring's attention was increasingly absorbed by his military responsibilities as Commander-in-Chief of the *Luftwaffe*. His role in the economy gradually diminished as the Four Year Plan Office was increasingly supplanted by the Reich Ministry of Armaments and Munitions under Fritz Todt and, later, ALBERT SPEER. He directed the operations of the *Luftwaffe* against Poland and France in 1939 and was made a Reich Marshal in June 1940; but the failure of the *Luftwaffe* to gain command of British air space during the Battle of Britain in the summer of 1940, to make an impact in the war against the Soviet Union from 1941 onwards and to defend Germany from British and American bombing raids led Hitler to hold him responsible for German military setbacks.

Göring continued to be involved in the

radicalization of Nazi anti-Semitic policy, and his order of late July 1941 to HEYDRICH to prepare a plan for a comprehensive solution to the 'Jewish problem' is seen by most historians as of central importance in the realization of the Nazi 'final solution' – the murder of the European Jews (*see* HOLOCAUST). By 1943 Göring's power and influence had declined sharply with the rise of BORMANN, GOEBBELS and Speer within the Nazi regime. By this stage, Göring was a shadow of his former self, drug-dependent, living in ostentatious luxury and increasingly politically marginal. As the Third Reich collapsed in April 1945, Göring sought to assume command of the armed forces from Hitler. Hitler interpreted this as treason, ordered his arrest, and expelled him from the Nazi Party, stripping him of all of his offices in his political testament. Detained briefly by the SS, Göring was captured by Allied forces in May 1945. At the NUREMBERG TRIALS Göring was found guilty of conspiracy to wage war, war crimes, crimes against peace and crimes against humanity. He committed suicide shortly before he was due to be hanged in October 1946.

R. J. Overy, *Goering: The 'Iron Man'* (1987)

**Gorlice-Tarnow, Battle of.** *See* FIRST WORLD WAR.

**Gorshkov, Sergei** (1910–88). Soviet admiral and naval Commander-in-Chief. Born in the Ukraine, he attended the Frunze Higher Naval School. He saw distinguished war service in the Azov and Black Seas during the Second World War, becoming Chief of Staff then commander of the Black Sea fleet. In 1956 he was appointed Commander-in-Chief by KHRUSHCHEV, a post held for almost 30 years. Gorshkov oversaw a huge expansion of the Soviet submarine and surface fleets in which the Soviet navy was transformed from a coastal defence force to a well equipped 'Blue Water' navy capable of representing the Soviet Union's interests world-wide. Gorshkov's achievement has to be seen in the context of the humiliation inflicted on the Soviet Union by the American naval blockade of Cuba and its lack of ability to influence events beyond Europe. He was appointed to take the navy into the age of nuclear submarines

and missiles. With the backing of BREZHNEV (with whom he had served in the war) he was able to build up the submarine fleet until it soon equalled that of the US navy; furthermore, he also established a huge destroyer and cruiser building programme and ordered the construction of the first Soviet aircraft carriers. By 1973 the Soviet navy was able to achieve local superiority over its American counterpart in the Mediterranean during the Yom Kippur War and built up an ocean-going presence and a network of overseas bases during the rest of the decade. Gorshkov's writings on Soviet sea power became widely known in the West, contributing to pressures for increases in Western arms expenditure. When Gorshkov stepped down in 1985 he was widely regarded as the founder of the modern Soviet navy. *See also* COLD WAR.

S. G. Gorshkov, *Red Star Rising at Sea* (1974)
——, *The Sea Power of the State* (1976)

**Gosplan.** Abbreviation for the state general-planning commission set up in the Soviet Union on 22 February 1921 to 'work out a single general state economic plan and methods and means of implementing it'. Its main purpose was to assist the Council of Labour and Defence (STO), a commission of the Council of Peoples' Commissars, effectively the major economic-military committee, and which appointed the members of Gosplan. In August 1923 its name was altered to 'state planning commission' and its duties redefined and extended giving it a co-ordinating role for the work of other state agencies. In its early years during the NEW ECONOMIC POLICY it had no direct control over the economy as a whole, its major function being the production of figures on which basis decisions could be taken about investment decisions and economic priorities. With the beginning of the programme of industrialization, Gosplan's role became much more important. In June 1927 a decree of the Council of People's Commissars called for the creation of 'a united all-union plan'. The role of Gosplan was strengthened and planning bodies in the republics placed under its control. It was then given the task of producing the first FIVE YEAR PLAN. As the Plan developed, Gosplan was given wider functions and placed directly under the Council of People's Commissars, effectively taking over all economic planning functions and becoming one of the most important organs of Soviet industrialization. Although Gosplan's role was to be overshadowed by the changes in emphasis of Soviet economic policy after Stalin, it played a crucial role in pioneering the production of national economic statistics and, ultimately, producing the plans which attracted much foreign interest in Soviet 'planning'. *See also* INDUSTRIALIZATION DEBATE, SOVIET.

A. Nove, *An Economic History of the USSR* (1969)
R. W. Davies, *The Industrialisation of Soviet Russia* (1980)

**Gottwald, Klement** (1896–1953). Czech communist leader. He was the founder member of the CZECHOSLOVAK COMMUNIST PARTY in 1921, becoming its General Secretary in 1929 as Stalin's protégé. He acquiesced in the purge of many of its members from 1929, and declared outright opposition to the Czech state. With a seat in parliament, Gottwald was put up as a presidential candidate in 1934 in opposition to MASARYK, but switched from opposition to the POPULAR FRONT line the following year, as a result of the Soviet–Czech Treaty of Alliance of May 1935. As COMINTERN's representative he urged the creation of an antifascist Popular Front, but with the Nazi occupation of the SUDETENLAND and the outlawing of the Communist Party on 20 October 1938 he escaped to Moscow. He returned with the RED ARMY in 1945 to lead the coalition government which took power after the elections of 1946. As Premier under BENES he began the socialization of parts of the economy, backed by 114 deputies (out of 300) and half the cabinet posts. A coup in February 1948 was followed by elections in May which gave the communist-dominated National Front candidates 214 deputies. On 9 May Czechoslovakia became a People's Democracy, and Gottwald became President on 14 June after Benes resigned. Gottwald presided over the Stalinization of Czechoslovakia, including the nationalization of all property, collectivization, extensive purges and a struggle to eliminate rival sources of influence such as the Catholic Church. Show trials of leading opponents, including the General Secretary Rudolf Slansky and other leading party

members, led to their execution and the imprisonment and purging of many others. Gottwald died on 14 March 1953 after returning from Stalin's funeral.

J. Korbel, *The Communist Subversion of Czechoslovakia* (1959)
E. Taborsky, *Communism in Czechoslovakia, 1948–1960* (1961)

**GPU** (Gosudarstvennoye Politicheskoe Upravleniye). The Soviet state security service which replaced the CHEKA in 1922. It was used to gather evidence on party opposition in 1923 under the ex-head of the Cheka, Dzerzhinsky, and to investigate early opponents of Stalin in 1926–7. It broadened its activities to conduct the campaign against the KULAKS from 1929 and forced requisitioning amongst the collectivized peasantry. Renamed the OGPU in 1924 and in 1934 the NKVD.

B. Levytsky, *The Soviet Secret Police, 1917–1970* (1972)

**Graeco–Turkish War.** As one of the defeated powers in the First World War, Turkey was subject to a punitive settlement favouring many of her neighbours. With the approval of the victorious allies Greek forces were allowed to land at the Turkish port of İzmir (Smyrna) on the western coast of Anatolia on 19 May 1919 in anticipation of promises made to them at the PARIS PEACE CONFERENCE. By the TREATY OF SÈVRES (10 August 1920) Greece was given control of İzmir and its hinterland for five years after which a plebiscite on its future was to be held. As substantial Greek populations lived in the area, this was likely to result in a permanent annexation of part of the former Turkish mainland. In addition Greece acquired eastern Thrace and all the Turkish islands in the Aegean, apart from the Dodecanese and Rhodes, which were given to Italy. Turkey never ratified the treaty and Kemal Ataturk (1881–1938) from spring 1919 began an attempt to redress the terms of the treaty by military force. Although other powers attempted to mediate, the Greeks under the expansionist CONSTANTINE I attempted to extend their area of control into Anatolia, winning initial success at the battle of Sakarya (24 August 1921), threatening the Turkish capital at Ankara. A Turkish offensive in 1922, however, drove the Greek armies back into disorder, the Turks taking İzmir on 11 September and forcing the embarkation of the Greek troops and a mass evacuation of Greeks from the area. Following a confrontation between British forces and those of Ataturk, the CHANAK CRISIS, an armistice was signed in October, leading to a peace conference at Lausanne. By the TREATY OF LAUSANNE (24 July 1923) Greece relinquished İzmir and eastern Thrace, as well as the Aegean islands of Imbros and Tenedos. Both sides agreed a mutual exchange of populations, thus ending centuries of Greek settlement on the western coast of Anatolia. While the outcome of the war for Turkey was the avoidance of almost complete dismemberment and a nationalist resurgence under Ataturk's leadership, the effects for Greece were disastrous, losing all the gains she had achieved at the Paris Peace Conference and having to absorb over 1.25 million Greek refugees in an already impoverished country. The scale of the defeat drove the Greek King Constantine I into abdication and exile and left a legacy of bitterness in Graeco–Turkish relations over the Aegean.

M. Llewelyn Smith, *Ionian Vision* (1973)
P. C. Helmreich, *From Paris to Sevres: The Partition of the Ottoman Empire at the Paris Conference of 1919–20* (1974)

**Gramsci, Antonio** (1891–1937). Italian communist politician and theoretician. He was a founder member of the ITALIAN COMMUNIST PARTY in January 1921 when it split from the Socialists. He visited Moscow in 1922–3 and had his leadership of the party recognized in January 1926. In November 1926 he was arrested, and in May 1928 sentenced to 20 years in prison, where he produced his highly influential *Prison Notebooks*, the source of the Italian Communist Party's post-war tactics and the theory of EUROCOMMUNISM. His views were notable for dropping insistence on violent proletarian revolution, stressing the importance of cultural and other non-economic factors in shaping history, and for suggesting the need to adopt more flexible tactics in which the communists would ally with progressive forces. The party should seek to propagandize the whole of society thus winning acceptance of communism, rather than enforce it through the dictatorship of the

proletariat. The concepts of 'hegemony' within societies and of what came to be called 'socialism with a human face', owe much to him. The centre of an international campaign for his release, he died in a prison hospital on 27 April 1937. Gramsci is now regarded as Italy's leading Marxist philosopher, and has a wide following worldwide, among non-Marxists as well as Marxists.

J. M. Cammett, *Antonio Gramsci and the Origins of Italian Communism* (1967)
M. Clark, *Antonio Gramsci and the Revolution that Failed* (1977)

**Grand Coalition, German.** Formed in 1966 when ERHARD resigned following the withdrawal of support by the FREE DEMOCRATS. Kiesinger became Chancellor of a coalition of the CHRISTIAN DEMOCRATIC UNION (CDU) and the SOCIAL DEMOCRATIC PARTY (SDP). The SDP's abandonment of its commitment to Marxism in 1959 and adoption of a mixed economy made the coalition possible, its leader, BRANDT, serving as Foreign Minister. It succeeded in reducing unemployment but was faced with continuing neo-Nazi activity and student protest. In the General Election of October 1969, the Social Democrats under BRANDT took office for the first time.

**Graziani, Rodolfo** (1882–1955). Italian general. He joined the army in the 1890s and served in the First World War, emerging as the youngest Colonel. He then fought in wars against the Arabs in Tripolitania from 1921 and carried through brutal repression under orders of BADOGLIO. As Governor of Somalia he fought in the Ethiopian War (*see* ETHIOPIAN CRISIS) and succeeded Badoglio as viceroy. His savage reprisals following an assasination attempt on 19 February 1937 provoked widespread unrest, and he was replaced in November. Appointed to command in North Africa in June 1940 he was defeated by the British at Sidi Barrani on 9 December, losing 40,000 men. After further defeats he retired from army life, but following the armistice of September 1943, he became Defence Minister and Chief of Staff in the puppet Italian Socialist Republic in Northern Italy. He organized an apolitical armed force which fought against the partisans and anti-fascists. Arrested by the US Army in 1945, he was handed back to Italy and sentenced in 1950, to 19 years' imprisonment. He was released within months, becoming honorary President of the neo-fascist Movimento Sociale Italiano until his death.

**Greater German People's Party** (*Grossdeutsche Volkspartei*; GdVP). The party was formed by the amalgamation of a number of Pan-German groups in Austria in 1921. The groups originated from the nationalistic and anti-clerical movement which grew up in the late 19th century under the leadership of Georg Ritter von Schönerer. Although by far the smallest of the three ideological groupings in Austrian politics, electoral support for the GdVP was significant enough to prevent single party government in the First Republic, and the party provided Conservative coalitions with their electoral majorities. Most political support for the German Nationalists was transferred to the Nazis during the DEPRESSION.

**Greek Civil War.** The Greek Civil War grew out of the rivalry of the resistance groups within Greece during the AXIS occupation from 1941–4, growing into a struggle for control of Greece which, with intervals, lasted until 1949. Following the German invasion of the Soviet Union in June 1941, the Communist Party of Greece (KPP), formed a National Liberation Front (EAM) which recruited and trained a guerrilla army, the People's Liberation Army (ELAS), which it was hoped would provide the basis for a communist seizure of power. Fighting between ELAS and pro-royalist resistance groups was temporarily halted in April 1944 by the Lebanon agreement with the Greek government-in-exile and the formation of a national unity government with communist participation. When the Nazi withdrawal from Greece began in September 1944 there was renewed fighting, but the return of the Greek government in exile in October led to a meeting at Caserta in which ELAS and the National Republican Greek League (EDES) agreed to put their guerrilla forces under government control. By early December, however, this agreement had broken down and street clashes were followed by a full-scale communist insurrection in Athens from 3 December. The Greek government called on British troops to assist them, and ELAS was defeated in Athens by mid-January 1945. On 12 February a cease-fire was signed, the Varkiza Agreement, granting an amnesty to all those who surrendered their weapons and a plebiscite on the future of the monarchy.

Although subject to savage presecution EAM remained strongly entrenched in northern Greece where it could draw on communist support from Albania, Yugoslavia and Bulgaria and the terrain offered opportunities for a successful guerrilla campaign. The war was reopened with armed attacks on 31 March 1946, the day of general elections under UNITED NATIONS auspices which the communists boycotted. It had become a full-scale struggle by October 1946 when the ELAS commander, Markos Vafiadis, established a 'Democratic Army of Greece' in the northern countryside, aiming to establish control over a broad swathe of territory and set up a rival government in Konitsa, which they twice attempted to seize.

A crucial development came with the intervention of the United States, responding to Britain's inability to continue to support the Greek royalists, by the enunciation of the TRUMAN DOCTRINE in March 1947, offering military assistance to any government threatened by communist aggression. The United States took the view that, as ELAS was being supplied from beyond Greece's borders, the Greek Civil War fulfilled the requirements of an outside attack and on this basis United States aid was offered to the Greek government on 12 March 1947. The Greek Communist Party was officially outlawed on 24 December 1947 after it announced the formation of a rebel government under the presidency of Vafiadis. American military assistance began to have effect, especially after February 1948 when the American General James Van Fleet arrived and began to organize counter-guerrilla operations, including a series of sweeps against guerrilla bases. In Operation Dawn in April 1948 20,000 Greek National troops attacked communist bases in the Roumeli Mountains north of the Gulf of Corinth, killing or capturing over 2,000 guerrillas in a decisive campaign which freed central Greece from communist control. Faced with growing resistance, disagreements opened up among the communist forces. Vafiadis was overruled in his preferrence for a return to a purely guerrilla war, expelled from the Communist Party, and replaced in control of military affairs by the Moscow-backed head of the Greek Communist Party, Zachariadas, who proceeded to form a Democratic Army, capable of holding territory and maintaining a rival government. Accordingly, the communists appointed a Prime Minister in January 1949 and declared 1949 the 'Year of Victory'. However, the appointment of a veteran of the Albanian War of 1940, General PAPAGOS, to command the Greek armies in January 1949 marked the beginning of the end for the communist forces as they suffered a series of defeats. In July 1949 TITO announced the gradual closure of the border with Greece as his defection from COMINFORM led him to seek more peaceful relations with his neighbours and concentrate on rebuilding his shattered country. The final campaigns by the Greek armies at Mounts Vitsi and Grammos in August 1949 drove the last remnants of the communist forces across the borders into Albania, Yugoslavia and Bulgaria. On 16 October 1949 the Democratic Army announced that it had ceased fighting, allowing Truman to announce victory in Congress on 28 November 1949.

The Greek Civil War cost 55,000 casualties amongst Government forces, with at least 38,000 communists killed and some 40,000 captured. Civilian casualties are not known with accuracy, but at least 4,000 were executed in reprisals carried out by both sides, large numbers of hostages, including children, were abducted, and 750,000 people were made homeless. The war ensured that Greece would remain in the western camp in the post-war period, a member of the NORTH ATLANTIC TREATY ORGANISATION (NATO) and eventually a member of the EUROPEAN ECONOMIC COMMUNITY. The war, however, left a legacy of bitterness which continued to mark Greek politics into the post-war era. The struggle for control in the Civil War had its origins in the turbulent politics of the inter-war years when Greece was prey to civil strife and ended the period under the dictatorship of METAXAS. Civil strife and dictatorship were to feature again in the rule of the

GREEK COLONELS as fears of communist subversion resurfaced in Greek politics. The most important long-term consequence of the Greek Civil War, however, was in the enunciation of the TRUMAN DOCTRINE and the commitment of American support against a potential communist takeover. The crisis provoked by Britain's inability to carry the burden of defending Greece beyond early 1947 brought the United States directly into the struggle to maintain a non-communist southern flank agaisnt communist aggression. The victory of the anti-communist forces was internationally significant, as the first state where an attempted communist 'war of liberation' was successfully resisted. Locally, it left Greece as part of a tier of pro-Western states, with Turkey and Iran, who were seen as essential to American global strategy in protecting the Middle East oilfields, while apparently offering lessons for the containment of communism by similar means elsewhere.

E. O'Ballance, *The Greek Civil War, 1944–49* (1966)
C. Woodhouse, *The Struggle for Greece, 1941–1949* (1976)
H. Jones, *'A New Kind of War': American Global Strategy and the Truman Doctrine in Greece* (1989)

**Greek Colonels.** Army junta which ruled Greece from 21 April 1967 until 23 July 1974. Army officers acting in the name of King CONSTANTINE II seized power and suspended parliamentary government. Troops under Colonel Georgos Papadopoulos seized government buildings in the capital and proclaimed martial law. Claiming to be acting to save Greece from 'internal enemies', the leading spirits in the coup, Papadopoulos and Stylianos Pattakos, were explicitly anti-communist and traded upon the virulent hatreds which still survived in Greece as a legacy of the GREEK CIVIL WAR. Although Constantine remained on the throne for six months, he was forced to flee after a botched attempt at a counter-coup on 13 December 1967. His departure allowed the Colonels to convert their regime into a dictatorship. The regime was marked by widespread persecution of left wing and liberal opponents, with many instances of torture brought before international tribunals. An undercurrent of royalist plotting led the Colonels to declare

Greece a Republic in June 1973, with Papa-dopoulos as President. His attempt to gain domestic and international legitimacy by gradually liberalizing the regime backfired, however, when a major explosion of student unrest in Athens in November was followed by a coup against Papadopoulos by intransigent officers led by General Dimitrios Ioannides who rejected the liberalization policies. The deepening crisis in Cyprus in July 1974, when Ioannides followers were implicated in the overthrow of Archbishop MAKARIOS and blamed for the subsequent TURKISH INVASION OF CYPRUS, brought about the Colonels' downfall. Moderate army leaders joined with moderate political leaders and called on Constantine KARAMALIS to form a government on 23 July 1974, three days after the Turkish invasion. Subsequently the leading figures in the junta were put on trial, Papadopoulos, Pattakos and Ioannides being sentenced to death, though this sentence was later commuted to life imprisonment.

The Colonels' regime demonstrated the fragility of liberal democracy in a country frequently prey to dictatorial regimes in the 20th century. The resolution of the position of the monarchy was one lasting result, a referendum on 8 December 1974 deciding that Greece would remain a Republic, codified in a new constitution adopted in June 1975.

R. Clogg and G. Yannopoulos (eds.) *Greece under Military Rule* (1972)

**Green Party, Austrian** (VGÖ). The Green movement in Austria is considerably more conservative and middle-class than its German counterpart (*see* GREENS, GERMAN). It runs a joint list in elections with the so-called 'alternatives', who are more radical, and whose ideological outlook resembles more closely that of the West German Greens. The two parties first entered a provincial diet in Vorarlberg in 1984 and first entered parliament in 1986 with nine members. Its most prominent public personality, Frieda Meissner-Blau campaigned unsuccessfully for the presidency against KURT WALDHEIM in 1986.

**Green Party, British.** Founded in 1973 as the People's Party, becoming the Ecology Party in 1975, the party adopted its present name in September 1985. The party campaigns to raise public consciousness about environmental and peace issues and promote an 'ecological' or 'green' perspective on economic matters. By 1987 the Green Party had an estimated 6,000 members and had almost 100 parish or community councillors, plus three district councillors. They fielded 133 candidates in the 1987 general election, compared with 53 in 1979, polling 89,854 votes but losing their deposit in every seat. The Green Party's influence extends much wider than its parliamentary performance, with the activities of the Greenpeace organization to alert public attention to environmental hazards. The party achieved a major breakthrough in the 1989 European elections, when it achieved its best ever results, with 15 per cent of the vote, and took second place in many Euro-constituencies, though obtaining no MEPs. The party benefited from growing environmental concerns aroused by CHERNOBYL, ACID RAIN, the 'Greenhouse effect' and pollution. Its members also rose rapidly, making it an effective force in local politics. The party retains a loose structure and has no leader, only 'spokespersons'. It had consistently achieved over 4 per cent of support in National Opinion Polls since the summer of 1989 into 1990 but fell thereafter.

S. Parkin, *Green Parties: An International Guide* (1989)

**Greens, German** (Die Grünen). The German *Die Grünen* evolved from the West German Ecology Party, first emerging as a political force in the Bremen elections of October 1979 when the 'Green list' candidates, representing a number of environmentalist and anti-nuclear groups, won 59 per cent of the votes for the Land Parliament. In the *Bundestag* elections of October 1980 this vote fell away, probably because of the markedly left-wing programme the Greens had adopted, but in the 1983 elections the Greens again performed exceptionally well, gaining more than the necessary 5 per cent of votes (5.6 per cent) for representation in the *Bundestag*. In the Schleswig-Holstein elections of March 1986, they took over 7 per cent of the vote, reflecting growing concern over green issues. The *Grünen* went on to win 8.3 per cent in the January 1987 *Bundestag* elections, achieving 42 seats. Although excluded from the national governing coalition, in early March 1989 they joined with the SOCIAL DEMOCRATIC PARTY (SPD) to form a left coalition to govern West Berlin, seen as a potential prototype of future co-operation between Greens and socialists. The German Greens are to the left of most other similar parties in Europe, drawing many leaders from the student protests of 1968. They developed mass support as a result of protests against nuclear energy and against CRUISE MISSILES during the 1970s and early 1980s. Serious splits and conflicts within the party have somewhat hampered its influence.

W. Huelsberg, *The German Greens: A Social and Political Profile* (trans., 1988)
S. Parkin, *Green Parties: An International Guide* (1989)

**Grey, Edward** (1862–1933). British statesman. He was Liberal MP for Berwick-on-Tweed, 1885–1916 and served as Foreign Secretary, 1905–16. He concluded the Anglo–Russian Entente of 1907 and supported British obligations to France and Belgium in August 1914, which brought Britain into the First World War. German apologists sometimes argued that Grey had left Britain's position unclear prior to 1914 and that this was a contributory cause of war. In fact Britain was not bound to stand by France, and Belgian neutrality might have been infringed in so minor a way that war was unnecessary. However, the scale of German demands in their ultimatum to Belgium provided Grey with the public support to act as he had always wanted to in support of France, to whom he felt morally bound. He left the Foreign Office when ASQUITH resigned as Prime Minister in December 1916; he then became Viscount Grey.

Grey of Falloden, *Twenty-Five Years* (1925)
K. Robbins, *Sir Edward Grey* (1971)
M. Brock 'Britain Enters the War', in R. J. W. Evans and H. Pogge von Strandman (eds.), *The Coming of the First World War* (1988)

**Groener, Wilhelm** (1867–1939). German soldier and politician. He trained as a professional soldier and was attached to the General Staff from 1899; placed in charge of war production in 1916, in October 1918 he became second-in-command of the German army, succeeding LUDENDORFF as first Quartermaster-General. Groener

advised WILHELM II that he should abdicate on 9 November. He supported the Republican government in accepting the TREATY OF VERSAILLES and made a pact with the socialist leader Ebert in November 1918 guaranteeing army support for the government's crushing of the SPARTACISTS. Groener sponsored the formation of the FREIKORPS. He served as Minister of Communications, 1920–3 and was appointed Minister of Defence January 1928, serving until May 1932. During 1931–2 he served as Minister of the Interior under BRUNING. He attempted to keep the army above politics, but was undermined by the NAZIS. His attempt to ban the SA in April 1932 earned a bitter attack from GOERING. He resigned in May 1932, depriving the WEIMAR REPUBLIC of one of its major defenders. *See also* WEIMAR REPUBLIC.

J. W. Wheeler-Bennett, *The Nemesis of Power: the German Army in Politics, 1918–45* (2nd edn., 1980)
F. L. Carsten, *The Reichswehr and German Politics, 1918–33* (1966)

**Gromyko, Andrei** (1909–89). Soviet statesman. He became a member of the Communist Party in 1931. He was Ambassador to the United States, 1943–6; chief permanent Soviet delegate to the United Nations, 1946–8; Ambassador to Great Britain, 1952–3; deputy Soviet Foreign Minister, 1947–52, 1953–7. Appointed Foreign Minister in 1957, he was also elected First Deputy Premier in 1983 but only relinquished the foreign portfolio in 1985 when he was named Soviet President. His appointment to a largely honorific office was widely interpreted as paving the way for the 'new look' foreign policy of MIKHAIL GORBACHEV and his loyal supporter and new foreign minister Edward Shevardnadze. Gromyko's almost 30 years in charge of foreign affairs earned him a reputation as a tough negotiator and able representative of the Soviet Union's interests as a superpower. His memoirs, published shortly before his death, gave little insight into his rise under Stalin.

A. B. Ulam, *Expansion and Coexistence* (1968)
T. W. Wolfe, *Soviet Power and Europe, 1945–70* (1970)
A. Gromyko, *Memories* (1988)

**Grossdeutsche Volkspartei.** *See* GREATER GERMAN PEOPLE'S PARTY.

**Grünen, Die.** *See* GREEN PARTY, GERMAN.

**Guderian, Heinz** (1886–1954). German general and pioneer of tank warfare. He came from an army background and was commissioned in 1907. He became interested in battlefield mobility during the First World War and read the works of other likeminded theorists. He worked with motorized troops and was given command of Second Panzer Division in 1936. By 1938 a Corps Commander with overall command of mobile troops, he demonstrated the BLITZKRIEG tactics of the use of armour during the war against Poland. In 1940 he approved the plan to attack France through the Ardennes and led XIX Panzer Corps in the defeat of France in May–June 1940. He commanded an Army Group, Panzergruppe 2, in the assault on Russia in June 1941. Originally deployed in the centre, he was diverted to the south, encircling a Soviet force of over 1 million men in the Kiev area, taking 665,000 prisoner. The Kiev encirclement demonstrated the potential for rapid armoured thrusts backed up by other arms. He quarrelled with HITLER on strategic matters and was relieved of his command in December 1941. He was recalled to supervise tank production in 1943 and on 23 July 1944 returned to active service as Chief of Staff of the Army. After a final quarrel with Hitler in March 1945 he was sent on indefinite sick leave. He surrendered to the Americans.

H. Guderian, *Panzer Leader* (1952)
J. Erickson, *The Road to Stalingrad* (1975)

**Guernica.** A small town in northern Spain, associated with Basque claims to independence and nationhood, Guernica became a symbol of the cruelties of the SPANISH CIVIL WAR following its destruction on 26 April 1937. After being bombed repeatedly with high explosives and incendiaries, mainly by planes of the German CONDOR LEGION, fleeing survivors from the normal population of 7,000–10,000 and refugees from the Nationalist advance were machinegunned from the air. Though of some strategic importance as a communication centre, the manner of the attack provoked an immediate and persistently emotive polemic. Embarrassed Nationalists sought to blame retreating government forces, while supporters of the Republican side focused on the episode as an example of the barbarity of their opponents. Under FRANCO, while attempts to establish the truth of events continued, the image of Guernica, perpetuated most strongly in the painting by Picasso, remained as a powerful symbol for the opposition of the loss of liberty, both Basque and Spanish. The return of Picasso's work to Madrid in 1981 was consequently a sign of renewed democracy.

G. Thomas and M. Witts, *Guernica* (1975)
H. R. Southworth, *Guernica! Guernica!: A Study of Journalism, Diplomacy Propaganda and History* (1977)

**Gulag.** Russian acronym for the Chief Administration of Corrective Labour Camps, used generally to refer to the Soviet system of penal colonies and LABOUR CAMPS. The term obtained wide currency following the publication in the West in 1973 of the first part of ALEXANDER SOLZHENITSYN's *The Gulag Archipelago*, which documented the expansion of forced labour camps under the BOLSHEVIKS and STALIN. The Russian title of the book evokes the image of an enormous number of 'islands', the Gulag archipelago, with thousands of 'natives' existing within the borders of the Soviet Union. As an exposé of the vast network of penal institutions and labour camps and of the apparatus of police oppression, bureaucracy and terror which maintained them, the book became a major indictment of the whole Soviet system. Solzhenitsyn's decision to publish in the West was the culmination of a freezing out of his works from the officially sanctioned press in the Soviet and their circulation in SAMIZDAT editions. The search for a foreign press was prompted by the arrest, interrogation and suicide of a Leningrad woman entrusted with part of the manuscript. He pointedly dedicated the book to 'all those who did not live to tell it'. Publication was followed in 1974 by his arrest and deportation from the Soviet Union. *See also* PURGES.

D. Dallin and B. Nicolaevsky, *Forced Labour in the Soviet Union* (1948)
A. Solzhenitsyn, *The Gulag Archipelago* (1973–6)
R. Conquest, *Kolyma: The Arctic Death Camps* (1978)

**Gulf War.** War between UN-backed Coalition of the United States, European powers, and Arab countries and Iraq for control of Kuwait. On 2 August 1990 the leader of Iraq, Saddam Hussein, ordered his forces into Kuwait following disputes between him and the Gulf States over cuts in the price of oil, disputes with Kuwait over islands in the northern Gulf, and over extraction from an oilfield shared between Iraq and Kuwait. UN resolution 660 demanded immediate withdrawal of Iraq's forces from Kuwait and on 6 August the UN imposed a complete trade embargo on Iraq. On 16 August Iraq ordered foreign nationals in Kuwait and Iraq to report to hotels and the next day proposed deploying them as a 'human shield' against 'aggression'. On 28 August Kuwait was declared to be the 19th province of Iraq. During September British and French troops joined a growing United States military build-up in the Gulf, creating the largest deployments of American troops abroad since Vietnam and the largest British and French extra-European efforts since the SUEZ CRISIS. On 29 November, the UN authorized 'all necessary means' to drive Iraqi forces from Kuwait if they had not withdrawn by 15 January 1991. Piecemeal release of western hostages was followed by the announcement on 6 December of the release of all hostages, but high-level talks to resolve the crisis had broken down by early January 1991. On the night of 16–17 January the Coalition forces began a systematic air assault on Iraqi military pos-itions and defence infrastructure, Operation 'Desert Storm'. In spite of some retaliation from Scud missile attacks on Israel and Saudi Arabia by Iraq, complete air supremacy over Kuwait and Iraq was obtained by 30 January. The biggest anxiety on the Coalition side concerned restraining Israel from participating in the war and threatening the break-up of the Coalition. Iraqi peace proposals sent via Moscow on 19 and 21 February 1991 were declared insufficient by President Bush and on 22 February he imposed a deadline of 5 pm on 23 February for Iraqi forces to leave Kuwait. On 24 February the Coalition forces launched a massive assault into Kuwait and southern Iraq, routing and encircling most of the forces in the area. On 28 February the Allied offensive was suspended and a provisional ceasefire agreed between Coalition and Iraqi forces. Allied casualties were light, 119 killed, but Iraqi losses were estimated at almost 100,000. In spite of a crushing defeat, Saddam Hussein retained sufficient power to defeat revolts in the Shi'ite areas of southern Iraq and a Kurdish rebellion in the north, the latter precipitating a mass exodus of Kurds to Turkey and Iran. A formal ceasefire agreed in the UN in April 1991 imposed on Iraq the obligation to destroy its weapons of mass destruction, pay compensation to Kuwait, and accept a UN peace-keeping force on the Iraq-Kuwait border.

# H

Haig, Douglas (1861–1925). British general. The son of a Scottish distiller, Haig was commissioned in the Seventh Hussars in 1885, and distinguished himself in the Boer War. He was principal military adviser to the reforming war minister, Haldane, from 1906 to 1908. He led the First Army Corps of the BRITISH EXPEDITIONARY FORCE to France in 1914, and fought at Mons, on the Meuse and at Ypres. In 1915 he succeeded Sir JOHN FRENCH as British commander-in-chief on the WESTERN FRONT. Haig has been fiercely criticized for the way in which he conducted the battles of attrition of the Somme, 1916, and Ypres, 1917, but his determination and self-confidence stood him in good stead in resisting the German assaults in March 1918, and he ably conducted the final battles which brought about the defeat of Germany in the autumn of 1918. In 1919 Haig was made an earl and given £100,000 by Parliament. He was President of the British Legion from 1921 until his death and launched the 'Poppy Day' appeal fund for ex-servicemen which still carries his name. Haig infuriated those who felt, like LLOYD GEORGE, that the great attritional battles were simply a waste of lives, and he was often judged in post-war writing as an unimaginative, inflexible commander. A more balanced judgement sees him as struggling to solve the same riddle which defeated other commanders on the Western Front, of overcoming the defensive strength of modern weapons. However, he did show an obstinate unwillingness to bring attacks to an end when they had clearly failed to achieve a breakthrough.

C. Falls, *The First World War* (1960)
J. Terraine, *Douglas Haig* (1963)
——, *The Western Front, 1914–18* (1964)

Halifax, Edward, 1st Earl of (1881–1959). British statesman. He was Conservative MP for Ripon, 1910–25; Viceroy of India, 1926–31; Lord President of the Council, 1937–8; Foreign Secretary, 1936–40; and Ambassador to the United States, 1941–6. As Indian Viceroy he dealt with unrest on the North West Frontier and Gandhi's campaign of civil disobedience; he reached agreement with Gandhi, March 1931. As Foreign Secretary he was one of the major exponents of the policy of APPEASEMENT, reconciled to some revival of German political dominance in Europe as she revived economically. His meetings with HITLER and the MUNICH AGREEMENT gradually turned him to a policy of isolating Germany diplomatically and standing up to her if necessary. He was a possible candidate for Prime Minister in 1940 on CHAMBERLAIN's resignation, but supported CHURCHILL's accession.

Earl of Halifax, *Fullness of Days* (1957)

Hallstein Doctrine. Foreign policy doctrine pursued by the FEDERAL REPUBLIC OF GERMANY between 1955 and 1967. Named after one of Chancellor ADENAUER's senior foreign policy advisors, and first stated in 1955, the doctrine sought to prevent international recognition of the GERMAN DEMOCRATIC REPUBLIC by threatening to sever diplomatic relations with any country which recognized the East German state. The doctrine thus sought to maintain the claim of the Federal Republic, stated in the preamble to the Basic Law, alone to speak for the whole German nation until free elections for a government of both West and East Germany. The wisdom of adhering to the doctrine was increasingly challenged by critics within the Federal Republic from the early 1960s onwards: not only did it deprive the Federal Republic of all diplomatic influence on the communist states of central and eastern Europe and prevent the resurrection of historically important trade links, but also enabled the communist governments to justify their rule by portraying the Federal Republic as a hostile revisionist power. The doctrine was effectively abandoned in 1967 by the 1966–9 'Grand Coalition' government, when West Germany established diplomatic relations with Yugoslavia and Rumania, states which had long recognized the DDR: yet the comprehensive normalization of relations between the Federal Republic and its communist eastern neighbours had to await the 'Eastern Policy' (*See* OSTPOLITIK) developed by the BRANDT government after 1969.

W. Griffith, *The Ostpolitik of the Federal Republic of Germany* (1978)

H. A. Turner, *The Two Germanies since 1945* (1987)

**Hammarskjöld, Dag** (1905–61). Swedish politician and Secretary-General of the United Nations, 1953–61. A former economics professor at Stockholm University, 1933–6, he entered the service of the Swedish government and became Deputy Foreign Minister, 1951–3. He was elected Secretary-General of the United Nations in 1953 in succession to TRYGVE LIE and re-elected in 1957. During the SUEZ CRISIS and in the Congo he earned a reputation for impartiality. He was killed in an air crash while engaged in negotiations between the Congo and the secessionist province of Katanga. He was posthumously awarded the 1961 Nobel Peace Prize.

**Haughey, Charles** (1925–). Irish politician; Taoiseach (Prime Minister) of the Irish Republic 1979–81, 1982, and since 1987. He has been the leader of FIANNA FAIL since 1979, and served as Finance Minister, 1966–70. His earlier career suffered an eclipse when he was implicated in an alleged 'gun running' scandal to assist the IRISH REPUBLICAN ARMY. In spite of the traditions of his party, he attempted to improve the relationship with the British government under Mrs THATCHER in his first term of office. In May 1980 an agreement was reached on a 'new and close political co-operation' over Northern Ireland, and at the end of the year there was an undertaking to establish Anglo–Irish studies on matters of common concern. The joint studies, reporting in November 1981, recommended the establishment of an 'Intergovernmental Council' of ministers to renew Anglo–Irish policy towards Northern Ireland. But Haughey also protested at the treatment of the republican hunger strikers in the North in 1981 and attacked British policy over the occupation of the Falkland Islands – a return to the more traditional role of his party as a staunch critic of British policy in the North and elsewhere in the world. Haughey's defeat in the election of December 1982 kept him from power until March 1987, when he was elected Prime Minister on the casting vote of the speaker of the Dial (Irish Parliament). Although it was widely anticipated that his election might lead to a more stormy period in the operation of the ANGLO–IRISH AGREEMENT signed by his predecessor Dr FITZGERALD in 1985, Haughey has maintained the regular meetings required by the agreement, although he has felt free to criticize openly aspects of British policy in the North.

**Havel, Vaclav** (1936–). Czech playwright, DISSIDENT and politician. Born into a family of architects who lost wealth and status after the communist seizure of power in 1948, he entered the theatre in 1960 and achieved his first hit in 1965. He broadcast on Free Czech Radio during 1968 and had his work banned. During the period of 'normalization' under HUSAK he was forced to work as a labourer. He was co-founder of CHARTER 77 and was gaoled for four months; he was also tried as a member of the Committee for the Defence of the Unjustly Persecuted and sentenced to four and a half years in prison. In 1986 he was awarded Holland's Erasmus Prize, but was sentenced in January 1989 to imprisonment for taking part in demonstrations to commemorate the suicide of the student Jan Palach in 1969; he was released in May as a result of an international campaign. He became the co-founder of the reform group, Civic Forum, on 19 November 1989, and took a leading part in the demonstrations which forced the resignation of the communist leadership in December. He was elected President of Czechoslovakia on 29 December 1989 in succession to Husak. A noted liberal playwright whose works are concerned with the corruption of life under a totalitarian system, Havel emerged as the leader of the new democratic forces in Czechoslovakia.

**Heath, Edward** (1916–). British politician and Prime Minister, 1970–74. He was Conservative MP for Bexley, 1950–74, and Sidcup, from 1974. A liberal Conservative, he served as chief whip, 1955–9 and as Lord Privy Seal, 1961–3, when he conducted Britain's unsuccessful first attempt to join the EUROPEAN ECONOMIC COMMUNITY (EEC). He defeated Reginald Maudling (1917–79) in 1965 to become leader of the Conservative Party, and was leader of the Opposition from 1965–70 to WILSON's Labour governments. A surprise victor in the June 1970 general election, becoming Prime Minister with a majority of 30 seats, Heath undertook a programme of economic liberalization, foreshadowed by a meeting of senior shadow politicians at Selsdon Park prior to the election. Under the Chancellor of the Exchequer appointed in July 1970, Anthony Barber (1920–) the so-called 'Barber-boom' led to rapid growth in the economy at the price of higher inflation, balance-of-payments difficulties and increased industrial unrest. Heath successfully reopened negotiations for Britain's entry into the EEC, achieved in 1973. His attempt to establish a new legal framework for industrial relations led to bitter opposition from the trade unions. A serious confrontation with the National Union of Mineworkers early in 1972 led to the declaration of a state of emergency and a return to work in February on terms favourable to the mineworkers. During 1972 Heath was also forced to impose direct rule in Northern Ireland, suspending the Stormont Parliament. A new Northern Irish Assembly based on proportional representation was established in 1973 and a power-sharing agreement reached with the major Northern Irish parties, but in May 1974 a General Strike by the Protestant Ulster Workers' Council led to the resignation of the Northern Ireland executive and forced the reimposition of direct rule. Heath's government, however, was faced with its most serious crisis when it attempted to rein in pay awards by an incomes policy; a

miners' strike led him to put industry on a THREE-DAY WEEK. Heath called a general election on the issue in February 1974, but failed to gain a majority and resigned, leaving the Labour Pary under WILSON to form a government. He was defeated in the election for the Conservative Party leadership by MARGARET THATCHER in 1975. Heath remained on the back benches during Mrs Thatcher's governments from 1979, occasionally expressing dissent at her government's economic policies or those shown towards the EEC.

R. Blake, *The Conservative Party from Peel to Thatcher* (1985)

P. Henessy and A. Seldon (eds.), *Ruling Performance: British Governments from Attlee to Thatcher* (1987)

**Heimwehr.** See AUSTROFASCISM.

**Helsinki Agreement.** Final Act of the Helsinki Conference on Security and Co-operation in Europe (CSCE), 1 August 1975, signed by 35 European and North American states. The Act established a number of commitments and a code of behaviour for more open relationships between governments of east and west. It contained undertakings about security, respect for human rights, and co-operation in economic, humanitarian and other matters. Meetings to review the application of the Helsinki Agreement took place in Belgrade (1977–8), Madrid (1980–83) and Vienna 1987–89). The Madrid Conference also set up in Stockholm in 1984 a Conference on Confidence- and Security-Building Measures and Disarmament in Europe, as well as subsidiary meetings on other matters, such as human rights (Ottawa, 1985) and culture (Budapest, 1985). Further measures to improve the implementation of the Helsinki Final Act were taken at Vienna in January 1989 in the field of human rights, including freedom of religion, and human contacts, including the free movement of citizens. A series of subsidiary meetings on such matters as the environment, information, the Mediterranean, economic co-operation and cultural heritage preceded the Helsinki Conference in 1992. Three annual conferences on the Human Dimension in 1989–91 have reviewed the implementation of commitments on all aspects of human rights, humanitarian contacts and similar topics.

The Stockholm conference in 1986 produced an agreement of 35 CSCE states, the Stockholm document, for advance warning of military manoeuvres and provisions for verification, and from 1987 CSCE observers attended NATO and WARSAW PACT exercises. The Vienna CSCE Conference became the vehicle for talks beginning in March 1989 for further confidence building measures, based on the Stockholm document, and between members of NATO and the Warsaw Pact for mutual force reductions. At the Paris summit of CSCE in November 1990 they agreed the CONVENTIONAL ARMED FORCES IN EUROPE TREATY, substantially reducing conventional forces in Europe maintained by NATO and the Warsaw Pact, eliminating disparities and the potential for surprise attack, and verification procedures.

The initial Helsinki Agreement provided a basis for the defence of human rights and raised the question of DISSIDENTS. Increasingly, however, the CSCE has become a major forum for easing east–west tension and managing the transition brought about by the ending of the COLD WAR.

**Helsinki Human Rights Group.** Formed in the Soviet Union in May 1976 following the Helsinki Conference on Security and Cooperation in Europe (30 July–1 August 1975; *see* HELSINKI AGREEMENT) where the USSR agreed to 'respect for human rights and fundamental freedoms'. The group was set up to monitor the provisions and contained a number of prominent Jewish dissidents and the distinguished physicist ANDREI SAKHAROV. It called for an amnesty for political prisoners, but in 1978 its leader Dr Yuri Orlov was sentenced to seven years' detention, and his co-founders, Alexander Ginsberg and Anatoly Shcharansky, were also given lengthy sentences on trumped-up charges. Sakharov was sentenced to internal exile in Gorky in 1980. Other members in the UKRAINE and the BALTIC STATES also received prison sentences. Many were released following the thaw in Soviet attitudes brought about with the accession of MIKHAIL GORBACHEV in 1985, who has subsequently reaffirmed the Soviet Union's adherence to the Helsinki agreement.

J. Rubinstein, *Soviet Dissidents: Their Struggle for Human Rights* (1980)

M. Shatz, *Soviet Dissent in Historical Perspective* (1980)

**Henderson, Arthur** (1863–1935). British Labour politician and cabinet minister. He had an elementary education before becoming an ironmoulder. At 16 he was converted to Methodism, which remained his leading principle. By the 1890s he was a leading trade unionist and a Liberal agent, but in 1903 he became the LABOUR PARTY's fourth MP. He became the party's General Secretary (1911–34), and in 1914 succeeded Ramsay MACDONALD as party leader on the outbreak of war. In 1915 he entered ASQUITH's coalition cabinet, and in 1916 joined LLOYD GEORGE's war cabinet, being forced to resign in 1917. Impressed by the dangers to freedom posed by Bolshevism he set out to make Labour, through the 1918 constitution (the first to include a socialist commitment), in his words 'the best bulwark against revolution and reaction'. Losing his seat at the 1918 election, he concentrated on party organization and (although he was Home Secretary in the 1924 government) on foreign affairs, becoming Foreign Secretary in 1929. His popularity in the party increased, especially after his resistance to benefit cuts in 1931, and he succeeded MacDonald as leader when the latter formed the NATIONAL GOVERNMENT. However, he was upset by the party's leftward drift, and after losing his seat in 1931 concentrated on his work as President of the abortive World DISARMAMENT CONFERENCE, for which he received the Nobel Peace Prize in 1934. He died in 1935 after many years of indifferent health.

Henderson was always a moderate. He has been seen as a heroic figure and as the builder of the modern Labour Party. Certainly his long partnership with MacDonald was very fruitful, and although their relations were never good, he believed until 1931 that no one else would be as effective a leader. However, he was somewhat narrow-minded and old-fashioned by the later 1920s, and a poor leader of the party in 1931. His foreign-policy achievements were, ultimately, pyrrhic. But he knew his limitations and served Labour well over many years.

F. Leventhal, *Arthur Henderson* (1988)
C. J. Wrigley, *Arthur Henderson* (1990)

**Henlein, Konrad** (1898–1945). Leader of the German population in the SUDETEN-LAND. Born in Bohemia of Czech mother and German father, he served in the Austrian army in the First World War. He became a gym instructor in the Sudeten German Club in Asch in 1925, and was appointed leader of the German Gymnastic Union in Czechoslovakia in 1931. He founded the Sudeten German *Heimatfront* (Patriotic Front) in 1933 as a front for pro-Nazi activity. In 1935 it changed its name to the *Sudetendeutsche Partei* (SDP), demanding autonomy for the Sudetenland within the Czech state. The Party obtained 44 seats in the Czech elections of 1935, representing about half the German population. In receipt of German subsidies from 1935, the SDP was used by HITLER to destabilize the Czech state. At a secret meeting between Henlein and Hitler on 28 March 1938 it was agreed to increase demands in such a way that compromise would prove impossible. Czech offers of autonomy were spurned, and Hitler made increasingly threatening preparations for war to 'protect' the Sudeten Germans. A rising took place with the formation of a Sudeten FREI-KORPS, and when martial law was declared Henlein fled to Germany. With the cession of the Sudetenland to Germany by the MUNICH AGREEMENT on 30 September 1938, Henlein returned. When German troops moved against the rest of the Czech state in March 1939, Henlein was appointed head of the civil administration in the Sudetenland and GAULEITER. Captured in 1945, he committed suicide in an Allied prisoner-of-war camp in May.

**Herriot, Edouard** (1872–1957). French politician and statesman. President of the RAD-ICAL PARTY (1919–57); Prime Minister, 1924–25, 1926, and 1932; member of the Senate, 1912–19; member of the Chamber of Deputies, 1919–40; Mayor of Lyon, 1905–41 and 1945–57. He was one of the leading politicians of the later Third Republic, leading the Radical party. As President of the Chamber of Deputies in 1940 he called on the French to rally to Marshal PÉTAIN. Herriot became an opponent of the VICHY régime, he was placed under restriction in 1942 and deported to Germany in 1944. Herriot was a respected President of the National Assembly, 1947–54. *See also*: RADICAL PARTY, FRENCH; VICHY.

P. Larmour, *The French Radical Party in the 1930s* (1964)

**Hess, Rudolf** (1894–1987). German Nazi politician and deputy to HITLER. Born in Alexandria, Egypt, Hess joined a Bavarian infantry regiment in 1914 before transferring to the German air force. Having been a member of a paramilitary FREIKORPS unit in 1919, Hess joined the NAZI PARTY (NSDAP) in January 1920. Participating in the MUNICH PUTSCH, Hess was imprisoned with Hitler in 1924–5 and acted as his secretary as Hitler wrote MEIN KAMPF. In December 1932 Hess was appointed head of the Political Central Commission of the NSDAP and, in April 1933, Hitler's deputy for party affairs. In June 1933 he was given permission to attend all cabinet meetings, and in December 1933 appointed a Minister without Portfolio. Introverted and insecure, Hess was blindly loyal to Hitler, who extended his powers in 1935 and used him as an instrument for the involvement of the party in all prospective legislation and personnel policy within government. In February 1938 he was made a member of the Secret Cabinet Council and, in August 1939, of the Ministerial Council for the Defence of the Reich. In 1939 he became successor designate to Hitler and Göring. With the outbreak of war, Hess's real importance within the Nazi regime diminished, though the Staff of the Führer's Deputy served as the initial power base for his successor as Hitler's secretary, MARTIN BORMANN. In May 1941 Hess embarked on an unofficial peace mission, flying to Britain in the hope of persuading the British establishment to conclude peace with Germany. Imprisoned in Britain, he was portrayed as insane in Germany. During his imprisonment Hess's mental health deteriorated sharply. Sentenced to life imprisonment by the tribunal during the NUREMBERG TRIALS, Hess subsequently retreated into a half-crazed world of illusion. From 1969 onwards, he was the sole prisoner in Spandau Prison in Berlin, detained at the insistence of the Soviet authorities. He committed suicide in Spandau in 1987.

M. Broszat, *The Hitler State* (1981)

**Heydrich, Reinhard** (1904–42). Leading functionary of the Reich Security Head Office in Nazi Germany, and a leading architect of the 'Final Solution' (*see* HOLOCAUST). A career naval officer from 1922 to 1931, Heydrich joined the NAZI PARTY and SS (*see* SS) in July 1931. Rising rapidly through the SS, he became head of the security service (SD) of the SS in July 1932 and, after the Nazi seizure of power, an SS Lieutenant-General following the purge of the SA (*see* SA in the 'NIGHT OF THE LONG KNIVES'. Deputy to HIMMLER after the latter's appointment as head of the political police in Bavaria in April 1933, he shared in the expansion of the power of the SS, becoming head of a new security police apparatus established by Himmler after his appointment as Chief of the German Police in June 1936. In January 1939 Heydrich was appointed head of the 'Reich Central Office for Jewish Emigration', and in September 1939 head of the Reich Security Head Office, with responsibility for the GESTAPO, the criminal police and the SD. In his capacity as head of the Reich Central Office for Jewish Emigration, he was responsible for the deportation of Jews from areas of pre-war Poland annexed by Germany to German-occupied Poland; together with his subordinate EICHMANN, he was engaged in 1940 in drawing up plans for the deportation of European Jews to Madagascar. He was responsible for briefing the EINSATZGRUPPEN (special task forces), which were to carry out the murder of Soviet Jews, before the invasion of the USSR; and, at the end of July 1941, he was charged by Göring with overall organizational responsibility for implementing the Nazi 'Final Solution' to the 'Jewish Question'. He summoned the Wannsee Conference of January 1942 to co-ordinate the deportation and murder of the European Jews. Appointed Deputy Reich Protector of Bohemia and Moravia in September 1941, he was the object of an assassination attempt in May 1942 by Free Czech agents trained in Britain, and died of his wounds in early June 1942.

H. Krausnick *et al.*, *Anatomy of the SS-state* (1968)
J. Noakes and G. Pridham (eds.), *Nazism, 1919–1945*, vol. 3: *Foreign Policy, War and Racial Extermination* (1988)

**Hillsborough Agreement.** *See* ANGLO–IRISH AGREEMENT.

**Himmler, Heinrich** (1900–1945). German Nazi police chief. Born in Munich, Himmler served as a cadet officer at the end of the First World War, joining the NAZI PARTY whilst an agricultural student in Munich. He participated in the MUNICH PUTSCH and was appointed *Reich* leader of the SS (*see* SS) in January 1929. He was elected a Nazi member of the REICHSTAG in September 1930. He established the security service (SD) within the Nazi party in August 1931 and, together with his subordinate HEYDRICH sought to use his power base within the SS–SD complex to take control of the political police after the Nazi seizure of power. In March 1933 he was appointed Police President in Munich, becoming Political Police Commander of Bavaria in April of the same year. In September 1933 he became commander of the political police in all states except Prussia; and was appointed head of the Prussian police and GESTAPO in April 1934. His position strengthened by the part played by the SS in the 'NIGHT OF THE LONG KNIVES' purge, Himmler increasingly asserted his independence of his nominal superior, GÖRING. HITLER resolved continuing friction between Himmler and the Ministry of the Interior by appointing Himmler Chief of the German Police in June 1936: although nominally still subordinate to the Minister of the Interior, Himmler now exercised authority over the police throughout Germany, a position he exploited to build an independent power base. In October 1939 he was appointed by Hitler 'Reich Commissar for the Strengthening of Germandom', charged with resettling central and east European ethnic Germans in areas annexed by Germany after 1939. As head of the SS, Himmler was responsible for the implementation of the Nazi 'Final Solution', the murder of the European Jews (*see* HOLOCAUST), personally witnessing a mass shooting of Jews near Minsk in August 1941 and specifically ordering the murder of the Jews in occupied Poland in early autumn 1941. The coercive role of the SS within Germany expanded significantly after 1941, a process which was to reach its climax after Himmler's appointment as Minister of the Interior in August

1943. By this stage Himmler was, after Hitler, perhaps the most powerful man in Nazi Germany. An insipid and pedantic character, his rise to this position of power is attributable not only to the internal logic of the regime's development but also to his assiduous exploitation of the possibilities opened up by the bureaucratic chaos of government in Nazi Germany for the extension of the power of the SS. Strikingly credulous, he accepted at face value much of the Ayran racial 'science' nonsense spawned by pseudo-scientific institutes established by the regime, and saw the SS as the core of the future racially based empire to be set up in the occupied eastern territories. Less the incarnation of evil than a total moral vacuum, Himmler raised bureaucratic diligence without regard for the content of the policies he was implementing to its apogee. Following the JULY BOMB PLOT in July 1944, Himmler's position was strengthened further when he was appointed Commander-in-Chief of the Reserve Army. Convinced of the imminent collapse of Nazi Germany, Himmler approached the Swedish Red Cross early in 1945 with a view to negotiating a separate peace settlement with the Western Allies. Informed of this betrayal, an enraged Hitler stripped Himmler of all of his offices in late April 1945. With the final defeat of Nazism, Himmler went into hiding: captured by British soldiers in May 1945, he committed suicide.

R. Manvell and H. Fraenkel, *Himmler* (1965)
H. Krausnick *et al., Anatomy of the SS State* (1968)

**Hindenburg, Paul von Beneckendorff und von** (1847–1934). German field marshal and Reich President, 1925–34. From 1903 to 1913 Hindenburg was General commanding the Fourth Army, from August 1914 General commanding the Eighth Army, and responsible for the German victories at the battle of Tannenberg (late August 1914) and the Masurian lakes (early September 1914), which repelled the invading Russian armies. Idolized by the German public, he was made a Field Marshal in November 1914. In August 1916 he was appointed Chief of Staff of the Army High Command, in the wake of the battles of Ypres and the Somme and of Romanian entry into the war on the side of the Entente. Despite the hope of the Reich Chancellor, BETHMANN-HOLLWEG, that his appointment would strengthen the hand of the government in resisting extreme annexationists and in working for a negotiated peace settlement, Hindenburg rapidly became a strong advocate of the introduction of unrestricted submarine warfare and the pursuit by the government of annexationist war aims; he also fell increasingly under the sway of his nominal subordinate LUDENDORFF. With Ludendorff, he played a major role in the introduction of unrestricted submarine warfare in February 1917, the dismissal of Bethmann-Hollweg in July 1917 and the imposition of harsh annexationist peace settlements with Rumania and the Soviet Union through the TREATY OF BUCHAREST and the TREATIES OF BREST-LITOVSK in 1918. Following the failure of the March 1918 offensive on the WESTERN FRONT, in September 1918 Hindenburg accepted the necessity of an armistice. Surviving the GERMAN REVOLUTION, he resigned his command in June 1919 after the acceptance by the government of the TREATY OF VERSAILLES. Through his appearance in November 1919 at the REICHSTAG commission of enquiry established to determine the origins and conduct of the war and through the publication of his memoirs, he contributed to the dissemination of the myth of Germany's defeat in the war arising from a 'stab in the back'.

Following the death of EBERT in February 1925, Hindenburg agreed to stand as a candidate for the presidency with the support of the right-wing parties, following the failure of the first ballot to produce a clear majority for any candidate. He was elected by a narrow margin in April 1925. From the outset, Hindenburg was determined to minimize the participation of the SOCIAL DEMOCRATIC PARTY (SPD) in government and maximize that of the right-wing nationalist DNVP (*see* DNVP). Given the fragile nature of coalition politics in the WEIMAR REPUBLIC and the difficulty experienced by successive chancellors in establishing a stable basis of support in the *Reichstag*, he was able to bring his political preferences to bear in a manner which had not been anticipated by those who drafted the constitution when the presidency was invested with wide-ranging powers. Hindenburg was intent on making the fullest possible use of the most important of these powers, the right to support government by emergency decree under Article 48 of the constitution, which he interpreted as granting him virtually dictatorial powers. In the governmental crisis which occurred in December 1926 Hindenburg worked tirelessly for the construction of a new coalition government including the DNVP. Following the collapse of the centre-left coalition formed after the May 1928 elections, he seized the opportunity to attempt to bypass the *Reichstag* and move towards an authoritarian presidential form of government. From April 1930 until December 1932, Hindenburg, increasingly under the influence of the illiberal and anti-democratic circle which surrounded him, used his emergency powers under Article 48 of the constitution to support the minority governments of BRÜNING, PAPEN and SCHLEICHER. Under the impact of the polarization of German politics brought about by the DEPRESSION, Hindenburg was able to secure re-election to the presidency in April 1932 only with the support of the SPD and CENTRE PARTY and in the face of a challenge from both the DNVP and the NAZI PARTY (NSDAP). From July 1932 onwards even government by emergency decree under Article 48 of the constitution became increasingly difficult and, under the influence of Papen and the camarilla which surrounded the president, Hindenburg appointed HITLER Reich Chancellor on 30 January 1933. His hope that Hitler and the NSDAP could be contained by an essentially conservative nationalist cabinet was rapidly proved to be an illusion; and the presidency increasingly lost authority during 1933–4 to the new Reich Chancellor. Hindenburg's approval of the Röhm purge ('NIGHT OF THE LONG KNIVES') of June 1934 paved the way for the abolition of the presidency following his death on 2 August 1934, and the assumption by Hitler of supreme authority.

A. Dorpalen, *Hindenburg and the Weimar Republic* (1964)

J. Wheeler-Bennett, *Hindenburg: The Wooden Titan* (1967)

M. Kitchen, *The Silent Dictatorship: The Politics of the German High Command under Hindenburg and Ludendorff, 1916–1918* (1976)

E. Kolb, *The Weimar Republic* (1988)

**Hitler, Adolf** (1889–1945). *Führer* of the National Socialist movement and Reich Chancellor of Germany from 30 January 1933 until his suicide on 29 April 1945. Born at Braunau-am-Inn on 20 April 1889, Hitler attended a grammar school in Linz before moving to Vienna in 1909, hoping to pursue a career as an artist. Disappointed in this ambition, he led a socially marginal existence, absorbing Pan-German, Social Darwinist and anti-Semitic political ideas. On the outbreak of war in 1914 Hitler enlisted in a Bavarian infantry regiment and served on the WESTERN FRONT, receiving the Iron Cross and ending the war as a corporal. Convalescing from a gas attack which temporarily blinded him, Hitler ended the war in a military hospital, and was soon recruited by the army as a political agitator for the nationalist right. In September 1919 he joined the Bavarian-based German Workers' Party (Deutsche Arbeiterpartei), which transformed itself into the National Socialist German Workers' Party (Nationalsozialistische Deutsche Arbeiterpartei, NSDAP, the NAZI PARTY) in February 1920. He became the leader of the party in August 1921, largely as a consequence of his oratorical abilities and contacts with the army. In November 1923 Hitler led the abortive MUNICH PUTSCH, seeking to exploit the chaos arising from the Franco–Belgian occupation of the Ruhr (*see* RUHR OCCUPATION) to overthrow the WEIMAR REPUBLIC. He turned his trial for treason following the failure of the putsch into a major propaganda exercise; and secured his pre-eminence amongst radical nationalists and anti-Semites throughout Germany. The NSDAP was dissolved and Hitler was sentenced to five years' imprisonment. In the event, he served less than one year of his sentence, using his imprisonment to dictate *MEIN KAMPF*, a statement of his rabidly anti-Semitic and extreme nationalist political philosophy and objectives. Hitler consolidated his position as undisputed leader of the NSDAP during this period. The onset of the world economic crisis in 1929–30, following hard on the heels of the agricultural depression of 1927–8, coincided with a crisis within the established conservative and liberal parties to facilitate the Nazi electoral breakthrough of 1930. By July 1932 the NSDAP had become the largest party in the REICHSTAG, and in the succeeding six months, Hitler's efforts were concentrated on seeking his appointment as Reich Chancellor, an objective he achieved in January 1933. Although Nazis were a minority in the new cabinet and the post of vice-chancellor was held by a non-Nazi, PAPEN, Hitler skilfully exploited the *Reichstag* fire of 27–8 February 1933 to secure the acceptance by the Reich President, HINDENBURG, of a decree suspending basic civil liberties enshrined in the Weimar Republic. The campaign for the *Reichstag* elections of 5 March 1933 and the seizure of power in the federal states by the NSDAP enabled Hitler to out-manoeuvre his conservative nationalist coalition partners, and accelerated the monopolization of political power by the NSDAP. By July 1933 a one-party state had been established, and followed his purge of the SA (*see* SA) paramilitary in late June 1934 (*see* NIGHT OF THE LONG KNIVES) Hitler was to become Reich Chancellor and Führer on the death of President Hindenburg in August 1934.

His domestic political position unassailable, Hitler was to concentrate after August 1934 largely on foreign affairs and on forcing the pace of German rearmament, intervening only rarely in domestic policy issues. Initially, his foreign policy initiatives aimed at disrupting the European alliance system and overturning the TREATY OF VERSAILLES seemed to meet little success, and by the spring of 1935 Germany was diplomatically isolated. The ANGLO–GERMAN NAVAL AGREEMENT of June 1935, the remilitarization of the RHINELAND (March 1936) and closer ties with Italy throughout the period from summer 1935 to summer 1937 marked the process whereby Germany broke out of diplomatic isolation; from the autumn of 1937 German foreign policy under Hitler's direction was to become increasingly expansionist. German occupation of Austria in the ANSCHLUSS of March 1938 was followed by absorption of the SUDETENLAND in October 1938 and of the remainder of Czechoslovakia in March 1939. In pursuing his expansionist policy, Hitler was aided by widespread reluctance in the Western democracies to contemplate resort to war to preserve the international status quo, British doubts about the United Kingdom's ability to fight a continental war whilst

protecting imperial interests in the Mediterranean and Far East, the hostility of Western governments towards the Soviet Union and general underestimation of the scope of Hitler's ambitions. A sense that the strategic balance was moving against Germany and, perhaps, anxieties amongst the Nazi leadership about the state of the economy and possible domestic discontent served to maintain the dynamic of German foreign policy in 1939 during a dispute with Poland over the status of DANZIG (Gdansk); the NAZI–SOVIET PACT of August 1939 seemed to clear the way for a war which Hitler hoped would remain localized. Following the outbreak of war with Poland, France and Britain in September 1939, the German armed forces quickly overran Poland and, in a series of brilliant campaigns in the spring and summer of 1940, most of western and north-western Europe. The invasion of Yugoslavia and Greece in spring 1941 was followed by the invasion of the Soviet Union in June 1941, setbacks in which led Hitler to assume personal command of the army in the field in December 1941. Despite German successes against Soviet forces in the course of 1942, the tide of the war began to turn against Germany; and in 1943 and 1944 the German military was forced increasingly onto the defensive. The success of the Normandy landings in June 1944 signalled that the Nazi regime's days were numbered; and in July 1944, Hitler narrowly escaped assassination in a plot led by disillusioned army officers and conservative civilians (*see* JULY BOMB PLOT). By spring 1945 large areas of Germany had been occupied by Soviet and Anglo–American forces. Trapped in Berlin, Hitler chose suicide, having raffirmed his extreme nationalism and anti-Semitism in his political testament dictated shortly before his death on 29 April 1945.

Hitler's political career has been the subject of very thorough investigation by historians, and it is unlikely that the account which has been built up will be radically altered by new documentary material. In recent years the attention of historians of the THIRD REICH has concentrated on the role of Hitler within the regime. Debate has centred chiefly on the extent to which the gradual radicalization of the regime's domestic and foreign policies may be explained principally – or even exclusively – by reference to Hitler's intentions, and the extent to which wider, structural features of the regime, and decision-making processes within it, need to be considered in seeking to explain its trajectory. The extent to which Hitler was able to act more or less free of constraint within the regime, the extent to which he alone was responsible for the formulation and conduct of foreign policy and the extent to which the evolution of the regime's anti-Semitic policies and actions have been at the heart of this discussion.

Whilst it would be premature to speak of a clear consensus, perhaps a majority of specialists are now inclined to insist on the need to see Hitler's intentions and objectives within the wider framework of the power cartel which made up the Nazi regime and the way in which decisions were made within this regime. It is now widely acknowledged, for example, that, whilst Hitler retained overall control of the conduct of German foreign policy during the 1930s and often undertook inititatives which were viewed with scepticism by other important institutions within the regime, such as the Foreign Office and the army, his radical revisionist foreign policy must also be seen as compatible with the interests of many of the non-Nazi élites. Similarly, Hitler's role as the *sole* driving force in the steady radicalization of Nazi anti-Semitic policy has now come to be questioned. Recent research into popular opinion in the Third Reich and into popular perceptions of Hitler as Führer have highlighted the extent to which his political authority was legitimated in charismatic terms. The unstable nature of this form of political authority is now commonly seen as a major contributory factor in the gradual disintegration of bureaucratic decision-making processes and the cumulative radicalization of the regime. *See also* HOLOCAUST; SECOND WORLD WAR.

A. Bullock, *Hitler: A Study in Tyranny* (2nd edn, 1964)
J. Fest, *Hitler* (1977)
W. Carr, *Hitler: A Study in Personality and Politics* (1978)
M. Broszat, *The Hitler State* (1981)
I. Kershaw, *The 'Hitler Myth': Image and Reality in the Third Reich* (1987)
'——, *The Nazi Dictatorship: Problems and Perspectives of Interpretation* (2nd edn, 1989)

**Hitler Youth** (Hitler Jugend, HJ). Youth organization of the NAZI PARTY, established in 1926 as a Nazi counterpart to the confessional and political youth organizations which had flourished in Germany since the turn of the century. Before the appointment of HITLER as Chancellor in January 1933, the main function of the Hitler Youth was to assist in the dissemination of Nazi propaganda. With a membership of only 55,000 – or a mere 1 per cent of the total membership of all youth organizations in Germany – the HJ was a fairly insignificant organization in 1933. Its subsequent expansion may be traced back to the Nazis' attempt to monopolize control of all features of social and political life in Germany: in July 1933 its leader, Baldur von Schirach, was appointed 'Youth Leader of the German Reich', charged with the supervision of all youth activities in Germany under the Reich Ministry of the Interior. By the end of 1933 the HJ had absorbed all youth organizations in Germany with the exception of those which were explicitly Catholic – these remain protected for a while by the Concordat of July 1933 between the regime and the Vatican. Whilst membership of the HJ for boys aged between 14 and 18 remained in theory voluntary until March 1939, increasing pressure was brought to bear on young people to join the organization, especially through the schools. By early 1939 HJ membership had expanded to 1.7 million: with its affiliate organizatons for boys aged 10–14, for girls aged 10–14 and girls aged 14–18, the Hitler Youth embraced 7.7 million young Germans out of a total population of 8.9 million 10–18 year olds. Given the status of an independent organization subordinate only to Hitler in December 1936, the Hitler Youth took over many of the recreational and educational functions performed by the youth organizations before 1933; but also added to these political indoctrination and pre-military training. After the outbreak of war in 1939 the function of the HJ was increasingly to become one of pre-military training; as the war progressed, members were involved in, for example, anti-aircraft units. The formation in September 1944 of a militia embracing all able-bodied males aged between 16 and 60 (*Volkssturm*) led Hitler Youth members to fight against the invading Allied armies in the final stages of the war. The impact of the HJ and its associated youth organizations on young Germans is difficult to assess, and seems to have varied from area to area and over time. Poor leadership limited the effectiveness of the organization as an agent of indoctrination, and the common picture of a generation of young people transformed into fanatical Nazis, acknowledging no allegiance save that to Hitler, is an absurd exaggeration. Nevertheless, whilst the growing militarism of the HJ alienated some and led to the formation of unofficial youth gangs, membership of the organization probably served to strengthen cultural features, such as glorification of militarism and a stress on obedience and loyalty functional to the maintenance of the Nazi regime.

H. W. Koch, *The Hitler Youth* (1975)
D. J. K. Peukert, *Inside Nazi Germany: Conformity, Opposition and Racism in Everyday Life* (1989)

**HJ**. Hitler Jugend. *See* HITLER YOUTH.

**Hoare–Laval Pact.** Secret agreement devised by Samuel Hoare, the British Foreign Minister, and PIERRE LAVAL, the French Prime Minister in December 1935 to resolve the ETHIOPIAN CRISIS following the Italian invasion in October 1935. It was proposed that Italy would receive two-thirds of Ethiopia, enlarging the existing Italian colonies in East Africa and giving further scope for Italian settlement and economic development. In return, Ethiopia was to receive a narrow strip of territory and access to the sea. When news of the pact reached the press on 10 December it was widely denounced as APPEASEMENT of Italian aggression, forcing both Hoare and Laval to resign.

H. Gatzke, *European Diplomacy between the Two World Wars* (1972)
D. Waley, *British Public Opinion and the Abyssinian War, 1935–6* (1975)
N. Rostov, *Anglo–French Relations, 1934–6* (1984)

**Hohenzollern.** Ruling dynasty of Prussia from 1701 to 1918 and imperial family of the German Empire from 1871 to 1918. The last Hohenzollern King-Emperor was WILHELM II.

**Holocaust.** The mass murder of European Jews carried out by the Nazi regime during

the SECOND WORLD WAR. Explanations of the Holocaust must start with the pathological hatred of the Jews evinced by HITLER from the earliest stages of his political career and manifest in MEIN KAMPF. Virulent ANTI-SEMITISM played an important role in holding together the otherwise heterogeneous membership of the NAZI PARTY but seems to have been relatively unimportant in attracting electoral support for the party before 1933. Whilst anti-Semitism was at the core of Nazi ideology and formed an article of faith for the activists within the Nazi movement, and whilst they were determined to remove Jews from public life in Germany, the Nazis did not have a detailed programme for the attainment of this objective before Hitler's appointment as Chancellor in January 1933. The development of Nazi anti-Semitic 'policy' between 1933 and 1939 thus often took place on an *ad hoc* basis: the gradual radicalization of the Nazi regime's measures against German Jews during this period was often surprisingly unco-ordinated and accompanied by only sporadic interventions by Hitler.

During the Nazi seizure of power in spring 1933, German Jews were not the principal target of grass-roots Nazi activism, which was focused on the destruction of the left-wing political parties. The necessity of maintaining his alliance with President HINDENBURG and the economic and military élites forced Hitler to seek to control the anti-Semitic rampages of the Nazi rank and file and SA (*see* SA) which followed the March 1933 elections; and on 1 April 1933 a rather unsuccessful one-day national boycott of Jewish shops was held in an attempt to channel Nazi anti-Semitism in a relatively orderly direction. Similarly, legislation in April 1933 to dismiss Jews from the civil service contained many exemptions inserted at Hindenburg's insistence. Thereafter, whilst Jews constantly ran the risk of being subjected to verbal and physical abuse, faced discrimination in schools and were gradually excluded from some professions (e.g. journalism), a relative calm descended on Nazi anti-Semitic activity.

In spring 1935, however, grass-roots anti-Semitism re-emerged, spearheaded once again by the Nazi rank and file. There is little evidence that renewed outbursts of violence and vandalism were co-ordinated or planned beyond the local level. Rather, this recrudescence of Nazi activism in the 'Jewish Question' seems to have been related to the disappointment of many party members at the limited gains they had made from the Nazi seizure of power; and may have been exploited by regional party chiefs to divert the disgruntled rank and file and to deflect attention from a mounting economic crisis. Hitler appears to have played a largely responsive if sympathetic role, accepting by summer 1935 that the campaign must be brought to an end in the interests of both economic recovery and maintenance of diplomatic relations with foreign states, yet also realizing that he could not afford to terminate the campaign without some gesture towards 'action' against the German Jews. The Nuremberg Laws of September 1935, prohibiting relations between Jews and other Germans, forbidding Jews to fly the German flag and depriving them of German citizenship, were announced by Hitler at the annual party rally and, whilst heightening discrimination against the German Jewish population, brought the grass-roots violence of spring and summer 1935 to an end.

Despite continuing piecemeal extension of discriminatory measures against the Jews, the years 1936–7 were to witness another period of relative calm for German Jews: the regime sought to dampen down anti-Semitic propaganda and activity by the party rank and file in order to avoid the danger of an international boycott of the 1936 Berlin Olympic Games and of disruption to businesses as full-scale rearmament got under way. From the autumn of 1937, however, the cumulative radicalization of Nazi anti-Semitic measures regained momentum. At the September 1937 Nuremberg rally, Hitler attacked the Jews publicly for the first time in two years.

The growing ascendancy of GÖRING within the economy after the launch of the FOUR YEAR PLAN led to a campaign to 'Aryanize' the German economy by forcing the sale of Jewish-owned businesses to 'Aryan' (i.e. German) competitors at rates well below market prices. The radicalization of Nazi anti-Semitic policy during 1937–8 cannot be divorced from the general radicalization of the regime in both the domestic and foreign policy spheres. This period witnessed a wide-ranging purge of 'conservatives' within the regime, such as SCHACHT, which opened the way for more radical anti-Semitic measures, a development which received new impetus from the German annexation of Austria through the ANSCHLUSS of March 1938. In April 1938 Jews were obliged to register all property with a value of more than 5,000 marks and were forbidden to sell or lease such property without permission. In June and July 1938, further restrictions on the activities of Jewish professionals were announced, and all German Jews were required to adopt either Israel or Sarah as an additional first name. From October 1938 the passports of all German Jews were stamped with the letter J.

Throughout this period, emigration of German Jews remained the Nazis' principal objective: by the end of 1937, however, only 129,000 Jews had emigrated, barely a quarter of the 1933 German Jewish population of 503,000. Jewish emigration increased in 1938, when a further 40,000 Jews left Germany; and 45,000 of the 190,000 Austrian Jews emigrated in a six-month period after the *Anschluss*. The confusion and lack of co-ordination in the regime's anti-Semitic policies at this stage is apparent from the fact that whilst one agency – the Security Service (SD) – was seeking to accelerate emigration, others were hampering this process by confiscation of German Jews' property.

The climax of the radicalization of Nazi anti-Semitic policy in 1937–8 came in early November 1938 when GOEBBELS secured Hitler's approval for the unleashing of a pogrom following the murder of an official in the German embassy in Paris by a young Jewish émigré: on the night of 9–10 November rampaging SA men and party activists murdered 91 Jews (a further 20,000 Jewish men being summarily arrested and thrown into concentration camps), burned synagogues and looted Jewish property throughout Germany. In the wake of the KRISTALL NACHT which was greeted with almost universal disapproval by ordinary Germans, Göring seized the opportunity to levy an enormous fine on the German Jewish community and to issue the 'Decree excluding Jews from German Economic Life' of 12

November, which extended and formalized the 'Aryanization' campaign. Fatefully, in January 1939, he was to delegate to REIN-HARD HEYDRICH, head of the SD, responsibility for the promotion of Jewish emigration and to establish a 'Reich Central Office for Jewish Emigration' within the Reich Ministry of the Interior. Thus, on the eve of the Second World War, effective control of anti-Semitic policy passed into the hands of functionaries of the SS (see ss).

The outbreak of the Second World War in September 1939 marked an important turning-point in Nazi policy towards the Jews. Through an ominous psychological projection, Hitler blamed the Jews for the outbreak of war. In a speech to the REICHS-TAG in January 1939 he had threatened that: '. . . if the international Jewish financiers in and outside Europe should succeed in plunging the nations once more into a world war, then the result will not be the bolshevizing of the earth, and thus the victory of Jewry, but the annihilation of the Jewish race in Europe.' Subsequently, Hitler often postdated this speech to 1 September 1939, merging the outbreaks of war with his 'mission' to destroy the Jews. The outbreak of war also created a new context for Nazi anti-Semitic policy. The regime was now largely able to disregard foreign opinion, an important restraining influence in the pre-war period. The rapid German conquest of Poland also increased dramatically the number of Jews under German control, and hence the dimensions of the 'Jewish problem', whilst emigration became more difficult. Finally, the conditions of war made morally possible in the minds of many Nazi functionaries a more brutal treatment of Jews under German control.

In late October 1939 HIMMLER ordered the deportation to occupied Poland (the 'General Government') of all Jews in those areas of pre-war Poland which were to be incorporated into Germany: in the interim, Polish Jews were to be concentrated in ghettos and obliged to carry out forced labour. Throughout 1940, forced emigration and deportation were still seen by most Nazi leaders as the instruments whereby a 'solution' to the 'Jewish problem' would be brought about. Yet the deportations of Jews to occupied Poland were

halted in March 1940 at the insistence of the governor-general, Hans Frank; and British control of the sea lanes made unworkable a plan widely discussed by the Nazi leadership to deport Jews from German-occupied territory in both Eastern and Western Europe to the island of Madagascar (a plan which was finally abandoned only in early 1942).

As the standard of living of the Jews in the Polish ghettos deteriorated horrifyingly during late 1940, the Nazi leadership was finalizing its plans for the invasion of USSR. Conceived of by Hitler as an ideological war of annihilation – a view widely shared by the Nazi leadership and the officer corps of the German armed forces – the invasion of the USSR in June 1941 was to lead directly to the mass murder of the bulk of the Jewish population of Europe. The invasion was preceded by a complex of orders – some oral – to the armed forces and special task forces (EINSATZGRUPPEN) of the SS to shoot Russian Jews, Soviet political commissars and other categories of Soviet citizens falling into German hands.

In late July 1941, Göring authorized the SS to plan '. . . a complete solution of the Jewish question within the German sphere of influence in Europe'. Whilst no written order from Hitler ordering the mass murder of the Jews survived the war, and Hitler's precise role in the development of the mass-murder programme remains shadowy, it is almost certain that Göring's initiative stemmed from a decision on Hitler's part, taken sometime shortly after the start of the invasion of the USSR, to begin the physical destruction of the European Jews.

In September 1941 restrictions on the freedom of movement of Polish Jews were extended to German Jews, who were now obliged to wear a yellow Star of David and were forbidden to leave their area of residence without permission. In October 1941 Himmler banned any further Jewish emigration from German-controlled Europe. In all likelihood, Hitler approved in late October or November 1941 an extermination plan which Göring had charged the SS with preparing in July. In late November 1941 the first massacres of German Jews deported eastwards took place in Kovno (Lithuania) and Riga. In January 1942 Heydrich chaired a meeting of senior SS and security police figures and officials from the Ministry of Justice and occupied Poland, held in the Berlin suburb of Wannsee: the business of the meeting was the detailed planning for the mass murder of the European Jews. Whilst work on the construction of the extermination camps at Belzec and Auschwitz-Birkenau had begun in December 1941, it was to be accelerated after the Wannsee conference. In the Soviet Union, Jews were murdered by shooting; perhaps 0.75 million men, women and children being shot by the *Einsatzgruppen* between June 1941 and April 1942 alone. Occupied Poland became the site of the mass gassings of Jews from the whole of Europe in specially constructed extermination camps: camps at Belzac, Sobibor and Treblinka all began their industrial mass murder in spring and early summer 1942, Auschwitz-Birkenau having begun operating slightly earlier.

A special department within the German Foreign Ministry, which collaborated closely with EICHMANN's department within the SS-Police headquarters, was established to press Germany's allies and satellites to deport their Jewish populations to eastern Poland to be murdered. In Italy, deportations of the Jewish populations began in earnest only after the German occupation of September 1943; in Hungary, only after the Germans took control in March 1944. In occupied Europe, the extent to which the Germans were able to pursue the deportation of the indigenous Jewish populations depended on a range of factors, the most important being the extent of German control and the attitude of the authorities and non-Jewish populations towards their Jewish compatriots. In Poland, Czechoslovakia, Holland, Latvia, Yugoslavia, Greece and Germany itself, over 80 per cent of the pre-war Jewish populations had been murdered by 1945. In the USSR, Hungary, Romania, Italy, Belgium and France, more than half the pre-war Jewish populations survived the war. In Denmark, at another extreme, the small Jewish populations survived almost intact, largely because of the uncompromising resistance of the non-Jewish population towards the Nazis' policies. In all, at least 4.2 million and perhaps as many as 5.7 million European Jews were murdered by the Nazi

regime in the course of the Second World War.

Sophisticated studies of the development of popular opinion in Nazi Germany have now demonstrated beyond doubt that the mass murder of the European Jews did not stem from any genocidal hatred on the part of the bulk of the German population. Whilst Nazi discriminatory measures and propaganda had some success in isolating Jews socially from the rest of the German population, German attitudes towards the 'Jewish Question' were generally characterized by indifference before 1939, indifference which easily and quickly turned to outright disapproval of grass-roots Nazi violence and vandalism in 1933, 1935 and 1938. After 1939 German civilians were generally preoccupied by day-to-day and family concerns arising from the war. Knowledge of the mass shootings in the USSR, largely conveyed by soldiers on leave from the Eastern Front, was certainly more widespread than most Germans were willing to concede in the post-war decades. The mass gassings of Jews in the extermination camps of Poland seem to have been the subject of only vague rumour. The principal charge which might be raised against most Germans is that of indifference and apathy towards progressively more savage measures against a minority of their Jewish compatriots. As for those members of the SS, German army and civilian bureaucracies which were so deeply implicated in the Nazi 'Final Solution' of the 'Jewish Question', their participation in genocide seems to have been made possible less by evil and murderous conviction than by their regarding those they murdered as somehow less than human beings: time and again, even the most senior figures participating in the Holocaust made clear their understanding of their monstrous activities as an at times unpleasant duty to be carried out in as professional and detached a manner as possible.

During the last 15 years or so, research has once again turned to the central figure of Hitler and to the fundamental question of how his obsessive hatred of the Jews came to be translation into genocidal practice by a modern state apparatus. Here, two main lines of approach have emerged.

Some historians have argued that the

Nazi mass murder of the European Jews can be explained largely with reference to Hitler's intentions. On this understanding, Hitler contemplated from a very early stage in his political career the physical destruction of the Jews and seized the opportunity to realize this long-term goal afforded by the Second World War and especially the invasion of the USSR. The gradual escalation of discrimination against Jews in Germany before 1939 is thus seen as part of a planned process, co-ordinated to a greater or lesser extent by Hitler, and forming a prelude to the terrible events of the war years.

Other historians, by contrast, have placed greater emphasis on the confused and fragmented decision-making processes in Nazi Germany; and have stressed the *ad hoc* character of discriminatory measures before 1939 and of the radicalization of Nazi anti-Semitic policy after the outbreak of war. On this reading, the cumulative radicalization of Nazi anti-Semitic policy cannot be traced back to Hitler's intentions alone. Rather, it arose from local initiatives taken by individuals in the certain knowledge that they were carrying out Hitler's wishes, initiatives which, more often than not, did not stem from clear guidance from above. Initially planning the deportation of the Jews to a 'reservation' beyond the Urals, the Nazi leadership was taken by surprise by the stiffening of Soviet resistance in the autumn of 1941, resistance which now made the 'reservation' plan unworkable. The resumption of deportations of Jews to the East in October 1941 led to over-crowding and massive logistical problems on the ground, which local SS leaders sought to solve by resorting to *ad hoc* massacres. In October or November Hitler was informed by Himmler of this gradually spreading practice, a practice which he endorsed and proposed should be extended to the European Jewish population as a whole. Whilst in no way reducing Hitler's ultimate moral and political responsibility for genocide, this line of interpretation does shift the immediate explanation of the terrible radicalization of Nazi anti-Semitic policy which took place in summer and autumn 1941 away from Hitler and on to those responsible for local initiatives within an increasingly brutal bureaucracy of terror.

Whilst it would be premature to speak of a consensus amongst historians of the Third Reich on this central question, a number of points now command general assent. The first concerns the decisive radicalization of policy which occurred with the orders to the *Einsatzgruppen* in spring 1941 to murder Soviet Jews in the course of the invasion of the USSR. Second, it is apparent that this dramatic development could not have taken place without Hitler's knowledge and without his sanction. Finally, it is generally agreed that the extension of the mass-murder programme to the non-Soviet European Jews was being planned from at least late July 1941 onwards and that this plan received Hitler's approval in late October or November 1941. Whilst Hitler's direct interventions in the planning and direction of Nazi anti-Semitic policy are often difficult to chart, the centrality of his paranoid hatred of the Jews in bringing about the Holocaust cannot be doubted. His maintenance of this obscene obsession, in conjunction with the fragmented decision-making processes of the Nazi regime and the ideological nature of the war against the Soviet Union, led directly to the systematic mass murder of the bulk of the Jewish population of Europe.

L. S. Davidowicz, *The War against the Jews* (1976)
R. Hilberg, *The Destruction of the European Jews* (1983)
G. Fleming, *Hitler and the Final Solution* (1986)
J. Noakes and G. Pridham (eds), *Nazism, 1919–1945*, vol. 3: *Foreign Policy: War and Racial Extermination* (1988)

**Home, (Sir) Alec, Douglas** (1903–). British politician; Prime Minister, 1963–4. As a Scottish peer, Lord Douglas, he entered the House of Commons in 1931, serving as Parliamentary Private Secretary to Prime Minister NEVILLE CHAMBERLAIN, 1937–9. Upon succeeding his father as 14th Earl of Home in 1951, he resigned his seat in the Commons. He served as Minister of State, 1951–5; Minister for Commonwealth Relations, 1955–60; Leader of the House of Lords, 1957–60; and Foreign Secretary, 1960–63. Following MACMILLAN's resignation in 1963 he was a surprise choice as Prime Minister, seen as a representative of a more traditional brand of Conservative politics and a less accomplished television and public performer than his Labour opponent, WILSON. In order to take up the premiership he had to relinquish his peerage and fight a by-election to the House of Commons. Following his defeat in the 1964 General Election he became Leader of the Opposition until 1965, when he stood down and was replaced by EDWARD HEATH. In 1970–74 he served as Foreign Secretary under Heath, taking a life peerage after the Conservative defeat in the 1974 election. *See also* CONSERVATIVE AND UNIONIST PARTY.

R. Blake, *The Conservative Party from Peel to Thatcher* (1986)

**Home Rule.** The establishment of devolved powers of government, usually applied exclusively to the question of Irish agitation for self-government short of full independence. The Home Rule Association was founded by Isaac Butt in Dublin in 1870. Under the leadership of Charles Stewart Parnell (1846–91) the Irish Nationalist MPs represented in Parliament induced Gladstone to introduce two Home Rule bills. The first, in 1886, provided for a legislative body in Dublin with full control of administration, save for the budget, foreign policy and defence. It was defeated in the Commons. A second bill, in 1892, was defeated in the House of Lords. Following the two 1910 general elections which left the Home Rulers, now led by REDMOND, as a balancing force in the House of Commons and the limitation of the powers of the House of Lords in 1911, a third Home Rule bill was introduced by ASQUITH in 1912. Offering self-government to the whole of Ireland, including Ulster, it was strongly opposed by Ulster Protestants, who feared Roman Catholic domination, backed by the Conservatives. Amidst mounting tension, with both Irish Nationalists and Ulster Protestants threatening to resort to arms, the bill passed the Commons in May 1914. Negotiations continued on the eve of the First World War to find a compromise on the Ulster question and avert civil war. The outbreak of war in August 1914 led to the Bill's enactment, but suspended in effect.

From 1916, after the EASTER RISING, the Home Rule issue became radicalized, with SINN FEIN threatening to implement Home Rule unilaterally and capitalizing on grow-ing Irish discontent over British rule. An Irish Convention was organized in 1917 by LLOYD GEORGE to discuss the future government of Ireland but was increasingly overtaken by Sinn Fein's ability to command support. Two Sinn Fein candidates were elected MPs at Roscommon and Longford in 1917, and in 1918 attempts to extend conscription to Ireland met with almost universal opposition and proved a complete failure. Although Sinn Fein was declared illegal and its leaders detained, the party obtained 73 seats in the 1918 general election. Sinn Fein members refused to sit at Westminster and set up a provisional government of the Irish Republic, the Dail Eireann, which met in January 1919. DE VALERA escaped from British custody and was elected President. Both the Dail and Sinn Fein were declared illegal as clashes between British forces and republicans gathered pace. The older IRISH VOLUNTEERS was reconstituted as the IRISH REPUBLICAN ARMY, which now carried on a virtual guerrilla war with the British regular troops, the Royal Irish Constabulary and the specially-recruited BLACK AND TANS.

In December 1920 the Government of Ireland Act divided Ireland into two: 'Northern Ireland' based on the six counties of Ulster, and 'Southern Ireland', consisting of the remaining 26. Each part was to have its own parliament, but accept the supremacy of the British parliament at Westminster, where both would retain representatives. A Council of Ireland would be set up to co-ordinate matters relating to the whole of Ireland. Ulster politicians accepted the Act and a Northern Irish Parliament was elected on 24 May 1921, sitting at Belfast. Southern politicians refused to implement it, however, returning Sinn Fein candidates for 124 of the 128 southern seats, but refusing to take them up, forcing the adjournment of the parliament. Guerrilla warfare, terrorist attacks and reprisals continued, including the assassination of Field Marshal Henry Wilson, Chief of the Imperial Staff, at his London home in June 1921. Eventually, on 6 December 1921 a treaty was signed between LLOYD GEORGE and MICHAEL COLLINS, the Irish leader, by which Ireland accepted dominion status subject to the right of Northern Ireland to opt out. This right was exercised by the

North, where elections produced an over-whelming UNIONIST majority. In 1922 the Southern Irish *Dail* approved the treaty with Britain by 64 votes to 57. De Valera led the anti-treaty 'Republican' faction and resigned as President. A general election in the south confirmed majority support for the pro-treaty group.

Following the IRISH CIVIL WAR between pro- and anti-treaty factions, a cease-fire was accepted by De Valera and the Repub-lican group in 1923. In December 1925 a tripartite agreement was signed between Britain, Northern Ireland and the Irish Free State, subsequently ratified by all three par-liaments, fixing the boundary between Northern Ireland and the Irish Free State, relieving the Irish Free State of responsi-bilities for any part of the British National Debt, and transferring the powers of the Council of Ireland relating to Northern Ire-land to the Northern Irish Government. In 1937 a new constitution was promulgated in the south, changing the name of Southern Ireland to Eire. Eire's association with the BRITISH COMMONWEALTH OF NATIONS by virtue of the External Relations Act of 1936 was severed by the Republic of Ireland Act of 1948, which ended the last constitutional links with Britain.

A trajectory which passed from demands for Irish local self-government or DEVOL-UTION to the partition of Ireland and the complete separation from Great Britain of its larger southern half has attracted enor-mous attention. Broadly, debate concerns the 'inevitability' of these processes, 'nationalist' historiography concentrating on Irish independence movements in the past and the development of Irish national-ism as the chief theme of events from the Home Rule era before 1914. Other accounts stress the attempts at compromise which existed both before and after 1914 and the imminent passage of a Home Rule bill onto the statute book designed to satisfy the moderate Irish nationalists. The effects of the First World War in delaying implementation of Home Rule and the seiz-ure of the initiative by the more extreme nationalists, especially after 1916, trans-formed the situation from one where self-government was being sought within the framework of the United Kingdom to a demand for *de facto* independence for all

or part of Ireland. The Treaty of December 1921 was a compromise, the product of mutual exhaustion by the parties in the Anglo–Irish conflict, but one which left a permanent legacy of opposition to partition and to Dominion status amongst a section of the Southern Irish population. The estab-lishment of Northern Ireland as a self-gov-erning entity (on terms similar to those offered to the Irish Nationalists in 1892 and 1914), firmly under the control of a Union-ist majority opposed to the unification of Ireland, sowed the seeds of the ULSTER CON-FLICT which erupted after 1968.

F. S. L. Lyons, *Ireland since the Famine* (2nd edn, 1973)
C. Townshend, *The British Campaign in Ireland, 1919–1921* (1979)
R. Forster, *A New History of Ireland* (1988)

**Honecker, Erich** (1912–). German com-munist politician. Born the son of a coal-miner in the Saarland, Honecker joined the youth organization of the Communist Party at the age of ten and the party at the age of 17. In 1931 he became a functionary of the youth organization; after the Nazi seiz-ure of power he carried out underground work on behalf of the party within Germany until his arrest and imprisonment in 1935. With the collapse of the Nazi dictatorship, Honecker joined ULBRICHT in the work of re-establishing the Communist Party in Germany, and was charged with building up the party's youth organization, the Free German Youth. Rising rapidly through the SED (*See* SED) apparatus, Honecker became a candidate member of the Polit-buro in 1950 and a full member in 1958. Ulbricht's protégé, Honecker was elected by the People's Chamber Ulbricht's suc-cessor as chairman of the National Defence Council in June 1971. In this office he reversed Ulbricht's policy and began once more appointing party functionaries rather than technocrats to key positions in state and society. Head of the party secretariat (later retitled 'General Secretary of the Party'), Honecker added the chairmanship of the Council of State to his range of offices in 1976, thus ensuring his complete domi-nation of the central party and state machinery in the GERMAN DEMOCRATIC REPUBLIC. Honecker's assumption of leader-ship of the party and state was accompanied by a reversal of the cautious economic decentralization policies pursued by Ulbricht during the 1960s, and in 1972 most remaining private concerns in agriculture and industry were socialized. Whilst Honecker's government initially welcomed the diplomatic recognition of the GDR which the BRANDT government's OSTPOLITIK brought about, it soon came to resort to repressive measures against domestic critics and to seek to reduce contacts between East German citizens and visitors from the Federal Republic. Honecker's postponement in October 1980 of a long-planned visit to the GDR by the West German Chancellor, HELMUT SCHMIDT, highlighted his cautious attitude towards closer relations between the two German states. Finally meeting Schmidt in December 1981, Honecker secured the West German Chancellor's recognition of the 'sovereignty and statehood' of the GDR; and, despite the poor relations between the USA and the USSR which characterized the early and mid-1980s, relations between the two German states gradually improved, culminating in a visit to the Federal Republic by Honecker in September 1987. From spring 1989 onwards, Honecker's personal position, as well as the dominant position in state and society in the GDR occupied by the SED, came under pressure as unofficial emigration to the West increased following the dismantling of the IRON CURTAIN between Hungary and Austria in May 1989. Demonstrations demanding political reform continued to grow even as Honecker acted as host to President GORBACHEV during celebrations in October 1989 to mark the 40th anniversary of the establishment of the GDR. Shortly thereafter, Honecker resigned his offices on grounds of ill-health. *See also* GERMANY, FEDERAL REPUBLIC OF.

E. Honecker, *From My Life* (1981)
M. McCauley, *The German Democratic Republic since 1945* (1983)
H. A. Turner, *The Two Germanies since 1945* (1987)

**Horthy, Miklos** (1886–1957). Hungarian admiral and Regent. Coming from a landed family but trained for the Austrian–Hungarian navy, he served with distinction in the Adriatic during the First World War and became Commander-in-Chief of the Imperial Navy. He led the counter-revolution against BÉLA KUN based on the town

of Szeged, and finally entered Budapest in November 1919. In March 1920 he became Regent for the absent Habsburg King, whose restoration was often discussed, but never in fact implemented, Horthy refusing to surrender his powers to King CHARLES in 1921. Governing a small state, he sought to maintain social order while obtaining revision of the TREATY OF TRIANON. His regime was dictatorial, but allowed some forms of parliamentary democracy to survive, including a free press and political parties, although the communists were banned and the Jews subjected to harassment and persecution by the Hungarian fascist movement, the ARROW CROSS. Gradually drawn into the diplomatic orbit of the AXIS powers, Horthy was rewarded for his support by the Feldvidek region of Czechoslovakia in the First VIENNA AWARD on 2 November 1938, the award of the eastern tip of Czechoslovakia, Ruthenia, in March 1939 and in August 1940, the return of much of Transylvania from Romania in the second Vienna Award. Horthy attempted to keep Hungary out of the war with the West but was forced to join the TRIPARTITE PACT of Germany, Italy and Japan on 20 November 1940. In spite of a Treaty of Eternal Friendship between Hungary and Yugoslavia on 12 December 1940, ratified in February 1941, under its pro-German Prime Minister, Bardossy, Hungary joined the German invasion of Yugoslavia on 11 April 1941, occupying a territory of 11,000 square kilometres, containing a minority Magyar population. With Axis assistance, by June 1941 Hungary had acquired 80,000 square kilometres of territory and 5 million people, including 2 million Magyars. Divisions within Hungary over joining Hitler's attack on the Soviet Union were resolved when planes with Soviet markings bombed the Hungarian towns of Kassa and Munkacs. Although probably flown by German pilots or Slovakian dissidents, the incident prompted Hungary's declaration of war on the Soviet Union on 27 June 1941. By December 1941 Hungary was also at war with the United States and the United Kingdom. Heavy German exactions of food and raw materials, high inflation and growing losses on the Eastern Front led Horthy to have his son, Istvan, elected Vice-Regent and appoint a more neutral Prime Minister, Miklos Kallay. The loss of 110,000 men, either killed or captured, of the Hungarian Second Army at Voronezh in January 1943, decisively tipped Horthy towards developing contacts with the Western Allies and refusing German requests for more Hungarian troops. In reaction, the Germans sent eight divisions to occupy Hungary on 19 March 1944, forcing Horthy to dismiss Kallay and appoint a right-wing puppet government dominated by the Arrow Cross movement. Moreover, while Horthy had been able so far to resist the wholesale destruction of the Jewish population in Hungary, though accepting new anti-Semitic laws, over 450,000 Hungarian Jews were now sent to the concentration camps with the assistance of the virulent anti-Semites of the Arrow Cross. A similar fate befell all other opponents of National Socialism, including the leaders of rival parties, intellectuals and journalists, while the press was gagged and non-fascist political parties dissolved. Encouraged by the D-Day landings in Normandy in June 1944 and Romania's defection to the Allies on 23 August, Horthy began serious attempts to make a separate peace, dismissing the pro-German government on 24 August and appointing the trusted General Geza Lakatos on the 29th. Only with the entry of Soviet troops onto Hungarian territory, however, did the negotiations bear fruit, with a tentative armistice signed with the Soviets on 11 October 1944. His attempt to announce the armistice on 15 October resulted in a coup by the Arrow Cross, backed by German troops. Horthy was arrested and deported to Austria, the government being taken over by the Arrow Cross leader, Szalasi, who carried out further deportations of Jews and opponents before Hungary fell to Soviet forces on 4 April 1945. Horthy was eventually released by the Americans, escaping further punishment, going into exile in Portugal, where he died in 1957.

C. A. Macartney, *History of Modern Hungary, 1929–45* (2 vols., 1956)

J. K. Hoensch, *A History of Modern Hungary, 1867–1986* (Eng. edn, 1988)

**Hossbach Memorandum.** The record of a meeting between HITLER, the commanders-in-chief of three German armed services,

the German Foreign Minister von Neurath and the Minister of War von Blomberg on 5 November 1937, at which Hitler outlined his foreign policy plans for German expansion in Europe. The memorandum derives its name from that of Colonel Friedrich Hossbach, the senior military adjutant on Hitler's personal staff, who was present and took a note of the meeting.

The immediate background to the meeting was the growing shortage of steel which was hampering German rearmament. The commanders-in-chief sought a meeting with Hitler in which they expected him to adjudicate between the competing claims being made on the limited steel supply. In fact, this issue was touched upon only towards the end of the meeting, the bulk of which was absorbed by a lengthy exposition by Hitler of Germany's racial, economic and strategic position, in which he stressed the inevitability of expansion in Europe by 1943–5 at the latest. For the first time Hitler made clear his commitment to war in terms of specific goals – the absorption of Austria and the destruction of Czechoslovakia – and outlined a provisional timetable for this.

The Hossbach memorandum was presented to the Nuremberg Tribunal (*see* NUREMBERG TRIALS) as evidence of the existence amongst the Nazi leadership of a plot to wage war and as a blueprint for expansion. The significance of the document has, however, been a matter of debate amongst historians. Some have seen it as merely the record of a rhetorical attempt on Hitler's part to avoid making a clear decision about military-economic priorities. Others have pointed out that, if the document *was* a blueprint for aggression, both the timing of subsequent diplomatic developments and the manner of German expansion at the expense of Austria and Czechoslovakia departed markedly from Hitler's intentions as set out in the memorandum, and that it fails to record any mention by Hitler of what was undoubtedly his most important long-term foreign policy ambition – German expansion to the east at the expense of the Soviet Union. Nevertheless, the document is now regarded by the majority of historians as a reliable indication of Hitler's determination to pursue a more aggressive foreign policy – initially against Austria and Czechoslovakia –

before the diplomatic and military situation changed to Germany's disadvantage; of his awareness of accumulating economic difficulties as a consequence of the pursuit of rapid and massive rearmament; of his concern to persuade senior military and diplomatic figures within the regime of the necessity of an accelerated tempo in German foreign policy; and of his abandonment by late 1937 of his earlier belief in the necessity of an agreement with Britain as a prerequisite to German expansion in continental Europe. *See also* ANSCHLUSS; SECOND WORLD WAR; SUDETENLAND.

W. Carr, *Arms, Autarky and Aggression: A Study in German Foreign Policy 1933–1939* (2nd edn, 1979)
J. Noakes and G. Pridham (eds.), *Nazism 1919–1945: A Documentary Reader*, vol. 3 (1988)

**Hoxha, Enver** (1908–85). Albanian communist leader. A former schoolteacher, he spent part of his life in France. He returned to ALBANIA in 1936 and maintained an underground existence there. With the coming together of various communist groups in November 1941 to form the Albanian Communist Party (PKSH) he became its General Secretary and led the National Liberation Movement against the German occupation and rival anti-fascist groups. In May 1944 he became head of the Antifascist Council of National Liberation as well as commander-in-chief of the National Liberation Army. He was elected Prime Minister in October 1944 when a Provisional Democratic Republic was established following German withdrawal from the Balkans. He fashioned a Stalinist People's Republic, proclaimed on 12 January 1946, but came under increasing pressure from pro-Yugoslav elements in the party led by Koci Xoxe and Pandi Kristo which almost led to his removal as party leader. The Soviet-Yugoslav split, however, allowed Hoxha to strengthen his position as a loyal supporter of Stalin and an opponent of TITO. In November 1948 he carried out a purge of all pro-Yugoslav elements, estimated in total at about 12,000 members, approximately one-quarter of the total. Hoxha steered the party during KHRUSHCHEV's DE-STALINIZATION phase, seizing the opportunity to purge further opponents and resisting Soviet rapprochement with Yugoslavia as a potential threat to Albanian

independence. With the Sino–Soviet rift from 1960 Hoxha allied Albania with China, openly attacking the Soviet Union and being cut off from Soviet aid and technical assistance in retaliation. Combined with further purges of pro-Soviet members of the Politburo and a series of show trials in May 1961 of those charged with plotting against the regime, Hoxha effectively severed relations with the Soviet Union. Diplomatic ties were finally cut by Moscow in 1961 and Albania was banned from the activities of the WARSAW PACT and the following year, COMECON. Hoxha maintained the isolation of Albania during the next 25 years, leaning for support upon China until that relationship was severed in July 1977 by Peking. Hoxha's determination to retain his hard-line grip on the party and the country was reaffirmed by the suicide of the Prime Minister, Mehmet Shehu, in December 1981, accused of being a foreign agent, and purges of Shehu's supporters in 1982. Remaining General Secretary of the Party until his death in April 1985, when he was succeeded by Ramiz Alia, Hoxha's aim was to maintain a rigidly Stalinist independent Albania. The most persistent feature of his regime from the end of the Second World War was to ensure Albanian independence and pursue socialist self-sufficiency. A series of Five Year Plans were inaugurated, of which the sixth (1981–5) claimed to be founded on 'the revolutionary principle of self-reliance'. In spite of large increases claimed in production, Albania remained under Hoxha the poorest and most isolated country in Europe.

N. C. Pano, *The People's Republic of Albania* (1968)
P. R. Prifti, *Socialist Albania since 1944* (1978)
A. Schnytzer, *Stalinist Economic Strategy Practice: The Case of Albania* (1982)

**Hungarian Uprising.** KHRUSHCHEV's attack on Stalin's legacy at the 20th Party Congress in 1956 and the unpopularity of RÁKOSI's regime led to his replacement by Erno Gerö as First Secretary in June 1956. Moves to rehabilitate the principal victim of Rákosi's purges, Laszlo Rajk, executed in 1948, and to push forward more liberal policies associated with IMRE NAGY were met by resistance from hard-line sections of the Communist Party and security apparatus. Peaceful demonstrations by students, workers and others on 23 October led to attacks on the secret police and party headquarters, becoming a general national uprising against Gerö's leadership and Soviet occupation. After lengthy debates the Central Committee on 24 October supported Nagy's assumption of the premiership. On 27 October Soviet forces withdrew from Budapest. Carried along by the popular revolution, Nagy was unable to adopt the same course as GOMULKA in Poland and retain Communist Party control. A general strike and popular sentiment forced an increasingly liberal line, leading to the denouncing of the WARSAW PACT and an attempt to declare Hungarian neutrality. By the end of October the Hungarian Communist Party had dissolved itself and admitted more democratic elements into a broader party. On 4 November Soviet troops which had surrounded Budapest entered the city and suppressed the uprising after bitter fighting. Resistance continued until 14 November, by which time over 3,000 Hungarians and 1,500 Soviet troops had been killed. The Soviets installed JANOS KADAR as head of a 'revolutionary workers' and peasants' government'. Kadar claimed that a legitimate revolution on 23 October had been seized by counter-revolutionary elements; he acted swiftly to arrest the leaders of the rising and the Nagy government and re-establish one-party rule. After initial attempts to compromise with the powerful workers' groups who supported the uprising, Kadar reimposed a stern Stalinist-style regime, including the execution of an estimated 2,000 people, the imprisonment of 20,000 others, and the secret trial and execution of Nagy and the other leaders of the revolt. Some 200,000 Hungarian refugees fled to the West.

The suppression of the Hungarian uprising was the most decisive action by the Soviet Union to quell discontent in Eastern Europe between the post-war seizure of power and the crushing of the 'PRAGUE SPRING' in 1968. It defined the limits of Soviet tolerance of liberalization which was permitted under the auspices of Communist Party control under Gomulka in Poland, but which appeared to be passing out of control under Nagy and threatened the loss of Hungary from the Soviet bloc. Party centralists such as Kadar undoubtedly connived

at Soviet intervention in the face of what they saw as a counter-revolutionary, nationalistic movement. The West, distracted by the SUEZ CRISIS, was unable to intervene; and Soviet action of 'sending in the tanks' was a clear signal to other satellites.

The event was written up in official communist historiography as an attempted counter-revolution, Western and liberal Hungarian writers preferring to see it as a genuinely popular uprising or 'revolution'. As the Hungarian communist regime lessened its grip in 1988–9 one of the principal issues was the interpretation of the events of 1956. The victory of more liberal forces was marked by the demotion of the symbol of the Soviet suppression, Kadar, in 1989 and the public rehabilitation and reburial of Nagy.

F. Fetjo, *A History of the People's Democracies: Eastern Europe since Stalin* (2nd edn, 1974)
J. K. Hoensch, *A History of Modern Hungary, 1867–1986* (trans., 1988)

**Hunger Marches.** Name given to demonstrations by the unemployed in Britain during the inter-war years. Organized, in the main, by the communist-led NATIONAL UNEMPLOYED WORKERS' MOVEMENT (NUWM) they took the form of marches on London and provincial centres to protest about unemployment and unemployment relief. Major marches occurred in 1922, 1929, 1930, 1932, 1934 and 1936. The marches of 1932, 1934 and 1936 were 'national' marches converging on London and holding mass demonstrations. The 1932 march carried a million-signature petition protesting against the MEANS TEST, but was prevented by police baton charges from conducting a mass lobby of parliament. The 1934 march aroused concern that the authorities were acting to provoke disturbances, and led to the founding of the National Council of Civil Liberties to safeguard the rights of demonstrators. Local demonstrations and marches in the early part of 1935 contributed to the government halting its implementation of a new unified system of unemployment relief, the Unemployment Assistance Board. The best-known hunger march was the 'Jarrow Crusade' of autumn 1936, the only one not organized by the NUWM, undertaken by the town council of the Tyneside unemployment blackspot

Jarrow and led by the town's Labour MP, Ellen Wilkinson. 200 men marched to London bearing a petition to the House of Commons seeking assistance for the town. The marchers' quiet dignity earned them widespread sympathy although the march achieved few practical results. The 'Jarrow March' became the symbol of the plight of the unemployed in the 1930s, whereas the larger and more persistent campaigns of the NUWM were viewed as a threat to public order and met with hostility and harassment by the authorities. They achieved some local successes in forcing local authorities to revise relief scales and provided one of the few visible protest movements by the unemployed in Britain between the wars.

C. Cook and J. Stevenson, *The Slump: Politics and Society in the Depression* (1976)
P. Kingsford, *The Hunger Marches* (1987)

**Husak, Gustav** (1913–). Czech politician; President of Czechoslovakia from 1975 to 1989. He was appointed First Secretary of the CZECHOSLOVAK COMMUNIST PARTY in April 1969 following the ending of the 'PRAGUE SPRING', displacing DUBČEK, who had been coerced into reimposing hard-line communist policies. He supervised the 'normalization' process of screening and mass purges of the party membership, harassing and imprisoning DISSIDENTS and members of CHARTER 77. Combining the positions of President and First Secretary from 1975 he gave the appearance of maintaining a stern hold upon Czechoslovakian politics until a wave of mass demonstrations in November and December 1989 forced the admission of members of the non-communist Civic Forum into Government in early December. He was forced to resign as President and First Secretary, being replaced on 29 December by the former dissident VACLAV HAVEL.

A. G. Skilling, *Czechoslovakia's Interrupted Revolution* (1976)

**hydrogen bomb.** *See* NUCLEAR WEAPONS.

# I

**Ibarruri, Dolores** (1895–1989). Spanish communist leader. Born at Gallarta into poor Basque family, she began writing articles in 1918 under the *nom de plume* 'La Pasionara'. She joined the SPANISH COMMUNIST PARTY and in 1930 was elected to its Central Congress. Imprisoned on several occasions, she was elected deputy for the Asturias in 1936. Following the Nationalist rising she made radio broadcasts and is most famous for the phrase 'No pasaran' ('They shall not pass') used to stiffen the defence of Madrid. She made numerous broadcasts to boost morale on the Republican side and became widely known abroad. She left for exile in Russia just before the fall of the Republic in March 1939 and became Secretary-General of the Communist Party from 1942 to 1960, subsequently its President. One of her two surviving sons was killed fighting at Stalingrad. She returned to Spain in 1976 and was elected to the Cortes for the Asturias in 1977. Somewhat out of sympathy with the more moderate role of the Communist Party in post-Francoist Spain, she remained widely respected until her death.

**ILO.** See INTERNATIONAL LABOUR ORGANISATION.

**ILP.** See INDEPENDENT LABOUR PARTY, BRITISH.

**Independent Labour Party, British** (ILP). Founded in 1893 by the socialist pioneer Keir Hardie in 1900, the ILP was one of the founding bodies of the Labour Representation Committee. Although affiliated to the LABOUR PARTY, the ILP held its own conferences, sponsored its own candidates and maintained its own policies, even after the 1918 revision of the Labour Party Constitution. Throughout the 1920s differences with the Labour Party grew and the 37 ILP members among the 288 Labour MPs elected in 1929 were strong critics of MACDONALD's government. Indeed, the 1930 ILP Conference decided to vote against the policy of the Labour government where it contradicted the ILP line. In 1932 the Labour Party Conference disaffiliated the ILP. Accordingly, all 17 ILP candidates stood against Labour candidates in the 1935 election, and four were returned for various Glasgow divisions. In 1945 the ILP ran five candidates and three were successful, but after the death of the party's leader, James Maxton, in 1946, the ILP MPs joined the Labour Party. In the 1950 and 1951 elections the ILP ran three candidates, in the 1955 and 1959 elections, two. All lost their deposits, a tale repeated in the cases of the three ILP candidates who stood at by-elections in the 1960s. There were no ILP candidates at the 1964 and 1966 general elections, and in the 1970 general election, the one ILP candidate lost his deposit. There were no ILP candidates in the 1974 and subsequent elections.

**Independent Social Democratic Party of Germany.** See USPD.

**Indo-Chinese War.** Following the surrender of Japan in 1945, the Vietnamese communist leader, Ho Chi Minh, proclaimed the Democratic Republic of Vietnam at Hanoi on 2 September 1945 in what had formerly been French Indo-China. French and British forces regained control in Saigon, and after negotiations French troops entered Hanoi on 16 March 1946. After French naval forces shelled the Vietnamese quarter of Haiphong on 13 November 1946 an abortive Viet Minh (communist) uprising took place in Hanoi on 19 December. Guerrilla warfare grew into a full-scale conflict between French regular troops and the Viet Minh, commanded by General Giap. By 1947 communist guerrilla forces were fighting the French not only in Vietnam but throughout Laos and Cambodia, the other former French territories in South East Asia. French attempts in 1949 to set up independent states with ties to France failed to halt the war. Supplied by Communist China after 1949, the Viet Minh forces proved an elusive enemy which denied the French forces command of the bulk of the countryside. In France the war was debilitating to the economy and so unpopular that conscripts could not be used. Initially opposed to the French attempt to hold on to power, the United States was then distracted by the war in Korea from providing assistance until it was too late. On 20 November 1953 the French established a forward base at Dien Bien Phu to invite the Viet Minh into a set-piece battle, but found the tables turned against them when the Vietnamese forces under Giap beseiged the base using heavy artillery and anti-aircraft guns manhandled through miles of 'impassable' terrain. The French outposts were gradually wiped out and the air strip upon which supply depended was rendered unusable. After 56 days of siege an all-out assault on 6–7 May 1954 overwhelmed the remainder of the 15,000-strong French garrison. 2,293 French soldiers were killed, over 5,000 wounded and the rest taken captive. The defeat ended French hopes of maintaining the former empire in Asia. On 8 May discussions opened in Geneva to bring an end to the war. A cease-fire came into effect on 21 July 1954. Laos and Cambodia were recognized as independent and neutral states by the GENEVA AGREEMENTS on 20–21 July; Vietnam was divided at latitude 17° north, between a communist North and a democratic South with provision for future unified elections. On 5 October the last French troops left Vietnam. The major effect of the Indo-Chinese war lay in providing the first stage of the protracted war carried on by American forces against North Vietnamese-inspired insurgency against the South. For France, the war marked a decisive defeat, contributing to the turmoil of the

FOURTH REPUBLIC. One of its most significant features was the growing independence and even insubordination of the armed forces. Bloodied and, as some felt, betrayed, the army was increasingly contemptuous of the politicians, feelings which were to spill over into open revolt during the ALGERIAN WAR.

G. Kelley, Lost Soldiers: The French Army and Empire in Crisis, 1947–62 (1965)

J. S. Ambler, The French Army in Politics, 1945–1962 (1966)

A. Short, The Origins of the Vietnamese War (1989)

J. Dalloz, The War in Indo-China (trans., 1990)

**industrialization debate, Soviet.** LENIN and the BOLSHEVIKS assumed that socialism required an industrial society. The question of how this was to be achieved became a central issue in the debates which occurred in Lenin's last years and following his death. One school envisaged a process of state planning diverting resources from the private sector to build heavy industry. The main spokesman for this programme, Evgeny Preobrazhensky, backed by TROTSKY, argued that this process of 'primitive socialist accumulation' would mostly affect only the 'bourgeois' section of the economy and would eventually produce benefits for society as a whole. A process of rapid industrialization would also offer the prospect of mechanizing agriculture and drawing the peasants into collective farms with the benefits of greater productivity and none of the unpleasant capitalist side-effects with which peasant proprietorship under the NEW ECONOMIC POLICY (NEP) had become associated. The opponents of this view broadly supported the current path of development which accepted the New Economic Policy and pursued slower, balanced growth in which the growing prosperity of the peasantry would provide the capital and food surpluses required. Its leading exponent was BUKHARIN, who spoke at one point of 'riding into socialism on a peasant nag'. The arguments became a part of the political factionalism of the period after 1924. The proponents of the more rapid development of heavy industry were sometimes known as the 'LEFT OPPOSITION', mainly supported by Trotsky, but were later joined by ZINOVIEV and KAMENEV. STALIN initially backed Bukharin's line but was to emerge later as having adopted the opposition's priorities.

It has been pointed out that the distinction between the eventual programme of rapid industrialization inaugurated in the first FIVE YEAR PLAN from 1928 and the gradualist, pro-NEP policies of Bukharin and, initially, Stalin can be drawn too sharply. All accepted the need to industrialize and the shared aspiration of a collectivized agriculture (*see* COLLECTIVIZATION, SOVIET), the differences were more of emphasis and of timing. Hence in 1925 the 14th Party Conference passed resolutions favouring industrialization with little controversy, while, two years later the 15th Congress declared in favour of collectivizaion and a Five Year Plan, the latter resolution introduced by one of Bukharin's chief supporters, RYKOV. One important influence lay in the development of the techniques of the state planning commission or GOSPLAN which enabled it by 1925 to draw up projections for the national economy in the year ahead and to begin to draft longer-term growth plans. Another lay in developments abroad. The sense of military vulnerability inherited from the past and memories of allied intervention in the RUSSIAN CIVIL WAR were sharpened by the crushing of the Chinese communist uprising in 1927, the revival of Japanese militarism and Britain's breaking off of diplomatic relations. These factors influenced Stalin in backing the programme of large-scale investment in heavy industry in 1928 put forward by the so-called 'Teleological School' of planners. Three years later he was to justify it dramatically as a need to catch up the Western powers before 'we go under'. Stalin now turned on his previous allies in the debate, Bukharin, Rykov and Tomsky, accusing them of being a 'RIGHT OPPOSITION' or 'deviation'. The first Five Year Plan, intended to operate from October 1928, was, in fact, only confirmed in April 1929 at the 16th Party Conference. By that time Stalin had removed many of his opponents, forcing them to recant. Once the plan was begun, Stalin sought further upward revisions. The more cautious members of Gosplan were dismissed in 1931 and several of them were tried for retarding the country's development. Stalin's adoption of the earlier position of the 'Left Opposition'

and its emphasis on almost impossibly high targets also had consequences for the other parts of the economy. Integral to the opposition of Bukharin and others had been the need to retain good relations with the peasants and encourage prosperous peasant proprietorship. Implicitly, Stalin's targets left little time for the slow process of peasant savings and rising consumption to work through. In early 1928 Stalin launched in the Urals and Siberian regions a policy of grain seizures which reverted to the days of WAR COMMUNISM. This 'Urals–Siberian Method' was repeated in 1928–9, foreshadowing a process of depressing peasant living standards which was to lead to rapid collectivization from the autumn of 1929.

The industrialization debate was to have profound implications for the Soviet Union. The problem of developing a still largely peasant society became entangled with both the power struggles of the party and ideological debates about the proper relationship between private and public sectors. By 1928 Stalin had outmanoeuvred his rivals by switching sides in the debate and adopting a programme of rapid industrialization which placed its major emphasis on heavy industry. It was already clear that this was only possible at the expense of a considerable squeeze upon peasant proprietors and the virtual end of the New Economic Policy. By 1929 the declaration of the programme of collectivization was to ensure that the peasantry would supply the resources necessary to support industrialization.

A. Nove, *An Economic History of the USSR* (1969)
R. W. Davies, *The Industrialisation of the Soviet Union* (1980)

**INLA.** *See* IRISH NATIONAL LIBERATION ARMY.

**Intermediate Nuclear Forces Treaty.** A treaty signed in Washington on 8 December 1987 between the United States and the Soviet Union. It provided for the withdrawal and destruction of all land-based nuclear missiles in Europe with ranges of between 500 and 5,500 kilometres, including American Pershing II and CRUISE MISSILES and Soviet SS-20s. The treaty was a breakthrough in the arms control talks conducted between the United States and the Soviet Union under President REAGAN and Premier GORBACHEV, and was anticipated as forming a component of larger arms control talks to embrace strategic weapons and conventional forces. A major feature was the strict verification procedures laid down by each side for the removal and destruction of the weapons, including 'on-site' inspection. Agreement to the latter marked an important shift in Soviet policy, which had previously resisted the presence of inspection teams. The treaty laid down the scrapping of 1,752 Soviet and 859 American missiles within a three-year period.

**International Brigades.** Volunteers who enlisted to fight on the Republican side in the SPANISH CIVIL WAR. In total, almost 36,000 took part, playing a significant part in the early battles which prevented the Republic from being overrun. Recruited largely from communists and left-wing sympathizers, most were brought into Spain on networks organized by local communist parties. The Brigades included 10,000 French, 5,000 Germans and Austrians, 5,000 Poles, 3,400 Italians, 3,000 Americans, 2,000 British, 1,500 Yugoslavs, 1,500 Czechs, 1,200 Canadians and 1,000 Hungarians. Two Brigades saw action in defence of Madrid in the winter of 1936–7 and in March 1937 fought at the battle of Guadalajara. Most Brigades saw action at Brunete outside Madrid in July 1937, causing heavy casualties, as did the assault on Belchite in August and the Ebro offensive in October 1937. The Brigades were also caught up in the retreat caused by the Nationalist advance in Aragon in March 1938. The non-intervention agreements (*see* NON-INTERVENTION COMMITTEE) prevented further enlistments, and by late July 1937 the Brigades were only 30 per cent foreign. In the summer of 1938 the Republican government withdrew the volunteers from the line, and the survivors, numbering 12,763, were repatriated from September, the last groups leaving in January 1939. The Brigades were one of the most important symbols of anti-fascist feeling in the 1930s, drawing upon the prevailing 'POPULAR FRONT' enthusiasm and a broad range of left-wing sentiment and commitment. The Brigades included poets, writers and intellectuals, trade unionists, ordinary workers, students and anarchists. Large numbers of them were to remain active in socialist or left-wing politics and play a part in the resistance during the Second World War.

G. Orwell, *Homage to Catalonia* (1938)
V. Brome, *The International Brigades* (1965)
V. B. Johnson, *Legions of Babel: The International Brigades in the Spanish Civil War* (1967)

**International Labour Organisation** (ILO). Founded in 1919 an an autonomous organization of the LEAGUE OF NATIONS, but not limited to League members. Its aim was to improve labour conditions through international action and investigation, paying particular attention to working conditions, wage rates, health care and employment levels. At its inception the ILO consisted of the International Labour Conference, meeting at least once a year, and the International Labour Office, controlled by a governing body composed of 16 government representatives, eight employers' representatives and eight workers' representatives. The Conference could make Draft Conventions or Recommendations, the former obliging the state concerned to approach the competent authority and seek action. The ILO had 24 sessions between 1919 and 1939, adopting 63 Draft Conventions and 56 Recommendations. The ILO did much valuable work in regulating and investigating working conditions under its first director, the French socialist Albert Thomas (1878–1932). When the League of Nations was dissolved, the UNITED NATIONS recognized its role and it became a specialist UN agency which continues to investigate working conditions. An annual conference decides policy and each member state sends two delegates to it, one representing employers, one employees. Nine governments have permanent seats because of the level of their industrial production (Canada, China, France, India, Italy, Japan, Britain, the USSR and West Germany). The other 38 places are filled by representatives elected by the conference. In 1960 the ILO won the Nobel Peace Prize. In 1977 the USA withdrew from the ILO, after accusing it of supporting left-wing political groups.

S. R. Gibbons and P. Morican, *The League of Nations and UNO* (1970)

**intervention, Allied.** *See* RUSSIAN CIVIL WAR.

**IRA.** *See* IRISH REPUBLICAN ARMY.

**IRB.** *See* IRISH REPUBLICAN BROTHERHOOD.

**Irish Civil War.** The split within the Irish nationalists over ratification of the treaty agreed between plenipotentiaries of the Dail and the British government in December 1921, creating an Irish Free State with Dominion status and permitting the separation of the six counties of Ulster, broke into open warfare from February 1922. The Republican faction led by DE VALERA refused to acknowledge the treaty and accept an oath of allegiance to the British Crown. The anti-treaty group within the Irish Republican Army began raids into the North and a series of armed raids and ambushes were carried out in the South. In April a force led by Rory O'Connor seized the Four Courts building in Dublin. The Free State government then besieged the Four Courts and other positions in Dublin seized by the anti-treaty forces, recapturing it in June at the cost of over 60 dead and the destruction of the building. MICHAEL COLLINS took command of the Free State Army, but was shot himself in an ambush in Cork. Under new leaders, Kevin O'Higgins and W. T. Cosgrave, the Free State forces gradually hunted down the anti-treaty groups and carried out executions. In May 1923 the anti-treaty forces sued for a cease-fire. The bitter struggle in which many of the leaders of the Irish nationalist movement died polarized opinion in the South for many years, determining the shape of party politics for generations. The pro-treaty forces set up a new party, CUMANN NA NGAEDHAEL, in 1923, which became FINE GAEL in 1933. Although 44 members of a Sinn Fein party had been elected to the Dail in 1923, they did not take their seats. Only in 1927 when De Valera set up a new party, FIANNA FAIL, splitting from the most extreme anti-treaty groups, did the losing side in the Civil War take up its seats and swear the oath of allegiance. Fianna Fail maintained a more consistently anti-British and Republican policy.

C. Younger, *Ireland's Civil War* (1968)

**Irish Nationalist Party.** Formed from the supporters of the Home Rule League (*see* HOME RULE) who constituted themselves into a separate party in 1874. Split over the divorce case of their leader, Parnell, in 1890, only in 1900 did they reunite under REDMOND's leadership. 82 Nationalists were returned in 1900, 83 in 1906. In 1910 they found themselves again holding the balance between Liberals and Conservatives, having over 80 seats, and pressed ASQUITH to remove the House of Lords' veto, thus opening the way for a Home Rule Bill to pass. But the First World War prevented implementation of the Act, and divisions over the war and the 1916 Easter Rebellion broke the hold of the party on the Irish electorate. In 1918 only seven of its 58 candidates were elected, compared to Sinn Fein's 73, although T. P. O'Connor (the solitary Irish Nationalist MP for an English seat) was returned unopposed for Liverpool Scotland division until his death in 1929.

**Irish National Liberation Army** (INLA). Established in December 1974 by members of the official IRISH REPUBLICAN ARMY who opposed the cease-fire declared by the official chief of staff in May 1972. In 1973 it also recruited from PROVISIONAL IRISH REPUBLICAN ARMY men who were disillusioned by their own movement's cease-fire. The INLA promoted a completely ruthless campaign of terror against British and Protestant targets, especially in the border areas of south Armagh. It numbers less than 100, and was disrupted by a feud in 1986. It was responsible for the killing of three worshippers at a Pentecostal service in November 1983, and has participated in the execution of informers.

P. Arthur and K. Jeffery, *Northern Ireland since 1968* (1988)

**Irish Republican Army** (IRA). Traditionally the army which has fought for a 32-county Irish Republic, although its personnel, methods and other aims have changed significantly over a period of years. Formed in 1919 as the army of SINN FEIN and DE VALERA, it became illegal under the different governments of the Irish Free State, reappearing at irregular intervals with bombings in Northern Ireland and Great Britain. As normal politics continued in both parts of Ireland it had all but petered out by the mid–1960s. However, the Civil Rights Movement of the late 1960s revived traditional Catholic aspirations in Ulster which the IRA was eager and successful in exploiting. A division occurred within the IRA in the late 1960s between the 'provisionals' (see PROVISIONAL IRISH REPUBLICAN ARMY) with the more traditional aims of republicanism, greater armoury and financial backing, and the 'officials' with a Marxist orientation and who have refrained in recent years from the armed struggle. Both sides have a political party, each known as Sinn Fein, in support.

**Irish Republic Brotherhood** (IRB). The IRB grew out of the Fenian movement of the 19th century; several of its leaders were represented in the IRISH VOLUNTEERS formed in 1913 and in the minority which retained the name when the Volunteers split in September 1914, the majority under REDMOND forming the National Volunteers. The IRB opened talks with German leaders, and delegates visited Berlin, planning an insurrection for Easter 1916. The IRB aimed to use a Volunteer Parade on Easter Sunday 1916 to mount the rising. Although the leader of the Irish Volunteers banned the parade, the Military Council of the IRB, joined by members of the Volunteers sympathetic to the insurrection, went ahead with it (see EASTER RISING). Although the rising was crushed, the IRB reformed the Volunteers in 1917, eventually reconstituted into the IRISH REPUBLICAN ARMY in 1919.

**Irish Volunteers.** An organization formed in November 1913 by an informal committee of younger nationalists, drawing many recruits from the Gaelic Athletic Association and the Gaelic League. Its leaders included PATRICK PEARSE and Eoin Mac-Neill. The force had no clear policy other than to further the independence of Ireland, but many of its leaders were members of the IRISH REPUBLICAN BROTHERHOOD (IRB) who saw it as a vehicle for educating public opinion in a nationalist direction. In March 1914 the Irish Parliamentary leader REDMOND decided to bring the movement under his control by insisting on the enlargement of the committee by including members of the parliamentary party; in June the committee was reconstructed. By September 1914, the Volunteers had 180,000 members, but split over Redmond's recruiting for the British forces through the organization. The consequence was the formation of a minority Irish Volunteers led by MacNeill, while the Redmondite body became known as the National Volunteers. In 1916 the rump Irish Volunteers, perhaps 15,000 strong, were seen by some as providing the means to mount an insurrection by the IRB, but their chief-of-staff MacNeill remained committed to a defensive stance. As a result only a portion of the Volunteers participated in the EASTER RISING of 1916. MacNeill, discovering the plans for the insurrection, sought to prevent its occurring, but was disobeyed by the Military Council of the IRB, supported by Volunteers who rejected MacNeill's policy, like Pearse himself. Some Irish Volunteers in the provinces rose to accompany the Easter Rising, but the failure of the insurrection disrupted the movement. It reformed in November 1917 and in early 1919 was reconstituted as the army of the Irish Republic, the IRISH REPUBLICAN ARMY.

**Iron Curtain.** A term first used in February 1945 by JOSEF GOEBBELS, the Nazi Minister of Enlightenment and Propaganda. However, it was the repetition of the phrase in a speech by WINSTON CHURCHILL at Fulton, Missouri on 5 March 1946 that first brought it to public attention and introduced it to general use. It denoted the border between Soviet-dominated Eastern Europe and the West and, more specifically, the restraints placed on ideology and movement by communist regimes in Bulgaria, Czechoslovakia, Hungary, Poland, Romania and Albania.

**Iron Guard.** Romanian nationalist and fascistic organization led by Corneliu Codreanu (1899–1938). Influenced by the anti-Semitic philosophy of A. C. Cuza, a professor at the University of Jassy (Iasi), Codreanu and his supporters organized a number of Nationalistic Leagues from 1920, including the National Christian Anti-Semitic League (LANC), set up in 1923 in response to the government's extension of citizenship to all resident Jews. The League pursued a campaign of terror combined with a movement of moral restoration which attracted considerable support. In

June 1927 Codreanu left the League and founded the Legion of the Archangel Michael, organized on parliamentary lines and dedicated to manual labour, comradeship and moral regeneration. In 1932 the movement, now known as the 'Iron Guard', obtained four deputies in Parliament and built up a large following amongst Moldavian (see MOLDAVIA) peasantry by assisting in the repair of buildings, roads and schools. In December 1933 the Liberal Premier Son Duca ordered the Legion dissolved; three weeks later he was assassinated and the leaders of the Legion sentenced for his murder. Codreanu was released and set up a Legion Labour Corps, reforming the Iron Guard as the 'All-for-the-Fatherland' Party which obtained 16 per cent of the votes and 66 deputies in the 1937 elections. The establishment of CAROL II's royal dictatorship in 1937–8, however, led to the dissolution of the Iron Guard and the arrest and murder of its leaders, including Codreanu. When members of the movement assassinated the Minister of the Interior, Carol ordered the execution of hundreds of the imprisoned legionnaires. The surviving members led the rising which forced Carol's abdication in September 1940, and formed a government with the army under the Premier, General Antonescu, with Codreanu's heir and 'Commander' of the Legion, Horia Sima, as Vice-Premier. Tensions between the army and the legion erupted into full-scale insurrection in Bucharest in January 1941 when Antonescu tried to remove legionary ministers and prefects. During the insurrection, the Legion carried out a slaughter of thousands of Jews and other enemies, the captured radio station transmitting the slogan 'Long Live Death'. But after four days the Legion's power was broken by German and Romanian forces and its leaders killed, captured or exiled. Some were eventually released from prison by the Germans in 1944 as Romania fell to the Russians and were spirited away to form a short-lived fascist Romanian government in exile at Vienna. At once populist, anti-Semitic and intensely nationalistic, the Iron Guard had many of the characteristics of contemporary fascist movements elsewhere in Europe. Anti-communism had particular force for the Romanians, who shared a border with Bolshevik Russia, intensifying the nationalism of the Iron Guard and for some of its leaders, elevating the Christian element and fashioning a reformist populism which aimed at a moral regeneration. In practice many of the Iron Guard were violent anti-Semites, drawing support from Moldavia, where Jewish settlement from Poland and Russia was most heavy. See also SECOND WORLD WAR.

E. Weber, 'Romania', in Varieties of Fascism (1964)
S. Fischer-Galati, Twentieth Century Rumania (1970)

# J

**Jajce Congress.** A meeting of delegates to the Anti-Fascist National Liberation Committee organized by TITO's partisans and held on 29–30 November 1943 at the liberated town of Jajce in Bosnia. The congress set up a National Committee of Yugoslavia as a rival communist-led government to the royalist government-in-exile in London. It resolved to create a federal Yugoslavian Republic after the war and gave the committee the powers of a provisional government with Tito as President. Tito was also awarded the title of 'Marshal of Yugoslavia' in recognition of his military leadership of the partisans against the German occupying forces. The resolutions of the congress paved the way for the communist takeover of YUGOSLAVIA at the end of the war.

**Jaruzelski, Wojciech** (1923–). Polish soldier and politician. He had a long and distinguished army career; he became Chief of the General Staff, 1965; Minister of Defence, 1968; member of the Politburo of the Polish Communist Party, 1971; Prime Minister following the resignation of Pinkowski in 1981, and Party leader from October 1981. He declared martial law on 13 December 1981 to tackle a mounting economic crisis and to counter the growth of the SOLIDARITY movement. His introduction of martial law followed discussions with Moscow and was widely seen as the only alternative to direct Soviet intervention which could preserve a semblance of independence and avoid a futile and bloody anti-Soviet uprising. Jaruzelski claimed to be acting 'patriotically', using the prestige of the Polish armed forces to prevent a civil war. Solidarity was banned and thousands of its members and those of the Workers' Defence Committee arrested, including LECH WALESA. For the next few months

General Jaruzelski acted to suppress the once apparently unstoppable Solidarity movement, but by the end of 1982 he had suspended martial law and released Walesa from detention. An effective stalemate with Solidarity unable to recapture the momentum of its early years and the government unable to secure agreement to much-needed economic reforms led gradually in 1987–8 to a rapprochement between Walesa and Jaruzelski. In September 1986 the still illegal Solidarity announced its willingness to work with the Communist Party, but the decisive influence was the failure of Jaruzelski to secure approval in a referendum held in November 1987 for radical economic reform, opposed by Solidarity, and demonstrating its ability to frustrate any progress in the economic sphere. During 1988 a renewed wave of strikes over wage restraints and price rises strengthened Walesa's hand in calling for talks with the government. In December Jaruzelski agreed to an offer of 'round-table' discussions, followed in January 1989 by agreement by the Communist Party to lift the ban on free trade unions. Talks opened in February led to an agreement in April to legalize Solidarity, to allow opposition parties to contest partly free elections, and to create the office of President. Following Solidarity's sweeping victory in the seats it was allowed to contest in June, Jaruzelski was elected President of Poland by a one vote margin. His attempts to maintain a communist-led Government under General Kiszczak on the basis of the 299 seats allocated to the Communist Party and its allies was defeated when these allies withdrew their support on 14 August. Jaruzelski was left with no alternative but to agree to accept a Solidarity Prime Minister. Although clearly uncomfortable in his role as titular head of a country run by a government led by the movement he had sought to suppress eight years earlier, Jaruzelski made attempts to enlist Solidarity in the attempt to remedy Poland's chronic economic problems. The uneasy constitutional compromise of a freely elected upper house (Senate) and a lower house (Sejm) with a third of its seats freely elected and the remainder filled by communist appointees and their allies permitted the Communist Party considerable power. Jaruzelski, too, represented, in a new guise, the often complex role of the Polish Army in Polish politics. His term as President ended with the election of Walesa in December 1990.

T. Garton Ash, *The Polish Revolution: Solidarity, 1980–82* (1983)

**Jellicoe, John** (1859–1935). British admiral. He entered navy in 1872 and became a gunnery expert, receiving the patronage of Admiral JOHN FISHER. Jellicoe was appointed second-in-command of the Grand Fleet in November 1911 and Commander on 3 August 1914. He fought the battle of Jutland on 31 May – 1 June 1916. He was criticized for breaking off the action as night fell, but was concerned to fight the German fleet to best advantage, which he believed would accrue from daylight; instead the German fleet evaded him and steamed for its home port. He became First Sea Lord on 22 November and was replaced as Commander by his Jutland subordinate Sir David Beatty (1871–1936). Jellicoe opposed the introduction of convoys and was replaced by Admiral Webster-Wemyss in November 1917. His reputation has always hinged upon the action at Jutland which has been more generously interpreted in recent studies than by contemporaries, who expected a crushing defeat of the German battle fleet.

A. J. Marder, *From the Dreadnought to Scapa Flow: The Royal Navy in the Fisher Era, 1904–1919* (1961–70)

A. Temple Patterson, *Jellicoe: A Biography* (1969)

**Jenkins, Roy** (1920–). British politician; first British President of the EEC COMMISSION (1977–81). Educated at Balliol College, Oxford, he was elected Labour MP for Southwark Central and from 1950 until 1976 represented Stechford (Birmingham). He has held the following governmental posts: Minister of Aviation, 1964; Home Secretary, 1965–7; Chancellor of the Exchequer, 1967–70; Home Secretary, 1974–6. He was deputy leader of the Labour Party from 1970–72. On the right of the Labour Party, Jenkins had proved an effective Chancellor of the Exchequer and Home Secretary. On his return from Europe in 1981 he was instrumental in setting up the SOCIAL DEMOCRATIC PARTY and was its first leader. As a close ally of DAVID STEEL he supported the formation of THE ALLIANCE with the LIBERAL PARTY formed the same year. He won a by-election victory in Glasgow Hillhead in 1982 and led the SDP to a high point in the opinion polls. He was displaced as leader by DAVID OWEN in 1983. He lost his seat in the 1987 election, but remains an influential figure in the House of Lords, where he now sits as Lord Jenkins of Hillhead.

**Joffre, Joseph** (1852–1931). French general. Born near Perpignan, he entered the army in 1870, serving with a battery in defence of Paris. He served in Indo-China and North Africa, earning distinction for the capture of Timbuktu in 1894. He was Chief of the General Staff in 1911 and led the French armies in 1914. He ordered the counter-offensive on 4 September 1914 against the German right wing in the Marne area, halting the thrust on Paris. His later career was clouded by lack of obvious success in the Somme battles of 1916. On 31 December 1916 he was made a Marshal and was succeeded as Commander-in-Chief by General Nivelle, removing him from active command. Joffre served as President of the Allied War Council in 1917 and remained at the Ministry of War from 1918 to 1930. FOCH was an important protégé.

A. Horne, *The Price of Glory: Verdun* (1962)

H. Isselin, *The Battle of the Marne* (1966)

**John XXIII, Pope** (1881–1963). Pope, 1958–63. Born Angelo Giuseppi Roncalli, son of a Lombard peasant farmer, he attended a seminary in Bergamo, going to Rome in 1900 and ordained in 1904. He served as an army chaplain in the First World War and entered the papal diplomatic service, serving in Bulgaria, Greece and Turkey between 1925 and 1945. He was papal nuncio to liberated France where he worked to reconcile the state with those bishops who had collaborated with the VICHY government. He was made a Cardinal in 1953 and appointed Archbishop of Venice. When elected Pope on 28 October 1958 in succession to PIUS XII, he was seen by many as a caretaker figure, already aged seventy-seven. To widespread surprise he announced in 1959 plans for the SECOND VATICAN COUNCIL to meet in 1962. The Council was the first for 94 years and was seen by the Pope as part of a process of bringing the Church into more effective relationship with the twentieth century. Key features of the Council's agenda were the opening of dialogue with other faiths, a modernization of liturgy and devotional practice, and the addressing of major issues such as nuclear war and the COLD WAR. He presided over the first session which met in October 1962 with more than 2,300 bishops, but much of the Council's work had to be pursued by his successor, PAUL VI, following his death in June 1963. Nonetheless, Vatican II marked a revolutionary change in Church's attitudes towards other churches and faiths, as well as instituting far reaching changes in liturgy, most strikingly in the adoption of the vernacular for the mass and a more collaborative style of service. John XXIII also played a major part in improving relations between the Catholic Church and the eastern bloc, seeking peaceful coexistence with the Communist regimes of the east. This was the major theme of his major encyclical *Pacem in Terris* (Peace on Earth). During the CUBAN MISSILE CRISIS he issued a personal call for restraint to the superpowers. His warmth, humanity and pious humility earned him enormous popular affection and widespread respect.

**John Paul II, Pope** (1920–). Pope, 1978–. Born Karol Wojtyla at Wadowice, near Cracow, Poland, he entered university at Cracow in 1938 and was a forced labourer under the German occupation. Ordained a priest in 1945, he studied in Rome before returning to Cracow as a parish priest. An auxiliary bishop in 1958, he became Archbishop in January 1964 and Cardinal in 1967. Extensively travelled and a gifted linguist, he was elected Pope in October 1978 following the sudden death of John Paul I

after 33 days as Pontiff. The first non-Italian Pope since 1522, he was formally invested on 22 October 1978. His pontificate has been noted for his extensive travelling, visiting far more countries than any previous Pontiff. In his interpretation of Church doctrine he has proved conservative, refusing to accept changes in such matters as the bans on artificial contraception, abortion and the celibacy of the clergy. He has also shown himself a vigorous critic of communism and is opposed to the more extreme notions of 'liberation theology' associated with some Third World churches, notably in Latin America. He worked for the reconciliation of the breakaway traditionalist movement led by Archbishop Lefebvre in France, conceding permission for the performance of the Latin rite. Seriously wounded in an assassination attempt in May 1981 in Rome, he made a full recovery, and was unharmed when a further attempt was made at Fatima in Portugal. In May 1982 he became the first Pope to visit the British Isles, and participated in ecumenical services at Canterbury. He attempted mediation in the FALKLANDS WAR, visiting Argentina immediately after his visit to Britain. As well as occasional outspoken comments about human rights abuses, his most important political role came with his visits to Poland in June 1982 and again in June 1987. His first visit provided an opportunity for pro-SOLIDARITY demonstrations when the movement was under a ban following the introduction of martial law in 1981. His second visit in 1987 came when Solidarity was at a low point; he gave his blessing to the movement, stating that it was legitimate for Poles to fight peacefully for human rights. These visits and his granting of a personal audience to LECH WALESA undoubtedly leant great moral weight to the pro-Solidarity movement in Poland, putting the Catholic Church firmly behind the forces for change and ensuring that its leaders could not simply be suppressed.

**Juan Carlos, of Spain** (1938–). King of Spain from 22 November 1975. The grandson of King ALFONSO XIII, he began his education under FRANCO's tutelage in 1948 as the latter's potential successor. Named as future King in 1969, he took the throne in 1975, shortly before Franco's death. He played a crucial role in the restoration of democracy in Spain and established himself as a constitutional monarch with effective power being placed in the hands of the Prime Minister. He signed the new constitution on 27 December 1978. He acted decisively to resist the coup attempt by a section of the Guardia Civil led by Lieutenant-Colonel Antonio-Tejoro de Molina on 23 February 1981, broadcasting to the nation in full military uniform and ordering the armed forces to 'take all necessary measures' to put down the revolt. Extremely popular among all social groups, Juan Carlos seems to have succeeded in restoring legitimacy to the formerly much disputed Spanish monarchy.

R. Carr and J. P. Fusi, *Spain: Dictatorship to Democracy* (1979)

D. Gilmour, *The Transformation of Spain* (1985)

**July Bomb Plot.** The attempted assassination of HITLER on 20 July 1944. The most spectacular attempt by the liberal-conservative German resistance to overthrow the Nazi regime, the abortive coup was launched by the conspirators when it became clear that the GESTAPO was close to uncovering them. Count Claus von Stauffenberg, chief of staff to the commander of the Army Reserve, smuggled a bomb into a briefing meeting at Hitler's East Prussian headquarters in Rastenburg. It was planned that, following the death of the dictator, army leaders active in the conspiracy (von Witzleben and von Beck) should seize power in Berlin, install a conservative government led by Carl Goerdeler (a former Lord Mayor of Leipzig) and seek a negotiated peace with the Western Allies. Crucial to the failure of the attempted coup was the survival of Hitler, who was only slightly injured: not only was the briefing at which the bomb was planted held above ground rather than in the usual concrete

bunker, but also the bomb was moved away from Hitler before it exploded. The conspirators co-ordinated their activities poorly, and the attempt to seize power in Berlin did not begin until after Stauffenberg had flown back to the capital. GOEBBELS acted quickly, telephoning Hitler and putting the latter in contact with Major Remer, the commander of the guards battalion in Berlin who had undertaken to seal off the government quarters: on hearing of Hitler's survival, Remer acted to suppress the coup and arrest the conspirators. In Paris General von Stulpnagel, the military governor of France and one of the conspirators, initially succeeded in seizing the Paris headquarters of the police, SS (*see* ss) and Gestapo. Yet, learning of Hitler's survival, the commander-in-chief of the German forces in the west, Field Marshal von Kluge, cancelled all measures taken against the SS, thus ensuring the failure of the conspirators' plan to seize control of Paris. Stauffenberg was shot on the evening of 20 July and, in the succeeding weeks, other leading conspirators were either arrested and subsequently executed or chose suicide: in all, perhaps 5,000 opponents of the regime were executed in the aftermath of the abortive coup. Perhaps the most important long-term consequence of the coup was the decimation of the conservative elites which Hitler unleashed in revenge; a purge which, once and for all, broke the political will of the Prussian nobility. Undertaken by the conspirators with only limited expectation of success, the coup's true significance is perhaps a moral one – the determination of the conspirators to resist Nazi barbarism and inhumanity even at the cost of their lives. *See also* SECOND WORLD WAR.

H. Graml *et al.*, *The German Resistance to Hitler* (1970)

**Jutland, Battle of.** *See* FIRST WORLD WAR; JELLICOE, JOHN.

# K

**Kadar, Janos** (1912–89). Hungarian communist leader. He was born in Rijeka (Fiume), formerly part of the Austro-Hungarian empire (now Yugoslavia). A toolmaker and trade union leader, he became a member of the HUNGARIAN COMMUNIST PARTY in 1932 and was imprisoned under HORTHY DE NAGYBANYA. He joined the party's Central Committee in 1942 and organized resistance to the Nazis. He took control of the police and the Budapest organization under RÁKOSI, replacing his former friend Rajk as Minister of Internal Affairs when the latter was purged in 1948. Kadar was imprisoned and subjected to torture himself in 1951, but was released in 1954 when the more moderate IMRE NAGY became Premier. Kadar rejoined the Politburo. He initially welcomed the first stages of the HUNGARIAN UPRISING of late October 1956, but disappeared from view when events radicalized, re-emerging to head the Soviet-backed regime on 4 November as the rising was crushed. At first he acted sternly to suppress the supporters of the revolt, executing 2,000 people, and carried out the secret trial and execution of Nagy and other leaders. In 1958–9 he enforced collectivization and consolidated one-party rule. Thereafter, he gradually liberalized the regime under his slogan of 1961, 'He who is not against us is with us'. 'Kadarism' combined support for Soviet foreign policy (as in the action to invade Czechoslovakia in 1968) with greater economic relaxation. Under his rule Hungary emerged as the freest of the East European satellites, encouraging a mixed economy and a return to peasant proprietorship. By 1988 he was increasingly regarded as an unnecessary impediment to further reform welling up within the party and the country. In May 1988 he was relegated to a largely honorific position and in June 1989 was stripped of most of his remaining offices, including membership of the Central Committee. He died on 9 July. A sincere communist, he always claimed to be acting in his country's interests. His role in the events of 1956 earned him the hatred of many Hungarians, but his generally mild and enlightened rule from 1961 to 1988 to some extent redeemed his reputation.

P. E. Zinner, *Revolution in Hungary* (1962)
J. K. Hoensch, *A History of Modern Hungary, 1867–1986* (trans., 1988)
C. Gati, *Hungary and the Soviet Bloc* (1988)

**Kadets.** *See* CONSTITUTIONAL DEMOCRATIC PARTY, RUSSIAN.

**Kamenev, Lev** (1883–1936). Russian Bolshevik politician. He joined the Russian Social Democratic Workers' Party in 1901 and returned to Petrograd from Siberia after the February Revolution. Although he opposed LENIN's seizure of power he joined the seven-man Politburo formed to carry out the coup. He was opposed to Lenin's exclusivity, and in November 1917 resigned from the Central Committee of the Party and from his presidency of the Central Executive Committee of the Soviets. Re-elected to the Central Committee and to the Politburo in 1919, he became leader of the Moscow party and chairman of the Moscow Soviet. He formed part of the triumvirate which took over during Lenin's last illness. In the power struggles which followed Lenin's incapacity and death he sided first with STALIN against TROTSKY and then with Trotsky and ZINOVIEV, thus earning the opposition of Stalin. Expelled from the party in 1927, in 1935 he was sentenced to five years' imprisonment; retried the next year he was sentenced again and executed.

Another of the early Bolshevik leaders destroyed by Stalin, Kamenev had attempted to follow his own course but was fatally compromised by his support for Zinoviev. *See also* PURGES.

R. Conquest, *The Great Terror* (1968)

**Kapp Putsch.** An abortive attempt in March 1920 by a group of right-wing conspirators with military support to overthrow the centre-left government of the WEIMAR REPUBLIC. The putsch takes its name from that of one of its leaders, Wolfgang Kapp, a former East Prussian official and founder-member of the wartime right-wing Fatherland Party. The immediate cause of the insurrection was the government's order at the beginning of March 1920 that the Erhardt Marine Brigade, a FREIKORPS paramilitary formation stationed in Berlin, be dissolved in keeping with the terms of the TREATY OF VERSAILLES. The putsch occurred against the background of widespread right-wing and military discontent with defeat during the First World War and with the outcome of the GERMAN REVOLUTION of 1918–19. A group of extremists headed by Kapp and General LUDENDORFF had formed the intention as early as July 1919 of overthrowing the Weimar government; forming the National Association in October 1919 was the organizational core of their conspiracy. The National Association actively sought the support of right-wing politicians and army officers for their conspiracy; it established close ties with General von Lüttwitz, commander of all German troops east of the River Elbe and of units in Hanover, Saxony and Thuringia. Reduction in the size of the German army in compliance with the terms of the Versailles settlement from autumn 1919 onwards led to growing anti-government sentiment amongst the officer corps and members of the *Freikorps* formations which Kapp and his associates sought to exploit to overthrow the government.

On 10 March 1920 Lüttwitz demanded that a halt be called to further dissolutions of *Freikorps* formations, that the President and government resign and that new elections to the REICHSTAG be held. When the government dismissed him from his command he led the Erhardt Brigade in an occupation of the government district of Berlin on 13 March, proclaiming Kapp the

new Chancellor. Only the commander-in-chief of the army, General Reinhardt, was willing to deploy it against the putsch; and the army, following the position of the chief of the general staff General Seeckt, remained aloof from developments, leaving the government defenceless against the rebels. The President and government fled Berlin for Dresden and then Stuttgart.

Despite its initial success and the sympathy of many military commanders throughout Germany, the putsch soon collapsed. The Prussian and national civil service refused to carry out the orders of Kapp's government, and the trade unions called a general strike against the rebel government. Unable to administer the country or establish its authority, the Kapp government collapsed within four days and on 18 March the conspirators fled to Sweden.

Only in Bavaria had the putsch met any real success. Here it led to the resignation of the coalition government led by a Social Democrat and its replacement by a right-wing government sympathetic to anti-republican elements. The long-term significance of the Kapp putsch lies in its demonstration of the – at best – lukewarm attitude of much of the officer corps and army leadership towards the liberal-democratic republican order.

G. A. Craig, *The Politics of the Prussian Army, 1640–1945* (1955)
F. L. Carsten, *The Reichswehr and Politics, 1918–1933* (1966)
E. Kolb, *The Weimar Republic* (1988)

**Karamanlis, Konstantinos** (1907–). Greek statesman, and dominant political figure in post-war Greece. Born in eastern Macedonia, he practised as a lawyer in Athens. He entered government in 1946 and worked on good terms with the Americans in the MARSHALL PLAN programme and in rebuilding the country after the GREEK CIVIL WAR. Appointed Prime Minister on the death of the veteran soldier and politician ALEXANDER PAPAGOS in October 1955, he set up a new conservative grouping, the National Radical Union (ERE) which secured comfortable victories in elections in 1956, 1958 and 1961. He resigned in protest over the Royal State Visit to Britain in June 1963, a legacy of the bitterness aroused over the CYPRUS EMERGENCY. During his time in office Greece benefited considerably from American aid and its position as a bulwark of the NATO alliance in the eastern Mediterranean (see NORTH ATLANTIC TREATY ORGANISATION). During the GREEK COLONELS regime he was in exile in France, but returned in June 1974 to form a caretaker administration after their fall. Karamanlis's New Democratic Party won an overwhelming victory in the elections of November 1974. For the next six years he presided over Greece's successful transition to democracy, and a period of considerable social and economic growth that culminated in the EEC's acceptance of Greece's application for full membership. His main objectives having been achieved, Karamanlis resigned as Premier in May 1980 and he became President. He occupied the presidency until March 1985, when the Premier, ANDREAS PAPANDREOU, and his majority PASOK party gave their support to Christos Sartzetakis, a Supreme Court Judge. After the expiry of Sartzetakis's five-year term, Karamanlis again became President in May 1990 since his New Democracy once again had a majority in the Greek parliament.

C. A. M. Woodhouse, *Karamanlis: the restorer of Greek Democracy* (1982)

**Karelian Isthmus.** The creation of an independent Finnish state in 1917 made the Karelian Isthmus a critical strategic area, both for the Soviet Union and Finland, as the shortest land route between Leningrad and the major centres of Finnish population. The border established between the Soviet Union and Finland in October 1920 drew a line only 20 miles from Leningrad and 60 from the major Finnish city of Viipuri. The new border was fortified on the Finnish side by the MANNERHEIM LINE from the late 1920s. Soviet demands for adjustment of the frontier in the Soviet Union's favour and for the demilitarization in 1939 were resisted by the Finns. As a result of the RUSSO-FINNISH WAR of 1939–40 the Soviet Union gained the whole of the Karelian Isthmus and the Finnish second city of Viipuri. The former Finnish territories were reoccupied by the Finns in the CONTINUATION WAR of 1941–4, but were returned to the Soviet Union at the conclusion of

hostilities. The Isthmus remains part of the Soviet Union.

**Károlyi, Mihály** (1875–1955). Hungarian statesman. Born of one of the ancient Hungarian landowning families, he entered Parliament in 1905 as a liberal, but in 1911 became Chairman of the Independence Party. In 1916 he broke with them in order to pursue his own more radical policies, including electoral reform and the division of the great estates. He was appointed Prime Minister by Emperor CHARLES on 30 October 1918 in the hope of stemming a growing national revolt. He obtained from Charles his freedom from his oath of allegiance two days later and sought an armistice with the Entente Powers. On 11 November he proclaimed the Hungarian Republic, becoming its Provisional President five days later. He attempted to introduce land reforms but his position was undermined by opposition from conservatives and from the left by both communists under BÉLA KUN and Social Democrats. Faced with the threat of a communist demonstration on 23 March 1919 to free their leaders arrested on 21 February and the prospect of further losses of Hungarian territory from the PARIS PEACE CONFERENCE, Károlyi surrendered power on 22 March to a Revolutionary Governing Council led by the communists and went into exile. He returned to Hungary in 1946 after the overthrow of HORTHY DE NAGYBANYA's dictatorship. He served as a diplomat in 1946–9 before increasing communist domination forced him into a final exile.

M. Károlyi, *Memoirs: Faith Without Illusion* (1956)
J. K. Hoensch, *A History of Modern Hungary, 1867–1986* (trans., 1988)

**Kars, Treaty of.** Signed in 1921 between the Armenian Socialist Republic and the Russian Soviet Government with the Turkish Government. By the treaty the disputed area of Kars province, ceded to Russia in 1878, annexed by Turkey by the TREATY OF BREST-LITOVSK, then part of the Republic of ARMENIA, was returned to Turkey following its conquest by the 'Young Turk' armies under Karabakir Pasha.

**Katyn Massacre.** In April 1943 German troops discovered the mass graves of 4,500

Polish officers at Katyn Wood, near Smolensk. The bodies bore evidence of systematic execution. The discovery was immediately seized on by German propaganda to accuse the Russians of having carried out a massacre of Polish officers captured during the Soviet occupation of western Poland in September 1939. Russia denied the charge, but considerable circumstantial evidence suggested that they were, in fact, responsible. For the Germans the most important result was the outrage amongst the Polish government-in-exile in London and the serious friction caused between them and the Soviet Union, now Britain's allies in the war against Germany. STALIN used the furore as an opportunity to sever relations with the London Poles, setting up his own puppet Polish government. Subsequently the Katyn site fell into Russian hands. The International Red Cross were denied access and a Soviet commission laid the blame on the German forces, but no prosecutions were conducted at Nuremberg (see NUREMBERG TRIALS) or subsequently. The Katyn affair remained a potent focus of anti-Soviet feeling amongst those opposed to the Soviet domination of Eastern Europe after 1945. Demands for a full investigation of the Katyn massacre resurfaced during the COLD WAR and following the rise of the SOLIDARITY movement in Poland in 1980–81. As part of GLASNOST, MIKHAIL GORBACHEV promised a full investigation of the Katyn incident in 1988. The most likely explanation lies in Stalin's ruthless determination to destroy the Polish ruling class as a possible source of opposition to Soviet rule, analogous to the forced deportations from the BALTIC STATES in 1941.

W. Anders, *The Crime of Katyn* (1965)
J. K. Zawodny, *Murder in the Forest* (1972)

**Kautsky, Karl** (1854–1938). German Social Democratic politician and political theorist. Having joined the Austrian Social Democratic Party in 1875, Kautsky served in London as Engels's private secretary between 1885 and 1890. From 1883 until 1917 he was editor of the social-democratic newspaper *Die Neue Zeit*. A major contributor to the formulation of the 1891 Erfurt programme of the GERMAN SOCIAL DEMOCRATIC PARTY (SPD), Kautsky became the leading Marxist theoretician within the

party and a prominent figure in the Second International. He upheld the orthodox Marxist analysis which informed the Erfurt programme against the 'revisionist' challenge mounted by Eduard Bernstein at the turn of the century, yet seemed to many radicals within the SPD, such as ROSA LUXEMBURG, to place too great an emphasis on the economically determinist elements within Marx's work at the expense of political will as a means of bringing about socialist revolution. In *The Road to Power* (1907), Kautsky argued that the SPD's main tasks lay in the organization of the working class and political agitation: the ruling class would lose the confidence of the mass of the population as the contradictions within the political, economic and social systems became progressively more apparent. During the FIRST WORLD WAR, Kautsky became increasingly disillusioned with the SPD's continuing support for the Imperial government's war effort despite the evidently annexationist aims pursued by the government, and left the party to join the breakaway pacifist Independent GERMAN SOCIAL DEMOCRATIC PARTY (USPD) in 1917. In the early stages of the GERMAN REVOLUTION of 1918–19 Kautsky was a deputy minister in the Foreign Office and was charged with the publication of German diplomatic documents relating to the outbreak of the First World War. Settling in Vienna in the 1920's, Kautsky published political-theoretical writings, fleeing to the Netherlands in 1938 on the eve of the ANSCHLUSS.

C. E. Schorske, *German Social Democracy, 1905–1917* (1955)
D. Geary, *Karl Kautsky* (1986)

**Kekkonen, Urho Kaleva** (1900–1986). Finnish President, 1956–81; and dominant political figure in post-war Finland. Active in student politics during the 1920s, a period characterized by intense nationalism with distinctly Russophobic tendencies, he became a member of the Agrarian Union Party and entered parliament in 1936. He was appointed Minister of Justice in the centre-left Kallio government in 1937. During the CONTINUATION WAR of 1941–4 with Russia Kekkonen gradually aligned himself with those such as PAASIKIVI who advocated the necessity of coming to terms with the realities of the great-power status of Finland's eastern neighbour. Always a controversial figure – his part as Minister of Justice in supervising the trial of those adjudged culpable of leading Finland into war as a co-belligerent of Germany in 1941 aroused much resentment amongst the old guard of his own party – Kekkonen nevertheless proved to be an indispensable figure in politics during the early 1950s, when he headed five governments. Elected President in 1956 by the narrowest of margins (151 to 149 votes in the electoral college), he had to deal with a general strike during his first days of office. The turning-point of his presidential career was in 1961, when he successfully defused a potentially serious crisis in relations with the Soviet Union, a triumph which ensured his easy re-election for a further term of office in 1962. The forging of good relations with the Soviet Union, which Kekkonen believed was the best guarantee of Finnish neutrality, was his main achievement, not least in terms of domestic politics. By the 1970s all the major political parties supported the Paasikivi-Kekkonen line of foreign policy; the consensual nature of recent Finnish political life owes a great deal to this unanimity. The staging of the European Security Conference in Helsinki in 1975 was a tribute to Kekkonen's tireless promotion of a policy of active neutrality, though his regional initiatives, most notably suggestions for a Nordic nuclear-free zone, were less successful. Ill-health eventually obliged him to resign in October 1981.

U. Kekkonen, *Neutrality: The Finnish Position* (1973)
K. Korhonen, (ed.), *Urho Kekkonen: A Statesman for Peace* (1975)

**Kellogg Pact.** Popular name for the Pact of Paris, signed on 27 August 1928, also known as the Kellogg-Briand Pact from the initiators ARISTIDE BRIAND, French Foreign Minister, and the United States Secretary of State, Frank B. Kellogg (1856–1937). Briand proposed to the United States in April 1927 that France and America should sign a pact renouncing war and expressing an intention of seeking settlement of disputes by peaceful means. To widen support a nine-power conference was called in Paris on 27 August 1928 attended by Belgium, Britain, Czechoslovakia, France, Germany, Italy, Japan, Poland and the United States.

Eventually 65 states signed the pact, but provided no machinery to restrain aggression should it occur. In 1931 Japan cynically evaded the pact by declaring her invasion of Manchuria an 'incident', and the pact was soon rendered ineffective by the rise of international tensions thereafter. For a time, however, it expressed the good intentions of a relatively peaceful and hopeful era of international relations. *See also* LOCARNO TREATIES.

R. Albrecht-Carrie, *A Diplomatic History of Europe from the Congress of Vienna* (1961)
H. Gatzke, *European Diplomacy between the Two World Wars* (1972)

**Kennedy, John Fitzgerald** (1917–63). American statesman. Born 29 May 1917 in Boston, Massachusetts, the son of Joseph Kennedy, a successful businessman, ambassador to the United Kingdom and a Roman Catholic, John Kennedy graduated from Harvard University in 1940 and served in the US Navy. He was elected to the House of Representatives in 1946. He defeated Henry Cabot Lodge for one of the Massachusetts Senate seats in 1952, and in November 1960 defeated Richard Nixon in the presidential election by a narrow margin. On 22 November 1963 he was assassinated in Dallas, Texas. A commission under the Chief Justice of the United States Supreme Court, Earl Warren, concluded that he had been killed by one Lee Harvey Oswald, acting alone. He was succeeded by the Vice President, Lyndon Baines Johnson, on the afternoon of his death. His short period as President witnessed the CUBAN MISSILE CRISIS. His style and charisma made him one of the most admired and popular Presidents of modern times.

**Kennedy Round.** Four year-long negotiations to encourage world trade through reductions of tariffs on industrial and agricultural imports, particularly between the United States and Europe. They were named after President KENNEDY's message to Congress on 25 January 1963, which urged greater freedom of trade. A final agreement was reached at Geneva on 15 May 1967. The agreements were part of a process of ensuring the maintenance of free trade and preventing the development of the protectionism and bilateral agreements which it was felt had contributed to the inter-war DEPRESSION. The growth of the EUROPEAN ECONOMIC COMMUNITY as a major economic power with external tariffs played a major part in promoting the need for agreement.

W. Feld, *The European Community in World Affairs* (1976)

**Kerensky, Alexander** (1881–1970). Russian statesman and Prime Minister of the PROVISIONAL GOVERNMENT in 1917. A middle-class lawyer, he was an active opponent of the autocracy in the courts and was elected to the Duma in 1912, siding with the moderate socialists of the SOCIAL REVOLUTIONARY PARTY. A member of the Provisional Committee appointed by the DUMA, he held the positions of Minister of Justice, then of War and the Navy (16 May), before becoming Prime Minister on 20 July. Kerensky was undoubtedly the most vigorous of the members of the Provisional Government. This led both to his rapid promotion and a renewal of the war effort in spring 1917. More prepared to see a further development of socialism than some of his colleagues, he was Deputy Chairman of the Petrograd Soviet as well as Minister in the Provisional Government, but turned on the Bolsheviks following their abortive coup in July. While his socialist leanings alienated conservatives, his attempt to prosecute the war and his failure to deliver significant reforms alienated the population at large. Threatened from both Right and Left, he was increasingly isolated, with no firm basis of support, especially after the virtual disintegration of the army following the 'Kerensky offensive' in July. Hence, having requested the new Commander-in-Chief KORNILOV to move troops against the capital, he became fearful of Kornilov's intentions and had to call on the Bolsheviks to deal with Kornilov's advance on Petrograd in early September. Only two days before the Bolshevik seizure of power a meeting of representatives of various party and public organizations refused to give him powers to deal with the incipient Bolshevik threat, urging him instead to implement a programme of revolutionary reforms. Escaping the Bolshevik forces who seized the Winter Palace on the night of 7 November, his

attempt to retake the capital with scratch forces was defeated at Pulkovo on 12 November. Forced to leave Petrograd and eventually the country, he spent the rest of his life in exile in Europe and the United States.

Kerensky is usually treated harshly in the pro-Marxist historiography and little less generously by opponents of the Bolshevik regime. It is still difficult to see how the Provisional Government might have controlled the forces of national disintegration which offered LENIN his opportunity, although the failure to achieve a speedy peace and satisfy peasant aspirations for land reform undoubtedly assisted the fall of the Provisional Government. Deluded by his own successes in rallying the front-line troops in the spring of 1917, he overestimated their readiness to make further sacrifices and the war-weariness on the home front. *See also* RUSSIAN REVOLUTION.

A. Kerensky, *The Kerensky Memoirs: Russia and History's Turning Point* (1965)
L. Shapiro, *1917: The Russian Revolutions and the Origins of Present-day Communism* (1984)

**Keynes, John Maynard** (1883–1946). British economist. Born and educated in Cambridge, he worked in the Treasury during the First World War and was a chief representative at negotiations prior to the TREATY OF VERSAILLES. He criticized the REPARATIONS plans in *The Economic Consequences of the Peace* (1919). His radical proposals for dealing with mass unemployment by deficit financing and state intervention influenced Lloyd George's ORANGE BOOK of 1929 and OSWALD MOSLEY's proposals to the SECOND LABOUR GOVERNMENT. His full theoretical position was published in *The General Theory of Employment, Interest and Money* (1936), which inspired the 'Keynesian Revolution' in economic thinking during and after the Second World War. This rejected the classical belief in the self-regulating economy, arguing the benefits of government expenditure and economic management by the state to maintain maximum output and full employment. He acted as an economic adviser in the Second World War and co-operated with BEVERIDGE over the funding of the welfare state as envisaged in the Beveridge Report. He was the chief British delegate at the BRET-

TON WOODS CONFERENCE in 1944 and in the discussions leading to the creation of the International Monetary Fund and the World Bank. His economic ideas proved immensely influential until the rise of MONETARISM in the 1970s and the apparent inability of 'Keynesianism' to cope with the simultaneous onset of stagnation and inflation. See also DEPRESSION.

L. Klein, *The Keynesian Revolution* (1966)

**KGB.** Abbreviated Russian name of the Committee of State Security, the Soviet secret police. Following the fall of BERIA, who had reamalgamated all the branches of the security forces under his control, the Communist Party moved to detach the secret police and place them under firmer party control. Subordinated to the Council of Ministers and, in effect, the Central Committee, the KGB increasingly came to be headed by party officials rather than those, like Beria, who had come up through the security services. The KGB is the branch of the state security apparatus which maintained surveillance on DISSIDENTS and other opponents of the Soviet regime. It is also responsible for foreign espionage and maintains an extensive establishment of several hundred thousand employees.

R. Hingley, *The Russian Secret Police* (1970)
B. Levytsky, *The Uses of Terror: The Soviet Secret Service, 1917–1970* (1971)

**Khrushchev, Nikita** (1894–1971). Russian statesman and First Secretary of the Soviet Communist Party, 1953–64. A party member from 1918 he rose in 1934 to Second Secretary, and then in 1935 to First Secretary of the Moscow Party Organization under STALIN. One of the young party members to be advanced by the PURGES, he was appointed First Secretary of the Ukrainian Party in 1938, a Politburo member in 1939 and a political officer in the Second World War. He became Prime Minister of the Ukrainian Soviet Republic from its liberation until 1947, and was appointed by Stalin to reorganize Soviet agricultural production in 1949. He became First Secretary of the COMMUNIST PARTY OF THE SOVIET UNION after Stalin's death as part of the 'collective leadership'. From 1958 he was also Chairman of the Council of Ministers, replacing BULGANIN and combining

the supreme posts in both state and party until 1964. His leadership was most notable for his attack upon Stalin in the 'secret speech' to the 20th Party Congress in 1956, beginning the process of DE-STALINIZATION and having important effects on the rest of the communist world, notably in provoking a breach with China and hard-line allies such as Albania. Domestically, however, it marked a move towards a less harsh regime, including a revised criminal code and legal reforms to remove the worst excesses of Stalinism, reforms of the party structure, and attempts to improve living standards, housing and education. But Khrushchev also pursued a harsh policy of de-Christianization, put down the HUNGARIAN UPRISING, and was responsible for introducing some disastrous experiments to improve agricultural output. The last, including the VIRGIN LANDS CAMPAIGN, proved clumsy failures, provoking bread riots in the cities in 1962 and forcing the Soviet Union to make foreign purchases of grain. As agriculture had been considered his major area of expertise, Khrushchev found himself increasingly isolated. In foreign policy, his attempt to test the resolve of the American administration under Kennedy by placing Soviet missiles in Cuba in 1962 forced an embarrassing retreat, exposing the Soviet weakness in naval power. The disappointing harvest of 1963, falling 40 per cent short of its planned target, helped to provoke an indictment of Khrushchev's policies at a plenum of the Central Committee in October 1964, at which he was voted out of office. It was nonetheless symptomatic of the changes he had wrought that he was permitted to live out the rest of his life in obscure retirement. See also DE-STALINIZATION.

C. Linden, *Khrushchev and the Soviet Leadership, 1957–64* (1966)
M. McCauley, *Khrushchev and the Development of Soviet Agriculture: The Virgin Lands Programme, 1953–64* (1976)
R. and Zh. Medvedev, *Khrushchev: The Years in Power* (1977)

**Kilbrandon Report.** See DEVOLUTION.

**Kinnock, Neil** (1942–). British Labour politician. A Labour MP since 1970 and a member of the LABOUR PARTY's National Executive Committee from 1978, he was elected leader of the Labour Party in 1983 following the resignation of MICHAEL FOOT. His attacks upon Militant Tendency and extremist influence in the party were seen as an attempt to moderate the party's image after the 1983 defeat. He promoted attempts to improve the Labour Party organization, especially at Walworth Road headquarters. He led the Labour Party to defeat in what was widely regarded as a highly dynamic and professional campaign in the 1987 general election. Following the defeat he inaugurated a widespread policy review, abandoning firm views on UNILATERALISM and modifying policies on NATIONALIZATION. Internal party reforms continued, with alteration to the selection procedure for parliamentary candidates and commitments to amend the 'block vote' enjoyed by trades unions at the Labour Party conference. He is widely seen as trying to moderate and modernize the Labour Party's platform and image.

K. O. Morgan, *Labour People: Leaders and Lieutenants: Hardie to Kinnock* (1985)
H. Pelling, *A Short History of the Labour Party* (8th edn, 1988)

**Kirov, Sergei** (1886–1934). Russian Bolshevik politician. He joined the party in 1905, and after the RUSSIAN REVOLUTION worked to establish Soviet power in the Caucasus. Party secretary in Leningrad from 1924, he joined the Politburo in 1930. A popular member of the party who favoured some moderation towards opponents to STALIN, he was assassinated on 1 December 1934 at the party headquarters in Leningrad by a disillusioned young communist. The evidence suggests that Stalin at least connived at the assassination, which removed a potential rival and provided the pretext for the inauguration of a major purge of opponents. A decree was immediately passed permitting arbitrary arrest, trial and execution of those committing terroristic acts. Three weeks later the assassin was announced to have been working for a 'Leningrad opposition centre', leading to the arrests of ZINOVIEV, KAMENEV and several other leading opponents of Stalin. Zinoviev and Kamenev were tried in January 1935 and imprisoned for general responsibility for the murder, and finally executed following 'confession' to the murder at their

retrial in August 1936. The Kirov affair also sparked a widespread purge of almost 0.5 million party members in the course of the next two years (*See* PURGES).

B. D. Wolfe, *Khruschev and Stalin's Ghost* (1957)
R. Conquest, *The Great Terror* (1971)
——, *Stalin and the Kirov Murder* (1989)

**Kitchener, Horatio** (1850–1916). British general. Kitchener joined the Royal Engineers in 1870. He served in the Sudan and Egypt, 1882–5, and was Governor-General of East Sudan, 1886–8. As Commander-in-Chief ('Sirdar') of the Anglo-Egyptian Army in the 1890s he undertook the reconquest of the Sudan, defeating the dervishes at Omdurman on 2 September 1898. On becoming Commander-in-Chief in South Africa he broke the resistance of the Boers by the use of blockhouses and concentration camps. He was then Commander-in-Chief in India, 1902–9, and British Agent and Consul-General in Egypt, 1911–14. On 5 August 1914 he was appointed War Minister. One of the few to envisage that the war might prove prolonged, he sought to build up large, new armies which he hoped would take the field in the latter years of the war and allow Britain to arbitrate the final peace settlement. His enormous prestige as Britain's Imperial hero was utilized in the recruiting campaigns which raised over 1 million volunteers by Christmas 1914 – known as 'Kitchener's Armies'. He was drowned on a mission to Russia on 5 June 1916 when the cruiser HMS Hampshire struck a mine off the Orkney Islands. He was awarded a peerage in 1898, made a viscount in 1902, and an earl in 1914.

P. Magnus, *Kitchener* (1958)
P. Simkins, *Kitchener's Army* (1988)

**Kohl, Helmut** (1930–). West German politician and Chancellor of the FEDERAL REPUBLIC OF GERMANY from 1982. Born in the Rhineland, Kohl was active in the CHRISTIAN DEMOCRATIC UNION (CDU) from the age of 17. He became a member of the regional parliament for the Rhineland-Palatinate in 1959 and was the chairman of the parliamentary CDU from 1963 until 1969, and of the regional party from 1969 to 1976. In 1969 he became Prime Minister of Rhineland-Palatinate and Deputy Chairman of the CDU throughout Germany. Replacing Rainer Barzel as chairman of the Federal CDU in 1973, he was the party's candidate for Chancellor in the 1976 elections to the Federal Parliament (*Bundestag*). Despite the gains made by the CDU in those elections, his party chose to put up FRANZ-JOSEF STRAUSS against HELMUT SCHMIDT as candidate for Chancellor in the 1980 *Bundestag* elections. Strauss's poor performance revived what had seemed to many to be Kohl's flagging political career. In September–October 1982, he played a key role in persuading the FREE DEMOCRATIC PARTY to abandon its coalition with Schmidt's SOCIAL DEMOCRATIC PARTY (SPD) and in initiating a no-confidence vote in Schmidt. Becoming Chancellor in October 1982, Kohl arranged the loss of a no-confidence vote in his own government in order to precipitate elections. In the March 1983 *Bundestag* elections, the CDU-CSU won a resounding victory, emerging with more seats than at any time since 1957. In an at times uneasy coalition with the FREE DEMOCRATIC PARTY (FDP), the Kohl government embarked on an austerity programme of reducing taxes and public expenditure, despite the persistence of high unemployment throughout the period 1983–5. In foreign affairs Kohl's government adhered to the NATO DUAL TRACK POLICY and accepted the installation of US medium-range missiles in West Germany in 1984. Its policy towards East Germany and its other communist neighbours was less clear, building on the gradual normalization of relations which had taken place since the late 1960s but also hinting at continuing hopes for German unification. In the January 1987 *Bundestag* elections, the CDU-CSU, wracked by internal dissension and tainted by a long-running scandal about clandestine political funding from a large industrial concern, sustained heavy electoral losses, of which the FDP and the environmentalist GREENS were the main beneficiaries. After the election, with economic recovery clearly well-established, the Kohl government adhered to its 'No Experiments' election slogan in domestic affairs. Kohl has continued to play an important role in promoting greater economic integration within the EUROPEAN ECONOMIC COMMUNITY (EEC), maintaining the Franco-German alignment on most

EEC issues established by Schmidt in the late 1970s. However, Kohl's clumsiness and lack of diplomatic sensitivity had often meant that his government had been unable to make the most of closer relations with East Germany. Following the opening of the BERLIN WALL in November 1989, Kohl surprised commentators by immediately raising the issue of unification of the two German states, proposing a ten-stage plan by which this might be realized. He campaigned actively in the East during the first free elections in spring 1990 and supervised the economic and political reunification of the two Germanies by October 1990, securing victory in the December all-German elections.

H. A. Turner, *The Two Germanies since 1945* (1987)

**Kolchak, Alexander** (1874–1920). Russian admiral and White leader in the RUSSIAN CIVIL WAR. The son of a high-ranking naval officer, he entered the navy, serving with distinction in the Russo-Japanese War and with the Baltic and Black Sea fleets in the First World War. Initially supporting the PROVISIONAL GOVERNMENT, he gave up his command in the summer of 1917 and was sent to the United States to discuss naval co-operation. Receiving word of the October Revolution while returning via Japan, he spent almost a year in the Far East before re-entering Siberia and becoming War Minister for the White provisional government based on Omsk. Supported by the Allies and the more conservative elements, he became 'Supreme Ruler' after a coup overthrew the Provisional Government. Aided by the CZECH LEGION Kolchak's forces advanced westwards in 1919, crossing the Urals and attacking as far west as the Volga, but RED ARMY counter-attacks drove back the White armies, precipitating a rout, and Kolchak was forced to quit his 'capital' at Omsk in November 1919. As well as the military defeat of his forces, Kolchak had secured little support for his government of Siberia, failing to make any concessions to the national minorities. As a result, his government dissolved with defeat and he was handed over to the Bolsheviks by the disillusioned Czech Legion in January 1920. He was executed the following month.

D. Footman, *Civil War in Russia* (1961)
P. Fleming, *The Fate of Admiral Kolchak* (1963)

kolkhoz. *See* COLLECTIVIZATION, SOVIET.

**Kommunistische Partei Deutschlands (KPD).** *See* COMMUNIST PARTY, GERMAN.

**Kommunistische Partei Österreichs (KPÖ).** *See* COMMUNIST PARTY, AUSTRIAN.

**Komsomol.** (All-Union Leninist Communist Union of Youth). Soviet youth organization founded in 1918 under the direction of the COMMUNIST PARTY OF THE SOVIET UNION. The Komsomol embraces virtually all young people between the ages of 14 and 28. Although only a small proportion of its members join the party, the Komsomol has frequently been seen as the source of energetic volunteers and activists, as in SOVIET COLLECTIVIZATION and the VIRGIN LANDS CAMPAIGN.

A. Kassof, *The Soviet Youth Program: Regimentation and Rebellion* (1965)

**Komunisticka Strana Československa (KSC).** *See* COMMUNIST PARTY, CZECHOSLOVAK.

**Koniev, Ivan** (1897–1973). Soviet Marshal. The son of a farmer, he fought in the Tsarist army in the First World War and was promoted to corporal. He joined the Communist Party after the Bolshevik revolution in November 1917, and fought in the RED ARMY during the RUSSIAN CIVIL WAR against KOLCHAK and in suppressing the KRONSTADT MUTINY. He attended Frunze Military Academy and commanded a division in the Far East, 1931–8, escaping the PURGES. In the SECOND WORLD WAR he played a key role in the defence of Moscow in 1941–2, and was subsequently involved in every major Soviet campaign. He led the counter-attack in 1943 which followed the German defeat at Kursk and the advance across Poland to the Vistula in 1944. With ZHUKOV he participated in the battle for Berlin. Originally given the secondary role, his troops entered Berlin on 2 May 1945. From 1946–66 he held the post of Commander-in-Chief, Land Forces, then that of Soviet Minister of Defence. Used as a counter-weight to the dominant Zhukov by STALIN, he was to supplant him in the immediate post-war years.

J. Erickson, *The Road to Stalingrad* (1975)
——, *The Road to Berlin* (1983)

**Korneuburg Oath.** The declaration by Austrian *Heimwehr* leaders at Korneuburg, Lower Austria on 18 May 1930. It was the movement's most explicitly fascist statement of its ideology. The 'oath' rejected not only Marxism, but Western parliamentary democracy as well, and expressed a determination to replace the Austrian Republican system with government by corporations (*Stände*).

**Kornilov, Lavr** (1870–1918). Russian soldier and commander-in-chief of the PROVISIONAL GOVERNMENT, 1917. He served in the Russo-Japanese war and was captured in the Austro-German offensive at Gorlice in May 1915. On his escape and return to Russia he became a national hero. He was appointed commander of the Petrograd Military district by the Provisional Government but his authoritarian attitude led to his resignation and return to the front, where he served with distinction in the 'Kerensky offensive' of July 1917. Created Supreme Commander in August he again called for draconian measures to halt the disintegration of the army. Massing troops near Petrograd on KERENSKY's orders he was suspected of a plot to overthrow the government when he moved them against the capital in early September. The movement of his troops was halted by Bolshevik forces and strikes of railwaymen and he was arrested in mid-September. After the RUSSIAN REVOLUTION he fled to the Don to rally anti-Bolshevik forces, but was killed in a skirmish at Ekaterinodar on 13 April 1918. *See also* RUSSIAN CIVIL WAR.

A. Kerensky, *Prelude to Bolshevism: The Kornilov Rising* (1919)
G. Katkov, *Russia 1917: The Kornilov Affair* (1980)

**Kosygin, Alexei** (1904–80). Soviet politician; Chairman of the Council of Ministers of the USSR and effective Prime Minister, 1964–80. Born in Leningrad, he rose to power there through local party committees. He became a member of the Central Committee of the Communist Party in 1939 and was given responsibility for the textile industry. He served as Commissar for Finance and Minister for Light Industry, 1948–53, and as a member of the Politburo. He was Minister for Economic Planning, 1956–7, Chairman of the State Economic

Planning Commission and First Deputy Prime Minister in 1960. In 1964 he succeeded KHRUSHCHEV as Prime Minister, heading the Council of Ministers, but was increasingly overshadowed by BREZHNEV. Acting as Soviet Foreign Minister from 1957, Kosygin occasionally acted as an important arbitrator in world affairs, notably in securing the Tashkent Agreement between India and Pakistan over Kashmir in January 1966, following the armed conflict between the two states in 1965. In domestic affairs he sought greater decentralization of industry and agriculture, but the influence of Brezhnev frustrated major initiatives. Ill-health forced his resignation in October 1980.

**KPD**. Kommunistische Partei Deutschlands. See COMMUNIST PARTY, GERMAN.

**KPÖ**. Kommunistische Partei Österreichs. See COMMUNIST PARTY, AUSTRIAN.

**Kreisky, Bruno** (1911–90). Social Democratic Chancellor of Austria, 1970–83. Kreisky was born in Vienna in 1911, and studied at Vienna University where he graduated with a doctorate in law. He joined the SOCIAL DEMOCRATIC WORKERS' PARTY (SDAP) in 1926, and was imprisoned by the Austrofascist regime (see AUSTROFASCISM) for his political activities in 1936. Doubly exposed as a socialist and a Jew, Kreisky fled to Sweden when the Nazis invaded Austria in 1938 and worked there as a journalist until the end of the war, when he stayed on as a diplomat in Stockholm. He returned to the Foreign Ministry in Vienna in 1950 and was elected to parliament in 1956. In 1959 he became both Deputy Chairman of the Socialist Party of Austria (SPÖ) and Foreign Minister. Following the Party's election defeat of 1966 Kreisky became the leader of those in favour of party reform and, with the victory of that faction, assumed the party leadership in 1967. When the SPÖ won a relative majority of parliamentary seats in the 1970 election Kreisky dissolved the Grand Coalition of the SPÖ and the CHRISTIAN SOCIAL PARTY (ÖVP), which had governed Austria for 20 years, and led a minority administration until new elections the following year gave the SPÖ an absolute

majority. The 'Kreisky years' were characterized by social and welfare initiatives and a relatively high degree of economic stability and prosperity at a difficult time for the international economy. Austria's international standing was enhanced by the pursuit of a successful foreign policy based on active neutrality, despite Kreisky's often controversial initiatives.

**Kremlin.** Russian term for a citadel or fortress, most usually applied to the Moscow Kremlin, a walled complex of religious buildings and palaces dominated by the Great Kremlin Palace built in 1839–40. The Kremlin became the seat of Soviet power when LENIN transferred the government to Moscow in 1918. Lenin and STALIN both lived in the Kremlin, the latter being the last Soviet leader to do so. It is to Stalin, who closed the area to the public, that the term owes its connotations of secrecy and oppressiveness. 'The Kremlin' is now used as a synonym for the Soviet Government as a whole, as with 'the White House' or 'Downing Street'.

**Kristall Nacht.** German for 'crystal night', 9–10 November 1938, when the NAZI PARTY organized the destruction of Jewish property littering the streets with glass. See also HOLOCAUST.

**Kronstadt Mutiny.** Revolt amongst the Soviet sailors at Kronstadt, the naval base in the Gulf of Finland in March 1921. The mutiny followed a series of strikes and riots in Petrograd and elsewhere caused by food shortages and a growing discontent with the economic and political authoritarianism of the Bolsheviks. Strongly influenced by anarchist ideas of a self-governing soviet, the Kronstadt sailors made contact with workers in Petrograd and demanded fresh elections to the SOVIETS, freedom to campaign openly and economic reforms. The Soviet government declared the Kronstadt movement a 'counter-revolutionary conspiracy' and troops led by MIKHAIL TUKHACHEVSKY stormed the mutineers' headquarters in the Kronstadt fortress on 17 March with heavy loss of life on both sides. Many of those involved were arrested and shot by the CHEKA. The immediate effects of the Kronstadt Mutiny were to strengthen

Bolshevik control. At the tenth Party Congress, LENIN obtained resolutions condemning the principal opposition grouping, the WORKERS' OPPOSITION, and ordering that all factions of the party operate in the open on pain of expulsion. Lenin made it clear that he regarded the party as the sole vehicle for determining the future of the Soviet Union, irrespective of popular opinion, and the suppression of the Kronstadt Mutiny has often been interpreted as marking the increasing divorce between the party and the masses it claimed to represent. The popular discontent of which the Kronstadt Mutiny was a symptom, however, played a part in encouraging Lenin to reconsider the direction of economic policy seen in the NEW ECONOMIC POLICY.

P. Avrich, *Kronstadt 1921* (1970)
I. Getzler, *Kronstadt, 1917–21: The Fate of a Soviet Democracy* (1983)

**KSC.** Komunisticka Strana Československenska. *See* COMMUNIST PARTY, CZECHOSLOVAK.

**Kulaks.** Wealthy peasants, many of them the beneficiaries of Stolypin's land reforms prior to the First World War. The wealthier peasantry were largely expropriated by the Soviet Decree on Land on 8 November 1917, which abolished all private land-ownership without compensation and left it to village and rural land committees to share out land on an egalitarian basis. Identified during the RED TERROR as one of the groups to be seen as 'class enemies', they had virtually been eliminated by the time LENIN launched the NEW ECONOMIC POLICY (NEP) in 1921. A prosperous peasantry began to reappear during the next few years but a drive against 'Kulaks' was revived in 1928 to provide grain for the state. Better-off peasants were forced to deliver grain, private marketing was banned, and the free trade in food prohibited. Committees of Poor Peasants were formed, and all villagers classified according to three categories of 'poor peasant', 'middle peasant' and 'Kulak', the last being subjected to penal targets for grain delivery. With the decision to implement full-scale collectivization in 1929 (*See* COLLECTIVIZATION, SOVIET), the first stage of the campaign was designated as 'de-Kulakization', in which Stalin referred to the necessity to liquidate the Kulaks as a class. As a result, almost any peasants resisting requisitions or showing opposition to collectivization were likely to be branded as 'Kulaks' and forced to give up grain or other goods, and in many cases be forcibly deported to remote regions or sent to labour camps. In some areas there was open resistance which was put down by force. De-Kulakization formed the prelude to wholesale collectivization, virtually wiping out the class of wealthier peasants who had survived the Civil War or had been encouraged into existence under the NEP. It has been estimated that between 5 and 10 million people underwent de-Kulakization.

M. Fainsod, *Smolensk under Soviet Rule* (1958)
M. Lewin, *Russian Peasants and Soviet Power* (1968)

**Kun, Béla** (1886–1937). Hungarian communist leader. He served in the Austro-Hungarian army in the First World War and was captured by the Russians. Following the Bolshevik Revolution in November 1917 he returned to Hungary as a communist activist. He helped to build up support for the newly founded HUNGARIAN COMMUNIST PARTY (KMP) amongst the workers and soldiers in the capital and the provinces. The arrest of Kun and other KMP leaders on 21 February led to the threat of a mass demonstration on 23 March against the KÁROLYI government. A fusion of Social Democrats and communists on 21 March forced Károlyi to surrender power to a Revolutionary Governing Council, numerically dominated by the Social Democrats, but led by Béla Kun. On 22 March 1919 the new Government proclaimed the Soviet Hungarian Republic with Kun as Foreign Minister. Kun introduced a Soviet-style regime, creating a Hungarian Red Army and revolutionary courts, and carried through the nationalization of all medium-sized and major economic enterprises. A radical land reform on 3 April expropriated without compensation the medium-sized and larger estates, and Soviet-style single-list elections were held on 7–10 April. Placed under economic blockade by the West, Kun was also forced to fight a war with Romanian and Czech forces. Although initially successful in preventing further dismemberment of Hungary, Kun's government was faced by a strong counter-revolutionary movement based on the town of Szeged, which was under the control of French occupation forces. On 3 June 1919 a rival government was set up at Szeged under Count Gyula Károlyi as Chairman and Admiral HORTHY DE NAGYBANYA as minister of war. Growing disenchantment with Kun's regime and its increasingly brutal 'Red Terror' led to growing opposition, and an attempted insurrection on 24 June was put down by Kun's Red Guard units. By then, however, a major uprising had broken out backed by the Szeged government, and the intervention of Romanian forces at the end of July signalled the end of Kun's

Soviet experiment. His Social Democrat allies demanded that he relinquish power, which he did on 31 July 1919. Kun was able to make his escape to Austria and a short-lived Social Democrat government succeeded before a counter-revolutionary regime was set up as Romanian forces occupied Budapest. In November Admiral Horthy took over the reins of government. Kun eventually sought refuge in the Soviet Union, where he perished in the PURGES of 1936–7.

M. Károlyi, *Memoirs: Faith Without Illusion* (1956)
R. Tokes, *Béla Kun and the Hungarian Soviet Republic* (1967)

**Kursk, Battle of.** *See* SECOND WORLD WAR.

# L

**labour camps, Soviet.** The first Soviet labour camps were 'concentration camps' set up during the RED TERROR and the initial stages of the RUSSIAN CIVIL WAR in 1918 to detain counter-revolutionary groups. In April 1919 they received formal authorization when the Soviet state enacted the exploitation of forced labour for state economic projects under the control of the Commissariat of the Interior, the NKVD (*see* NKVD). Although they were used to receive many of the victims of the CHEKA and many thousands of people were killed, they retained some element of the idea of 'corrective labour'. By 1922 it has been estimated that there were 190 camps with about 85,000 inmates. The prison camps had expanded from the late 1920s to accommodate hundreds of thousands of Kulaks and political victims of the PURGES who were not executed. Increasingly they were used to provide labour in the remoter parts of the country. Thus, in 1930 GOSPLAN was instructed to build into plans the work of prisoners. A special department of the NKVD, the Chief Administration of Camps or Gulag, was established to run the penal enterprises which began to develop a huge network of camps in the remoter parts of Siberia and the Arctic to carry out mining, forestry and construction projects. Whereas earlier political prisoners had been exempted from 'corrective labour', during the FIVE YEAR PLANS all camps were set quotas and groups of prisoners were obliged to work to set targets in order to earn their daily rations. By the end of 1937 an estimated 11 million people had been deported as part of the 'de-Kulakization (*see* KULAKS) and SOVIET COLLECTIVIZATION campaigns, and the purges which followed the assassination of KIROV. To these were added between 5 and 7 million people arrested in the major wave of purges in 1937–8, of whom as many as 6 million may have ended up in the prison camps. These were joined by the mass deportations from the UKRAINE, the BALTIC STATES, BELORUSSIA, and POLAND in the first years of the war, followed by the mass transfer of ethnic minorities, such as the Soviet Germans and Crimean Tatars, to Siberia during the Russo-German war. With the war's end, the Soviet areas occupied by the Germans yielded up as many as a further 6 million prisoners, to whom were added another 1 million imprisoned in Stalin's last years. These enormous totals have led to suggestions of as many as 12 million people in the prison camps by 1939, reaching as high as 15 or 17 million after the war. Very high mortality rates, particularly in the harsh conditions of the remoter camps in the Arctic, and an almost continuous flow of fresh detainees have led to estimates of as many as 12 million deaths in the camps between 1936 and 1950.

From the late 1940s general conditions appear to have improved, although political detainees were kept on a harsher regime. Strikes and mutinies in camps were recorded, particularly following Stalin's death and the execution of BERIA. Under Khrushchev increasing numbers were released from camps, and many were coming to the end of their sentences without fresh waves of detainees to follow. Although hard labour remained the fate of many DISSIDENTS into the Brezhnev era, the numbers involved were tiny compared with the years of Stalin's terror. Nonetheless, campaigns to end the Soviet labour camp system and to release political detainees remained a major feature of the campaigns to uphold the HELSINKI AGREEMENTS of 1975 and a recurrent part of the propaganda campaigns of the West in the last years of BREZHNEV. The widespread attention attracted by the writings of ALEXANDER SOLZHENITSYN and his exposé of the GULAG 'archipelago' of labour camps did much to publicize the record of the labour camps. Under GORBACHEV there has been a much greater frankness about the worst features of the labour camps, with Soviet historians investigating the Stalinist legacy and publishing their findings abroad.

E. Ginsburg, *Into the Whirlwind* (1967)
R. Conquest, *The Great Terror* (1968)
A. Solzhenitsyn, *The Gulag Archipelago* (3 vols., 1974–8)
R. Medvedev, *Let History Judge: The Origins and Consequences of Stalinism* (2nd edn, 1989)

**Labour Party, British.** The Labour Party had its origins in the development of trade unions and socialist societies in the late 19th century. In 1900 the INDEPENDENT LABOUR PARTY (ILP), the Marxist-based Social Democratic Federation (SDF), the FABIAN SOCIETY and trade union organizations formed the Labour Representation Committee (LRC). The aim of the LRC was to establish a Labour Group in Parliament. In 1906 the Labour Party was formed from the 29 LRC members elected to the House of Commons. In 1918 the Party's Constitution was drafted, laying down the objectives and principles of the party. In the same year *Labour and the New Social Order* established the party's policy aims as being the pursuit of the 'National Minimum', the democratic control of industry, progressive taxation and the creation of better living conditions for the working class.

In 1923 JAMES RAMSAY MACDONALD became Labour's first Prime Minister, presiding over a minority Labour government which was dependent upon Liberal support. Labour's first administration lasted for ten months. During the 1920s the influence of trade unions in the party's organization increased, most of the party's MPs being trade union sponsored. A minority Labour government held power from 1929 to 1931 (*see* SECOND LABOUR GOVERNMENT). In 1931 the international monetary crisis led the Prime Minister, Ramsay MacDonald, to agree to adopt policies which were incompatible with those of the Labour movement. The trade unions and majority of the party refused to co-operate with the proposed

introduction of reductions in unemployment benefit and public expenditure cuts. Instead of resigning MacDonald formed a NATIONAL GOVERNMENT which secured a huge majority over Labour in October.

Labour was out of office for the remainder of the decade under the leadership of ARTHUR HENDERSON, George Lansbury and CLEMENT ATTLEE. In 1932 the ILP disaffiliated from the party and attempts to persuade the party leadership to coalesce with the COMMUNIST PARTY and ILP to form a united front against fascism failed. *For Socialism and Peace* (1934) advocated the NATIONALIZATION of most major industries and financial institutions; it also proposed a radical overhaul of the existing social services.

During the Second World War the party joined the all-party coalition led by CHURCHILL. Labour urged the early implementation of the wartime reformist reports and white papers, which were eventually incorporated in the party's 1945 manifesto *Let us Face the Future*. Labour won 393 seats in the 1945 general election, an overall majority of 146. Labour's first majority government under Attlee's premiership implemented most of its legislative programme. Labour obtained a narrow victory in the general election of 1950 but was defeated in 1951. During the following 13 years in opposition, the party was beset by internal disputes, particularly when HUGH GAITSKELL was leader. The party was divided over nuclear disarmament and CLAUSE FOUR of the Constitution.

In 1963 HAROLD WILSON became leader. Labour won the general elections of 1964 and 1966. During the party's period in office, capital punishment was abolished and the laws relating to divorce, homosexuality and abortion were liberalized. In 1969 the government abandoned its proposed industrial relations legislation in the face of opposition from the trade unions and left wing of the party. Labour was defeated in the 1970 general election but was returned to power in February 1974. The formation of a social contract with the trade unions and renegotiations of the terms for British membership of the EUROPEAN ECONOMIC COMMUNITY (EEC) became important issues. Labour obtained an overall majority in the October 1974 general election. The creation of a National Enterprise Board, the granting of political DEVOLUTION to Scotland and Wales and the nationalization of the ship-building and aircraft industries occupied the attention of the government. Britain's first ever referendum, on EEC membership, was held in June 1975. Approximately two-thirds of the voters favoured Labour's renegotiated entry terms. Harold Wilson resigned the party leadership in March 1976 and JAMES CALLAGHAN became leader and prime minister.

The party lost the 1979 election and went through a profound internal debate under its new leader from the end of 1980, MICHAEL FOOT. The breakaway SOCIAL DEMOCRATIC PARTY in 1981 reflected increasing divisions in the party and a drift to the left in policy which culminated in a crushing defeat in the 1983 general election. Foot resigned as leader and was replaced by NEIL KINNOCK, who set out to purge the Militant Tendency left-wingers in the party and restore its credibility. He was defeated in the 1987 general election, but then initiated a widespread policy review which steered the party much nearer to the middle ground, abandoning opposition to the EEC, dropping the traditional form of nationalization, and loosening the commitment to UNILATERALISM. The party, which had appeared to be in danger of serious decline in the early 1980s, is generally considered to have improved its image and credibility.

C. Cook and I. Taylor (eds.), *The Labour Party* (1980)
H. Pelling, *A Short History of the Labour Party* (8th edn, 1989)

**Labour Party, Irish.** Founded in 1921 as political wing of the Irish trade union movement. By refusing to contest the 1918 election to the first Dail, it effectively avoided participation in the constitutional debate at the cost of remaining the peripheral party in a heavily divided polity. The attraction of FIANNA FAIL's populism has also tended to deprive Labour of its 'natural' support amid a growing industrial proletariat. It participated in the 1973–7 coalition with the FINE GAEL. Despite the coalition's defeat in the 1977 election, Labour lost little support which could reflect the strength but more likely the inertia of its electoral base. As the only major Irish party of 'leftish' tendencies it has also tended to attract intellectual sympathizers.

**Lancaster House Agreement.** *See* UDI.

**Largo Caballero, Francisco** (1869–1964). Spanish socialist politician. He was elected to parliament in 1918, and became leader of the Spanish trade union movement (UGT) in 1925. He served as Minister of Labour in several governments in 1931–3. He was a proponent of extremist socialist policies in the months leading up to the SPANISH CIVIL WAR, calling in March 1936 for the 'dictatorship of the proletariat', which helped to precipitate schism in the SOCIALIST WORKERS PARTY and provoke a right-wing reaction. He reaffirmed his ultra-left wing policy after the outbreak of war. But once he became Prime Minister of a left coalition government and Minister of War on 4 September 1936, he increasingly committed himself to winning the war at the expense of revolutionary aims. He yielded to Soviet military advice to set up a regular army, abolishing soldiers' councils and introducing normal discipline and ranks. He also reorganized the police into a National Republican Guard and replaced popular tribunals with more regular forms of justice. He refused, however, to give way to the communists on removing General José Asensio, instead making him Under-Secretary of War. This display of independence led the communists to seek to undermine him. Street-fighting in Barcelona between communists and the radical Marxists of the PARTIDO OBRERO DE UNIFICACIÓN MARXISTA in early May 1937, the MAY DAYS, led the communists to demand the suppression of POUM. He refused, and the communist ministers resigned from his government, bringing down the coalition and leading to his replacement on 17 May 1937 by Juan Negrin. In October he was ousted from the presidency of the UGT; his attempts to denounce the communists were prevented by removing him from control of socialist newspapers. In February 1939 he went into exile in France. He was imprisoned in Dachau by the Germans, 1942–5, but survived, returning to Paris in 1946, where he died.

B. Bolloten, *The Spanish Civil War* (1991)

**Lateran Pacts.** Agreements reached on 11 February 1929 between MUSSOLINI and Pope PIUS XI under which the sovereignty of the Vatican City State was recognized and a substantial indemnity paid to it in respect of papal possessions confiscated during Italian unification in 1870. A concordat was signed between the church and state regulating their relations. The pacts were signed after two and a half years of negotiations conducted on behalf of the papacy by Francesco Pacelli, later PIUS XII. Agreement in principle on the three documents, a treaty, a concordat and a financial convention, was reached early but negotiations were protracted by Mussolini's desire to limit the territorial scope of the Pope's sovereignty, for which he was prepared to concede considerable spiritual privileges to the church in educational and cultural fields. Mussolini's threats to disband the Catholic youth body, Catholic Action, finally produced a concession of part of the Pope's claim to territory and the signing of the pacts. The gain to Mussolini was considerable, consolidating his support amongst conservative Catholics, but his concession, in turn, of autonomy to Catholic Action led to renewed clashes between church and state in 1930–31 when Catholic Action members were harassed by fascists. As a result a supplementary agreement was reached in August 1931, confirming that Catholic Action centres would be reopened, but would confine themselves to spiritual and religious matters. The agreement followed upon a Papal Encyclical on fascism, *Non abbiamo bisogno*, published on 29 June 1931, which attacked fascism as 'a pagan statolatry'. As a result the papacy finally gained autonomy and a privileged place in secondary education and youth work. The financial agreement also assisted the Vatican to escape bankruptcy. It did, however, appear to commit the papacy to friendly relations with fascism, and was later to prove a source of embarrassment.

D. A. Binchy, *Church and State in Fascist Italy* (1941)
H. Daniel-Rops, *A History of the Church of Christ: A Fight for God, 1870–1939* (trans. 1966)

**Lattre de Tassigny, Jean de** (1889–1952). French general. He served and was wounded in the French cavalry in the First World War. He continued his army career, becoming General and Chief of Staff to the French Fifth Army in 1939. During the German invasion he took command of the 14th Division. He remained in the army after the capitulation and was sent to command the VICHY GOVERNMENT forces in Tunisia. He was sentenced to ten years' imprisonment for pro-Allied sympathies and hostility to the German occupation of the FREE ZONE, but escaped to England in 1943 and placed himself under DE GAULLE's command, one of a growing number to do so. Lattre de Tassigny organized the First French Army in North Africa for the invasion of southern France in 'Operation Dragoon' in August 1944. On 9 May 1945 he signed the German surrender on behalf of France in Berlin. He became the first commander of the NORTH ATLANTIC TREATY ORGANISATION (NATO) land forces in Europe in 1948, but in November 1950 was given command of the French forces in Indo-China and the post of High Commissioner. He waged a vigorous campaign against the Vietminh in the Red River Delta, but left at the end of 1951, dying a few months later. He has been described as a non-political General, typical of many of the old officer corps who remained loyal to Vichy in the hope of utilizing the forces maintained in the Free Zone. Its occupation by the Germans in November 1942 forced him to recognize that only de Gaulle offered any real prospect of national salvation. *See also* FREE FRENCH.

**Lausanne, Treaty of.** Treaty of settlement of Turkish frontiers following the repudiation of the TREATY OF SÈVRES (10 August 1920) by the Turks under Kemal Ataturk. The treaty, which was signed on 24 July 1923, followed the lines of the agreement signed between the commander of the British forces in Turkey, General Harrington, and the Turkish representative Ismet Bey at Mundania in October 1922. That agreement pledged the return to Turkey of Eastern Thrace, lost to Greece under the Treaty of Sèvres, and the demilitarization of the Dardanelles and the Bosphorus. These points were confirmed in the Treaty of Lausanne. Turkey surrendered its claim to territories of the Ottoman Empire occupied by non-Turks, whilst retaining Constantinople and Eastern Thrace in Europe. The Greeks surrendered Izmir (Smyrna) but were confirmed in possession of all the Aegean Islands except Imbros and Tenedos, which were returned to Turkey. Turkey recognized the annexation of Cyprus by Britain and of the Dodecanese by Italy. The Bosphorus and the Dardanelles were declared to be demilitarized. (By the Montreaux Convention of 20 July 1936 Turkey was permitted to refortify the Straits.)

**Laval, Pierre** (1883–1945). French statesman. He was born in the Auvergne and trained as a lawyer. He joined the Socialists in 1903 and was elected deputy for the working-class district of Aubervilliers near Paris in May 1914. He served as a member of the Chamber of Deputies, 1914–19, 1924–7; from 1927 to 1936 he was Senator for the Seine, and from 1936 to 1944 for the Puy-de-Dome. Anti-war activity in 1917–18 almost led to his imprisonment, and he left the Socialists after 1920 to pursue an increasingly independent line. He served as Minister of Public Works in 1925, of Justice in 1926 and of Labour in 1930, becoming Prime Minister on 27 January 1931 until February 1932. Foreign Minister from 13 October 1934 until 24 January 1936, and Prime Minister from June 1935 to January 1936, he was forced to resign following his attempted appeasement of MUSSOLINI in Ethiopia in the HOARE-LAVAL PACT. He returned as Foreign Minister of the VICHY GOVERNMENT on 24 October 1940 for two months, then became Prime Minister and Foreign Minister from 18 April 1942 until September 1944, when the Vichy Government fell. Arrested by the Nazis, he fled to Spain in 1945, returning to France to face trial for treason. Found guilty, he was shot at Fresnes Prison on 15 October 1945. Laval's career was notable prior to the Second World War for his role in the foreign policy of France, including the negotiation of the Hoare-Laval Plan of December 1935 to partition Ethiopia and appease Mussolini. It led to his fall from office, but he remained a proponent of closer ties of France with Italy and Germany. Following the fall of France he pursued a collaborationist line which he justified as necessary to preserve France from civil war and complete German domination. He sought to avoid a formal military

alliance with Germany, and after the Normandy landings attempted to reconvene the National Assembly. His trial in 1945 raised almost all the issues about the collaboration of the majority of the French nation after 1940 with the Nazis. Seen as an even more enthusiastic collaborator than Pétain, he was shown less mercy. He remains a controversial figure.

R. Aron, *The Vichy Regime, 1940–4* (1958)
G. Warner, *Pierre Laval and the Eclipse of France* (1968)
R. Paxton, *Vichy France* (1972)

**Law, Andrew Bonar** (1858–1923). British Conservative politician and Prime Minister, 1922–3. Born in Canada, the son of a Presbyterian minister, he left Canada for Scotland in 1870 and was educated in Glasgow. He worked in the iron trade before being elected MP for Glasgow Blackfriars, 1900–6; Dulwich, 1906–10; Bootle (Liverpool), 1911–18; and Glasgow Central, 1918–23. He served as Parliamentary Secretary to the Board of Trade, 1902–5, but won rank and file support to gain the leadership of the party in 1911. During the pre–1914 'Ulster Crisis' he strongly supported the Ulster Unionists, but entered the wartime coalition government led by ASQUITH in 1915, serving as Colonial Secretary, 1915–16, then as Chancellor of the Exchequer, 1916–19. In the post-war coalition government led by LLOYD GEORGE he was Lord Privy Seal and Leader of the House of Commons until 1921. In 1922 he became leader of the Conservative Party again. Following the revolt of Conservative backbenchers against Lloyd George's handling of the CHANAK CRISIS and the latter's resignation, he became Prime Minister on 23 October 1922. In the General Election in the following month, he won a comfortable Conservative majority, forming a government with BALDWIN as Chancellor of the Exchequer and Curzon as Foreign Secretary. In May 1923 ill-health forced his resignation and replacement by Baldwin. He died the same year. The first Conservative Prime Minister since 1906, Bonar Law began the establishment of Conservative political domination of inter-war politics in Britain. His earlier opposition to the terms of Irish HOME RULE had helped to prevent a settlement of the Irish question by 1914 and had seemed to bring the country to the brink of civil war, postponing a solution until 1921. See also CONSERVATIVE AND UNIONIST PARTY.

A. T. Stewart, *The Ulster Crisis* (1967)
M. Kinnear, *The Fall of Lloyd George* (1973)
J. Ramsden, *The Age of Balfour and Baldwin, 1902–40* (1978)
R. Blake, *The Conservative Party from Peel to Thatcher* (1986)

**League of Nations.** International organization set up as part of the peace settlement ending the First World War. The League was an association of states which pledged themselves, through signing the Covenant (the constitution) of the League, not to go to war before submitting their disputes with each other, or states not members of the League, to arbitration or enquiry and a delay of from three to nine months. Furthermore, any state violating this pledge was automatically in a state of outlawry with the other states, which were bound to sever all economic and political relations with the defaulting state. Both LLOYD GEORGE and President THOMAS WOODROW WILSON suggested some form of international organization before the end of hostilities, one of Wilson's FOURTEEN POINTS referring to 'a general association of nations' to guarantee independence and security to all states. There were differing views as to whether the League would simply replicate the work of the Congress system after 1815, with meetings of the Great Powers at regular intervals to deal with individual disputes, or be a broader organization working actively to develop international co-operation in a wide range of areas. The latter concept, articulated by Jan Smuts in *The League of Nations: A Practical Suggestion*, published at the end of 1918, was the form actually taken up with enthusiasm by Wilson and given a key place at the PARIS PEACE CONFERENCE. The Covenant of the League was written into the peace treaties signed with the defeated powers. As a result the League formally came into existence on 10 January 1920, at the same time as the TREATY OF VERSAILLES.

The seat of the League was Geneva, Switzerland, and the organization had four primary organs: the Council, the Assembly, the Secretariat, and the Permanent Court of International Justice (which sat at the Hague). The Council was originally composed of four permanent members (the British Empire, France, Italy and Japan) and four non-permanent members to be elected every year by a majority of the Assembly. With the approval of the Assembly, the Council could admit new permanent and non-permanent members. At the Assembly of September 1926 Germany was admitted to the League and given a permanent seat on the Council, further non-permanent seats were added in 1922, 1926 and 1936, bringing the total to 11.

Every state member of the League was entitled to be represented by a delegation to the Assembly, composed of not more than three delegates and three substitute delegates, but it had only one vote. It met annually at the seat of the League (Geneva) in September. It could meet at places other than Geneva, and extraordinary sessions could be called to deal with urgent matters. The President was elected at the first meeting of the session, and held office for the duration of the session. The Assembly divided itself into the seven principal committees, on each of which every state member of the League had the right to be represented by one delegate: Juridical, Technical organizations, Disarmament, Budget and staff, Social questions, Health, and Intellectual co-operation. Decisions had to be voted unanimously in the Assembly, except where the Covenant or the Peace Treaties provided otherwise. The Secretariat was a permanent organ composed of the Secretary-General and a number of officials selected from among citizens of all member states and from the United States of America. The Permanent Court of International Justice at The Hague was created by an international treaty, the Statute of the Court, which was drafted in 1920 by a committee appointed by the Council of the League of Nations and revised in 1929 with amendments which came into force in 1936. The revised Statutes adopted at the tenth Assembly provided for 15 judges for the Court, and stipulated that the Court should remain permanently in Session. The judges were elected jointly by the Council and the Assembly of the League for a term of nine years. On the dissolution of the League of Nations and the establishment of the

United Nations Organisation, the Court was superseded by the International Court of Justice. The League had a large number of secondary organs dealing with specific matters, broadly divided into Technical Organizations (Economic and financial, Health, Communications), Advisory Committees (Military, European Union, Mandates, Opium, Social, Slavery), Committees for Intellectual Co-operation, International Institutes (at Paris and Rome), and the Administrative Organization for the Free City of DANZIG. In addition the INTERNATIONAL LABOUR ORGANISATION was set up in 1919 as an autonomous organization of the League of Nations.

The League began to work with 42 member states, rising to 54 by 1923, the most notable absentees being the United States, the Soviet Union and Germany. Almost from the outset there were examples of states acting without reference to the League, Poland engaging in the RUSSO-POLISH WAR in 1920 and seizing Vilna from Lithuania in 1920 (see VILNA DISPUTE); while Lithuania took MEMEL from League control in 1923. In 1926 Germany was readmitted to the League and the League began to build up a respectable record of arbitration in international relations, organizing a loan for Austria in the early 1920s to overcome its economic problems, settling a dispute over the Aaland Islands between Sweden and Finland in 1921, and resolving an armed conflict between Greece and Bulgaria in 1925. The League supervised plebiscites in accordance with the peace treaties and administered efficiently those areas placed under its control. As well as resolving conflicts outside Europe it began to develop a body of useful work in the social and educational spheres, especially in areas such as health and refugees. Its Disarmament Commission organized two international Disarmament Conferences, meeting in 1926 and 1932, but little progress was made. Although envisaged as the body that would bring about a general reduction in armaments, it was evident that no agreement could be reached that satisfied all parties. Moreover, the League's ability to control aggression was limited, as shown in the CORFU INCIDENT of 1923. However, it

was in the 1930s that the League's reputation was most severely damaged.

The Japanese invasion of Manchuria in 1931 was met by a slow response from the League. Its eventual condemnation of Japan simply led to her withdrawal from the League and the consolidation of her conquests in China. Similarly, China's appeal to the League for assistance against Japan in 1937 met with little practical response. The ETHIOPIAN CRISIS exposed the League's frailties still further. Initially recommending negotiation to Ethiopia, the Italian invasion in October 1935 led the League to impose economic sanctions and condemn Italy as the aggressor, but as the sanctions were not adhered to, they had little effect. Faced with a *fait accompli* of Italian conquest by May 1936, the League was forced to abandon sanctions. The League could do little to prevent Italian intervention in the SPANISH CIVIL WAR, and Italy itself left the League in December 1937. The League was unable thereafter to prevent the Italian takeover of Albania in April 1939. In October 1933 Germany had withdrawn from the International Disarmament Conference and also left the League of Nations. The League was powerless to prevent German rearmament and to control states who sought agreement with HITLER. Thus the ANGLO-GERMAN NAVAL AGREEMENT of 1935 revised the Treaty of Versailles, increasing the permitted size of the German navy. Although the League condemned the German reoccupation of the RHINELAND, there was nothing it could do as a body to prevent it, nor the subsequent ANSCHLUSS with Austria. By the time of the Munich crisis (see MUNICH AGREEMENT) the League had little direct role to play in the diplomacy of the major powers. Following the outbreak of the Second World War, its last significant act was to expel Russia from membership for its attack on Finland in December 1939. The League did not meet formally thereafter. In 1946 the League was dissolved and replaced by the UNITED NATIONS, which took over its major technical and welfare functions. The early desire to replace the League with a more effective organization reflected a widespread recognition of its weaknesses. From the beginning the League was handicapped by the failure of the United States and the Soviet

Union to participate. Thereafter it found itself unable to overcome the rivalries and suspicions of the major states which prevented effective progress on disarmament. The League's Covenant was vague on the powers available to control aggression, and its only effective weapon, economic sanctions, was vitiated by non-compliance and the withdrawal of states from the League. Even in the 1920s much of the major diplomacy took place outside the orbit of the League. After the rise of the Nazis and military rule in Japan, the League was shouldered aside, powerless to resolve the major disputes that arose. Increasingly, these had to be dealt with by traditional diplomacy, and attempts to limit the use of force in international disputes had palpably failed by 1939. The League, however, embodied much idealism and in its attempt to seek a more rational approach to settling international disputes it provided a forerunner of the United Nations. In one sense the League's greatest achievement lay in the desire to replace it with a similar, but more effective body. *See also* MUSSOLINI, BENITO.

F. P. Walters, *A History of the League of Nations* (1960)
S. R. Gibbons and P. Morican, *The League of Nations and UNO* (1970)
S. Marks, *The Illusion of Peace, 1918–33* (1977)

**Leagues, French.** Right-wing organizations in inter-war France, variously nationalistic, anti-Republican, and anti-Semitic. Many of them supported the older ACTION FRANÇAISE, led by its sub-organization the Camelots du Roi (the King's newsvendors), and included Solidarité Française, the Francistes and the most successful, the Croix de Feu (Fiery Cross) led by Colonel Count de la Rocque. The Leagues embraced a variety of attitudes on the right of French politics, their only common feature being their opposition to the THIRD REPUBLIC. The Croix de Feu was anti-communist and ultra-conservative, the Francistes more self-consciously national socialists, and the Camelots du Roi overtly monarchist. But the character of the Leagues was also paramilitary, the Camelots du Roi acting as uniformed street fighters, recruited to sell the *Action Française* journal. On 6 February 1934 the Leagues demonstrated in Paris at the Place de la Concorde and threatened to march on the Chamber of Deputies where

DALADIER was presenting a new administration for approval. The police were forced to fire, killing 14 demonstrators. With a larger demonstration threatened for the next day, Daladier resigned. The attempted *coup* by the Leagues provoked mass counter-demonstrations in defence of the Republic on 12 February, backed with a general strike by the CGT. The most significant feature of the demonstrations was the common response by communists, socialists and republicans to the threat from the right. The first moves towards the establishment of the Popular Front followed with a United Action Pact signed between socialists and communists in July 1934 and extended to the Radicals later in the year. Born out of opposition to the Leagues, the Popular Front had their dissolution as part of its programme. Although several League candidates put up in the 1936 elections they failed to achieve the electoral success of the NAZI PARTY, being largely swept away in the crushing electoral victory of the POPULAR FRONT. The Front banned the Leagues, but their influence remained and was to re-emerge under the VICHY GOVERNMENT. One right-winger who survived the 1936 landslide was the ex-communist deputy, Jacques Doriot (1898–1945). An opponent of Stalinism, he founded the French Popular Party in 1936, which drew in many neo-fascist supporters from the Leagues and Action Française. After 1940 Doriot was to become one of the leaders of collaboration under Vichy. Another who moved across from socialism to fascism was Marcel Deat (1894–1957), a revolutionary syndicalist who preached an authoritarian anti-capitalism and founded the Rassemblement National Populaire in 1941 with Nazi support. Several of the leaders of the Leagues and right-wing groupings were tried and executed after liberation in 1944 for collaboration with the Nazis.

C. A. Micavel, *The French Right and Nazi Germany* (1972)
P. Paxton, *Vichy France* (1972)
W. D. Irvine, *French Conservatism in Crisis* (1979)

**Lebensraum.** German term meaning 'living space', adopted by German nationalists and the NAZI PARTY, referring to the need for the German people to expand territorially in the East at the expense of inferior races, the Slavs and the Jews. Signs of the implementation of *Lebensraum* have been seen in German war aims in the First World War and discussed in the Fischer Thesis (*see* FISCHER CONTROVERSY), the TREATIES OF BREST-LITOVSK and the theories articulated in Hitler's MEIN KAMPF. Germany's experience of food and raw material shortages in the First World War were amalgamated with racial theories to make *Lebensraum* an important component of Nazi foreign policy, referred to in the HOSSBACH MEMORANDUM, and apparently implemented in the diplomatic conquests and military operations of 1938–41. HITLER's determination to turn against the Soviet Union even at the point of his greatest triumph has been seen as representing the importance of these ideas to his foreign policy.

**Leclerc, Philippe** (1902–47). French general in the FREE FRENCH forces. *Nom de guerre* of Jacques Philippe de Hautecloque, a professional soldier serving as an army captain in May 1940. He twice escaped from German hands, and was one of the small group to join DE GAULLE in London, which he reached via Spain and Portugal in July 1940. He was given command of French forces loyal to de Gaulle in sub-Saharan Africa. Leclerc led Free French forces in an epic march across the Sahara in December 1942 to join the British forces advancing under Montgomery. He fought in the final campaign in Tunisia, then formed the Second Armoured Division, which joined Patton's Third Army and fought in Normandy. Leclerc led the Free French forces into Paris on 25 August 1944 and formally received the surrender of the city. He took Strasbourg in ALSACE-LORRAINE after a swift armoured advance in late November 1944. He then took his forces into Germany and was the first to reach Hitler's famous retreat at BERCHTESGADEN. After the war he served in Indo-China and was known to favour negotiations with the Vietminh. He was killed in an air crash in Indo-China on 28 November 1947.

**Left Communists, Russian.** Group of radical communists identified primarily with BUKHARIN. They were opposed to LENIN's policy of securing peace at Brest-Litovsk (*see* BREST-LITOVSK, TREATIES OF) on the grounds that it betrayed the revolutionary movements elsewhere in Europe and that the continuation of revolutionary war by Russia was the correct path to follow. At the centre of their thinking lay a belief in the pursuit of the class struggle on an international scale in which the specific needs of the Russian party were secondary. Lenin, on the other hand, considered it necessary to secure the proletarian revolution in one country. They extended this critique beyond the immediate issue of the Treaty of Brest-Litovsk to demand a radical socialist programme, abandoning pragmatic arrangements and compromises, to inaugurate workers' control, the full nationalization of industry, the rejection of any cooperation with Russian or foreign capitalists, and communal farming of the land. Fearful of being identified with the LEFT SOCIALIST REVOLUTIONARY PARTY after their attempted rising in July 1918, Bukharin and RADEK admitted their 'errors' and conformed to Lenin's policy, though their early opposition was later to be resurrected as charges against them during the PURGES, when Bukharin and other Left Communists would be charged with plotting with the Left Socialist Revolutionaries against Lenin. In fact, their opposition had always been open and had been largely forsaken for lack of support by 1919.

R. V. Daniels, *The Conscience of the Revolution: Communist Opposition in Soviet Russia* (1960)
L. Shapiro, *The Origin of the Communist Autocracy* (1965)

**'Left Opposition'.** Name given to those within the Russian Communist Party who believed in the need to develop heavy industry rapidly and were disposed against Lenin's NEW ECONOMIC POLICY. They were prepared to attempt a more radical, forced industrialization at the expense of the peasantry and social harmony. Many of the most significant followers of this view were supporters of TROTSKY and found themselves opposed by STALIN, who sided with the more moderate advocates of the pace of industrialization to discredit Trotsky and his followers. Once they had been removed from influence or banished, Stalin inaugurated an even more extreme pace of industrialization himself, which led, in turn, to criticisms of the 'RIGHT OPPOSITION'.

Amongst the notable figures discredited amongst the Left Opposition were ZINOVIEV, and about a hundred supporters within the party were expelled by 1927. *See also* INDUSTRIALIZATION DEBATE, SOVIET.

**Left Socialist Revolutionary Party, Russian.** The left wing of the RUSSIAN SOCIALIST REVOLUTIONARY PARTY, who offered support for the BOLSHEVIKS and after the October Revolution formed a separate political party. In December 1917 they formed a coalition with the Bolsheviks thus giving LENIN the illusion of support amongst the peasantry. They were initially won over by the Bolsheviks' firm stand on the war and the land issue and alienated by their own party's support for the war. In May 1917 the Left group demanded a programme of immediate peace, non-cooperation with bourgeois parties, and socialization of land, policies close to those of the Bolsheviks as expressed in Lenin's APRIL THESES. They voted to disobey their party leaders in supporting the PROVISIONAL GOVERNMENT in late October 1917, and seven members joined the MILITARY REVOLUTIONARY COMMITTEE. Their final break with the Social Revolutionaries came when they refused to walk out of the Second All-Russian Soviet Congress on 7 November, and effectively joined in sanctioning the Bolshevik seizure of power. The Left Socialist Revolutionaries heavily influenced the shape of Lenin's Decree on Land which followed closely on the lines of a Peasant Congress held in June 1917. Gradually, however, the Left Socialist Revolutionaries became alarmed at the policy of confiscations pursued against the peasantry and they quarrelled with the Bolsheviks over the degree of terror used by the CHEKA. They opposed Lenin over the TREATY OF BREST-LITOVSK and resigned from the Council of People's Commissars on 19 March. Thereafter several groups of Left Socialist Revolutionaries attempted to overthrow the Bolshevik leadership in the local Soviets of the provinces and attempted to revive the war against the Germans. One group assassinated the German ambassador in Moscow in July 1918, accompanied by a rising in several northern towns. The rising, however, was put down and its leaders executed. The party was not outlawed, but its press was closed down and its members hounded out of local positions to which they had been elected. The July revolt split the party, some members going underground, others joining the communist party, and some going into exile. By 1919 it was virtually ineffective.

L. Shapiro, *The Origin of the Communist Autocracy* (1965)

**Lend-lease.** A system used by President ROOSEVELT to permit Britain to obtain war supplies and necessary goods without paying for them. By early 1941 Britain had virtually exhausted her credit for purchasing goods abroad. The Lend-lease Act of March 1941 allowed Britain to receive as much as she wished without worrying about repayment. The goods totalled nearly £8 billion by the end of the war. Lend-lease was terminated by President TRUMAN on 2 September 1945, causing immense difficulties in Britain. The supplies of goods were essential to Britain's war effort, allowing her to concentrate and specialize her war production without having to find goods for export.

S. Pollard, *The Development of the British Economy, 1914–1980* (3rd edn, 1983)

**Lenin, Vladimir** (1870–1924). The First Soviet leader and Marxist theorist. His real name was Vladimir Ilyich Ulyanov. He was born on 23 April 1870 in Simbirsk on the Volga, the son of a schools inspector. His elder brother, Alexander, was hanged in 1887 for attempting to assassinate Alexander III. Expelled from Kazan University for his political activities, he graduated in law in 1891 as an external candidate at St Petersburg University, becoming influenced by Marxism before he moved to the capital to practice law in 1893. He made his first journey abroad to Switzerland in 1895, but was arrested shortly after his return for his participation in a revolutionary group known subsequently as the St Petersburg Union of Struggle for the Emancipation of the Working Classes. In exile in Siberia from February 1897 to February 1900, he married Nadezhda Krupskaya in July 1898. Leaving Russia in July 1900, he lived in Brussels, Paris, London and Geneva, producing his newspaper, *Iskra* (The Spark) and building up support for his militant faction of the RUSSIAN SOCIAL DEMOCRATIC

LABOUR PARTY. At the second Party Congress in 1903 he assumed the leadership of this group, who assumed the title BOLSHEVIKS from their temporary majority at the Congress. He published his own newspaper *Vpered* (Forward) in January 1905, but his attempt to convene a purely Bolshevik Party Congress met with no success. Returning to Russia in October 1905 he organized the Petersburg Soviet but was forced to flee to Finland, returning to Switzerland in 1907. In 1914 Lenin was based near the Russian border in Galicia, closely monitoring events in St Petersburg. Arrested by the Austrian authorities at the outbreak of the war, he was permitted to return to Switzerland, where he concentrated on writing, including *Imperialism: The Highest Stage of Capitalism* – his analysis of the war as the outcome of the rivalry of finance capitalism, and propaganda aimed at transforming an 'imperialist' war into a revolutionary struggle.

Lenin remained on the sidelines during the February Revolution, but was assisted by the German foreign ministry to return to Russia, where it was hoped that his antiwar agitation would contribute to the demoralization of the Russian armies. Lenin was returned in a sealed train provided by the German General Staff, arriving in Petrograd in April 1917. He immediately set out an extreme revolutionary programme in the APRIL THESES, committing the Bolsheviks to peace and a radical social revolution while promoting widespread propaganda amongst the troops and workers. In July the Bolsheviks attempted to seize power with mass demonstrations in the capital; they failed, but Lenin was able to escape to Finland, where he remained in hiding until the eve of the October Revolution. As the PROVISIONAL GOVERNMENT moved into crisis and the power of the SOVIETS grew, Lenin urged the Bolshevik central committee to prepare to seize power.

The actual Bolshevik seizure of power on 7 November was accomplished with remarkable ease and was ratified by the second All-Congress of Soviets almost immediately; Lenin was made Chairman of the Council of People's Commissars on 9 November. As effective head of the Soviet government his task was to turn a virtually bloodless *coup d'état* into a stable regime.

He immediately implemented decrees socializing land and introducing workers' control in industry, followed swiftly by the abolition of ranks in the army and the introduction of elected people's courts to replace the old judicial system. He acted ruthlessly to suppress the CONSTITUENT ASSEMBLY which met in January 1918 and introduced the CHEKA to deal with counter-revolutionary activity. Lenin also insisted that peace was necessary to consolidate Bolshevik power in Russia and to promote revolution abroad, accepting the punitive terms of the TREATIES OF BREST-LITOVSK in March 1918. Shot and wounded by a Socialist Revolutionary terrorist, Fanny Kaplan, in August 1918, Lenin nonetheless steered the Bolshevik state through the RUSSIAN CIVIL WAR. In his policies of WAR COMMUNISM and RED TERROR he brought the same single-minded ruthlessness to the conduct of the war which ensured the survival of the Bolshevik state as he had to seizing power. The divisions this caused within the ranks of his erstwhile supporters were dealt with severely. Opponents were rounded up by the Cheka, opposition newspapers suppressed, and the KRONSTADT MUTINY in 1921 crushed.

The conclusion of the Civil War and the failures of War Communism provided the context for the adoption of the NEW ECONOMIC POLICY, an apparent retreat from communist policy by the reintroduction of a free trade in agriculture and the return of small capitalist enterprises. In poor health by early 1921 he was forced to convalesce at Gorki, a few miles outside Moscow, where he continued to play an active role in government. In May 1922 he suffered his first stroke. He made his last public speech in November of that year. A second stroke on 16 December left him partially paralysed. A further stroke in March left him virtually an invalid, and he died on 21 January 1924, his embalmed body being placed in the Lenin mausoleum in Red Square.

One immediate bequest to the Soviet state was his 'testament', written on 20 December 1922, assessing the various leaders and his warning of STALIN's potentially harmful effects as General Secretary, suggesting that means might be found to remove him. Publication of the 'testament' was suppressed because of the embarrassment it would cause to those who had assumed the leadership on his becoming incapacitated. It was not made public until the DE-STALINIZATION period under Khrushchev in the early 1960s.

Lenin proved a very effective political leader in the context of the events in Russia in 1917. His theoretical development of Marxism, known later as MARXIST-LENINISM, elevated the role of the party as the vehicle of the proletarian revolution, and all his energies were devoted to creating a tightly-organized revolutionary party. Prior to 1917 this had led to Lenin's isolation and feuding with other Marxist groups, but from April 1917 he was able to give direction to the popular movements represented in the soviets. Having seized power, he provided determined and ruthless leadership to the early Bolshevik state, ensuring its eventual victory in the Civil War. Critics of Lenin have argued that his single-minded pursuit of power and suppression of all non-Bolshevik opposition laid the foundations for the highly centralized and authoritarian features which became consolidated in the Soviet Union under Stalin. Others have n STALINISM as a perversion of the Revolution created by Lenin, and there has been a tendency for reformers such as KHRUSHCHEV and GORBACHEV to base their case for change on a return to 'Leninist' principle. Considerable debate surrounds the implications of the introduction of the New Economic Policy and whether this represented an alternative path to that later associated with Stalin. Current evidence suggests that Lenin saw the NEP as a tactical retreat, but that he was prepared to consider a more gradual and balanced development of collective agriculture and industrialization than that brought about by Stalin. Many now consider that his legacies of the 'dictatorship of the party' and his record of intolerance of opposition outside it are obstacles to political growth in the Soviet Union. But although current reassessments of Soviet history have increasingly questioned the role of Stalin, they have still to grapple fully with the question of whether a more capitalistic and pluralistic society will bear any recognizable resemblance to what Lenin sought to achieve. In practice, Lenin's supreme talent as a revolutionary ideologue and tactician did not prepare him for the failure of revo-

lutions elsewhere in the world or for the longer-term problems of governing the sole socialist state in peace-time conditions. *See also* RUSSIAN REVOLUTION; SOVIETS.

A. B. Ulam, *Lenin and the Bolsheviks* (1965)
D. Shub, *Lenin* (1966)
H. Shukman, *Lenin and the Russian Revolution* (1977)

**Leningrad.** *See* ST PETERSBURG.

**Leningrad, Siege of.** *See* SECOND WORLD WAR.

**Le Pen, Jean-Marie** (1928–). French politician. From 1972 he built up the right-wing Front National (FN), voicing concern over immigration, with occasional anti-Semitic overtones. The FN won 35 seats and almost 10 per cent of the vote in the 1986 elections, mainly based on the south. Le Pen entered the presidential race in May 1987, focusing on the alleged threat to French national identity and social stability from coloured immigrants. He promised a tough stance on immigration, to strengthen family values and provide strong defences. In the first round of the presidential elections in April 1988 Le Pen took over 14 per cent of the vote, not only in the south, but also in eastern France, drawing support both from working-class voters and former POUJADISTS. Le Pen's success forced CHIRAC to make a bid for his supporters in the run-off with MITTERRAND in the second-round elections a fortnight later by an aggressive stance in foreign policy. Mitterrand's victory was followed by decline for the FN in the June 1988 elections, in which the party lost all but one of its 33 seats, including that of its leader in Marseilles. In spite of this set-back, Le Pen has continued his anti-immigrant platform, winning municipal seats in March 1989 from the centre-right parties. With the rapid growth of mainly Arab immigration in France, Le Pen has been able to graft some of the traditional policies of the Poujadist right onto the new concerns of a wide range of voters, many of them working class.

**Liberal National Party, British** (National Liberal Party after 1948). The Liberal National Group was formed in 1931 by 23 Liberal MPs who split from the LIBERAL PARTY to join the ranks of the National

Government. In the 1931 general election they were opposed by Liberals, but not by Conservatives. They won 35 of the 41 seats they contested. In 1932 the 'Samuelite' Liberals left the National Government in protest at its protectionist policies, but the other Liberal Nationals, the 'Simonites', remained. In 1935, 33 of the 44 Liberal National candidates were returned. Between joining the National Government in 1931 and 1945 the Liberal Nationals were only opposed twice by Liberals (Denbigh 1935 and St Ives 1937). They were not opposed by a Conservative until 1946 (Scottish Universities). In 1940 E. Brown succeeded Sir John Simon as Leader. In the 1945 election Brown was defeated, and only 13 of the Liberal Nationals' 51 candidates were returned. The Woolton-Teviot agreement of May 1947 urged the constituency parties of the Conservatives and Liberal Nationals to combine, and in 1948 the party adopted the name National Liberal Party. One of the many damaging splits to affect the Liberal Party after the First World War, it formed part of the fusion of ex-Liberals and their supporters with the Conservatives.

C. P. Cook, *A Short History of the Liberal Party, 1900–1988* (3rd edn, 1989)

**Liberal Party, British.** The party was at the height of its power during the period 1905–14. In the 1906 General Election it won 400 seats, an overall majority of 230. It introduced several reform measures, notably in the field of social policy, including old age pensions and national insurance. The National Insurance Act of 1911 and the Parliament Act of the same year which reformed the House of Lords remain the most important testaments to the 20th-century Liberal Party. The decline of the party was rapid after the First World War. By 1923 it was the smallest of the three main parties. Its decline was due to a split between the supporters of LLOYD GEORGE and ASQUITH, the rise of the LABOUR PARTY and an ideology which was unable to attract the support of either capital or labour. A section joined the National Governments of MACDONALD, BALDWIN and NEVILLE CHAMBERLAIN during the 1930s and played an active role in the coalition politics of the Second World War. In the post-war period

the decline continued almost to extinction during the 1950s. The party held only six seats in Parliament throughout the 1950s. A Liberal revival under the leadership of Jo Grimond was marked by the by-election victories at Torrington in 1958 and Orpington in 1962, since when the Liberal share of the vote has increased, although the party has been unable to win sufficient seats to threaten the dominance of the Labour and Conservative Parties. In the two general elections of 1974, the party won 14 and 13 seats respectively. Under DAVID STEEL, its leader from 1976, the party entered the LIB-LAB PACT supporting the minority government of JAMES CALLAGHAN. The Pact caused discontent at the grass roots and was abandoned in 1978. The party was little further forward in the 1979 general election, winning 11 seats. The formation of the SOCIAL DEMOCRATIC PARTY (SDP) in 1981 and Labour's internal splits led to the formation of THE ALLIANCE of the Liberals and SDP and an immediate rise in support and several major by-election victories. The Alliance obtained almost a quarter of the vote in the 1983 and 1987 general elections, but Steel's call for a merger following the 1987 election led to a serious split in the SDP. Although the majority of the SDP and Liberal Party agreed to merge as the Social and Liberal Democrats, formed in 1988, the merger process and the defection of the 'continuing' SDP led by DAVID OWEN brought about a collapse in popular support. The new party, known as the Liberal Democrats since 1989, has struggled to recapture a mass following being increasingly challenged by the revival of Labour and the rise of the GREEN PARTY. The Party has still considerable strength in local government. *See also* ORANGE BOOK.

C. P. Cook, *A Short History of the Liberal Party, 1900–1988* (3rd edn, 1989)

**Lib-Lab Pact.** An agreement formed between the LIBERAL PARTY and the LABOUR PARTY on 23 March 1977. Weakened by by-election losses and the defection of two Labour MPs to form a breakaway Scottish Labour Party, the Labour Government of JAMES CALLAGHAN was faced with defeat in a no-confidence motion scheduled for debate on 23 March 1977. Few Liberals wanted an early election and a Conservative victory, while their leader DAVID STEEL wished to give his party the experience of sharing government. A joint statement by Callaghan and Steel on the 23rd outlined an agreement in which the Liberals would support the Labour Government and the establishment of a joint Consultative Committee to examine policies prior to their presentation to Parliament, as well as regular joint meetings between the party leaders and between their economic spokesmen. Only vague promises were exacted to consider proportional representation for the European elections, but clearer ones were made over DEVOLUTION and a Housing Bill supported by the Liberals. As a result the Labour Government survived the no-confidence vote by 322 votes to 288. Grass-roots Liberal opinion was hostile to the Pact, believing the terms were insufficient, and when many Labour MPs voted against proportional representation for European elections in November 1977 opposition became more vocal. Although the Pact was endorsed at a special Liberal Assembly in January 1978, the Liberals prepared to withdraw themselves from it pending the outcome of the referendums on Scotti... and Welsh DEVOLUTION in March 1979. The failure of these referendums embittered Scottish and Welsh nationalists, and with Liberal withdrawal from the Pact, the Labour Government was exposed to defeat in a vote of no confidence on 28 March 1979, precipitating a general election and Mrs THATCHER's Conservative victory.

C. Cook, *A Short History of the Liberal Party, 1900–88* (3rd edn, 1989)

**Lie, Trygve** (1896–1968). Secretary-General of the United Nations, 1946–53. He was a Norwegian Social Democratic politician serving in every government, 1935–46. Elected the first Secretary-General of UN in 1946, he was an early but unsuccessful advocate of the admission of communist China to the UN. He took the initiative in organizing UN forces to assist South Korea check aggression by North Korea in 1950. He resigned in 1953 and later re-entered Norwegian politics.

**Liebknecht, Karl** (1871–1919). German socialist politician. A lawyer by training, Liebknecht was elected to the Prussian par-

liament in 1908 and to the REICHSTAG in 1912. Politically he stood on the extreme left of the SOCIAL DEMOCRATIC PARTY. Having voted against war credits in August 1914, Liebknecht became one of the most outspoken of the Social Democratic opponents of the war effort. Early in 1916 he left the SPD and, together with ROSA LUXEMBURG, founded the revolutionary and internationalist SPARTACIST LEAGUE. Arrested on 1 May 1916 after publicly distributing leaflets calling for the overthrow of the government and an end to the war, Liebknecht was sentenced to two and a half years' imprisonment. Pardoned and released from prison in October 1918, Liebknecht took part in the GERMAN REVOLUTION, demanding the establishment of rule by workers' and soldiers' councils within Germany and an alliance with the Soviet Union. Whilst the Spartacists remained organizationally part of the USPD (*see* USPD) until December 1918, Liebknecht and Luxemburg failed to win significant support in the councils and turned to demagogic leadership of street demonstrations in November and December 1918. Leaving the USPD with the merger of the Spartacist League with other radical groups and the establishment of the GERMAN COMMUNIST PARTY (KPD) on 1 January 1919, Liebknecht participated in the uprising in Berlin launched by the new party on 5 January. Together with Luxemburg, he was murdered by members of a paramilitary FREIKORPS group on 15 January 1919.

**Little Entente.** Term, first used pejoratively in a Hungarian newspaper on 21 February 1920, for a series of alliances between Yugoslavia and Czechoslovakia (1920), Czechoslovakia and Romania (1921) and Yugoslavia and Romania (1921), which were consolidated by the Treaty of Belgrade in May 1929. Their aim was to provide for mutual assistance in preventing Austria or Hungary from asserting claims to territory lost as a result of the TREATY OF ST GERMAIN and the TREATY OF TRIANON. Military talks were held between the states during 1929–37, and in February 1933 a permanent council and secretariat was established. The alliances were undermined by Yugoslavia's collaboration with Germany from 1935 and fatally damaged when the Western Powers failed to defend Czechoslovakia at Munich (*see* MUNICH AGREEMENT). The Little Entente was ended when the Yugoslavs and the Romanians withdrew in February 1939.

H. Seton-Watson, *Eastern Europe between the Wars* (1962)
J. Rothschild, *East Central Europe between the Two World Wars* (1974)

**Litvinov, Maxim** (1876–1951). Soviet diplomat of Jewish parents, real name Vallakh. He joined the Social Democrats in 1900 after a period in the army. He was arrested, but escaped from captivity and joined the *Iskra* editorial board in 1901 in Switzerland. In 1903 he returned to Russia, and participated in the 1905 revolution. Again fleeing abroad he spent ten years in London working as a clerk and maintaining his Bolshevik contacts. Following the October Revolution he was appointed Soviet representative in London but was deported in September 1918. He travelled on early trade delegations, becoming Deputy Foreign Commissar in 1921 and assisting in the normalization of relations with the Western powers. His appointment as full Foreign Commissar in 1930 formalized his growing role, and as one of the more Westernized of the Soviet leaders, married to an Englishwoman, he was associated with furthering better relations with the West after the Soviet Union joined the LEAGUE OF NATIONS in 1934, negotiating the FRANCO-SOVIET PACT in 1935. He was demoted in May 1939 and replaced by MOLOTOV. He was reappointed Deputy Foreign Commissar in 1941, serving also as ambassador to the United States from December 1941 until July 1943. He relinquished the position of Deputy Foreign Commissar in 1946. *See also* POPULAR FRONT; COMINTERN; APPEASEMENT.

W. H. McNiell, *America, Britain and Russia* (1953)
G. F. Kennan, *Russia and the West under Lenin and Stalin* (1961)

**Locarno Treaties.** The result of a conference which met at Locarno in autumn 1925 to ease international tensions. A series of agreements were produced, all signed on 1 December. One confirmed the inviolability of the Franco-German and Belgo-German frontiers as laid down by the TREATY OF VERSAILLES and confirmed the Rhineland as a demilitarized zone. A Treaty of Arbitration bound Germany and France to accept mediation in disputes and Germany concluded similar agreements with Belgium, Poland and Czechoslovakia. France made separate agreements with Poland and Czechoslovakia to protect them in the event of German aggression. Russia was brought into the framework by a renewal of the TREATY OF RAPALLO between Germany and the USSR, although Soviet fears of exclusion remained. The treaties were largely the work of ARISTIDE BRIAND, GUSTAV STRESEMANN and AUSTEN CHAMBERLAIN, and were seen as a major initiative in international co-operation and fulfilment of the peace treaties. They remained the basis for European security until Hitler's re-occupation of the RHINELAND in March 1936.

H. Gatzke, *European Diplomacy between the Two World Wars* (1972)

**Lomé Conventions.** Successive five-year trade accords signed between the EUROPEAN ECONOMIC COMMUNITY (EEC) and developing countries. The first was signed on 28 February 1975 and renewed in 1979 and 1985. Negotiations for a Fourth Lomé Convention were concluded in 1990. Originally embracing 46 states, now 66, members of the African, Caribbean and Pacific group of nations (ACP states), the Conventions grant tariff-free, unlimited entry for exports to the EEC. Other developing countries outside the Lomé framework are only able to export specified amounts of their manufactured produce with partial or total reduction of tariff duties. The Lomé trade accords are not based on the principle of reciprocity and are combined with aid and investment as a mechanism for economic development in the Third World.

W. Feld, *The European Community in World Affairs* (1976)

**London, Treaty of.** A secret treaty signed on 26 April 1915 between Britain, France and Russia, the 'Entente powers', and Italy, offering Italy territorial gains in return for entering the war within a month. The treaty promised Italy the Austrian provinces of Trentino, South Tyrol, Istria, Gorizia, Gradisca and Trieste, a large stretch of the Dalmatian Coast, part of Albania, control of the Turkish Dodecanese Islands, the Turkish province of Adalia in Asia Minor, and colonial gains in Africa. As a result Italy entered the war on 24 May 1915. The territorial acquisitions offered to Italy implied the substantial revision of Austria-Hungary's frontiers, making a negotiated peace less likely, and was the cause of conflict with the new state of YUGOSLAVIA after 1918. The terms of the secret treaty were revealed by the BOLSHEVIKS early in 1918 and were immediately seen as both annexationist and a denial of the principle of self-determination enshrined in President WILSON's FOURTEEN POINTS. Wilson's opposition to the full implementation of the treaty and the implied promises made to Yugoslavia led to Italy's not receiving all the territories promised. The denial of Italy's full share of the fruits of the victory helped to promote right-wing and nationalistic attacks on the post-war government of Italy, assisting the rise of MUSSOLINI, and creating long-running disagreements with Yugoslavia over TRIESTE and FIUME.

A. J. P. Taylor, *The Struggle for Mastery in Europe, 1848–1918* (1954)
A. J. Mayer, *The Policy and Diplomacy of Peacemaking* (1968)

**Lublin Committee.** Named after the Polish city to the south-east of Warsaw where the Moscow-backed Polish Committee of National Liberation was installed on 25 July 1944 as the nucleus of the communist government of Poland. The committee served as the executive organ of the National Council of the Homeland and served as a front for the Communist Polish Workers' Party (PPR). It was recognized by the Soviet Union as the provisional government of Poland in December 1944 in spite of protests from the West, with the communists Boleslaw Bierut as Premier and WLADYSLAW GOMULKA as Vice Premier. At the YALTA CONFERENCE in February 1945, the Western powers recognized the provisional government as the basis for a new Polish 'government of national unity', and it was joined on 28 June 1945 by members of the Polish government-in-exile from London. It was then re-established in Moscow as the Polish Provisional Government of National Unity and formally recognized by Great Britain and the United States on 6 July 1945. With pressure from

the Red Army and secret police the Polish Socialist Party was forced into a 'Democratic Bloc' with the PPR which secured 9 million of the 11.25 million votes in the elections of January 1947. In December 1948 the Polish Socialists were forced into a merger with the PPR, forming the Polish United Workers' Party (PZPR), which introduced a Soviet-style constitution in July 1952.

R. F. Staar, *Poland, 1944–1962: The Sovietisation of a Captive People* (1962)
J. Coutouvidis and J. Reynolds, *Poland, 1939–1947* (1986)

**Ludendorff, Erich** (1865–1937). German general. Commissioned as an infantry officer in 1882, Ludendorff was head of the Operational Division of the General Staff, 1908–12. In 1914 he became Chief Quartermaster to the Second German Army in the West and, from the end of August 1914, Chief of the General Staff of the German Eighth Army in the East under HINDENBURG. His partnership with Hindenburg continued when he became Chief Quartermaster-General in August 1916, being jointly charged with the conduct of the entire military conduct of the war. He participated in the formulation of the 'Hindenburg Programme' for total mobilization of German industry for the war effort and of the Auxiliary Service Law of December 1916 which introduced the direction of manpower within the economy. His authority gradually came to exceed that of the Reich Chancellor BETHMANN-HOLLWEG. Following the introduction of unrestricted submarine warfare, of which he was an advocate, he forced the dismissal of Bethmann-Hollweg in July 1917 by threatening to resign. Intervening in the peace negotiations at Brest-Litovsk (*see* BREST-LITOVSK, TREATIES OF) in 1918, he dominated the pursuit by the German negotiator of a wide-ranging annexationist policy. With the loss of the war on the Western Front, Ludendorff pressed strongly in September 1918 for the immediate formation of a parliamentary government and armistice negotiations. Resigning as Quartermaster-General on 26 October 1918, he fled to Sweden, where he remained until mid-1919. Appearing in November 1919 before a parliamentary commission charged with investigating the conduct of the war, he played a major role in disseminating the myth that Germany's defeat in the First World War was a consequence of betrayal by dissident groups on the home front (the 'stab in the back' myth). From July 1919 onwards he was associated with extremist right-wing anti-republican groups, and participated in both the KAPP PUTSCH and the Nazi MUNICH PUTSCH. A Nazi member of the REICHSTAG from 1924 to 1928, he stood as Nazi candidate for the presidency in 1925 but attracted only a small share of the popular vote. From 1928 onwards, he distanced himself from the NAZI PARTY and took little part in active politics.

D. Goodspeed, *Ludendorff: Genius of World War I* (1966)

**Luftwaffe.** The German air force. Germany was prohibited an air force under the TREATY OF VERSAILLES but began training and re-equipment secretly during the 1920s both in Germany and in the Soviet Union under the TREATY OF RAPALLO. The Luftwaffe was officially declared in existence on 9 March 1935 at the same time as Germany introduced conscription. Claims about the strength of the Luftwaffe played a considerable part in the pre-war diplomacy of HITLER's Germany, helping to build up an image of a powerful war machine to back up German demands. German rearmament did increase spending on the air force, with considerable attention to the development of close-support ground-attack aircraft which could assist in breaking enemy morale and a successful armoured thrust in BLITZKRIEG tactics. Long-range heavy bombers were neglected. The Luftwaffe played a decisive part in the opening campaigns in Poland, Norway and France, but failed to obtain air supremacy over southern England in summer and autumn 1940 during the Battle of Britain. Diverted to the BLITZ of British cities, for which it did not have the large bombers required, the Luftwaffe became absorbed in the massive operations in the Soviet Union from 1941 and increasingly in the defence of the German homeland from the ALLIED BOMBING OFFENSIVE. Ground down by war on several fronts and in the skies over Germany itself, the Luftwaffe was faced with a complex breakdown of fuel supplies, training and resources by the last months of the war. Until that point it was able to inflict heavy losses on Allied bombers, introduce revolutionary new equipment, such as the jet fighter-bombers, and hold its own on the Eastern Front. A complete loss of air supremacy in the West after D-Day was followed by increasing inability to contest Allied bombing of German cities. The mass destruction wrought on cities such as Hamburg, Berlin and Dresden was justified by the Allies as returning in kind what the Luftwaffe had done to Warsaw, Rotterdam, Belgrade and Coventry in the opening years of the war. See also GÖRING, HERMANN.

D. Irving, *The Rise and Fall of the Luftwaffe* (1973)
E. L. Homze, *Arming the Luftwaffe: The Reich Air Ministry and the German Aircraft Industry, 1919–39* (1977)

*Lusitania*, **sinking of the.** See FIRST WORLD WAR.

**Luxemburg, Rosa** (1871–1919). German-Polish Social Democrat and Marxist theoretician. Born of German-Jewish parentage in Russian-occupied Poland, she was educated in Warsaw and at the University of Zurich. She was a founder-member and leader of the Social Democratic party in the 'Polish Kingdom' before settling in Germany in 1898 and joining the SOCIAL DEMOCRATIC PARTY (SPD). She worked for a union of socialist groups in occupied Poland, and in 1905 took part in the upheavals in Poland during the Russian Revolution of that year. She contributed to the wide-ranging debate within the SPD at the turn of the century between those who wished to maintain the party's commitment to revolutionary action inspired by a Marxist analysis accepted by the party at its 1891 Erfurt Congress, and those around Eduard Bernstein who wished to revise the party's Marxist doctrine and revolutionary commitment in a reformist direction. In this debate Luxemburg assumed a radical position, both denouncing Bernstein's 'revisionism' and attacking the reluctance of the SPD leadership to transform its radical rhetoric into revolutionary practice. A critic of Lenin's model of the 'democratic-centralist' hierarchical revolutionary party, she emphasized the potential of the mass strike for raising workers' political consciousness and pressing for concrete political changes such as the reform of the Prussian property-related three-class franchise. At the level of Marxist theory she made important contributions to the analysis of imperialism. A revolutionary internationalist, she was highly critical of the SPD's decision to vote for war credits in August 1914 and, together with KARL LIEBKNECHT, published an open letter denouncing the war as a conflict between imperialist powers. Playing a leading role in establishing the SPARTACIST LEAGUE, a group of social democrats opposed to the First World War, Luxemburg spent most of the period between February 1915 and November 1918 in prison. Her 'prison letters' called on workers to undertake revolutionary action to bring the war to an end. She was also critical of Lenin and the Bolsheviks in her essay on *The Russian Revolution* for their dissolution of the CONSTITUENT ASSEMBLY in January 1918 and their incipient authoritarianism. Released from prison in 1918, in the debate over the future of the GERMAN REVOLUTION, she pressed for the extension of the revolution in a socialist direction; and was one of the founders of the GERMAN COMMUNIST PARTY (KPD). Although she regarded the 'Spartacist uprising' of 5 January 1919 as premature, she participated in this and, together with Liebknecht, was captured and murdered by the right-wing irregular FREIKORPS troops deployed by the Ebert government to crush the uprising. Since the 1960s, increasing attention has been paid both to her contributions to Marxist theory and to her writings on revolutionary politics. The latter have been seen by sections of the New Left as offering a model of revolutionary action retaining a commitment to basic freedoms and democracy within a socialist framework.

J. P. Nettl, *Rosa Luxemburg* (2 vols., 1966)
N. Geras, *The Legacy of Rosa Luxemburg* (1976)

**Lvov, Prince Georgi** (1861–1925). Russian reformer and first head of the RUSSIAN PROVISIONAL GOVERNMENT. A leader of the *Zemstvo* movement for local self-government and social reform, he was asked by the Provisional Committee of the DUMA in March 1917 to form a government. He failed to give strong direction to the Provisional Government, refusing to act decisively against disorders but antagonizing others by attempting to concentrate power at the centre and slow down revolutionary change. The abortive Bolshevik coup of 16 July sharpened divisions between Lvov and KERENSKY, leading to the former's resignation on 20 July. He went into exile in France after the October Revolution. *See also* RUSSIAN REVOLUTION.

**Lynch, Jack** (1917–). Taoiseach (Prime Minister) of the Irish Republic 1966–73, 1977–9. In 1957 Lynch became FIANNA FAIL Minister for Education and held various governmental positions until he succeeded Sean Lemass as Taoiseach in 1966. In many ways he personified the variety of strands of opinion in the Fianna Fail party; although a member of the Dail (T.D.) from the traditionally republican county of Cork, he was involved in promoting a more modern and less parochial outlook in Irish politics, particularly through the mechanism of the EUROPEAN ECONOMIC COMMUNITY. Lynch's greatest trial and success came during the ULSTER CONFLICT, when he tamed an upsurge of traditional nationalism within his party by disciplining members assisting the Republican forces in the North.

# M

**MacDonald, James Ramsay** (1866–1937). British Labour and National Prime Minister. The illegitimate son of a Scottish farmgirl, MacDonald had an elementary education before becoming a pupil teacher and then moving to England, where he became a clerk and later secretary to a Liberal MP. Thwarted in his attempts to advance in Liberal politics, he joined the INDEPENDENT LABOUR PARTY and in 1900 became secretary of the newly-formed Labour Representation Committee (the Labour Party from 1906), being supported financially by his marriage settlement. In 1906 he was elected to Parliament, one of a number of candidates benefiting from the secret pact that MacDonald and the Liberal chief whip had negotiated in 1903 to allow for electoral co-operation in some seats. In 1911 MacDonald took over as chairman (leader) of the parliamentary party, relinquishing the party secretaryship to ARTHUR HENDERSON. He also published a number of books which stressed his belief that socialism would evolve gradually from the economic success of capitalism. MacDonald opposed Britain's participation in war in 1914, however, and was forced to resign as leader. Henderson succeeded him. MacDonald, while accepting the need to defeat Germany, was nevertheless critical of Britain's conduct and became a leading figure on the Union of Democratic Control (of foreign policy). Largely as a result of his 'anti-war' stand, he lost his seat in 1918, but was re-elected to parliament and the leadership in 1922. In 1924 MacDonald formed the first Labour government, in which he also served as Foreign Secretary. Having proved that Labour was not 'unfit to govern', and weighed down by the cares of office and a series of difficulties, the government resigned and was heavily defeated at the 1924 election. During the 1920s he continued to ensure that Labour's policies appealed to the middle-ground voter. However, the SECOND LABOUR GOVERNMENT of 1929–31 fared disastrously; in 1931, following its split on the question of the reduction of unemployment benefits, he formed a NATIONAL GOVERNMENT in which a handful of Labourites were swamped by Liberals and especially Conservatives. He did so because he felt that his actions were in the best interests of the nation (including the working classes) and because he was persuaded to stay on by King GEORGE V and the opposition leaders. Expelled from the Labour Party, he led the government to a sweeping victory at the 1931 election. His prestige never stood higher, but soon he was under Conservative attack, and his performance increasingly suffered from physical and mental deterioration. In 1935 he was replaced by STANLEY BALDWIN, and took the post of Lord President of the Council, but on the succession of NEVILLE CHAMBERLAIN in 1937 he retired. He died shortly afterwards.

Few politicians have aroused such controversy as MacDonald. He certainly had his failings. Vain, rather arrogant, and aloof, he was a better party leader than Prime Minister. Yet the charges of treachery which surrounded him after 1931 were unfair. He continued to act honestly, if at times foolishly, throughout his career, buoyed up by a rather vague philosophy of socialism, and he helped make Labour a major party. Where he can be faulted, perhaps, is in not being receptive to new ideas, and in being more concerned with talk rather than action.

D. Marquand, *Ramsay MacDonald* (1977)
A. Morgan, *J. Ramsay MacDonald* (1987)

**Macedonia.** Balkan region under Turkish control for several centuries. Bulgarian claims to the area were disputed by Greeks and Serbs giving rise to the second Balkan War of 1913. In 1919 the TREATY OF NEUILLY placed most of Macedonia in Serbia (Yugoslavia from 1929), while southern Macedonia and Salonika were given to Greece. Bulgaria was left with the district around Petritch. Bulgarian attempts to obtain more of Macedonia continued during the inter-war years, with attacks by the Internal Macedonian Revolutionary Organisation (IMRO), which organized terrorist campaigns within Yugoslavia. After 1924 IMRO split into two rival factions which were involved in raids into Greece and Yugoslavia. They collaborated with the Croatian USTASE, also hostile to Serb-dominated Yugoslavia, and provided the assassin of King ALEXANDER in 1934. Bulgaria was able to occupy the Yugoslav and Greek portions of Macedonia as a result of the German invasion of the Balkans in 1941, but the TREATIES OF PARIS of 1947 restored the pre-war borders. Under the federal constitution of Yugoslavia in 1946 Macedonia was created a Federal Republic with its capital at Skopje and its ethnic identity encouraged. Considerable numbers of Macedonians live in Bulgaria where they maintain their cultural distinctiveness. In Greece, by contrast, cultural integration is further advanced.

**Macmillan, Harold** (1894–1987). British Conservative politician. He was Conservative MP for Stockton-on-Tees, 1924–9, 1931–45, and for Bromley, 1945–64. He served as Parliamentary Secretary to the Ministry of Supply, 1940–42; Under Secretary to the Colonial Office, 1942; minister resident at Allied HQ in North-West Africa, 1942–45; Secretary for Air, 1945; Minister of Housing and Local Government, 1951–4; Minister of Defence 1954–5; Foreign Secretary, 1955; Chancellor of the Exchequer, 1955–7; and Prime Minister, 1957–63. As early as the 1930s Macmillan revealed himself as an advocate of the Tory paternalist tradition in the Conservative Party (*see* CONSERVATIVE AND UNIONIST PARTY), a stance which suited the mood of the 1950s and facilitated his rise to the premiership. He pursued an expansive

housing policy, promising to build 300,000 houses a year, which was accomplished. His term in Downing Street was seen as something of a high point of post-war prosperity. He revelled in international diplomacy and concluded the NASSAU AGREEMENT with the United States in 1962 which ensured Britain's future as a nuclear power. He also made the 'Wind of Change' speech in South Africa in February 1960 which accepted the process of DECOLONIZATION. He received a setback with the veto on Common Market entry by DE GAULLE, and his final months in office were overshadowed by the PROFUMO AFFAIR. By the time of his resignation in October 1963 it appeared to many people that Macmillan's style of leadership was dated and out of touch with the new decade. He retired due to ill-health. In his later years he was associated with criticism of Thatcherite policies of social division and PRIVATIZATION, calling for a revival of 'one nation' Toryism. Created Earl Stockton in 1984.

H. Macmillan, *The Middle Way* (1938)
R. Blake, *The Conservative Party from Peel to Thatcher* (1985)

**Mafia.** Criminal organization of Italian origin based on family networks, later becoming an international criminal syndicate with its strongest presence in the United States. It developed in Sicily as an indigenous organization used to counter the oppression of rulers and landowners. After Italian unification, however, it allied itself with the local elites to control elections and to suppress labour protests. Sporadic attempts by the national government to eradicate the society were unsuccessful, but the fascists under MUSSOLINI pursued a vigorous campaign of suppression under Cesari Mori (1872–1942), appointed Prefect of Palermo from 1924 to 1929. Known as the 'Iron Prefect' he used secret tribunals, torture and banishment with some success to curtail the organization. It survived the fascists, reappearing strongly after 1945, and was increasingly assisted by the development of its family connections with the American Mafia, based upon Sicilian immigrants, which during the prohibition era had become a dominant force in organized crime. By the post-war era, the American and Italian Mafia were involved in highly sophisticated criminal operations controlled by a number of 'families', based upon a mixture of legitimate and illegitimate activities. Drugs, gambling and prostitution lay at the heart of the Mafia networks, but they increasingly involved themselves in property and construction. Determined efforts by the Italian state to deal with the Sicilian Mafia have led to a protracted series of trials, notable for breaking the code of silence (*omerta*) which is imposed on Mafia members, but also for a spate of assassinations of police chiefs and magistrates sent to conduct anti-Mafia investigations. In spite of renewed efforts to bring Mafia 'bosses' to justice, there is little sign that the organization has been eliminated from Italian life. The Mafia is believed to control crime syndicates in a number of major European cities, especially those on the drug trafficking routes through the Mediterranean, such as Marseilles.

A. Bloc, *The Mafia of a Sicilian Village* (1975)
C. Duggan, *Fascism and the Mafia* (1989)
C. Sterling, *The Mafia* (1990)

**Maginot Line.** Line of fortifications constructed between 1929 and 1938 on the eastern frontier of France from the Swiss border to the Ardennes, named after André Maginot (1877–1932), French Minister of War from 1922 to 1931. France's experience of invasion in 1870 and in 1914 and the need to defend the newly recovered provinces of ALSACE-LORRAINE on the frontier prompted French military planners to seek security in a system of fixed fortifications. There were also additional factors such as the experience of the huge losses incurred in the assault of fixed positions in the First World War and the demographic imbalance of France with Germany, which argued for France's standing on the defensive in a future clash with Germany in order to gain time to mobilize her reserves. Initially, there were different proposals. Marshall JOFFRE argued for a series of fortified zones stretching all the way from the North Sea to Switzerland with gaps through which offensives could be mounted; Marshall PÉTAIN favoured a continuous line of fortifications for the most vulnerable sector of the frontier. The scheme adopted in 1928 owed something to both. This was a continuous line of defences running from Switz-

erland to the Ardennes, of varying strength and depth. The line took ten years to build because of financial difficulties, but the result was a formidable chain of self-contained concrete and steel bastions, supposedly impregnable to frontal assault, capable of maintaining their garrisons for many months with their own power supplies, railways, lifts, stores and hospitals. The decision not to extend the line west of the Ardennes was deliberate, based on an assumption that the French army would advance into Belgium to engage the enemy, also because there were geological difficulties in siting large concrete fortifications in the local subsoil, and because of the proximity of vital centres such as Lille to the frontier.

For all its formidable strength, the Maginot Line's weakness lay in the possibility of its being outflanked and also in the defensive attitude it encouraged in French thinking, the so-called 'Maginot mentality'. Moreover, fixed fortifications of the type planned in the aftermath of the First World War were increasingly obsolescent with the development of more mobile arms of warfare, the armoured divisions, parachute and glider-borne forces, and the use of tactical airpower. In the event, the Maginot Line was outflanked by the German attack through the Ardennes in May 1940 and was surrendered virtually intact with its garrison of 200,000 men when France concluded the armistice with Germany on 22 June 1940 (*see* SECOND WORLD WAR).

The folly of the Maginot Line can be overplayed. It forced the Germans to consider an attack on France beyond its western extremity and France's fate was decided by the brilliant German plan to invade via the virtually undefended Ardennes, completely nullifying France's preparations and leaving her forces both in Belgium and the fortified line completely outflanked. Undoubtedly, however, French propaganda aimed at emphasizing the impregnability of the Maginot Line helped to inculcate some complacency in French public opinion and left it unprepared and vulnerable when a German breakthrough occurred.

J. Williams, *The Ides of May: The Defeat of France, May-June 1940* (1972)

J. Benoist-Mechin, *Sixty Days that Shook the West: The Fall of France* (trans., 3 vols., 1974)
A. Kemp, *The Maginot Line: Myth and Reality* (1981)

**Magyar Kommunista Part** (MKP). *See* COMMUNIST PARTY, HUNGARIAN.

**Major, John** (1943–). British Conservative politician and Prime Minister; succeeded Mrs. THATCHER as leader of the CONSERVATIVE PARTY and Prime Minister in November 1990. Major left school at 16 and worked in banking, Before entering local government in south London. MP for Huntingdon since 1983; served in junior posts, 1985–7; joining the Cabinet in 1987 as Secretary to the Treasury in charge of public spending; Foreign Secretary, July–October, 1989; then Chancellor of the Exchequer following Lawson's resignation. Took Britain into the European EXCHANGE RATE MECHANISM in October 1990. When Mrs. Thatcher withdrew from the leadership contest in late November 1991, he obtained the largest number of votes on the second ballot as the heir to the Thatcher legacy. He earned praise for his conduct in the Iraqi invasion of Kuwait and the GULF WAR, achieving very high poll ratings. He oversaw the replacement of the poll tax with a more acceptable system of local government taxation. Economic problems delayed an appeal to the country in 1991. *See also* THATCHER.

E. Pearce, *The Quiet Rise of John Major* (1991)
B. Anderson, *John Major: the making of the Prime Minister* (1991)

**Makarios III** (1913–77). Archbishop and President of the Cypriot Republic, 1960–77, except for a short interval in 1974. Born near Paphos of peasant stock, he was a monk from the age of 13. He was ordained priest in 1946, became Bishop of Kitium in 1948, and was head of Orthodox Church in Cyprus from 1950. The political as well as the spiritual leader of his people, he undertook negotiations with the British during the CYPRUS EMERGENCY during the 1950s; he was deported by them to the Seychelles in 1956, suspected of being the leader of the EOKA terrorist force. Returning to Cyprus in 1959 he became the first President of the independent Cypriot Republic on 16 August 1960. Several attempts were made on his life by those who sought 'enosis'

(union) with Greece, and saw Makarios as a traitor. He was forced into exile after an attack on the presidential palace by members of the Cypriot National Guard in July 1974. Widely believed to have been inspired by the GREEK COLONELS' regime in Athens, the attempted coup resulted in the TURKISH INVASION OF CYPRUS and its partition. He returned to a divided island and died of a heart attack on 3 August 1977.

**Makhno, Nestor** (1889–1935). Russian anarchist. Of Ukrainian peasant stock, he joined an anarchist group in 1907. He was sentenced to death for revolutionary activity in 1910 but was reprieved. Released from prison in 1917, he organized a Revolutionary Insurgent Army of the Ukraine which fought against the Central Powers, the Whites, the forces of PETLYURA and also against the Bolsheviks. He set up a regime based on councils of peasants, workers and soldiers which attempted to operate on anarchist lines. The RED ARMY defeated his forces by early 1921 and he was forced to flee abroad. He died in exile. *See also* ANARCHISM, RUSSIAN; SOVIETS; RUSSIAN CIVIL WAR.

P. Avrich (ed.), *The Anarchists in the Russian Revolution* (1973)
M. Malet, *Nestor Makhno in the Russian Civil War* (1982)

**Malenkov, Georgi** (1902–79). Soviet Prime Minister. He joined the Communist Party in 1920 and worked for the party's Central Committee and the party's Moscow Committee. He assisted in the SOVIET COLLECTIVIZATION campaigns and the PURGES, and was one of the party members to rise via the Secretariat under STALIN. During the Second World War Malenkov served on the State Defence Committee, the small war council chaired by Stalin. He became a Deputy Prime Minister and a member of the Politburo in 1946. Widely regarded as Stalin's natural successor, he became First Secretary to the Party and Prime Minister on Stalin's death in March 1953, but relinquished the former post to KHRUSCHEV within the month. He was eased out of the premiership in February 1955 when he was succeeded by BULGANIN, and placed in charge of electricity supply. In 1957 he was identified with the 'anti-party' group and expelled from the Central Committee and other party posts as part of Khrushchev's consolidation of power and process of DE-STALINIZATION. He was allowed to manage a small electrical concern before retiring to Moscow. He was one of the first Soviet leaders to survive deposition by his opponents.

M. Ebon, *Malenkov: Stalin's Successor* (1953)
F. Fejto, *A History of the People's Democracies: Eastern Europe since Stalin* (2nd edn, 1974)

**Malta.** Central Mediterranean island annexed by Britain in 1814 and developed into a major naval base. During the Second World War the island was under virtual siege between 1940 and 1943, being heavily bombed by Italian and German aircraft. It served as a vital naval base for attacks on German and Italian supply routes to North Africa. The island was awarded the George Cross on 16 April 1942. In 1947 the island received internal self-government. A referendum in 1956 voted for integration with the United Kingdom, but independence was granted in 1964. It remained a member of the Commonwealth until 1974, when it became a Republic. Its leading politician in the post-war era was Dom Mintoff of the Maltese Labour Party, who was in office 1947–58, and since 1971.

E. Bradford, *Siege: Malta, 1940–1943* (1985)

**Mandates.** Former colonies of Germany and the Ottoman Empire, excluding Turkish areas, for which the LEAGUE OF NATIONS assumed responsibility in 1919–20. The League gave certain of the ex-Allies a 'mandate' to administer the colonies and to make annual reports on conditions in them: these mandatories were Britain, South Africa, Australia, New Zealand, France, Belgium and Japan. There were three classes of mandate. A: those which would be administered for a short time only, as they prepared for full independence, for example Iraq, Palestine and Transjordan under British mandate, Lebanon and Syria under French; B: those to be administered indefinitely as separate territories because of the backward state of the peoples, for example all 'German Africa' except South-West Africa; C: those also to be indefinitely administered but which, because of their small size and contiguity to the mandatory

state could be treated as part of the mandatory's territory, for example South West Africa, New Guinea and Samoa. Any complex problems arising from the administrations were to be referred to the Permanent Commission of the League. In 1946 the Trusteeship Council of the UNITED NATIONS assumed the Commission's responsibilities.

**Manhattan Project.** Code name for the project of developing the first NUCLEAR WEAPON, an atomic bomb, begun in June 1942 under the US Army Corps of Engineers. A large community of American, Canadian, British and European refugee scientists eventually worked on the project, the co-operation of Britain and the United States on the project being formally agreed at Quebec in August 1943. Only the United States had the abundant resources of raw materials and energy which were required to test various means of obtaining fissile Uranium–235 from Uranium–238 and to pursue the two methods of making atomic devices using enriched uranium or plutonium. In the event, devices of both types were available by 1945. An experimental bomb was successfully exploded at Alamogordo, New Mexico, on 16 July 1945. On 6 August 1945 the United States Air Force bomber *Enola Gay* dropped the first atomic bomb on the Japanese city of Hiroshima, killing an estimated 78,000 people; a second bomb dropped on Nagasaki on 9 August killed a further 40,000 people. Between them the bombs wounded as many people again, many of them to die from radiation sickness and long-term effects long into the post-war era. In August 1946 President TRUMAN signed the Atomic Energy Act, restricting exchange of information with other nations on atomic energy, thus ending co-operation between Britain and America on nuclear weapons. As a result Britain decided to press ahead with her own atomic bomb programme, testing her first bomb in Western Australia on 3 October 1952.

R. G. Hewlett and O. E. Anderson, *The New World* (1970)
M. Gowing, *Britain and Atomic Energy* (1974)

**Mannerheim, Carl** (1867–1951). Finnish soldier and statesman. Born at Villnaes of Finno-Swedish descent, he was commissioned in the Russian Imperial Army in 1889 and served in the Russo-Japanese War in 1904–5, rising to the rank of Major-General in the First World War. Following the RUSSIAN REVOLUTION and the Finnish declaration of independence in December 1917 he led the 'White' forces, supported by a German expeditionary force, to victory over the Left, supported by the Soviets, in the Finnish Civil War of January to April 1918. He advocated Finnish intervention in support of the 'White' Russian forces in the RUSSIAN CIVIL WAR, but was defeated in the presidential elections of July 1919. Following the Soviet Union's recognition of Finnish independence on 14 October 1920 he retired from active service with the rank of Field Marshal. In retirement he maintained an active interest in the military readiness of Finland for any future war, including the fortification of the Karelian frontier with the Soviet Union. As the Chairman of the National Defence Council from 1931 he supervised the improvement of the line of defences across the Karelian Isthmus, which became known as the MANNERHEIM LINE. Recalled to active service in 1939, he commanded the Finnish forces in the RUSSO-FINNISH WAR of 1939–40 and advised the government to seek peace in March. He also commanded Finnish forces in the CONTINUATION WAR of 1941–4 when the Finns joined the attack on the Soviet Union launched by Hitler in June 1941. Faced with certain defeat by the summer of 1944, the Finns elected Mannerheim President (4 August 1944); he secured an armistice with the Russians in September 1944. He retired from office on 9 March 1945.

D. Kirby, *Finland in the Twentieth Century* (1979)
A. F. Upton, *The Finnish Revolution, 1917–18* (1980)

**Mannerheim Line.** 88-mile long line of fortifications on the KARELIAN ISTHMUS built by Finland to guard its most vulnerable border with the Soviet Union. Begun in the 1920s it was strengthened under the direction of Marshal MANNERHEIM, Chairman of the Finnish National Defence Council, in 1931–2, when 100,000 unemployed were set to work on it, and again in 1939, when student and volunteer labour was employed. The strength and impregnability of the Mannerheim Line was much exaggerated by Soviet propaganda during the

RUSSO-FINNISH WAR of 1939–40 to explain the slowness of their advance. It was largely composed of machine gun nests and anti-tank obstacles, many of which were obsolete or ineffective, and lacked the depth and sophisticated emplacements of the MAGINOT LINE. Sited 20 to 30 miles from the border, the line was used as the main defence position in the Winter War of 1939–40 to which Finnish forces made a planned retreat before inflicting heavy losses on Soviet attacks in December 1940. The breach of the line in March 1940 spelled the end of Finnish resistance, and the line was surrendered as part of the terms of the Treaty of Moscow which ended the war.

R. W. Condon, *The Winter War: Russia against Finland* (1972)
V. Tanner, *The Winter War* (1974)

**Maquis.** Name for the French resistance groups who took to the hills from 1943 to escape conscription for labour in Germany. Loosely controlled by the National Council of the Resistance led by DE GAULLE, some 40,000 Maquisards were operating by 1944. Lightly armed, they received equipment dropped by Allied airforces in June and July 1944 to enable them to delay German efforts to reinforce northern France. The name was derived from the resistance groups which liberated Corsica in 1943.

M. R. D. Foot, *Resistance* (1976)

**March on Rome.** A projected occupation of Italy's capital by the Italian fascists. With Italy on the verge of civil war in the autumn of 1922, MUSSOLINI demanded the formation of a fascist government to save the country. Inspired by D'ANNUNZIO's seizure of FIUME, the FASCI DI COMBATTIMENTO had seized several provincial capitals in the summer of 1922. A plan was drawn up in Naples on 24 October for a three-stage movement: the occupation of public buildings in northern and central Italy, the concentration of three columns of fascists on the main roads leading to Rome, and the occupation of the ministries and centre of government in the event of resistance. Rome was, however, defended by regular troops, and martial law was declared on 28 October. When the fascists began to assemble on 27/8 October they were disrupted by heavy rain and lacked arms and supplies. Although provincial occupations occurred, most of the larger cities were unaffected. The putsch only succeeded because of the atmosphere of crisis built up by Mussolini and because of deep divisions within the ruling groups. Mussolini offered to compromise; with many army commanders divided in their loyalties and the Facta government paralysed, the King, backed by advice from the army and leading businessmen, invited Mussolini to form a government. He arrived in Rome on 30 October and was made Prime Minister, ruling initially through a coalition. The 'March on Rome' was subsequently played up as a seizure of power, which, in fact, never occurred. It provided a key element in the future depiction of the Italian fascist movement as one which had seized power, rather than having obtained it through royal decision.

A. Lyttleton, *The Seizure of Power* (1973)

**Marne, Battles of.** The first battle of the Marne was fought in September 1914 and marked a turning point in the FIRST WORLD WAR. Responding to the German offensive of northern France, JOFFRE ordered an attack on the German right in the Marne area to deflect the threat to Paris. The counter-offensive opened a gap between the German 1st and 2nd Armies, forcing a German retreat. The battle ended the threat of a rapid German victory in accordance with the SCHLIEFFEN PLAN, forcing an extension of the battlelines to the Channel coast and the development of a continuous trench line on the Western Front. The second battle was fought in July 1918 when LUDENDORFF launched a final offensive in the West in the Rheims area. The attack was repulsed by FOCH on part of the front, but a successful thrust west of Rheims by the German armies was only halted by the use of British, American and Italian divisions in support of the French. A counter-attack on 17 July, assisted by tanks and spearheaded by American troops, eliminated the German salient and prepared the way for a successful advance against the demoralized German forces.

**Marshall Plan.** A plan devised in response to a speech by US Secretary of State General George C. Marshall in June 1947,

offering economic assistance for the recovery of the war-devastated economics of Europe. The plan led to the European Recovery Programme (1948) under which 17 nations in Western Europe received $15 billion in grants and loans between 1948 and 1952. The plan was at least partly designed to diminish the growth of communist influence in Western European politics. The plan was rejected by the Soviet Union, who exerted its influence to prevent acceptance by the countries of Eastern Europe. The Western Powers organized a conference at Paris in July 1947 to discuss the allocation of aid and in April 1948 set up the ORGANISATION FOR EUROPEAN ECONOMIC CO-OPERATION (OEEC), representing 18 European countries, plus the United States and Canada. The OEEC administered the programme with the United States Economic Co-operation Administration. With the assistance of the aid all the participating nations had, by 1951, raised their production capacities beyond pre-war levels. In contrast to the DEPRESSION which followed the First World War, the Marshall Plan added a crucial margin of investment resources which enabled European economic reconstruction to proceed without greater austerity, thereby assisting political stability. In total the plan represented only a fraction of the resources involved in the reconstruction of the European economy. There seems little doubt that the growth of the FRENCH COMMUNIST PARTY and ITALIAN COMMUNIST PARTY and the development of a Soviet bloc in Eastern Europe acted to stimulate United States economic intervention, though this was combined with strong humanitarian and cultural sympathies for the plight of post-war Europe. *See also* COLD WAR; NORTH ATLANTIC TREATY ORGANISATION; TRUMAN DOCTRINE.

A. S. Milward, *The Reconstruction of Western Europe, 1945–51* (1984)

M. J. Hogan, *The Marshall Plan: America, Britain and the Reconstruction of Western Europe, 1947–1952* (1987)

**Martignon Agreement.** See BLUM, LÉON.

**Martov, Yuli** (1873–1923). Menshevik leader. He was born in Constantinople of Jewish background. His real name was Tsederbaum. With LENIN he founded the Union for the Struggle for the Emancipation of the Working Class in October 1895 and *Iskra* (the 'Spark'), and helped to create the RUSSIAN SOCIAL DEMOCRATIC LABOUR PARTY. Martov broke with Lenin over the role of the party and revolutionary strategy, and led the MENSHEVIK wing of the Social Democrats. During the First World War he edited the Russian 'internationalist' newspaper *Goles* (Voice) with TROTSKY and ANTONOV-OVSEYENKO. Returning to Russia on 23 May 1917 he opposed Menshevik participation in the coalition PROVISIONAL GOVERNMENT of 19 May, but failed to gain majority support. He opposed the renewal of the military offensive in July 1917 but was increasingly isolated between growing BOLSHEVIK strength and the Mensheviks in the Provisional Government. His attempts to end co-operation with the 'bourgeois' parties and to form a broad socialist government were defeated at a Menshevik Congress on 27 September. Following the Bolshevik seizure of power he was elected leader of the Menshevik opposition. While opposing the 'White' forces and the allied intervention, he attacked the use of terror. Forced into exile in 1920, he edited the *Socialist Messenger* and attempted to resist Bolshevik influence over other socialist parties in Europe. Perceptive about the dangers inherent in the regime set up by Lenin, he nonetheless refused to countenance action against it. Often seen as the 'conscience' of Russian communism, he died in Germany in 1923.

I. Getzler, *Martov: Political Biography of a Russian Social Democrat* (1967)

**Marxist Leninism.** Official doctrine of the BOLSHEVIKS and of the Soviet Union. LENIN developed classical Marxism in three principal directions; the role and nature of the Communist Party; the nature of the forthcoming revolution; and the nature of the state. Lenin's most original contribution was in the role of the party. In *What is To Be Done?* (1902) Lenin formulated the idea that the workers alone could not bring about the revolution but would have to be led by professional full-time revolutionaries acting as a vanguard of the working class, opening the prospect of a revolution brought about by a revolutionary élite. As far as the course of revolution was concerned, after 1906 Lenin envisaged a 'revol-

utionary democratic dictatorship of the workers and peasants' following the first-stage 'bourgeois revolution' of orthodox Marxist theory, but from his arrival in Russia in April 1917 declared in favour of 'all power to the Soviets', effectively an immediate proletarian revolution, breaking with the course of development Marx had outlined. Lenin foresaw the dictatorship destroying the opposition of the bourgeoisie and landlords, introducing complete 'democratization', radical alternatives of land tenure, and kindling of revolution elsewhere in Europe. The state Lenin claimed to have set up in November 1917 was a 'dictatorship of the proletariat', whose theoretical foundation was expressed in his *State and Revolution*, written in September 1917 and published early in 1918. Lenin viewed the dictatorship of the proletariat as the transitional phase from the socialist revolution to the final phase of communism, in which the proletariat creates a proletarian state of its own after destroying the previous bourgeois state. Although dictatorship and violence would be required initially, Lenin envisaged the need for the apparatus of dictatorship and repression to lessen and, in time, for the state to wither away.

Critics of Lenin have argued that his formulation of Marxism effectively elevated the role of the party in a way which fatally compromised Marx's wider vision of a whole class coming to power, and that in fashioning the revolutionary instrument of a vanguard party and the dictatorship of the proletariat he laid the foundations of a narrowly based autocracy based on repression. Others argue that Lenin was forced to modify Marxist principles to suit Russian conditions of an under-developed working class, although Lenin's justification for a vanguard seemed to deny that the workers as a class were ever capable of revolutionary consciousness and bringing about a revolution. Russia's condition after November 1917 as a sole, beleaguered communist state meant that the dictatorship of the party in the name of the proletariat had to be prolonged, awaiting eventual revolution elsewhere.

L. Shapiro, *The Origins of the Communist Autocracy* (1965)
——, *The Government and Politics of the Soviet Union* (rev. edn, 1967)

**Masaryk, Jan** (1866–1948). Czechoslovak diplomat and Foreign Minister. The son of TOMAS MASARYK, he attended PARIS PEACE CONFERENCE, 1919–20. He was Czech diplomatic envoy to London 1925–38, but resigned after the MUNICH AGREEMENT. He spent the war years in London as Foreign Minister and Deputy Prime Minister of the Czech government-in-exile, 1941–5. On the liberation of Czechoslovakia he continued as Foreign Minister although he was out of sympathy with an increasingly pro-Soviet policy. He remained in office after the communist coup in February 1948 but died a few days later on 10 March in suspicious cirmumstances. Anti-communists claimed he was murdered, as one of the prewar leaders of democratic Czechoslovakia; the communists claimed he commited suicide.

**Masaryk, Tomas** (1850–1937). Czech politician. Born in Moravia, he was educated at Brno, Vienna and Leipzig. He was a professor at Prague, 1882–1914. He displayed strong pro-Slav feelings and escaped to London in December 1914, where he cultivated intellectual contacts in support of Czech independence. He became chairman of the Czech national council and published the periodical *The New Europe*. In 1917 he travelled to Russia and obtained permission to organize the CZECH LEGION amongst prisoners-of-war taken by the Russians, aiming to bring them to France and fight in the war against the Central Powers. He went on to the United States, where he influenced President WILSON who recognized him as leader of an independent state on 3 September 1918. As president-elect he returned to Czechoslovakia to become its first President when the independent state was founded on 14 November 1918. Twice re-elected, he remained a non-party figure, standing aside from the more extreme nationalism of his fellows. He made way for BENES on 13 December 1935. He is widely revered as the founder of the nation.

S. B. Winters, R. B. Pynsent, H. Hanak (eds.), *T. G. Masaryk (1850–1937)* (3 vols., 1990)

**Massive Retaliation.** The name given to a defence doctrine announced by JOHN FOSTER DULLES in January 1954, which laid down that the United States would meet local communist aggression by responding 'vigorously at places and with means of our own choosing'. The implied threat was that the United States would use her full nuclear capability against the Soviet Union in response to acts of communist aggression anywhere in the world and as part of the operational doctrine of the NORTH ATLANTIC TREATY ORGANISATION forces in Europe. The advantage of the policy was that it meant a saving on conventional forces, but there was a problem of credibility, as it would be extremely difficult to convince the Russians that the United States would initiate nuclear war to counter all minor acts of aggression. It was in response to these dilemmas that the doctrine of FLEXIBLE RESPONSE was adopted from the 1960s.

**Masurian Lakes, Battles of the.** *See* FIRST WORLD WAR.

**Matteoti Crisis.** A crisis in the early Italian fascist regime caused by the kidnapping and murder of the socialist deputy Giacomo Matteoti (1885–1924) on 10 June 1924 by fascist thugs acting on their own initiative. An outspoken critic of the fascist regime, Matteoti had attacked the illegalities and violence of the fascist gangs or *squadristi*, and his death followed a speech on 30 May condemning the elections which had taken place on 6 April for the violence and intimidation of the fascists. The murder provoked a major crisis, with public denunciations of MUSSOLINI in the Chamber and mass demonstrations in the streets. Mussolini, fearing that the King might intervene, reacted by sacking all those whom he suspected of complicity in the crime, including the Minister of the Interior. The King refused to act, and in spite of the withdrawal of 120 non-fascist deputies from the Chamber, in the so-called 'Aventine secession' (taking their name from the protest of Gaius Gracclus and his followers in the early Roman Republic in withdrawing to the Aventine Hill), Mussolini was able to bring some opposition politicians into his cabinet and obtain a vote of confidence in the Senate. Although the Aventine carried out a vigorous press campaign and obtained the defection of GIOLITTI and some other members, Mussolini turned the crisis to his advantage, unleashing a wave of fascist violence against opponents in January 1925, gagging the press and banning socialist meetings. Matteoti became a martyr to the left and the anti-fascist movement, but no direct involvement by Mussolini in the murder has ever been proved.

A. Lyttleton, *The Seizure of Power* (1973)

**Max, Prince of Baden** (1867–1929). German statesman. From 1907 the heir-apparent to the Grand Duchy of Baden, Prince Max was widely considered by liberals a possible Reich Chancellor after the July 1917 crisis which had led to the dismissal of BETHMANN-HOLLWEG. With the collapse of the German army on the Western Front in September 1918 and the acceptance by the German High Command and Kaiser of the inevitability of suing with the Allies for an armistice, Prince Max was appointed Reich Chancellor and Prussian Foreign Minister on 3 October 1918, charged with negotiating an armistice, introducing domestic political reform and parliamentary government, and preventing German military defeat developing into revolution. Whilst he succeeded in the first and second of these tasks, his government proved unable to contain the spread of a naval mutiny in Kiel and Wilhelmshaven to army units in North Germany. His attempts to preserve the HOHENZOLLERN dynasty by persuading Kaiser WILHELM II to abdicate proved fruitless. Nevertheless, confronted by the outbreak of revolution in Berlin, he announced both his resignation as Chancellor and the Kaiser's abdication on 9 November 1918, handing over power to the leader of the SOCIAL DEMOCRATIC PARTY (SPD), FRIEDRICH EBERT. See also GERMAN REVOLUTION.

A. Rosenberg, *The Birth of the German Republic, 1871–1918* (1931)
A. J. Ryder, *The German Revolution of 1918* (1967)

**May Days, Spanish.** Period of street-fighting in Barcelona on 3–7 May 1937 between anarchists, communists and Catalan separatists. The occasion for the fighting was the attempt by the Republican government of LARGO CABALLERO, backed by communists, and Catalan separatists to assert control over the revolutionary forces of the anarcho-syndicalist CNT-FAI (*see* CONFEDERACIÓN NACIONAL DE TRABAJO) and the revolutionary Marxis POUM (*see* PARTIDO

OBRERO DE UNIFICACIÓN MARXISTA). The latter groups resisted attempts to regularize military discipline, government control of war industries, and the creation of a single Republican army. The Republic police were ordered to seize the central telephone exchange on the afternoon of 3 May and general fighting spread throughout the city. Leading anarchists were assassinated and their forces disarmed. The fighting signalled the end of the broad left popular front coalition and the subordination of the revolutionary wing of the left to the aim of winning the war under communist control. The communists used the events to demand the final suppression of the POUM; this Premier Caballero refused, leading to the break-up of his coalition government and its fall from power on 17 May. Thereafter the war effort on the Republican side was dominated by the communists, who systematically destroyed their opponents and organized the full militarization of the Republican war effort. The events have frequently been seen as marking the end of the genuinely revolutionary phase of the Civil War and the assertion of Soviet control.

G. Orwell, *Homage to Catalonia* (1938)
B. Bolloten, *The Spanish Civil War* (1991)

**May events.** *See* ÉVÉNEMENTS DE MAI.

**means test.** Survey of income and resources to test eligibility for welfare benefits. Introduced as an emergency measure by the British NATIONAL GOVERNMENT in autumn 1931 for those in receipt of employment insurance beyond the statutory period of six months under the National Insurance Acts. Hundreds of thousands of unemployed had exhausted their entitlement to benefits during the DEPRESSION, and a variety of *ad hoc* regulations to prevent them having to apply to the Poor Law had been introduced, including a system of 'transitional payments' for those unemployed for over six months. Under the new regulations, these claimants had to undergo a 'household means test' carried out by the local Public Assistance Committees, the successors to the Poor Law Guardians, who assessed the circumstances of the claimant and determined the rate of relief received. Any form of income, including pensions, contributions from sons or daughters, lodgers or charities could be taken into account, as well as savings, furniture or other effects. The enquiries brought many of the respectable unemployed into contact with the Poor Law authorities for the first time; household enquiries were demeaning and often carried out with officiousness and meanness. By January 1932 an estimated 1 million people were coming within the scope of the 'tests'. Several local councils rebelled against carrying them out, but were forced to comply by the threat of commissioners from London doing the work instead of local people. Within a year 180,000 people were removed from the receipt of Unemployment Insurance and a half of those applying for 'transitional payments' received less than the full amount, saving £24 million. The means test remained in operation for the rest of the decade, although its operation was somewhat relaxed. The means test, however, left a legacy of bitterness which did much to fuel the desire for a more humane and guaranteed system of social security in the future. The Beveridge Report of 1942 assumed that the major benefits covering sickness, unemployment and old age would be paid as of right. Estimations of means, however, remained part of the machinery for paying National Assistance to those who fell outside other state benefits. Moreover, as state benefits proliferated after the Second World War, governments began to introduce thresholds for their receipt, such as housing benefit, income support, rates rebates, and supplementary benefit. Although rarely policed as intrusively as the original means test, they were nonetheless 'means-tested' benefits and the principle is now an integral part of 'targeting' benefits.

B. B. Gilbert, *British Social Policy, 1914–1939* (1973)
D. Fraser, *The Evolution of the British Welfare State* (2nd edn, 1975)

**Mein Kampf.** A book written by ADOLF HITLER during his imprisonment in 1924–5 following the failure of the 1923 MUNICH PUTSCH. Its title, 'My Struggle', refers to Hitler's early attempts to establish himself as a politician. Turgid, repetitive and stylistically crude, it nevertheless became a standard work following the Nazi seizure of power, and sold millions of copies. Its prin-

cipal interest lies in the insight it provides into Hitler's mental world and in its programmatic character. Three themes emerge from the book: Hitler's belief that all human life is made up of conflict and that the history of the world is the history of struggle between races; his virulent anti-Semitism; and his concern to re-establish German great-power status as a prelude to the establishment of a racially-based empire in Central and Eastern Europe.

Hitler's belief in conflict as the essence of human life was derived from Social Darwinist theories current in Europe in the early 20th century. He believed, moreover, that this principle governed the behaviour of social groups as well as that of individuals, and saw conflict between races of differing cultural value as the key to world history. Aryans constituted the only valuable race since only they were truly creative; Germans constituted the most valuable component within the Aryan race. Jews were seen as the polar opposite of the Aryan race – parasitic, the fomentors of Bolshevism, and committed to the destruction of the Aryan race. The key to the survival of races was the amount of living space (*Lebensraum*) at their disposal and their physical health. Since Hitler rejected contraception or internal colonization as solutions to growing population, his concern with 'living space' inevitably entailed the acquisition by Germany of more territory.

*Mein Kampf* also contains the key elements of the foreign policy which Hitler was to seek to pursue after he attained power in 1933. Since, by the time he came to write *Mein Kampf*, Hitler had concluded that France posed the greatest threat to German territorial integrity and expansionism, and since France could only be contained by an alliance with Britain and Italy necessitating the abandonment by Germany of pursuit of a colonial empire, German territorial expansion must inevitably be principally at the expense of her eastern neighbours – above all, at the expense of the Soviet Union.

If the central elements in *Mein Kampf* may be separated for expository purposes, it should not be forgotten that they were inseparable in Hitler's mind. His obsession with racial purity and the life-and-death struggle between Jews and Aryans both necessitated and legitimated his commitment to territorial expansion eastwards. Whilst some historians have argued that *Mein Kampf* cannot be seen as amounting to a political programme, and point to the areas in which Hitler failed after 1933 to secure the diplomatic objectives outlined in the book, most historians accept it as a clear statement of Hitler's ideological obsessions, obsessions whose realization were to form the cornerstone of Nazi foreign policy after 1933, and were to inform the conduct of the war against the Soviet Union after 1941 and the mass murder of European Jews. *See also* HOLOCAUST; HOSSBACH MEMORANDUM; SECOND WORLD WAR.

A. Hitler, *Mein Kampf* (trans., 1969)
E. Jaeckel, *Hitler's Weltanschauung* (1972)
I. Kershaw, *The Nazi Dictatorship* (2nd edn, 1989)

**Memel.** Port in East Prussia put under LEAGUE OF NATIONS control by the TREATY OF VERSAILLES in 1919, but seized by Lithuania in 1923. In March 1939 it was seized by Germany. Left as part of German East Prussia by the NAZI-SOVIET PACT, it was absorbed into the Soviet Union after 1945.

**Mendés-France, Pierre** (1907–82). French politician. Born in Paris of Jewish parentage, he trained as a lawyer in Paris and joined the RADICAL PARTY in 1923, entering the Chamber in 1932. He served as a Treasury minister in 1938, then joined the French Air Force, escaping to join DE GAULLE in 1941. He acted as financial adviser to de Gaulle and represented France at the BRETTON WOODS CONFERENCE. To the left of de Gaulle, he went into opposition after 1945, but on 19 June 1954 formed a broad-based coalition government brought about by widespread discontent over the INDO-CHINESE WAR, especially after the fall of Dien Bien Phu in May 1954. He negotiated an end to the war in the cease-fire agreement signed at Geneva on 27 July and opened talks for the independence of the North African protectorates. However, his dispatch of further troops to Algeria (*see* ALGERIAN WAR) and his failure to back the EUROPEAN DEFENCE COMMUNITY lost him support, forcing his resignation on 5 February 1955. Seen initially as new blood who might be able to break free of the indecisive and weak governments endemic in the FOURTH REPUBLIC, he was able to make only a beginning on domestic reforms before he lost office. His attempts out of office to weld the Radical Party into an effective force proved fruitless, serving merely to divide it between his supporters and those opposed to him. He served as a minister again in 1956, but returned to opposition thereafter, opposing de Gaulle's return in 1958 and his policies in the FIFTH REPUBLIC. The career of Mendés-France represented the failure of the old Radical Party to create an effective basis for support in post-war France. Although he was widely admired, he lacked the parliamentary support to achieve a permanent power base. *See also* DECOLONIZATION.

D. Pickles, *France and Algeria* (1963)
P. Williams, *Crisis and Compromise* (1964)
A. Short, *The Origins of the Vietnam War* (1989)

**Mensheviks.** Before 1917 the non-Leninist faction of the RUSSIAN SOCIAL DEMOCRATIC LABOUR PARTY, their name referring to their temporary 'minority' status in a vote taken by the party in 1903. Although working with the Bolsheviks prior to 1914, the Mensheviks were divided between those who were prepared to seek representation in the DUMA and assist the PROVISIONAL GOVERNMENT after the Russian Revolution in fighting the Germans, and those, led by MARTOV, who opposed this policy. Many were increasingly repelled by the Bolsheviks, and attempts to reunite Bolshevik and Menshevik factions also foundered on Lenin's uncompromising position. Although the Mensheviks contained many of the most internationally-minded and Europeanized of the Russian Marxists, they had far less popular support than either the Bolsheviks or the SOCIALIST REVOLUTIONARY PARTY. Their divisions were revealed at the Second All-Russian Congress on 7 November 1917, when many Mensheviks withdrew from the Congress rather than support the Bolshevik seizure of power. Although a handful of Mensheviks were represented on the new Central Executive Committee of the Soviet Congress and 16 were elected to the Constituent Assembly in January 1918, their influence was increasingly marginalized. Although there was some revival of Menshevik support in the spring of 1918 and the party was reunited under Martov's leadership in May, in June they were expelled from the Central Executive Committee and from all Soviets throughout the country, while also being harassed by the arrest of members and the closure of their press. A further wave of arrests followed in spring 1919, then, following Menshevik support for the strikes and protests in Petrograd in 1921, Lenin set out finally to crush them as a counter-revolutionary group. By then Martov had already gone abroad and there were no leaders to replace his influence. Thereafter the term 'Menshevik' was associated with counter-revolution and used as a charge against individuals in the purges.

L. H. Harrison, *The Russian Marxists and the Origins of Bolshevism* (1955)
A. Ascher (ed.), *The Mensheviks in the Russian Revolution* (1976)

**Merger Treaty.** Treaty of 1965 which established a single COUNCIL OF MINISTERS and a single Commission for the EUROPEAN ECONOMIC COMMUNITY, the EUROPEAN COAL AND STEEL COMMUNITY and EURATOM (*see* COMMISSION OF THE EUROPEAN COMMUNITY).

**Metaxas, Joannis** (1871–1941). Greek soldier and dictator. He served with distinction in the Graeco-Turkish War, 1897, and the Balkan Wars, 1912–13. He was Deputy Chief of Staff of the Greek army at the outbreak of the First World War and pro-German in sympathies, reinforcing the position of the monarch, CONSTANTINE I, in opposition to the pro-Entente premier, VENIZELOS. Acting as liaison between Constantine and the Central Powers, he connived at the Bulgarian seizure of Greek outposts, purged pro-Entente officers from the army, and tried to persuade the King to leave Athens and rally the army to him in the north of the country. Removed to a junior posting by Allied pressure in August 1916, he organized pro-royalist paramilitary and guerrilla forces in preparation for Greece's entry to the war on the side of the Central Powers. He went into exile when Constantine was forced to abdicate in June 1917. Following the declaration of a Republic in 1924, Metaxas led the Monarchist Party in opposition to his old opponent Venizelos. Following the abortive coup by Venizelos's supporters in March 1935 he was instrumental in bringing George II (reigned 1935–47) to the throne in November. In March 1936 he was made Minister of War and became Prime Minister on 13 April. Parliamentary deadlock caused by the coalition of 15 communist deputies with the liberal opposition in a 'popular front' and a series of strikes and revolts in Salonika in May led Metaxas to adjourn parliament indefinitely. A call for a political general strike on 4 August, led by the communists, demanding a popular front government, led Metaxas to proclaim a dictatorship. Although his regime showed some fascist elements, he improved the army, developed agriculture, and built up the infrastructure of the country through public works. His army reforms and his own generalship contributed to the humiliating reverses inflicted on the Italian armies in their invasion of Greece in the autumn of 1940. He died in Athens on 29 January 1941 after a short illness, leaving no obvious successor.

M. Cervi, *The Hollow Legions: Mussolini's Blunder in Greece, 1940–1941* (1971)
D. Close, 'Conservatism, authoritarianism and fascism in Greece, 1915–45' in M. Blinkhorn (ed.), *Fascists and Conservatives* (1990)

**MGB.** Abbreviated Russian name for the Ministry of State Security responsible for the security police under STALIN after 1946. Its functions were separated from the MVD, the Ministry of Internal Affairs, responsible for the police forces, public order and the labour camps. Headed by V. S. Abakumov (to 1951) and then S. D. Ignatiev, it was responsible for the PURGES of Stalin's later years. Following Stalin's death, BERIA, the head of the MVD, amalgamated it with the MGB bringing all the security forces under his control, a manoeuvre which contributed to his downfall and arrest in July 1953. The security functions were then taken over by the KGB (*see* KGB) and placed under firmer party control. *See also* NKGB.

R. Hingey, *The Russian Secret Police* (1970)
B. Levytsky, *The Uses of Terror: The Soviet Secret Service, 1917–1970* (1971)

**MI5.** Division 5 of the British Directorate of Military Intelligence, established in 1916 to take over counter-espionage work from the former MO5 (Military Operations

Directorate), which was established in 1904. Since 1916 MI5 has been active in counter-espionage both within and outside Britain. MI6, the Secret Intelligence Service (SIS), is responsible for intelligence work in foreign countries. It is, however, well known for its failures, particularly its failure to stop the defection to the USSR of two communist spies, Guy Burgess and Donald MacLean, in May 1951, both of whom had worked for a number of years in MI5 and MI6. MI5 then investigated Harold (Kim) Philby, another employee who was known to be close to the defectors. They failed to establish that Philby was also a spy, and he defected on 23 January 1963. They were, however, successful in identifying a fourth man, Anthony Blunt, but he was granted immunity from prosecution. His identity was revealed in 1979.

C. Andrew, *The Mobilization of British Intelligence for Two World Wars* (1980)
N. West, *MI5* (1983)

**MI6.** See MI5

**Milice Française.** Paramilitary body formed early in 1943 from a right-wing group, Joseph Darnand's Service d'Ordre Légionnaire, to provide counter-terrorist forces in Vichy France. At its peak it had 45,000 members who were engaged in policing their own areas against resistance groups and operating to suppress armed attacks. *See also* VICHY GOVERNMENT.

D. Littlejohn, *The Patriotic Traitors* (1972)
R. O. Paxton, *Vichy France* (1972)

**Military Revolutionary Committee** (MRC). Body set up by the Petrograd Soviet on 25 October 1917 to monitor troop movements in the capital and prepare for the seizure of power. Although dominated by the BOLSHEVIKS and chaired by TROTSKY as head of the Petrograd Soviet, it also contained membership from other revolutionary parties. Operating from the same headquarters as the Bolshevik Central Committee at the Smolny Institute, it directed the seizure of key points by the RED GUARDS. The MRC was also charged with protecting the new Bolshevik government once the seizure of power had taken place, organizing the resistance to KERENSKY's counter-offensive on 12 November. The MRC then took over civil administrative functions such as the supply of food to Petrograd by the use of forced requisitioning, the enforcement of the press decrees of the Bolshevik government, and the control of exit and residence permits. The MRC, numbering as many as 82 members at one point, was finally dissolved on 18 December 1917, and its functions distributed amongst various bodies. *See also* RUSSIAN REVOLUTION.

E. H. Carr, *The Bolshevik Revolution, 1917–23* (3 vols., 1966)
R. Service, *The Bolshevik Party in Revolution, 1917–1923* (1979)

**Mindszenty, Joseph** (1892–1975). Cardinal and Primate of Hungary, ordained 1915; Monsignor 1937; Bishop 1944. Anti-Nazi views led to his arrest in 1944–5. Installed as Primate of Hungary, 1945; made a Cardinal, 1947. He was arrested in December 1948 by the Communist régime on charges of treason and currency offences and was sentenced to penal servitude for life in February 1949; this was commuted to house detention in July 1955. Freed during the HUNGARIAN UPRISING, he took refuge in the American Legation when it was suppressed. He remained there until 1971, refusing to accept the reconciliation between the Vatican and the Hungarian government in 1964. In 1971 he left Budapest for Vienna, eventually retiring to Rome. A stubborn opponent of Communism and for long a symbol of resistance in Hungary, his pro-Habsburg, conservative views became an embarrassment in a period of rapprochement between the Vatican and the Communist régimes of eastern Europe.

**Mir.** Name for Russian village communities which provided peasant self-government in rural areas and were in charge of collecting taxes and the administration of land following the emancipation decree of 1861. The *mir* was at the centre of populist and SOCIALIST REVOLUTIONARY PARTY proposals for the peasantry. The adoption by the Bolsheviks of the Socialist Revolutionary proposal for the socialization of all land in their Land Decree of November 1917 and its distribution on an egalitarian basis by the *mir* breathed new life into an institution which had suffered erosion with the growth of peasant proprietorship and larger landholdings under the Stolypin land reforms prior to 1914. In spite of the effects of WAR COMMUNISM and famine, the years after 1917 have been called the 'hey-day of the *mir*'. The very slow growth of state and collective farms, the weakness of the Bolsheviks in rural areas, and the adoption of the NEW ECONOMIC POLICY meant that the *mir* remained the basis for local administrative duties and tax collection under the rural soviets. It was only with the campaign of 'de-Kulakization' and wholesale COLLECTIVIZATION in 1928–9 that the *mir* structure was effectively dismantled through the liquidation of village notables and the breakup of the peasant landholdings established since 1917 (*see* KULAKS).

M. Lewin, *Russian Peasants and Soviet Power* (1968)
D. J. Male, *Russian Peasant Organisation before Collectivization* (1971)

**Mitterrand, François** (1916–). French politician, the fourth President of the Fifth Republic. Born at Angoulême, he was educated at the University of Paris. His war service was distinguished; he was taken prisoner-of-war in 1940, but escaped to join the RESISTANCE; he was sent to London in 1943, later to Algeria, and awarded the Croix de Guerre. He entered politics as a Socialist deputy for Nièvre *département*, serving as a deputy until 1980 with a three-year break as Senator in 1959–62. He gained experience as a minister in various coalition governments from 1947, emerging in 1965 as the Left's presidential candidate against DE GAULLE. Although defeated, he gained almost 45 per cent of the vote, and his success led to further moves to create a more united party of the Left. Hindered by Mitterrand's lack of an organizational base, the divisions caused by the events of 1968, and personal rivalries, the Left fared badly in the legislative elections of 1968, and the Socialists even worse in the 1969 presidential elections, taking only 5 per cent of the vote. The result was the creation of the Parti Socialiste (PS, *see* SOCIALIST PARTY, FRENCH) in 1971 as a federation of the Left with Mitterrand as First Secretary. He undertook a *rapprochement* with the Communists and signed a joint manifesto with them in 1972 (*see* COMMUNIST PARTY, FRENCH). His candidature in the 1974 presidential elections saw him ahead on the first

ballot; in the final ballot he obtained 49 per cent of the vote. The Socialists had already proved themselves a revived force in the 1973 legislative elections, taking over 20 per cent of the vote for the first time since 1946. When the Communists withdrew from the common programme in 1978, the Socialists were able to poll more than their former allies in the Assembly elections shortly afterwards. In May 1981 Mitterrand secured a clear victory in the presidential elections over GISCARD D'ESTAING, followed quickly by elections for the Assembly which secured a decisive victory, the Socialists obtaining an absolute majority for the first time in their history. Although four Communist ministers came into the cabinet of Pierre Mauroy, the Communists had suffered a serious decline in their fortunes. Mitterrand was able to inaugurate the Socialist programme of NATIONALIZATION, but ran into serious economic difficulties as the depression of the early 1980s affected France. Soaring imports, rising inflation, the franc under pressure, and growing government debts forced a choice between austerity and socialist commitments. In March 1983 Mitterrand acted decisively, reshuffling the cabinet and imposing a crisis economic package which increased taxes and slashed government spending under the direction of JACQUES DELORS as Minister of Finance. Mitterrand's major achievement was to keep the Socialists united behind the policy of *rigueur*. The withdrawal of the Communist ministers in July 1984 exposed him to an all-out attack from the Left; he reacted by adopting expansionist policies of economic liberalism and tax cuts and the appointment of a young technocrat, Laurent Fabius, to replace Mauroy on 15 July 1984. The 1986 elections saw Mitterrand's Socialists lose seats, but not as savagely as expected; they remained the largest party, with 206 seats. Mitterrand was, nonetheless, forced to accept a Gaullist Prime Minister, CHIRAC, thus beginning almost two years of 'cohabitation'. Mitterrand stood by his presidential powers while his Prime Minister's popularity declined, faced by public-sector strikes and student unrest. Mitterrand had kept open the question of his candidature in the 1988 presidential elections, and was the last to enter the race on 22 March 1988. He campaigned on a programme which now owed little to socialism and appealed to the centre voters, calling for European integration, economic modernization and increased investment in welfare and education. Increasingly offering himself as a candidate for a 'united France', he secured a landslide victory on 8 May in the run-off against Chirac, securing over 50 per cent of the votes in 77 of the 96 metropolitan departments. He appointed the Socialist Michel Rocard Prime Minister, then dissolved the Assembly to seek a majority. In the May 1988 elections the PS failed to obtain an overall majority but was able to govern with the support of the centre. Since 1988 Mitterrand has been able to remain above minor scandals affecting the Socialist government and led the party to fresh successes in the 1989 municipal elections.

Mitterrand has achieved a position enjoyed by few other French Socialist politicians in France this century. Assisted by the decline of the Communists and the rise of the PS to be the major party of the Left he has been able to broaden its appeal to the centre voters by abandoning much of the distinctively socialist programme while retaining France's nuclear defences, a strong presidency and a liberal economic regime. Current debate centres around whether Mitterrand's successes are largely personal and whether his 'de-ideologized' PS can maintain power after he has gone.

D. S. Bell and C. Coates, *The Left in France* (1983)
J. W. Friend, *Seven Years in France: François Mitterrand and the Unintended Revolution 1981–1988* (1989)

**MKP.** Magyar Kommunista Part. *See* COMMUNIST PARTY, HUNGARIAN.

**Mola, Emilio** (1887–1937). Spanish general. He organized the conspiracy which brought about the SPANISH CIVIL WAR. Born of a military family, he was commissioned into the infantry in 1907, serving with the Moorish forces after 1910. He was promoted Brigade General in 1927, and served as Director of General Security, then as garrison commander in Morocco, but was recalled to command Pamplona under the Popular Front. Initially a lukewarm Republican, he became involved in plots against the Popular Front, which he hoped to replace by more orderly but still Republican

government. Recognized as the director of the plot, he sought support from the FALANGE, Carlists (*see* CARLISM) and other right-wing groups. On 19 July 1936 he issued a proclamation for a revolt in northern Spain in conjunction with FRANCO's arrangements to ferry the Army of Africa across the Straits of Gibraltar. His Army of the North seized control of the principal towns of Navarre and Castile. He formed the Junta de Defensa Nacional which approved Franco as Generalissimo, but he was unhappy at Franco's being proclaimed head of state. His forces seized Irun on 4 September, cutting the Republican Basque country off from contact with France. His attempts to mount a converging attack on Madrid from the north proved a failure, and he turned his attention in March 1937 to subduing the Basque country. His army was still engaged in the campaign when he was killed in an air crash on 3 June. He was one of the potential rivals to Franco with a strong basis of support in the army; his death removed one of the Nationalists' more effective generals.

H. Thomas, *The Spanish Civil War* (1977)

**Moldavia.** Ancient principality and one of the 'Danubian Principalities' which were amalgamated into the state of Romania in the 19th century, leaving part of the Moldavian population living in the Russian Empire. On 12 October 1924 the Soviet Union created the Moldavian Autonomous Soviet Socialist Republic with its boundary with Romania on the River Dniester. The former Moldavian Soviet Socialist Republic included the earlier Autonomous Republic and areas of Bessarabia ceded by Romania to the USSR on 28 June 1940 with a largely Moldavian population. Since 1985 there had been open agitation for greater national autonomy on the part of the Moldavians within the Soviet Union, leading in August 1991 to a declaration of an independent 'Moldova'. The population of the Soviet Republic in 1984 was just over 4 million people, of whom 64 per cent were Moldavians. *See also* BESSARABIA.

**Mollet, Guy** (1905–75). French Socialist politician. A schoolteacher in Arras before the Second World War, he served in the RESISTANCE. He became Socialist Deputy for Pas-de-Calais in October 1945, and was Secretary-General of the French Socialist Party, 1946–68. He was Premier from January 1956 to May 1957 in the longest-lasting government of the FOURTH REPUBLIC, heading a centre-left coalition of Radicals and Socialists. Mollet's ability to act decisively was limited by the large bloc of 147 Communist seats in the Assembly (a quarter of the deputies), and the presence of over 50 POUJADISTS. The influence of the Algerian settlers also acted as a brake upon movement towards a settlement of the ALGERIAN WAR, which was one of Mollet's chief ambitions. Mollet visited Algiers in February 1956, where he was met by hostile demonstrators and soon gave up any positive attempts at reconciling the conflict. He continued the policy of repression, losing the support of MENDÉS-FRANCE in May and several Socialists who either resigned or were expelled. Virtually a prisoner of the more conservative forces in the Assembly, Mollet was seen increasingly as a reactionary figure, a view confirmed by his authorization of the Suez invasion in November 1956 (*see* SUEZ CRISIS). He was brought down, however, not over Suez, but over tax reform proposals to finance the Algerian War. After his resignation, he was involved in attempts to organize an effective Socialist opposition to de Gaulle, largely unsuccessful. He retired from active politics in 1971.

D. Pickles, *Algeria and France* (1963)
P. M. Williams, *Crisis and Compromise* (1964)
H. Thomas, *The Suez Affair* (1967)

**Molotov, Vyacheslav** (1890–1986). Soviet statesman. His family name was Skriabin, but he adopted 'Molotov' ('hammer') as a cover. He joined the Bolsheviks in 1905, served a period of exile in 1909–11, then assisted in editing PRAVDA. A leading member of the Petrograd party he was a member of the MILITARY REVOLUTIONARY COMMITTEE at the time of the October Revolution, becoming head of the party organization in the Ukraine, 1921–5, Second Secretary of the Central Committee, 1921–30, and a member of the Politburo from 1921. He sided with STALIN over the SOVIET INDUSTRIALIZATION DEBATE and helped to undertake the FIVE YEAR PLANS, becoming Chairman of the Council of People's Commissars, 1930–41. In May 1939 he took over as Commissar for

foreign affairs from LITVINOV, negotiated the NAZI-SOVIET PACT of August 1939, and the negotiations with Finland which preceded the RUSSO-FINNISH WAR of 1939–40. A member of the State Defence Committee 1941–5, he remained Commissar for foreign affairs until March 1949, conducting negotiations with the Western Allies and then building up the Eastern bloc during the early COLD WAR. His influence declined following Stalin's death, but he resumed the conduct of foreign affairs, negotiating the AUSTRIAN STATE TREATY in 1955. He quarrelled with KHRUSHCHEV's policy of reconciliation with TITO. He became Minister of State Control in June 1956, but was expelled from his party posts as part of the 'anti-party opposition' in 1957 and was made ambassador to Mongolia, 1957–60. In 1960 he was appointed as the Soviet delegate to the International Atomic Energy Agency in Vienna and retired shortly afterwards. Immensely able, and once the youngest member of the Politburo, Molotov was a staunch Stalinist who played a key role in the rise of the Soviet Union as a superpower. *See also* SECOND WORLD WAR.

G. Kennan, *Russia and the West under Lenin and Stalin* (1961)
W. H. McNeill, *America, Britain and Russia: Their Co-Operation and Conflict, 1941–46* (1970)
V. Mastny, *Russia's Road to the Cold War* (1979)

**monetarism.** Term which acquired general currency from the 1970s for policy of controlling the money supply in order to influence the operation of the economy. In contrast to the policies associated with JOHN MAYNARD KEYNES, money supply was seen as the central feature in managing the economy and drew upon the ideas of the American economist Milton Friedman (1912–). Monetary targets were set by the International Monetary Fund for the British Labour Government in 1976 as a condition of granting credit facilities. The adoption of monetary targets meant that the Public Sector Borrowing Requirement and money supply measures became important economic indicators, and these policies were adopted by the THATCHER government from 1979 to control inflation. Monetarist policies led to major cuts in government spending, greater reliance upon market forces, and setting of targets for future reductions in government borrowing. Some relaxation of strict adherence to monetary control was noted by commentators during Mrs Thatcher's second term of office, as doubts accumulated about the practical and theoretical aspects of the monetary policy. Less weight was attached to formal monetary targets and a wider range of economic policies and indicators employed to manage the economy, although money supply remained as an important aspect of economic management.

K. Minogue and M. Biddiss (eds.), *Thatcherism: Personality and Politics* (1987)

**Monnet, Jean** (1888–1979) French economist and diplomat. Born in Cognac, France, he began his working life in North America representing his family brandy firm. In the First World War he proposed and organized the joint Anglo-French Supply Commission, so that Britain and France could co-operate, not compete, to obtain badly needed raw materials. In 1919, aged 31, he became Deputy Secretary of the LEAGUE OF NATIONS. In 1923 he returned to the family business, and thereafter until the Second World War pursued a varied business career, including two years in China. In 1939 he became Chairman of the Franco-British Committee for Economic Co-ordination, and in 1940 proposed to CHURCHILL and DE GAULLE a scheme for political union between Britain and France. He served as a member of the British Supply Council in Washington, and then in Algiers as a member of the French National Liberation Committee. In 1945 he devised and presided over the setting up of French planning, one of the major post-war French economic and administrative achievements. As head of French planning he produced, in 1950, and persuaded ROBERT SCHUMAN to adopt, the SCHUMAN PLAN. He became the first President of the High Authority of the EUROPEAN COAL AND STEEL COMMUNITY on its foundation in 1952. He resigned in 1955 to set up the Monnet Action Committee for the United States of Europe, comprising major political figures from all the non-communist parties and from the non-communist trade unions. By 1969 it had been enlarged to include representatives of the political parties in the countries that had applied for membership. Monnet, with this committee, played a most important role in the development of events and ideas that led to the foundation of the EUROPEAN ECONOMIC COMMUNITY and EURATOM, and to their subsequent enlargement. His name is frequently linked with the notion that economic integration will develop an impetus that will lead to increased unity, possibly under supra-national institutions, and to eventual political union. By the 1970s Monnet himself admitted that this was not necessarily the inevitable way forward for the European Community.

R. Mayne, *The Recovery of Europe: From Devastation to Unity* (1970)

**Montenegro.** Independent Balkan principality under Nicholas Petrovic Njego, as King Nicholas I, 1910–18. Montenegro supported Serbia in the conflict with Austria in 1914 but was overrun with Serbia by the combined offensive of the Central Powers in 1915, forcing Nicholas into exile. In 1918, an assembly at Podgorica deposed the dynasty and voted for union with SERBIA. Montenegro therefore became absorbed in the new Kingdom of Serbs, Croats and Slovenes, proclaimed in December 1918 and renamed Yugoslavia in 1929. Montenegrin identity was recognized when Montenegro was named as one of the six federal republics under the 1946 constitution.

**Montgomery, Bernard** (1887–1976). British general. The son of a bishop, he joined the Royal Warwickshire Regiment from Sandhurst in 1908. Although wounded in the chest in 1914 he returned to France in 1916. He rose to the rank of Lieutenant-Colonel and battalion commander by the end of the war. In 1940 he was evacuated from Dunkirk with the 3rd Division which he was commanding. By December 1941 he was head of South-Eastern Command and a Lieutenant-General. Montgomery was chosen to command the 8th Army in North Africa in 1942. He transformed the army so that it was able to halt ROMMEL's attack at El Alamein then move onto the offensive, beginning 24 October. The battle, well planned and methodically accomplished, was a British victory. He led the invasion of Sicily and Italy, then was appointed land commander for the invasion of Europe ('Operation Overlord'). He came into conflict over personal and strategic matters with his American allies, especially over the question of 'narrow' or 'broad' front assault into Germany in 1944–5. After the war he was chief of the imperial general staff and deputy commander of NATO forces (*see* NORTH ATLANTIC TREATY ORGANIZATION). He was created Viscount Montgomery. *See also* EISENHOWER, SECOND WORLD WAR.

E. Belfield and A. Essame, *The Battle for Normandy* (1965)
R. Lamb, *Montgomery in Europe, 1943–5* (1983)

**Morgenthau Plan.** Proposal made by US Secretary of the Treasury Henry Morgenthau (1891–1967) at the Quebec conference between ROOSEVELT and CHURCHILL on 13–16 September 1944. Roosevelt and Churchill accepted his suggestion that Germany should be 'pastoralized' – that all industry be removed from the country – but both the US State Department and the British Foreign Office considered the idea absurd, seeing no point in subsidizing a rural Germany after the war. The Nazis made much of the proposal in their attempts to encourage resistance to the Allied armies.

**Moro, Aldo** (1916–78). Italian politician. A Christian Democrat deputy from 1948 and leader of the party from 1959, he served as Foreign Minister, 1965–6, 1969–72, 1973–4, and Prime Minister, 1963–8, 1974–6. He played a leading role in the EUROPEAN ECONOMIC COMMUNITY and helped to construct the 'historic compromise' by which the communists gave their support to the CHRISTIAN DEMOCRATIC PARTY to combat ITALIAN TERRORISM. On 16 March 1978 he was abducted in Rome by members of the Red Brigade, followed by a series of letters allegedly written by him, pleading with the government to exchange him for Red Brigade prisoners. The government refused and on 9 May Moro's body was found in Rome.

**Morrison, Herbert** (1888–1965). British Labour politician and cabinet minister. The son of a drunken policeman, Morrison became secretary of the London Labour Party in 1915. Both there and nationally in the 1920s he led the fight to exclude communists from the party. From 1922 he was a member of London County Council (LCC),

and he was an MP, 1923–4, 1929–31 and 1935–59. In the SECOND LABOUR GOVERNMENT he was Minister of Transport and a loyal admirer of RAMSAY MACDONALD, whom he almost followed into the NATIONAL GOVERNMENT. Defeated at the 1931 election, Morrison concentrated on London, and in 1934, under him, Labour won control of the LCC for the first time. In 1935 he hoped to become Labour leader, but was defeated by CLEMENT ATTLEE, and his efforts to oust Attlee in 1939 and 1945 also met with failure. During the Second World War he was an effective Home Secretary. In 1945 he became Lord President of the Council, and masterminded the Labour government's nationalization programme. He ensured that the public corporation form, by which industries were run by autonomous boards without trade union representation, was the one adopted. By 1950 he was concerned to 'consolidate' Labour's achievements, but this was an unexciting cry for most Labourites, and his waning fortunes were confirmed by an unsuccessful spell as Foreign Secretary (1951). He hoped to succeed Attlee as party leader, but the latter stayed on until 1955, partly to block his old rival's ambition, and in the leadership election which followed, Morrison came a humiliating third behind HUGH GAITSKELL and ANEURIN BEVAN. He then largely withdrew from Labour politics, received a life peerage in 1959, and wrote rather misleading memoirs.

Morrison had a long, distinguished and effective career, but was seen as arrogant, and aroused the distrust and even hatred of many colleagues. He often seemed too concerned about London. In addition, his favoured form of nationalization produced an inefficient state sector, which added to the arguments of Labour's critics.

Lord Morrison of Lambeth, *An Autobiography* (1960)
B. Donoughue and G. W. Jones, *Herbert Morrison: Portrait of a Politician* (1973)

**Mosley, Oswald** (1896–1980). British politician. After fighting in the First World War he became Conservative MP for Harrow, 1918–22, but sat as an independent 1922–4 before becoming Labour MP for Smethwick, 1926–31. He was appointed Chancellor of the Duchy of Lancaster in the SECOND LABOUR GOVERNMENT in 1929 but was frustrated by the refusal of the leadership to adopt his policies to deal with mass unemployment. He resigned and founded the NEW PARTY, which proved unsuccessful in the 1931 general election. He formed the BRITISH UNION OF FASCISTS in 1932, which adopted fascist-style uniforms and rallies. Its policies were explicitly anti-communist, also advocating protection, and modernization of British institutions and economy. The brutality of the behaviour of his followers at the Olympia meeting in 1934 lost him support and the backing of the influential *Daily Mail*. He increasingly turned to ANTI-SEMITISM to build up a following, but obtained only limited backing and earned considerable opposition. The Public Order Act of 1936 restricted the wearing of uniforms, and Mosley had little success in developing the movement thereafter. In 1940 he was interned, but was released in 1943. He returned to politics after 1945, leading the Union Party and opposing coloured immigration. An intelligent and in some ways progressive figure, Mosley's adoption of fascism isolated him from mainstream politics, leaving him waiting to take power in a crisis which never occurred. The stability of British politics under the NATIONAL GOVERNMENT and the recovery from the depression further limited his appeal. Anti-Semitism proved a double-edged policy, earning Mosley the contempt of the liberal, educated classes and making his career a study in political failure.

O. Mosley, *Greater Britain* (1932)
R. Skidelsky, *Oswald Mosley* (1975)
R. Thurlow, *Fascism in Britain* (1988)

**Motor Tractor Station.** *See* COLLECTIVIZATION, SOVIET.

**Moulin, Jean** (1899–1943). French resistance hero. The youngest Prefect in France in 1939, based at Chartres, he quarrelled with the Germans over his duties and attempted to commit suicide in June 1940. Dismissed from office, he retired to Provence. He contacted the RESISTANCE groups in the south and went to London in 1941 to contact DE GAULLE. Accepting de Gaulle's leadership he returned to France on 1 January 1942 and travelled through France persuading the resistance groups in the south to unite in the Mouvement Unis de Résist-

ance in March 1943. By May he created the national body, the Conseil National de la Résistance, pledged to support de Gaulle. On 21 June he was captured at Lyons and died under torture without revealing any information. He had performed the crucial feat of unifying the French resistance movement under de Gaulle's leadership leading to his emergence as *de facto* head of state after the Liberation. *See also* FREE FRENCH.

H Michel, *Jean Moulin l'unificateur* (2nd edn, 1971)
M. R. D. Foot, *Resistance* (1976)

**Mountbatten, Louis** (1900–1979). British naval commander. At the outbreak of the Second World War Mountbatten was commanding the Fifth Destroyer Flotilla. In 1941 his ship, HMS *Kelly*, was sunk in the Mediterranean and he was nearly drowned. He was appointed adviser on combined operations. His largest operation was the Dieppe Raid in August 1942, which, though a failure, taught valuable lessons. Mountbatten was then appointed Supreme Commander in South-East Asia, arriving in India in October 1943 to find a diversity of problems, but overseeing eventual victory over the Japanese. After the war he was viceroy of India and presided over the partition of the subcontinent and the independence of India and Pakistan. He later returned to a naval career. In 1955 he was First Sea Lord and in 1959 Chief of the Defence Staff. He was assassinated by Irish extremists in 1979.

P. Ziegler, *Mountbatten* (1985)

**Mouvement Républicain Populaire** (MRP). French Christian Democrat organization, constituted in 1944 at Lyons and drawing support from members of the Catholic Resistance and the expansion of catholic trade union and social organizations prior to the Second World War. Its aims were to regenerate French political life. By August 1945 it had 100,000 members and in the October 1945 elections it secured 4.75 million votes, 25 per cent of the total, and 141 deputies. Its success in part lay as a bulwark against communism, and it obtained further advances in 1946, reaching a peak of 28 per cent of the vote and 160 deputies. Increasingly, however, its support was attracted by DE GAULLE's Rassemblement du Peuple Français (RPF) founded on

7 April 1947. Although the MRP forbade its members to join, many of its voters deserted it for the RPF. In the municipal elections of October 1947, the MRP had fallen to 10 per cent of the vote, compared with 25 per cent the previous year. The MRP was permanently reduced as a political force, returning 82 deputies with just over 12 per cent of the vote in 1951, a strength it largely maintained until 1962 when it fell to 37 seats with 9 per cent of the vote. Squeezed between the Gaullists of the UDR, which leaned towards the Catholic Church in its legislation, and the reorganizing forces on the Left, the MRP finally dissolved itself in 1967. As a party, it had participated in every government of the FOURTH REPUBLIC, providing five Prime Ministers and two foreign ministers. From the rise of Gaullism, however, it was confined to a minor electoral role. *See also* GAULLISM.

P. Williams, *Politics in Post-War France* (1954)
R. E. M. Irving, *Christian Democracy in France* (1973)

**Munich Agreement.** Signed on 29 September 1938 as a settlement of the SUDETENLAND problem. Following the successful accomplishment of the ANSCHLUSS Hitler brought pressure to bear in late March on Czechoslovakia through the leader of the Sudeten Germans, HENLEIN, urging him to make such demands on the Czech state as would break it up. When war between Czechs and Germans seemed imminent in May, Britain feared that French support for the Czechs would precipitate a general war. On 3 August Britain sent Lord Runciman on a mission to arbitrate between the Sudeten Germans and the Czechs. When Hitler rejected the settlement proposed and both France and Germany stood mobilized, Chamberlain flew to meet Hitler at BERCHTESGADEN on 15 September. An agreement on discussions on self-determination for the Sudeten Germans was agreed. But a second visit to Hitler on 22 September was met by Hitler's demand for almost immediate German occupation of the Sudetenland. With the two sides deadlocked and Britain mobilizing for war, Hitler on 28 September agreed to an international conference at Munich. On 29 September the Munich Conference met, attended by HITLER, MUSSOLINI, CHAMBERLAIN and DALADIER. On the 30th an agreement was signed, transferring the Sudetenland to Germany, including most of the Czech frontier defences and providing for other minor territorial concessions to Poland and Hungary at Czechoslovakia's expense. The Czechs, who were not consulted, were compelled to accept, but had their remaining frontiers guaranteed. Chamberlain also unilaterally obtained Hitler's signature to a piece of paper in which war was renounced between the two states in favour of negotiation.

The agreement was met with great relief in the West and in Germany, where it appeared war had been averted. Chamberlain flew back to London in triumph. Misgivings about the morality of the agreement were widespread but were undermined by the case the Sudeten Germans had for self-determination and the threat of war. The remnants of Czechoslovakia soon crumbled, Slovakia was granted autonomy on 6 October and proclaimed itself a Slovak 'Free State' under its leader, Josef Tiso (1887–1947) on 14 March 1939. A day later German troops marched into the rest of Czechoslovakia and occupied Prague. Chamberlain and the West averted war, but at considerable cost to the Czechs. For Britain and France the most valuable outcome was the clear evidence, especially from March 1939, that Hitler was totally untrustworthy, and a breathing space for increasingly hectic rearmament. On the debit side, a potentially defensible barrier to Hitler had been surrendered, and in such a way as to convince Hitler (and also Stalin) that the West was unwilling to fight. As a result one outcome of the Munich agreement was the NAZI-SOVIET PACT of August 1939.

Munich has been endlessly debated, Chamberlain was the key initiator of attempts to prevent a war, and it formed the high point of his APPEASEMENT strategy. It was justifiable in his terms as an alternative to a war which his defence chiefs told him Britain was unready to fight. It was also a consistent attempt to bring Hitler into a peaceable framework of negotiated settlement. CHURCHILL called it 'a defeat without a war'.

K. Robbins, *Munich* (1968)
R. Overy and A. Wheatcroft, *The Road to War* (1989)

**MRC.** *See* MILITARY REVOLUTIONARY COMMITTEE.

**MRP.** *See* MOUVEMENT RÉPUBLICAIN POPULAIRE.

**multilateralism.** *See* UNILATERALISM.

**Munich Putsch.** An abortive attempt by HITLER and the NAZI PARTY on 8–9 November 1923 to seize power in Bavaria as a prelude to the overthrow of the national government of the WEIMAR REPUBLIC through a 'March on Berlin', imitating Mussolini's successful MARCH ON ROME. The background to the putsch was formed by the Franco-Belgian RUHR OCCUPATION in January 1923, the hyper-inflation and collapse of the German economy which this promoted, and the apparent polarization of Weimar politics and loss of authority by the central government as communist-dominated paramilitary units were formed in Saxony and Thuringia. Although the right-wing Bavarian authorities were sympathetic to Hitler's plans to overthrow the Weimar state and install a conservative government headed by Ludendorff, they were reluctant to support him openly until they could be certain of the support of right-wing groups in North Germany and of the Army. Hitler, who feared that the STRESEMANN government was getting a grip on the crisis by early November 1923, was also under pressure to go ahead with the planned uprising from activists within the Nazi Party; and decided to force the situation. Yet the support he seemed to have secured from the Bavarian State Commissioner (Kahr), the commander of the Bavarian Military District (von Lossow) and the commander of the Bavarian paramilitary police (von Seisser), at a stormy meeting in a Munich beer-hall on the evening of 8 November, had evaporated by the following morning: when Hitler, together with Ludendorff, led a march into the centre of Munich, a gun battle with the police ensued in which 16 marchers were killed and the leaders of the putsch arrested. The significance of the abortive putsch became clear when Hitler, Ludendorff and other conspirators were tried in February 1924. Hitler was able to turn the trial into a propaganda triumph and to establish his reputation as the most promi-nent of the extreme right-wing nationalist opponents of the Weimar Republic. The right-wing judges acquitted Ludendorff, despite clear evidence of his involvement in the uprising, and gave Hitler the minimum possible sentence of five years' imprisonment, with the clear indication that he would be released on probation after a few months.

H. J. Gordon, *Hitler and the Beer Hall Putsch* (1972)
J. Noakes and G. Pridham (eds.), *Nazism, 1919–1945*, vol. 1: *The Rise to Power* (1983)

**Mussolini, Benito** (1883–1945). Italian politician and dictator. Born near Forti in the Romagna, he was the son of modest parents, and was influenced by his father's socialism. He took a teaching certificate but emigrated to Switzerland in July 1902, where he worked as a labourer and came into contact with quasi-socialist ideas, though of an élitist and anti-democratic nature. Expelled from Switzerland in November 1904, he performed military service before becoming a teacher and editor of a socialist weekly. He became involved with agitation in the Austrian-controlled region of the Trentino and in the campaign against the war in Libya, and was imprisoned. He became one of the leading members of the left wing of the ITALIAN SOCIALIST PARTY and was active in the expulsion of moderate elements. He was editor of the party newspaper *Avanti!* from November 1912. He broke with the Socialist Party over the question of intervention in the First World War, resigning from *Avanti!* and founding his own pro-interventionist newspaper *Il Popolo d'Italia* in November 1914. Mussolini was drafted into the army following Italy's entry into the war in May 1915. He served on the front, where he was wounded; he returned to edit the paper in Milan. He used the newspaper as a vehicle to unite nationalist and anti-socialist elements. On 23 March 1919 he founded the first FASCI DI COMBATTIMENTO in Milan, committed to a part-leftist, part-nationalist programme, demanding the full implementation of Italy's demands at the PARIS PEACE CONFERENCE. It supported D'ANNUNZIO's seizure of FIUME. In 1920 the Fasci co-operated with GIOLITTI to establish themselves in Parliament, and during 1920–21 spread rapidly in the countryside as a counterweight to socialist agitation. The Fascist Party was formed in November 1921 and Mussolini was able to threaten a seizure of power in the MARCH ON ROME, which led King VICTOR EMMANUEL III to appoint him Prime Minister on 30 October 1922.

Mussolini's first government was a coalition of Fascists, Christian Democrats, Liberals, and Nationalists. In July 1923 he obtained passage of the Acerbo Law, granting two-thirds of all seats in the Chamber to the party with the largest vote: only socialists and communists opposed, with some Christian Democrats abstaining; many conservatives saw it as a means of ensuring stability. In the elections held on 6 April 1924, accompanied by much fascist brutality, Mussolini secured 374 deputies, leaving the opposition to divide up the remaining 161 seats. In June the MATTEOTI CRISIS led to the secession of most of the opposition deputies from the Chamber, but Mussolini retained the support of the King. From January 1925 Mussolini began the construction of a fascist regime with himself as *Il Duce* (leader). A group of laws and decrees on 6 November 1926 – the 'Exceptional Decrees' – dissolved all political parties and anti-fascist organizations, suppressed non-fascist newspapers, cancelled passports, introduced domestic exile for political offences and created a political police. Three days later the fascist majority in the Chamber declared the seats of the absent deputies annulled. The Fascist Grand Council, originally created as a consultative body in December 1922, became the principal organ of the government by a law of 9 December 1928. Presided over by Mussolini and controlled by him, it selected the list of candidates for election to the Chamber and drew up statutes for implementation. Parliament was reformed on 17 May 1928 so that all 400 Deputies were elected by plebiscite as a single list prepared by the Fascist Grand Council. Later, in 1939, the Chamber of Deputies was replaced by the Chamber of Fasces and Corporations, drawing its membership from the Fascist Party National Council, members of the National Council of Corporations, and members of the Fascist Grand Council. Trade unions were dissolved and replaced by fascist institutions which arbitrated between employer and employee. In 1929 a national plebiscite supported the regime and legitimized the transformation of the country into the first fascist state.

Mussolini's policies embraced the agreement with the Catholic Church in the LATERAN PACTS of 1929, which gave the church a privileged position in education, but restricted its role in the social sphere to religious education. A major public works programme was introduced, notably in the construction of railways and roads, electrification, public monuments, urban renewal and land reclamation, spending 25 billion lire from 1922 to 1932, a huge increase on the pre-fascist budgets. Although spending fell after 1932 with the onset of the DEPRESSION, specific projects were commenced to assist the unemployed. In social policy, pro-natalist and health campaigns were introduced, lowering the rate of infant mortality. From 1929 there was increasing emphasis on economic autarky, including a decree of January 1929 requiring all government agencies to purchase only national goods and a decree of September 1931 introducing increased tariff duties. The 'Battle for Grain', begun in 1925 to increase food production and promote peasant life, was intensified.

With visions of recreating a Roman empire in the Mediterranean, Mussolini conducted an agressive foreign policy, seen from an early stage in the Corfu incident of 1923. Relatively quiescent until the mid-1930s, Mussolini launched the conquest of Ethiopia in 1935 which provoked sanctions from the LEAGUE OF NATIONS and his isolation (*see* ETHIOPIAN CRISIS). After Mussolini's initial hostility towards HITLER over the South Tyrol (*see* SOUTH TYROL DISPUTE), their mutual interests in revising European frontiers in their favour drew the two dictatorships together in what became the AXIS in 1936. Attempts at APPEASEMENT of Mussolini were made in the HOARE-LAVAL PACT and during the SPANISH CIVIL WAR, where Mussolini's involvement was disliked but not prevented by Britain and France. He was used as a go-between and was a signatory in the MUNICH AGREEMENT of 1938, but his involvement in the Spanish Civil War pushed him deeper into the alliance with Hitler, as well as seriously weakening the economy. Mussolini remained watchful for gains, and in spring 1939 annexed Albania, but declared non-belligerency in September 1939 because of the weakness of the armed forces. With the incipient fall of France he declared war on Britain and France on 10 June 1940, obtaining Nice. He invaded Greece on 28 October 1940, but suffered severe reverses, followed by defeats in North Africa and in East Africa. The failures of the war and the imminent invasion of the Italian mainland led Victor Emmanuel and Marshal BADOGLIO to force Mussolini's resignation on 25 July 1943. Imprisoned in the Appennines at Gran Sasso, he was rescued by German airborne troops on 12 September 1943 and installed in a puppet republic in northern Italy, known as the Italian Socialist Republic or Republic of Salo. Under virtual German control, it enunciated an anti-capitalist, collective, labour-based economy. Its army under GRAZIANI conducted operations against partisans and anti-fascists. Mussolini attempted to obtain promises from Hitler for better treatment for Italian workers and prisoners in Germany, but the nationalization of essential industries, mass conscription, and anti–Jewish and anti-partisan operations alienated support. Controlling only Milan by April 1945, he was arrested while attempting flight at Lake Como and shot on 28 April 1945, his corpse being publicly displayed in Milan.

Until the rise of Hitler to prominence in the early 1930s, Mussolini was the prototype fascist. He gave the word currency as an activist, authoritarian, and nationalistic movement which proclaimed itself to be both anti-capitalist and anti-communist. He developed the concept of the CORPORATE STATE, with its emphasis on forms of social institution transcending class barriers and representing vertically-integrated interests which were to impose social discipline and work harmoniously in the national interest. ANTI-SEMITISM was not an original component of Italian fascism, although anti-Semitic elements existed within Italian Catholicism and extreme nationalists. Anti-Semitism was introduced by Mussolini in a manifesto of July 1938 distinguishing between Jews and Italians on racial lines, forbidding intermarriage, and removing Jews from government, banking and education. The fascist state did not go beyond discrimination laws, but many Italian Jews fell under Nazi control from 1943, and 8,000 were ultimately killed. Mussolini's foreign policy made early gains, particularly in Africa, creating an East African Empire and developing Libya with Italian colonists. With a powerful modern fleet, Mussolini's Italy was treated with caution and respect by the West. But Mussolini's growing collaboration with Hitler tempted him into war in 1940 when Italy was barely capable of sustaining a campaign of any length. The survival of Great Britain and her ability to reverse his African conquests, the disasters in Greece, and the widening war with the United States and the Soviet Union brought about his downfall. He existed thereafter only as a German puppet.

F. W. Deakin, *The Brutal Friendship* (1966)
M. Gallo, *Mussolini's Italy* (trans., 1973)
A. Lyttleton, *The Seizure of Power* (1973)
——, *Italian Fascism from Pareto to Gentile* (1973)
D. Mack Smith, *Mussolini's Roman Empire* (1977)

# N

**Nagy, Imre** (1896–1958). Hungarian political leader. He fought in the First World War and was captured by the Russians. He became a communist. After his return to Hungary he was forced underground following the fall of the BÉLA KUN regime and the subsequent 'White Terror' by HORTHY DE NAGYBANYA. Nagy spent most of the inter-war years in Moscow, returning with the Soviet army to Hungary in 1944. As Minister of Agriculture in the Hungarian People's Republic, he carried out a major land reform in 1945–6, breaking up the large estates. He served briefly as Minister of the Interior, but was removed by RÁKOSI. With Soviet backing he succeeded Rákosi as Premier on 4 July 1953 and instituted a more liberal regime. Owing to the fall of his supporter in Moscow, MALENKOV, he was removed from the premiership in February 1955 and expelled from the Communist Party eight months later. His popularity, however, led to his return to head the government during the HUNGARIAN UPRISING on 24 October 1956, aiming to support a mixed economy and a neutral Hungary by withdrawing from the WARSAW PACT. His government was overthrown by Soviet forces on 4 November and he was replaced by JANOS KADAR. Nagy took refuge in the Yugoslav embassy, but was tricked into surrender, arrested and executed after a secret trial on 17 June 1958, and buried in an unmarked grave. In June 1989 during the liberalization of the Hungarian regime he was officially rehabilitated and re-buried with full honours.

F. Fejto: *A History of the People's Democracies: Eastern Europe since Stalin* (2nd edn, 1974)

J. K. Hoensch, *A History of Modern Hungary, 1967–1986* (1984)

**Nassau Agreement.** Agreement signed between President KENNEDY and British Prime Minister HAROLD MACMILLAN on 18 December 1962 on nuclear co-operation. The United States agreed to supply Britain with submarine-launched POLARIS nuclear missiles to replace her ageing and obsolescent V-bomber force and plans for the purchase of an American sky-launched nuclear attack missile, Skybolt. The cancellation of the latter threatened Britain with the loss of her capacity to remain as an 'independent' nuclear power, and the Polaris agreement provided a substitute on extremely favourable terms. The agreement was partly the outcome of the good relations enjoyed by Macmillan with Kennedy, but antagonized DE GAULLE, who interpreted it as evidence of Britain's continuing relationship with America. He vetoed British entry to the Common Market a month later.

**National Democratic Party, German** (Nationaldemokratische Partei Deutschlands: NPD). West German neo-Nazi party. Established in the early 1960s, the NPD combined radical right-wing populist anti-capitalism with anti-republicanism and hostility towards foreign workers in the FEDERAL REPUBLIC OF GERMANY. In the 1965 elections it gained only 2 per cent of the vote and so failed to gain any representation in the West German parliament. With the onset of a short-lived economic recession in 1966, however, it gained 8 per cent of the vote and representation in the regional parliaments of Hesse and Bavaria. Alarmed by the spectre of fascism apparently represented by the NPD, the major parties in West Germany combined against it. Its support in national parliamentary elections fell steadily after 1969, when it gained 4.3 per cent of the vote. *See also* NAZI PARTY; REPUBLICAN PARTY, GERMAN.

**Nationaldemokratische Partei** (NPD). *See* NATIONAL DEMOCRATIC PARTY, GERMAN.

**National Front, British** (NF). The National Front was formed in early 1967 following the merger of the League of Empire Loyalists, the British National Party and members of the Racial Preservation Society. Shortly afterwards the Greater Britain Movement merged with the Front. The party's aims included an end to all coloured immigration, repatriation of immigrants living in Britain, withdrawal from the Common Market, support for Ulster Unionists and stronger penalties for criminals.

In the 1970 municipal elections the NF won 10 per cent of the poll in some places, but in the General Election all 10 NF candidates lost their deposits despite an average NF vote of 3.6 per cent of the poll. The Front ran 36 candidates in the 1974 GLC elections and 54 in the February general election. All 54 lost their deposits, but won an average of 3.3 per cent of the votes. 90 candidates were run in October of that year, all losing their deposits. In the same year Kingsley Read replaced John Tyndall as leader. In 1975 membership of the NF began to fall: Read, again voted head of the Directorate, expelled Tyndall who was reinstated by court action. A split occurred, with Read and others leaving to form the National Party. At the 1979 general election, the Front ran 303 candidates; they polled 190,747 votes, and shortly afterwards further internal rifts occurred. In 1982 a breakaway faction, led by John Tyndall, merged with other groups to form a new version of the British National Party. The party's vote fell back in 1983 to 0.1 per cent of the votes cast. It put up no candidates in 1987.

The National Front was once feared as an anti-immigration movement, achieving some successes in the early 1970s. Tighter immigration controls and splits have undermined the party, and have combined with the unfavourable electoral system in Britain for minor parties to reduce its impact. Its parades and demonstrations have sometimes occasioned serious public disorder, as

at Red Lion Square, June 1974 and Southall, April 1979.

M. Walker, *The National Front* (1977)
R. Thurlow, *Fascism in Britain, 1918–1985* (1986)

**National Front, French** (NF). *See* LE PEN, JEAN-MARIE

**National Government.** British administrations, 1931–40. First formed by RAMSAY MACDONALD on 24 August 1931, following the collapse of the SECOND LABOUR GOVERNMENT. Most of the Labour party went into opposition, although a few Labourites, including SNOWDEN and J. H. Thomas stayed in the government; the Liberals and Conservatives supported it. Originally a temporary arrangement to balance the budget, it failed to keep Britain on the GOLD STANDARD but decided in October to fight a general election against Labour, winning the biggest victory in British electoral history, with 554 seats (470 Conservative) against Labour's 46. After the election the cabinet of 10 (4 Labour, 4 Conservatives and 2 Liberals) was restored to full size, with 11 Conservatives, 4 National Labour, 3 free trade Liberals and 2 pro-tariff Liberal Nationals. The government became, in time, almost totally Conservative, the free trade Liberals and Snowden resigning over protection and imperial preference in September 1932, and others being replaced by Conservatives when they left.

During 1931–5 the government faced a series of difficulties especially over the economy, unemployment benefit, India (where there was a substantial but unsuccessful Conservative revolt over the government's liberal policy) and MacDonald's increasing decrepitude, but by mid-1935 most had been overcome, especially when BALDWIN, the Conservative leader, succeeded MacDonald in June 1935. The cabinet he formed with 15 Conservatives, 4 Simonites and 3 National Labourites, reflected the trend towards the Tories.

At the 1935 election the government won a convincing victory against weak opposition, but soon faced crises: the HOARE–LAVAL PACT regarding Abyssinia, which led to the Foreign Secretary's resignation, the budget leak scandal, which resulted in Thomas's departure, and the ABDICATION CRISIS. However, Baldwin's successful handling of the latter restored his position, allowing him to resign in a blaze of glory after the coronation of George VI in 1937. His successor, NEVILLE CHAMBERLAIN, was to pursue APPEASEMENT vigorously. By this stage the National Government was Conservative in all but name.

Chamberlain's government, while making some useful domestic reforms, was increasingly beset with foreign policy difficulties which resulted in the alienation of many Conservatives and ended in the declaration of war on Germany in September 1939. (Even so, few observers had expected the government to lose the next election.) Although opinion rallied to the government at first, its lacklustre handling of the war effort aroused criticism, and the disastrous failure of the Norway campaign led to a bitter debate in Parliament on 7–8 May 1940. Many Conservatives opposed the government or abstained, and Chamberlain was forced to resign. Churchill then formed a more wide-ranging Coalition including Labour. Most of the leading figures of the National Government were excluded from Churchill's administration by the end of the year. What had been intended as a purely temporary expedient had, in fact, lasted for nearly nine years.

The National Governments have suffered severe criticism, especially over Appeasement and their failure to deal more vigorously with unemployment. This was the prevailing view among historians until the late 1960s, but recent years have seen a more sober reassessment, recognizing the scale of the difficulties faced. In many ways they were dull, unimaginative and pessimistic governments, but they did preside over a period of unprecedented prosperity for some, and also helped to preserve parliamentary democracy in Britain at a time when it was under fierce attack in most of Europe. They also ensured that Britain entered war united and reasonably well prepared in civil administration and airpower.

C. L. Mowat, *Britain Between the Wars, 1918–1940* (1955)
M. Cowling, *The Impact of Hitler* (1976)
J. Stevenson and C. Cook, *The Slump* (1977)

**National Health Service, British.** Set up by the National Health Service Act of 1946 under the ATTLEE government. The Health Service was foreshadowed by pre-war concern about the patchy and varying systems of health care available in Britain, some of them based on voluntary hospitals, some on local authority-run health services, and others on private insurance systems. Several recommendations from pressure groups urged the creation of a unified system. Wartime experience of the emergency pooling of hospital and health service to meet the effects of bombing and strong political pressures for improved social welfare led to a firm commitment by 1945. The negotiations setting up the service were conducted by ANEURIN BEVAN, the first Minister of Health. As finalized, the Act provided for a Health Service free at the point of access, covering doctors, hospital treatment, dental and optical care, paid for out of general taxation. When it came into effect in 1948, it gave Britain the most comprehensive free medical service in the world. Under pressure from doctors and consultants, it was agreed that they should have considerable independence under the system and be free to take on private patients. The principle of a completely free service was breached in 1951 when economic constraints forced the introduction of the first treatment charges, leading to Bevan's resignation from government. The Health Service has remained a commitment of governments of all shades of opinion, generally thought to be an issue on which the LABOUR PARTY has the advantage over the Conservative Party (*see* CONSERVATIVE AND UNIONIST PARTY). Under Mrs THATCHER attempts have been made to privatize some elements of administration and to boost the private sector, as well as to reorganize the way services are delivered, including allowing hospitals to 'opt out' of health service control. These changes have proved a matter of much controversy in the 1980s.

**Nationalities Question, Soviet.** The presence of large non-Russian minorities has been one of the endemic political problems of the Russian and then the Soviet state. Under the Russian Empire, Russians proper made up only 45 per cent of the total population. Prior to 1917 a policy of RUSSIFICATION had been applied to the national minorities, though somewhat relaxed after the revolutionary uprisings of

1905, a period which saw the development of stronger national minority movements. The FIRST WORLD WAR and the RUSSIAN REVOLUTION had profound effects on the national minorities. The creation of Finnish and Polish states, as well as separate republics in the BALTIC STATES reduced the land area of the former Russian Empire, but still left within its borders significant non-Russian populations, amounting to 41 per cent of the total population, 22 per cent non-Slavs. The Bolsheviks had accepted the right of 'self-determination for all nations forming part of the state' which LENIN had made a clause in the programme of the Russian Social Democratic Labour Party in 1903. When the Revolution broke out the Bolsheviks championed the liberation of the national minorities in the territories of the former Russian Empire. In 1917 STALIN was charged with drawing up a Report on the National Question on the basis that 'oppressed nations forming part of Russia must be allowed the right to decide for themselves whether they wish to remain part of the Russian state or separate and form an independent state'. The first step was the recognition of Finnish and Polish independence, but in the course of the RUSSIAN CIVIL WAR the right of secession was modified and increasingly viewed as a theoretical rather than an operative right. Both Lenin and Stalin believed it impractical for independent small states to secede when they could only serve as bases for counter-revolutionary activity or deprive the Soviet state of vital raw materials. As a result the Soviet government adopted a position in which the right of secession was allowed to remain, though this was on the understanding it would not be exercised. Having, in fact, destroyed the independent republics set up in places such as the UKRAINE, ARMENIA and GEORGIA, the new Soviet Constitution of 1923 created a federal system of republics, formally enacted in January 1924. Union Republics, Autonomous Republics and Autonomous Regions were bound together in a voluntary federation. The Soviet Socialist Republics of BELORUSSIA and the Ukraine, later joined by others, were set up with maximum publicity for their independent sovereignty. Under the slogan 'National in Form, Socialist in Content', the early Soviet state granted the minorities extensive linguistic autonomy and organization on national-territorial lines. At the same time the key structure of the Soviet state remained the Communist Party, which while attempting to draw on national minorities almost always maintained a large Russian and Ukrainian influence. Moreover, the division of powers between Moscow and the republics left the major areas of finance, defence, foreign affairs, external trade, transport and heavy industry in the hands of the central government. With little economic autonomy, the Union Republics were left with largely limited powers over local agriculture, justice and health.

Nonetheless the Soviet 'federal' experiment, while preserving the centralized control of the major functions of government and maintaining the primary authority of the Communist Party, did permit considerable cultural autonomy and enshrined the multi-ethnic character of the Soviet state in its early years. The rise of Stalin to supreme power was accompanied by an increasing 'Sovietization' of the Soviet Union. COLLECTIVIZATION and the FIVE YEAR PLANS did much to transform the economic character of all the constituent republics, sweeping away the traditional landholding systems and village leaders. De-Christianization and the propagation of 'Soviet' culture was accompanied by a clamp-down on expressions of national and ethnic culture. The Russian language was increasingly used as the vehicle of education and in central Soviet institutions such as the military.

Even after Stalin's death, the Soviet state maintained a strong grip upon the expression of national sentiment. Although there was some relaxation of Stalinist rigour, KHRUSHCHEV in 1961 still spoke of a 'fusion' (sliyanie) of the nations of the USSR in a supranationalist socialist community as the ultimate aim. In practice, the more overt features of what was seen as 'Russification' were reduced, with increased freedom for native languages at primary level, greater cultural respect for minority culture and history, and more economic autonomy. At the same time local party bosses were allowed greater economic and cultural latitude, and by the BREZHNEV era reference to eventual 'fusion' had largely been dropped. It was not, however, until the GORBACHEV era that the national minorities began to agitate openly for greater autonomy. Attempts to embrace these demands in a new All-Union Treaty were overtaken by local nationalist demands, especially in the Baltic States, and the failed coup of August 1991. As a result the Baltic States left the Union and several Republics declared independence.

A. Cobban, *The Nation State and National Self-Determination* (1969)
R. Conquest (ed), *Soviet Nationality Policies and Practices* (1978)
J. Dunlop, *The Faces of Contemporary Russian Nationalism* (1983)

**nationalization.** The taking into state control of economic enterprises. Nationalization has formed a part of the doctrine of socialist and communist movements in many parts of Europe in the 20th century, while temporary nationalization has been practised for emergency conditions such as wartime. Many social democratic and labour parties have included nationalization as part of their programmes. The BRITISH LABOUR PARTY interpreted CLAUSE FOUR of its constitution to mean the nationalization of key sectors of the economy, a programme carried into fulfilment by ATTLEE after 1945 and again under HAROLD WILSON after 1964. Under communist regimes, nationalization has usually taken the form of outright expropriation, as opposed to the compensation systems operated in democratic countries, including the socialization of agriculture. After 1945 several European countries which were not explicitly socialist, such as France and Italy, undertook extensive nationalization of major industries and transport in order to facilitate reconstruction under state control. This non-doctrinaire form of state ownership was also evident in the creation of public corporations to carry on essential services which were not seen as appropriate for private control, such as broadcasting, airlines and strategically important industries in armaments and the nuclear sector. Since the 1960s there has been growing disenchantment with nationalization, although this has been for differing reasons on various points on the political spectrum. The revival of economic liberalism has induced a wave of PRIVATIZATION in Britain and France, as well as amongst the Eastern bloc countries. Left-wing socialists have often argued that both communist and social democratic regimes never fulfilled the aspirations of true workers' control, setting up inefficient and monolithic enterprises run by managers rather than workers.

**National Liberal Party, British.** See LIBERAL NATIONAL PARTY, BRITISH.

**Nationalsozialistische Deutsche Arbeiterpartei (NSDAP).** See NAZI PARTY.

**National Unemployed Workers' Movement (NUWM).** Organization of the unemployed set up in Britain under the auspices of the BRITISH COMMUNIST PARTY in 1921. Its aim was to politicize the unemployed and to campaign for higher benefits. Led by Wal Hannington, an engineer and early party member, the NUWM took the lead in organizing protests and HUNGER MARCHES from 1922. The movement had two peaks of activity: in the early 1920s, when unemployment reached a peak in 1921–2, and during the trough of the depression from 1929–35. The NUWM mounted a series of national marches in 1929, 1932, 1934 and 1936, which were often represented by the authorities as a threat to public order, and led to the arrest of activists and clashes with the police. Agitation against the MEANS TEST in 1931 failed to deter the government's action, but some influence was exercised on local Public Assistance Committees to improve benefits. Marches organized by the movement led to serious rioting in Birkenhead, Manchester, Belfast and London in 1932, and the government was widely criticized for its tactics, leading to the formation of the National Council for Civil Liberties in 1934. A major campaign against the standardization of unemployment relief undertaken by NEVILLE CHAMBERLAIN in 1934–5 in the Unemployment Assistance Board regulations forced the government to issue a standstill order in early 1935, suspending its measures. The NUWM suffered from the suspicion from the TRADES UNION CONGRESS and the LABOUR PARTY, who viewed it as a 'front' organization of the Communist Party, and which had participated in attacks on them in 1929–33 when the NUWM joined the Party's militant 'class against class' campaign against 'reformist' bodies. Many unemployed joined temporarily to gain assistance in dealing with benefit claims, one of the most valuable services provided by the NUWM, but few remained permanent members. On the whole, the NUWM failed to achieve the objectives set for it of mobilizing and politicizing the unemployed of inter-war Britain. Although as many as 400,000 may have passed through its ranks, its peak membership at any one time was just over 20,000 members, and was generally far less. Shortly after the outbreak of the Second World War in 1939 the organization was wound up.

W. Hannington, *Unemployed Struggles, 1919–1936* (1936)
——, *Never on Our Knees* (1967)
C. P. Cook and J. Stevenson, *The Slump: Society and Politics during the Depression* (1977)
R. Croucher, *We Refuse to Starve in Silence: A History of the National Unemployed Workers' Movement, 1920–46* (1987)

**National Volunteers, Irish.** *See* IRISH VOLUNTEERS.

**NATO.** *See* NORTH ATLANTIC TREATY ORGANIZATION.

**Nazi Party** (Nationalsozialistische Deutsche Arbeiterpartei; NSDAP; National Socialist German Workers' Party). German extreme nationalist right-wing party. The NSDAP grew out of the German Workers' Party (DAP), founded in 1919, and was established in February 1920. Its 25-point programme committed it to agitation against the TREATY OF VERSAILLES, a populist radicalism and anti-Semitism. HITLER assumed leadership of the party in August 1921. Before November 1923, the NSDAP was largely confined to Bavaria, where it co-operated with other exteme-right nationalist groupings and planned the overthrow of the WEIMAR REPUBLIC. After the abortive MUNICH PUTSCH of November 1923 the NSDAP disintegrated. It was refounded in February 1925 and, between 1925 and 1929, extended its organizational infrastructure to areas beyond Bavaria. Yet during this period the NSDAP, now committed to the pursuit of a 'legal path' to power, made apparently little headway, winning only 2.6 per cent of the vote in May 1928 REICHSTAG elections. With the onset of a world agricul-

tural crisis in 1928, shortly to be followed by the industrial DEPRESSION of 1929, however, membership of the party grew rapidly from 100,000 in October 1928 to 130,000 in September 1930. During the period 1928–30, the NSDAP concentrated on trying to win the support of sections of the middle class, especially the peasantry, artisans and small retailers. Its electoral breakthrough came in September 1930, when it gained 18.3 per cent of the vote in the *Reichstag* elections and emerged as the second largest party, with 107 seats. After 1930 the party sought to broaden its electoral base further, seeking to appeal to industrial workers and sections of the 'new' lower-middle class such as civil servants and white-collar workers. To this end, it developed new and striking forms of propaganda, including the selective use of political violence by its paramilitary SA (*see* SA). In the July 1932 *Reichstag* elections it won 37.4 per cent of the popular vote, though it suffered a set-back in the November 1932 elections when its share of the vote fell to 33.1 per cent. Its electoral success was largely at the expense of right-wing and economic-interest splinter parties, the liberal DDP and DVP (*see* DDP; DVP) and the conservative DNVP: it thus functioned as a 'rallying party' for the discontented middle and lower-middle classes, stressing its nationalism and propagating a charismatic 'Führer-myth' around Hitler, seeking thereby to transcend the political divisions which had plagued the parties representing the middle classes. It was less successful in winning the support of industrial workers, who were under-represented in both its membership and electorate, though it made some headway in gaining the allegiance of non-unionized workers, agricultural workers and state employees. It also failed to make much headway in largely Catholic areas, which were dominated by the CENTRE PARTY. Following Hitler's appointment as Chancellor, the grass-roots of the NSDAP, which now had a membership of 850,000, played an important role in the Nazi seizure of power, leading the often loosely co-ordinated 'revolution from below' in the provinces and localities. In July 1933 it was declared to be the only legal party in Germany. The relationship between the NSDAP and the state after 1933 was a complicated one, with party bodies enjoying quasi-official status, often duplicating the work of central, regional and local government organs: tension between party and state existed at every level of government and administration, and the extent to which party organs were able to gain the upper hand depended on the individual personalities involved, their skill at political infighting and their connections with key figures in the regime, especially with Hitler. The conflict between party and state organs was an important structural feature pushing the Nazi regime in a progressively more radical direction, a process exemplified by the cumulative radicalization of the regime's anti-Semitic policies. By 1944 the membership of the NSDAP had expanded to over 8 million and its presence was felt in almost all spheres of social life. With the collapse of the Third Reich in 1945, the NSDAP disintegrated. Declared illegal by the occupying powers, its revival is explicitly banned by the constitution of the Federal Republic of Germany. *See also* GAULEITER.

M. Broszat, *The Hitler State* (1981)
J. Noakes and G. Pridham (eds.), *Nazism, 1919–1945* (2 vols., 1983–4)

**Nazi–Soviet Pact.** Also known as the Nazi–Soviet Non-Aggression Pact or the Ribbentrop–Molotov Pact after the respective foreign ministers who negotiated the agreement. Signed on 23 August 1939, the first article declared mutual non-aggression, and was preceded on 19 August 1939 by a trade agreement offering credit to the Soviet Union of 200 million Reichmarks. By secret protocols Germany and the Soviet Union allocated to each other spheres of influence in Poland bounded by the lines of the rivers Narew, Vistula and San. Germany also allowed the Soviet Union a free hand in BESSARABIA, Finland and the BALTIC STATES. The Nazi–Soviet Pact followed attempts by the Western powers, France and Britain, to negotiate an alliance with the Soviet Union, but they proved unsuccessful as a result of mutual suspicions. The replacement in May 1939 of LITVINOV, a strong anti-Nazi with close connections in the West, by MOLOTOV, who took a more pragmatic line, was a decisive step. Although discussions both with the West and Nazi Germany pro-

ceeded in July, STALIN appears to have seen greater short-term security and more immediate territorial advantages from an alliance with Nazi Germany. The West appeared to Stalin unprepared to stand up to Hitler following the MUNICH AGREEMENT and the absorption of the rest of Czechoslovakia in spring 1939. Moreover, Stalin's exclusion from the Munich discussions and evidence of continued anti-communist feeling led him to fear an attack by Germany on the Soviet Union in which the West would either stand neutral or even intervene. Agreement with the Nazis offered the immediate prospect of reacquiring territory lost by the Soviet Union after the First World War and extending its frontier westwards as a buffer against German aggression. For HITLER the Pact allowed him to dismember Poland and seize DANZIG without risk of Soviet intervention and a war on two fronts. Without Soviet support the British and French guarantees to Poland were militarily worthless, even if they were acted upon, which Hitler suspected they might not be.

After almost a decade of virulent anti-communist propaganda by the Nazis and increasingly frantic attempts by the Soviet Union to engage the West in an anti-fascist alliance, the Pact was a major volte-face in diplomatic relations. Its direct effect was to leave Poland, the Baltic States, Finland and Romania vulnerable to attack by their giant neighbours. Moreover, via the COMINTERN the Soviet Union instructed local communist parties to desist from anti-fascist activities, weakening the opposition to fascist aggression in many countries until Germany turned against the Soviet Union in June 1941. The Pact was followed swiftly by the German invasion and conquest of Poland in September 1939 and the movement of Soviet forces into eastern Poland, and subsequently against Finland, the Baltic States and Bessarabia. Ultimately, the Pact appears to have lulled Stalin into a false sense of security, as he refused to believe reports in 1941 that German forces were preparing for an invasion. The German assault on the Soviet Union in 'Operation Barbarossa' on 22 June 1941 ended the Pact.

G. Kennan, *Russia and the West* (1961)

A. B. Ulam, *Expansion and Coexistence: Soviet Foreign Policy, 1917–72* (1968)

E. H. Carr, *German–Soviet Relations between the Two Wars* (1974)

**Negrín, Juan** (1887–1956). Spanish politician. A moderate socialist, he was Spain's last Prime Minister of the Republic during the SPANISH CIVIL WAR. A former Professor of Physiology, he became a socialist deputy in 1931, but did not devote his full time to political affairs until the outbreak of the SPANISH CIVIL WAR. He served as Minister of Finance (Sept. 1936–May 1937) in LARGO CABALLERO's government, then as Prime Minister from May 1937 until the end of the war, adding the Defence Ministry to his duties from April 1938 onward. Negrín was the Republican side's most important leader; even more than Caballero and Indalecio Prieto, Defence Minister until April 1938, he was responsible for converting the Republican army into a formidable opponent of FRANCO's Nationalist forces. Often denounced because of his close relations with the Communists, it is difficult to see what alternative Negrín had since Britain and France refused to help the Republic and the Soviet Union was its only active supporter. Convinced that a general European war was about to erupt, and that this would force the western powers to rescue the Republic, Negrín tried to keep the Spanish war going even after the fall of Barcelona in February 1939. This provoked a coup against him, led by Colonel Casado, which vainly sought favourable surrender terms from Franco. The falseness of the 'fellow traveller' charges against Negrín is suggested by his post-war actions; he never visited the Soviet Union, nor had any contact with the European communist parties. He lived out a lonely exile, shunned even by most of his own party, in France, apart from the years 1940–45, which he spent in England.

H. Thomas, *The Spanish Civil War* (1961)

G. Jackson, *The Spanish Republic and the Civil War* (1965)

**Nenni, Pietro** (1891–1980). Italian socialist. He joined the Republican Party in 1908, and in 1911 organized a general strike in protest against the Libyan War. He was imprisoned for his activities, and again in 1914 for promoting strikes. He collaborated with MUSSOLINI on *Il Popolo d'Italia* newspaper and advocated intervention in the First World War. He served in the army for a year, 1915–16, but became increasingly disillusioned by Republicanism and was involved in founding the first FASCI DI COMBATTIMENTO in Bologna, where he edited a journal. He became editor of *Avanti!* in 1922 and gradually adopted an anti-fascist stance. His attempts to create an anti-fascist alliance failed, and he went into exile in France in 1926. He supported co-operation between socialists and communists in the Pact of Unity of 1934, serving as the Socialist Party's Secretary. He fought in the INTERNATIONAL BRIGADES in Spain and was involved in clandestine work during the Second World War. Imprisoned by the Germans in 1943, he re-formed the Socialist Party on his release, becoming its Secretary-General, 1944–66, and President, 1966–9. In 1945 he was a candidate for the presidency, eventually serving as Vice-President to DE GASPERI. He retained an alliance with the communists but broke with them after the HUNGARIAN UPRISING. In June 1960 he helped to form the first centre-left government, serving as Vice-President of the Council of Ministers and Foreign Minister. In 1964 his support for MORO's Christian Democrats split his party. He served as Foreign Minister again in 1968 and stood unsuccessfully for the presidency in 1971. Nenni inherited a difficult post-war position for the Socialist Party, squeezed between a strong ITALIAN COMMUNIST PARTY and CHRISTIAN DEMOCRATIC PARTY. He pioneered the 'opening to the left', the *rapprochement* between Christian Democrats and Socialists, ending support for the Communists and by 1958 dropping socialist opposition to the NORTH ATLANTIC TREATY ORGANISATION and the EUROPEAN ECONOMIC COMMUNITY. Nenni's collaboration with the Christian Democrats led to the secession of the left wing, in part compensated for by a reunion with the Social Democrats in 1966, though this broke down in 1969. *See also* SOCIALIST PARTY, ITALIAN.

M. Clark, *Modern Italy, 1871–1982* (1984)

S. di Scala, *Renewing Italian Socialism: Nenni to Craxi* (1988)

**NEP.** *See* NEW ECONOMIC POLICY.

**Neuilly, Treaty of.** A treaty signed with Bulgaria on 27 November 1919 as a result of the PARIS PEACE CONFERENCE. Western Thrace was ceded to Greece and territory along Bulgaria's western boundary was ceded to Yugoslavia. The Bulgarian army was reduced to 33,000 men and reparations were set at £90 million. The Covenant of the League of Nations was written into the treaty. Bulgaria lost not only all the territorial gains she had made as a result of her entry into the war on the side of the Central Powers in 1915 but also access to the Aegean and hence directly to the Mediterranean.

A. J. Mayer, *The Policy and Diplomacy of Peacemaking* (1968)
H. W. V. Temperley, *The History of the Peace Conference* (1974)

**New Economic Policy** (NEP). Economic policy inaugurated by the Soviet Union in 1921 to replace the system of WAR COMMUNISM. Its main feature was the replacement of forced requisitioning by taxes in kind set at lower levels than under War Communism. It aimed to revitalize agriculture by giving the peasants greater incentives to increase production and implied the restoration of a degree of private trade and the supply of industrial and consumer goods for purchase. This led to the abolition of state control of the retail, service and manufacturing sectors other than heavy industry, banking and foreign trade. The policy produced a recovery of agricultural output to within 10 per cent of 1913 levels in 1926 and livestock production reached pre-war levels in the same year. Grain output per head, however, remained below pre-war levels, and there was growing concern with the failure of sufficient grain to come to market to meet the needs of the towns and industrial workers. Following LENIN's death in 1924, these factors led to a major debate on the future development of industry and agriculture, and the NEP was replaced by the first FIVE YEAR PLAN in 1928. The NEP has been viewed variously as a decisive move by Lenin in the direction of a more free market system following the rigours of War Communism, and as a mere temporary expedient to resolve the disastrous plunge in output in 1920–21. In fact, Lenin appears to have believed in the gradual replacement

of private plots by large-scale collective enterprises, some of which had been set up as early as the Russian Civil War, and his death only three years into the NEP leaves his long-term intentions unclear. The NEP was soon, however, to become the subject of intense debate about the future course of Soviet economic development and the role of collectivization (*see* COLLECTIVIZATION, SOVIET).

E. H. Carr, *Socialism in One Country, 1924–26* (1958–9)
M. Lewin, *Russian Peasants and Soviet Power* (1968)
——, *Lenin's Last Struggle* (1969)

**New Party, British.** Sir OSWALD MOSLEY resigned from the Labour government in May 1930 when the cabinet rejected his 'Memorandum' on unemployment. In October 1930 a resolution at the Labour Party Conference, calling upon the NEC to consider the Memorandum, was narrowly defeated. In December the main points of the Memorandum were published as the Mosley Manifesto. 17 Labour MPs signed the Manifesto, six of whom (Sir Oswald Mosley, Lady Cynthia Mosley, J. Strachey, O. Baldwin, W. J. Brown and R. Forgan) left the party to form the New Party in February 1931. Baldwin and Brown resigned from the New Party almost immediately and Strachey left four months later. But a Conservative MP (Allen) and a Liberal (Dudgeon) joined the party. In the 1931 general election the New Party's 24 candidates were all defeated, and only Mosley saved his deposit. The following year Mosely formed the BRITISH UNION of FASCISTS

R. Skidelsky, *Oswald Mosley* (1975)

**NF.** *See* NATIONAL FRONT, BRITISH.

**Ngorno-Karabakh.** Disputed region of the Soviet republic of AZERBAIJAN, part of ARMENIA prior to the Russian Revolution of 1917. Overwhelmingly Christian, it forms an enclave in a largely Shi-ite Moslem republic. Demonstrations in Armenia in February 1988 demanded the redrawing of boundaries between Armenia and Azerbaijan to conform more closely with ethnic and cultural divisions. GORBACHEV promised discussions to resolve Armenian grievances but refused to allow a unilateral revision of boundaries without central authority. The demonstrations in Armenia were followed shortly after by serious rioting in the Azerbaijani city of Sumgait in which the Soviet authorities admitted that 31 people had died in a 'pogrom' of the Armenian population. Soviet troops were sent into Sumgait, and a considerable armed presence remained in the area to prevent further violence, although further incidents took place through 1988–9. The Ngorno-Karabakh riots and the demonstrations in Armenia represented one of the most serious challenges for Gorbachev's process of liberalization. Alongside similar agitation in the BALTIC STATES, they tested the extent to which the Soviet Union would permit a redrawing of boundaries to emphasize ethnic groupings and permit greater self-expression for nationalities, thereby leading to the reawakening of separatist movements suppressed under the earlier Soviet regime. *See also* NATIONALITIES QUESTION, SOVIET.

**Nicholas II, of Russia** (1868–1918). Tsar of Russia, 1894–1917. Born 18 May 1968, the eldest son of Alexander III, he married shortly after his accession Alexandra of Hesse, the grand-daughter of Queen Victoria. Declaring his attachment to autocracy from his accession, he maintained a stubborn resistance to constitutional reform until his hand was forced in the aftermath of defeat in Russo-Japanese War of 1904–5 and the revolutionary unrest of 1905. Although agreeing to the setting up of a DUMA he remained distrustful of constitutionalism and remained in uneasy relationship with it up to the outbreak of the FIRST WORLD WAR. Unable to halt the slide to war, he assumed supreme command of the Russian forces in September 1915, but was blamed for the disastrous losses inflicted on the Russian forces and the growing discontent on the home front. Failing to make any positive political concessions to the opposition, his position was increasingly undermined by the influence of RASPUTIN at court, alienating many members of the ruling élite. Rasputin's murder at the end of 1916 did little to ease pressure on the Tsar, and he was urged, fruitlessly, to broaden the base of his government. In February 1917, as unrest mounted in Petrograd, he placed the capital under the command of General Khabalov, himself leaving for army headquarters at Mogilev on 7 March. As disorder spread and troops refused to disperse the crowds, Nicholas sought to suspend the Duma. On the 12th, however, it formed a Provisonal Committee to replace the Tsarist government. Attempting to return to the capital by train, he was stranded at Pskov where, receiving news that his commanders were unwilling to support him, on 15 March he signed an order of abdication, initially in favour of his son, Alexey, with his brother Grand Duke Michael as Regent, but then altered in favour of Michael as successor. Michael, however, refused the offer, by which time the PROVISIONAL GOVERNMENT was established. Placed under arrest, Nicholas and the Royal Family were despatched first to Siberia, and then to Ekaterinburg in the Urals. As the RUSSIAN CIVIL WAR developed, fear of the Tsar's becoming the focal point for counter-revolutionary forces led to the execution of the Tsar and his family on the orders of a local Bolshevik commander on the night of 16–17 July 1918.

Nicholas did little as Tsar to halt the disintegration of the Russian Empire through his misplaced faith in rigid autocracy, stiffened by the views of his wife and the influence of Rasputin. He repeatedly failed to answer calls for a broader-based government to meet the unprecedented strains of the war, and he eventually lost the confidence even of his natural allies, the aristocracy. As a result, the February Revolution represented as much the dissatisfaction of the ruling class with his conduct of the war as it did liberal and popular opposition from below. The complete collapse of his authority early in 1917 was initially replaced by a determination to carry the war on more effectively; it was only with the rise of rival sources of authority in the SOVIETS and the Provisional Government, followed by the Bolshevik seizure of power, that the Civil War became the likely outcome. *See also* RUSSIAN REVOLUTION.

B. D. Charques, *Twilight of Imperial Russia: The Reign of Tsar Nicholas II* (1965)

V. Alexandrov, *The End of the Romanovs* (1966)

R. Pearson, *The Russian Moderates and the Crisis of Tsarism, 1914–1917* (1977)

**'Night of the Long Knives'.** Purge of the paramilitary SA (*see* SA) leadership and other opponents of HITLER carried out on the night of 29–30 June 1934 and the succeeding two days. The background to the purge was formed by the growing problem that the SA presented to Hitler after the Nazi seizure of power in spring 1933. The SA contained many of the more socially radical members of the Nazi movement who were discontented with the limited gains that they had made in the Nazi 'revolution'. Throughout the period from the summer of 1933 to the summer of 1934, interference in local and regional administration and in businesses by grass-roots SA activists put the alliance between Hitler and the conservative élites within Germany under some strain. More worrying still from Hitler's point of view were the demands articulated by the SA leadership for the dissolution of the professional army and its integration into a militia which they would control, demands to which the army leadership was implacably opposed. Hitler sought to defuse the crisis in February 1934 by forcing the leader of the SA, RÖHM, to sign an agreement with the Minister of Defence, General von Blomberg, under which the SA would be responsible for pre- and post-military training under the supervision of the army. Yet tension between the army and the SA continued to mount thereafter, as the activities of the SA in areas demilitarized under the TREATY OF VERSAILLES threatened to bring about diplomatic complications for the regime, endangering its plans for cautious rearmament. The SS (*see* SS), which sought to displace the SA, fostered such tension, reporting SA activity to the army. In June 1934 the crisis became more acute as it became clear that President HINDENBURG was dying. Hitler, who wished to succeed Hindenburg, was aware that he would need the support of the army: yet the continuing antagonizing of the army and élites by the SA not only jeopardized the likelihood of a smooth succession, but threatened to bring about a military coup against the new regime. On 29 June Hitler summoned a meeting of SA leaders at Wiessee (Bavaria) for the following day. Having put the army and SS on alert, Hitler flew to Bavaria early on 30 June, where he supervised the murder of Röhm and other

SA leaders. The purge extended to other opponents of the regime and was used by Hitler to settle a number of old political scores. Hitler received the congratulations of the army leadership and President Hindenburg after the purge, which was legalized retroactively by the cabinet. Justifying his action to the REICHSTAG, on 13 July 1934, Hitler invoked the fiction of a planned coup by Röhm – the occasion on which he also coined the phrase 'Night of the Long Knives'. The main result of the purge was to cement the alliance between the army, élites and Hitler – who combined the offices of President and Reich Chancellor following Hindenburg's death on 2 August 1934.

J. Noakes and G. Pridham (eds), *Nazism, 1919–1945*, vol. 1: *The Rise to Power* (1983)

**NKGB.** Abbreviated Russian name for the People's Commissariat for State Security, the state security force after 1943 when the responsibilities of the NKVD (*see* NKVD) were divided. In 1946 the MGB (*see* MGB) became responsible as the Ministry of State Security for the secret police and its agents, while an MVD or Ministry of Internal Affairs became responsible for the ordinary police, public order and the labour camps.

R. Hingley, *The Russian Secret Police* (1970)
B. Levytsky, *The Uses of Terror: The Soviet Security Service, 1917–1970* (1971)

**NKVD.** Abbreviated Russian name of the People's Commissariat for Internal Affairs which supervised the GPU (*see* GPU), the Soviet Security Police, until 1923. Renamed OGPU, the security police became an independent ministry in 1923, but in 1934 OGPU was absorbed into a reorganized NKVD, which became the police organization in charge of state security and the secret police during the PURGES. In 1943 it was divided again into two commissariats, the BKVD and the NKGB (*see* NKGB), the latter being responsible for the secret police and the security apparatus.

R. Hingley, *The Russian Secret Police* (1970)
B. Levytsky, *The Uses of Terror: The Soviet Secret Service, 1917–1970* (1971)

**Non-intervention Committee.** Formed in September 1936 at Italian suggestion but with Great Britain taking the lead. Its aim was to 'quarantine' the SPANISH CIVIL WAR and to prevent it sparking off a European conflagration. On 16 December 1936 a protocol was signed in London by 27 powers agreeing to non-intervention in Spain. In practice the committee served to assist the Nationalist side as they continued to receive valuable German and Italian support during the conflict. Although the Soviet Union aided the Republic, the determination of Britain and France to confine the conflict denied the Republic access to its most likely sources of assistance. In 1937 at the Nyon Conference (10–14 September) the committee acted to develop a naval and air patrol of the Mediterranean when neutral ships were being attacked by Italian submarines. Eventually Germany and Italy resigned from the neutrality patrols. The committee held its last meeting in July 1938 before a wind-up meeting in April 1939. Dismissed by some as a propaganda exercise to mask the unwillingness of Great Britain to become involved in a war and to ensure that France was not implicated, the committee was only an instrument of larger policy. ANTHONY EDEN, its leading British member, was less ready to acquiesce in Italian breaches of non-intervention than NEVILLE CHAMBERLAIN, his Premier, who sought to appease MUSSOLINI. The rift between them came to a head in February 1938 with Eden's resignation over the question of the withdrawal of Italian 'volunteers' from Spain. Chamberlain brought pressure against the French government when intervention was proposed by the new Blum government in spring 1938. On 16 April 1938 the Anglo-Italian Mediterranean Pact stipulated only that Italy would withdraw its troops once the war was ended, after which Italy would help preserve the *status quo* in the Mediterranean. As a result the non-intervention agreements concluded by Britain, while ensuring that the war did not spread, allowed the Republic to bleed to death for lack of supplies and arms. Opposition to British policy grew in early 1939 even within government circles, but it was too late to reverse a policy which had won few friends.

Lord Avon, *Facing the Dictators* (1954)
J. Edwards, *The British Government and the Spanish Civil War* (1979)

**Normandy landings.** *See* D-DAY; SECOND WORLD WAR.

**North Atlantic Treaty Organisation** (NATO). Created by the North Atlantic Treaty of 4 April 1949. NATO came in response to Western fears about the power of the Soviet Union and the failure of the UN Security Council to operate in the face of the Soviet veto. The treaty states are obliged to take such action as they deem necessary to assist a fellow signatory subjected to aggression, although there is no obligation to fight. The original treaty states were Belgium, Luxembourg, the Netherlands, Britain, the United States, Canada, Italy, Norway, Denmark, Iceland and Portugal. These were joined later by Greece and Turkey (1952), West Germany (1955) and Spain (1985). The Paris Agreements of 1954 added a protocol to the treaty aimed at strengthening the structure of NATO and revised the TREATY OF BRUSSELS of 1948, which now includes Italy and West Germany in addition to its original members (Benelux countries, Britain and France). The Brussels Treaty signatories are committed to give one another 'all the military and other aid and assistance in their power' if one is the subject of 'armed aggression in Europe'. Since 1969 members of the Atlantic Alliance can withdraw on one year's notice; the Brussels Treaty was signed for 50 years. The organization's highest authority is the North Atlantic Council, which is made up of permanent representatives, meeting twice a year. A Military Committee consisting of chiefs of staff also meets at least twice a year. The organization is designed to make a military response to the threat of Soviet and Eastern bloc incursion into Western Europe which since 1955 has been represented by the WARSAW PACT. NATO maintains ground, sea and air forces which numbered almost 5 million in 1985, of which over 1 million were stationed in Europe, with more than 10,000 tanks, 2,500 combat aircraft and 7,000 tactical nuclear weapons. The Allied Command Europe (ACE) has its headquarters near Mons, in Belgium, known as SHAPE (Supreme Headquarters Allied Powers in Europe), and is responsible for the defence of NATO countries in continental Europe. Originally it was conceived that a Soviet violation of frontiers would be met by an immediate nuclear response, known as MASSIVE RETALIATION, but during the 1960s increasing emphasis was placed on the so-called FLEXIBLE RESPONSE, allowing a graduated response with appropriate levels of force, including ultimately nuclear weapons. In 1966 a Defence Planning Committee was formed to deal with the integration of military planning. At the same time two permanent bodies were established to deal with nuclear planning, and the Nuclear Defence Affairs Committee (NDAC), to associate non-nuclear members in the nuclear plans of the alliance, the Nuclear Planning Group (NPG), which deals with matters of detail.

Tensions developed between the aims of Europe and the EEC and those of the USA, the latter being particularly desirous of establishing an 'Atlantic Community' and committing the European members to a definite stance against Soviet aggression. French suspicion of the USA's aims led France to leave NATO in March 1966, at which time the North Atlantic Council's headquarters, its Military Committee and International Secretariat were moved from Fontainebleau to Brussels.

On 17 August 1964 Greek military forces were withdrawn from NATO due to tension with Turkey over Cyprus but Greece re-entered in October 1980. In the 1980s opposition to the siting of US CRUISE MISSILES in Europe, particularly in the Netherlands and Britain, led many American politicians to question the will of European nations to support NATO. It was suggested that NATO might collapse if Western Europe did not take a more active part in its own defence. That immediate crisis was overcome by the progress of arms talks between the United States and the Soviet Union, leading to the withdrawal of intermediate-range missiles from Europe from 1989, under the terms of the INTERMEDIATE NUCLEAR FORCES TREATY of 1987. The changes in Eastern Europe in 1989 led to the first talks, starting at Vienna in March under the CSCE framework and culminating in the treaty on Conventional Armed Forces in Europe in November 1990 between NATO and the Warsaw Pact.

NATO represented an important stage in the development of the COLD WAR and can be viewed either as a cause or a consequence of it. It was the first peacetime commitment to European defence by the United States and has underpinned the

Cold War and all superpower relations since the 1940s. The military confrontation of forces between the Warsaw Pact and NATO in Europe since 1948 has represented the largest concentration of military force anywhere in the world, except possibly the Sino-Soviet border. The balance of forces was regarded as a key to stability for more than 40 years, although critics had argued that it sought to defend against an imaginary threat.

R. Osgood, *NATO: The Entangling Alliance* (1962)
J. Schaetzel, *The Unhinged Alliance* (1975)
W. Hahn and R. Pfaltzgraff, *Atlantic Community in Crisis* (1979)
M. Kaldor, *The Disintegrating West* (1979)

**Northern Ireland Conflict.** *See* ULSTER CONFLICT.

**North–South Divide.** Phrase used in British politics in the 1980s to reflect growing concern about the increasing disparity between the older industrial regions of the north and the expanding sectors of the south, emphasized by the deep recession of 1981–2, the persistence of heavy unemployment in traditional manufacturing sectors, and the growth of 'high-tech' and financial employment near London. Although only crudely accurate, booming house prices and lower unemployment in southern England, especially the South-East, gave some credibility to the concept. It was widely referred to in the 1987 election campaign, often in association with the allegation of the creation of 'two nations' of a rich south and a poor north.

**Norwegian campaign.** *See* SECOND WORLD WAR.

**Novotny, Antonin** (1904–75). Czech communist politician; First Secretary of the Czech Communist Party, 1953–68, and President, 1957–68. A veteran communist who joined the party on its inception in 1921, he was a member of the Czech Party delegation to the seventh Comintern Congress in Moscow in 1935, where he called for a Popular Front in Czechoslovakia. When the party was declared illegal in 1938, he was arrested and spent the period 1941–5 in Mauthausen concentration camp. He was promoted amidst the purges of the

Communist regime in Czechoslovakia during the Stalin era, and after the death of GOTTWALD was appointed to carry on the work of the Party Secretariat (21 March 1953). On 4 September he was appointed First Secretary. He presided over a modest relaxation of the regime during the KHRUSHCHEV era and the disgrace of some former supporters of Gottwald, including his son-in-law, the Deputy Prime Minister and Defence Minister, Alexei Cepika. In general, however, Novotny sought to follow the Soviet line as closely as possible, claiming in November 1961 that the Soviet Communist Party's programme also represented that of the Czech Communist Party. A new constitution in 1960 proclaimed the attainment of socialism in the form of the Czechoslovak Socialist Republic. Economic stagnation and student unrest in 1963 forced the dismissal of some former hard-liners and the admission of some younger, more liberal figures to key positions. Under pressure for further reform, a new management system in industry was attempted in 1965. But faced by mounting unrest and criticism from the liberal communists, he was replaced as First Secretary by ALEXANDER DUBČEK in January 1968 and resigned the Presidency on 22 March.

E. Taborsky, *Communism in Czechoslovakia, 1948–60* (1961)

**NPD.** Nationaldemokratische Partei. *See* NATIONAL DEMOCRATIC PARTY, GERMAN.

**NSDAP.** Nationalsozialistische Deutsche Arbeiterpartei. *See* NAZI PARTY.

**Nuclear weapons.** Nuclear weapons use the energy released from the nuclei of atoms to create an explosive effect. The term 'atom bomb' is usually applied to those which work through nuclear fission – the splitting of the atom. The 'hydrogen bomb' uses the process of fusion in which atoms join together in order to make larger particles. Both fission and fusion release enormous amounts of energy, providing the huge destructive power of nuclear weapons.

In the atom bomb, energy is released by dividing the nuclei of Uranium–235 atoms. When bombarded with neutrons, the U–235 atom can be split so that other neutrons are released, creating a chain reaction. Another

readily fissionable substance is Plutonium–239 – a by-product of nuclear reactors. Both materials will start spontaneous chain reaction when assembled in a 'critical mass'. In order to achieve a practicable fission warhead or bomb, a critical mass of U–235 or Pu–239 has to be brought together in a controlled way, so that it does not initiate the chain reaction before it is wanted. The 'trigger' device in an atom bomb represents one technique for bringing subcritical blocks of the fissionable materials together. The earliest atomic devices, such as that dropped on Hiroshima, were of the 'gun type' in which a piece of cone- or bullet-shaped U–235 was 'shot' by a conventional explosion at a larger block just under the critical mass. Together the two blocks of U–235 produced a critical mass, and a nuclear explosion resulted. Plutonium fission devices, such as that dropped on Nagasaki, require a similar technology in which the critical mass has to be assembled. Although less Pu–239 is required for a critical mass, it must be brought together quickly by 'implosion', so that wedges of Pu–239 are driven together by conventional explosive to initiate a chain reaction.

The hydrogen bomb is even more powerful. The explosive force comes from fusing together the nuclei of light isotopes of hydrogen, such as deuterium and tritium. Because the nuclei would naturally repel each other, they have to be forced together at very high temperatures. In order to do this, hydrogen bombs use an atom bomb as the 'trigger'. The very high temperatures produced by the fission reaction fuse the nuclei together releasing energy in a 'thermonuclear' explosion. Thus, most practicable H-bombs are in fact 'fission–fusion' devices. The earliest H-bombs consisted of an A-bomb surrounded by some of the isotopes of hydrogen in liquid form. Because the liquid forms were unstable and did not store easily, many modern H-bombs use lithium deuteride, a solid compound of deuterium and lithium.

The force of a nuclear explosion is usually measured in terms of its equivalent of TNT. A kiloton (kt) equals 1,000 tons of TNT, and a megaton (mt) a million. The bombs dropped at Hiroshima and Nagasaki were in the 15–20 kiloton range. H-bombs are capable of a much greater 'yield' than A-bombs because the fusion materials are intrinsically lighter than those used in fission bombs. A fusion bomb of given weight is theoretically capable of producing three times the energy of a fission device of similar weight. Moreover, the fusion reaction is more efficient, continuing until all the fusion material is exhausted; by contrast, A-bombs cease to produce energy once the amount of material falls below the critical mass. As a result, thermonuclear devices can create the most devastating explosions known to man.

Nuclear weapons release energy in three main forms – blast waves, thermal radiation or heat, and various types of radioactivity. The blast effect of a nuclear weapon is similar in kind, but vastly greater than that achieved by any conventional explosive. Heat sufficient to ignite inflammable materials at distances of several miles is also released within seconds of an explosion. This can have the indirect effect of creating a 'firestorm', similar to those produced by saturation bombing in the Second World War, where fires create fierce winds and burn up the oxygen in the atmosphere, asphyxiating anybody in the area. Radiation is also released by nuclear explosions. Immediate radiation of gamma and neutron rays is produced within a minute of the explosion, while local 'fallout' consisting of radioactive debris is also produced, which can fall over large areas and remain dangerous for weeks or even years. Radiation affects the body mechanism immediately and over long periods. Exposure to intense radiation will prove fatal within days, but lower doses cause death over longer periods, as well as resulting in illnesses such as leukaemia and genetic damage over a number of years.

Virtually all the theory of atomic weapons was available by 1939. The difficulties lay in turning the ideas into practicable weapons of mass destruction. In France research was halted by the defeat in 1940, when most of its scientists fled to Britain or Canada. Soviet developments were also disrupted by the German invasion of 1941 and no programme was in place before the end of 1942. In Germany a group of scientists set up a research institute in Berlin in 1940 code-named 'The Virus

House' but their work was frustrated by the sabotage in April 1942 of the heavy water plant at Ryukan in Norway on which their work depended; thereafter the German atomic bomb project floundered with little backing from Hitler. In Great Britain an important step was the preparation of a memorandum by Professors Reierls and Frisch of Birmingham University which set out the main stages in making a nuclear bomb. In February 1941 the British Maud Committee reported favourably on the possibility of making an atomic weapon. Spurred on by the possibility of a German device being prepared, further research was carried out. With America's entry into the war, the MANHATTAN PROJECT was inaugurated in June 1942 and after initial difficulties from the Americans over Britain's involvement the project was pushed through to a successful conclusion with the explosion of the first atomic device in 1945 at Alamogordo Desert, New Mexico in 17 July 1945, followed by the bombing of Hiroshima and Nagasaki on 6 and 9 August 1945. Captured German documents in 1944 showed, in fact, that their programme was far behind.

From 1942 the Soviets were obtaining nuclear secrets from the spy Klaus Fuchs, but did not press ahead with developments until after 1945. Anglo-American co-operation broke down in 1946, so that after 1945 Britain, the United States and the Soviet Union each pursued independent programmes. The first hydrogen bomb was exploded by the United States in November 1952, a month after Britain tested her independently researched atom bomb. The Soviet Union tested its first A-bomb in 1949 and exploded an H-bomb in August 1953. Once the initial technology had been mastered, the major powers concentrated on developing more efficient and powerful weapons. Britain exploded its first H-bomb in 1957; France joined the nuclear powers in 1960 when she exploded a small nuclear device in the Sahara.

The earliest nuclear weapons were 'free fall' bombs dropped from aircraft. Strategic nuclear bombers became the backbone of nuclear forces built up in America, Britain and Russia during the post-war years. The British 'V-bomber' force was based primarily on the Vulcan bomber, while the Russians used various large long-range bombers such as the Tupalev-GS 'Bear'. These aeroplanes, though increasingly vulnerable to missiles, remained in service as nuclear delivery vehicles into the 1970s. Missile technology, pioneered by the Germans in the V-WEAPONS, provided a new range of nuclear weapons. From the 1950s an increasing number of land-based nuclear missiles were deployed by the United States and the Soviet Union. Rising from 90 in 1963, the Soviet Union deployed 1,618 by 1975; missiles remain the principal part of the nuclear armoury of the Soviet Union. The development of submarine-launched nuclear missiles has seen their development into a major part of the armoury of both the United States and Russia. Russia joined this field late, with under 200 submarine-launched missiles in 1970, but rapid expansion in the next decade took the total to 1,028 by 1978. Britain experimented with a solid-fuelled rocket, Blue Streak, but abandoned the programme in 1959, opting eventually for the POLARIS system of submarine-launched missiles to maintain an effective nuclear force. France's late entry to the nuclear race led to her initially using aircraft for her nuclear strike force, the FORCE DE FRAPPE. A land-based missile force on the Plateau d'Albion became operational in 1971, consisting of 18 missiles in silos. France also created a fleet for submarine-launched ballistic missiles, the first launched in 1971, reaching five in number in 1980, carrying a total of 80 warheads.

Moreover, in addition to the strategic forces, both the WARSAW PACT and the NORTH ATLANTIC TREATY ORGANISATION (NATO) deployed considerable numbers of intermediate-range nuclear weapons, either shorter-range missiles or medium-range bombers. In 1980 it was estimated that the Soviet forces had 900 bombers and missiles of this type, while NATO deployed 236. A new range of intermediate weapons fuelled the COLD WAR in the early 1980s with the deployment of the highly-mobile Soviet SS–20 missiles, based on tracked launchers, countered by the sending of American CRUISE MISSILES to bases in Europe in 1984 and preparations to deploy an updated missile, the Pershing II. Beneath them there was also the development of battlefield nuclear weapons such as short-range strike aircraft, nuclear howitzer shells, and short-range missiles such as the Soviet Scud or American Lance. Increasingly, following a NATO ministerial decision in 1957, a deliberate decision was taken to deploy large numbers of tactical nuclear weapons, mainly aircraft, as a means of countering a massive conventional force attack by the Warsaw Pact. These weapons grew considerably in numbers in accordance with the NATO strategy of FLEXIBLE RESPONSE – a graduated escalation from conventional weapons to tactical nuclear weapons. By 1978 these included over 1,000 nuclear strike aircraft and 7,000 tactical nuclear missiles.

C. Chant and I. Hogg, *The Nuclear War File* (1983)
J. Newhouse, *The Nuclear Age: A History of the Arms Race from Hiroshima to Star Wars* (1989)

**Nuremberg rallies.** Rallies of the NAZI PARTY held in the Franconian city of Nuremberg. Massively theatrical and organized on a huge scale after HITLER's appointment as Chancellor in January 1933, the rallies of the NSDAP held in September each year were stage-managed occasions for the acclamation by the party faithful of Hitler as *Führer* (leader). Hitler often used the rallies to announce major domestic and foreign policy initiatives: thus the 1935 rallies witnessed the announcement of a series of new anti-Semitic laws (the 'Nuremberg laws'), whilst the 1938 rally was exploited to convey the image of a people united behind Hitler during the crisis over the SUDETENLAND.

I. Kershaw, *The 'Hitler Myth': Image and Reality in the Third Reich* (1987)

**Nuremberg trials.** Trials of 22 leading members of the NAZI PARTY, the Nazi government, and the German armed forces, conducted by an International Military Tribunal in the Franconian city of Nuremberg from October 1945 to September 1946. The Tribunal was presided over by eight judges from America, Britain, France and the Soviet Union. The defendants were charged with conspiracy and crimes against peace, war crimes and crimes against humanity. Ten were sentenced to death and executed (including RIBBENTROP), two committed suicide (including GÖRING), seven were sentenced to periods of imprisonment (including HESS and SPEER) and three were acquitted (including VON PAPEN and SCHACHT). A number of trials of lower-ranking Nazis and industrialists took place between 1947 and 1949. *See also* GERMANY, ALLIED OCCUPATION OF.

A. Tusa and J. Tusa, *The Nuremberg Trial* (1983)

**NUWM.** *See* NATIONAL UNEMPLOYED WORKERS' MOVEMENT.

# O

**OAS.** *See* ORGANISATION DE L'ARMÉE SECRÈTE.

**October Revolution.** *See* RUSSIAN REVOLUTION.

**Oder-Neisse Line.** The boundary line of the river Oder and its tributary, the Western Neisse, which was established as a frontier between Poland and Germany after the Second World War. It was accepted by the UK, the USA and the USSR at the POTSDAM CONFERENCE on the understanding that a final determination would take place later. An agreement made between the DEMOCRATIC REPUBLIC OF GERMANY and Poland in 1950 described the line as a permanent frontier, and in 1955 the East German and Polish governments made a declaration to this effect. It was not accepted by the German Federal Republic, the UK and the USA. In pursuit of improved relations with Eastern Europe, the Chancellor of the German Federal Government, WILLY BRANDT, signed a treaty with Poland in December 1970 in which both countries accepted the existing frontiers. *See also* SECOND WORLD WAR; OSTPOLITIK.

**OECD.** Organisation for Economic Co-operation and Development. *See* ORGANISATION FOR EUROPEAN ECONOMIC CO-OPERATION.

**OEEC.** *See* ORGANISATION FOR EUROPEAN ECONOMIC CO-OPERATION.

**OGPU.** *See* GPU.

**Okhrana.** Tsarist secret police established in Russia in 1881 as the department for defence of public security and order. The first sections were established in the major cities but spread rapidly to district and local level to monitor revolutionary activity. The Okhrana's role was specifically defined as exposing political crimes, for which they developed branches abroad to keep track of Russian exiles and made extensive use of undercover agents and informers. The investigation of crimes was the responsibility of the special corps of Gendarmes, and the Okhrana formed only a branch of the Police Department of the Interior Ministry. Unlike the CHEKA it had no extraordinary judicial powers. The Okhrana was abolished by the PROVISIONAL GOVERNMENT in 1917.

A. T. Vasilev, *The Okhrana* (1930)
E. E. Smith, *The Okhrana, the Russian Department of Police: A Bibliography* (1967)

**Ombudsman.** Swedish term for an investigative officer dealing with complaints about maladministration; the role was introduced by the Swedish constitution in 1809. The idea was adopted by Finland in 1919, Denmark in 1954, Norway in 1962 and Britain in 1965. Appointed by Parliament after each general election, the Swedish ombudsman then has security of office until the next election. He has the power to call for persons and relevant documents relating to a complaint, and if he finds the complaint justified it is his duty to inform the parties to the case and to publicize his findings. Although he does not have the power to reverse a decision by the administration, nor to award damages, public opinion and the press are able to ensure that a government department takes notice of his recommendations.

In Britain the ombudsman's official title is Parliamentary Commissioner for Administration (PCA). He is appointed by the

Crown, yet is a servant of Parliament. He differs in that he acts only at the request of an MP; in other respects his powers closely approximate to those of the Scandinavian model. Investigations of the behaviour of local authorities and public corporations is beyond his remit. Specific ombudsmen have been created to deal with particular sectors, such as insurance.

**Orange Book.** The book *We Can Conquer Unemployment* published by LLOYD GEORGE and the BRITISH LIBERAL PARTY in 1929, named after its orange cover. It developed the proposals in an earlier title, sometimes known as the 'Yellow Book', proposing a massive programme of government expenditure and public works, including extensive road and house construction. The schemes were eventually to be self-financing, and it was claimed that the initial cost of starting them would be balanced by savings in the payment of unemployment benefit as employment increased. The proposals were heavily influenced by the work of JOHN MAYNARD KEYNES and have been seen as marking an attempt to break free from economic orthodoxy to combat the DEPRESSION. The book served as the election manifesto of the Liberal Party in the 1929 general election but achieved only limited success for the party, securing 59 seats and 23 per cent of the vote, insufficient to halt its decline.

T. Wilson, *The Downfall of the Liberal Party, 1914–35* (1966)
R. Skidelsky, *Politicians and the Slump* (1967)
J. Campbell, *The Goat in the Wilderness: Lloyd George, 1922–1931* (1977)

**Orange Order.** Irish society formed in Ulster in 1795 to uphold Protestantism, taking its title from William III, Prince of Orange, who defeated the Catholic James II at the Battle of the Boyne in 1690. Branches of the Order, or Lodges, were formed in Britain, particularly in cities such as Glasgow and Liverpool where there was a significant Irish population. The Orange Lodges remain an important social focus for Protestant UNIONISTS in Northern Ireland, organizing parades on important festivals, such as 12 July to celebrate the Battle of the Boyne, and have branches in a number of English-speaking countries.

**Organisation de l'Armée Secrète** (OAS). Organization of ex-Algerian colonists and soldiers opposed to DE GAULLE's attempts to bring an end to the ALGERIAN WAR by granting independence to Algeria. Led by General Salan (1899–1984), former commander-in-chief in Algeria and military governor of Paris, 1959–60, the OAS was organized in Spain from the end of 1959. Led by Salan and General Maurice Challe, it mounted a revolt in Algiers in April 1961 which was suppressed. It made several assassination attempts on de Gaulle before and after April 1961. Its leaders were either arrested or driven out of France by 1963. Salan was arrested in April 1962 in Algiers and sentenced to life imprisonment for treason, but pardoned by de Gaulle in June 1968.

D. C. Gordon, *The Passing of French Algeria* (1966)
A. Horne, *A Savage War of Peace* (rev. edn, 1988)

**Organisation for Economic Co-operation and Development.** The successor organization to the ORGANISATION FOR EUROPEAN ECONOMIC CO-OPERATION.

**Organisation for European Economic Co-operation** (OEEC). Organization formed on 16 April 1948 with most Western European states, including the three Western zones of Germany, and with Canada and the United States as associate members to supervise the economic reconstruction of Europe with the assistance of MARSHALL PLAN aid. Its headquarters were in Paris. The stated aim of the OEEC was to achieve the economic reconstruction of Europe by 1951 and to promote European economic co-operation amongst the member states. When Marshall Aid ceased in 1952, the OEEC continued to operate until 1960, when it was replaced by the Organisation for Economic Co-operation and Development (OECD). This continued the objectives of the OEEC to promote economic and social welfare, but added a commitment to contribute to the economic expansion of developing countries. As with the OEEC, it has a Council and Executive Committee who meet regularly, plus technical committees, and its headquarters are also in Paris.

R. Mayne, *The Recovery of Europe* (1970)

Orlando, Vittorio (1860–1952). Italian politician. Born in Palermo, where he became a Professor of Law, he entered the Chamber in 1897, and became Minister of Education, 1903–5, and Minister of Justice, 1907–9, under GIOLITTI. He returned to the Ministry of Justice in 1914 and supported intervention in the First World War. In June 1916 he became Minister of the Interior, and was criticized for not taking a stronger line with dissent. He became Premier on 30 October 1917, following the Italian defeat at Caporetto. He mobilized national resources and helped restore the situation by obtaining 15 divisions from France and Britain. He accepted FOCH's overall control of the Allied armies in June 1918 and promoted the successful offensive of October 1918 at Vittorio Vento. One of the leaders of the PARIS PEACE CONFERENCE, he found Italy's territorial demands compromised by President WILSON's view of self-determination. He walked out of the Paris negotiations on 24 April, but failed to obtain further advantages. In June 1919 his government collapsed in the face of growing industrial unrest and accusations of presiding over a 'mutilated victory'. He tried twice to form a government in the early 1920s, but without success. A tacit supporter of MUSSOLINI, he broke with him over his dictatorial measures in 1925–6. Orlando re-entered politics as President of the post-war constituent assembly in 1946, but was defeated for the presidency in 1948 and retired.

A. J. Mayer, *Politics and Diplomacy of Peacemaking: Containment and Counter-revolution at Versailles, 1918–19* (1967)
C. Seton Watson. *Italy from Liberalism to Fascism, 1870–1925* (1967)

**Österreichische Volkspartei (ÖVP).** *See* AUSTRIAN PEOPLE'S PARTY.

**Ostpolitik.** Literally 'Eastern policy' designed to improve relations between the FEDERAL REPUBLIC OF GERMANY and the communist states of central and eastern Europe, pursued by the coalition government between the SOCIALIST DEMOCRATIC PARTY (SPD) and FREE DEMOCRATIC PARTY (FDP) led by Chancellor BRANDT from October 1969. Having pressed the Kiesinger 'Grand Coalition' government (1966–9) to pursue a more positive policy

towards the GERMAN DEMOCRATIC REPUBLIC and other communist states than had been pursued by the intransigent ADENAUER, the SPD leadership finally abandoned the HALLSTEIN DOCTRINE of non-recognition of the GDR and sought to normalize relations with West Germany's communist neighbours. In August 1970 Brandt visited Moscow and signed an agreement between the Federal Republic and the USSR to respect existing frontiers – including the ODER–NEISSE LINE between Poland and the GDR and the border between the DDR and the Federal Republic. In December 1970, in the course of a visit to Warsaw in which Brandt knelt before a Polish war memorial, an agreement was signed between Poland and the Federal Republic in which the latter agreed to respect the Oder–Neisse line as Poland's western border. The replacement of the intransigent WALTER ULBRICHT as leader of the GDR in May 1970 removed an important obstacle to improved relations between the GDR and the Federal Republic; as did an agreement on the relationship between Berlin and the Federal Republic reached between the four occupying powers in September 1971. Brandt's *Ostpolitik* provoked bitter controversy within the Federal Republic, however, entailing as it did recognition of the borders imposed by the victorious powers in 1945, and led to an attempt by the CDU–CSU opposition (*see* CHRISTIAN DEMOCRATIC UNION, GERMAN; CHRISTIAN SOCIAL UNION, GERMAN) to topple the government through a no-confidence vote. Having gained a mandate for his 'Eastern policy' in the November 1972 elections, Brandt capped his foreign policy successes with a BASIC TREATY between the DDR and the Federal Republic signed in December 1972. Under the Basic Treaty (*Grundervertrag*), each of the German states agreed to recognize the other's authority and independence; accepted the frontier between them and foreswore the use of force in the event of disagreements; and abandoned any claim to represent the other internationally. Both German states agreed to respect the human rights set out in the UNITED NATIONS charter; and to seek admission to that body. In December 1973 the Federal Republic signed an agreement with Czechoslovakia paralleling the treaties concluded with the

USSR and Poland, and exchanged ambassadors with Hungary and Bulgaria. The agreements associated with Brandt's *Ostpolitik* have governed relations between the GDR and the Federal Republic, and between the Federal Republic and the other WARSAW PACT states, since 1974.

W. F. Griffith, *The Ostpolitik of the Federal Republic of Germany* (1978)
H. A. Turner, *The Two Germanies since 1945* (1987)

**Ottawa Conference.** Imperial economic conference held from 21 July to 20 August 1932 on the initiative of the Canadian Premier, R. B. Bennett; it attempted to meet the problems of the DEPRESSION by introducing a system of imperial preference which allowed goods to be traded within the British Empire on favourable terms. The system was maintained into the post-war era, but was gradually abandoned after Britain's accession to the EUROPEAN ECONOMIC COMMUNITY in 1973. The Ottawa agreements had some effect in the immediate aftermath of the conference, increasing the share of imperial trade with Britain, particularly in dairy products and meat, and increasing manufactured exports from Great Britain.

I. M. Drummond, *British Economic Policy and the Empire, 1919–1939* (1972)

**ÖVP**. Österreichische Volkspartei. *See* AUSTRIAN PEOPLE'S PARTY.

**Owen, David** (1938–). British politician. He trained as medical practitioner. He was Labour MP, 1966–81, and for the SOCIAL DEMOCRATIC PARTY (SDP) since 1981 for Plymouth Devonport. He served as Labour Foreign Secretary, 1977–9. Co-founder of the SDP with Roy Jenkins, Bill Rodgers and Shirley Williams, he became its leader from 1983 and advocated distinctive SDP views on defence and the 'social market'

economy, opposing full merger with the LIBERAL PARTY. He was joint leader of THE ALLIANCE, with DAVID STEEL, in the 1987 general election. Owen opposed calls for merger following the election and resigned the leadership in August 1987 after a ballot of his members showed a majority in favour of joining the Liberals in a single party. He was elected leader of the minority of the party which retained the SDP title. He was forced to limit the national activities of the party early in 1989 and then announce its demise in June 1990 as a result of loss of support.

**Oxford Union Debate.** Debate in the Oxford Union debating society on 9 February 1933, when a resolution was passed by 275 votes to 153 that 'This House will in no circumstances fight for its King and Country'. Taken by British and foreign opinion as a sign of the spread of pacifism and anti-war sentiment amongst the younger generation, the resolution attracted disproportionate attention in view of the unrepresentative nature of the debate and those participating. It was also not widely noticed that the phrase 'King and Country' referred to the more blinkered patriotism associated with the Great War which was subject to attack in a wave of anti-war literature and memoirs from the end of the 1920s. The debate was widely interpreted abroad as marking a decline in Britain's willingness to fight, a point reinforced by the victory of an anti-rearmament candidate at a by-election in East Fulham in October 1934. A Conservative majority of over 14,500 was overturned for a Labour majority of 4,800. With the results of the PEACE BALLOT the following year, these events were contributory factors in promoting APPEASEMENT by the British government.

M. Ceadel, *Pacifism in Britain, 1914–1945* (1980)

# P

**P2** (Propaganda Due). Powerful lodge of Italian freemasons whose members included leading Italian statesmen, industrialists, service chiefs and policemen. It became the centre of a political scandal in 1981 when it was accused of being involved in right-wing terrorism, kidnapping, murder, fraud, and tax evasion. Sr Forlani's government fell in May 1981 as a result of the exposures of its alleged crimes; other resignations extended to the Christian Democrat Minister of Justice, Sr Sarti, the Chief of the Defence Staff, Admiral Torrisi, and other heads of civilian and military intelligence. The Lodge was disbanded and its Grand Master, Licio Gelli, arrested on fraud charges.

**Paasikivi, Juho Kusti** (1870–1956). Finnish banker, politician, diplomat and President, 1946–56. His political career began in the early years of this century, when Finland was still part of the Russian Empire. A member of the Old Finn Party, he was head of the Senate's finance department in 1908–9 and headed the second government of independent Finland in 1918. As head of the Finnish delegation which concluded a peace treaty with Soviet Russia in 1920, Paasikivi fell out of favour with the right-wing nationalists of his party, now retitled the National Coalition, and he devoted much of his time to directing the affairs of a leading commercial bank. He returned to active political life in 1934 and, as chairman of the National Coalition, helped lead his party away from its close association with the fascist IKL party. In autumn 1939 he led the Finnish delegation in negotiations with the Soviet Union. These talks proved abortive, and in the ensuing Winter War (*see* RUSSO-FINNISH WAR) Paasikivi held the post of minister without portfolio in the coalition government. A strong advocate of a realistic approach to relations with the Soviet Union, Paasikivi was involved in diplomatic moves to restore peace between the two countries in 1943–4, and after the conclusion of an armistice in August 1944 emerged as the only man capable of steering Finland through the difficult transitional period leading up to the final peace with the Soviet Union in 1947. As prime minister (1944–6) and as president after the retirement of Marshal MANNERHEIM he strove to lay the foundations of a more durable relationship between Finland and its eastern neighbour. The signing of a treaty of friendship and mutual assistance with the Soviet Union in the spring of 1948, though widely feared at the time as the first step towards Soviet domination, has in the course of time come to be regarded as the foundation-stone of Finland's foreign policy. A conservative by conviction and inclination, Paasikivi often displayed evident impatience with those whom he believed had learnt nothing from the lessons of the past, though his conduct of foreign policy during his final presidential term (1950–56) was reserved and cautious, in contrast to the markedly more active policy of his successor, URHO KEKKONEN.

M. Rintala, *Four Finns: Political Profiles* (1969)
U. Tuominen and K. Uusitalo, *J. K. Paasikivi: A Pictorial Biography* (1970)

**Pact of Steel.** Name given to the military alliance between Nazi Germany and Fascist Italy on 22 May 1939 formalizing the Rome–Berlin AXIS and promising to support one another if attacked.

**Panhellenic Socialist Movement** (PASOK). *See* PAPANDREOU, ANDREAS.

**Pankhurst, Emmeline** (1858–1928). British leader of the SUFFRAGETTE movement. She was the joint founder and leader after 1898 of the Women's Franchise League and with her daughter Christabel (1880–1958) of the more militant Women's Suffrage and Political Union from 1903. Her discussions with the Prime Minister in 1906 led to disillusionment with the Liberals and resort to more violent tactics. She was arrested several times and sentenced to three years' penal servitude in 1913 after blowing up a house being built for Lloyd George, but was released on licence. On the outbreak of the First World War she turned to a campaign to encourage women to work in the war factories and prove their entitlement to the vote. She joined the Conservative Party in 1918 and was adopted as a Conservative candidate for Whitechapel just before her death.

A. Rosen, *Rise up Women! The Militant Campaign of the Women's Social and Political Union, 1903–14* (1974)
M. D. Pugh, *Women's Suffrage in Britain, 1867–1928* (1980)

**Papagos, Alexander** (1883–1955). Greek soldier and Prime Minister. Born in Athens, he served in the Balkan Wars, the First World War, and the GRAECO-TURKISH WAR of 1920–23. He was Minister of War in 1936, when METAXAS appointed him Chief of the General Staff. He proved an able commander in countering the Italian invasion in 1940, but fell back with his armies under the German invasion of the following year. He was given command of the Greek royalist armies in January 1949 at a decisive stage in the GREEK CIVIL WAR, supervising the reduction of the communist strongholds at Mounts Vitsi and Grammos in August, which brought the war to an end. In May 1951 he resigned his military appointments and founded a new conservative political party, the 'Greek Rally' which won the largest number of seats in the 1951 elections. Following an overwhelming majority in the elections of November 1952, he became Premier, serving until his death on 5 October 1955, when he was replaced by KARAMANLIS. A conservative, he helped to cement the alliance of Greece with the West and its reconstruction in the aftermath of the war.

E. O'Ballance, *The Greek Civil War* (1966)

C. M. Woodhouse, *The Struggle for Greece, 1941–49* (1976)

**Papandreou, Andreas** (1919–). Greek politician. The son of GEORGE PAPANDREOU, he became a naturalized American citizen in 1944 and taught economics in California. He returned to Greece in 1960 and entered his father's government in 1964, and through his extremist rhetoric contributed to the polarization of Greek politics from 1964 to 1967. Imprisoned under the GREEK COLONELS' regime, he was released in 1967 and went to America. He returned to Greece in 1973 and formed the Panhellenic Socialist Movement (PASOK) in opposition to KARAMANLIS. PASOK won an outright victory in the 1981 elections and Papandreou became Prime Minister on 21 October 1981. He pursued an anti-business policy which resulted in a stagnation of the Greek economy, and an anti-American policy which caused concern amongst Greece's NATO allies, but Greek entry into the EUROPEAN ECONOMIC COMMUNITY earlier in the year bound Greece more closely to the West. Following a further election victory in June 1985 he gradually modified his earlier commitments to withdraw from NATO, announcing in January 1987 that Greece would remain in the alliance. This cost him left-wing support, but also saw improved relations with Turkey, who sought to overcome Greek objections to their entry to the EEC. A financial scandal in which PASOK ministers were implicated in 1988–9 and the personal affairs of the Premier led to a vote of no confidence in the government in March 1989. The elections of June 1989 resulted in the loss of PASOK's overall majority but the rural New Democratic Party could not itself win a majority either then or in new elections in November 1989. On its third attempt however, on 8 April 1990, New Democracy secured a slim majority of one over all other parties, breaking nine years of PASOK or coalition rule. Scandal ridden, PASOK nevertheless continued to draw 40% of the vote.

**Papandreou, George** (1888–1968). Greek politician. Born in Salonika, he trained as a lawyer and entered politics as a moderate socialist. He was Minister of the Interior in 1923, and Minister of Education, 1929–33.

He founded the Democratic Socialist Party in 1935 but was exiled under METAXAS, 1936–40. Imprisoned during the Axis occupation of Greece, Papandreou escaped to head the Greek government-in-exile, concluding a short-lived truce with the communist guerrilla forces, before returning to head a coalition government from April 1944. He quickly went into opposition, distrusted by the right, as the country moved towards full-scale civil war (*see* GREEK CIVIL WAR). He founded the moderate socialist Centre Union Party in 1961 which obtained the largest number of seats in the elections of November 1963, allowing him to become Prime Minister for the first time in 17 years. Leaving office on 30 December 1963, he obtained an outright victory in the elections of February 1964. His government, however, was undermined by growing conflict with the army, the quarrels with Turkey over Cyprus, and clashes with CONSTANTINE II, leading to his fall from office in July 1965. The opening of a new election campaign in April 1967, in which it was believed that Papandreou and the Left would prove triumphant, provoked the GREEK COLONELS' coup on 21 April 1967. Briefly imprisoned, he died the following year. A controversial figure, but less so than his son, Andreas.

E. O'Ballance, *The Greek Civil War, 1944–1949* (1966)
R. Clogg, *A Short History of Modern Greece* (1979)

**Papen, Franz von** (1879–1969). German politician and Reich Chancellor in the WEIMAR REPUBLIC from June to December 1932. After a military career, Papen became a member of the Prussian lower house in 1920, attaching himself to the right wing of the CENTRE PARTY in the assembly. A monarchist who sought the restoration of the HOHENZOLLERN dynasty, Papen became editor of the Centre Party newspaper *Germania*. His links with the *Reichswehr* and his marriage to the daughter of a leading Saar industrialist established his connections amongst the largely anti-republican élites within the Weimar Republic. Despite lacking any significant political experience, Papen was appointed Reich Chancellor by President HINDENBURG following the dismissal of BRÜNING, not least as a consequence of the intrigues of General SCHLEI-

CHER, political advisor to the former *Reichswehr* minister in the Brüning cabinet.

Papen's cabinet, with its strong aristocratic tinge and its representation of industrial interests, soon became known as the 'cabinet of the barons'. It lacked the support of any of the major parties in the REICHSTAG and was bent on transforming the political system in an authoritarian direction. Utterly dependent on presidential emergency powers to maintain him in office, Papen immediately sought a dissolution of the REICHSTAG in the hope that new elections would return a parliament more congenial to the authoritarian right. In the event, the July 1932 Reichstag elections brought a massive upsurge of support for the NAZI PARTY (NSDAP) and a further erosion of support for those parties sympathetic to a presidential form of government. Papen's determination to break the power of the SOCIAL DEMOCRATIC PARTY (SPD) and labour movement was demonstrated by his implementation of further cuts in social security payments and his illegal deposition of the SPD-led Prussian government. Despite Nazi electoral gains, Papen refused to accede to HITLER's demand that he be appointed Reich Chancellor in return for Nazi support in the *Reichstag* for an authoritarian government; a decision in which he was supported by Hindenburg. Seeking to apply further pressure to the NSDAP, Papen called for another dissolution of the *Reichstag* in mid-September 1932 and fresh elections. In the November 1932 elections the NSDAP suffered substantial losses; yet, whilst the parties supporting the Papen government had enjoyed some electoral gains, the basis on which the government rested was extremely narrow and Hitler was no more willing than before to accept a subordinate place in government. Papen now planned a *coup d'état* to replace the Weimar constitution with an authoritarian presidential dictatorship. Whilst Hindenburg was willing to support this scheme, it was opposed by General Schleicher, Minister of Defence in the Papen government, who believed the army incapable of coping with both Nazi paramilitary and communist opposition to the planned coup. Schleicher's opposition to his plan forced Papen's resignation as Chancellor in early December 1932.

Determined to wreak his revenge on Schleicher, who replaced him as Chancellor, Papen now began a series of intrigues designed to secure the support of Hitler and the NSDAP for an authoritarian government in which he might play a leading role. Arranging financial support for the NSDAP from industry at a time when the party was in a state of financial crisis, Papen also concentrated on winning the support of Hindenburg for Hitler's appointment as Chancellor. This he finally achieved in late January 1933, and on 30 January Hitler was appointed Chancellor with Papen as Vice-Chancellor.

During the succeeding months the Nazi seizure of power proved how mistaken had been Papen's belief that Hitler and the NSDAP could be contained within an essentially conservative-authoritarian government. Papen's authority as Vice-Chancellor was rapidly undermined as he sought to articulate the anxieties of conservative circles at the radical course being assumed by the Nazi seizure of power from the summer of 1933 onwards. When Hitler finally acted to purge the leadership of the SA (*see* SA) in June 1934, Papen was placed under house arrest.

From 1934 to 1938, Papen was Ambassador to Vienna, becoming Ambassador to Turkey after the ANSCHLUSS. Acquitted by the Allies at the NUREMBERG TRIALS, he was sentenced in 1947 to eight years' imprisonment by a German court. He was released in 1949.

E. Kolb, *The Weimar Republic* (1988)

**Paris, Treaties of.** Treaties signed on 10 February 1947 following a peace conference of 21 nations which had fought against Hitler. The treaties were imposed on Italy, Hungary, Bulgaria, Romania and Finland, who were collectively required to disband their fascist organizations and limit their armed forces. All had to make REPARATIONS to Russia, Yugoslavia and Greece; Italy had to pay restitution also to Ethiopia. Italy was forced to abandon her claims to Albania and Ethiopia and cede parts of Istria, plus some Adriatic islands, to Yugoslavia. The Dodecanese islands were ceded to Greece; Nice was returned to France; and TRIESTE became a Free City. Italy also renounced her claims to her other, longer-established

African territories, Libya and Somalia. Bulgaria was returned to her frontiers of January 1941; Hungary was reduced to the frontiers decided at the TREATY OF TRIANON, and Romania recovered her inter-war frontiers apart from BESSARABIA and the northern BUKOVINA, which remained with the Soviet Union; Romania also lost the southern Dobrudja to Bulgaria. Finland was to revert to her frontiers of 1940, before the CONTINUATION WAR, losing the Arctic port of Petsamo.

**Paris, Treaty of.** The treaty establishing the EUROPEAN COAL AND STEEL COMMUNITY (ECSC), signed in Paris on 18 April 1951. It was subsequently amended by the 1965 Merger Treaty establishing a single Commission (*see* COMMISSION OF THE EUROPEAN COMMUNITY) and a single COUNCIL OF MINISTERS for the EUROPEAN ECONOMIC COMMUNITY (EEC), EURATOM and the ECSC; by the 1970 treaty amending certain of its budgetary provisions; and by the 1972 Treaty of Accession, under which Denmark, Ireland and the United Kingdom joined the European Community. The Treaty established a Coal and Steel Community with a common market, common objectives and common institutions. The aims of this Community were defined as the promotion of economic expansion, employment and improvements in living standards in the member states, and the rationalization of production. The treaty set up a High Authority as the main administrative body of the Community, with a Consultative Committee, a common assembly to allow for the expression of Parliamentary opinion, a Council of Ministers and a Court of Justice. From the foundation of the EEC and Euratom, the Assembly became the European Parliament, serving all three Communities, and the scope of the Court of Justice was similarly transformed. The European Commission took over the work of the High Authority and the Council of Ministers merged with those of the other Communities in 1965. A distinction between the Treaty of Paris and the TREATY OF ROME was that the former laid down detailed provisions for the operation of the Coal and Steel Community, provided the High Authority with considerable powers to achieve this, and ensured it from the

beginning of an independent income raised by levies on the industry, while the latter was an 'outline' treaty, which envisaged the subsequent working out of common policies in many fields. It did not immediately provide for independent financial resources and gave a larger place to the Council of Ministers in the decision-making process.
R. Vaughan, *Post-War Integration in Europe* (1976)

**Paris Peace Conference.** Congress of 'allied and associated powers' held at Paris between 18 January 1919 and 20 January 1920 to conclude a peace settlement following the First World War. The settlement was embodied in the TREATY OF VERSAILLES (with Germany), the TREATY OF ST GERMAIN (with Austria), the TREATY OF NEUILLY (with Bulgaria), the TREATY OF TRIANON (with Hungary) and the TREATY OF SÈVRES (with Turkey), all named after districts of Paris. The Conference was dominated by the Council of Ten, to which the United States, Britain, France, Italy and Japan each contributed two members. In effect, the proceedings were dominated by President WILSON, CLEMENCEAU, and LLOYD GEORGE, with lesser but important parts played by ORLANDO on behalf of Italy and the representatives of Romania, Greece and Yugoslavia. Germany was denied any effective influence on the settlement, and the Soviet Union was not represented. A Council of Ambassadors was used to finalize the frontiers of Turkey and Hungary. The major powers came with differing objectives. Clemenceau, who presided over the Conference, was primarily concerned with guaranteeing French security by a return of ALSACE-LORRAINE and limiting Germany's control over the Rhineland, thus ensuring France some territorial barrier to further German aggression. In the Versailles Treaty he was only partly successful, more extreme French demands for permanent annexation of the west bank of the Rhine or the creation of a puppet Rhineland state being soon seen as unrealistic in the face of the objections of Wilson and Lloyd George. Clemenceau was adamant, however, on the need to restrict German armaments and to secure heavy REPARATIONS. Lloyd George was also pledged 'to make Germany pay', eventually accepting a large reparations burden on Germany but concerned to see

a swift settlement in order to restore European prosperity. The end of the German naval threat and the surrender of the German colonies to MANDATES of the LEAGUE OF NATIONS were major objectives he obtained from the Versailles settlement. President Wilson's FOURTEEN POINTS had been the basis on which the armistice had been signed on 11 November 1918 by Germany, and he sought to ensure that the principles of self-determination were applied. Although this was a major feature of the settlements, making frequent use of the democratic instrument of the plebiscite to settle frontiers, the principle was not applied consistently, many Germans, Austrians, and Hungarians being placed under the control of other nationalities and denied the opportunity of determining their own futures. Wilson's Fourteen Points had also sought the end of secret diplomacy, but the agreements entered into with Italy to secure her entry into the war in 1915, as well as promises made to other powers, such as Romania, produced conflict. Italy, one of the victors, remained dissatisfied with her gains, while the satisfaction of Romania and the SUCCESSOR STATES in Eastern Europe stored up problems for the future. Underpinning the settlement was the creation of the LEAGUE OF NATIONS, seen by Wilson as a body which would help to ensure peace in the future and arbitrate injustices and grievances in a rational manner. The failure of the US Congress to ratify the Treaty of Versailles or sign the Covenant of the League removed one of the principal guarantees of the settlement.

The work of the Peace Conference has often been harshly judged. The task facing it was huge, no less than a major readjustment of European frontiers consequent not just on the end of the war but also the break-up of the Austro-Hungarian Empire, the fragmentation of parts of the old Russian Empire, the collapse of Ottoman power, and the claims of several new nation states which were coming into existence even as the Peace Conference met. The difficulties were reflected in the inability of the conference to produce a single treaty. The settlement nonetheless ratified a radical revision of European frontiers, especially in Eastern and Central Europe, forming the basis for political sovereignty and international diplomacy for the next 20 years. The setting up of the the League of Nations was a bold experiment in international affairs in which much idealism and optimism for the future was vested. The greatest weakness of the peace settlements lay in the challenge that could be offered to it by the defeated powers on the grounds that they had been discriminated against in the application of the principle of self-determination and the vindictive character of the 'war guilt' clauses and the reparations agreements. The unwitting damage caused to the European economy as a whole by the reparations settlement with Germany also attracted much adverse comment, particularly as the DEPRESSION began to threaten the survival of many of the newly established governments.

The historiography has reflected different phases in the reception of the settlement; favourable judgments on it in the light of the relatively peaceful atmosphere of the LOCARNO TREATIES and the KELLOGG PACT, harsher criticism as it seemed the occasion for the return of tension and crises during the 1930s. Something of a consensus existed by 1939 that Versailles required revision, that the League of Nations had 'failed' and that the opportunity for a long-lasting peace had been 'lost', apparently reinforced by the outbreak of the Second World War. Thereafter, a more balanced and neutral assessment re-emerged, which stressed the difficulties under which the peace-makers had laboured and the impossibility of satisfying the differing aims of the participants. Moreover, in spite of considerable revisions to boundaries after 1945, much of the settlement remained intact, principally in the new states of Eastern, Central and South-Eastern Europe.

H. Nicholson, *Peacemaking, 1919* (1933)
A. J. Mayer, *The Policy and Diplomacy of Peacemaking* (1968)
S. Marks, *The Illusion of Peace: International Relations in Europe, 1918–1933* (1976)
E. H. Carr, *The Twenty Years Crisis* (new edn, 1981)

**Parti Communiste Français** (PCF). *See* COMMUNIST PARTY, FRENCH.

**Partido Communista Española** (PCE). *See* COMMUNIST PARTY, SPANISH.

**Partido Obrero de Unificación Marxista** (POUM). Spanish TROTSKYITE group, approximately 100,000 strong in 1936, formed by opponents of Stalin who had returned to Spain with the establishment of the SECOND REPUBLIC. Led by Joaquin Maurin (1897–1973) and Andres Nin (1892–1937), it advocated collectivization of the means of production and believed in the necessity of a single transforming revolution advocated by TROTSKY in his idea of permanent revolution. Especially strong in Catalonia, it supported the Popular Front in February 1936 and was represented on the government of Catalonia from the first weeks of the war. Its militias were notable for their revolutionary zeal and lack of normal military discipline. It was starved of arms by the Soviet-dominated Socialist Party of Catalonia and attacked for its open opposition to Stalin's PURGES and support for Trotsky. The POUM representatives were ousted from government in Catalonia in April 1937 and conflict between it and the communists, Republicans and Catalan separatists erupted into fighting in the MAY DAYS. After a truce on 7 May the communists attempted to get Premier LARGO CABALLERO to suppress the organization; following his resignation, the POUM was subjected to a bitter propaganda campaign as the communists sought to bring all Republican forces under their control. In mid-June it was declared illegal and its leaders arrested. Nin died in a Soviet-run camp near Madrid on 20 June. Many of the rest of the leadership were tried in October 1938 and imprisoned. The action against POUM bred a growing distrust between communist and non-communist forces on the Republican side, the fate of the romantic idealism of the POUM coming to symbolize the end of the utopian phase of the Spanish conflict.

S. Payne, *The Spanish Revolution* (1970)
B. Bolloten, *The Spanish Civil War* (1991)

**Partido Republicano Radical.** Founded in 1908 by the flamboyant demagogue, Alejandro Lerroux, the Radical Republican Party played a crucial, though idiosyncratic, role in Spanish politics. Its original populist anti-clericalism and anti-monarchism failed to attract lasting working-class support, and it evolved as a vehicle for meritocratic republican criticism of the restrictive features of the Restoration and Dictatorship. Initially a pillar of the opposition San Sebastian Coalition of 1930, the party increasingly sought to represent conservative reaction to the social and economic reforms attempted during the early SECOND REPUBLIC. Consequently, when in government after 1933 with the support of the Catholic CONFEDERACIÓN ESPAÑOLA DE DERECHAS AUTÓNOMAS (CEDA), the Radicals presided over the destruction of reform and the repression of the ASTURIAN RISING that marked important stages on the road to the SPANISH CIVIL WAR. The party finally disintegrated before the 1936 elections under the combined effects of accumulated internal divisions, pressure from the political Right, and a series of financial scandals that completed public disillusionment in a corrupt leadership.

A. Lerroux, *La Pequena historia* (1945)
O. R. Manjon, *El Partido Republicano Radical* (1976)

**Partido Socialista Obrero Español** (PSOE). *See* SOCIALIST WORKERS' PARTY, SPANISH.

**Partidul Comunist Roman** (PCR). *See* COMMUNIST PARTY, ROMANIAN.

**partisans.** Armed groups of guerrillas acting behind enemy lines. The term was adopted in the 20th century by STALIN to describe the groups operating behind German lines following the Nazi invasion. The propaganda value of demonstrating both to his own subjects and to foreign governments that the Soviet people had not been beaten into subjection or had joined the Nazi conquerors was a necessary counterweight to the severe defeats suffered up to 1942 and the defection of many Soviet citizens to join the invading armies. Partisan warfare undoubtedly tied down hundreds of thousands of German and auxiliary troops whose activities and reprisals in anti-partisan operations often helped to alienate the local population from Nazi rule. Their full military significance is difficult to calculate, but they undoubtedly played a part in forcing the German armies to operate in occupied Russian territory with even greater ferocity. Partisan operations were also called on by the Soviet Union in other German-occupied countries in order to wear down the German war effort. COMINTERN instructed the Greek, Albanian and other Communist Parties to oppose actively the German occupiers by partisan warfare. The most famous partisan army of all, that led by TITO in Yugoslavia, was called on by Comintern on 1 July 1941. Members of the YUGOSLAVIAN COMMUNIST PARTY took command of 'people's liberation partisan detachments' formed into a National Liberation Army in November 1942. Based on their mountain strongholds in Bosnia and Herzegovina, the communist partisans waged a protracted and bitter war against the Nazi forces and against their non-communist rivals the CHETNIKS. The partisan army of Tito formed the basis for the communist government proclaimed in 1943 at the JAJCE CONGRESS. By the end of 1944 it had captured Belgrade and was one of the few partisan or RESISTANCE groups to succeed in liberating its own country. Elsewhere, as in Bulgaria and Romania, it was Soviet armies which finally defeated the German and other Axis forces. In Greece the communist partisans became engaged in the bloody and, ultimately, unsuccessful GREEK CIVIL WAR for control of the country which did not end until 1949. Less well known are the various national partisan movements which continued to operate in parts of the BALTIC STATES and the UKRAINE against the Soviet Union until the 1950s. *See also* SECOND WORLD WAR.

M. R. D. Foot, *Resistance* (1976)

**Partito Communista Italiano** (PCI). *See* COMMUNIST PARTY, ITALIAN.

**Partito Popolare Italiano** (PPI). First mass-based Catholic Party in Italian politics, founded in January 1919 with the prior authorization of the Catholic Church. Led by Luigi Sturzo (1871–1959), it aimed to support Christian principles and offer an alternative to socialism. The party promoted social reform, the rights to form unions, defence of property and the family, WOMEN'S SUFFRAGE and the LEAGUE OF NATIONS. It grew dramatically in the highly charged atmosphere of post-war Italy, winning 100 seats in the Chamber in November 1919 and had a minister in GIOLITTI's cabinet. It ran autonomously in 1921, increasing its seats to 108 in 1921, and refused to support a new Giolitti government. It remained out of the government formed by Luigi Facta (1861–1930) in February 1922, weakening its ability to deal with the rising fascist movement. Divided in its attitude to fascism, Sturzo resigned in July 1923 and the party collapsed into factions, obtaining only 39 seats in 1924. The Vatican issued an injunction against Catholic participation in the secession of deputies from the Chamber following the murder of Matteoti (*see* MATTEOTI CRISIS), and Sturzo went into exile. The party was banned by the Exceptional Decrees of 1926. The PPI was the forerunner of the CHRISTIAN DEMOCRATIC PARTY reformed after the fall of Mussolini, continuity being provided by ALCIDE DE GASPERI, Party Secretary of the PPI in 1923–5 and later leader of the Christian Democrats.

R. Webster, *Christian Democracy in Italy, 1860–1960* (1961)

**Partito Socialista Italiano** (PSI). *See* SOCIALIST PARTY, ITALIAN.

**Parti Socialiste** (PS). *See* SOCIALIST PARTY, FRENCH.

**Pasic, Nikola** (1845–1926). Serbian statesman and Prime Minister. Born at Zajecar in eastern SERBIA on the border of Bulgaria and Serbia, he trained as an engineer. He participated in the struggle which freed Serbia from the Turks in 1876–7 and entered the independent National Assembly in 1878. Although Prime Minister in 1891–2, he clashed with the Austrophile policies of the ruling Obrenovic dynasty and was imprisoned in 1897 and 1898. He regained power through the coup in 1903 which brought King Peter of the Karadjordjevic dynasty to the throne and was Prime Minister in 1904–8 and 1910–18. A strong Serbian nationalist, he presided over the enlargement of Serbia in the Balkan Wars of 1912–13. It is now believed Pasic bore little responsibility for the plot which led to the assassination of Archduke FRANCIS FERDINAND at Sarajevo on 28 June 1914. His reply to the Austrian ultimatum of 23 July, while conciliatory, stopped short of surrendering Serbian sovereignty and, assured of Russian support, suggests he was prepared to accept war with Austria as the outcome. When Serbian resistance was finally overcome in 1915 he led the Serbian govern-

ment-in-exile from Corfu. Initially he was cool to the overtures of the Yugoslav committee set up in London by ANTE TRUMBIC for the creation of a united South Slav state, but the collapse of Russia and the support of the Western Allies for Trumbic persuaded him to agree to the Corfu Pact of 20 July 1917, foreshadowing the creation of a Yugoslav state under the Serbian royal house. His views, however, still centred on an enlarged Serbia rather than a federal state envisaged by Trumbic, and he resisted giving pledges on a federal structure. He was increasingly outflanked by the momentum Yugoslav unity developed with the support of the Prince-Regent Alexander (*see* ALEXANDER I) and the collapse of the Austro-Hungarian Empire in the autumn of 1918. When the new state was created he was denied office and sent to conduct peace negotiations at the PARIS PEACE CONFERENCE, where he openly clashed with Trumbic, the new Foreign Minister. He returned as Prime Minister in 1921, influencing the assertion of Serbian nationalism within the new state against the opposition of the other ethnic groups. Pasic's role in the creation of YUGOSLAVIA has been disputed. Some have claimed him as a proponent of South Slav unity from the early 20th century. Most accounts suggest that his outlook remained dominated by Serbian nationalism, in which the idea of a genuinely federal Yugoslavia played little part. This half-hearted acceptance of the principle upon which other ethnic minorities entered the new state left a legacy of instability and bitterness which bedevilled Yugoslavian politics for the rest of the century. *See also* CROATIA.

A. N. Dragnich, *Serbia, Nikola Pasic and Yugoslavia* (1974)
M. B. Petrovich, *A History of Modern Serbia*, vol. 2 (1976)
B. and C. Jelavich, *The Establishment of the Balkan National States, 1804–1920* (1977)

**PASOK.** *See* PAPANDREOU, ANDREAS.

**Passchendaele, Battle of.** *See* FIRST WORLD WAR.

**Paul VI, Pope** (1897–1978). Pope, 1963–78. Born Giovanni Montini, near Brescia, he was ordained in 1920 and served in the papal secretariat, 1924–54. He was Archbishop of Milan for nine years and was made a Cardinal in 1958. He presided over the end of the SECOND VATICAN COUNCIL and continued its ecumenical thrust. He was the first Pope to travel beyond Europe, going on a pilgrimage to Jerusalem in 1964, to India, also in 1964, and visiting the United Nations in 1965. He visited Latin America and Africa, Australia and the Philippines. He pursued traditional policies in doctrine, notably on birth control, but promoted the vernacular liturgy introduced by Vatican II. He died on 6 August 1978. He is often seen as a consolidator of the work of JOHN XXIII.

**PCE.** Partido Communista Española. *See* COMMUNIST PARTY, SPANISH.

**PCI.** Partito Communista Italiano. *See* COMMUNIST PARTY, ITALIAN.

**PCF.** Parti Communiste Français. *See* COMMUNIST PARTY, FRENCH.

**PCR.** Partidul Comunist Roman. *See* COMMUNIST PARTY, ROMANIAN.

**Peace Ballot.** British house-to-house ballot conducted from late 1934 by an *ad hoc* body chaired by Lord Cecil and drawing support from the League of Nations Union. Those canvassed had to answer five questions about their attitude to war. The final results were published on 27 June 1935. The questions were: 'Should Britain remain a member of the League?'; 'Are you in favour of an all-round reduction in armaments by international agreement?'; 'Are you in favour of an all-round abolition of national military and naval aircraft by international agreement?'; 'Should the private manufacture and sale of arms be prohibited by international agreement?'; and 'Do you consider that, if a nation insists on attacking another, the other nations should combine to compel it to stop by (a) economic and non-military measures? (b) if necessary military measures?'. The referendum polled 11.5 million votes. To all the questions the answer was affirmative; over 10 million voted 'Yes' to the first, and around 10 million to the others; to the last question (b) 6,784,368 voted 'Yes', 2,351,981 voted 'No'. The Ballot was hailed as a high point of support for the League of Nations and

pacifist or pacific policies by the public. Although tendentiously worded, the Ballot helped to contribute to pro-appeasement policies (*see* APPEASEMENT) within the British government and other parties in the run-up to the ETHIOPIAN crisis and general election later in the year. *See also* PEACE PLEDGE UNION.

M. Gilbert, *The Roots of Appeasement* (1966)
M. Caedel, *Pacifism in Britain, 1914-1945* (1980)

**Peace Pledge Union.** Organization formed as a result of the initiative of Canon 'Dick' Sheppard of St Martin's-in-the-Fields Church in London. In October 1934 he appealed to men to pledge themselves against war by sending him a postcard saying they bound themselves to a pledge to renounce war and to persuade others to do the same. The Peace Pledge Union developed as a result of the response, and by mid-1936 had an estimated 100,000 members. The Union was an important pacifist organization which contributed to the pro-appeasement policies (*see* APPEASEMENT) of the NATIONAL GOVERNMENT and the LABOUR PARTY in the 1930s.

M. Gilbert, *The Roots of Appeasement* (1966)
M. Caedel, *Pacifism in Britain, 1914-1945* (1980)

**Pearse, Patrick** (1879-1916). Irish writer and patriot. Born in Dublin and educated at Royal University, he qualified as a barrister, but concentrated on work as a writer and educator. He was a member of the Gaelic League from 1896, an editor of Irish language and other nationalist literature, a founder-member of the IRISH VOLUNTEERS and joined the IRISH REPUBLICAN BROTHERHOOD in 1913. He was a fund-raiser on behalf of the Irish Volunteers in the United States in 1913 and led the group of Irish Volunteers who refused to support REDMOND's commitment of the movement to the British war effort. Deeply imbued with the sense of cultural nationalism and of a late romantic sense of the necessity for 'blood sacrifice', he determined on the EASTER RISING as a means of shattering British legitimacy and rousing the Irish people. Part of the group of 70 rebels who seized the General Post Office in Dublin on 24 April 1916, Pearse proclaimed the Irish Republic from the steps of the GPO and styled himself President of the Provisional

Government and Commandant-in-Chief of the army. Forced to surrender on 29 April, he was executed on 3 May. Pearse became the symbol of the 'martyrs' of the Easter Rising as initial Irish hostility to the destruction caused in Dublin was changed to anger at the execution of the leaders. As a writer and intellectual sincerely committed to the cause of Irish nationalism, his death caused widespread disquiet and contributed to the ends he sought.

R. Dudley Edwards, *Patrick Pearse: the Triumph of Failure* (1977)

**Perestroika.** From the Russian word for 'restructuring', *Perestroika*, with GLASNOST, has been the most frequently cited slogan of the GORBACHEV era since 1985. It has become synonymous with his attempt to regenerate the stagnant economy by encouraging market forces, decentralizing industrial management, and democratizing the Communist Party and government machinery. Initial steps towards the implementation of *Perestroika* also included greater devolution to the lower tiers of government and party apparatus, the introduction of open elections, and the promise of multi-party contests in future. Evidence of fundamental restructuring of the economic base of Soviet society was less evident by early 1991. Perestroika was overtaken by the rapid restructuring of the Soviet state and its constitution after the failed hard-line coup of August 1991.

M. Gorbachev, *Perestroika* (1988)

**Pétain, (Henri) Philippe** (1856–1951). French soldier and politician. The son of a peasant family, he entered the army and received his commission from Saint-Cyr in 1878. He lectured at the École de Guerre, where he stressed the importance of modern weapons to the defence. His somewhat unfashionable views meant that by 1914 he was nearing retirement after a not particularly successful career, having seen no active service. Appointed a Brigadier at the outbreak of war, he soon rose to command a division and then a corps. This led to his command of the Second Army which met the attack on Verdun by the Germans in 1916. His stout defence of Verdun, symbolized by the slogan 'They shall not pass' was backed by astute

manipulation of the forces at his disposal. Following the successful defence of Verdun, he was passed over as commander-in-chief, only to be given the task of repairing morale after the mutinies in the French army which followed the failure of the Nivelle offensive in April 1917. Appointed commander-in-chief in May, he had several mutineers executed, but also acted to improve conditions with better rations and leave, while scaling down offensives and re-instilling confidence in his men by limited attacks. With FOCH he developed a realistic strategy to suit the conditions of modern war, leading the French armies into 1918 in far better shape than he had found them. Initially his caution was viewed with some disfavour and he found himself second-in-command once Foch became Supreme Allied Commander, but following the counter-attack on the German armies in July 1918 he pressed home the offensive which finished the war in the West. Made a Marshal of France in December, Pétain remained on active service as joint Franco-Spanish commander suppressing the 'RIF REVOLT' in Morocco, and advising on the construction of the MAGINOT LINE on the Council of War.

In 1934 Pétain entered the Cabinet as Minister of War and in 1939 accepted the post of ambassador to Madrid. Recalled by REYNAUD on 15 May 1940 as Minister of State and Vice-President of the Council, Pétain joined WEYGAND in urging an armistice with the Germans. When Reynaud resigned on 16 June he named Pétain as his successor, who immediately sought an armistice with the Germans, concluded on 22 June. Two days later a separate agreement was signed with Italy.

The new French government took its name from the Spa town of Vichy in the Auvergne where it set up government to administer the third of France left under its control by the armistice (*see* VICHY GOVERNMENT). As well as supervising the immediate problems of the aftermath of the war, the Vichy regime under Pétain soon developed a momentum of its own. LAVAL persuaded the former representatives of the government to confer on Pétain autocratic powers as Chief of State on 11 July. Pétain embarked on the most controversial part of his career as head of the Vichy Government. Democratic and civil liberties were removed, trade unions dissolved and political parties banned. Local councils were nominated and a purge of government officials was carried out. Anti-Semitic legislation was passed in October 1940 and in June 1941, while arbitrary arrests placed almost 80,000 people in prison by 1942, including most of the former members of the government. Although 82 at the time of the assumption of the presidency and often betraying signs of senility, Pétain was sufficiently active to give a distinctly conservative and authoritarian stamp to the regime. Pétain's Vichy has been called 'a reactionary, authoritarian, Roman Catholic, chauvinist corporatist state'. He attempted to steer a course for France between a full military alliance with Germany and collaboration to obtain the return of French prisoners-of-war and exert such influence as he could to improve France's position. Initially Laval was his chief lieutenant and was nominated his successor on 12 July 1940. Disagreements with Laval led to the latter's dismissal in December 1940 and the appointment of Admiral DARLAN on 10 February 1941 as Deputy Prime Minister and Foreign Minister, followed a day later by his appointment as Pétain's successor. Darlan, however, also fell foul of Pétain for becoming too closely entangled in offering military support to the Germans, and was demoted in April 1942. Laval returned to succeed him with the post of Prime Minister, Foreign Minister and Minister of the Interior. Pétain's support, however, was eroded by the desperate material conditions in which most of the French were forced to live, the increasingly active RESISTANCE and drafts of forced labour to Germany. The German occupation of the FREE ZONE and the deportation of Jews from 1942 revealed the powerlessness of the regime to defend French interests even at the price of collaboration. With the Allied invasion in 1944, retribution for Pétain was inevitable. Although taken to Germany to carry on an émigré Vichy Government at Sigmaringen, he was brought back to stand trial for treason at a special High Court in July 1945. Sentenced to death, a recommendation for mercy was accepted, and he was imprisoned in the for-

tress on the Île d'Yeu off the west coast of France, where he died in 1951.

Had Pétain died in 1914 he would have been unknown, in 1919 or 1939 he would have been buried with the honours of the French nation. In 1940 he acted only as many wished to do, to end a war in which France was plainly beaten. But the attempts by Pétain to regenerate France along conservative authoritarian lines, his complicity in the death of thousands of French Jews and members of the Resistance and his compliance in the exploitation of France at German hands, condemned him in the eyes of many who had supported him in 1940. Pétain was more than a collaborator, he revealed reactionary and anti-Semitic attitudes which had remained beneath the instabilities of the Third Republic.

R. Aron, *The Vichy Regime, 1940–4* (1958)
S. Ryan, *Pétain and Soldier* (1969)
R. Griffiths, *Marshal Pétain* (1970)
R. Paxton, *Vichy France* (1972)

**Petlyura, Simon** (1879–1926). Ukrainian peasant and national leader. He helped to found the Ukrainian Social Democratic Workers Party in 1905, and after serving in the First World War was one of the leaders of the Ukrainian Central Council which negotiated terms with the Central Powers at Brest-Litovsk (*see* BREST-LITOVSK, TREATIES OF). As Minister of Defence in the Ukrainian People's Republic in the RUSSIAN CIVIL WAR, he fought to preserve Ukrainian independence against both the RED ARMY and the White Russian forces of General DENIKIN. His anti-Semitic pogroms did much to alienate Jewish support for an independent UKRAINE, and he was forced to move the Ukrainian government-in-exile first to Warsaw and eventually to Paris, where he was assassinated in 1926 by a communist agent.

M. Bulgakov, *The White Guard* (1925)
J. S. Reshetar, *The Ukrainian Revolution, 1917–20: A Study in Nationalism* (1952)

**Petrograd.** See ST PETERSBURG.

**Phoney War.** Name given to the relatively inactive phase of the Second World War between the invasion of Poland by Germany on 1 September 1939 and the German occupation of Denmark and invasion of Norway in April 1940. The French dubbed the period 'la drôle de guerre' and the British also called it the 'Bore War', 'Funny War' or, as Churchill termed it in his work *The Second World War*, the 'Twilight War'. The phrases reflected the absence of major land or air assaults after the fall of Poland. Following the fall of Norway and Denmark, then of France, the Phoney War formed part of the indictment of the pre-war leaders, such as NEVILLE CHAMBERLAIN and DALADIER, who had survived into the first phase of the war for lack of preparedness and determined war-leadership.

E. S. Turner, *The Phoney War on the Home Front* (1961)

**Pilsudski, Josef** (1867–1935). Polish soldier and statesman. Born near Vilna, then under Russian rule, he studied at Kharkov and was exiled in Siberia for his socialist views, 1887–92. He combined nationalist and socialist views in his underground newspaper, *Robotnik* and founded the Polish Socialist party. He was re-arrested in 1900 but escaped in 1901, and in 1904 travelled to Japan. On his return to Poland he began from 1908 to organize a private army, hoping for Austro-Hungarian support against Russia in order to liberate Poland. By 1914 7,000 of Pilsudski's followers were employed by Austro-Hungary, Pilsudski commanding his own Legion of 3,000 men. In November 1916 the Central Powers proclaimed the independence of Poland, and Pilsudski was named Minister of War. The new Polish state was of limited geographical extent and treated as a puppet regime by the Central Powers, leading to the refusal of his men to swear loyalty, and to his arrest in July 1917. Imprisoned at Magdeburg by the Germans, he was released in autumn 1918 and on 11 November 1918 proclaimed Polish Head of State and first Marshal of Poland. He led the Polish forces in the RUSSO-POLISH WAR of 1919–20, defending Warsaw and turning back the invading RED ARMY in 'the miracle of the Vistula' in August 1920. Groups fearful of his influence curbed the powers of the presidency in the new constitution enacted in March 1921, and Pilsudski refused to stand for election and went into retirement. The growing disarray of parliamentary government led Pilsudski to stage an armed demonstration on 12 May 1926 to pressure the President to stop the formation of a centre-right government, which he believed would precipitate a left-wing revolt. The President refused to concede and fighting broke out between Pilsudski's supporters and government forces. Assisted by the support of the Polish Socialist Party and a railway strike, Pilsudski became the arbiter of power. He held the post of Prime Minister in 1926–8 and 1930, remaining Minister of War from his coup until his death in 1935. Exercising influence from behind the scenes, he allowed the forms of parliamentary government to continue, but with restrictions on the parliament's ability to hold up the budget or overthrow the government, and granting the President power to dissolve parliament. Moving away from the Left's demands for social reform and then flirting with the Conservatives, he eventually founded in 1928 a Non-party Bloc for Co-operation (BBWR) with the government, which secured the largest number of seats in March 1928. Growing opposition from the Left and Centre Parties led to the dissolution of parliament in 1930, followed by the arrest of many of their supporters and a further victory for the BBWR in the elections of 1930. Thereafter Pilsudski ruled increasingly through a group of ex-Legionnaires, known as the Colonels, and became remote and autocratic. A new constitution in April 1935 reduced the powers of parliament further. Pilsudski died in May 1935.

Although his dictatorship began in a relatively relaxed manner, by the time of his death the character of his regime, the Sanacja as it was called, had become stagnant and bankrupt of new ideas. Pilsudski's death was followed by restrictions on the electoral system which led the opposition to boycott the elections in 1935 and 1938. Pilsudski's dislike for the politicians and growing inability to operate a fair electoral system undermined an already fragile democracy beset by economic difficulties and international tensions. In international affairs the major achievement was the Polish–German Non-aggression Pact of January 1934, the culmination of attempts to improve relations with Germany, but even this was to bequeath a dangerous legacy to his successors, whose adherence to it blinded them to the dangers inherent in Nazi Germany.

A. Polonsky, *Politics in Independent Poland, 1921–39* (1972)
R. M. Watt, *Bitter Glory: Poland, 1918–39* (1982)

**Pius XI, Pope** (1857–1939). Pope, 1922–39. Born Achille Ratti at Brianza, he entered senior seminary in 1875, took a doctorate in canon law at Gregorian University, in theology at Rome, and another at the Academy of St Thomas. He worked in Milan and as Prefect in the Vatican library. As Pope he promoted Catholic social work and attacked fascism in his encyclicals *Non abbiamo bisogno* (1931) and *Mit Grennender Sorge* (1937). He also condemned ACTION FRANÇAISE in 1922. His encyclical *Quadragesimo anno* (1931) was a striking denunciation of the unfair distribution of goods and called for just and adequate wages, workers' participation and access to capital ownership. He nonetheless authorized the settlement of disputes with the Italian state in the LATERAN TREATIES, and made a concordat with Nazi Germany. His encyclical of 1937, *Divini Redemptoris*, condemned communism. He died on 10 February 1939.

R. Webster, *Christian Democracy in Italy, 1860–1960* (1961)
H. Daniel-Rops, *History of the Church of Christ: A Fight for God* (1963)

**Pius XII, Pope** (1876–1958). Pope, 1939–58. Born Euginio Pacelli, in Rome, he was educated there and ordained in 1899. He joined the papal secretariat in 1901 and served as a papal diplomat for the next 38 years. He was Nuncio to Bavaria in 1917 and later to the WEIMAR REPUBLIC. He negotiated the LATERAN TREATIES with MUSSOLINI and was responsible for the concordat with Nazi Germany in 1933. He was made a Cardinal in 1930. As Pope he was condemned for not speaking out vigorously enough against the persecution of the Jews, although he made many private efforts to aid them and other refugees.

**Plaid Cymru** (Welsh National Party). The party was founded in 1925 by John Saunders Lewis with the aim of obtaining independence for Wales. It ran candidates at every general election and at numerous by-elections, but without success until its president, Gwynfor Evans, won the 1966 Carmarthen by-election. In 1970 the Plaid ran 36 candidates and polled 175,000 votes, although none was elected. The party tended to attract a new influx of working-class support from South Wales to supplement the 'hard core' membership of the Welsh-speaking rural North Wales region. It also broadened its appeal by pursuing economic regeneration for the Welsh economy, encouragement for Welsh cultural activities, as well as full self-government for Wales. The adverse publicity attracted by the activities of the 'Free Wales Army' may have injured the party's prospects for a time, but in the February 1974 election it won two seats (Caernarvon and Merioneth) and in October 1974 Gwynfor Evans added a third, by again winning at Carmarthen. The lack of support for DEVOLUTION in the Welsh referendum in early 1979 was taken as marking some decline in enthusiasm for Welsh nationalism. In the 1979 general election the party fielded 36 candidates, polling 132,000 votes and retaining two seats, with Evans again losing Carmarthen. Its vote in 1983 and 1987 fell back to about 125,000 votes, but electing three MPs in the latter poll. Prior to the 1987 election, Plaid signed an agreement of co-operation with the SCOTTISH NATIONALIST PARTY.

A. Butt-Phillips, *The Welsh Question: Nationalism in Welsh Politics, 1945–70* (1975)
K. O. Morgan, *Rebirth of a Nation: Wales, 1880–1980* (1981)

**PNF.** Partito Nazionale Fascista. *See* FASCIST PARTY, ITALIAN.

**Poincaré, Raymond** (1860–1934). French politician. Born at Bar-le-Duc, Lorraine, the son of an engineer, he trained as a lawyer and was elected a Deputy in 1887, serving until 1903, thereafter a Senator, 1903–13 and 1920–29. He served as Minister of Education, 1893–5, and Finance Minister in 1906. He led a pre-war Republican–Radical Coalition for 12 months from January 1912. On 18 February 1913 he became President of the THIRD REPUBLIC, strengthening the Franco-Russian Entente by his visit to St Petersburg in July 1914. He attempted to raise the authority of his office, one largely lacking in real substance since the early years of the Republic, taking an active part in choosing the Premier and the Ministers and presiding over the Council of Defence for the duration of the war. He also played a part in making the wartime cabinets more broadly based, representing socialists and moderates as well as Radicals. Although the military proved increasingly independent, Poincaré was instrumental in backing Nivelle's plans for an offensive in 1917. Following Nivelle's disgrace, Poincaré's influence was reduced. The appointment of CLEMENCEAU as Premier in November 1917 meant Poincaré had less opportunity to interfere, and although he backed FOCH's views for an even more punitive peace than that arrived at, it was Clemenceau's views that prevailed at the PARIS PEACE CONFERENCE. His presidential term over in 1920, he returned to head a government in January 1922 in which he acted as his own Foreign Minister. A strong nationalist, he backed the RUHR OCCUPATION. In January 1924 his government broke up, but he returned to office in July 1926 as part of a 'Government of National Unity'. Although forced to carry through economy measures in order to stabilize the currency, he also oversaw the preparatory planning and inauguration of the MAGINOT LINE before his retirement in July 1929.

J. King, *Generals and Politicians: Conflict between France's High Command, Parliament and Government, 1914–1918* (1951)
G. Wright, *Raymond Poincaré and the French Presidency* (1967)

**Polaris.** Submarine-launched ballistic missile system, formerly part of the 'triad' of American strategic forces, and the basis of the British independent nuclear deterrent from 1962 until the introduction of the Trident system in the 1990s. Submarine-launched missiles began to be developed from the late 1950s. The possibility of launching nuclear missiles from submarines offered several advantages: it was very difficult to carry out an effective pre-emptive strike against submarine-launched ballistic missiles (SLBMs) compared with existing strategic bombers which were becoming vulnerable to a new generation of ground-to-air missiles; they could be fired quite close to the enemy's coast and needed only intermediate range; and, even with advances in anti-submarine warfare, submarines were likely to remain the least vulnerable of all delivery systems. The A-1

Polaris system was the first to be developed, and the American government ordered a fleet of 41 submarines, to be capable of firing 16 missiles, each carrying a thermonuclear warhead. The more advanced A-2 and A-3 Polaris systems were offered to Britain for use in submarines of its own construction and fitted with its own warheads following the NASSAU AGREEMENT of December 1962. 'Polaris' provided the principal British nuclear force from the late 1960s, consisting of a fleet of four submarines, each capable of carrying 16 missiles. The A-3 Polaris missile was fitted with British warheads which carried three nuclear weapons, giving each submarine a total of 48. While the United States began to develop the more powerful Poseidon missile, the United Kingdom undertook the top secret 'Chevaline' project to increase the effectiveness of its warheads. Deployment of the improved system, costing an estimated £1,000 million was announced as completed in January 1980. Meanwhile the United States was developing the even more powerful Trident system, capable of carrying more warheads over a longer range. With the imminent obsolescence of the Polaris-carrying submarines, the British government in 1986 announced the decision to replace Polaris with Trident missiles, bought from the United States and carried in four new nuclear submarines. The first vessels will go into service in the mid-1990s.

Polaris has been at the centre of the debate about Britain's maintenance of nuclear weapons since the 1960s. The secret decision to upgrade the Polaris system by CALLAGHAN's Labour government caused a storm of protest amongst its left wing and contributed to the swing towards UNILATERALISM by the LABOUR PARTY in the 1983 general election. The future of Polaris and the role of Trident was also a major divisive issue in the Liberal–SDP ALLIANCE and in the Labour Party in the 1987 general election.

C. Chant and I. Hogg, *The Nuclear War File* (1983)
C. McInes, *Trident: The Only Option?* (1986)
J. Newhouse, *The Nuclear Age: A History of the Arms Race from Hiroshima to Star Wars* (1989)

**Polish Corridor.** The TREATY OF VERSAILLES decided that the new Polish state should have direct access to the sea. In order to provide this a large area of West Prussia and Posen, containing many Germans, was assigned to Poland. The 'Corridor' also had the effect of cutting East Prussia off from the rest of Germany. DANZIG, standing at the mouth of the Vistula and the natural artery of Polish trade, but a German city and formerly part of Germany, was placed under League of Nations control, Poland remaining responsible for her foreign relations. The creation of the 'Corridor' was bitterly resented by German nationalists, and Hitler's demands for the return of Danzig and parts of the 'Corridor' formed part of the crisis which brought about war in September 1939.

**Polish Workers' Uprising.** Reactions to KHRUSHCHEV's secret speech at the 20th Party Congress in 1956 (*see* DE-STALINIZ-ATION) sparked off optimism in Poland about a change in the style of the regime. Intellectual responses were followed by strikes at the ZISPO engineering works in Poznan against increases in production norms. On 28 June demonstrators marched into the town centre calling for better economic conditions and more freedom. Others joined in with anti-Soviet slogans and placards supporting the imprisoned Cardinal Wyszynski. Attacks took place on the radio and police stations. The protests were suppressed by the Polish security forces, resulting in 53 dead and 300 injured. Sympathetic strikes in other industrial centres followed, backed by demands within the Communist Party for a new course in policy and the return of the popular WLAD-YSLAW GOMULKA. After negotiation between the Soviet government and the Polish Communists, Gomulka was readmitted to the Party in August and elected First Secretary and the Plenum of the Central Committee of the Party in mid-October. Gomulka embarked on a more liberal 'national communism', reversing collectivization, freeing Cardinal Wyszynski and making a concordat over religious education, and setting up workers' councils.

N. Bethel, *Gomulka, his Poland and his Communism* (1972)

**Pompidou, George** (1911–74). French politician, the second President of the FIFTH REPUBLIC. Born in the Auvergne, he taught as a schoolmaster before joining the RESIST-ANCE, eventually becoming DE GAULLE's adviser in 1944 on economic and educational matters. He served as a director of the Rothschild Bank and adviser to de Gaulle on the latter's return to power in 1958. He acted as chief negotiator with the Algerian nationalists and brought about the EVIAN AGREEMENTS which ended the ALGER-IAN WAR. Appointed Prime Minister by de Gaulle on 15 April 1962, Pompidou was seen initially as a stolid functionary for de Gaulle, but emerged more fully into public view with his responses to the student and trade union protests of 1968. Having been Prime Minister for six years, he was dismissed by de Gaulle in July 1968. For long seen as de Gaulle's heir apparent, Pompidou announced his candidature for the next presidential elections. Following de Gaulle's resignation in April 1969 Pompidou was elected President on 15 June 1969 with the backing of the Gaullists and centre parties. He continued the consolidation and stabilization of the Fifth Republic on the basis of a crushing Gaullist majority, although it began to fray at the edges as Pompidou's health began to fail in 1973 and rivalries over his succession developed. Pompidou showed himself a capable President, one of his most important acts being to lift the ban imposed by de Gaulle on British entry into the EUROPEAN ECONOMIC COMMUNITY following negotiations with Prime Minister HEATH in 1971. *See also* GAULLISM.

P. M. Williams and M. Harrison, *Politics and Compromise: Politics and Society in de Gaulle's Republic* (1971)
M. Anderson, *Conservative Politics in France* (1974)

**Poplarism.** British term for support for local control over welfare payments and for fairer distribution of resources between rich and poor areas. The phrase derives from the campaign from 1921 of the poor London borough of Poplar, led by its mayor George Lansbury and other socialists, to seek 'equalization of the rates' between the London boroughs in order to support the larger numbers of unemployed and poor within its area. On 31 March 1921 the borough refused, as a protest, to levy the rates they were obliged to for the overall London authority, the London County Council. As a result the leaders of the borough, including Lansbury, were imprisoned in September. They remained in prison for six weeks until a compromise was arrived at which made important concessions in the allocation of rate income to the poor areas. There were renewed conflicts in 1922 over the level of relief scales being allocated under the Poor Law by sympathetic local authorities, leading to the imposition of government orders on the councillors concerned. Similar conflicts also occurred over the use of Poor Law expenditure to relieve strikers in the prolonged aftermath of the GENERAL STRIKE in 1926, leading the government to pass an Audit Act in 1927 which threatened disqualification and surcharge on any councillors disobeying official guidelines on expenditure.

N. Branson, *Poplarism, 1919–1925* (1979)

**Popular Front.** Name adopted by coalitions of communists, socialists and centre parties in the mid-1930s. They were brought about by the growth of unity on the left to resist fascism, especially after the rise of HITLER in 1933. A crucial ingredient was the adoption by COMINTERN of a Popular Front strategy, abandoning its earlier attacks on social democratic and reformist trade unions in favour of electoral support for broad-based anti-fascist coalitions. In France the term *front populaire* was actually the suggestion of the Comintern liaison agent, Eugen Fried, and it became used to describe the government formed by LÉON BLUM in June 1936 on the basis of a common electoral programme of communists, socialists and Radicals, although the last mentioned did not use the term regularly. A Popular Front was also formed in Spain under MANUEL AZAÑA in February 1936 under the SECOND REPUBLIC. As a result the mid-1930s is sometimes referred to as the 'Popular Front era', brought to an end with the signing of the NAZI–SOVIET PACT of August 1939. The phrase has been used subsequently by left coalitions elsewhere in the world.

H. Graham and P. Preston (eds.), *The Popular Front in Europe* (1987)

**Portuguese Revolution.** The right-wing dictatorship which under SALAZAR and CAETANO had ruled Portugal for more than forty years was toppled by a nearly bloodless military coup on 25 April 1974. The conspirators, organized into the Armed Forces Movement (MFA), were mainly young officers who had been radicalized during the gruelling colonial wars going on since 1961 in Mozambique and Angola, but their revolt was jubilantly welcomed by almost every other sector of society. An explosive situation was created which, over the next nineteen months, brought Portugal closer to full-scale social revolution than any European nation has been since Russia in 1917 or Spain immediately after the outbreak of the Civil War in 1936. The revolution can be divided into four stages: (i) from April to September 1974, moderates under General Antonio Spinola predominated; their goal was liberal capitalism and parliamentary democracy of the European kind; they restored full civil liberties and promised elections; (ii) September 1974 to April 1975: Spinola was ousted by left-wing elements of the MFA who, in alliance with the Communist party, increasingly moved toward a 'popular democracy', with major sectors of the economy nationalized and the MFA assuming a permanent 'guiding role' not subject to electoral control. This movement gained impetus, especially after an attempted countercoup by Spinola in March was defeated. Banks and large businesses of all kinds were nationalized, and in southern Portugal, where large estates predominated, peasants organized by the Communists began to seize land. The radicals also tried to sabotage the elections scheduled for 25 April 1975 by urging blank ballots, but did not dare cancel them entirely; (iii) April to November 1975: as blank ballots and the Communist vote combined did not exceed 20% of the vote, the relative isolation of the radicals was revealed. They nevertheless sought to impose their vision, on society as a whole by refusing to surrender power and by using various means to undermine the autonomy and freedom of expression of all rival groups, especially the Socialists, who had emerged as the largest party, and the Catholics. An intense war of nerves began which by July had turned to violence, especially in the centre and north, the most populous regions of Portugal, where opposition groups burned down Communist party headquarters and defied the central government. The threat of civil war receded somewhat in September, when the left-wing government under Vasco Goncalvez resigned, but did not end completely until November when a final attempt by military extremists to stage a coup was crushed under the leadership of General Eanes; (iv) November 1975 to 1989. The radical stages of the revolution were now ended, but its legacy lived on for much longer. The victory of the moderates was incomplete, so anti-capitalist and anti-parliamentary clauses were accepted in the constitution that was devised during 1976. The nationalization of businesses and expropriation of landed estates could not be reversed overnight. Nor could the political role of a now-truncated MFA be abruptly ended. These were changes that came gradually, over the next fifteen years. The main leaders in the revisionary process were the Socialist leader MARIO SOARES, the centre-right leader Sa Carneiro (killed in an air crash in 1980), and the moderate military chief, Eanes, first President of the Republic. Major dates were 1979, when the centre-right parties won a parliamentary majority for the first time; 1986, when Portugal was admitted to the EEC and the trend towards Europeanization was thus strongly reinforced; 1989, when the last of the socializing provisions of the 1976 constitution was dropped under the joint sponsorship of Soares, as President, and Cavaco Silva, Sa Carneiro's disciple who had been Prime Minister since 1975. Portugal's revolution had wider implications. It brought rapid independence to Mozambique and Angola; it affected Spain's transition to democracy the following year; and for a while in 1975 it served as a beacon to the radical left everywhere as it seemed to be bringing to fruition the worldwide revolutionary promise which had been frustrated in the ÉVÉNEMENTS DE MAI of 1968.

T. Gallagher, *Portugal: A twentieth-century interpretation* (1983)

**Potsdam Conference.** Last of the wartime summit conferences, held from 16 July to 2 August 1945 in the Berlin suburb of Potsdam. TRUMAN and STALIN represented the USA and USSR respectively and were present throughout the conference. CHURCHILL and EDEN led the British delegation during the first week of the conference. With the announcement of a Labour victory in the

1945 general election, they were replaced by ATTLEE and BEVIN. The conference discussed many issues, ranging from Poland to Spain and Greece to Libya. But the most important issue discussed was the future of Germany. The participants agreed that Germany should be de-Nazified and democratized. They also agreed that Germany should pay reparations, in kind rather than monetary form: each occupying power received authorization to seize industrial plant, the Soviet Union agreeing to ship agricultural produce from eastern Germany in return for a portion of the reparations from the industrialized western part of the country. Germany was to be administered as an economic unit by a four-power Allied Control Council, yet executive authority was assigned to the American, British, French and Soviet controllers of the four occupation zones into which Germany was divided; and the controllers were to be responsible only to their governments (*see* GERMANY, ALLIED OCCUPATION OF). The Western powers also accepted the territorial alterations made by the USSR in East-Central Europe: the new German–Polish border was to be the ODER–NEISSE LINE, whilst the USSR absorbed territory contained within Poland's pre-1939 borders. All of the participants at the conference designated these arrangements as provisional, and charged their foreign ministers with convening a peace conference to make final dispositions. In the event, no such conference ever met, and the borders accepted as Potsdam have remained in place since: the division of Germany into separate occupation zones foreshadowed the establishment of two separate German states. The Potsdam conference also witnessed a commitment by the Soviet Union to enter the war against Japan, and Truman's revelation to Stalin of the existence of the atom bomb. The conduct of the American and British participants in the conference has often been criticized as excessively accommodating towards Stalin, facilitating the establishment of Soviet hegemony over East Central Europe. It seems clear, however, that whilst Truman might have exploited Soviet dependence on continuing US aid to force some concessions from Stalin, a generally tougher Anglo-American position at Potsdam would merely have hastened the outbreak of the COLD WAR: short of the deployment of armed force, unthinkable in the circumstances, there was little that the Western powers could do to dislodge the USSR from the territories it had occupied in 1944–5. *See also* TEHERAN CONFERENCE; YALTA CONFERENCE.

T. Sharp, *The Wartime Alliance and the Zonal Division of Germany* (1975)

A. de Zauas, *Nemesis at Potsdam* (1975)

**Poujadists.** Followers of Pierre Poujade (1920–) a bookseller from Lot in central-southern France, former member of French fascist youth movement; he was later a sergeant in the FREE FRENCH air force. In 1954 he formed the Union de Défence des Commerçants et Artisands (Union for the Defence of Small Shopkeepers and Artisans), initially complaining about taxes on small businesses and shops. The Poujadists attacked tax inspectors, bought back goods distrained by the authorities, and provided legal aid. It developed into an anti-socialist, anti-intellectual movement of the 'small man', recruiting mainly from the lower middle class and shopkeepers. Poujadists won 52 seats in the 1956 elections to the National Assembly, attracting some support from North African settlers and right-wing elements. Unable to force through legislation of their own, they stood for 'traditional' values and caused a considerable stir through Poujade's demagoguery and rallies. The return of DE GAULLE in 1958 led to the decline of the movement as many of its followers turned to support of the new leader. Many of them were disappointed with him, particularly over Algeria, and voted against him in the 1969 referendum which brought about his resignation. By then, Poujadism was virtually dead, although some of its former members continued to support right wing causes, such as LE PEN's Front National.

S. Hoffman, *Le Mouvement Poujade* (1956)

**POUM.** *See* PARTIDO OBRERO DE UNIFICACIÓN MARXISTA.

**PPI.** *See* PARTITO POPOLARE ITALIANO.

**'Prague Spring'.** A brief period of reform in Czechoslovakia from 5 January 1968 when ALEXANDER DUBČEK was elected First Sec-

retary of the CZECHOSLOVAK COMMUNIST PARTY to the Soviet invasion of 20–21 August. The reform movement began with a quickening pace of liberalization from within the Communist Party which resulted in the replacement of NOVOTNY by the pro-reform Dubček in January. This was followed by a Central Committee report on a more pluralistic political system, published as the Action Programme of the Communist Party in April 1968. Following in part the lines of thought developed by Yugoslav communists such as DJILAS, it proposed guarantees of 'socialist legality' and stressed the need to decentralize political and economic power. It suggested the revival of a People's Front, with political groupings permitted some autonomous existence while retaining a major role for the Communist Party. Press censorship and all control over artistic and intellectual life were to be abolished. By the spring of 1968 several autonomous political groupings had been set up, some calling for the re-establishment of pre-communist political parties. On 10 August the new draft statutes of the Communist Party outlined a liberalization and democratization of the party structure, including secret ballots, rotation of offices and the formation of legitimate minority groupings within the party structure. The growing unease on the part of the Soviets at the loosening of the leading role of the party and the ending of the principles of party discipline upon which communist parties operated in the Eastern block were unallayed by Dubček's professions of continued commitment to socialism and to membership of the WARSAW PACT. There was increasing concern that events in Czechoslovakia were moving out of control with the relaxation of censorship and the setting-up of independent groupings such as the Union of University Students and the Club of the Politically Non-aligned (KAN). Disconcerting economic reforms were also pursued by the Czechoslovak deputy Prime Minister Ota Sik, aiming to decentralize economic planning and decision-making, and introducing experiments in elected workers' councils.

The trigger for Soviet intervention was the need to forestall the meeting of the 14th Congress of the Czechoslovak Communist Party due in September, when it was anticipated that the reform process would be consolidated by the removal of hard-liners and the election of reformers. On the night of 20–21 August several hundred thousand Warsaw Pact troops crossed the Czechoslovak borders or were airlifted into the main airports, encountering only sporadic violent resistance, though met with angry crowds of demonstrators and impromptu barricades in the major cities. Within a matter of hours Czechoslovakia was under effective Soviet control. Dubček and President Lidvik Svoboda were spirited away to Moscow, where an agreement was exacted that they would accede to Soviet demands for the reversal of the reform process and the 'normalization' of society. Press censorship was reimposed on 6 September and when a clandestine 14th Party Congress met in a Prague factory Dubček had to denounce its decision to continue the reform process. Restrictions on independent political organizations were introduced and the moves towards decentralization in the economy, codified into a draft law by early 1969, were effectively nullified. A widespread purge of the party took place, approximately a third of its 1.5 million members being expelled after a thorough screening process which involved every member. Prominent supporters of the liberalization were removed from positions of responsibility, many being transferred to menial employments or forced into exile. Dubček himself, having been used to curtail the reform process, was replaced by GUSTAV HUSAK as First Secretary of the party in April 1969 and eventually demoted to the job of Forestry Inspector.

Soviet justification for the invasion appeared in *Pravda* on 28 September 1968. Soon dubbed the BREZHNEV DOCTRINE by Western commentators, it implied the right of the Soviet Union to intervene where one of its satellites was seen to be damaging 'socialism' in their own country or other satellites. A clear signal from the Soviet Union of the limits of its tolerance of deviations from the Soviet model of communism, it effectively forestalled reform in large parts of the Eastern bloc, including Czechoslovakia, for almost 20 years. Thereafter the shadow of Soviet intervention hung over any attempt to relax in significant ways

the leading role of the Communist Party or central planning.

R. Remington (ed.), *Winter in Prague: Documents on Czechoslovakia: Communism in Crisis* (1969)
G. Golan, *Reform in Czechoslovakia: The Dubček Era, 1968–9* (1973)
H. Gordon Skilling, *Czechoslovakia's Interrupted Revolution* (1976)
V. Fisera (ed.), *Workers' Councils in Czechoslovakia, 1968–9* (1978)

***Pravda.*** The daily newspaper of the COMMUNIST PARTY OF THE SOVIET UNION since 1912; its title means 'Truth'. The newspaper has a huge circulation of over 10 million, facilitated by printing in more than 40 cities. Its editorials and letters have often been used to announce or anticipate party policy, as well as denounce or correct deviations.

**Primo de Rivera, José Antonio** (1903–36). Founder of the Spanish fascist movement, the son of the dictator, MIGUEL PRIMO DE RIVERA. Trained as a lawyer, his early political position was monarchist, but in 1933 he edited the periodical *El Fascio*, opposed to the Republican government. In October 1933 he founded the FALANGE, also entering the Cortez. Although soon closed down, *El Fascio*, was replaced by two other short-lived newspapers, *Fe* (1934) and *Arriba* (1935). His ideas leaned heavily on Italian fascism, aiming for a strong government, the integration of the Church and Army into political life and a paternalistic attitude to the lower classes. Although personally reluctant to act against the Republic, the Falange had attracted some 40,000 members by July 1936, many of them young conservatives who adopted paramilitary style and supported violent opposition. Primo de Rivera was arrested at Alicante on 6 July, found guilty of crimes against the state and executed on 20 November 1936. He became the martyr of the Nationalist movement, becoming the source of a political cult under FRANCO. Many of his works were reprinted and he was extolled as the unofficial philosopher of Francoist Spain. *See also* FALANGE.

S. G. Payne, *Falange: A History of Spanish Fascism* (1961)
H. Thomas, *Selected Writings of José Antonio Primo de Rivera* (1972)

**Primo de Rivera, Miguel** (1870–1930). Spanish dictator, 1923–30, his authoritarian regime attempted a series of social-economic and political experiments that proved highly influential examples for the radical Right of the 1930s, and often became established features of the FRANCO era. Born into a landed military family in Cadiz, a disrespectful and bohemian personality did not prevent Primo advancing steadily through the officer corps and holding brief political office as a senator for the Conservative Party under the RESTORATION REGIME. During the period of unrest after 1917 he was Captain-General in, successively, Cadiz, Valencia and Madrid, before taking command in Barcelona in 1922. In the city he became a staunch defender of local empoyers, terrified at the waves of strikes launched by the anarcho-syndicalist CONFEDERACIÓN NACIONAL DEL TRABAJO (CNT) and the terrorism that accompanied them. Convinced that the ineffective parliamentary government was incapable of effectively preserving law and order, offering firm leadership defending the army and monarchy against the attacks of Republicans, he rose on 13 September 1923 in a successful bloodless coup, supported by the economic and military élites.

Once in power, politically naive and with very little sign of having preconceived policies, Primo and his advisors had to confront the need firmly to establish his regime and to deal with accumulated economic and social problems. Many of the attempted solutions – in the form of the creation of the Unión Popular as a mass party, a corporate system of labour relations, economic *dirigisme* and a strong executive ruling through plebiscites – aped fashionable fascism. In contrast, a restrained foreign policy, that largely solved Spain's entrenched Moroccan difficulties, and attempts to forge an alliance with the working class through the Socialist Party raised pragmatism over any ideological purity. Even so, anarchism and communism were severely repressed, and freedom of expression was curtailed.

Political miscalculation and the onset of an economic depression that ruined all attempts at promoting social and economic renewal led to the downfall of the regime. Primo's resignation in January 1930, and death shortly thereafter in exile, was preceded by the gradual withdrawal of support by all his original influential backers among the army and landed and industrial classes who had become alienated by attempts at reform that struck at their privileges. A return of labour discontent broke the alliance with the Socialists, and with no truly independent political base to support him, Primo was forced from power as peacefully as he had originally attained it. A short period of 'soft' dictatorship followed while the monarchy unsuccessfully tried to save itself, paving the way to the SECOND REPUBLIC.

C. P. Boyd, *Praetorian Politics in Liberal Spain* (1979)
S. Ben-Ami, *Fascism from Above: The Dictatorship of Primo de Rivera in Spain, 1923–30* (1983)
J. H. Rial, *Revolution from Above* (1985)

**Princip, Gavrilo** (1894–1918). The assassin of Archduke FRANCIS FERDINAND at Sarajevo on 28 June 1914. Born in a small village of Bosnia, the son of poor parents, he was the first literate member of his family. He attended school at Sarajevo, where he was influenced by Russian revolutionary literature and joined secret societies seeking to unify the South Slavs. Expelled from school for political activities in 1912, he volunteered for the Serbian army in the Balkan war but was rejected. Supplied with weapons by the BLACK HAND organization, he and two other young men participated in the attempt on the life of the heir to the Austrian throne in the hope of bringing about the downfall of the Empire and the freeing of Slavs from its control. Princip shot Francis Ferdinand and his wife while his car was halted in the confusion caused by an earlier unsuccessful attack by one of the co-conspirators. Arrested and tried in October 1914, he was excused the death sentence on account of his age and sentenced to 20 years' hard labour. He died of tuberculosis on 28 April 1918, aged 23. Buried in an unmarked grave, he was reinterred at Sarajevo in 1920.

J. Remak, *Sarajevo: The Story of a Political Murder* (1959)
Z. A. B. Zeman, 'The Balkans and the Coming of War', in R. J. W. Evans and H. Pogge von Strandmann (eds.), *The Coming of the First World War* (1988)

**privatization.** The policy of reducing the role of the state and extending the operation of free-market forces associated with the 'new right' philosophies of the 1970s and 1980s, particularly with Mrs THATCHER in Great Britain and JACQUES CHIRAC in France. More specifically, the policy became identified with the sale of shares in publicly owned or partly owned corporations. The British Conservative administration elected in 1979 was publicly committed to changing the boundary between the public and private sectors. It encouraged the contracting out to private firms and the offering to competitive tender of work previously undertaken by public bodies, such as municipal cleansing and hospital cleaning, and relaxed monopoly control in such areas as buses, telecommunications and broadcasting. The government also sold all or part of its share in a number of public enterprises, including, by 1983, a majority stake in British Aerospace and Britoil. In 1984 over half the shares in British Telecom were sold, and in 1986 almost all the shares in British Gas. Sales also took place of Jaguar, British Airways, the Trustee Savings Bank and other concerns. In the 1987 general election campaign the Conservatives announced plans for further privatization of water and electricity supply. Criticized in some quarters as 'selling off the family silver' (Earl Stockton), the programme of asset sales allowed the government greater flexibility in budgetary matters, while emphasizing the ideological merits of private as opposed to public ownership. Similar policies were pursued in France under the premiership of Jacques Chirac during the period of 'cohabitation' with President MITTERRAND in 1986–8. The French privatization programme was disrupted, however, by the stock exchange collapse of 1987. Reformed governments in Eastern Europe, especially in Hungary and Poland, have shown interest in these policies as they consider the de-nationalization of their economies. *See also* NATIONALIZATION.

P. Henessy and A. Seldon (eds.), *Ruling Performance: British Governments from Attlee to Thatcher* (1987)
K. Minogue and M. Biddiss (eds.), *Thatcherism: Personality and Politics* (1987)

**Profumo Affair.** British political scandal, leading to the resignation of the Conservative War Minister, John Profumo, on 4 June 1963. Profumo had initially denied his involvement with a prostitute who was also having relations with the Soviet naval attaché. As the press enquiry developed, Profumo had to admit he had lied to the House of Commons and resigned. Although a subsequent enquiry claimed that national security had not been endangered, the affair attracted enormous publicity and became the butt of much satire which helped to discredit the Conservative government in a pre-election year.

**Prolekult.** Abbreviation for the Proletarian Cultural and Educational Organizations established after the October Revolution in Russia, combining cultural and educational roles. It grew out of a conference of Cultural–Educational Societies which met in Petrograd in October 1917, adopting the title the next month. Drawing support from FACTORY COMMITTEES and labour organizations, it attempted to evoke a genuinely proletarian culture in theatre, painting and music. By 1919 it had enrolled 80,000 students and drew mainly on working class participants. Although it employed avant-garde writers and designers, much of Prolekult's work was directly educational in providing libaries, art classes, literary and theatrical performances, and courses in history, literature and other subjects, often drawing upon traditional or folk elements. From 1920 its funding was cut as the Communist Party sought to bring educational and cultural affairs more directly under its control. LENIN's suspicions about the direction in which Prolekult movement's leader, Alexander Bogdanov (1873–1928), was taking the organization led to its being brought under direct monitoring by the Communist Party, although not finally abolished until 1932. During the 1920s its role was increasingly taken over by the semi-official Russian Association of Proletarian Writers (RAPP), which was drawn more directly from the professional classes. They attempted to enforce party ideology, attacking non-communist writers, before they were themselves suppressed in preparation for the more tightly-organized system of artistic control by the Union of Writersand the propagation of SOCIALIST REALISM.

S. Fitzpatrick, *The Commissariat of Enlightenment* (1970)

**Provisional Government, Russian.** The government of Russia between the abdication of Nicholas II in March 1917 and the seizure of power by the Bolsheviks on 7 November 1917. Called into being by a Provisional Committee of the Duma following the Tsar's order for its dissolution on 12 March, it became the *de facto* government on 15 March on his abdication. The Provisional Government was intended to exercise authority until a CONSTITUENT ASSEMBLY could be called to draw up a constitution. Its first government from 16 March to 18 May was dominated by Kadet ministers (*see* CONSTITUTIONAL DEMOCRATIC PARTY, RUSSIAN) and led by Prince LVOV as Prime Minister. Disputes over the annexionist nature of Russian war aims against the central powers culminated in demonstrations and mutinies in the 'April days' and a reconstitution of the provisional government.

In the first coalition government, formed on 18 May, the socialist revolutionary KERENSKY moved from the justice ministry to the war ministry while the former foreign affairs minister, Milynkov, was toppled in a move which shifted the government to the left. The failure of the offensive mounted by Kerensky in July and the concession of autonomy to the UKRAINE led the remaining Kadet ministers to resign, followed by the attempted coup by the BOLSHEVIKS in the 'July days' of 16–18 July 1917. The provisional administration was increasingly squeezed by the leftward pressures exercised on it by the Petrograd Soviet, and was forced both to agree to the loss of its Minister of Justice (who had released documents purporting to show that Lenin was in the pay of the German government) and its Prime Minister, Prince Lvov.

On 20 July Kerensky became Prime Minister of a truncated socialist coalition which lasted until 3 August, when Kerensky resigned. Following a conference between the rival middle-class and working-class leaders, a second coalition government was formed on 9 August with Kerensky as Prime Minister and strong representation in the ministry for MENSHEVIK and Socialist Revolutionary ministers, including CHERNOV, the SR's leader, with the agricultural portfolio. An attempted reconciliation of the political factions at the Moscow State Conference (25–28 August) failed and was exacerbated

by the growing authoritarianism of the Supreme Commander, KORNILOV, which increasingly threatened to turn into a right-wing putsch. As a result Kerensky brought about the end of the Second Coalition on 9 September and assumed what were in effect dictatorial powers as Prime Minister and Supreme Commander, co-opting a 'Directory' of two ministers and two military commanders to assist him. He was, however, forced to call on the Bolsheviks to prevent Kornilov's advance on Petrograd.

Increasingly isolated by the growing support for the Bosheviks and viewed with growing suspicion by the moderate socialists and Socialist Revolutionaries, Kerensky postponed forming a Third Coalition until the outcome of a meeting of a Democratic Conference of democratic, socialist, and working class organizations, which met on 27 September. The Conference failed to reconcile Kadet and socialist factions, leaving Kerensky to create a Third Coalition. The Third Coalition formed on 10 October was directly threatened by the prospect of a Bolshevik coup and attempted to govern in a state of incipient political, economic and military collapse. Attempts to obtain support from a Council of the Russian Republic (or 'pre-parliament' as it was known), which convened on 20 October, failed to resolve any of the questions necessary to ensure the broadening of the basis of its support. Having postponed the elections for the Constituent assembly from 30 September to 25 November, the Coalition attempted to hang onto power until the Constituent Assembly could meet. Its attempts to do so were ended by the Bolshevik seizure of the Winter Palace on 7 November and the arrest of the ministers. An attempt by Kerensky to recapture Petrograd with loyal troops was finally defeated five days later.

The Provisional Government had initially aimed to continue the war against the CENTRAL POWERS, but differences over war aims and the growing demand for peace undermined its stability. With rival sources of allegiance to it in the SOVIETS, especially the Petrograd Soviet, an unreliable army, and growing discontent amongst workers and peasants, the failure of the July offensive left its only strong leader, Kerensky, increasingly isolated. By September the authority of the Provisional Government was in tatters, forcing Kerensky into increasingly desperate measures. The Bolshevik seizure of power was the death blow to a government which was already virtually powerless. *See also* RUSSIAN REVOLUTION.

A. F. Kerensky, *The Kerensky Memoirs: Russian and History's Turning Point* (1965)
M. Ferro, *The Russian Revolution of February 1917* (1972)
W. G. Rosenberg, *Liberals in the Russian Revolution: The Constitutional Democratic Party, 1917–21* (1974)
M. Ferro, *October 1917: A Social History of the Russian Revolution* (1980)

**Provisional Irish Republican Army.** Northern Ireland-based terrorist organization which is from time to time active on the British mainland. It was established during 1969 to protect the Catholic areas in Northern Ireland from attacks from Protestant extremists. Its principal objectives became resisting the British Army's internment operations and alleged harassment of Catholics. In addition to military operations mounted against the British army in Northern Ireland, the Provisionals have carried out bombing campaigns in Britain. The principal objective of the Provisional Sinn Fein, its political wing, is the complete independence of the 32 counties of Ireland. It is more militaristic in outlook than the Official Sinn Fein, whose main political objective is to establish a united socialist Ireland. *See also* ULSTER CONFLICT.

P. Bishop and E. Mallie, *The Provisional IRA* (1987)
P. Arthur and K. Jeffery, *Northern Ireland since 1968* (1989)

**PS.** Parti Socialiste. *See* SOCIALIST PARTY, FRENCH.

**PSI.** Partito Socialista Italiano. *See* SOCIALIST PARTY, ITALIAN.

**PSOE.** Partido Socialista Obrero Español. *See* SOCIALIST WORKERS' PARTY, SPANISH.

**Purges.** A general term applied to STALIN's elimination and liquidation of opponents, which reached its high point after 1934, also referred to as 'the Terror', 'Great Purge' and 'Yezhovshchina'. Stalin's struggle for supremacy in the Soviet Union from 1926 had already seen demotions and expulsions of leading figures from the Communist Party, mainly for alleged deviations from

the party line and the exile of TROTSKY in 1929. These had extended to include up to a hundred followers of the 'LEFT OPPOSITION' and was followed in 1929 by similar demotions and expulsions of the 'RIGHT OPPOSITION'. Already there was a tendency for Stalin to proclaim any deviation from his own chosen course of action as a cause for discipline by the party, and the first examples of leading opponents making abject recantations of error. Following the neutralization of the Right Opposition, Stalin had weathered the difficulties surrounding the pace of SOVIET COLLECTIVIZATION by purging 'saboteurs' and GOSPLAN and taking a firm grip upon the security apparatus.

At the 17th Party Congress in January–February 1934, the so-called 'Congress of Victors' celebrating the 'victories' of collectivization and the first FIVE YEAR PLAN, Stalin received fulsome praise as the heir to Lenin from KAMENEV and BUKHARIN, the most prominent leaders of the early oppositions. Stalin, however, followed this apparent triumph with a purge of quite unprecedented scale and ferocity. Mass arrests of party members followed the assassination of KIROV on 1 December 1934. While the evidence is only circumstantial that Stalin authorized the murder, it was used as a pretext to pass emergency decrees which ordered rapid investigation and trial of those suspected of 'terroristic organizations or acts' which could be held *in absentia* by special courts and without benefit of appeal. On 21 December a 'Leningrad opposition centre' was identified, justifying the arrest of Kamenev and ZINOVIEV. Tried in January 1935 they accepted a general responsibility for Kirov's murder and were imprisoned. During 1935 the rest of the Left Opposition was arrested and a purge of party members inaugurated in which almost half a million members were denounced and expelled from the party. The first phase of the purges culminated in a 'show trial' in Moscow in August 1936, at which Zinoviev and Kamenev, with others, confessed to a 'Trotskyist' conspiracy to murder Stalin and other Soviet leaders and of having directly organized the murder of Kirov. Their testimony implicated the other leading opponents of Stalin, Bukharin, RYKOV and TOMSKY (who immediately committed suicide). A second show trial early in 1937 led to sentences on RADEK and others for self-confessed links with Trotsky and foreign agencies, sabotage, and the setting up of terrorist groups. The last of the trials in March 1938 saw the conviction of Bukharin, Rykov and others, including a former head of the NKVD (*see* NKVD), for belonging to a 'Trotskyist–Rightist Bloc' in league with foreign intelligence services for the purposes of invading the country. Both Rykov and Bukharin were executed immediately afterwards.

The 'show trials' were the most public face of the purges, but only accounted for a tiny fraction of those arrested and punished, some 70 people. They served as a public justification for Stalin's actions. The 'confessions' obtained from the defendants were the only evidence of actual 'crimes' available and were the product of intensive interrogation, beatings, threats to families, and a quasi-religious willingness of the defendants to accept their own errors. Behind the public facade of the show trials, Stalin had cut an enormous swathe through the higher echelons of the party. Of the 139 members and candidate members of the Central Committee elected at the 1934 Congress, some 110 had been arrested by 1939, of whom 98 were executed. Of 1,966 delegates, 1,108 were arrested and only 59 remained available to attend the next Congress. But denunciations and executions reached out widely throughout the party and beyond, with estimates of some 5 million people arrested in 1936–8, of whom several hundred thousand were executed or imprisoned. The purge also reached into the armed forces, starting in 1937 with Marshal TUKHACHEVSKY. By 1940 it had led to the arrest of three out of five Soviet Marshals, all but seven of the 82 leading army commanders, and some 70 per cent of the officer corps. The security services were themselves purged: Yagoda (1891–1938), head of the NVD from 1934–6, and Nikolai Yezhoz (1895–1939), his successor, fell victims to the purge, the latter giving rise to the name for its most intense phase (Yezhovschina). Arrests also extended to touch the professions, the arts, industry, the COMINTERN and the diplomatic corps.

The extent and nature of the purges still arouse great controversy, not least in the Soviet Union itself, where they form a central part of the debate about Stalin's place in the evolution of communism in the Soviet Union. Where some have estimated up to 20 million dead as a result of Stalin's terror, others have moderated the figure for the purges alone to perhaps only a few hundred thousand. A high figure seems more realistic, however, given the huge numbers arrested in 1936–8 and the harsh conditions in the SOVIET LABOUR CAMPS, from which many did not return. Stalin's immediate objective of destroying his former and potential opponents appears to have developed a momentum of its own, seen in the readiness of party members and others to save themselves by denouncing others. Opportunities to fill the posts of those removed and the necessity to show no evidence of reluctance to act against counter-revolutionaries help to explain the self-fuelling character of the denunciations, accusations and self-confessions of 1935–8. Stalin, himself, perhaps with BERIA, the new head of security, seems to have recognized that the process had gone far enough by the end of 1938, when the purges on a large scale came to an end. At the 18th Party Congress in March 1939, held two years late because of the frenzied activity of the past three years, Stalin conceded that 'serious errors' had been made. It was left to Stalin's successors to open up the full scale of the blood-letting that had occurred. The purges left a legacy of 'terror' in the Soviet regime to be resumed sporadically and more selectively after 1938. It also transformed the Soviet labour camps into a vast and permanent apparatus holding a significant subsection of the population. The most direct effect of the purges was to strengthen Stalin's position, but this was at an appalling cost to a country already short of experienced administrators and professionals. The losses in the armed forces did much to limit their effectiveness in the RUSSO-FINNISH WAR of 1939–40 and in the first campaigns of 1941–2 and, more seriously, to lead Germany to underestimate the degree of resistance the Soviet Union would provide to invasion.

E. Ginsburg, *Into the Whirlwind* (1967)
R. Conquest, *The Great Terror* (1968)
R. C. Tucker, *Stalinism: Essays in Historical Interpretation* (1977)
R. Medvedev, *Let History Judge: The Origins and Consequences of Stalinism* (2nd edn, 1989)

# Q

**Quisling, Vidkun** (1887–1945). Norwegian leader of the Nasjonal Samling (National Unity) movement, founded in 1933 in imitation of the German Nazi Party. In December 1939 Quisling met Hitler and discussed a possible *coup d'état* in Oslo. In April 1940 he revealed details of Norwegian defences to the Germans and became head of a puppet government after the German invasion of that month. He was executed for treason 1 October 1945. The term 'Quisling' is commonly used to describe a collaborator with foreign enemies.

O. K. Hoidal, *Quisling: A Study in Treason* (1989)

# R

**Radek, Karl** (1885–1939). Russian Bolshevik and journalist. Born in Poland, and of Jewish ancestry, he became a journalist writing for the German social democratic press in Poland and Germany. He met Lenin in Switzerland during the First World War and fought in the RUSSIAN REVOLUTION. A LEFT COMMUNIST, he went to Germany in 1918 to help organize the GERMAN COMMUNIST PARTY. Returning to Russia in 1920 he became a leading member of the COMINTERN but lost influence as a result of the failure of the Comintern to promote revolution in Europe. Expelled from the Communist Party in 1927 for having supported TROTSKY, he was banished to the Urals. Readmitted to the party in 1930, he wrote for a time for *Izvestiya*, but in 1937 was tried for 'Trotskyist' activities and sentenced to ten years' imprisonment. He died in prison.

K. Radek, *Portraits and Pamphlets* (1935)
W. Lerner, *Karl Radek: The Last Internationalist* (1970)

**Radical Party, French.** The Radical or Radical-Socialist Party was the pivotal party of the THIRD REPUBLIC. Its ideological basis was broadly conservative in economic and social matters, but also fiercely anti-clerical (*see* ANTI-CLERICALISM) and ardently republican. Acting as a centre party they secured a major bloc of seats in all the elections of the Third Republic; this bloc was usually large enough for them not to be ignored in forming governments but never large enough to form a stable one-party government themselves. Although they had a left-wing tradition as the founding party of the Republic, enemies of excessive executive power and opposition to clericalism, most of their great battles were won by the end of the First World War, leaving them with little around which to unite. Disinclined to commit themselves to the Socialists who in turn were fearful of being outbid by the Communists, the strength and the weakness of the Radicals contributed to the impermanence of French governments between the wars. The Radicals also found themselves increasingly exposed, as over the STAVISKY AFFAIR, to charges of corruption and complacency under the Third Republic. The riots of 1934 and the threat of fascism led to the POPULAR FRONT alliance of 1936, but even here the Radicals were only interested in those parts of the programme – press reform, secular education, and banning the fascist LEAGUES – which formed part of their traditional liberal republicanism; they were far less enthusiastic about liberal economic policies, social security and concessions to workers. DALADIER, their President from 1925, was to play a significant part in breaking up the Blum government in May 1937 when he expressed concern about increasing disorder and economic disarray.

In 1939 the Radicals were still the dominant force electorally, usually able to command the premiership and the Ministry of the Interior, with a large following from peasants and the lower middle class, those who 'wore their hearts on the left and their wallets on the right'. Its loose organization and discipline opened it to a wide membership and its semi-permanent hold on power made it a natural avenue of advancement for ambitious young politicians. Most of its leaders and deputies supported APPEASEMENT and voted for Pétain's assumption of power. Although some former Radicals, such as Daladier, were deported by the Germans, many participated in the VICHY GOVERNMENT and relatively few played an active part in THE RESISTANCE. In 1945 its prestige was seriously diminished by its association with Vichy and the failures of the Third Republic. The rising forces of the FRENCH COMMUNIST PARTY and the Catholic MOUVEMENT REPUBLICAIN POPULAIRE also faced it with better organized rivals. The Radicals remained a major force in the FOURTH REPUBLIC although more limited in their voting strength, often providing the Prime Minister and determining the fate of governments. Increasingly overshadowed by the rise of GAULLISM, an independent Republican Party led by GISCARD D'ESTAING supported de Gaulle but retained its independence. The Radical Party is no longer a major electoral force in its own right, most of its support being attracted to new centre groupings such as those led by Raymond Barre, the UNION POUR LA DÉMOCRATIE FRANÇAISE or to the FRENCH SOCIALIST PARTY. See also CAILLAUX, JOSEPH; MENDÉS-FRANCE, PIERRE.

P. Larmour, *The French Radical Party in the 1930s* (1964)
P. M. Williams, *Crisis and Compromise: Politics in the Fourth Republic* (1964)

**Radoslavov, Vasil** (1854–1929). Bulgarian politican. Born in Lovec in northern Bulgaria, he studied in Prague and Heidelberg before becoming a journalist and entering politics. As Minister of Justice at the age of 30 and leader of the government in 1899–1901 he earned a reputation for brutality in putting down peasant unrest. His pro-Austrian and pro-German views fitted in well with FERDINAND I's expansionist aims and he was instrumental in swinging Bulgaria away from her traditional alignment with Russia in diplomatic affairs. Appointed to head the government in July 1913, he skilfully manipulated Bulgarian neutrality in 1914–15 to obtain maximum concessions from the belligerents, finally agreeing to an alliance with the CENTRAL POWERS in September 1915 in return for territorial concessions in Serbian MACEDONIA. Following the successful conquest of SERBIA he faced increasing opposition as a result of the use of Bulgarian troops against Romania and growing food shortages. A hungry winter in 1917–18 and the failure to obtain territorial compensation in the Treaty of Bucharest between Romania and the Central Powers in May 1918 left him politically exposed, and he was replaced by the pro-Entente Malinov in June 1918. He was

forced into exile with Ferdinand in October 1918 and tried *in absentia* by the STAMBOLISKI government after the war. Although amnestied in June 1929, he died in exile in Berlin on 21 October. See also FIRST WORLD WAR.

**RAF.** See ROTE ARMEE FAKTION.

**Rákosi, Mátyás** (1892–1971). Hungarian communist leader. He served in the First World War in the Austro-Hungarian armies and was captured by the Russians. On his return to Hungary he became a communist, rising to command the Red Guard under BÉLA KUN. He escaped to Austria in 1919 after the fall of the regime and eventually reached the Soviet Union. He worked as a party secretary for COMINTERN with French and Italian communists before being sent to reorganize the Hungarian Party in 1924. Arrested in 1925 and sentenced to eight years in gaol in 1927, he was rearrested in 1935 and sentenced to life imprisonment. As a result he escaped the Stalinist PURGES, which killed many of the Hungarian communist leaders, including Béla Kun. Exchanged with Moscow in November 1940, he returned to Hungary in 1945 to become General Secretary of the HUNGARIAN COMMUNIST PARTY with STALIN's support. He purged rival communists and expanded party membership in the communists' drive to dominate the post-war coalition, by June 1948 achieving overall control. Non-Stalinist communists were eliminated in 'anti-Titoist' purges in autumn 1948. He also embarked on a programme of industrialization and collectivization. Prime Minister from August 1952 as well as Party Secretary, Rákosi was forced by the Party Presidium to turn over the premiership to the more moderate IMRE NAGY on 4 July 1954, but he retained control of the police and party apparatus. The apparent setback to anti-Stalinist forces in the Soviet Union in early 1955 allowed Rákosi to retain power, but in July 1956 he was forced to resign as General Secretary in the build-up of pressure which led to the HUNGARIAN UPRISING in October 1956. Bitter memories of his regime meant that he was left out of the KADAR government which was imposed by the Soviets after the rising. He lived out most of the rest of his life in the USSR, being deprived of his party membership in 1962 and repeatedly being refused his requests to return to Hungary.

M. Molnar, *A Short History of the Hungarian Communist Party* (1978)

J. K. Hoensch, *A History of Modern Hungary, 1867–1986* (trans., 1988)

**Rapacki Plan.** A Polish initiative, proposing the creation of a central European nuclear free zone presented by the Polish Foreign Minister, Adam Rapacki, at the UN General Assembly on 2 October 1957. The zone was to include Poland, Czechoslovakia, East and West Germany. It was to be supervised by member states of the WARSAW PACT and the NORTH ATLANTIC TREATY ORGANISATION. It was rejected by the United Kingdom and the United States because it was thought to favour the Warsaw Pact countries with their superiority of conventional weapons.

**Rapallo, Treaty of.** A treaty signed between Germany and the Soviet Union in 1922. Following the abortive Genoa Conference which met early in that year to discuss the economic reconstruction of Europe, the German representative, RATHENAU, and the Russian, Chicherin, made an agreement at nearby Rapallo on 16 April. The treaty was a diplomatic breakthrough for LENIN, securing the recognition of the Soviet Union by Germany and the re-establishment of commercial relations. Germany and the Soviet Union mutually renounced financial claims arising from the First World War, and in secret clauses the Soviets undertook to assist Germany to test and develop weapons forbidden by the TREATY OF VERSAILLES. The Treaty was reinforced by the Treaty of Berlin in 1926 and by further conciliation machinery in 1929. The 'embrace of two pariahs', the Treaty of Rapallo gave the Soviet Union a breakthrough in diplomatic recognition, followed by that of Great Britain and France in 1924, and the United States in 1933, while it provided Germany with a useful training ground for her armed forces. Initial reactions in France, however, were hostile, seeing a revival of German power which combined with German default on its REPARATIONS payments contributed to the Franco-Belgian occupation of the RUHR.

The Rapallo agreement lapsed with the accession to power of the NAZI PARTY in 1933.

A. B. Ulam, *Expansion and Coexistence: Soviet Foreign Policy, 1917–72* (1968)

H. Gatzke, *European Diplomacy between the Two World Wars* (1972)

**Rasputin, Grigori** (1872–1916). Siberian 'holy man' who exercised considerable influence at the court of Tsar NICHOLAS II through his ability to ease the sufferings of the heir, Alexey, a haemophiliac, earning him the unswerving devotion of Tsaritsa Alexandra. Denounced as an imposter by the church in 1912 and sent back to Siberia, he returned in 1914, and with the departure of the Tsar for army headquarters in autumn 1915 he resumed a powerful position at a court now dominated by the Tsaritsa. Rasputin interfered in political appointments and influenced an uncompromising stand against the DUMA's demands for reform. Although a known drunkard and debauchee, there is no hard evidence to support the allegation that he was in the pay of the Germans. The rumours, however, were symptomatic of the poisonous atmosphere he helped to create and which did much to discredit the court and undermine the Tsar's personal authority in the course of 1916. By the autumn of that year, various plots aimed at the removal of the Tsar or of Rasputin in order to forestall national defeat or revolution. Eventually Rasputin was assassinated by a group of conspirators led by Prince Felix Yusupov, Grand Duke Dmitry Pavlovich and the right-wing Duma deputy V. M. Purishkevich on the night of 30 December 1916. Behind the plot, however, lay many members of the ruling circle and the Duma, some of whom hoped that ridding the court of Rasputin's influence might allow more sensible counsels to prevail and save the dynasty. But although government reshuffles followed the assassination, the damage to the reputation of the Tsar was already too great and the war situation too grave for Rasputin's removal to save the situation. The assassination of Rasputin has been seen as a last desperate attempt by pro-monarchist forces to prevent the fall of the Tsar.

M. J. Minney, *Rasputin* (1972)

A. de Jonge, *The Life and Times of Grigori Rasputin* (1982)

**Rathenau, Walter** (1867–1922). German industrialist and politician. Born of Jewish parentage in Berlin, Rathenau studied engineering before becoming president of the AEG electrical trust, which his father had founded, in 1915. An ardent advocate of economic planning in wartime, Rathenau was responsible for the establishment of the War Raw Materials Office in August 1914 under the aegis of the Prussian Ministry of War: by 1918 the Department had expanded into a large bureaucracy which supervised the work of over two dozen companies responsible for the acquisition and allocation of strategic raw materials. In 1918 he popularized the idea of a *levée en masse* in response to impending German defeat. He entered politics after the German defeat as a founder-member of the German Democratic Party (*see* DDP), took part in the PARIS PEACE CONFERENCE as an economic adviser to the German delegation, and served on a commission to consider socialization of leading sectors of the German economy in 1920. An early advocate of an essentially corporatist approach to economic management within a capitalist economic framework, Rathenau was appointed Minister for Reconstruction in 1921. He played a conciliatory role in the reparations conferences of London, Paris and Cannes, advocating fulfilment of the TREATY OF VERSAILLES, but was also keenly aware of the trading opportunities which existed for German industry in Eastern Europe. Appointed Foreign Minister to the WEIMAR REPUBLIC in January 1922, Rathenau was largely responsible for the negotiation of the TREATY OF RAPALLO (April 1922) between the Weimar Republic and the Soviet Union, establishing diplomatic relations between the two states, normalizing relations and promoting trade; it thereby overcame German diplomatic isolation. Rathenau was assassinated by right-wing anti-Semitic nationalists in June 1922.

J. Joll, *Three Intellectuals in Politics* (1960)
H. Pogge von Strandmann (ed.), *Walter Rathenau: Industrialist, Banker, Intellectual and Politician: Notes and Diaries* (1985)

**Reagan, Ronald** (1911–). United States President, 1981–9. He was a film star who entered politics as a Republican, serving as Governor of California, 1967–74. In the 1980 presidential election he defeated Jimmy Carter, becoming President at the age of 70. Although many in Washington doubted his ability and stamina, his skill in communicating with ordinary Americans made him one of the most popular and successful Presidents in recent times. His second term of office, following a sweeping victory in 1984, was marked by a thaw in his previously strained relations with the USSR, helped by summits with GORBACHEV in Geneva, Rejkavik and Washington, and by controversy concerning arms sales to Iran and support for the Contra rebels in Nicaragua.

**Red Army.** Originally the Bolshevik army formed to fight the RUSSIAN CIVIL WAR. Initially the Bolsheviks had only the RED GUARDS and a few units of ex-Tsarist troops, such as the Latvian Rifle Brigade under the command of TROTSKY, and detachments of Baltic sailors. The first Workers' and Peasants' Red Army of 1918 had no insignia of rank, units were run by elected committees who chose its officers, and only recognized military discipline when on active service, following the model of a workers' militia like the early Red Guards. Faced with the exigencies of the Civil War, Trotsky remodelled the force, disbanding the Red Guards, recruiting ex-Tsarist officers to lead and train the forces, and raised men by conscription through a network of military committees in Soviet-controlled territory. By the end of 1918 the Red Army numbered half a million men and by the end of the conflict well over a million. Increasingly professionalized, with full military discipline, the unit committees gave way to 'political COMMISSARS' of equal rank to officers, appointed by the party, to safeguard political orthodoxy and raise the political education of the troops. Directed with great *élan* by Trotsky, the Red Army proved a highly disciplined and motivated force, many veterans of the army going on to join the Communist Party or see command in the Second World War. Behind the military organization, however, lay a highly effective centralized system of requisitioning, known as WAR COMMUNISM, which seized whatever supplies were needed for the front armies, especially grain.

Alongside Trotsky, the other decisive influence on the Red Army's early development was Mikhail Frunze (1885–1925), a successful Red Army commander in the civil war; he became Deputy Commissar for War in 1924, succeeding Trotsky in January 1925. Resisting attempts to restore a militia style army, he advocated the need for a professional, standing army. His view prevailed, and, although much reduced after the Civil War, the Red Army was maintained as a regular force. With the extension of military service of from two to three years to all Soviet citizens, the army was greatly expanded under Stalin to almost 5 million men by 1939. Unlike under the Tsars, national minorities were no longer excluded, and as part of a policy of 'Sovietization' from 1939 ethnically based units were abandoned and a deliberate attempt made to mix units from different regions and impose Russian as the universal military language. The creation of a standing army after 1922 also saw the retention of the dual command system of 'political commissars' responsible for political education and the military commander responsible for normal military matters. Redefined several times between the wars, the balance in this system was tilted first one way and then the other.

Although Stalin expanded the army and reintroduced a full military hierarchy and discipline, he remained deeply suspicious of the Red Army as a possible source of opposition. As a result the Red Army was savagely purged in 1937–8 (*see* PURGES), losing many of its ablest commanders, including Marshal TUKHACHEVSKY, shot or imprisoned. This experience partly explained the poor performance of the Red Army in the RUSSO-FINNISH WAR in 1939–40 and the initial collapse in the face of the German invasion of 1941 (*see* SECOND WORLD WAR). One result was a reimposition of officer privileges, including separate uniforms for officers and lavish dispersals of decorations.

After the Second World War, the Red Army's name was changed to the Soviet Army. Still based on conscription, with a core of professional soldiers, the Soviet Army has continued to become more like regular armies elsewhere in Europe, although it retains the political commissar and its role as a major Sovietizing institution. The enormous prestige gained by the army in the Second World War has elevated it to a major symbol of national survival. Although firmly under Communist Party control, it retains an enormous influence on the political structure of the Soviet state, an essential bulwark of communist power.

E. O'Ballance, *The Red Army* (1964)
M. McKintosh, *Juggernaut: A History of the Soviet Armed Forces* (1967)
T. J. Colton, *Commissars, Commanders and Civilian Authority: The Structure of Soviet Military Politics* (1979)

**Red Army Faction.** *See* ROTE ARMEE FAKTION.

**Red Brigade.** *See* TERRORISM, ITALIAN.

**'Red' Clydeside.** A period of strikes and socialist unrest in the Glasgow area of Scotland from 1915 to 1919. Strikes were organized by the Clyde Workers' Committee against the 'dilution' of skilled labour tasks by the use of unskilled and semi-skilled labour in 1915–16 which led to the arrest of strike leaders and the suppression of left-wing journals by government. Attempts to form a Workers' and Soldiers' Soviet in 1918 were prohibited by the government. A 40-hour strike in January–February 1919 led to mass demonstrations and the mobilization of troops and tanks. The events of 1918–19 have been seen as a high point of British socialist militancy in the aftermath of the First World War and the Russian Revolution. Although there was a militant leadership, they did not seek an open confrontation with the authorities and the strike wave ebbed away.

B. Pribicevic, *The Shop Stewards Movement and Workers' Control, 1910–1922* (1959)
J. Hinton, 'The Clyde Workers' Committee and the dilution struggle', in A. Briggs and J. Saville (eds.), *Essays in Labour History, 1886–1923* (1971)
I. McLean, *The Myth of Red Clydeside* (1983)

**Red Guards.** Contingents of armed workers formed from FACTORY COMMITTEES and SOVIETS during the RUSSIAN REVOLUTION. Gradually assuming the name 'Red Guards', they controlled the industrial areas largely beyond the control of the PRO-

VISIONAL GOVERNMENT and played a decisive part as the armed wing of the Bolshevik party in helping to frustrate KORNILOV's attempted putsch. Mobilized under the MILITARY REVOLUTIONARY COMMITTEE of Petrograd, as well as elsewhere, they provided the forces which seized power in November 1917. The Red Guards were mobilized to disperse the CONSTITUENT ASSEMBLY when it met in January 1918 and formed an initial component of the first Workers' and Peasants' Army with which Bolsheviks began the RUSSIAN CIVIL WAR. Most of the Red Guard detachments were disbanded during 1918 when TROTSKY remodelled the armed forces of the Soviet State into the RED ARMY. The most reliable party members were drawn from the Red Guards to form the nuclei of Red Army regiments.

V. Robert, *Red October: The Bolshevik Revolution of 1917* (1968)

**Redmond, John** (1856–1918). Irish nationalist leader. The son of an Irish Catholic family, he was Irish Nationalist MP for New Ross, 1881–5; North Wexford, 1885–91; Waterford, 1891–1918; and leader of reunited Nationalist Party from 1900. He worked for HOME RULE by constitutional means and negotiated the Home Rule Bill which was awaiting the royal signature in 1914. He insisted on bringing his Irish Nationalist Party members into the IRISH VOLUNTEERS and urged Irishmen to fight for Great Britain as loyal subjects. He was increasingly outflanked by the extreme· nationalists of SINN FEIN, and after the EASTER RISING he was increasingly bypassed.

**Red Terror.** A period of repression, imprisonment and executions proclaimed in Russia by the Bolsheviks on 5 September 1918 after an attempt on Lenin's life. The decrees urged the necessity of defending the revolution against its 'class enemies'. Carried out by the CHEKA, the Red Terror turned into an open, systematic policy of suppressing anyone not obviously of the proletariat by arbitrary means, including executions and imprisonment. Trotsky referred to the 'terror' as 'no more than a continuation . . . of armed insurrection'. The legacy of authoritarianism bequeathed to the Soviet Union has often been blamed upon the early use and even open avowal of such policies.

G. Leggett, *The Cheka: Lenin's Political Police* (1981)

**'Red Vienna'.** In 1918 the population and economic resources of the newly created – and overwhelmingly agricultural – AUSTRIAN REPUBLIC were disproportionately concentrated in the industrial and commercial city of Vienna. The capital city was also overwhelmingly Social Democratic, and its status under the constitution as an autonomous federal province enabled it to pursue policies independent of, and often opposed to, those of the federal government, particularly in the fields of housing and social policy. Although these successes in social policy were founded on sound capitalist economics and constitutional methods, 'Red Vienna' was a thorn in the flesh of the Austrian right, and its success contributed significantly to the political tensions of the First Republic.

**Regional Development Fund of the European Community.** A fund established in March 1975 to provide assistance to the poorest areas of the European Community. From the early 1970s regional policy was regarded as important because national regional policies may be affected by Community limitations on state aid to industries, and because the development of ECONOMIC AND MONETARY UNION could have damaging consequences on outlying regions. The setting up of the Regional Development Fund was hampered by difficulties over the provision of finance for the fund, and over the renegotiation of the United Kingdom's terms of entry to the European Community in 1975. The Fund was constituted with 130 million 'units of account' over the three years 1975 to 1977. The two basic principles of the fund are additionality – the help provided by the fund must be additional to what would have been available had the fund not existed – and concentration – the help provided by the fund must be concentrated in areas of greatest need.

**Reichstag.** German parliament, established through the constitution of the North German Confederation of 1867 and incorporated into the Imperial German constitution of 1871 and that of the WEIMAR

REPUBLIC of 1919. In Imperial Germany, the powers of the *Reichstag* were strictly limited: its role was largely confined to debate and the approval of legislation initiated and presented to it by the *Bundesrat* (federal council). Ministers were not accountable to the *Reichstag*, which was directly elected by all male citizens aged 24 or over, nor might members of the *Reichstag* become ministers and retain their seats. Elections were triennial to 1893, then quinquennial. The limited powers of the *Reichstag* exacerbated the pursuit of 'negative' interest-based politics in Imperial Germany. Following the GERMAN REVOLUTION of 1918–19, the constitution of the Weimar Republic extended the powers of the *Reichstag*, to which ministers were now accountable. From 1919 it was elected through a party-list system of proportional representation by all citizens aged 20 or over: elections were to take place at least once every four years. After the Nazi seizure of power in 1933, the *Reichstag* was formally maintained, yet seldom met, and then only to acclaim decisions taken by the regime. *See also* REICHSTAG FIRE; REICHSTAG PEACE RESOLUTION.

**Reichstag Fire.** The burning of the German parliament building on the night of 27–8 February 1933, a week before elections were due to be held. The police arrested a young Dutch communist, Marinus van der Lubbe, who was tried, convicted and executed. Deeming the *Reichstag* fire to be the signal for a communist uprising against the Nazis, the government also sought to implicate the visiting Bulgarian communist GEORGI DIMITROV, who was, nevertheless, acquitted by the court. The timing of the fire, and the fashion in which it was subsequently exploited by the Nazis, led many contemporaries to conclude that the Nazis themselves were responsible. This theory is now generally rejected by historians, who are inclined to believe that van der Lubbe acted alone. HITLER, GÖRING, GOEBBELS and the Reich Minister of the Interior, Frick, appear genuinely to have believed that the fire was a prelude to an attempt to overthrow the new government: the measures introduced by the regime in the immediate aftermath of the fire, such as the arrest of communist members of the

*Reichstag* and leading party officials, were often poorly co-ordinated and less successful than was subsequently claimed, as the government panicked and brought forward the suppression of the Communist Party it had hoped to postpone until after the March elections. The most important consequence of the fire was the promulgation by Reich President HINDENBURG of a 'Decree for the Protection of People and State' on 28 February 1933, a decree which, though hastily improvised, gave the government wide-ranging powers to suspend basic civil liberties and interfere in the government of the federal states. This decree, rather than the better-known Enabling Act of March 1933, provided the legal basis for the Nazi monopolization of political power which followed the fire.

F. Tobias, *The Reichstag Fire* (1964)
M. Broszat, *The Hitler State* (1981)

**Reichstag Peace Resolution.** Resolution passed by the German REICHSTAG on 19 July 1917, committing itself to the pursuit of a peace settlement to end the FIRST WORLD WAR based on 'understanding and permanent reconciliation of peoples'. The resolution declared forced territorial acquisitions to be incompatible with such a peace settlement. The background to the passage of the resolution was the growing anxiety of leading politicians in liberal parties and the CENTRE PARTY about the military deadlock in continental Europe and the entry of the USA into the war against Germany largely as a consequence of the pursuit by the German government of unrestricted submarine warfare. The resolution, which was supported by the SOCIAL DEMOCRATIC PARTY (SPD), Centre party and liberals, was unacceptable to the leaders of the Army High Command, HINDENBURG and LUDENDORFF, who had used its drafting to force the dismissal of the Chancellor, BETHMANN-HOLLWEG, and his replacement by their puppet Michaelis. Henceforth, real power in Imperial Germany lay with the military, which disregarded the resolution and pursued annexationist policies culminating in the peace TREATIES OF BREST-LITOVSK and the TREATY OF BUCHAREST. The longer-term significance of the resolution lay in the emergence of a coalition of SPD, Centre and left-liberal parties, committed to domestic political reform; a coalition which was to provide a democratic mainstay for the WEIMAR REPUBLIC.

A. Rosenberg, *Imperial Germany: The Birth of the German Republic, 1871–1918* (1931)
K. Epstein, *Matthias Erzberger and the Dilemma of German Democracy* (1959)

**Reith, Sir John.** *See* BRITISH BROADCASTING CORPORATION.

**Renner, Karl** (1870–1950). Austrian politician. A leading Austromarxist theorist, Renner was born in 1870 in Unter-Tannowitz, Moravia. As a law graduate from Vienna University he made a significant contribution to Marxist legal theory. His other principal intellectual concern was the nationalities problem in the Habsburg Empire. Renner adopted a patriotic position during the First World War, came to be acknowledged as the leader of the right wing of the AUSTRIAN SOCIAL DEMOCRATIC WORKERS' PARTY (SDAP), and in 1918 became the first chancellor of the First AUSTRIAN REPUBLIC. In June 1919 he succeeded OTTO BAUER at the Foreign Ministry, and continued to occupy both offices until the SDAP left the government in 1920. His reformist position put him in a minority within the SDAP between the wars, when Bauer became the effective leader of the party. Renner was President of the Second Austrian Republic from 1945–50, and foreign minister briefly for a second time from April to December 1945. Renner died in office in Vienna on New Year's Eve in 1950.

**Reparations.** In general, payments imposed on defeated powers, in the past often referred to as war indemnities. The term usually refers to reparations imposed on Germany as a result of the First World War. The 'war guilt' clause in the TREATY OF VERSAILLES was followed by an obligation on Germany to meet the costs of making good the damage and losses incurred in the war. The victorious allies did not ascertain a definite sum, but in April 1921 reparations were fixed at £6,600 million plus interest (132,000 million gold marks), and £50 million was paid almost immediately. However, hyper-inflation forced Germany to withhold payments in 1922, and in retaliation French and Belgian troops occupied the Ruhr. The DAWES PLAN, providing for annual payments of 2,000 million gold marks, was introduced in 1924. The payments were reduced under the 1929 YOUNG PLAN which gave Germany until 1988 to complete payment.

In 1931 the international DEPRESSION and financial collapse made it impossible for Germany to pay, and on 9 July it was decided at a conference in Lausanne to cancel all further reparations. By this time Germany had paid just over one-eighth of the sum originally demanded, but had received more than this in foreign loans. The extraction of enormous sums from defeated nations was criticized by leading economists, including JOHN MAYNARD KEYNES, who pointed out that the difficulties caused to Germany would dislocate the entire pattern of international trade. Reparations, greatly resented in Germany, proved a potent source of Nazi support in opposition to the Versailles settlement.

Following the fall of France in 1940 Germany exacted heavy reparations and occupation payments from France. In 1945 Germany was also forced to make payments to the USSR and the Western Allies, although the latter largely waived their demands in their desire to revive the German economy and their fears of a repeat of a depression and anti-democratic movements in Germany. The USSR's insistence on its demands and conflict with plans to reactivate German industry played a significant part in the rise of the COLD WAR.

J. M. Keynes, *The Economic Consequences of the Peace* (1919)
E. Mantoux, *The Carthaginian Peace – or the economic consequences of Mr Keynes* (1946)

**Republican Party, German.** The most recent of a series of extreme right-wing parties established in West Germany. Gaining prominence with its entry into the West Berlin parliament in 1989, the party currently claims a membership of around 25,000. Its strongholds are Bavaria and the Ruhr. The party's appeal lies in its nationalism, emphasis on law and order, and hostility to foreign workers and their families living in West Germany. It entered the European Parliament in June 1989, having gained 7 per cent of the votes cast in West Germany. Demanding a revision of the 1945 settlement to restore Germany's 1937 borders in both Western and Central Europe, the Republicans are extreme nationalist advocates of the unification of West and East Germany. See also NATIONAL DEMOCRATIC PARTY.

**Resistance, the.** General name for the opposition to the Nazis in occupied Europe during the Second World War. As early as the autumn of 1940 some groups began to organize in France, but it was with the entry of the Soviet Union into the war in June 1941 that resistance became more general as Communist groups began to play a major part. Rival resistance movements occurred in some countries, notably Yugoslavia and Greece, but in France they were united under DE GAULLE's leadership. Communist control of RESISTANCE and PARTISAN groups in Eastern Europe often gave them a key role in assisting the introduction of Soviet-backed regimes. In some countries, divisions provided the basis for conflicts which continued into the post-war period, as in the GREEK CIVIL WAR.

H. Michel, *The Shadow War: Resistance in Europe, 1939–45* (1972)
M. R. D. Foot, *Resistance* (1976)
H. R. Kedward, *Resistance in Vichy France* (1978)

**Restoration Regime, Spanish.** The regime was established in 1875, following 40 years of civil wars, military coups and the failure of the First Republic, when Canovas del Castillo engineered the restoration of the Alphonsine wing of the monarchy to the throne. Though Spain was a liberal constitutional monarchy with civilian control, separation of church and state, a parliament (Cortes) elected on a progressively widened male franchise, and freedom of political association and organization, power was effectively concentrated into the hands of a landed oligarchy. A narrow political class, strongly rooted in agrarian circles, was divided between two dynastic parties, the Liberals and Conservatives, which shared government office on an alternating basis known as the *turno pacifico*. Meanwhile, in the absence of intermediate social and economic organizations, localized interests and power brokers were integrated into the

regime through the operation of *caciquismo*, a mix of clientalist network and system of political bossism, which ensured the careful 'management' of elections and control of municipal affairs. Little could threaten the regime while civil society remained largely socially and politically demobilized, and the political class exercised firm control. However, the divisive and self-critical debate occasioned by the loss of Spain's final colonies in Cuba and the Philippines in 1898 paved the way for a period of almost endless crises.

By 1914 the regime appeared under siege. The 'social question' was becoming acute in the face of growing labour protest from rural labourers, miners and industrial workers affiliated to the Socialist UGT and Anarcho-syndicalist CNT union federations (*see* UNIÓN GENERAL DE TRABAJADORES; CONFEDERACIÓN NACIONAL DEL TRABAJO). Employers were pressing for protectionism and, in the case of industrialists, access to governing circles. Nationalism in Catalonia and the Basque country threatened the integrity of a Spanish state ruled from Madrid. Republican attacks on the monarchy and political corruption mounted. Within the officer corps, dissatisfaction at conditions of service and disgruntlement at a perceived lack of respect for the military soured relations with civilian politicians and threatened renewed intervention from soldiers. Encouraged by a church never totally at ease with the liberal elements of the Restoration, Catholics were increasingly entering public life in order to defend religion and to promote religious teaching. Some flexibility from the Restoration regime was evident in reaction to these complex pressures, mostly couched in the loosely formulated and widely used ideological language of national renewal, known as regenerationism. There were attempts at social reform and the modernization of the political system. However, the possibility for a purposeful response from within the political class was limited by the disintegration of the dynastic parties into warring factions and the ill judged interventions of the king, ALFONSO XIII.

An economic boom stimulated by wartime neutrality brought only temporary respite and eventually accelerated the vulnerability of the regime. From 1917 there followed a series of challenges to the regime – from militant army officers organized in the *juntas de defensa*, by the successionists of the Catalan Lliga Regionalista and revolutionary strikes largely associated with the anarchist agricultural south and industrial Barcelona – that taken together seemed to threaten its destruction. In practice, however, these movements were not mutually supporting, emerging from contradictory causes, allowing the government to divide and rule. Catalan industrialists were brought into a national government, splitting regionalism, while the army was appeased by strengthening officer privileges. Employers and military then combined to aid in the suppression of worker protest.

Survival did not bring a renewed lease of life. A vacuum opened up as the old mechanisms of manipulation failed, and increased criticism of the Monarchy, anticlerical sentiments and promises of reform, voiced by Socialists and Republicans within parliament, further alarmed the middle-class and military. Consequently, when General PRIMO DE RIVERA rose in September 1923 in a classic *pronunciamiento*, after carefully consulting employer and military opinion, the regime gave way peacefully to be replaced by a new authoritarianism.

R. W. Kern, *Liberals, Reformers, and Caciques in Restoration Spain* (1974)
G. H. Meaker, *The Revolutionary Left in Spain, 1914–23* (1974)
C. Boyd, *Praetorian Politics in Liberal Spain* (1979)
R. Carr, *Spain, 1808–1975* (1980)

**Rexists.** Belgian fascist party founded by Leon Degrelle (1906–). Degrelle was influenced by French right-wing thought and formed the Rex Party in 1930. Anti-Semitic, anti-capitalist, and anti-communist, the party drew upon Catholic pro-monarchical elements. Although of only limited success electorally, the party attracted considerable support and printed papers in both French and Flemish. It obtained 21 deputies (out of 202) in 1936 and 12 senators, but alienated support when it took the side of strikers in support of a 40-hour week. Degrelle also allied with Flemish nationalists, thus alienating Walloon support. He attempted to force new elections in early 1937, hoping to win a bargaining position, but lost a by-election against the Premier, Van Zeeland,

in February 1937. In 1939 the Rexists were reduced to four seats and Degrelle's insistence on neutralism and pacificism alienated patriots. After the defeat of 1940 Degrelle attempted to revive the party as a QUISLING-style government, but was opposed by conservative groups. He volunteered in 1941 for the SS Legion of Walloon volunteers which fought in Russia. Wounded five times and awarded the Knights Cross of the Iron Cross by Hitler, Degrelle was one of only a handful of the division to survive. He escaped to Norway and then to Spain in 1945, eventually retiring to Argentina. Belgian attempts to extradite him failed.

E. Weber, *Varieties of Fascism* (1964)

**Rey, Jean** (1902–). Belgian politician. A lawyer, he was a prisoner-of-war in Germany, 1940–45, and a liberal member of the Belgian Parliament, 1946–58. He was Belgian Minister of Reconstruction, 1949–50, and of Economic Affairs, 1954–8. He became a member of the Commission of the EUROPEAN ECONOMIC COMMUNITY (EEC) in 1958, with responsibilities for External Affairs. His most notable achievement was perhaps his successful conduct of the EEC's part in the KENNEDY ROUND of tariff-cutting negotiations. In 1967 he became the first President (Chairman) of the combined European Community Commission, a post which he held until 1970. He then took up senior positions in private business.

**Reynaud, Paul** (1878–1966). French politician. Born in the Basse-Alpes, he served in the First World War, winning Croix de Guerre. He served as a Deputy on the centre-right, 1919–24, 1928–40, and after 1946. He held several ministerial posts in the 1930s but formed his first ministry only on 21 March 1940. A consistent opponent of Nazism he was appointed as the PHONEY WAR was coming to an end and just before France was overwhelmed by the German invasion of 10 May 1940. He was responsible for replacing GAMELIN with WEYGAND as Commander-in-Chief on 19 May, something he had attempted to do on the eve of the German invasion, but which now served only to heighten the confusion and defeatism spreading through France and the French armies. Four days earlier he had asked Marshal PÉTAIN to return from his post in Madrid to join the government as Minister of State and Vice-President of the Council. Urged by both Pétain and Weygand to seek an armistice, Reynaud ordered the evacuation of Paris on 10 June. He resisted calls for an armistice for over a week, making a last appeal to the United States to enter the war on 14 June, and contemplating withdrawal to North Africa. Reynaud's hope of avoiding an armistice finally collapsed on the night of 15 June, when Roosevelt's reply to the request for assistance was negative. A final attempt to arrange an Anglo-French union failed to command Cabinet support and Reynaud resigned on 16 June, naming Pétain as his successor. Twelve days later he was injured in a car crash, preventing him from joining the FREE FRENCH movement where he would have been a better recognized leader than the virtually unknown DE GAULLE. Imprisoned under the VICHY GOVERNMENT, he was interned by the Germans in Austria, 1943–5. He returned to post-war politics as Minister of Finance in 1948, but was unable to command sufficient support to form a government in 1953. He remained President of the Finance Committee of the National Assembly into the Fifth Republic.

A. Horne, *To Lose a Battle: France 1940* (1969)

**Rhineland.** Area of western Germany. Under the TREATY OF VERSAILLES, the Rhineland and its eastern bridgeheads were to be occupied by British and French troops for 15 years and permanently demilitarized. With the improvement in Franco-German relations after 1923, culminating in the LOCARNO TREATIES of October 1925, the area around Cologne was evacuated. The conclusion of the YOUNG PLAN in 1929 paved the way for the early ending of the occupation, which was complete by the end of June 1930. Under HITLER the German government was to challenge the demilitarized status of the Rhineland (which had been reaffirmed at Locarno) after 1933. In early March 1936, Hitler exploited divisions between Britain and France, and their preoccupation with the Abyssinian War (*see* ETHIOPIAN CRISIS), to abrogate the Locarno treaties and remilitarize the Rhineland. A great diplomatic coup for the Nazi regime, and an important strategic move, the occu-

pation of the Rhineland by German troops and the failure of the British and French armies to intervene to uphold the Locarno agreements strengthened the prestige of the Nazi regime within Germany and encouraged Hitler to believe that his revisionist foreign policy would meet with British and French acquiescence.

G. Weinberg, *The Foreign Policy of Hitler's Germany: Diplomatic Revolution in Europe, 1933–36* (1970)
W. Carr, *Arms, Autarky and Aggression: A Study in German Foreign Policy* (2nd edn, 1979)

**Ribbentrop, Joachim von** (1893–1946). German Foreign Minister, 1938–45. Having served as a cavalry officer during the First World War and worked as a wine exporter during the 1920s, Ribbentrop joined the NAZI PARTY in 1932. With an entrée through marriage to the social élites of the WEIMAR REPUBLIC, Ribbentrop's villa was used during the backstage negotiations which preceded HITLER's appointment as Chancellor in 1933. Ribbentrop impressed Hitler with his knowledge of foreign countries, a knowledge of which Hitler himself was singularly lacking, and undertook a number of unofficial diplomatic missions to Britain and France after 1933. Hitler wished to reduce his reliance on advice from the conservative diplomats of the Germany Foreign Ministry, and in 1934 appointed Ribbentrop as representative for disarmament questions. Ribbentrop established his own bureau, which gradually developed into a diplomatic service paralleling that of the Foreign Ministry. He played a major role in negotiations leading to the ANGLO-GERMAN NAVAL AGREEMENT of June 1935 and the German–Japanese ANTI-COMINTERN PACT of November 1936 aimed against the Soviet Union.

Ribbentrop had been appointed Ambassador to London in spring 1936 and during the succeeding two years sought to persuade influential groups within the British élite of the necessity of an understanding with Germany based on mutual hostility towards the Soviet Union. Whilst Ribbentrop made some headway in strengthening the feeling amongst some sections of the British élite that an agreement with Germany was desirable, the British government refused to commit itself to an unequivocally pro-German and anti-Soviet policy. By

January 1938 Ribbentrop had come to see Britain as a likely future enemy and was emphasizing the need to cultivate closer relations with Italy and Japan.

Ribbentrop was recalled to Berlin and appointed Foreign Minister in February 1938 in succession to the conservative von Neurath, who had incurred Hitler's displeasure as a consequence of his scepticism concerning the accelerated tempo of German foreign policy outlined in the HOSSBACH MEMORANDUM. Whilst Hitler assumed more total control over the conduct of German foreign policy from 1938 onwards, Ribbentrop reached the peak of his career with his negotiation of the NAZI–SOVIET PACT, which he signed on 23 August 1939 and which paved the way for the German invasion of Poland on 1 September 1939.

After the outbreak of war in 1939 Ribbentrop's influence waned as the importance of diplomacy receded. He was active, however, in promoting German relations with Italy and Japan; a process which culminated in the signature of the TRIPARTITE PACT between the states in September 1940. Ribbentrop vainly sought to persuade Hitler to draw closer to the Soviet Union as a means of defeating Britain, and from the invasion of the USSR in June 1941 Ribbentrop's influence diminished. Arrested in June 1945, he was found guilty by the NUREMBERG TRIALS of crimes against humanity and peace and of war crimes, and was hanged in October 1946.

G. Weinberg, *The Foreign Policy of Hitler's Germany: Starting World War II* (1980)

**'Rif Revolt'.** From 1921 the Moroccan tribal leader Abd el Krim (1882–1963) led a revolt against Spanish forces in North Africa, defeating them in several engagements, including a crushing victory at Anual on 21 July 1921 in which the Spanish armies lost over 12,000 men. In 1922 Abd el Krim set up the 'Rif Republic' with the forms of Western-style government. He defeated another Spanish army at Sidi Messaod in 1924. The revolt was a contributory factor in the assumption to power of PRIMO DE RIVERA in Spain. He withdrew Spanish forces to the coast. In May 1924 Abd el Krim attacked the French positions in Morocco, and a joint offensive by Spanish and French troops led by Marshal Pétain finally defeated the revolt. Abd el Krim was captured in 1926 and sent into exile on the French island of Réunion. The revolt has been seen as the beginnings of nationalist movements in North Africa, and the 'Rif Revolt' was to provide an inspiration for Algerian and Tunisian aspirations later in the century.

D. Woolman, *Rebels in the Rif* (1968)

**'Right Opposition'.** The name given by STALIN in October 1928 to those who opposed his plans for rapid industrialization. Following the defeat of the so-called 'LEFT OPPOSITION' with the expulsions of ZINOVIEV, TROTSKY and about a hundred of their supporters at the end of 1927, Stalin turned on his erstwhile allies, notably BUKHARIN, RYKOV and TOMSKY. Stalin, having lulled them into believing that he had accepted their prescription of a slower pace of industrialization financed from the surpluses gained from a prosperous peasantry, advocated the establishment of SOVIET COLLECTIVIZATION, which would increase production, ensure grain deliveries to industry and the towns, and provide the basis for industrial development by depressing peasant living standards. In April 1929 Stalin attacked Bukharin, the most prominent member of the 'Right Opposition', and accused him of promoting a 'pro-Kulak' policy (*see* KULAKS). Bukharin was removed form the Politburo in November 1929, Tomsky in July 1930, and Rykov in December 1930; Rykov was also removed from the premiership. Although members of the opposition openly 'recanted' at the 16th Party Congress in June–July 1930 and again at the 17th Congress in 1934, when Bukharin praised Stalin as 'the best of the best', the opposition was effectively neutralized. Some of their views survived and were expressed in the so-called 'Ryutin programme' which was circulated amongst the Central Committee in 1932. No copy now exists, but it advocated the end of collectivization, a slow-down in investment to industry, and a revival of the retail and consumer goods sector. Ryutin, an official of the Central Committee, was exiled. His escape from the death penalty, at the behest of KIROV, may have prompted Stalin's connivance at Kirov's assassination and the most intense wave of PURGES, which was to see the deaths of all the leaders of the 'Right Opposition'. *See also* INDUSTRIALIZATION DEBATE, SOVIET.

R. W. Davies, *The Industrialisation of the Soviet Union* (2 vols., 1980)

G. A. Hosking, *A History of the Soviet Union* (1985)

**Rijeka.** *See* FIUME.

**Riom Trial.** The trial of the leaders of Republican France under the VICHY GOVERNMENT at Riom from 19 February 1942. DALADIER, BLUM and GAMELIN were charged with French unpreparedness for war, failure to use credits allocated for military purposes, and inefficiencies in the use of the armed forces. The attempt to lay the blame on the pre-war leaders rebounded when the accused were able to show that adequate weapons existed and had been misused by the military and pointed to misleading statements on possible German routes of attack by PÉTAIN himself. The trial proved an embarrassment to the Vichy regime and those it represented, and had to be suspended after two months; it was never resumed.

**Röhm, Ernst** (1887–1934). German Chief of Staff of the Nazi paramilitary SA (*see* SA). Having served during the First World War, Röhm remained an army officer after 1918, and was a political liaison officer for the army headquarters in Munich. Röhm's membership of the NAZI PARTY predated HITLER's assumption of leadership of the party. Röhm participated in the MUNICH PUTSCH of November 1923 and was imprisoned after its failure. Following his release he withdrew from politics and spent two years in Bolivia as a military instructor. Recalled by Hitler and appointed SA Chief of Staff at the beginning of 1931, Röhm played an important role in the rise to power of the Nazis, reorganizing the burgeoning SA and turning it into an effective street-fighting body and propaganda instrument. Following the appointment of Hitler as Reich Chancellor in January 1933, however, the SA presented an increasing problem for the new regime: containing many of the more socially radical elements within the Nazi movement, the SA was discontented with the limited gains it had made

during the Nazi 'revolution', and its grass-roots activities threatened to alienate the conservative élites on whose support Hitler was still dependent. Mounting tension between the army and the SA formed the background to the 'NIGHT OF THE LONG KNIVES' purge of the SA leadership of June 1934 in which Röhm was murdered.

**Rokossovsky, Konstantin** (1896–1965). Soviet Marshal. The son of a railway engineer, he fought in the Tsarist army in the First World War, then joined the RED GUARDS and the RED ARMY, in which he fought as a cavalryman. He was sent for staff training to the Frunze Military Academy. He saw service in Manchuria but was arrested during the PURGES, accused of spying for Japan and Poland. Released from a concentration camp he was reinstated to command of a corps in 1940. He distinguished himself in the opening days of the war and was promoted by ZHUKOV to command the 16th Army during the successful defence of Moscow in November–December 1941. In 1942 he was given command on the Don front and carried out the northern pincer movement in November which surrounded the German army at Stalingrad. At the battle of Kursk in July 1943 he commanded the Central Front, defeating Model's attack; then taking the offensive in 1944 he headed the drive into Poland which halted just outside Warsaw, refusing to link up with the rising of the Polish Home Army (*see* WARSAW RISING) on the grounds that his armies were exhausted. He finally took Warsaw in January 1945, then was moved to command the northern sector of the front, encircling the German armies on the Baltic and in East Prussia. He led the Victory Parade in Moscow on 24 June 1945 and was subsequently appointed Poland's Minister of National Defence. *See also* SECOND WORLD WAR.

**Rome, Treaty of.** Signed by Belgium, France, Italy, Luxembourg, the Netherlands and West Germany on 25 March 1957 creating the EUROPEAN ECONOMIC COMMUNITY (EEC).

**Rommel, Erwin** (1891–1944). German soldier. He served on the Romanian and Italian fronts during the First World War, then lectured at the War Academy and joined the NAZI PARTY in 1933. He commanded the 7th Panzer Division, which penetrated the Ardennes in May 1940. In 1941 he became commander of 'Afrika Corps', earning the nickname 'The Desert Fox'. He was defeated by the campaigns of MONTGOMERY, 1942–3. In 1944 he was given the task of strengthening defences in France, and was active in resistance to Allied landings in Normandy in June 1944. He was implicated in the JULY BOMB PLOT to assassinate Hitler, and was apparently forced to commit suicide in October 1944. A brilliant commander who led the crucial German breakthrough which defeated France in 1940 and almost drove the British out of Egypt. In the last resort his tactical abilities could not compensate for the material superiority of the Allies, which told heavily against him in North Africa and in Normandy.

A. Horne, *To Lose a Battle: France 1940* (1969)
D. Downing, *The Devil's Virtuosos: German Generals at War, 1940–45* (1974)

**Roosevelt, Franklin Delano** (1882–1945). United States President, 1933–45. Born into a wealthy political family, he was Democrat State Senator, New York, 1911–12; Assistant Secretary to the Navy, 1913–20. Crippled by polio in 1921, he was elected Governor of New York in 1928 and defeated Hoover in the 1932 presidential election. He instituted the 'New Deal' to counter the DEPRESSION with the 'Hundred Days' of legislation in 1933: he devalued the dollar and extended federal government role through public works, agricultural support, labour legislation and business protection. He was re-elected in 1936, 1940 and 1944 for a record fourth term. He was attacked for radicalism, and some of his legislation was declared unconstitutional by the Supreme Court in 1937. He maintained wartime neutrality in 1939–41, but supported Britain materially through LEND-LEASE. He brought the United States into the Second World War when the Japanese attacked Pearl Harbour on 7 December 1941 and Germany and Italy declared war on the United States on 11 December. He attended the major conferences with STALIN and CHURCHILL, helping to shape a war-winning strategy of defeating Germany,

then dealing with Japan. He relied heavily on his personal charm in dealing with Soviet leaders and was less suspicious of Russian intentions than Churchill. He helped to lay the basis for the post-war economic and political order with the ATLANTIC CHARTER and the BRETTON WOODS CONFERENCE. He died on 12 April 1945 a fortnight before the San Francisco conference which founded the UNITED NATIONS.

W. H. McNeill, *America, Britain and Russia* (1953)
H. Feis, *Churchill, Roosevelt, Stalin* (1957)
G. Kolko, *The Politics of War* (1968)

**Rosenberg, Alfred** (1893–1946). Nazi supporter and official, an early mentor of HITLER who became the semi-official 'philosopher' of anti-semitism, mainly through his book *The Myth of the Twentieth Century* (1930). Born in Estonia, he fled after the RUSSIAN REVOLUTION, joining nationalist and anti-semitic groups in Munich. An early member of the NAZI PARTY, he participated in the MUNICH PUTSCH and was temporarily Party leader while Hitler was in prison. His writings postulated a racial interpretation of world history, the Teutons representing a master-race of Aryans who had to combat Christian liberalism, Freemasonry and Judaism. Although obscure, muddled and pseudo-scientific, his book became second only to MEIN KAMPF as the bible of the Nazi movement. Given a Party post as head of the Foreign Affairs Department, he visited Britain in 1933 and entertained the Norwegian fascist leader QUISLING in December 1939, encouraging the invasion of Norway. From 1934 he was charged with supervision of ideological training of Party members. In 1940 he set up a task force to loot art treasures and Jewish property from occupied territories. Appointed Minister for Occupied Eastern Territories in July 1941, his protests at some of the aspects of Nazi policy were ignored and he remained in charge of the Ukraine until his arrest in 1945. He was tried at NUREMBERG for war crimes and hanged on 16 October 1946.

R. Cecil, *The Myth of the Master Race: Alfred Rosenberg and Nazi Ideology* (1972)

**Rote Armee Faktion** (RAF). A terrorist group, also known as the Baader–Meinhof group after two of its leaders, which emerged in West Germany following the wave of student protest in 1968. Its aim was to expose what it saw as reactionary forces in West German society and express opposition to the US military presence in Europe. Between 1968 and 1972 the German authorities believe that the group was responsible for at least six murders, 50 attempted murders, numerous bombings, bank raids and kidnappings. In 1968 Andreas Baader (1943–77) was arrested, but on 14 May 1970 was forcibly freed by Ulrike Meinhof (1934–76), a former television journalist. In June 1972 a large number of the group, including Baader and Meinhof, was captured again and committed for trial. On 9 May 1976 Meinhof was found dead in her prison cell in Stuttgart, allegedly having committed suicide. The suspicious circumstances surrounding her death led to a wave of protest from the extreme left. In April 1977 Baader and two associates were sentenced to life imprisonment, but after the failure of an attempted hijack to force their release they committed suicide in Stammheim prison in October. On 15 September 1978 one further member, Astrid Proll, was arrested in London and deported to stand trial in Germany. The RAF continued in existence with an estimated 'core' of 15–20 activists, allegedly responsible for a bomb attack at the Munich Beer Festival in September 1980 which killed 12 people and attacks on individuals representing the West German establishment. In 1985 the RAF issued a joint paper with the French terrorist group Action Directe, declaring the opening of a 'Bonn–Paris axis' to fight 'the military–industrial complex'. In West Germany in 1985 they assassinated two leading industrialists from the Siemens and MTU turbine group. In October 1989 the RAF activist, Helmut Pohl, warned from prison of a 'new phase in the struggle', followed in December by the blowing up of the car of Alfred Herrhausen, a banker, by a remote-controlled bomb. This action broke a four-year silence by the West German terrorists whom it had been believed had been rendered inoperative.

S. Segaller, *Invisible Armies: Terrorism into the 1990s* (rev. edn, 1987)

**ROVS.** *See* RUSSIAN ALL-SERVICES UNION.

**RSDRP.** *See* SOCIAL DEMOCRATIC LABOUR PARTY, RUSSIAN.

**Ruhr Occupation.** Occupation of Germany's main western industrial and mining region in January 1923 following the default of the government of the WEIMAR REPUBLIC on REPARATIONS deliveries imposed in 1921 under the terms of the TREATY OF VERSAILLES. The French government under POINCARÉ exploited the declaration of the Reparations Commission in December 1922 that Germany was in default on deliveries of coal and timber to seek to enforce reparations more rigorously and, perhaps more important, to try to create a political basis for pushing Germany's western frontier back to the Rhine and thus achieving the permanent political weakening of Germany which the French had sought in 1919. During the course of 1923, the French forces occupying the Ruhr were increased to 100,000 men; and the French sponsored ultimately unsuccessful separatist movements in western Germany, the Rhineland and the Palatinate. The German government responded to the occupation by suspending all reparations payments to France and Belgium and by calling on the population of the Ruhr to carry out a policy of passive resistance. As a consequence, industrial activity in the Ruhr came to a virtual standstill and the German government was obliged to expend virtually all of its foreign currency reserves for the importation of coal. Deprived of revenue from the Ruhr, making massive monetary payments and payments in kind to the population of the Ruhr and reluctant to impose high levels of taxation on the rest of the German population to fund this policy, the German government resorted to the printing press to fund its expenditure, accelerating hyperinflation and the collapse of the German currency. Confronted by this crisis, which threatened the political stability of the entire Weimar Republic, a broad-based coalition government under GUSTAV STRESEMANN revoked unconditionally the policy of passive resistance and resumed reparations payments in September 1923 calling on the Reparations Commission in October 1923 to carry out an investigation of Germany's economic situation. In November 1923 a new currency was introduced in Germany which eradicated hyper-inflation. Anglo-American pressure, stemming from anxiety about French attempts to establish economic hegemony in Western Europe, led to the ending of the occupation early in 1924; and the formulation of the DAWES PLAN for the future management of reparations payments, which was accepted by the German government in April 1924.

S. W. Halperin, *Germany Tried Democracy* (1946)

**Russian All-Services Union** (ROVS). Formed by the 'White' Russian general WRANGEL in Yugoslavia as an ex-serviceman's organization, but serving as a network of white emigrés through which former white generals and their units could remain in touch. After Wrangel's death in 1928, his two successors, Generals Miller and Kutepov, were abducted by Soviet agents and disappeared. *See also* RUSSIAN CIVIL WAR.

**Russian calendar.** Up to February 1918 the Soviet Union continued to operate on the Julian calendar, running 13 days behind the Gregorian calendar in use in most of the rest of Europe. 1 February 1918, Old Style, became 14 February, New Style, and dates thereafter followed the Gregorian calendar. As a result the 'October Revolution' actually occurred in November according to the Gregorian calendar in use in the West. Gregorian dates have been used for Russian events before 1918 throughout this volume.

**Russian Civil War.** War following the October Revolution (*see* RUSSIAN REVOLUTION) and the dissolution of the CONSTITUENT ASSEMBLY fought between the Bolshevik forces (the 'Reds') and anti-Bolshevik forces (the 'Whites'). Sporadic armed resistance to the Bolshevik revolution by supporters of the Tsar and of the Provisional Government began in December 1917, but the first large-scale actions against the Bolshevik government came in May 1918 with the refusal of the CZECH LEGION, composed of ex-prisoners-of-war, to disarm and their subsequent occupation of a large section of the Trans-Siberian Railway. As a result of the TREATIES OF BREST-LITOVSK the Allied powers were prepared to intervene on behalf of those forces who might resume the war against the Central Powers.

Thus, beginning in spring 1918, British, French, Japanese and American forces were landed in the north, at Murmansk and Archangel, in the south, in the Crimea and the Caucasus, and in the east, at Vladivostock. Until the armistice of November 1918, German, Austro-Hungarian and Romanian troops were involved in support of anti-Bolshevik forces in the Ukraine, while Finnish and German forces were active in the BALTIC STATES and the KARELIAN ISTHMUS. The situation was further complicated by the activities of semi-autonomous groups of national and ethnic armies. By the summer of 1918 anti-Bolshevik governments had been established at Samara, Omsk and Archangel, and Bolshevik control was restricted to a rump of territory around Moscow, Petrograd and the industrial areas west of the Urals. The war was conducted by the Bolsheviks by expanding the Communist RED GUARDS into the RED ARMY, organized and led by TROTSKY with the assistance of former Tsarist officers.

The civil war continued for almost three years, merging in the west into the RUSSO-POLISH WAR and covering a number of fronts. In the Caucasus, the Don COSSACKS rose in revolt in December 1917 under Hetman Kaledin but were overthrown by the Bolsheviks in the winter of 1917–18. Kaledin committed suicide in February 1918 and command passed to General DENIKIN, who with Allied support occupied the Ukraine and the northern Caucasus. The Red Army defeated Denikin's forces and he eventually fled the country, leaving command to General WRANGEL, who held out in the Crimea until November 1920. In the UKRAINE, resistance to the Bolsheviks was led by General Skoropadsky, appointed by the Germans after the Treaties of Brest-Litovsk as head of a puppet Ukrainian state. With the withdrawal of German forces in November 1918 Skoropadsky's regime was overthrown by the Ukrainian peasant leader PETLYURA who fought both the Bolsheviks and the forces of General Denikin. Denikin's forces occupied the Ukraine in the latter half of 1919 and there was Polish intervention in the first months of 1920, but the Bolsheviks suppressed all opposition by the summer of 1920. On the Baltic front the Bolsheviks were faced with anti-Soviet forces led by

General Yudenich which advanced on Petrograd in October 1919 but were repulsed. Anti-Soviet forces were also supplied by Latvia, Lithuania, Estonia and Finland, all of whom were forced to make peace with the Bolsheviks between February and October 1920. In northern Russia, British and French forces landed at Murmansk in June 1918 and seized Archangel, establishing a puppet government and attempting unsuccessfully to link up with the anti-Bolshevik forces near Petrograd. Their 'intervention' ended with the evacuation of their troops in October 1919. In Siberia, Admiral KOLCHAK set up a White government at Omsk with the aid of a Czech Legion and Japanese and American forces which had landed at Vladivostock in December 1917. The anti-Soviet forces controlled much of Russia east of the Urals and the central part of the Trans-Siberian Railway for almost a year, before the capture and execution of Kolchak in February 1920. Japanese forces held Vladivostock until November 1922.

The failure of the White forces to co-ordinate their activities, their internal divisions and lack of agreement upon a common objective, and the half-hearted support given by the Allies as they coped with the transition to peace, meant that the counter-revolutionary forces failed to capitalize upon the early weakness of the Bolshevik regime. In contrast, in spite of desperate shortages, a serious famine and peasant unrest, the Bolsheviks managed brilliant feats of improvisation. WAR COMMUNISM nationalized industry and trade, enforced labour service, and exacted supplies for the Red Army with great ruthlessness. Rigorous central direction and the enthusiasm of the early Red Army proved sufficient to give the Bolsheviks eventual military success against their strong but divided opponents.

The Russian Civil War left a legacy of economic devastation from which Russia only gradually recovered during the 1920s. Allied intervention against the Bolshevik government and the latter's repudiation of foreign debts deeply soured relations between the Bolsheviks and the Western powers, who only moved slowly to recognize the Bolshevik government (Britain, 1924; United States, 1933). Internally, the unpopularity and shortcomings of 'War Communism' were to influence Lenin in fashioning the NEW ECONOMIC POLICY, but the major outcome of the Civil War was the establishment of the Soviet regime and the extinction of effective challenge within Russia.

D. Footman, *Civil War in Russia* (1961)
R. Luckett, *The White Generals* (1971)
P. Kenez, *Civil War in South Russia, 1918–20* (2 vols., 1971–7)
G. A. Denikin, *The White Army* (1973)
I. Deutscher, *The Prophet Armed: Trotsky, 1879–1921* (1974)
D. V. Lehovich, *Denikin* (1974)
M. McCauley (ed.), *The Russian Revolution and the Soviet State, 1917–21* (1975)

**Russian Orthodox Church.** The largest church in pre-Revolutionary Russia, which came increasingly under state control from the 18th century. On 20 January 1918 the Bolshevik government published a decree depriving the church of all its legal rights and its property. Congregations could hire back buildings for use, but they were at the disposal of the local soviets. From 1919 an anti-Christian campaign was carried out, churches were desecrated, half the monasteries closed, and many clergy killed or imprisoned, leading one group to meet at Karlovtsy in Yugoslavia and endorse the anti-Bolshevik cause. In 1922 Metropolitan Veniamin was tried and executed for resistance to the seizure of church treasures for famine relief and Patriarch Tikhon was placed under house arrest. A year later a group of reformist clergy set up the 'Living Church', stripped Tikhon of his titles and reformed church administration. Tikhon then offered support for the state and was released from house arrest; three years later Metropolitan Sergei proclaimed full support for the Soviet state. In 1929 the state issued a new decree on 'religious associations', allowing religious activity only to registered congregations of 20 or more; all other religious activity was banned and evangelism prohibited. Under STALIN a large-scale purge of clergy took place in 1936; of 163 bishops active in 1930, only 12 were still at liberty in 1939. A major change, however, came with the Second World War. The Church pledged its support for the war effort and in 1943 Stalin re-established the patriarchate; ecclesiastical administration was revived, seminaries were set up and about half of the pre-1917 churches, some 20,000, were re-opened. Under KHRUSHCHEV a new wave of persecution began. The legislation of 1943–5 allowed the priest to administer the parish buildings as well as to provide services. In 1961 he was deprived of the administrative functions and some 10,000 churches were closed or converted to other purposes, as were most monasteries. After Khrushchev's fall the restrictions on the church were relaxed, but it was still supervised by a state department which ensured the conformity of clergy to state ideology. In 1988 the Orthodox Church had an estimated 40–60 million believers, of whom an estimated 10–20 per cent were regular churchgoers; 9,734 parishes were in existence, along with 35 monasteries, about a third of which had come into existence since 1985. A total of three seminaries operated in 1985, doubling to six by 1988.

W. Kolarz, *Religion in the Soviet Union* (1961)
W. C. Fletcher, *A Study in Survival: The Church in Russia, 1927–43* (1965)
P. Pascal, *The Religion of the Russian People* (1976)
C. Lane, *Christian Religion in the Soviet Union: A Sociological Study* (1978)

**Russian Revolution.** The origins of the Russian Revolution lay in the pre-war failures of the Russian monarchy under Tsar NICHOLAS II to make sufficiently effective constitutional and economic reforms to withstand the strains of the prolonged and intensive conflict which began in 1914. In spite of early enthusiasm for the war and a significant increase in industrial output, cripplingly high casualties and growing political discontent on the home front brought about a breakdown in government in early 1917. By then widespread defeatism and discontent in the army had rendered its loyalty suspect, and when riots and strikes broke out in Petrograd (the former St Petersburg) on 8 March (23 February by the old Russian calendar), the troops began to go over to the crowds in what became a largely spontaneous and bloodless revolution. The DUMA set up a PROVISIONAL GOVERNMENT on 12 March and the abdication of Nicholas II followed three days later.

The Provisional Government was intended to act as a caretaker administration until a CONSTITUENT ASSEMBLY could meet and establish a new government. Parallel to it, however, a Petrograd Soviet (*see* SOVIETS) was set up, which lost little time in exerting control over the armed forces. On 14 March it issued 'Army Order Number One' by which it turned itself into the 'Soviet of the Workers' and Soldiers' Deputies'. It decreed that representatives of the lower ranks of the armed forces should be elected to the Soviet, that in all political matters the military were under orders from the Soviet, and abolished military titles while emphasizing that military discipline should be retained. Although intended to apply only to the Petrograd garrison (confirmed in Army Order Number Two), the copies of the original order which reached the front line helped to precipitate a further crumbling of army morale and growing support for the Soviet.

With German connivance LENIN was returned from exile in Switzerland, arriving in Petrograd on 16 April, amply supplied with funds. In his APRIL THESES he set out a programme of immediate peace, noncooperation with the Provisional Government and 'all power to the soviets', which offered a radical platform quite distinct from the more moderate socialists as well as those who made up the Provisional Government. Although the Bolsheviks made up a minority in most of the soviets which had sprung into existence, their programme acted as an increasing challenge to all other parties. For its own part, the Provisional Government saw the revolution as the opportunity to pursue the war more effectively than the Tsar. In spite of having lost over 7 million casualties, the war was continued and a new offensive planned by the Provisional Government under its most effective leader, KERENSKY. The offensive proved unsuccessful, and its collapse in July served only to speed up the disintegration of the army.

The Bolsheviks made an abortive attempt to seize power on 16–17 July, which forced Lenin to seek temporary refuge in Finland, but in spite of Kerensky taking over the premiership on 22 July the Provisional Government remained weak. By failing to call a Constituent Assembly into being it lacked exclusive authority, there was no land reform to satisfy the peasantry, and it was unable to offer either the prospect of peace or a decisive victory on the battle-field. By September, it had little popular support and was faced by a Bolshevik group, now joined by TROTSKY, whose singleness of purpose, superior organiz-ation, active propaganda and armed RED GUARDS made them ready and willing to seize power when the occasion presented itself. Growing support for the Bolsheviks amongst soldiers and workers meant that when the commander-in-chief, KORNILOV, attempted a putsch against the Provisional Government in September, Kerensky was forced to call on the Bolsheviks for assist-ance. Bolshevik railway workers halted the movement of Kornilov's forces on Petrog-rad by train and pro-Bolshevik soldiers frat-ernizing with his troops induced them to lay down their arms.

During September the Bolsheviks had increased their support in the soviets, secur-ing majorities in Moscow and Petrograd, and squeezing out many of the more moder-ate socialists. On 23 October the Bolshevik Central Committee voted for armed insur-rection. A political bureau (Politburo) was formed and the Petrograd Soviet estab-lished a MILITARY REVOLUTIONARY COMMIT-TEE under the chairmanship of Trotsky to execute the attack. Having obtained the support of the Petrograd garrison on 3 Nov-ember and secured the main arsenal at the Peter and Paul Fortress, the assault on the headquarters of the Provisional Govern-ment in the Winter Palace was organized from the Soviet headquarters on the Smolny Institute for the night of 6–7 Nov-ember (24–5 October in the old calendar). During the 6th the Bolsheviks organized an alternative government headquarters in the Peter and Paul Fortress and took steps to secure the other major services in the capi-tal. At the same time Red Guards seized the major bridges, the telegraph office, the central news agency and the Baltic (Fin-land) station. Troops were then directed to seize the remaining major strategic points in Petrograd. On the morning of the 7th Lenin announced the transfer of power to the Military Revolutionary Committee and at 10 p.m. troops led by ANTONOV-OVSEY-ENKO attacked the Winter Palace at the signal of a shot from the cruiser *Aurora*, and arrested the Provisional Government. Meanwhile, the Second All-Russian Con-gress of Soviets meeting at the Smolny Insti-tute approved on the morning of the 8th the seizure of power and decreed the setting up of a Council of People's Commissars as the executive body of the new Soviet state.

The Bolshevik seizure of power was con-solidated in the next few days. Attempts by Kerensky, who had fled the Winter Palace, to retake Petrograd with scratch forces, were defeated by the 12th, and after heavy fighting control was established in Moscow by the 16th. The first official statement of the revolution was Lenin's *Appeal to the Workers, Soldiers and Peasants*, proclaim-ing that the Congress was taking power and that power throughout the country should pass into the hands of soviets of workers', soldiers' and peasants' deputies. Lenin also moved swiftly to deal with the two pressing issues of peace and land. A Decree on Peace was accepted by the Congress on the 9th proposing a peace without annexations and indemnities and offering a general armistice. By early December the Bolshe-viks had obtained a cease-fire and begun the negotiations which led to the TREATIES OF BREST-LITOVSK. A decree on land abol-ished private ownership for ever and redis-tributed land for the peasants' use. The decree redistributed some 540,000,000 acres of land, the royal family, the church, the large landowners and the richer peas-ants being the major losers. When early negotiations with other socialists, such as the MENSHEVIKS and the SOCIAL REVOL-UTIONARY PARTY about a coalition govern-ment failed, the Bolsheviks took it upon themselves to govern the country through the Soviet (council) of People's Commis-sars, headed by Lenin. The decree estab-lishing the executive also laid down that the new government was subject to the control of the All-Russian Congress of Soviets and its Central Executive Committee. In effect the early decree of the Congress became the constitution through which the Bolshe-viks governed the country. Consolidating power also meant silencing the liberal and right-wing press, the establishment of the CHEKA and the arrest of opponents. Forced to acquiesce in the meeting of the long-awaited Constituent Assembly on 18 Janu-ary 1918, the Bolsheviks withdrew follow-ing their first voting defeat and on the next day used Red Guards to disperse it.

The historiography of the revolution is enormous. Key themes concern the extent to which the revolution was primarily the product of the war rather than an event prefigured in 1905 and almost inevitable by 1914. Critics of this view point to the progress of the late Tsarist economy in industrial development and a measure of agricultural reform under Stolypin. The war, however, clearly imposed stresses of a new order and the Russian autocracy was only one of three well established dynasties to collapse as a result of the war. In a two-stage revolutionary process, the February revolution was virtually a bloodless abdication of power by the old order, in which dissatisfaction with the way the war was being conducted played at least as big a part as anti-war sentiment. Fatally, however, the Provisional Government failed to gauge the degree of war-weariness and deprivation affecting the army and the population at large, and lacked both the ideological coherence and the organization to create an effective bulwark against the communist forces. Marxist historiography inevitably concentrates on the central role of Lenin and the Bolsheviks. The wider picture involves a recognition that the Bolsheviks remained in a minority even amongst socialist groups right through the October revolution, but were able through their discipline and organization, as well as Lenin's tactical genius, to control events and form the first Soviet Government in an increasingly chaotic situation. Much recent work stresses the contingent features of Russian conditions in 1917–18, and the precarious position of the early Bolshevik government, for whom the decisive struggle for survival lay in the RUSSIAN CIVIL WAR which followed their seizure of power.

L. Shapiro, *The Origin of the Communist Autocracy* (1965)
A. B. Ulam, *Lenin and the Bolsheviks* (1965)
E. H. Carr, *A History of Soviet Russia: The Bolshevik Revolution* (3 vols., 1966)
H. Seton-Watson, *The Russian Empire, 1801–1917* (1967)
R. Service, *The Bolshevik Party in Revolution, 1917–23* (1979)

**Russification.** A term used to denote a policy of cultural assimilation and hegemony exercised over the non-Russian peoples and ethnic minorities of the Russian Empire, particularly associated with the latter years of the Tsars. Key features of Russification were discrimination against non-Russian languages and culture and the elevation of Russian, the assertion of the authority of the Russian Orthodox Church, and the repression of nationalist sentiment. The term has also been used, often by supporters of minority nations, as a pejorative description of the policies pursued within the Soviet Union since 1917, particularly under STALIN. In recent years, it has been noted that although the harshest manifestations of Russification were directed against the most alien ethnic groups within the empire, such as the Jews, Muslims, Finns and Poles, its most important target was the large Slav minorities, such as those of BELORUSSIA and the UKRAINE. Their assimilation was necessary to secure Slav ascendency in a situation where Russians proper accounted for only 45 per cent of the population in 1914. Under the Soviets, following the initially lenient terms with which the early leaders viewed the NATIONALITIES QUESTION, growing discrimination against ethnic and national groups under Stalin and later leaders should more accurately be seen as an attempt to promote 'Sovietization', a secular, Soviet culture which involved discrimination against expression of 'bourgeois' national culture and particularism. Combined with a growing process of centralization in the political and economic sphere, national minorities have frequently argued that 'Russification' has in fact been taking place, leading to clashes over the place of non-Russian languages in education, freedom of worship for minority religions, and the expression of cultural identity. Many of these grievances were more vocally expressed in the freer climate since the accession of MIKHAIL GORBACHEV in 1985. The Congress of People's Deputies which met in May–June 1989 offered the first opportunity for open expression of the grievances of the Soviet nations and ethnic groups.

J. Azarel, *Soviet Nationality Policies and Practices* (1978)
H. Carrere d'Encausse, *Decline of an Empire: The Soviet Socialist Republics in Revolt* (1979)
R. Pearson, *National Minorities in Eastern Europe, 1849–1945* (1983)
O. Glebov and J. Crowfoot (trans. and eds.), *The Soviet Empire: Its Nations Speak out* (1989)

**Russo-Finnish War** (Winter War). The Soviet Union attempted to gain agreement from Finland during exchanges in 1938 and early 1939 to accept Soviet assistance in the event of a German invasion and the concession of bases on islands in the Gulf of Finland neutralized under the TREATY OF TARTU. Finland refused to compromise her neutrality and strongly protested against attempts to include Finland in a Russian sphere of influence in negotiations which took place between Britain and France and the Soviet Union in spring 1939. The NAZI–SOVIET PACT of August 1939, however, contained secret clauses assigning Finland to Soviet influence. Following the German invasion of Poland in September 1939 and the Soviet entry into eastern Poland and the BALTIC STATES, the Soviet Union presented demands to Finland for a mutual assistance treaty, the lease of a naval base for 5,000 troops at the mouth of the Gulf of Finland, the occupation of islands in the Gulf of Finland, Finnish territory on the Arctic Ocean, the adjustment of the border on the KARELIAN ISTHMUS westwards in the Soviet Union's favour, and the mutual demolition of fortifications. These demands were rejected, but smaller concessions offered, and rejected in turn by Stalin.

On 26 November the Soviet Union claimed that the Finns were responsible for the deaths of Soviet troops at Mainila on the Karelian Isthmus and demanded the withdrawal of Finnish troops 25 kilometres westwards. An offer of mutual withdrawal of troops was rejected, and on the 29th the Soviet Union announced the severing of diplomatic relations and the renunciation of the non-aggression pact with Finland. This was followed by the bombing of Finnish cities on 30 November 1939 and an all-out attack by Soviet forces along the long eastern border of Finland and against the MANNERHEIM LINE on the Karelian Isthmus. Soviet forces at first made little headway against determined Finnish opposition which destroyed several Russian divisions. A huge Russian offensive in February 1940, massing over 45 divisions and nearly 1 million men on all fronts, breached the Mannerheim line in March and made landings on the north coast of the Gulf of Finland. After several weeks of bitter fighting and Western offers of assistance which proved insufficient to affect the situation materially, the Finns accepted peace terms with the Soviet Union on 12 March 1940. By the terms of the Treaty of Moscow, Finland lost 10 per cent of her territory, including the whole of the Karelian Isthmus and her second city Viipuri and islands in the Gulf of Finland, was forced to lease a naval base at Hanko Cape for 30 years, and to sign a defence pact with the Soviet Union. As a result of the treaty some 450,000 Finns had to be resettled from the Russian-occupied territories.

The material losses in the war were approximately 200,000 dead on the Soviet side and Finnish casualties of 25,000 dead or missing and another 43,000 wounded. The most important outcome of the war was the impression made abroad of the poor showing of the Soviet forces, whose overwhelming numerical and material preponderance had been stoutly rebuffed by the Finns for over three months. Deprived by the PURGES of some of her best commanders the Soviet forces proved unimaginatively led and slow to adjust to winter fighting and the guerrilla tactics adopted by the Finns. To the German military the war appeared confirmation of the poor quality of the opposition they would encounter in a war with the Soviet Union; as it turned out, this was an underestimation of the effects which Soviet reorganization following the Winter War and a fight on Russian soil would have in the ensuing war with the Soviet Union. Nonetheless, the conflict encouraged HITLER in his preparation of plans for an early invasion of the Soviet Union. For the Finns, the punitive terms of the Treaty of Moscow pushed them into informal co-operation with the German army following its occupation of Norway. When the German army finally invaded the Soviet Union in July 1941, Finnish troops joined in the assault to recapture their lost territories in the CONTINUATION WAR.

Another result of the war was to turn German attention to Norway. The half-hearted offers to assist Finland from France and Britain by transporting forces across Norwegian territory helped to determine Hitler's plans for the occupation of Norway, effected in April 1940.

M. Jakobson, *The Diplomacy of the Winter War* (1969)

R. W. Condon, *The Winter War: Russia against Finland* (1972)

V. Tanner, *The Winter War* (1974)

**Russo-Polish War.** The newly independent Poland was formally brought into existence by the TREATY OF VERSAILLES with the Germans on 28 June 1919 and the TREATY OF SAINT GERMAIN with Austria on 10 September. Article 87 of the Treaty of Versailles left the eastern border of Poland for settlement in due course, but in spring 1919 Polish forces had already seized Vilna (*see* VILNA DISPUTE) which the Soviet Union had ceded to Lithuania (*see* BALTIC STATES) and by July had occupied Eastern Galicia, which both Ukrainians and Russians considered part of the Ukraine. In spring 1920 PILSUDSKI, the Polish leader, made a bid to re-establish the borders of the Greater Poland which had existed in the 18th century, aiming to annex the Ukraine and Lithuania. A proclamation on 28 April called on Ukrainians to join a Polish 'federation', and by early May the Poles had occupied Kiev, the Ukrainian capital. An offensive by the RED ARMY drove the Poles from Kiev on 11 June 1920. Attempts by the British and French to persuade the Poles and Russians to adhere to a line of demarcation between ethnic and religious groups, the CURZON LINE, drawn up in December 1919, failed to prevent the Soviet armies under TUKHACHEVSKY advancing west of the Curzon Line and into the heart of Poland. Allied mediation secured a meeting of Russo-Polish peace delegations on 11 August, but they were overtaken by a counterattack on the 16th by Polish forces, now advised by French officers led by General WEYGAND, which rapidly drove back the Soviet forces, taking over 60,000 prisoners. The 'Miracle on the Vistula' led to the advance of Polish forces to the east of the Curzon Line, seizing Vilna on 10 October. Two days later an armistice and preliminary peace treaty was signed between Poland and the Soviet Union, con-firmed in a peace treaty at Riga on 18 March 1921. The outcome of the war as expressed in the treaty was the alteration of the Russo-Polish border considerably to the east of the Curzon Line, leaving Poland in occupation of Vilna and a large portion of Lithuanian territory, and an area of White Russia and the Ukraine containing 6 million inhabitants who were neither Polish nor Catholic. Although accepted by the Soviet Union at the time as an interim frontier agreement which would prove irrelevant once revolutions occurred elsewhere in Europe, in the secret protocols to the NAZI–SOVIET PACT of August 1939, Stalin laid claim to the territory surrendered at Riga and occupied it in September 1940 in his assault on Poland from the east. *See also* RUSSIAN CIVIL WAR.

D. Footman, *Civil War in Russia* (1961)

N. Davies, *White Eagle, Red Star: The Polish–Soviet War, 1919–20* (1972)

**Rykov, Aleksei** (1881–1938). Russian Bolshevik leader. The son of a peasant, he was an early member of the BOLSHEVIK faction of the SOCIAL DEMOCRATIC LABOUR PARTY. Relations with LENIN cooled after 1910 when he was more favourable to co-operation with the MENSHEVIKS. He returned from Siberia after the February Revolution and became a member of the Central Committee of the Bolshevik Party. He was appointed Commissar for internal affairs, 1917, and then chairman of the Supreme Council of National Economy, 1918–20, 1923–4. A member of the Politburo, 1923–9, he chaired the Council of People's Commissars (Sovnarkom), 1924–30. With BUKHARIN and TOMSKY a member of the 'RIGHT OPPOSITION' to collectivization, he was supplanted as chairman of Sovnarkom by MOLOTOV in 1930. In 1937 he was expelled from the party and arrested. In 1938 he was tried with Bukharin in the last show trial of the PURGES and executed.

E. H. Carr, *The Russian Revolution: From Lenin to Stalin* (1979)

# S

**SA** (Sturmabteilung). The paramilitary force of the German NAZI PARTY. The SA was established in October 1921 to protect Nazi Party meetings against attack by political opponents. It attracted a large number of ex-soldiers and ex-FREIKORPS members and rapidly became a uniformed quasi-military force. With a membership of 55,000 in 1923, it participated in the MUNICH PUTSCH. With the refoundation of the Nazi Party in 1925, the SA's main task came to be the dissemination of propaganda, though its participation in street fighting with communists and other political opponents also served to underline the Nazi Party's hostility to the Left in the minds of middle-class voters. Banned briefly by the WEIMAR REPUBLIC government in 1932, the SA had a membership of perhaps 500,000 on the eve of HITLER's appointment as Chancellor in January 1933, a membership which was young (over 80 per cent of members were under 30) and contained many unemployed workers. The SA played a key role in the Nazi seizure of power in spring 1933, intimidating political opponents of the regime and occupying the offices of the left-wing political parties and trade unions. With the consolidation of the Nazi dictatorship in summer 1933, the continuing disorderliness of the SA and its intervention in local government and interference with businesses presented a problem for Hitler, who was dependent on maintaining his alliance with the conservative élites. By early 1934 the SA numbered 2.5–3.0 million members. The threat to the regular army apparently posed by the SA leadership's ambitions to absorb the army into a political militia led Hitler to initiate a purge of the organization in the June 1934 'NIGHT OF THE LONG KNIVES'. After 1934, the significance of the SA declined sharply and its membership fell by 50 per cent between 1934 and 1937. Entrusted with no tasks of significance, the SA increasingly formed a pool of men on which the regional and local officials of the regime could draw at will to participate in demonstrations (as during the November 1938 anti-Semitic pogrom) or, after 1939, perform semi-military tasks. See also RÖHM, ERNST.

C. Fischer, *Stormtroopers: A Social, Economic and Ideological Analysis, 1929–1935* (1983)
R. Bessel, *Political Violence and the Rise of Nazism* (1984)

**Saar.** German industrial district on the left bank of the Rhine in the basin of the river Saar. It was put under League of Nations administration by the TREATY OF VERSAILLES for a 15-year period and its mines controlled by the French as a form of reparations. A plebiscite on 13 January 1935 voted for its return to German authority. The area was reoccupied by the French after the Second World War but was integrated into the FEDERAL REPUBLIC OF GERMANY on 1 January 1957.

**St Germain, Treaty of.** Treaty with Austria signed on 10 September 1919 as a result of the PARIS PEACE CONFERENCE. Austria and Hungary were separated and Austria lost control of the larger part of the former Austro-Hungarian Empire. Austria lost territory for the creation of the SUCCESSOR STATES of Poland, Czechoslovakia and Yugoslavia. The South Tyrol (*see* SOUTH TYROL DISPUTE), Trentino and Istria was ceded to Italy, and a plebiscite was to define the Austrian boundary in southern Carinthea. Article 88 forbade the union (ANSCHLUSS) of Austria with the German Republic. Austria was required to meet REPARATIONS, although the amount was unspecified. The Austrian armed forces were reduced to 30,000 men and her fleet was handed over to Yugoslavia, then distributed amongst the victorious powers. The Covenant of the League of Nations was written into the treaty. Austria was left a shadow of her former greatness, already overtaken by the creation of new states even before the Paris Peace Conference had met. In fact, Austria was reduced in size to about two-thirds even of its former German territories. As with the TREATY OF VERSAILLES there were ample grounds for grievance. Austrian 'self-determination' to join the new German Republic was forbidden, while over 3 million Germans were surrendered without plebiscite to Czechoslovakia and another 0.25 million in the South Tyrol handed over to Italy. Austria, too, was fixed with the blame of 'war guilt' and required to recompense her former enemies, although only a few small repayments in kind were able to be exacted from the virtually destitute new AUSTRIAN REPUBLIC.

Z. A. B. Zeman, *The Break-up of the Habsburg Empire, 1914–18* (1961)
A. J. Mayer, *The Policy and Diplomacy of Peacemaking* (1968)

**St Petersburg** (Petrograd, Leningrad). Before 1914 the Russian capital was known by its German form, Sankt Petersburg. At the outbreak of the First World War its name was Russified to Petrograd, but on Lenin's death in 1924 it was renamed in his honour. In 1991 resumed former name.

**Sakharov, Andrei** (1921–89). Soviet nuclear physicist and leading DISSIDENT. The Deputy Director of the Soviet H-Bomb programme and the youngest ever member of the Academy of Sciences, he became an important advocate of reform and intellectual freedom in the Soviet Union during the late 1950s. He gained international attention in 1968 with a manifesto outlining peaceful steps towards a world community. He co-founded the Committee for Human Rights in 1970 and received the Nobel Peace Prize in 1975. From 1980 to 1986 he was in internal exile in Gorky with his wife Yelena Bonner, and was the target of much world pressure for the better treatment of Soviet dissidents in accord with the HELSINKI AGREEMENT on Human Rights. In the more liberal climate under GORBACHEV he was encouraged to return to Moscow, where he played a prominent part in movements for greater freedom and democracy in the USSR, becoming a member of the Soviet Congress.

A. Sakharov, *Sakharov Speaks* (1974)
——, *My Country and the World* (1975)

**Salan, General Raoul.** *See* ALGERIAN WAR.

**Salazar, Antonio** (1889–1970). Portuguese dictator. Appointed Minister of Finance by the military dictatorship headed by General Carmona in 1928, he showed considerable skill at a time of political and economic crisis and soon established his ascendency over the military leaders. Although he preferred to rule from behind the scenes throughout his life, he accepted the position of Prime Minister in 1932. In 1933 he formally established the 'New State', a quasi-fascistic, 'clerical corporate' dictatorship which nevertheless permitted nominal opposition in periodic elections. Following austere fiscal policies, Salazar put Portugal's chaotic finances in order; during World War II, because of its neutrality, the country even prospered. Salazar's regime was exempted from the general post-war repugnance toward dictatorships, and was even admitted into NATO because of the military importance of the Azores. Major difficulties did not begin until the late 1950s, when a Portuguese ocean liner was seized in a spectacular act of piracy by Capitan Galvao to focus world opinion on the dictatorship and when a former ally, General Delgado, challenged Salazar's candidate in the 1958 presidential elections; these acts forced the regime to become more openly repressive. Still more severe troubles emerged after 1961, when the African colonies – Guinea-Bissau, Angola, Mozambique – rebelled against Portuguese rule. Unwilling to follow the English example of decolonization by negotiation, unable to learn from the French experiences in Vietnam and Algeria, Salazar condemned his nation to increasingly costly colonial wars. Also resistant to socio-economic change, Salazar allowed Portugal to fall behind its neighbours in modernizing itself. By 1968, when Salazar became incapacitated in a trivial household accident, the upper classes remained prosperous but Portugal was nearly in ruins: economically backward, locked in hopeless colonial struggles which consumed half the state budget and caused tens of thousands of young men to flee abroad to avoid conscription (Portugal's population actually decreased between 1960 and 1970). The courtly gentleman who in the early 1950s was sometimes lauded as a 'philosopher king' ended his long dictatorship (matched in duration within Europe only by Spain's FRANCO) politically bankrupt. Since his successor, CAETANO, lacked the courage to change his policies drastically, the PORTUGUESE REVOLUTION would in 1974 sweep away the regime Salazar had created. Always paternalistic, never openly brutal, Salazar's was nevertheless one of Europe's more harmful dictatorships.

P. Fryer and P. MacGowan Pinheiro, *Oldest Ally: A portrait of Salazar's Portugal* (1961)

H. Kay, *Salazar and Modern Portugal* (1970)

**Samizdat.** Literally 'self-publishing'. Russian term for the circulation of manuscript and carbon copies of works so as to avoid official censorship. A parody of the official Gosizdat (State Publishing House), Samizdat appeared under Khrushchev to facilitate the transmission of literature which was banned or had no hope of publication. A brief thaw in publishing critical literature was ended in 1963, and Samizdat subsequently became the means by which a wide range of material including novels, religious works, political statements and the human rights journal, the *Chronicle of Current Events*, begun in 1968, reached a wider audience. Illegal under the Soviet criminal code, it remained evidence of the extensive network of DISSIDENTS working within the Soviet Union.

**Sarajevo, assassination at.** *See* FRANCIS FERDINAND; PRINCIP, GAVRILO.

**SALT.** *See* STRATEGIC ARMS LIMITATION TALKS.

**SAP.** *See* SOCIAL DEMOCRATIC LABOUR PARTY, SWEDISH.

**SAS.** *See* SPECIAL AIR SERVICE.

**Savez Komunista Jugoslavije** (SKJ). *See* COMMUNIST PARTY, YUGOSLAVIAN.

**Saxe-Coburg.** Family name of sovereigns in Britain from 1901 to 1917. Albert (1819–61), Prince Consort of Queen Victoria, was prince of the Duchy of Saxe-Coburg and Gotha in Germany; his family name was Wettin. Their son, Edward VII (1841–1910), the first sovereign of the Saxe-Coburg dynasty, ruled between 1901 and 1910. He renounced his rights to Saxe-Coburg and Gotha which passed to his younger brother in 1893. Edward's second son GEORGE V (1865–1936) succeeded him in 1910 and reigned until 1936. However, he changed his name to Windsor in 1917 in deference to anti-German feeling generated by the First World War.

**Schacht, Hjalmar** (1877–1970). German banker. Born in Schleswig-Holstein, Schacht was brought up in the United States before he returned to Germany to complete his university studies in economics. He then pursued a career in banking before being appointed Reich Currency Commissioner in November 1923, charged with establishing a new currency backed by foreign loans to halt hyper-inflation. In December 1923 he was appointed head of the Reichsbank, a post he occupied until 1930 and in which he participated in negotiating the rescheduling of REPARATIONS through the DAWES PLAN and the YOUNG PLAN. Initially a supporter of the left-liberal German Democratic Party, Schacht turned sharply to the right at the end of the 1920s and joined the Harzburg Front, a conservative-nationalist grouping which sought an alliance with the NAZI PARTY, in 1931. In November 1932, together with several other industrial leaders, he petitioned President HINDENBURG, urging the latter to appoint HITLER Chancellor. Following the Nazi seizure of power, Schacht was reappointed head of the Reichsbank in March 1933. In August 1934 he was appointed Minister for Economics. From 1933 until 1937 Schacht occupied a central place in the formulation of economic policy in the Third Reich. Exploiting deficit financing policies which had been pursued timidly by his predecessors at the Reichsbank, he made a major contribution to financing the Nazi rearmament programme and was appointed Pleni-potentiary-General for the War Economy in May 1935. Establishing strict foreign exchange regulations and bilateral trade treaties, Schacht subordinated German trade to the political objectives of a rearma-ment and German economic penetration of south-eastern Europe: within Germany, however, he was successful in resisting party interference with the business com-munity. An opponent of the increasing pressure within the Nazi regime for a more autarkic economic policy, Schacht increas-ingly fell out of favour with Hitler and proved powerless to resist the establishment of the FOUR YEAR PLAN under GÖRING. Increasing conflicts of authority with Göring led him to resign as Minister of Economics in November 1937. He remained Minister without Portfolio until 1943 and President of the Reichsbank until January 1939. Arrested and imprisoned after the JULY BOMB PLOT, he was acquitted by the tribunal at the NUREMBERG TRIALS. In the 1950s he resumed his financial career as an advisor to developing countries.

H. Schacht, *My First Seventy-Six Years* (1955)
R. J. Overy, *The Nazi Economic Recovery, 1932–1938* (1982)
H. James, *The German Slump: Politics and Economics, 1924–1936* (1986)

**Schleicher, Kurt von** (1882–1934). German general and the last Chancellor of the WEIMAR REPUBLIC before HITLER's seizure of power. A career army officer, Schleicher enlisted in 1900 and served as a General Staff officer during the First World War. Playing a key role in the negotiation of an agreement between the Weimar Republic and the USSR, under which German mili-tary personnel might be trained in the USSR, Schleicher was appointed head of the political office in the Ministry of Defence in 1929. A subtle and unscrupulous political intriguer, he was a central figure in the presidential cabinets which governed Germany after March 1930. Claiming to speak for the army, and thus exercising a powerful influence over President HINDEN-BURG, he was instrumental in the appoint-ment and dismissal of Chancellors BRÜNING and PAPEN: in so far as his influence streng-thened the determination of Hindenburg to bypass the REICHSTAG and rule through

emergency decrees, he may be said to have helped undermine Weimar democracy. He planned the coup against the Prussian regional government which took place in July 1932. He was also a key exponent of the idea of 'taming' the NAZI PARTY, believ-ing that the NSDAP might provide the mass support necessary for an authoritarian nationalist government based on the army. Minister of Defence in the Papen govern-ment, he negotiated to try to secure the support of the Nazis. Succeeding Papen as Chancellor in early December 1932, he antagonized powerful élite groups by pro-posing land reform and offering concessions to the trade unions in an attempt to secure mass left-wing support. He also sought to split the Nazi party and to attract its 'left wing' under GREGOR STRASSER. Losing the support of President Hindenburg, he was compelled to resign as Chancellor in late January 1933, paving the way for the appointment of Hitler as Chancellor in a coalition government between the Nazi Party and the DNVP (*see* DNVP). Having retired from political life, Schleicher was murdered by Nazi assassins during the 'NIGHT OF THE LONG KNIVES' in June 1934.

A. J. Nicholls, *Weimar and the Rise of Hitler* (2nd edn, 1979)
E. Kolb, *The Weimar Republic* (1988)

**Schlieffen Plan.** German military plan for offensive action in the west, designed in December 1905 by the Chief of the German General Staff, General Count Alfred von Schlieffen (1833–1913). Although con-stantly revised over the next nine years, it formed the basis for the German attack in the west in August 1914 at the start of the FIRST WORLD WAR. Schlieffen postulated that a coming war between the CENTRAL POWERS and France, Russia and Britain would be decided in the west; that if France was rapidly defeated, Britain and other other allies would sue for peace, leaving the German forces to turn east for an attack on Russia; that for the requisite period for action in the west the Russians could be held off by defensive operations; and that the way to defeat France quickly was to bypass her forts near the German border by a march through Holland, Belgium and Luxembourg. The declared neutrality of Belgium was to be ignored.

Schlieffen's successor Moltke (1848–1916) modified the plan by restricting the flanking movement to Belgium and Luxembourg. The plan had great initial success in 1914 but eventually failed because of insufficient manpower. The line contracted and Moltke swung east, not west, of Paris, thus failing to take the enemy capital with the necessary speed. The contraction of the line was a result of defects in the plan: underestimation of the effectiveness of the BRITISH EXPEDITIONARY FORCE and of Belgian resistance, and a miscalculation of the speed at which the French could mobilize. However, the main factor in its failure was probably panic in Berlin occasioned by Russia's advance into East Prussia, which led to the transfer of divisions from the western to the eastern front.

The plan has been seen as part of the interlocking network of alliances and military plans which, almost automatically, brought about the First World War and, in particular, by invading Belgian neutrality made Britain's entry into the war virtually inevitable. The latter, however, was the result of the final form of the plan used in 1914 which involved the wholesale invasion of Belgian neutrality, not a minor infringement, as British statesmen thought possible, and Belgium's resistance to the German ultimatum, itself dependent on the scale of incursion threatened. In practice, the Schlieffen Plan, as operated, helped to bring Britain into the war by swinging public opinion behind Britain's existing moral commitment to France. *See also* FISCHER THESIS.

G. Ritter, *The Schlieffen Plan* (1958)
M. Brock, 'Britain Enters the War', in R. J. Evans and H. Pogge von Strandmann (eds.), *The Coming of the First World War* (1988)

**Schmidt, Helmut** (1918–). German politician and Chancellor of the FEDERAL REPUBLIC OF GERMANY, 1974–82. Born in Hamburg, Schmidt served in an anti-aircraft battery as an artillery officer during the Second World War. He joined the SOCIAL DEMOCRATIC PARTY (SPD) in 1946 and played a leading role in the Hamburg economic management and transportation authority between 1949 and 1953. He became a member of the West German parliament (*Bundestag*) in 1953 and, with the exception

of the years 1962–5, when he was representative for central Hamburg in the upper house (*Bundesrat*), has remained a Deputy since then. From 1967 to 1969 he was chairman of the SPD's parliamentary party. With the formation of the SPD–FDP coalition government under BRANDT in 1969, Schmidt became Minister of Defence, a position he held until 1972. In 1972 he moved to the finance ministry and was also briefly head of the economics ministry. With Brandt's fall in May 1974 Schmidt became Chancellor, taking office just at the moment when the worst effects of the recession produced by the 1973–4 'oil shock' were becoming apparent. Domestic politics were dominated by the abrupt ending of the post-war German 'economic miracle' and the strain this placed on welfare-state expenditure. Faced with the need to curtail government expenditure and bring it into line with government revenue if the currency were to be maintained (the West German constitution obliges governments to balance their budgets), the stabilization of welfare-state expenditure at a time of rising unemployment was also forced on the Schmidt government by pressure from its FDP coalition partners and the CHRISTIAN DEMOCRATIC UNION majority in the upper house. The only significant social policy achievement of Schmidt's first chancellorship was the passage in 1976 of an Act extending workers' participation in large businesses. In foreign policy, Schmidt cautiously continued the OSTPOLITIK inaugurated by Brandt, visiting a number of communist states and seeking further to normalize relations with East Germany: the provision of interest-free credit to the Democratic Republic was extended after 1974 and the West German government began to pay hard currency for the release of political prisoners. The active participation of West Germany in the Helsinki Conference (*see* HELSINKI AGREEMENT) in 1975 signalled the full integration of the Federal Republic in the European states system. Largely as a consequence of the austerity programme pursued by the government at home, the 1976 *Bundestag* elections witnessed significant losses by the SPD and the FDP to the CDU–CSU. Schmidt's second Chancellorship (1976–80) saw a gradual improvement in the economic situation, as growth recovered and unemployment began to fall. Schmidt's firm handling of the upsurge in terrorism in 1977 led by the Baader–Meinhof gang (*see* ROTE ARMEE FAKTION) earned him respect from all sections of West German society. Yet it was on the international stage that Schmidt's status as a leading European statesman was to be established. He acted as host to the first major Western summit held in Bonn in 1978 and joined President Carter, President GISCARD D'ESTAING and Prime Minister CALLAGHAN at the 1979 Guadeloupe summit. He also took a leading role in formulating the response of NATO (*see* NORTH ATLANTIC TREATY ORGANIZATION) to the deployment of short- and medium-range nuclear weapons by the WARSAW PACT from 1977 onwards, which threatened Western Europe and seemed to endanger the unity of NATO. Largely at his insistence, in 1979 NATO adopted its DUAL TRACK POLICY to go ahead with the development of US medium-range nuclear missiles but to dismantle these if the Warsaw Pact were to remove its newly deployed weapons. Schmidt's hard-headed approach to defence issues, his government's commitment to an extensive nuclear power programme (initiated in the wake of the 1973 oil crisis), and the persistence of high unemployment, generated much criticism within his own party and was instrumental in the formation of the environmentalist GREENS. Yet the SPD and the FDP made important gains in the 1980 *Bundestag* elections, not least because of the CDU–CSU's selection of the Bavarian right-winger FRANZ-JOSEF STRAUSS as its candidate for Chancellor in the elections. Schmidt's last period as Chancellor (1980–82) was dominated by renewed economic recession and rising unemployment in the wake of the second oil crisis of 1979–80 and by mounting protest from the Greens and opponents of his defence policy. In September 1982 the FDP sought to restore its credibility with centre-right voters by demanding major cuts in welfare expenditure. These were unacceptable to the SPD, and Schmidt ended the coalition, forming an SPD minority government. In early October 1982 Schmidt's chancellorship came to an end when the FDP joined the CDU–CSU in tabling and winning a no-confidence vote in his government.

J. Carr, *Helmut Schmidt: Helmsman of Germany* (1985)
H. A. Turner, *The Two Germanies since 1945* (1987)

**Schuman, Robert** (1886–1963). French statesman. Born in Luxembourg of a family from Lorraine, he studied in German universities and practised law in Metz. He was conscripted into the German army in the First World War. In 1919, following the return of Alsace and Lorraine to France, he became a French citizen. He became Deputy for Moselle in 1919 and, apart from the Second World War, served until 1960. He joined the French government as junior Minister for Refugees in March 1940, but soon broke with the VICHY GOVERNMENT. After his arrest and deportation to Germany, he escaped to France and worked with the RESISTANCE. In 1944 he helped to found the Christian Democratic MOUVEMENT RÉPUBLICAIN POPULAIRE. He was Finance Minister in 1946, then Prime Minister from November 1947 to July 1948 and Foreign Minister from 1948 to 1952. As such he accepted MONNET's plan to found a EUROPEAN COAL AND STEEL COMMUNITY, achieved the French Cabinet's assent to it, and played a vital role in the negotiations which led to the TREATY OF PARIS. He served as minister several times more under the Fourth Republic. He was the first President of the European Parliament from 1958 to 1960. *See also* EUROPEAN ECONOMIC COMMUNITY; SCHUMAN PLAN.

R. Capelle, *The MRP and French Foreign Policy* (1963)
D. Urwin, *Western Europe since 1945* (3rd edn, 1981)

**Schuman Plan.** A plan announced on 9 May 1950 by ROBERT SCHUMAN, the French Foreign Minister, outlining proposals for the establishment of a EUROPEAN COAL AND STEEL COMMUNITY (ECSC). The vital place of the coal and steel industries in industrial development, and the position of some of the coal and iron resources on the borders of West Germany and France in the Saar and Lorraine contributed to the notion that if political integration within Europe was to be sought by economic means, then coal and steel was the sector with which it should begin. The plan was worked out by JEAN MONNET and a few collaborators; Schuman accepted it enthusiastically, procured the French Cabinet's authorization to proceed, and announced it publicly the same day. He proposed putting all German and French coal and steel production under a common High Authority, and spoke of this as the first step towards a European Federation, which alone could ensure the maintenance of peace in Europe. Upon the basis of this announcement the negotiations which resulted in the foundation of the ECSC were undertaken.

F. Roy Willis, *France, Germany and the New Europe* (rev. edn, 1968)
R. Mayne, *The Recovery of Europe* (1976)

**Schuschnigg, Kurt von** (1897–1977). Austrian dictator. Born in 1897 at Riva del Garda, now in Italy, he made his career as a lawyer in Innsbruck after the First World War and was first elected to parliament in 1927 as a CHRISTIAN SOCIAL PARTY (CSP) delegate of monarchist sympathies. He became Minister of Justice in 1932 and Minister of Education in 1933 before succeeding ENGLEBERT DOLLFUSS as chancellor, following the latter's assassination. Schuschnigg was threatened from two sides, and although he succeeded in containing the *Heimwehr* he was less successful with the Nazis. The assertive *Heimwehr* leader Ernst Rüdiger von Starhemberg was forced from his state offices in 1936, and the *Heimwehr* itself was disbanded a few months later. However, no substantial steps were taken towards dismantling the Austrofascist system (*see* AUSTROFASCISM) set up by his predecessor, and considerable concessions were made to the Nazis. Under the Austro-German 'July Agreement' of 1936 Nazis were amnestied and 'national' ministers taken into the Austrian government. In return HITLER recognized Austria as a 'second German state'. During the following two years Nazis infiltrated and undermined the Austrian state apparatus and other organizations. At a meeting with Hitler at BERCHTESGADEN in February 1938 Schuschnigg was forced to make further concessions, which included the appointment of the Nazi leader ARTHUR VON SEYSS-INQUART as Interior Minister. Despite last-minute pleas for national unity, Schuschnigg was not prepared to make any concessions to labour leaders, preferring ultimately to see Austria annexed by Germany. The Austrian military was ordered to offer no resistance to the German invasion of March 1938 (*see* ANSCHLUSS). Schuschnigg himself was arrested and spent the war in prison. After the war he pursued an academic career in the United States, retired to Austria in 1967, and died in Innsbruck in 1977.

K. von Schuschnig, *Farewell Austria* (1938)

**Scissors Crisis.** The name given to the Russian economic crisis of 1923–4, so called because of the shape of the divergent parabolas of industrial and agricultural prices. By 1923 shortages of industrial goods and a resumption of agricultural output meant that industrial prices were rising while those of agriculture were falling. The fear was that, as agricultural prices fell, peasants might cut back on agricultural production. It raised the issue of the relative role of agricultural consumption and industrial output which was to recur in the SOVIET INDUSTRIALIZATION DEBATE and process of SOVIET COLLECTIVIZATION.

A. Nove, *An Economic History of the USSR* (1969)

**Scottish National Party** (SNP). The party was formed in 1934 as a merger of two earlier groups: the National Party of Scotland founded in 1928 and the Scottish Party in 1930. From 1929 onwards the National Party contested elections, but it was not until 1945 that the SNP won its first seat. R. D. McIntyre won the Motherwell by-election, but was defeated at the general election three months later. In 1964 the party contested 15 seats, and in 1966 23 seats, but with no success. Then in 1967 Mrs W. Ewing won the Hamilton by-election. This encouraged the SNP to field 65 candidates in the 1970 general election, but of these only one, in the Western Isles, was elected, and 43 lost their deposits. It appeared that the SNP was again in decline, yet in 1973 Mrs MacDonald won the Glasgow Govan by-election. In 1974 the party won seven seats in the February general election and in October won 11 seats. Poor performances in the Hamilton by-election and the 1978 local elections signified a wane in Scottish nationalism. In 1979 the country voted only narrowly for DEVOLUTION, thus relinquishing the possibility of devolution under the terms of the Act. In the 1979 general election the SNP won only two seats; the same number in 1983, but three in 1987. In 1987 its vote was 417,000, compared to 840,000 at its peak in October 1974. Prior to the 1987 election the SNP signed an agreement to co-operate with PLAID CYMRU in the next parliament.

C. Harvie, *Scotland and Nationalism: Scottish Society and Politics, 1707–1977* (1977)
——, *No Gods and Precious Few Heroes: Scotland, 1914–1980* (1981)
J. G. Kellas, 'Scottish and Welsh Nationalist Parties since 1945', in A. Seldon (ed.), *UK Political Parties since 1945* (1990)

**SDAP.** *See* SOCIAL DEMOCRATIC WORKERS' PARTY, AUSTRIAN.

**SDLP.** *See* SOCIAL DEMOCRATIC AND LABOUR PARTY, NORTHERN IRISH.

**SDP.** *See* SOCIAL DEMOCRATIC PARTY, BRITISH.

**Second International.** Formed in Paris in 1889 to organize international socialist solidarity. The movement was badly disrupted by the outbreak of the First World War, when the International's plans to prevent war by united action of the working-class parties was almost a complete failure. Overtaken by the communist-led Third International or COMINTERN organized by the Bolsheviks in March 1919, the Second International attempted to reform in 1923 as the Labour and Socialist International, drawing upon moderate socialist parties. In 1951 it became the SOCIALIST INTERNATIONAL, to which socialist and social democratic parties adhere.

J. Joll, *The Second International, 1889–1914* (1955)
G. Lichtheim, *A Short History of Socialism* (1970)

**Second Labour Government.** British government formed by RAMSAY MACDONALD in June 1929, following the 1929 general election: Labour 287 seats, Conservatives 260, Liberals 59. It made a bright start, particularly in foreign affairs, where its record remained impressive, and there were some useful reforms in housing and transport, but world slump from autumn 1929 destroyed its position. The LABOUR PARTY had promised to reduce unemployment, but it increased from 1.1 million to 2.8 million during its term of office. Labour tried various ineffective expedients to reduce the figure, but more radical alternatives of deficit-financed public works, as suggested

by Sir OSWALD MOSLEY in 1930, were rejected as SNOWDEN at the Treasury stuck to orthodox economics – free trade, the GOLD STANDARD and a balanced budget.

By June 1931 early and conclusive defeat looked likely. Left-wingers were alienated by the failure over unemployment; trade unions were angered by the government's inability and apparent unwillingness to deliver the reforms they wanted; the cabinet was ill, ageing and acrimonious; and by-elections since February 1930 had seen a widespread collapse in Labour support. Meanwhile the LIBERAL PARTY, whose rather wayward support had helped sustain the minority government, was beginning to break up, with right-wing rebels moving towards the Conservatives.

The manner of the government's fall was unexpected, though. In July 1931 the May committee on national expenditure predicted a budget deficit of £120 million unless taxes were increased and spending cut by £96 million, including substantial reductions in unemployment benefits and public servants' salaries. Coinciding with a general European financial crisis, this produced a severe crisis of confidence and flight from sterling. The cabinet set up a high-powered economy committee to recommend means of balancing the budget: it suggested cuts of £78 million. On 19 August this was accepted, with the exception of economies on benefits, by the full cabinet, which thus agreed to economies of £56 million. However, the government now found itself the victim of conflicting forces: the opposition leaders (whose parliamentary support would be necessary) and bankers wanted larger cuts; the trades union congress, whose support was necessary to maintain the integrity of the Labour movement, wanted none at all. A shaky compromise, to go ahead regardless, was reached on 21 August, but the insistence of opposition and bankers that only larger cuts would restore confidence forced MacDonald to recall his cabinet. After two days of meetings the cabinet voted by 11 to 9 to accept a 10 per cent cut in unemployment benefit, but the size and importance of the minority (including HENDERSON) meant that the government had to resign.

MacDonald, convinced he was right and persuaded by GEORGE V and the opposition leaders, formed a NATIONAL GOVERNMENT largely comprising Conservatives and Liberals, which went on to win a landslide victory over Labour at the general election in October. At the election the disastrous record of the second Labour government, the conduct of the Labour ex-ministers in 'running away' from the crisis, and unfair charges of 'trade union dictation' were used against Labour candidates, and continued as effective barriers to Labour throughout the 1930s. Labour allegations that MacDonald had conspired against his own government, or that the bankers had set out to destroy it, were similarly ill-founded.

The Labour government achieved little. Its minority position inhibited it somewhat, but there was little idea as to how to deal with the slump. It is debatable, though, whether more radical policies would have been effective: they could have made matters worse. Labour had always assumed that socialism would evolve from the success of capitalism; it had no idea of what to do in an economic crisis. However, weak leadership by MacDonald and Snowden's orthodoxy at the Treasury exacerbated a difficult situation by ruling out any meaningful short-term response. However, the world slump swept most Western governments out of office: thus the government's experience was by no means unique.

R. Skidelsky, *Politicians and the Slump: The Labour Government of 1929–1931* (1967)
D. Marquand, *Ramsay MacDonald* (1977)

**Second Republic, Spanish.** The Second Republic was established on 14 April 1931 following the abdication of King ALFONSO XIII. He had been forced to go by the results of municipal elections two days earlier, which had indicated widespread hostility to a monarchy long marked by corruption and inefficiency. This had reached its nadir during the dictatorship of General MIGUEL PRIMO DE RIVERA, whose attempt to shore up the monarchy had ended in humiliating resignation. The new republic was greeted with euphoria amongst progressive liberal and leftist groups who saw its arrival as an opportunity to embark upon a much-needed programme of modernization in social, political and economic spheres.

The initial government of the Republic was made up of a coalition between various disparate Republican groups, temporarily united through MANUEL AZAÑA's Izquierda Republicana, and the SOCIALIST WORKERS PARTY (PSOE). The new regime faced enormous socio-political and economic problems from its inception. A crippled economy, marked by major regional imbalances and devastated by mismanagement under the Primo dictatorship, was further damaged by the impa of the 1929 Wall Street crash and resultant DEPRESSION. Economic rationalization involved confronting the issue of agrarian reform, one of Spain's critical structural handicaps. Spanish agriculture remained backward and inefficient, divided into massive estates in the south and central western parts of the country, and smallholdings in the north. In socio-political terms, the key problem surrounded the drafting of a constitution which would generate widespread acceptance and political involvement whilst avoiding antagonizing the two principal pillars of the monarchy: the SPANISH CATHOLIC CHURCH and the military. The intractability of these issues was to be central to the Republic's collapse. Indeed, it could be argued that the failure to resolve them successfully directly culminated in the outbreak of the SPANISH CIVIL WAR.

The main feature of the Republic's failure and ultimate collapse was the counterpoint which developed between Left and Right, and which assumed ever more extreme manifestations between April 1931 and July 1936. Essentially, the Republic can be characterized as undergoing a series of pendulum swings as follows:

*April 1931 – November 1933* Republican–Socialist coalition government. This was a period of great hope which turned rapidly to disillusion. Reform measures, most clearly associated with the Socialist Minister of Labour, FRANCISCO LARGO CABALLERO, were dashed by the efficiency of rightist forces in organizing effective opposition to their implementation. The antagonism of the Right was exacerbated by Prime Minister Manuel Azaña's response to the church, whose monopoly of religious and educational life he was determined to smash. From the outset of the Republic, the Right began to organize in defence of its own interests, and the inability of the government, which lacked effective state machinery, to ensure respect for its legislation led to increasing frustration and divisions. In particular, Largo Caballero began to lose faith in the reforming possibilities of the Republic, foreshadowing his later shift to a radical Marxist stance. The government's problems were compounded by anarchist-led insurrectionary efforts, as well as an abortive coup in 1932 by General José Sanjurjo. By the end of 1933, when the deteriorating political situation forced elections, the Socialists had broken their alliance with the Republicans despite an electoral law which favoured coalitions. As a result the Right was able to take power.

*November 1933 – November 1935* Radical–CEDA government. During the *bienio negro* ('two black years'), the Right ruled in the shape of the PARTIDO REPUBLICANO RADICAL of Alejandro Lerroux, an ambitious, populist demagogue who had shifted during the course of the century from left to right on the political spectrum. The Radicals were supported by the CONFEDERACIÓN ESPAÑOLA DE DERECHAS AUTÓNOMAS (CEDA), an authoritarian right-wing coalition with close links to the Catholic Church, founded earlier in the year and headed by José María Gil Robles. For many in the PSOE the CEDA represented the thin end of a Spanish fascist wedge. When the government, which had quickly set about repealing much of the reformist legislation of its predecessor, offered ministerial posts in October 1934 to three CEDA members, the Socialists took this as a signal to launch an insurrectionary general strike. Poorly prepared, it soon collapsed everywhere except in Asturias (*see* ASTURIAS RISING), where it was brutally suppressed by troops led by General FRANCISCO FRANCO. Disputes over how to interpret the failure of the 1934 rising led to a split within the PSOE: a reformist wing, associated principally with Indalecio Prieto, aimed to re-create the Socialist–Republican coalition, while a more radical wing, led by Largo Caballero, engaged in ever more maximalist Marxist rhetoric against the government. Dubbed the 'Spanish Lenin', Largo Caballero became the figurehead of an increasingly extremist wing which opened out towards other Marxist groups in Spain. Prieto, however, sought to re-build links with Azaña in a move which led to the genesis of the Popular Front electoral coalition. In the meantime, Lerroux's Radical–CEDA coalition government was forced to resign in November 1935 following discovery of its involvement in a series of financial scandals.

*November 1935 – July 1936* From Popular Front to Civil War. New elections held in February 1936 brought to power the Popular Front coalition, a broad-ranging alliance of Republican and leftist parties initiated by Prieto and Azaña. Fear of political marginalization had induced more radical groups to join the expressly reformist coalition which narrowly defeated the Right in a highly disputed contest. As the Popular Front government, composed solely of Republicans, attempted to re-enact reformist legislation, the Right's increasingly open opposition to the Republic was fuelled by unrest amongst landworkers seeking revenge for the hardships endured under the *bienio negro*. The counterpoint of violence between Right and Left, represented at the extremes by the activities of Falangists (*see* FALANGE) and anarchists (*see* ANARCHISM, SPANISH), moved beyond political resolution. Conspiratorial moves by leading military figures were increasingly supported by right-wing civilian politicians. The murder by anarchists on 13 July of the right-wing leader, José Calvo Sotelo, provided the conspirators with a timely excuse to launch their rising against the Republic. On the night of 17 July, General Franco staged a coup which would develop into a three-year civil war.

The key to understanding the failure of the Second Republic lies in the divisions which affected both Left and Right in Spain. The PSOE, able to take advantage of its controversial collaboration with the Primo dictatorship to present a united organizational front, acted as the effective linchpin of the new regime. However, it was precisely the centrality of the Socialist Party which was to sow the seeds of its political instability. PSOE leaders misinterpreted both the political significance of the Republic and the role of their party within it, believing the new regime to be the consummation of a long-overdue bourgeois revolution. The Republicans were seen as a progressive bourgeois force, whilst rightist elements were equated with feudal remnants doomed to political oblivion. Both of these assessments were wrong: the former group was made up of liberal individualists without a solid social base, while the latter organized quickly and effectively in defence of their own interests. Crucially, the role of the PSOE itself remained ambiguous, with support for the Republic predicated upon the belief that it represented the harbinger of socialist revolution and must therefore be opposed in the long term. This ambiguity lay at the heart of the critical divisions within the Socialist Party which so damaged the new regime.

Divisions of the Right were more clear-cut between 'accidentalists' and 'catastrophists'. The former, associated mainly with Gil Robles and the CEDA, professed respect for the legal structures of the Republic whilst working to ensure that it remained unable to institute radical reforms. The latter, comprised of Carlists (*see* CARLISM), Alfonsine monarchists and – after 1933 – Falangists, sought the immediate destruction of the Republic and its replacement by some form of monarchical regime. Initially, after Sanjurjo's abortive coup and the success of Gil Robles in the 1933 elections, the accidentalists held sway – albeit uneasily. After the victory of the Popular Front, however, the tactic of accidentalism was discredited and catastrophists moved into the driving seat of rightist politics. Their plots against the Republic, now supported by many former proponents of accidentalism, culminated in the July 1936 rising and plunged Spain into a bloody civil war.

Historiographical debate on the Second Republic has centred on the issue of 'responsibility' for its collapse. In particular, attention has focused on two related questions: what role did divisions in the PSOE, especially during its so-called radicalization, play in destabilizing the Republic, and how genuine were the accidentalists in their professed respect for the new regime? There exists little consensus, although recent research suggest that the PSOE was far less radical in its aims and

the CEDA far more hostile to the Republic than has often been argued.

G. Brenan, *The Spanish Labyrinth* (1950)
G. Jackson, *Republic and Civil War in Spain* (1966)
R. Carr (ed.), *The Republic and the Civil War in Spain* (1971)
P. Preston, *The Coming of the Spanish Civil War* (1978)
M. Blinkhorn (ed.) *Spain in Conflict, 1931–1939* (1986)

**Second Vatican Council.** Second ecumenical council of the Roman Catholic Church in modern times, summoned by Pope JOHN XXIII in January 1959. Its purpose was to consider increased collaboration with other churches and renewal of the faith. Over 8,000 bishops attended in Rome when the council opened on 11 October 1962, including many observers from other churches. The council lasted a year and published 16 decrees pointing towards a closer relationship with non-Catholic churches, the use of the vernacular rather than Latin in the liturgy and a greater humanism in Catholic doctrine. Many people expected that the tone of the council presaged a relaxation of the church's position on artificial birth control, but the 1968 encyclical *Humanae vitae* condemned its use. The Council marked a major turning-point in the church's relations with other faiths, giving a spur to dialogue with the Anglican and Orthodox communions and removing barriers to groups such as the Jews and non-Christian faiths.

**Second World War.** On 31 March Britain and France offered a guarantee to Poland in the event of a threat to Polish independence. Attempts to form an agreement with the Soviet Union by France and Britain were overtaken by the NAZI–SOVIET PACT of 23 August, leaving HITLER with a free hand to attack Poland without fear of Soviet intervention. Hitler demanded satisfaction of the questions of DANZIG and the POLISH CORRIDOR. NEVILLE CHAMBERLAIN warned Hitler that Britain would stand by her guarantee to Poland but offered negotiation on the Danzig question. The Poles refused to enter negotiations and Hitler brought forward the date for preparations to invade Poland from 1 September to 26 August. On 25 August an Anglo-Polish mutual assistance pact was signed in London. Hitler made a 'last offer' on Poland and postponed his attack again until 1 September. From

26 August Britain and France urged direct negotiations between Germans and Poles which the Poles refused.

On 31 August, Hitler gave the orders for an attack on Poland. Using a faked incident to claim that Polish troops had attacked Germany, on 1 September German forces invaded Poland and annexed Danzig. Britain and France demanded withdrawal of German troops and on 2 September Britain delivered an ultimatum to Germany. When no reply was received, on 3 September Britain and France declared war on Germany. The declaration of war by the Western powers did not halt the German assault, which used BLITZKRIEG tactics to advance into Poland, defeating the Polish armies in 18 days. Soviet troops advanced into eastern Poland on 17 September and by the end of the month Germany and the Soviet Union had agreed a partition of Poland between them. Britain and France could do nothing to assist Poland. Instead France mobilized her forces for defence of the MAGINOT LINE and for an advance to the line of the River Dyle in Belgium in anticipation of a German attack, supported by the BRITISH EXPEDITIONARY FORCE, the last of which arrived in France on 30 September. On 30 November the Soviet Union invaded Finland, thus beginning the RUSSO-FINNISH WAR.

The winter of 1939–40 was relatively quiet, giving birth to the description of it as the period of PHONEY WAR. From November plans were discussed in Britain for obstructing German supplies of Swedish iron ore being shipped via Norwegian waters. CHURCHILL received permission to mine Norwegian waters and to send 'volunteers' to aid Finland. To forestall this Hitler ordered an invasion of Norway and Denmark. On 9 April German forces landed at the Norwegian ports of Kristiansand, Stavanger, Bergen, Trondheim and Narvik. Oslo fell on 10 April and Denmark capitulated. Although French and British troops were landed at Namsos, Andalsnes and Narvik on 14–19 April, they proved ineffective and the first two forces had to be evacuated on 1–2 May. The repercussions of the campaign were felt on 10 May with the resignation of NEVILLE CHAMBERLAIN after a heavy fall in his majority in the House of Commons and his

replacement by Churchill. The last allied troops were withdrawn from Narvik on 8–9 June.

On 10 May Germany invaded the Low Countries, forcing the surrender of the Dutch army four days later after the bombing of Rotterdam. As the Anglo-French armies swung their forces into Belgium to meet a German advance, German forces breached the Ardennes and crossed the Meuse, racing for the English Channel. The Allied army in the north was forced back to Dunkirk, while the French forces to the south were left in disorganized retreat. From 29 May to 3 June 338,226 British, French and Belgian troops were evacuated from Dunkirk, abandoning most of their equipment.

On 10 June Italy declared war on Britain and France and moved its forces into southern France. On 14 June Paris fell and on the 22nd France signed an armistice with Germany. On 3 July Britain took action to disable the French fleet at Mars-el-Kebir, sinking three ships and killing 1,300 French sailors. On 5 August Britain signed an agreement with the Polish government-in-exile in London and with the FREE FRENCH led by de Gaulle recognizing them as the governments of their respective countries.

From July the German air force began to engage the Royal Air Force over the English Channel and English coast in the protracted period of aerial warfare known as the BATTLE OF BRITAIN. The Germans sought to establish air supremacy over the Channel and wear down Royal Air Force (RAF) strength in order to permit an invasion of Britain – codenamed 'Operation Sealion'. The heavy losses inflicted on the Luftwaffe forced a recognition that air supremacy had not been obtained. On 12 October Hitler called off his invasion plans, although THE BLITZ on British cities continued.

Italy's entry into the war was followed on 28 October 1941 by an attack on Greece and an advance against British positions in North Africa. Both proved disastrous; the Greeks repulsed the Italians, driving them back into Albania, while the Italians were defeated in North Africa at Sidi Barrani on 9–15 December. Italian naval power was also severely curtailed by the sinking of major elements of her fleet at Taranto by carrier-borne aircraft on 11 November.

Britain remained undefeated but by early 1941 was already virtually bankrupt and unable to pay for war materials. On 6 January President ROOSEVELT sent the first LEND-LEASE Bill of Congress, which from March permitted Britain unlimited access to war material. In February the first German troops under ROMMEL were sent to North Africa, taking the offensive in early April. On 6 April a German ultimatum was delivered to Yugoslavia and Greece, forcing Britain to divert troops from North Africa to Greece. Yugoslavia capitulated on 17 April and Britain was forced to evacuate Greece on 22–8 April. Crete was seized in an attack by German parachute troops in just over a week of bitter fighting at the end of May.

On 22 June Hitler launched his offensive against the Soviet Union, 'Operation Barbarossa'. Taking STALIN and the Soviet forces by complete surprise, the German armies took Smolensk on 16 July, beseiged Leningrad by 8 September and took Kiev by the 19th. An advance on Moscow took the German forces to within 20 miles of the city by 15 November, where they were halted by the deteriorating weather and Russian counter-attacks.

On the other side of the world the Japanese attacked Pearl Harbour on 7 December, followed the next day by British and American declarations of war on Japan and, on the 11th, by German and Italian declarations of war on the United States. These events transformed the Second World War into a genuinely global conflict. On 12 July Britain and the Soviet Union signed a mutual aid agreement and on 11 August Churchill and Roosevelt signed the ATLANTIC CHARTER stating their war aims. The German forces were now locked into a war with the Soviet Union, while the huge resources of the American economy were now available for war against all three AXIS powers.

Early in 1942 saw the Axis forces at the height of their power; in the Pacific the Japanese captured the colonial possessions of Britain, the United States and Holland. The fall of Singapore on 15 February and Rangoon on 10 March marked the destruction of British power in South-East Asia.

In Russia the Germans defeated a Soviet offensive at Kharkov in May, inflicting heavy losses, and in their summer offensive advanced on Stalingrad and the Caucasus. In North Africa the British were driven back by Rommel to the border of Egypt. In late October the Axis forces were defeated by MONTGOMERY at El Alamein (23 October–4 November). Anglo-American landings in November, 'Operation Torch', and pursuit across North Africa by Montgomery forced the surrender of 250,000 Axis troops in Tunisia on 12 May 1943. By then the German forces at STALINGRAD under von Paulus had suffered Germany's most serious defeat, destroying an army of 270,000 men. On 5 July 1943 the Germans launched their last major offensive in Russia at Kursk but were halted by stubborn resistance and then overwhelmed by a massive counter-offensive which retook Smolensk and Kiev by November. In the Mediterranean, Allied landings in Sicily on 10 July forced the resignation of MUSSOLINI on 26 July and Italy's surrender and co-belligerancy with the Allies on 8 September.

During 1943 the ALLIED BOMBING OFFENSIVE begun against Germany by the RAF was developed into a regular aerial bombardment of all major German cities by the use of United States Air Force planes for daylight raids and RAF bombers for night attacks. The BATTLE OF THE ATLANTIC to keep open the sea routes to Britain was also reaching a decisive stage as the use of radar and long-range escort planes increased German losses.

In January 1944 the Allies attempted to outflank the German defence line in Italy at Anzio, but remained locked in a bitter battle to open the route to Rome at Monte Cassino which did not fall until March. From December 1943 Soviet forces mounted a major advance which carried them to the pre-war Russo-Polish border by January. Leningrad was relieved on 27 January after a siege of almost 900 days. By the summer of 1944 German forces had advanced almost 400 miles to the Vistula where they halted. The Polish Home Army mounted the WARSAW RISING on 1 August but were unable to obtain assistance from the Soviet forces and had to surrender on 2 October.

On 6 June 1944 Anglo-American landings took place in Normandy, opening the second front in the west. After bitter fighting, the Americans broke out at Avranches on 1 August, and German forces in France were destroyed in the Falaise Pocket (13–20 August). Allied landings took place in southern France on 11 August and Paris was entered on the 25th. On 5 September Brussels was liberated, but an attempt on 17 September to seize the river crossings at Arnhem, 'Operation Market Garden', proved a failure. On 16 December Hitler launched his last offensive in the west, the 'Battle of the Bulge', driving through the Ardennes in an attempt to seize Antwerp. The attack was held and by 3 January 1945 the Anglo-American forces had begun to counterattack.

In the east, renewed Russian offensives from late September took Soviet forces deep into German-held territory. A fresh offensive on 12 January 1945 by 1,350,000 men smashed through German lines and Warsaw was finally taken on 17 January. On 13 February Budapest fell, and by mid-April Russian forces were poised for the drive on Berlin, opening a huge offensive on 16 April along the Oder and Neisse rivers, reaching the outskirts of Berlin four days later.

The Americans crossed the Rhine at Remagen on 23 March, eventually linking up with Soviet forces at Torgau on 26 April. A week earlier all German forces in the Ruhr, 325,000 men, surrendered. The final battle for Berlin was still taking place when Hitler committed suicide on 30 April. On 2 May 1 million German troops in Italy surrendered and on 7 May the German High Command surrendered unconditionally to General EISENHOWER. On the next day the war in Europe was declared over.

British and American forces remained engaged in the war against Japan. In Burma the British defeated a Japanese attempt to invade India and went on to defeat Japanese forces by early 1945. The American 'island-hopping' campaign brought American forces within range of Japan. Mass bombing raids had brought Japan to the brink of surrender when the dropping of atomic bombs on 6 and 9 August forced her unconditional surrender on 14 August.

The causes of the Second World War have been seen as bound up with interpre-

tations of the TREATY OF VERSAILLES and the role of APPEASEMENT. Research into Nazi foreign policy has suggested that Hitler himself bears much of the blame for the conflict. The war in September 1939 may not have been the war Hitler wanted or when he wanted it, but his ambitions in the east brought about a series of crises from 1938 which made war likely at some point. The human cost of the Second World War was even greater than that of the First World War. An estimated 14,904,000 people died in battle, and civilian deaths totalled 38,573,000, of whom almost 6 million were Jews murdered in the HOLOCAUST. Britain lost 271,000 military dead and 90,000 civilian dead; Germany lost 3,300,000 military dead and 2,300,000 civilians killed; Poland lost 1,000,000 military dead and over 6,000,000 civilians; Russia lost 13,600,000 military dead and 7,720,000 civilians; France lost 205,000 military (and resistance) dead and 173,000 civilians.

The effects of the Second World War were immense, bringing about the dominance of the two superpowers of the United States and the Soviet Union, and the division of Europe into two opposed blocs, with Germany subjected to occupation (see GERMANY, ALLIED OCCUPATION OF). Unlike the First World War, there was no wholesale boundary revision in Europe, the major changes being in the Polish–Russian and Polish–German frontiers. Territorial claims by Russia on Finland were also fulfilled and the BALTIC STATES and BESSARABIA were absorbed into the Soviet Union. Eastern Europe fell under communist control and an attempted communist take-over in Greece led to the GREEK CIVIL WAR. Within three years of the victory in Europe the COLD WAR had become the dominant political motif.

The Second World War was a war of movement and technology. Blitzkrieg tactics, dependent on the use of aircraft and tanks, were joined by heavy bombers, radar, jet and rocket propulsion, and NUCLEAR WEAPONS. It also witnessed barbarity on a scale unprecedented in the First World War, the systematic destruction of European Jewry, gypsies and homosexuals, as well as the adoption of mass terror bombing and punitive operations against civilians. Mass ill-treatment of prisoners-of-war and the use of slave labour reached levels unmatched in the earlier conflict. Politically, however, there was an advance for progressive forces as a result of the Allied victory. The NUREMBERG TRIALS attempted to impose a condemnation of Nazi brutality and of inhuman conduct in general. Mass mobilization enhanced the status of organized labour and led to the growth of both communist and social democratic parties in the West. Welfare policies and a mixed economy became a *sine qua non* for most Western democracies after 1945, whatever their pre-war complexion.

A. Werth, *Russia at War* (1965)
G. Kolko, *The Politics of War* (1968)
A. Calder, *The People's War* (1969)
P. Calvocoressi and G. Wint, *Total War* (1972)
M. R. D. Foot, *Resistance* (1976)
A. S. Milward, *War, Economy and Society, 1939–1945* (1977)
P. M. Bell, *The Origins of the Second World War* (1986)
D. Cameron Watt, *How War Came: The Immediate Origins of the Second World War, 1938–9* (1989)
R. Overy and A. Wheatcroft, *The Road to War* (1989)

**Section Française de l'Internationale Ouvrière (SFIO).** *See* SOCIALIST PARTY, FRENCH.

**SED** (Sozialistische Einheitspartei; Socialist Unity Party). Communist-dominated East German political party. Following the collapse of Nazi Germany, former members of the GERMAN COMMUNIST PARTY returned to Germany from exile or were liberated from concentration camps. In the Soviet zone of occupied Germany, the Communist Party (KPD) was refounded in June 1945, alongside a reconstituted SOCIAL DEMOCRATIC PARTY (SPD) and liberal and moderate conservative parties. Initially, the KPD stressed that conditions in the Soviet zone would not permit the introduction of a Soviet-style economy: rather, a mixture of nationalization of key industries and private enterprise was to be encouraged. Throughout autumn 1945 the KPD leadership hoped that communist majorities might be obtained in free elections, and resisted calls from the SPD leadership in the Soviet zone for the formation of a united working-class party. Yet, by the end of 1945, it had become clear that such majorities would not be forthcoming, and the KPD now pressed the SPD for merger. When negotiations for such a merger opened in December 1945 the SPD leadership was placed under con-

siderable pressure from the Soviet occupying authorities, who effectively forced the merger of the two parties to form the SED in April 1946.

In the September 1946 local elections held in the Soviet zone, the SED gained narrow majorities in many areas, largely as a consequence of the handicaps imposed on the conservative and liberal parties' campaigns by the Soviet authorities. Yet, in the regional elections held in October, such handicaps on the other parties notwithstanding, the SED failed to gain an absolute majority in any of the five regions.

Initially composed equally of former KPD and former SPD members, the SED executive gradually came under communist domination. With the development of the COLD WAR, the conservative and liberal parties were 'synchronized' and compelled to acknowledge the primacy of the SED. The SED underwent a steady 'Stalinization' in 1947–8, paralleling the experience of other communist parties in the Soviet sphere of influence during the clash between STALIN and TITO. In January 1949, the SED was proclaimed a 'new-type party' which adhered to Marxist–Leninist principles.

With the establishment of the GERMAN DEMOCRATIC REPUBLIC in October 1949, the SED assumed a hegemonic position in the new state in the constitution of which its 'leading role' was enshrined. Under ULBRICHT and HONECKER, the SED was a pliant tool of the East German regime: criticism of the regime, which emerged within the party in the wake of the EAST GERMAN WORKERS' UPRISING of 1953 and the HUNGARIAN UPRISING of 1956, was repressed through show-trials and purges. The party's refusal to tolerate criticism of the East German state and social system persisted into the 1970s and the 1980s, as is attested by the trial and imprisonment of the dissident intellectual (and long-time SED member) Rudolf Bahro in 1977.

With the opening of the IRON CURTAIN by the Hungarian government in May 1989, facilitating emigration from East Germany, the Honecker government and the position of the SED within the regime came under increasing pressure. In December 1989 the new government headed by the reformist Hans Modrow announced the holding of free elections in May 1990. By late January 1990, however, confronted by the disintegration of its residual authority, the loss of over half its membership and continuing pressure for rapid reform, the SED was compelled to accept power-sharing with the other East German parties and brought forward democratic elections to mid-March 1990. Renamed as the Party of Democratic Socialism, the communists were overwhelmed by a landslide victory for the Conservative Alliance for Germany, campaigning for economic and political unification and backed by the West German CDU. The former SED retained 65 out of 400 seats in March 1990 but the first all-German elections in December saw it reduced to only 17 seats in the Bundestag.

M. McCauley, *The German Democratic Republic since 1945* (1983)

H. A. Turner, *The Two Germanies since 1945* (1987)

**Seipel, Ignaz** (1876–1932). Austrian Roman Catholic prelate, university professor and Christian Socialist Chancellor during the First Republic. Born in Vienna in 1876, he was ordained as a priest in 1899 and taught moral philosophy at the universities of Salzburg and Vienna until the end of the First World War. By 1918 he was a leading figure in the conservative CHRISTIAN SOCIAL PARTY (CSP) and was important in reconciling differences between its monarchist and republican wings. Seipel formed his first government in 1922 at the peak of the post-war inflation crisis, and successfully negotiated a loan of $100 million in return for draconian financial and administrative reforms to be implemented under Allied supervision, which provoked hostile reactions both from the opposition and from his own party. Wounded in an assassination attempt in June 1924, he resigned in November of that year, only to return to form a second administration (1926–9), in which he occupied the positions of Chancellor and Foreign Minister. His use of the fascist paramilitary *Heimwehr* during this second period of office, and particularly in 1927, is generally held to have strengthened fascism in Austria. Seipel himself was also now increasingly sympathetic to radical authoritarian solutions, and advocated a 'corporate' constitution with strong presidential

powers. He resigned in ill health and died at Pernitz, Vienna, in 1932.

V. Reimann, *Zu gross für Österreich: Seipel und Bauer im Kampf um die erste Republik* (1968)

**Serbia.** An independent principality from 1878, ruled by the royal house of Karajordjevic from 1903 following a military coup. Serbia was greatly enlarged as a result of the Balkan Wars of 1912–13 and was the base for secret societies such as the BLACK HAND which sought to 'liberate' the Slavs living under Austrian rule. The Austrians believed the Serbs connived at these activities and issues came to a head with the assassination of the Austrian Archduke FRANCIS FERDINAND at Sarajevo in Bosnia on 28 June 1914. The Austrian ultimatum to Serbia on 23 July 1914, ostensibly concerned with dealing with the terrorists, was almost designed to bring about war. The Serbian Premier, PASIC, although conciliatory, appears too have regarded a conflict with Austria as inevitable at some point and refused to yield to that part of the ultimatum which would have virtually ended Serbian sovereignty. His reply to the ultimatum (25 July 1914) led to the Austrian declaration of war on Serbia on 28 July. Serbia resisted Austrian assaults for almost a year, inflicting heavy defeats on the Austrian armies. In October 1915 a joint German-Austrian-Bulgarian offensive overran Serbia, forcing the Serbian army and government to seek refuge on the island of Corfu. Premier Pasic and Prince Regent Alexander (*see* ALEXANDER I) became the centre of plans developed by the Chairman of the Yugoslav Committee in London, ANTE TRUMBIC for the creation of a South Slav (Yugoslav) state. After some resistance from Premier Pasic, an agreement was reached at Corfu in June 1917 for the creation of a united state of Serbs, Croats and Slovenes under the royal house of Serbia. The new state was proclaimed on 1 December 1918. Serbia retained a dominant place within the new state, renamed Yugoslavia in 1929, and the source of continuing ethnic conflict up to the Second World War and beyond. The adoption of a Federal Constitution in November 1945 was an attempt to overcome the legacy of rivalry, although tensions still remain between the Serbs as the largest national group and

the other Yugoslav peoples. *See also* FIRST
WORLD WAR.

M. Petrovich, *A History of Modern Serbia, 1804–1918*
(2 vols., 1976)
F. Singleton, *A Short History of the Yugoslav Peoples*
(1985)

**Sèvres, Treaty of.** A treaty signed by the
Sultan of Turkey on 20 August 1920 at the
conclusion of the First World War. The
Sultan gave up all claims to non-Turkish
territory formerly part of the Turkish
Empire and recognized the independence
of Hejaz, Yemen and ARMENIA. Of former
Turkish territories, Syria and Alexandretta
were to become mandates of France; Palestine and Mesopotamia (Iraq) were to
become mandates of Great Britain; the
Dodecanes islands and Rhodes were to be
held by Italy; and other Turkish islands
ceded to Greece. The Straits of the Bosphorus and the Dardanelles were to be
internationalized and the adjoining territory
demilitarized. Izmir (Smyrna) and its hinterland were to be administered by Greece
for five years, after which a plebiscite was to
be held to decide their future. The punitive
nature of the treaty outraged Turkish
nationalists; the new Turkish President,
Kemal Ataturk, refused to ratify it and
began military action to overturn the settlement, leading to the GRAECO-TURKISH WAR
and operations against the Armenian and
Kurdish minorities, as well as against the
forces of Italy, France and Britain. By 1923
the Turks under Ataturk were able to
secure the more favourable TREATY OF LAUS-
ANNE.

P. C. Helmreich, *From Paris to Sèvres: The Partition of
the Ottoman Empire at the Paris Conference of
1919–20* (1974)
D. Fromkin, *A Peace to End All Peace: the Fall of
the Ottoman Empire and the Creation of the Modern
Middle East* (1990)

**Seyss-Inquart, Arthur von** (1892–1946).
Austrian politician and Nazi fellow-travel-
ler. Born in Stannern/Iglau in 1892, he was
the leader of the moderate faction of the
Austrian Nazis in the 1930s. In the hope of
winning these so-called 'legal' Nazis to the
government side Chancellor SHUSCHNIGG
appointed him to the State Council in 1937,
and was then forced by Hitler to appoint
him Interior Minister in February 1938.
Seyss-Inquart used this powerful position

to undermine the Schuschnigg regime from
within before the German invasion of 11
March 1938 (*see* ANSCHLUSS). Following
the occupation of Austria he became its
'governor' until the end of April, by which
time it had become clear that Austria was
to be completely absorbed into the Reich.
From Austria he was moved to occupied
Poland, before becoming Governor of the
Netherlands. He was executed by the Allies
as a war criminal at Nuremberg in 1946.

**SFIO.** Section Française de l'Internationale
Ouvrière. *See* SOCIALIST PARTY, FRENCH.

**Shakty Affair.** Trial of a group of Soviet
and foreign engineers working in the Donbass region accused of 'wrecking'. Their
highly publicized trial in Moscow in May
1928 was the first of a series of trials and
PURGES up to 1931 of technicians and
experts accused variously of 'wrecking',
'sabotage' and 'spying'. STALIN used the
trials to coerce technicians and experts who
might oppose the SOVIET COLLECTIVIZATION
campaign and the first FIVE YEAR PLAN. Five
'Shaktyites' were executed and a widespread campaign was launched against the
'bourgeois intelligentsia' accused of opposition to 'developing socialism'. Further
purges took place amongst the members of
GOSPLAN in 1931, as well as amongst agro-
nomists, scientists, academics and teachers.
Many of those imprisoned or dismissed
were replaced by more pliable Communist
Party members. The trials and accusations,
largely ended by 1931, neutralized a significant stratum of opposition to Stalin's
dictatorship and his economic plans. While
there was opposition to Stalin's plans,
almost all the charges were fabricated. The
use of show trials, the allegation of a widespread conspiracy against the Soviet state,
and the development of a climate of fear
and suspicion foreshadowed the purges
after 1934.

R. Conquest, *The Great Terror* (1968)
K. Bailes, *Technology and Society under Lenin and
Stalin* (1978)

**Shells Scandal.** British political crisis prompted by articles by the military correspondent of *The Times*, Colonel à Court Reping-
ton, who published a story on 14 May 1915
on lack of British shells causing an advance

to be checked. The story was partly abetted by the British commander-in-chief in France, Sir JOHN FRENCH, who felt he was not being properly supplied. Coming after the first heavy British casualties and with growing disquiet at ASQUITH's conduct of the war, the article triggered a demand for more effective prosecution of the war effort and the formation of a coalition. On 17 May Asquith was virtually presented with no alternative by LLOYD GEORGE and BONAR LAW, and he accepted the recommendation publicly on 18 May to form a coalition government. Asquith remained as Premier, with Lloyd George taking over a newly formed Ministry of Munitions. Bonar Law became Colonial Secretary and BALFOUR went to the Admiralty to replace CHURCHILL. Lloyd George undoubtedly saw the coalition and the Ministry of Munitions as important stepping stones for his ambitions. In the event, he also turned the office into a success, improving the war effort and demonstrating his own abilities.

J. M. Bourne, *Britain and the Great War, 1914–1918* (1989)

**shop stewards' movement.** Term for the growth of shop-floor organization in British trade unions, particularly in the engineering industry, before, during and after the First World War. Shop stewards were a reaction to the increasing remoteness and bureaucratization of the trade unions and drew upon the syndicalist ideas of trade-union-based activity (*see* SYNDICALISM). The First World War stimulated opposition to the directives of trade union leaders, especially over dilution, the substitution of semi-skilled and unskilled labour to replace skilled workers in order to increase war production. Shop stewards were active in the strike movements which developed in industrial centres such as Glasgow from 1915, forming a Clyde Workers' Committee, and subsequently in the strikes of 1917–19. Shop stewards became a common feature of most union organizations after the First World War, acting as the lowest tier of the union organization. In most unions, committees of shop stewards are the effective union representatives with employers. Increasingly, however, unions have asserted control over their shop stewards as the union structures have become more disciplined and well organized. *See also* 'RED' CLYDESIDE.

B. Pribicevic, *The Shop Stewards Movement and Workers' Control, 1910–1922* (1959)

H. Clegg, *A History of British Trade Unions since 1889*, vol. 2: *1911–33* (1985)

**Siegfried Line.** Originally, the defences between Lens and Rheims on the German 'Western Front' in September 1918; later, the defences built to emulate the MAGINOT LINE, which the Nazis believed invulnerable. Not as extensive as the Maginot Line, it was strong enough around Saarbrucken to resist French attacks at the beginning of the SECOND WORLD WAR. American forces reached this German line of defence in the west on 1 February 1945; British and Canadian forces broke through it the same month, on 8–9 February crossing the Rhine near Millingen in the northern sector where the line was weaker.

**Sikorsky, Wladyslaw** (1881–1943). Polish general and politician. Born in Galicia, he studied engineering at the universities of Cracow and Lvov. He served under PILSUDSKI in the RUSSO-POLISH WAR. Sikorsky retired from the armed forces in 1926 after a period leading a non-parliamentary coalition in which he earned the suspicions of Pilsudski and right-wing groups. His offer of service in 1939 was turned down, but he was able from Paris to organize a government-in-exile and a Polish army after Poland's defeat. As Prime Minister and Commander-in-Chief of the Free Polish Forces, he had 100,000 men under his command by the spring of 1940; these he brought to Britain after the fall of France. Following the German invasion of the Soviet Union in 1941 he concluded an alliance with the Soviets, repudiating the partition of Poland, re-establishing the pre-war frontiers and permitting the recruitment of a Polish army from Polish prisoners in Soviet hands. Disagreement over the use of this force, the 'Anders Army', led to its being transferred from Russia via Iran to Italy. Disputes about the future settlement of Polish frontiers also soured relations between the London-based government and Moscow. Soviet–Polish relations were shattered, however, by the revelations of the KATYN MASSACRE of Polish officers and

Polish accusations of Soviet responsibility, leading Stalin to sever diplomatic relations on 25 April 1943. Sikorski was killed in an air crash at Gibraltar on 4 July when travelling to inspect Polish forces in the Mediterranean. He was succeeded as Prime Minister by Stanislaw Mikolajczyk (1901–66), former Peasant Party leader. Sikorski's death has been seen as removing the one Polish leader with sufficient stature to act as an effective intermediary between his countrymen, the Western Allies and Stalin over Poland's future.

J. Coutouvidis and J. Reynolds, *Poland, 1939–1947* (1986)

**Single European Act.** Act creating a single European market by 1992. It was agreed in December 1985 at the Luxembourg Summit of European Community leaders and subsequently ratified by the member states. The Act agreed to steps to establish a complete internal market by 31 December 1992; deregulation to help small businesses; the goal of monetary union to be 'progressively realized'; reduction of disparities between richer and poorer regions or 'cohesion'; a technological research programme; action to improve the environment; and co-operation in the sphere of foreign policy to promote the development of a European identity. The Act also provided for a system of qualified majority voting in the Council of the EEC. Issues can be decided by a weighted system of voting for the member countries, each country having a number of votes up to ten according to its size, from ten for Britain, France and West Germany to two for Luxembourg. On fiscal issues a national veto remains. The Act was ratified in some countries, such as Denmark and Ireland, by referendum, elsewhere by the national parliaments. At its centre lay the creation of a unified market, seen by many integrationists as the first step towards full economic and political union. The act came into force on 1 July 1987.

R. Owen and M. Dynes, *The Times Guide to 1992* (rev. edn., 1989)

**Sinn Fein.** Gaelic term for 'Ourselves'. Irish nationalist party founded in 1902 by Arthur Griffiths (1872–1922) and formed into the Sinn Fein League in 1907–8 when it absorbed other nationalist groups. The group rose to prominence in the 1913–14 HOME RULE crisis, when many Sinn Feiners joined the IRISH VOLUNTEERS and many Dublin workers joined the organization. Sinn Fein members were involved in the EASTER RISING in 1916 and one of the battalion commanders, EAMONN DE VALERA took over as leader in October 1917. It successfully contested by-elections in 1917, and in 1918 won 73 out of 105 Irish seats, but its members refused to take their seats at Westminster, setting up an Irish parliament (Dail) in Dublin. Banned by the British, Sinn Fein provided the main political organization in the campaign against British forces from 1919 to 1921. In 1922 it split over the treaty with Britain, setting up the Irish Free State, de Valera leading the breakaway group who refused to accept the oath of allegiance. After the IRISH CIVIL WAR between 'Free-Staters' and 'Republicans' in 1922–3, Sinn Fein continued to contest elections, but its elected representatives refused to take their seats in the Dail and take the oath of allegiance to the Crown. In 1926 de Valera formed a new party, FIANNA FAIL, abandoning the fundamentalist Sinn Feiners to a minority role, as a consequence of which they failed to return any seats in the general election of September 1927. Sinn Fein continued in existence as the 'political wing' of the IRISH REPUBLICAN ARMY, winning four seats in the 1957 general election and operating as a fund-raising and propaganda body into the 1970s.

In 1980 and 1981 Provisional Sinn Fein (PSF) put up hunger strikers as candidates both for Westminster and the Dail. Bobby Sands was elected in a Westminster by-election in 1981, as were two candidates for the Dail, though none took their seats. This success led to the joint politico-military strategy 'The Armalite in one hand, and the ballot in another', with Sinn Fein contesting the Northern Irish Assembly seats in 1982, gaining five seats and 10 per cent of the vote. Sinn Fein's leader, Gerry Adams, was elected to Westminster in 1983 for Belfast West, but as with other Sinn Fein candidates refused to take his seat. In 1986 Sinn Fein took the controversial decision to take any seats it won in the Irish Dail, ending its long-standing boycott of southern Irish politics. In 1983 it appeared that Sinn Fein was challenging the SOCIAL

DEMOCRATIC AND LABOUR PARTY (SDLP) for the Catholic vote, taking 15 per cent as opposed to the SDLP's 18 per cent, but its support fell back in 1987.

F. S. Lyons, *Ireland since the Famine* (2nd edn, 1973)
C. Townshend, *The British Campaign in Ireland, 1919–1921* (1979)

**Six, the.** Name given to the original six members of the EUROPEAN ECONOMIC COMMUNITY (EEC): France, West Germany, Italy, Belgium, the Netherlands and Luxembourg. Later enlarged to 'the Nine' with the addition of Britain, Ireland and Denmark in 1973, and to 'the Twelve' with the addition of Greece, Portugal and Spain.

**SKJ.** Savez Komunista Jugoslavije. *See* COMMUNIST PARTY, YUGOSLAVIAN.

**Slovakia.** Region formally under Austro-Hungarian control until the end of the First World War. In 1919 it awaited formal incorporation into the Czechoslovak Republic by the Paris Peace Conference. Following the BÉLA KUN rising in Hungary, a group of military units and ex-prisoners-of-war declared a Slovak Soviet Republic on 16 June 1919 and appointed a revolutionary executive committee. Calling on aid from Hungary against 'imperialist Czechoslovakia' they appointed their own head of government. The regime proved short-lived, collapsing after Kun's flight. Hungarian units were removed and the Czech army took control by 7 July. During the inter-war years a Slovak People's Party led by Monsignor Hlinka and then by Josef Tiso (1887–1947), also a priest, sought to affirm Slovak independence. In October 1938 Tiso was appointed Prime Minister of an autonomous Slovak government set up as the Czech state crumbled in the aftermath of the MUNICH AGREEMENT. After the Nazi occupation of the rest of the Czech state in March 1939, Slovakia became the Slovak Republic with Tiso as President. He proved a willing collaborator with the Nazi war effort against the USSR, but fell with the Soviet advance. Arrested in May 1945, Tiso was sentenced to death in April 1947, and executed on the 18th, in spite of protest from Slovak and Catholic sources. Slovakia was permitted to retain some separate identity within the communist system, the state being officially a federal socialist republic consisting of two nations of equal rights. The Federal Assembly had 75 delegates from each grouping, Czech and Slovak, in a Chamber of Nations, as well as a Chamber of 200 deputies elected on a communist list system. The Communist Party of Slovakia was a constituent part of the CZECHOSLOVAK COMMUNIST PARTY and tame Slovak Parties formed part of National Front governments dominated by the Communists. Many leading politicians, such as DUBČEK have been Slovaks. Following the democratic upheaval in Czechoslovakia at the end of 1989 a Slovak counterpart to the Czech Civic Forum was formed as Public Against Violence. With CIVIC FORUM it gained 169 seats out of 300 in the bicameral federal parliament elections in June 1990, though Slovakia also gave support to Christian Democrat and Slovak parties.

**Slovenia.** A region inhabited by South Slav people and until 1918 under Austrian rule. The principal city, Ljubljana, was formerly known as Laibach. The Slovenes became part of the state of YUGOSLAVIA after the First World War, but retained distinctiveness as one of the more developed and sophisticated parts of the new state. The Federal Constitution of Yugoslavia in 1946 recognized the People's Republic of Slovenia as one of the federal units and of the six 'leading nations'. Stirrings of Slovenian independence became apparent after the death of TITO, fuelled by fears of Serbian dominance and their own distinctively Central European and Catholic background. The Slovenian Communist Party seceded from the Yugoslav Communist Party in January 1990. Slovenia's Parliament declared the Republic independent in March 1990, and following the success of the non-communist Demos coalition in elections in April opened negotiations with the Yugoslav government for complete separation.

F. Singleton, *Twentieth Century Yugoslavia* (1976)
L. J. Cohen, *Political Cohesion in a Fragile Mosaic: The Yugoslav Experience* (1983)

**Snowden, Philip** (1864–1937). British Labour (later National) politician and cabinet minister. Born in west Yorkshire, whose radical nonconformity and absence of trade unionism shaped his outlook, he became a civil servant before a crippling spinal disease forced his retirement. Joining the INDEPENDENT LABOUR PARTY (ILP) he soon became its leading propagandist and speaker. As a Labour MP (1906–18, 1922–31), he established himself as the leading spokesman on finance. His anti-war line in the First World War cost him his seat, but in 1924 and again in the SECOND LABOUR GOVERNMENT of 1929–31, he became Labour Chancellor of the Exchequer. But the leftward drift of the ILP and his dislike of the trade unions' power within the LABOUR PARTY led to his increasing detachment. Thoroughly orthodox in his economics (believing that only in that way could capitalism be made prosperous and the advance to socialism be continued), he opposed radical economic policies at the Treasury and pressed for severe curbs on public expenditure. In 1931, believing such cuts to be essential, he followed RAMSAY MACDONALD into the NATIONAL GOVERNMENT. At the 1931 election he made bitter and effective attacks on Labour. Ennobled after the election, he became Lord Privy Seal, but resigned from the cabinet in 1932 in opposition to the adoption of protection. Thereafter he attacked MacDonald, most notably in his memoirs (1934). He died in 1937, having spent most of his life in pain and precarious health. Snowden was old-fashioned, personally ascetic and often arrogant, but he always believed sincerely that his actions and opinions were in the best interests of the working classes. His main faults were refusal to accept the sincerity of his opponents, and a belief that he was always right.

Viscount Snowden, *An Autobiography* (2 vols., 1934)
K. Laybourn, *Philip Snowden* (1988)

**SNP.** See SCOTTISH NATIONAL PARTY.

**Soares, Mario** (1924–). Portuguese politician. Jailed 12 times for his opposition to the SALAZAR and CAETANO governments and exiled in France, 1970–74, he became secretary-general of the Socialist Party in 1973 and returned to Portugal following the coup in 1974. Breaking with the Communists and the radical military officers who dominated the government after they refused to honour the election results of April 1975, Soares emerged as the most important leader of the coalition that brought about the defeat of revolutionary radicalism in November 1975. He served as Foreign Minister from May 1974 to March 1975 and negotiated the independence of Portugal's African colonies. He then served as Prime Minister of two coalition governments, 1976–8 and 1983–5. During the latter he undertook an austerity programme and obtained legislation to return sectors of the economy nationalized after 1974 to private ownership. The escudo was devalued and preparations were made for Portugal's entry to the EUROPEAN ECONOMIC COMMUNITY on 1 January 1986. The withdrawal of his Social Democratic coalition partners in May 1985 precipitated a general election on 6 October which saw the socialists halved in number from 101 to 57 seats. Soares was replaced by a coalition led by Cavaco Silva in October 1985. Soares was elected President in January 1986 by a narrow margin, and in that office once again won great popularity, being re-elected to it by a wide margin in 1990. Following his election the Socialist Party chose Vitor Constancio as its new leader. *See also* PORTUGUESE REVOLUTION.

T. Gallagher, *Portugal: a Twentieth Century Interpretation* (1983)

**Social Contract.** An agreement negotiated between the British Labour government and the TRADES UNION CONGRESS in 1974, whereby the trade unions would support the government's anti-inflation measures by accepting wage restraint in return for controls over prices, rents and more egalitarian social policy measures. The breakdown of the social contract and the ensuing 'WINTER OF DISCONTENT' in 1978–9 helped to bring about the defeat of the Labour government in the 1979 general election.

**Social Democratic and Labour Party, Northern Irish** (SDLP). The SDLP, formed in 1970, grew out of the civil rights campaign of the late 1960s. Its first leader was Gerry Fitt, who sat for Belfast West. He stood down in 1983 and was replaced by John Hume, who was elected for the Londonderry seat of Foyle. The SDLP is the major Catholic party of Ulster and has played an important part in all the attempts to create an acceptable political structure in Ulster, including the power-sharing executive of the early 1970s and the ANGLO-IRISH AGREEMENT (Hillsborough Agreement) of 1985. Since 1981 the SDLP's electoral position in the Catholic community has been under challenge from SINN FEIN, and in 1983 its vote was only 3 per cent ahead. Since 1983 the party has gained support at the expense of Sinn Fein. In 1987 it had two MPs and one MEP.

W. D. Flackes, *Northern Ireland: A Political Directory, 1968–83* (1983)
P. Arthur and K. Jeffery, *Northern Ireland since 1968* (1988)

**Social Democratic Labour Party, Russian** (RSDRP). Founded in 1898 in Minsk by Russian Marxist activists. Divisions emerged between the followers of LENIN organized around his newspaper *Iskra* ('the spark') which argued for a highly centralized, disciplined party of dedicated revolutionaries and those who sought to work through the trade unions and see the co-operation of liberals. Lenin's views were fully articulated in *What is to be Done?* (1902) and at the Second Party Congress held in Brussels and London, he adopted the term BOLSHEVIK (the 'majority'), as opposed to the MENSHEVIKS (the 'minority'), when his group obtained a temporary ascendency. The congress, however, was a failure for Lenin's attempt to determine the shape of the party in his direction, and in 1903 he resigned from *Iskra*. Party activists in Russia continued to co-operate, and when Lenin in 1905 held a Bolshevik Third Congress, attempts were made to reunite the divisions. Lenin remained determined to preserve Bolshevik domination and a small 'Sixth' Party Conference at Prague in 1912 declared itself an all-party conference of the RSDRP.

By 1914 Lenin was in chronic dispute with the other members of the RSDRP, including the majority of those elected to the Fourth DUMA. In 1913 the pro-Bolshevik RSDRP deputies had been formed into a separate 'fraction' by Lenin from abroad. Although they had co-operated in opposing the voting of war credits in early August 1914 with Mensheviks and members of the SOCIALIST REVOLUTIONARY PARTY, their attempt to propagate Lenin's 'Theses on War' led to the trial and exile of the Bolshevik Duma deputies in February 1915. From his base in Switzerland Lenin continued to denounce the Menshevik wing of the party until he had the opportunity to return to Russia in April 1917. Prior to that the Mensheviks remained the dominant wing of the RSDRP within Russia. Operating within the Duma and in various other groups they formed the Petrograd Soviet following the February Revolution and controlled with the Socialist Revolutionaries the majority of soviets. They took a greater share in power when after the April crisis of the PROVISIONAL GOVERNMENT they joined it in May. As a result the Menshevik group became increasingly embroiled in the struggles of the Provisional Government to survive, and was reduced to a small minority in the Second Congress of Soviets which met on 7 November 1917. Earlier attempts to form a broad socialist government foundered on Bolshevik intransigence, and with the Bolshevik seizure of power to coincide with the Second Congress, the Mensheviks found themselves outmanoeuvred by the Bolsheviks. Under the leadership of YULI MARTOV they attempted to form a 'third force' in the growing drift to civil war, but found themselves forced to side with the Bolsheviks against the 'White' forces when fighting broke out. In spite of this, in 1921 the Menshevik opposition was suppressed by the Bolsheviks and driven into exile. There they attempted to keep alive some of the traditions of the RSDRP, co-operating with other socialist groups and publishing a newspaper, the *Socialist Messenger*, based first in Berlin, from 1921, then later in Paris and New York until its demise in 1963.

J. L. A. Keep, *The Rise of Social Democracy in Russia* (1960)
A. Ascher, *The Mensheviks in the Russian Revolution* (1967)
I. Getzler, *A Political Biography of a Russian Social Democrat* (1967)

**Social Democratic Labour Party, Swedish** (SAP). Founded in 1880 as a democratic socialist party, the SAP developed into the largest party in the Lower House by the First World War. It formed coalition governments with the Liberals in the war. The coalition extended the franchise and introduced the 40-hour week in 1919. The coalition then broke up over socialist demands for NATIONALIZATION, tax reform and unemployment insurance. The SAP remained in government alone under Karl Branting (1860–1925), but it lost seats in the 1920 election and was replaced by a non-party cabinet. An electoral reform trebling the electorate necessitated another election, and in 1921 the SAP recovered ground and formed another government, but fell in 1923. Branting returned in 1924, but died the following year. He was replaced by Richard Sandler (1884–1974) who reduced the length of military service but fell in 1926. The SAP supported a minority Liberal government in passing an Education Act in 1927 but resisted the strengthening of arbitration tribunals to interpret collective wage agreements, and the SAP again lost seats in 1928. A financial scandal and the resignation of the Liberal government in 1932 led to the SAP taking office under Per Albin Hansson (1855–1946). He began a period of almost unbroken rule for the SAP which lasted for nearly 50 years.

Under Hansson, Sweden developed the elements of a WELFARE STATE and acted to counter the DEPRESSION. He abandoned free trade, previously part of the SAP programme, raised minimum prices for agricultural products, controlled imports, devalued the krona, and directed grants and subsidies to the unemployed. Unemployment insurance was introduced in 1935 and old age pensions increased in 1936. After a few months out of office, he formed a coalition with the Agrarian Party to support him in return for assistance to agriculture. In 1937 family allowances were introduced, the eight-hour day was extended to land workers and paid holidays for all introduced in 1938. In the same year the Saltsjobaden Agreements were arranged between the Employers' Federation and the Unions, setting up binding long-term contracts. In foreign affairs they signed a joint declaration of neutrality with Denmark and Norway in 1936.

At the Russian attack on Finland on 30 November 1939 Sweden declared non-belligerency. A coalition cabinet was formed at the end of 1939. Sweden was forced to accept German requests to allow unarmed German troops rights of transit after the fall of Norway; the coalition restricted press criticism of its policy. The government also took full control of the economy, and rationing was introduced. From 1943 the transit traffic was stopped and Sweden operated as a haven for Jewish and other refugees from occupied Europe.

In July 1945 the coalition ended and the SAP ruled alone. A new Premier, Tage Erlander (1901–), accepted MARSHALL PLAN aid but maintained rationing until 1949 and rent controls. Increasing need for rearmament and inflation eroded the SAP's majority and they formed a coalition with the Agrarians in 1951. A socialist compulsory pension scheme was defeated in 1957 on a referendum although it was finally passed in 1964. This followed further welfare reforms, three weeks' paid holidays (1953), a raised and indexed basic pension (1959), non-means-tested family allowances (1947), a national health service (1955) with free hospital treatment and part payment of doctor's fees; and free, nine-year comprehensive schooling (from 1950). Erlander retired in 1969, and was replaced by Olof Palme (1927–86). The party lost office in 1976–82, but returned to power with Palme at its head in October of 1982. It remained in power until early 1990 when a government crisis led to its resignation.

M. Childs, *Sweden: The Middle Way* (1936)
S. Oakley, *The Story of Sweden* (1966)

**Social Democratic Party, British** (SDP). The SDP originated on 25 January 1981 as the Council for Social Democracy, an organization led by four disillusioned Labour politicians, the 'Gang of Four': Shirley Williams, DAVID OWEN, William Rodgers and ROY JENKINS. The broad aims of the new party were set out in the 'Limehouse Declaration' of 25 January, followed on 26 March by the setting up of the Social Democratic Party as a separate political party. Its leading members expressed support for electoral reform through proportional representation, continued membership of the EEC, multilateral disarmament and a reflationary economic strategy. In September 1981 the party joined THE ALLIANCE with the LIBERAL PARTY to fight the next general election and to reach mutual agreement on the fighting of by-elections and local government elections. Party membership in October 1981 stood at 66,000. The first SDP MP, Shirley

Williams, was elected at the Crosby by-election in November 1981. Roy Jenkins won Glasgow Hillhead in 1982 and was subsequently elected leader of the party. In the 1983 general election the SDP campaigned in alliance with the Liberals, each fighting approximately half the seats, but returning only six MPs. In June 1983 David Owen succeeded Roy Jenkins as leader, unopposed. In 1986 serious rifts with the Liberal Party developed over defence policy, but the Alliance was relaunched early in 1987, and the SDP and Liberals campaigned under joint leadership in the subsequent general election. In June 1987 the party returned only five MPs, only David Owen of the 'Gang of Four' being returned to parliament. Liberal calls for a merger in the wake of the election led to fierce controversy within the SDP, and there was a ballot of SDP members about opening merger talks with the Liberals. On 6 August a vote of 57 per cent in favour of merger talks led to David Owen's resignation as leader, and a major split within the SDP appeared imminent. Owen was succeeded as leader by Robert MacLennan. On 30–31 January 1988 the SDP voted in favour of a merger with the Liberals to form the Social and Liberal Democratic Party, launched in March. On 8 March the SDP was relaunched and elected Owen its leader. The party in early 1989 gave up full-scale national campaigning as its membership had fallen to around 12,000. In June 1990 the party was wound up because of lack of support, though retaining three MPs at Westminster. Its continued existence following the merger was widely perceived as having reduced support for the centre as a whole.

C. P. Cook, *A Short History of the Liberal Party, 1900–1988* (1989)
G. Daly, 'The Social Democratic Party, 1981–88', in A. Seldon (ed.), *UK Political Parties since 1945* (1990)

**Social Democratic Party, German.** (Sozialdemokratische Partei Deutschlands; SPD). Political party of the FEDERAL REPUBLIC OF GERMANY. The SPD was the successor party to the Sozialistische Arbeiterpartei Deutschlands (SAP), founded in 1875 and harassed under Bismarck's anti-socialist law (1878–90). In 1890 it adopted its new name and committed itself to a Marxist analysis

of society and a revolutionary political programme in the following year at its Erfurt congress. Closely allied with the mainstream of the trades union movement, the SPD had become the largest party in the REICHSTAG by 1912 with over one-quarter of the seats and the support of one-third of the electorate. With more than 1 million members, it was also by far the largest socialist party in the world.

Despite its internationalist and pacifist proclamations before 1914, the party supported the war effort in Germany during the FIRST WORLD WAR. Growing hostility to the continuation of the war led to a split in the party in 1917 and the formation of an Independent Social Democratic Party (*see* USPD) alongside the 'Majority' Social Democrats (MSPD). With the GERMAN REVOLUTION of 1918–19 the MSPD and USPD formed a transitional coalition government which ruled Germany until elections to a constituent national assembly in January 1919. The SPD absorbed the rump of the USPD in October 1922 and, during the WEIMAR REPUBLIC, the party was a mainstay of parliamentary democracy, usually in coalition with the CENTRE PARTY and the left-liberal DDP (*see* DDP). Controlling the important Prussian *Land* (regional) government between 1920 and 1932, it nevertheless headed Weimar coalition governments only in 1919–20 and 1928–30. Drawing its electoral support increasingly from the 'respectable' working class and white-collar workers, it was outflanked on the left by the GERMAN COMMUNIST PARTY during the DEPRESSION years. Its share of the vote fell from 28.7 per cent (1928) to 20.4 per cent (1932), and it seemed increasingly powerless in the face of an authoritarian presidential government after 1930 and the rise of the NAZI PARTY. Crippled by mass unemployment amongst trade union members, it was unable to resist the Nazi seizure of power after January 1933 and was banned, along with all other non-Nazi political parties, in July 1933. Its leadership fled into exile. During the Nazi dictatorship, SPD-inspired resistance activity was small-scale and politically insignificant.

With the collapse of the Nazi regime in 1945, the party re-emerged in occupied Germany. Absorbed into the SED (*see* SED) in East Germany, the SPD became a major political force in the Western occupation zones and, later, the Federal Republic, gaining 29.9 per cent of the popular vote in elections to the Federal Parliament (*Bundestag*) of the new state in August 1949. Yet the party was to remain out of office until 1966. During the 1950s it continued to advocate nationalization of basic industries, despite the catastrophic economic situation in East Germany. It also opposed West German rearmament and membership of NATO, and was easily portrayed by its conservative opponents as unduly sympathetic to West Germany's communist neighbours. In 1958, the SPD revised its programme at its Bad Godesberg congress, abandoning Marxism and proclaiming its conversion to only essential economic planning within a free-market economy. In 1960 it accepted West German membership of NATO. Making major gains in the 1965 *Bundestag* elections, it entered a 'Grand Coalition' with the CHRISTIAN DEMOCRATIC UNION and CHRISTIAN SOCIAL UNION in 1966 during a short-lived economic recession. During the 1960s the SPD's membership both increased and became socially more diverse as it sought to transform itself into a party capable of appealing to broader sections of German society. In coalition with the FREE DEMOCRATIC PARTY after the 1969 *Bundestag* elections, it was the governing party under Chancellors BRANDT and SCHMIDT until 1982. With the break-up of the Schmidt government in 1982 it returned to opposition, suffering significant electoral losses in 1983 and 1987, and coming under increasing pressure from the environmentalist GREENS. Following the democratic upheaval in the GERMAN DEMOCRATIC REPUBLIC, an East German SDP was founded with West German support. It won 87 seats in March 1990, but in the December all-German elections, following unification, the combined SDP did poorly with only 239 seats.

S. Miller and H. Potthoff, *A History of German Social Democracy* (1986)
R. Fletcher (ed.), *Bernstein to Brandt: A Short History of German Social Democracy* (1987)

**Social Democratic Workers' Party, Austrian** (SDAP). The Social Democratic Workers' Party was founded in 1889 at Hainfeld, Lower Austria. Although it was influenced by the German SPD, the SDAP was forced to respond to the particular problems of the Habsburg monarchy, above all the nationalities problem. The party's distinctive 'Austromarxist' ideology was rather more radical than that of other Social Democratic parties, and this may have helped inhibit the development of a strong Communist Party in Austria after the First World War. During the revolutionary upheavals of 1918–19 the SDAP, led by KARL RENNER and OTTO BAUER, emerged as the strongest single political force in Austria, but failed to gain an overall majority in parliament. It left the ruling coalition in 1920 and remained in opposition until it was banned after the brief AUSTRIAN CIVIL WAR of February 1934. However, throughout the First Republic the party retained control of Vienna, which had gained the status of an autonomous federal state under the new constitution. The party's educational and social policies in the capital made 'RED VIENNA' a model of municipal socialism and an unassailable electoral stronghold. Following the party's dissolution in 1934 an exile organization (*Auslands-organisation Österreichischer Sozialisten*, ALÖS) was formed, while of those remaining in Austria many defected to the AUSTRIAN COMMUNIST PARTY, while others formed the Revolutionary Socialists, a resistance group of underground activists. The two groups were reunited as the Socialist Party of Austria (Sozialistische Partei Österreichs; SPÖ) after the Second World War. A moderate social democratic party, the SPÖ obtained an absolute majority in parliament in 1971 under the leadership of Bruno Kreisky, and remained in sole power until 1983.

T. Bottomore (ed.), *Austro-Marxism* (1978)
J. Duczynska, *Workers in Arms* (1978)
M. Sully, *Continuity and Change in Austrian Socialism: The External Quest for the Third Way* (1982)

**'Socialism in one country'.** A theoretical development of Marxism associated with STALIN which justified concentrating on the preservation and furtherance of the revolution in the Soviet Union. This was in contrast to the view espoused by TROTSKY and others of 'world revolution'. According to standard interpretations of Marxist theory the revolution was expected to occur in more industrially advanced countries.

Lenin, Trotsky and other Russian Marxists gradually accepted the idea that the revolution could occur in a country such as Russia and that its character might be a so-called 'permanent' or 'interrupted' revolution which might combine the stages of bourgeois and proletarian revolution because of the uneven and backward character of its development. The security of such a revolution, occurring in a society where the peasantry still formed a large conservative force, would depend upon the organization and dictatorship of a vanguard party like the BOLSHEVIKS and the spread of 'world revolution' to the more advanced states. Accordingly, Trotsky, like Lenin, looked to the revolution in the other European states after 1917 to bring about the fulfilment of the socialist revolution. The formation of the new International, or COMINTERN, in March 1919 soon had to face the reality that further revolutions had been postponed for the immediate future and led to a theoretical debate about the future course of revolution. In this Stalin's position became defined as that of 'Socialism in one country', envisaging the possibility of building socialism in a single country and removing the need to look to world revolution for the transition to socialism. Stalin increasingly used his own theoretical position to discredit his opponents. In articles in December 1924 Stalin opposed his view to that of Trotsky as part of his campaign to wrest leadership of the Soviet Union and to undermine his rival. Stalin's view was accepted as the orthodox inheritance of Leninism at the 14th Party Conference in April 1925. Thereafter 'Socialism in one country' became official doctrine. Its implications went beyond the power struggle between Stalin and Trotsky, for it implied the need to preserve and further the Russian Revolution by strengthening the Soviet state, justifying both the rapid processes of industrialization and COLLECTIVIZATION and the subservience of the members of the Comintern to the needs of Soviet foreign policy. Rather than seeing the state 'withering away', the 'building of socialism' required the state to take a leading role in society and to become strong enough to resist internal and external enemies.

E. H. Carr, *Socialism in One Country, 1924–26* (2 vols., 1958–9)

R. C. Tucker, *Stalin as Revolutionary, 1879–1929* (1973)
B. Knei-paz, *The Social and Political Thought of Leon Trotsky* (1978)

**Socialist International.** An organization of social democratic parties formed in 1951 as heir to the SECOND INTERNATIONAL. It grew out of the Committee of the International Socialist Conference (Comisco) which met between 1947 and 1951 and called for socialist unity. In 1948 it declared that socialism was incompatible with suppression of democratic rights and approved the concept of a united Europe. It denounced the socialist parties of Hungary, Bulgaria, Czechoslovakia and Romania for uniting with communists, expelled the pro-communist wing of the Italian socialists led by NENNI and admitted exiled social democrats from Eastern Europe, the GERMAN SOCIAL DEMOCRATIC PARTY and the Italians under Saragat and Lombardo. It has 40 affiliated social democratic parties.

I. Campbell and W. Paterson, *Social Democracy in Post-war Europe* (1974)

**Socialist Party, French** (Parti Socialiste; PS). The French Socialist Party was originally founded in 1905 as the French section of the Workers' International (Section Française de l'Internationale Ouvrière, SFIO), continuing under this title until 1969. Under its most prominent leader, Jean Jaures (1859–1914), it developed a powerful organ in the nationally distributed newspaper, *L'Humanité*, founded in 1904, but it refused to participate in governments following the ruling of the SECOND INTERNATIONAL in 1904 that socialists should not participate in bourgeois governments. Jaures's assassination in July 1914 deprived the socialists of their most prominent leader, but the socialists joined the government of national unity in 1914. Increasing tensions within the party and the RUSSIAN REVOLUTION produced a major split in December 1920, when a majority at the SFIO's 18th Congress voted three to one in favour of affiliating to COMINTERN, thereby forming the FRENCH COMMUNIST PARTY (PCF). They took with them two-thirds of the membership, the newspaper *L'Humanité*, the party headquarters and two-thirds of the assets, but only 13 of the 67 deputies elected as Socialists in 1919.

The SFIO took time to recover from this

setback and, although it had an alliance with the Radicals (the Cartel des Gauches), the opposition of its rank and file to participation in government and the preference of the Radicals for coalitions with Conservatives kept it out of office until the victory of the POPULAR FRONT coalition of Socialists, Radicals and Communists in May 1936. Under the premiership of LÉON BLUM the Popular Front sought to implement a programme of economic expansion, social reform and support for the LEAGUE OF NATIONS. Born in the midst of a tumultuous strike wave in May–June 1936, the Popular Front struggled against a deepening economic crisis and the impact of the SPANISH CIVIL WAR. By spring 1937 it had been forced to rein in most of its reforms and abandon the Spanish Republic.

After Blum's resignation in June 1937, the party was beset by divisions, leading a large section to support APPEASEMENT and ultimately the VICHY GOVERNMENT. Almost three-quarters of the socialist deputies in 1940 voted to confer full powers on Marshal PÉTAIN. Following the Second World War, the SFIO was overtaken electorally by the PCF, and was returned as only the third largest party in 1945 with 134 deputies and 24 per cent of the vote, thus falling behind the Christian Democratic MRP and the communists. They were forced to maintain minority governments which both alienated their supporters and left them powerless to impose their own policies. Eventually the socialists, now led by GUY MOLLETT, withdrew from government in 1951.

The socialists remained electorally squeezed between the communists and the Gaullists (see GAULLISM), obtaining about 15 per cent of the vote in the elections of 1951, 1956 and 1958. Although Mollet served in several governments and became Prime Minister in 1956–7, the socialists remained a weak force as an independent electoral organization. In opposition from 1959, their candidate for the presidency in 1965, MITTERRAND, was only able to make a respectable showing with communist support. Organizational and personal rivalries, however, continued to weaken the Left, who faced a crushing Gaullist victory in 1968, while in the presidential elections of 1969 the socialists obtained only 5 per cent

of the vote. This signalled the end of the SFIO and the Left began to draw together.

In 1971 an electoral federation was formed of the SFIO, the Radical Socialists and the Convention of Republican Institutions (CIR), with Mitterrand as First Secretary. Initially, the new Parti Socialiste (PS) campaigned on the basis of a common programme with the communists, but it allowed the socialists to gain over 20 per cent of the vote in the 1973 elections and Mitterrand to mount a strong challenge to GISCARD D'ESTAING in the 1974 presidential elections. When the PCF withdrew from the common programme in 1978 the PS was able to develop both organizationally and electorally.

On 10 May 1981 Mitterrand triumphed in the presidential elections over Giscard d'Estaing, becoming the first socialist head of state since 1953. The Assembly elections held in June were a further socialist triumph, winning an absolute majority for the first time in their history, with 285 seats. The decline of the PCF, foreshadowed in the presidential elections, and now reduced to 44 seats, was equally striking: for the first time in recent French history, the socialists were able to act independently of the PCF, although four communists entered Pierre Mauroy's cabinet. In government the PS proved itself able to grapple with the consequences of the depression of the early 1980s, introducing an austerity programme in March 1983 and reversing many of its spending plans. Party unity was maintained, even when the communists withdrew their ministers in July 1984. Mitterrand then sought to adopt a new policy of economic liberalization and tax cuts with a new cabinet from July 1985 under Laurent Fabius.

The PS went into the 1986 Assembly elections fearing heavy losses, but emerged as still the largest single party with 206 seats, elections which also saw the PCF reduced to only 35. The socialist President, Mitterrand, was now forced to work with a conservative government led by JACQUES CHIRAC, so-called 'cohabitation'. In 1988 Mitterrand retained the presidency, convincingly defeating Chirac, by appealing to the centre voters. His triumph was followed by the Assembly elections in which the PS failed to gain overall majority but was able to govern through a centre-left coalition.

The PCF retained 27 seats, partly through PS support, emphasizing the extent to which under Mitterrand the socialists had become the dominant party of the Left in contemporary French politics. They have done so by increasing their appeal to centre voters; Mitterrand deliberately setting out to show the socialists as 'fit to govern', retaining France's nuclear forces and abandoning many of the older socialist commitments to NATIONALIZATION. The economic reversal of March 1983 under finance minister DELORS and the appointment of the young technocrat, Fabius, demonstrated a commitment to economic realism. The continuing weakness and disarray of the PCF gave the socialists the possibility of capturing permanently support from the former majority party of the Left.

N. Greene, *Crisis and Decline: The French Socialist Party in the Popular Front Era* (1969)
D. S. Bell and B. Criddle, *The French Socialist Party* (1988)
J. W. Friend, *Seven Years in France: François Mitterrand and the Unintended Revolution, 1981–1988* (1989)

**Socialist Party, Italian** (Partito Socialista Italiano; PSI). Founded in 1892, the party quickly distinguished itself for its intellectual vigour and organizational skills. Very moderate at first, it became radicalized in the early 1910s, partly due to the influence of MUSSOLINI, then the radical young editor of the chief newspaper, *Avanti*. The PSI proposed neutrality in the First World War, and remained officially neutral after the country entered the conflict in 1915, when many socialists led anti-war campaigns in 1915 and 1917. The party became the largest party in the Chamber after the 1919 elections and briefly dominated much of northern Italy, both through control of local government and through their strong labour unions, which operated in rural as well as urban areas. The verbal extremism of the dominant 'Maximalists' combined with their unwillingness actually to attempt revolution caused many of the elites to support the Fascist movement created by the ex-Socialist, Mussolini, in its violent attacks against them. Increasingly divided, in 1921 the party split, with the formation of a separate ITALIAN COMMUNIST PARTY. Further splits occurred in 1922, when the most moderate elements were expelled and formed the Partito Socialista Unitario (PSU). Unable to combat fascism, the socialists were officially suppressed, but participated in the émigré Concentrazione Antifascista from 1927, leading to the uniting of the two bodies. They were joined by the communists from 1934 as a POPULAR FRONT. Following the outbreak of the Second World War the socialists supported the Allies and in July 1943 formed the Partito Socialista Italiano di Unita Proletaria (PSIUP) and participated in government. Disagreement about fusion with the Communists led to a breakaway group, the Partito Socialista dei Lavoratori Italiani (PSLI) which supported the Christian Democrats and took office in cabinet. A further split led to a group joining the PSLI to form the Partito Democratico Italiano (PSDI). After the early collaboration, increasingly the party, under its longtime leader, Pietro Nenni, removed itself from the possibility of fusing with the communists. By 1959 the newly named PSI was exploring forming centre-left coalitions, the first being that of Fanfani in 1962–3, then that of ALDO MORO in 1963. This led to a breakaway of a left group taking the old name PSIUP. Further splits led to the breakup of the centre-left coalition by 1968. The PSI has consistently trailed the Communist Party in the polls since the late 1940s, its splits and shifts in position reducing its support, so that by 1976 it had less than 10 per cent of the vote and only 57 deputies, compared with the PCI's 35 per cent and 228 deputies. From 1979 the PSI has inched up in elections to reach 94 seats in the 1987 elections and hold the balance of power as the third party behind the Communists and Christian Democrats, with 177 and 234 seats, respectively. Much of the improvement in the PSI's position has been due to the powerful new leadership of BETTINO CRAXI, who was Prime Minister from 1983 to 1987. During that time too, Sandro Pertini, an octogenarian PSI militant, who had survived long years in Mussolini's prisons, served as perhaps Italy's most popular President in history.

A. Tasca, *The Rise of Italian Fascism* (1938)

**Socialist Party of Austria.** *See* SOCIAL DEMOCRATIC WORKERS' PARTY, AUSTRIAN.

**Socialist Realism.** The approved method of art and literature in the Soviet Union under Stalin. Following the highly experimental phase of artistic expression in the years immediately following the revolution, there were growing pressures on artists of all kinds to bend their efforts towards more distinctly political objectives. A certain amount of freedom was maintained while the Commissariat of Enlightenment (Narkompros) remained under the control of the intellectual Anotoli Lunarcharsky (1875–1933), but his departure in 1929 left the way open for STALIN and his son-in-law, ANDREI ZHDANOV, to interfere more directly in artistic affairs. During the First FIVE YEAR PLAN, Stalin had already interfered with the editing of films such as Eisenstein's *The General Line* (1929), and 'individualist' writers, artists and directors found their work subject to boycott and criticism.

In 1932 Stalin dissolved all existing artists' groups, including PROLEKULT and RAPP, replacing them with unions for each artistic discipline. Socialist Realism was codified by Zhdanov and Maxim Gorky (1868–1936) at the first All-Union Congress of Writers in 1934. Socialist realism was to be an organ of class struggle and the artist 'an engineer of human souls' (Stalin). Under its precepts socialist realism was the culminating form of all artistic forms, representing MARXIST-LENINISM in the presentation of reality and identifying the party as the embodiment of the socialist state. The approved style was defined as 'revolutionary romanticism', totally subservient to propagating the approved philosophy of the party. While some artists continued relatively untroubled, Eisenstein had work on his *Bezhin Meadow* halted in 1937 for its emphasis on moral rather than realist qualities and Dmitri Shostakovich was harshly criticized in 1936 for his opera *Lady Macbeth of Mtsensk*, described as 'un-Soviet' and 'leftist'. The approved style was enforced by the control of the cultural unions over the origination, production and publication of artistic work; expulsion from the appropriate union meant the end to artistic output, and during the PURGES a large number of artists were sent to labour camps or killed. Others were forced to recant publicly after criticism and conform to the dictates of the artistic unions.

While a greater degree of freedom was permitted during the Second World War, Zhdanov reiterated the policy in the postwar era, maintaining an unflinching control over evidence of 'bourgeois individualism' in artistic output. Following Stalin's death there was a thaw under KHRUSHCHEV, and during his DE-STALINIZATION campaign the high-water mark came with the publication of ALEXANDER SOLZHENITSYN's *A Day in the Life of Ivan Denisovich* in *Novy mir* in 1962. But the other most famous writer of the era, Boris Pasternak (1890–1960) died with his later works unpublished in the Soviet Union and circulating in foreign editions or SAMIZDAT. The brief thaw ended in 1963 when an Ideological Commission restated the doctrines of socialist realism as 'party-mindedness, ideological maturity and a popular outlook'. Under BREZHNEV the Soviet Union remained closed to the most vital artistic currents in the West and forced Solzhenitsyn to continue publishing abroad and, ultimately, to go into exile in 1974. In the freer atmosphere of GLASNOST under GORBACHEV many of the restraints in the artistic and cultural fields have been relaxed, although the Writers' Union and other cultural organizations continue to maintain a relatively conservative stance in defence of official artistic standards. Increasingly bureaucratic and staffed by approved writers and artists, they still maintain a powerful influence on Soviet cultural life.

H. Swayze, *Political Control of Literature in the USSR, 1946–1959* (1962)
H. Ermolaev, *Soviet Literary Theories, 1917–1934: The Genesis of Socialist Realism* (1963)
J. C. Vaughan, *Soviet Socialist Realism* (1973)

**Socialist Revolutionary Party, Russian.** The heir to the egalitarian socialism associated with the populist movement of the 19th century, the Socialist Revolutionary Party was founded in 1902. It derived most of its support from the peasantry. At its first Congress in 1906 it adopted a programme of land expropriation and socialization, the convocation of a Constituent Assembly, the setting up of a federal republic with self-determination for the national minorities, the separation of church and state, full political liberties and minimum hours of work. Confined by the electoral laws to only a few deputies in the DUMA, the party enjoyed mass support in rural areas, as shown by its vote in the Constituent Assembly elections in 1917. Lacking decisive leadership, however, the party split, with the formation of the LEFT SOCIALIST REVOLUTIONARY PARTY, who were alienated by the parent party's support for the war. The Socialist Revolutionaries found themselves increasingly outmanoeuvred by the BOLSHEVIKS with their determined leadership and support in the urban centres. Represented on many rural soviets, the Socialist Revolutionaries withdrew from the All-Russian Congress of Soviets on 7 November 1917 and repudiated the Bolshevik coup. Failing to take any direct action, they pinned their hopes on the coming elections to the CONSTITUENT ASSEMBLY (25 November), which confirmed them decisively as the largest party, securing 15 million votes and 370 delegates, compared to the Bolshevik's 10 million votes and 168 delegates. They decided, however, not to resist the Bolsheviks' dissolution of the Assembly, effectively destroying the party as a serious political force. Their press was closed down in 1918 and, instead of Bolshevik power crumbling as they had anticipated, they were themselves expelled from elected bodies, arrested and driven underground.

The TREATIES OF BREST-LITOVSK in 1918 brought about a major change in the policy of the surviving Socialist Revolutionaries towards outright opposition to the Bolsheviks for having 'betrayed democracy, Russia, the Revolution and the International'. By this time the party was hopelessly disunited, some throwing in their lot with the Bolsheviks, some fighting against them, and others turning to conspiracy. During the RUSSIAN CIVIL WAR, one group convened a Committee of Members of the Constituent Assembly at Samara on the Volga, attempting to reconstitute the Constituent Assembly and establish a middle position between 'Red' and 'White' forces on the basis of a radical land programme. Attempts to form a joint Directory with a Kadet-led Provisional Government, however, were suppressed by the 'White' forces who found their proposals too revolutionary. With the Bolshevik victory in the Civil War the Socialist Revolutionaries ceased to be a major force.

The failure of the majority socialist grouping to mobilize support was one of the major features of the course of the RUSSIAN REVOLUTION. Consistently outflanked by LENIN and the Bolsheviks, their lack of support in the towns amongst industrial workers and the split with the Left Socialist Revolutionaries rendered them increasingly ineffective. Not wishing to be associated with counter-revolution, but viewing the Bolsheviks with a mixture of fellow-feeling for them as socialists and distrust of them as adventurists for the October Revolution, they gravely miscalculated the Bolsheviks' ability to establish effective rule and their ruthlessness in suppressing the CONSTITUENT ASSEMBLY. Once the Civil War began, the Socialist Revolutionaries were crushed between the Bolsheviks and the genuinely counter-revolutionary forces of the Whites, never recovering. The victory of the Bolsheviks left them as a broken force. Subsequent Bolshevik attempts were made to brand the Socialist Revolutionaries as ruthless counter-revolutionaries. A 'show trial' in Moscow in June–July 1922 accused leading Socialist Revolutionaries of complicity in the attempt on Lenin's life in August 1918, and most of them were imprisoned. In fact, the Socialist Revolutionaries were often indecisive, genuinely reluctant to abandon their Russian patriotism or their plans for land socialization, leading them to be less ruthless in opposition to the Bolsheviks than was necessary for their survival.

L. Shapiro, *The Origins of the Communist Autocracy* (1965)

**Socialist Unity Party, German.** *See* SED.

**Socialist Workers' Party, Spanish** (Partido Socialista Obrero Espanol; PSOE). Founded in 1879, the PSOE led a precarious existence for decades, not electing its first deputy until 1910. It gained importance during and after World War I, but the PSOE first emerged as a truly key force in the elections of 1931, which made it the largest party of the new SPANISH REPUBLIC. Its support of AZAVA enabled his coalition, rather than a more conservative alternative under LERROUX, to exercise power between 1931 and 1933, and to include in its agenda significant measures of social and agrarian reform. As obstacles appeared to the full implementation of these reforms, however, and as the extraordinary growth of its trade union, the UGT, and the political polarization sweeping Europe during the early 1930s both exerted radicalizing influences, the PSOE under LARGO CABELLERO's leadership began to move away from its collaboration with the left republicans. This led to a breakup of the Azaba coalition, with disastrous consequences in the November 1933 elections for Socialists as well as the middle class leftist parties. Against the new centre-right governments usually headed by Lerroux, the UGT engaged in a fierce battle to preserve the organizational gains it had made in 1931–33, while the PSOE, convinced that the Catholic CEDA party was a fascist organization that would seize power, threatened insurrection if the CEDA were given seats in the cabinet. This happened in October 1934, but the Socialists could make their threat effective only in one northern province. The defeat of the ASTURIAS RISING split the party between followers of Indalecio Prieto, who wanted a return to reformism, and of Caballero, who advocated further radicalism. Although the moderates prevailed in getting the PSOE to join the POPULAR FRONT coalition that won the February 1936 elections, the radicals refused to co-operate with the new Azaza government and thus created fissures which helped weaken the centre-left prior to the outbreak of the CIVIL WAR. The divisions among the Socialists were intensified during the war, partly by conflicts over whether to revolutionize society immediately or concentrate exclusively on the war effort, partly by differences as to what relations to maintain with the increasingly dominant Communists. Caballero's views prevailed until May 1937 when he was ousted; Prieto's turn to be dropped came in April 1938. Only NEGRIN, a pragmatist, continued to hold significant power until the end of the war, and he was denounced by most of his fellow Socialists as a Communist tool. Socialist disunity continued well into the post-war era, among the large exile communities in both Mexico and France.

A new and very different chapter began in 1974 when, led by FELIPE GONZALEZ, young Socialists who had operated clandestinely within Franco's Spain, seized control of the PSOE from aging exiles. They forged close ties with the SOCIALIST INTERNATIONAL and projected an image of a fully modernized democratic socialist party which won them second place in the 1977 elections. In 1982 the PSOE won an absolute majority in both houses of parliament, an unprecedented feat which it repeated in 1986 and again in 1989. During its first decade in power, the PSOE consolidated the transition to democracy begun by ADOLFO SUAREZ in 1976, gave high priority to economic growth, carried out some social reform as well as changes in the educational system. It oversaw Spain's entry into the EEC in 1986 and obtained a successful referendum vote on NATO membership. The pronounced moderation of the PSOE, which Gonzalez had consolidated in 1979 by defeating the radical factions at party congresses, led to charges that it had ceased to be a socialist party, and to great tensions, especially in 1988–9, with the UGT, which felt that worker benefits were being sacrificed to capitalist interests. There was also concern that the PSOE had established a semi-monopoly over political life, as no opposition parties capable of challenging it appeared after 1982. The world had indeed been turned upside-down for the PSOE: from a worker's party it had become primarily a bastion of the middle classes, from excessive factionalism it had become perhaps too monolithic, from repeated failure it had gone on to seeming limitless success.

C. Malefakis, *Agrarian Reform and Peasant Revolution in Spain* (1970)
P. Preston, *The Coming of the Spanish Civil War* (1979)
R. Gillespie, *The Spanish Socialist Party: A History of Factionalism* (1989)

**Solidarity.** Polish trade union and political organization, founded in 1980. The attempt in the summer of 1980 by the Polish government led by EDWARD GIEREK to break the economic deadlock in the country by cutting subsidies and raising food prices provoked a wave of opposition, as similar measures had in 1970–1 and 1976. As before, one of the major sources of unrest was the industrial area along the Baltic coast, including the large Lenin Shipyard at Gdansk. There a strike was called on 14 August against a general background of unrest, but specifically provoked by the sacking of a crane operator who was also a popular workers' leader. The strike led to the formation of a new organization, known as Solidarity (Solidarnosc), led by a shipyard electrician, LECH WALESA. Initial demands included the legalization of 'free' trade unions and the right to strike, but were widened by the support of intellectual dissidents, including the Workers' Defence Committee (KOR) which had supported and assisted strikers in 1976, the backing of the Catholic Church, and even of some Communist Party members. On 31 August the Polish Government signed the Gdansk Agreement with Walesa, legalizing independent trade unions, sanctioning the right to strike and better conditions, and also making commitments about freedom of speech and the broadcast of religious services.

In September Gierek was replaced by Stanislaw Kania, an experienced trade union official who it was hoped would be able to deal with the new conditions. Solidarity, however, began to take on more of the character of a mass movement. Its formal establishment in September by 250 delegates of unofficial trade unions was overtaken by the formation of Solidarity groups in almost every walk of life, including the creation of a 'peasant Solidarity' and mass support amongst the young and middle-class professionals. By September the movement had an estimated 3 million adherents; intensely patriotic, its symbol used the red and white colours of the Polish flag, and was closely identified with and supported by the Catholic Church, so that its rallies and demonstrations represented an often emotional outpouring of Polish nationalism. On 16 December a huge monument was unveiled at Gdansk to the workers killed in the riots of December 1970, attended by representatives of the state, the church and Solidarity.

But during 1981 there was an effective stalemate; Solidarity demanded the full implementation of the Gdansk agreement while the government dragged its feet and attempted to contain an explosion of independent activity which gave the Solidarity movement an estimated 9 million adherents by the middle of the year. Further strikes and unrest in the summer did not bring about an effective political solution to Poland's problems. Solidarity could veto vir-

tually any political initiative on the part of the government, but did not itself possess or have means of obtaining governmental power. Meanwhile the Polish economy was on the verge of collapse, with foreign debts of $20 million, crippling shortages of food and fuel, and increasing disorganization in the factories, where some Solidarity unions had begun to take over management. Amidst growing tension in which Soviet intervention was being widely canvassed, the new Communist Party leader General JARUZELSKI, who had taken over from Kania in October, attempted to prohibit Solidarity gatherings and accused them of a plot to overthrow the government. It is clear that Jaruzelski had obtained Moscow's support, if not its instructions, for an attempt to restore 'order', gambling on the prestige of the Polish army to command allegiance and forestall major resistance.

On 13 December 1981 martial law was declared, Solidarity and kindred organizations were banned, and leading dissidents, including Walesa, were detained. Jaruzelski's actions proved effective in the short term in defusing a growing crisis of legitimacy for the Polish communist leadership. The Solidarity movement was effectively decapitated, driven underground and demoralized. Attempted demonstrations in Gdansk, Warsaw and Cracow in August 1982, the second anniversary of Solidarity, were broken up by police, but by the end of the year conditions were sufficiently calm for Walesa to be released from detention and martial law to be lifted.

Now much weakened and still illegal, Solidarity attempted to organize a boycott of government plans to set up 2,500 legally registered workplace-based unions in January 1983, but found it difficult to recapture the mass support of 1980–81. Solidarity was kept alive by its clandestine organization and by the support of the Catholic Church. The Pope's visit to Poland in June 1983 was used as an occasion to show the Solidarity emblem, and Walesa himself received international recognition by the award of the Nobel Peace Prize at the end of the year. The killing of the pro-Solidarity priest Father Popieluszko by two secret policemen in October 1984 served to reinforce the link between the Catholic Church and Solidarity, further emphasized when Walesa was granted a personal audience with the Pope, effectively putting him under papal protection. By the time of the Pope's return to Poland in June 1987 the blessing he gave to the movement was a much-needed boost to morale when strife had arisen between different factions. In September 1986 Walesa had announced his willingness to work within the system, but his pragmatic, trade unionist outlook was at odds with some of Solidarity's more intellectual and dogmatic supporters who sought to overthrow the communist-dominated system.

By 1987 the suppression of Solidarity had not solved any of Poland's fundamental difficulties. The advent of GORBACHEV in the Soviet Union suggested there was more room to manoeuvre than in the past, and foreign support for Solidarity from the United States and West Germany indicated that any further assistance with credits and Poland's debt crisis might require concessions. Moreover, Solidarity played a major part in frustrating Jaruzelski's attempt to obtain a positive referendum vote in November 1987 on a package of reforms. When this was rejected, the Polish government was faced with little option in the long term but to open talks with the banned organization. Strikes in spring and summer 1988, not only in the usual Baltic cities, but also in the hitherto peaceful Silesian coalfields, led to the first approaches. In December the Polish government finally indicated it would open serious talks with Solidarity. Formal discussions began on 6 February 1989, and on 5 April Solidarity and the government signed an agreement legalizing Solidarity and setting out terms for its participation in the forthcoming elections. Under the agreement Solidarity would be allowed to contest the minority of seats open to free election in the Sejm lower house of Parliament and all the seats for a freely-elected Senate.

In May 1989 Solidarity effectively began to campaign as a political party, with Walesa launching an election rally at Gdansk. In the two-tier elections to the new National Assembly of Senate and Sejm in June 1989, Solidarity won a landslide victory, taking 260 of the 261 seats it was allowed to contest. Although General Jaruzelski retained the presidency on 19 July by a one-vote margin, his attempts to set up a

communist-led government were defeated. At the end of August a Solidarity-led government was formed, led by an ex-journalist and activist Tadeuz Mazowiecki. Walesa took no formal position in the government, but soon adopted the role of its spokesman, travelling to Britain and the United States to appeal for economic support for Poland. He was re-elected Chairman of Solidarity in Spring 1990 and declared his intention to run for President. An acrimonious campaign split Solidarity into factions, but Walesa was elected in December 1990, defeating his former colleague Mazowiecki.

N. Ascherson, *The Polish August* (1981)
T. Garton Ash, *The Polish Revolution: Solidarity, 1980–1982* (1982)

**Solzhenitsyn, Alexander** (1918–). Soviet writer and DISSIDENT. He studied mathematics at Rostov University, but also obtained a degree in literature. He served as an artillery officer in the Second World War and was twice decorated for bravery. Arrested in February 1945 for his criticism of STALIN, he was sentenced to eight years in exile in Siberia, before returning to teaching in 1956. He was rehabilitated in 1957, and at the height of Khrushchev's DE-STALINIZATION campaign in 1962 he published *A Day in the Life of Ivan Denisovich*, his account of life in the labour camps, which caused a sensation both in the West and in the Soviet Union. In the subsequent reaction he was criticized for his other novels which depicted the corruption of Soviet life; he was forced to publish abroad or in SAMIZDAT. He was awarded the Nobel Prize for Literature in 1970 but was expelled from the Writers' Union and deported in 1974 following the publication in the West of his account of the history of the labour camps, *The Gulag Archipelago* (1971–3). He then lived in Switzerland and later in America. Acknowledged as one of Russia's greatest living writers, Solzhenitzyn was one of the most prominent non-Jewish dissidents, belonging to a current of Russian thought which looked to a reawakening of spiritual values and a revival of the Russian Orthodox Church. His *Letter to the Soviet Leaders* published in 1974 in the West calls for the return to an essentially Russian tradition and a rejection of Western, secular values.

Zh. Medvedev, *Ten Years after Ivan Denisovich* (1973)
G. Hosking, *Beyond Socialist Realism: Soviet Fiction since 'Ivan Denisovich'* (1980)
J. Dunlop, *The Faces of Contemporary Russian Nationalism* (1983)

**Somme, Battle of the.** FIRST WORLD WAR battle on the WESTERN FRONT, launched by HAIG on 1 July 1916. Planned as a largely British offensive, with French support, the operation was delayed by the VERDUN battle. Meticulous preparation and a seven-day artillery bombardment failed to prevent the German defenders inflicting massive casualties on the attackers. By the end of the first day, the British had lost 57,000 casualties, 19,000 of them killed – the heaviest loss by British forces in any single day of fighting. Subsequent attacks failed to achieve the objective of breaking the German lines, the deepest penetration being only five miles. Further offensives degenerated into costly battles for major German strongholds. When the battle ended on 18 November it had cost the British 420,000 casualties, the Germans, 400,000 and the French, 195,000 for no tangible gain. Led by Haig with stubborn faith in an eventual breakthrough and comprising many of the volunteer battalions raised by KITCHENER in the first months of the war, the Somme became synonymous with the futility of the conflict on the Western Front. *See also*: HAIG.

A. H. Farrar-Hockley, *The Somme* (1964)
M. Middlebrook, *The First Day on the Somme* (1971)

**South Tyrol Dispute.** By the terms of the TREATY OF ST GERMAIN between the Allies and Austria-Hungary the southern part of the Tyrol, including a sizeable minority of German speakers, was transferred to Italy. The South Tyrol question has remained a bone of contention between Austria and Italy ever since. Despite good relations with MUSSOLINI neither DOLLFUSS nor HITLER was able to resolve the issue in Austria's favour, and the Nazis even evolved plans for resettling the South Tyrolese Germans in Burgundy, Poland or the Soviet Union. After the Second World War Austrian hopes of a reunification of the Tyrol were dashed, and although the terms of an Austro-Italian agreement provided Bozen (Bolzano) province with autonomous powers, these were largely cancelled by the incorporation of the area into the Italian province of Trentino–Alto Adige, created by the Italian constitution of 1948, in which Italians outnumbered German speakers by two to one. After Austria achieved independence in 1955 Vienna attempted to persuade the Italians to review the situation, and took the matter to the United Nations in 1960. In 1961, against the background of a bombing campaign in the area, Italy set up a committee to deal with the situation. This committee reported in 1964, and its recommendations were incorporated into an agreement of 1969, which extended Bozen's autonomous powers and permitted the use of German as an official language. The agreement was ratified by both parliaments in December 1969.

A. E. Alcock, *The History of the South Tyrol Question* (1970)
M. Toscano, *Alto Adige – South Tyrol* (1975)

**Soviets.** Soviets (or Councils) had sprung into existence in Russia during the 1905 Revolution as virtually spontaneous bodies to express and organize working-class support in particular localities. Usually known as Soviets of Workers' Deputies, they were elected by factory assemblies; in rural areas these were paralleled by peasant soviets. Prior to 1914 most Marxists and socialists saw the soviets as having a crucial part to play in representing workers' interests in any future revolution, though only a faction, the Socialist Revolutionary 'Maximalists', seem to have envisaged them as the basis for power. Most soviets which had emerged in 1905 had, in fact, sought the calling of a Constituent Assembly and had acted as a form of local trades union council to press their economic and social demands.

With the February Revolution in Russia in 1917 soviets sprang up in hundreds of towns, cities and rural regions. The most important were in Petrograd and Moscow. The former was convened by a Provisional Executive Committee of intellectuals, Duma deputies and socialists, who called on workers and soldiers to send delegates to the Tauride Palace. Known as the Petrograd Soviet of Workers' and Soldiers' Deputies, it was in session by 12 March, acting as a parallel representative of lower-

class interests to the PROVISIONAL GOVERN-
MENT. Although later to be identified with
Bolshevik power, the early soviets were
dominated by the SOCIALIST REVOLUTIONARY
PARTY and MENSHEVIKS. Initially the soviets
were seen as representing working-class
interests while awaiting the next stage of
the revolution. An important and novel
component, however, was the presence of
soldiers' representatives, giving the soviets
direct access to armed force in what was an
increasingly confused political situation.

The first All-Russian Congress of Soviets,
which met in June 1917, represented over
400 soviets and confirmed the authority of
the Petrograd Soviet, paralleled by a congress of peasant soviets. The most important political development was the enunciation by Lenin in the APRIL THESES of the
doctrine of 'All power to the soviets', a
radical call which began a lengthy battle for
control of the soviets between the Bolsheviks and the other Marxist and socialist factions. As late as June the Mensheviks and
SRs held a clear majority even in Petrograd,
but as they became compromised by their
support for the Provisional Government the
Bolsheviks gained the ascendency. By September there were as many as 900 soviets
in all and, as significant, Bolsheviks had
increased their support to something near
a majority in the Petrograd and Moscow
bodies.

The second All-Russian Congress of Soviets, which met on 7 November, secured
majorities to legitimize the Bolshevik seizure of power on behalf of the Soviets of
Workers, Soldiers and Peasant Deputies.
On the 8th an all-Bolshevik Council of People's Commissars (Sovnarkam), responsible
to the Congress and its Central Executive
Committee, was set up with Lenin as chairman, to exercise 'government power'. In
effect, rule by the soviets was now to be
carried on very largely by the Bolsheviks,
with other groups either refusing to participate or being expelled. Nonetheless, the
soviets were the essential organs in the constitution confirmed at the fifth All-Russian
Congress of Soviets on 10 July 1918. The
Congress was defined as the supreme legislature and was to be elected indirectly by
urban and rural soviets. The Central Executive Committee was to hold supreme power
in between meetings of the Congress, while

the Council of People's Commissars was
entrusted with the 'general direction' of
public affairs. Local soviets were to be
directly elected and were given their own
executive committees. As a result the soviets had been transformed from *ad hoc*
workers' councils to the governing institutions of the new Soviet state, although
clearly under firm political direction from
the Bolsheviks.

See also RUSSIAN REVOLUTION; LENIN,
VLADIMIR.

L. Shapiro, *The Government and Politics of the Soviet
Union* (2nd edn, 1967)
M. Fainsod and J. Hough (eds.), *How the Soviet Union
is Governed* (1979)

**Soviet Union.** *See* UNION OF SOVIET SOCIALIST
REPUBLICS.

**Sozialdemokratische Partei Deutschlands
(SPD).** *See* SOCIAL DEMOCRATIC PARTY,
GERMAN.

**Sozialistische Einheitspartei.** *See* SED.

**Sozialistische Partei Österreichs (SPÖ).** *See*
SOCIAL DEMOCRATIC WORKERS' PARTY, AUS-
TRIAN.

**Spaak, Paul-Henri** (1899–1972). Belgian
statesman. A socialist member of the
Belgian Parliament, he first became a Minister in 1935. He served both as Foreign
Minister and as Prime Minister before the
outbreak of the Second World War, and
after the war was Foreign Minister again
from 1944–9, 1954–7 and 1961–5. He thus
played a vital role in the shaping of all the
European bodies of which Belgium formed
a part, the BENELUX, TREATY OF BRUSSELS
and WESTERN EUROPEAN UNION. He strongly
supported the idea of European unity,
becoming an honorary President of the European Movement in 1946 and the first President of the Consultative Assembly of the
EUROPEAN COAL AND STEEL COMMUNITY in
1952. He played a particularly important
role in the developments which led to the
creation of the EUROPEAN ECONOMIC COM-
MUNITY and EURATOM, and presided over
the meetings in which the TREATY OF ROME
and the Euratom Treaty were drafted.

**Spanish Civil War.** The Spanish Civil War broke out on 17 July 1936 when the Spanish army in Morocco rose as part of a pre-arranged plan. Under the command of General FRANCISCO FRANCO it was able to cross the Straits and take firm control of most of southern Spain by early August. In northern Spain the rebel General MOLA declared martial law in Pamplona and quickly (20–21 July) seized control of Valladolid, Segovia and much of the north, but attempted risings in Madrid and Barcelona were put down by pro-Republican forces. By September 1936 the rebels held much of southern, western and northern Spain, approximately half of the country, but had failed to take the capital, the Basque region, Catalonia and much of eastern Spain. On 1 October Franco was declared Generalissimo and Head of State, and as 'Nationalist' forces moved on Madrid, the Republican government was moved to Valencia. Militarily the situation was that of an army putsch which had been only partly successful. Franco consolidated his position by taking Malaga on 8 February 1937, but failed in repeated attempts to take Madrid between November 1936 and the battle of Guadalajara in March 1937. Instead the Army of the North under Mola turned against the BASQUES, bombing GUERNICA on 26 April and capturing Bilbao on 19 June. Republican forces went over to the offensive at Teruel to avert a new threat to Madrid on 15 December 1937, but were eventually defeated in a gruelling battle that continued until 23 February 1938. In March a Nationalist advance to the sea at Valencia was planned to cut the Republican area in half. On 15 April the Nationalists reached the coast at Vinaroz, cutting Catalonia off from the rest of Republican Spain. During July and August Republican offensives on the Ebro forced Franco to suspend his attack on Valencia. The Battle of the Ebro became an epic struggle in which the two sides struggled savagely against each other until November. Now exhausted, the Republicans gave way at the end of the year before the offensive Franco opened against Catalonia. On 26 January 1939 Barcelona fell to the Nationalist forces, followed a fortnight later by the collapse of resistance in Catalonia. After a period of upheaval in the Republican camp in which attempts were made to obtain peace terms, Valencia and Madrid fell on 28 March. Three days later all fighting ceased.

Sometimes seen as the last great cause, the Spanish Civil War assumed a significance in the international politics of the 1930s which it would be difficult to exaggerate. The effective non-response of the democracies to overt intervention in the Spanish conflict by the fascist and communist powers, part of a desperate attempt to avoid a European conflagration, in fact encouraged HITLER's war plans. It is for this reason that the Spanish Civil War has often been described as the first battle of the SECOND WORLD WAR.

Nonetheless, for all its international ramifications, the civil war was above all a Spanish war, or rather, as has been emphasized in recent historiography, a series of Spanish wars. At root a class struggle, its long-term origins lay in historic divisions between landowners and landless labourers, industrialists and workers, militant Catholics and anti-clericals, military centralists and regionalists. These divisions found their most intense expression during the SECOND REPUBLIC of 1931–6, a reformist experiment which quickly polarized Spanish society between the forces of progress and reaction, and ultimately culminated in General Franco's uprising of July 1936.

There are four inter-related factors – international, political/ideological, military and economic – which explain why Franco and his insurgent forces were eventually able to prevail over the legally constituted Republic. The war assumed an international dimension when Franco's rising, intended as a swift military coup, met unexpectedly determined resistance by Republican forces. With many of his troops trapped in Morocco, the rebel general was forced to call upon Hitler and MUSSOLINI for logistical and military aid. Both dictators responded: Mussolini agreed after initial reluctance to sell twelve bombers, while Hitler readily provided transport aircraft, followed by fighters and volunteer pilots from the LUFTWAFFE. German intervention escalated over the following months, reaching its apogee in April 1937 with the deliberate destruction by the CONDOR LEGION of Guernica in the Basque country.

Officially, such intervention did not exist. The Non-Intervention Agreement of December 1936 involving 27 nations (*see* NON-INTERVENTION COMMITTEE), was designed to ensure that the conflict did not spread beyond Spain. Promoted principally by the British, it worked to the advantage of the rebel insurgents, who were viewed by the Conservative government as less threatening to commercial interests than the Republicans. Britain's position, which was not unanimous, reflected a genuine fear of communist infiltration in Spain, together with instinctual caution and a desire to see German expansionist aims turn eastwards to the Soviet Union. The Republic expected more from France, where LÉON BLUM led a Popular Front coalition government. Blum's personal sympathy, however, foundered on divisions within his own government, which forced him to drop plans to supply the Spanish Republicans with arms. The Republic was therefore forced to turn to the Soviet Union for assistance against the rebels.

The Soviet position, though, was complex. Fearing an attack by Hitler, the Russians were attempting to promote a policy of alliances with Western democratic powers. They were therefore at pains to avoid antagonizing the Germans and also to play down revolutionary aspirations. The Spanish conflict thus emerged as a political embarrassment: Stalin needed to avoid the emergence of another fascist state, but wished to avoid alienating Western powers should he be seen to support a social revolution. He therefore decided, behind the cloak of neutrality provided by the Non-Intervention Agreement, to provide enough arms to keep the Republic alive while sending Soviet agents to Spain to help extinguish any revolutionary aspirations. There thus arose the remarkable historical irony by which the revolutionary elements in the Republican camp were opposed with equal vigour by both fascist-backed and communist-backed forces.

This highlights the second factor in Franco's victory: the political and ideological splits which bedevilled the Republic. Whilst the insurgent rebels were united in what they were fighting against, the Republican forces were divided over what they were fighting for. Some sought to defend the constitution and political institutions of the Second Republic, while others saw the war as a point of departure for social revolution. This led early in the war to a situation of 'dual power', whereby although the Republican state retained formal power, real power lay with a variety of extra-state bodies, peopled by revolutionary elements such as the anarcho-syndicalist CNT and the dissident marxist POUM (*see* CONFEDERACIÓN NACIONAL DEL TRABAJO; PARTIDO OBRERO DE UNIFICACIÓN MARXISTA). Revolutionary experiments in collectivization throughout the Republican zone drastically undermined the government's authority. Collectives embraced land, industry and even the retail trade. In practice, though, they were often marked by indecision and inefficiency, with damaging effects on the Republican war efforts.

Against the revolutionaries stood the Republicans, moderate socialists and the communists, obeying STALIN's orders. The SPANISH COMMUNIST PARTY (PCE), which soon emerged as the one force which could restore order, grew massively as middle-class professionals, smallholders and small businessmen hurried to join it. With the advantage of Stalin's military backing, the PCE was able to impose its wishes on Republican politics, especially in the last months of the term as Premier of the Socialist FRANCISCO LARGO CABALLERO. Although Largo agreed with the objective of dismantling the collectives, he opposed the methods used and was eventually himself forced out of power in May 1937. His position underlines the Republic's central political conundrum, about which bitter debate still rages.

Essentially, the issue hinges on whether victory over Franco was a necessary precursor to revolution, or whether revolution was the only means by which to achieve that victory. While the popular enthusiasm associated with the revolutionaries was a major factor in the Republic's initial resistance, there is no proof that such enthusiasm could have been channelled into victory over Franco. The evidence of the first ten months of the war, during which the Republic lost far more territory than in the remaining 33, suggests that at one level the communists were right to seek the creation of a disciplined army. At another level, however, the brutal means by which they achieved it contributed to widespread disillusionment on the Republican side. In a sinister replication of Soviet anti-Trotskyist PURGES, the POUM revolutionaries were persecuted, culminating in the Barcelona MAY DAYS of 1937.

Largo's refusal to acquiesce in the purge of the POUM led to his replacement by another socialist, Dr JUAN NEGRÍN. Convinced that discipline and Soviet supplies were the only hope of defeating France, Negrín had little option but to follow the communist line of centralization and anti-revolutionary repression. The impact on Republican morale was devastating. Ironically, the first tangible evidence of Soviet involvement, the establishment of the INTERNATIONAL BRIGADES, had acted as a massive boost to morale. The military impact of the Brigaders has often been exaggerated: although they provided much needed manpower, most of their members – in total, some 40,000 volunteers from 53 countries – had no experience of warfare and received only rudimentary training on arrival in Spain. The true importance of the International Brigades lay in counteracting the Republic's sense of isolation.

In fact, however, the very existence of the Brigades highlights the third factor which contributed to Franco's victory: the insurgents held a distinct military advantage in terms of the composition and nature of their troops. Although it is now clear that many regular generals initially claimed loyalty to the Republic, such claims were met with suspicion on account of incidents such as that in Seville, where General Queipo de Llano posed as a loyalist before revealing his true colours in a bloody repression of the city on behalf of the rebels. The Republican war effort was hindered as checks on loyalty were conducted before enlistment to the cause could be sanctioned. Moreover, the makeshift militia units which sprang into existence to defend the Republic were marked by indiscipline and inefficiency. An insistence on democratic decision-making often led to situations in which vital hours were lost in debate; there were even instances of militiamen going home for the weekend while on active service.

Ultimately, the communists were able to seize the military initiative and organize the Popular Army, which became the backbone of the Republican war effort. In spite of its discipline, however, its effectiveness was undermined by the political rivalries endemic to the Republican cause. To maintain their dominance, the communists denied the CNT militia columns adequate weaponry. Moreover, although the Republicans, especially under Chief of Staff Vicente Rojo, often demonstrated superior tactical awareness, the rebels had the advantage of greater manpower and better military equipment. In early 1938 Franco managed to cut off Catalonia from the rest of the Republican zone, compounding the logistical difficulties faced by the legal government. By this stage the Republic was effectively doomed to what was to become a war of attrition which would drag on for another year.

The final factor contributing to Franco's victory was financial. The economic imbalance between the two sides is often underplayed, but the rebels enjoyed several advantages in spite of the Republic's possession of Spain's national gold reserves. These were transferred in October 1936 to the Soviet Union to be held as credit against future arms purchases. This action was largely forced, since other countries refused to deal with the Republic, and the international financial community was firmly on the side of the insurgents. A variety of obstacles, such as refusing to honour or cash cheques and grant exchange, was placed in the way of official Republican arms purchasers. Moreover, Franco was granted extensive credit facilities by both Germany and Italy, while certain individuals, such as the millionaire smuggler and financier, Juan March, provided hefty donations to his cause. Several international companies, such as Texas Oil, Shell and Texaco, did illegal, but lucrative, business with Franco throughout the war. The insurgents were also able to export wheat and other foods in return for foreign exchange, whilst the Republicans, physically concentrated in areas normally dependent on manufacturing, were deprived of raw materials and therefore had nothing to trade.

There has been a vast amount written on the Spanish Civil War, much of it of an extremely partisan nature. A continuation of the war in words, often generating more heat than light, was ensured by Franco's lack of accommodation to Republican sympathizers throughout his 36-year dictatorship. 'Official' regime histories were rebutted by supporters of the Republic, in turn themselves bitterly divided over the role of the communists during the war. The 50th anniversary of the outbreak of the war produced a considerable outpouring of literature, but little in the way of consensus on the central issues. See also AZAÑA, MANUEL, SECOND REPUBLIC, SPANISH.

H. Thomas, *The Spanish Civil War* (3rd edn, 1977)
R. Fraser, *Blood of Spain* (1979)
P. Preston 'War of Words: The Spanish Civil War and The Historians', in P. Preston (ed.), *Revolution and War in Spain, 1931–39* (1984)
R. Carr, *The Civil War in Spain* (1986)
P. Preston, *The Spanish Civil War* (1986)

**Spartacist League.** Radical political grouping, led by ROSA LUXEMBURG and KARL LIEBKNECHT, within the USPD (*see* USPD) following the latter's split from the GERMAN SOCIAL DEMOCRATIC PARTY in April 1917. Containing internationalist and extreme left-wing members of the pre-war SPD, the Spartacist league opposed the SPD's continuing support for the German war effort and called for peace and domestic revolution. With the GERMAN REVOLUTION of 1918–19, the League emerged as the most left-wing of the political groupings in November 1918, pressing for an alliance of revolutionary Germany with the USSR, the transfer of power to the workers' and soldiers' councils and the socialization of large industrial concerns as well as of big agricultural estates. With a tiny membership, the League enjoyed little support amongst the workers' and soldiers' councils and turned to the organization of street demonstrations. The League merged with Bremen-based left-wing radicals in late December 1918 to form the GERMAN COMMUNIST PARTY, which led an abortive uprising in January 1919 against the German transitional government. The suppression of the uprising, and the murder of Luxemburg and Liebknecht by a FREIKORPS unit, was to leave a bitter legacy of division within the German labour movement throughout the WEIMAR REPUBLIC.

J. P. Nettl, *Rosa Luxemburg* (2 vols., 1966)

A. J. Ryder, *The German Revolution of 1918* (1967)

**SPD.** Sozialdemokratische Partei Deutschlands. See SOCIAL DEMOCRATIC PARTY, GERMAN.

**Special Air Service** (SAS). A specialized unit of the British army involved in anti-terrorist and other clandestine activity, formed out of the Long Range Desert Patrol Group of the Second World War and the Artists' Rifles. The regiment came to public prominence in August 1980 when it successfully stormed the Iranian embassy in London, which had been taken over by 7 gunmen who took 24 people hostage. Six gunmen were killed and one captured. Members of the SAS were also engaged in recapturing the Falkland Islands from the Argentinians in 1982. In 1988 they were involved in the controversial killing of three Irish terrorists in Gibraltar, giving rise to the claims of a 'shoot to kill' policy on the part of the British anti-terrorist forces.

T. Geraghty, *Who Dares Wins* (1980)

**Speer, Albert** (1905–81). German architect and Minister for Armaments and War Production in Nazi Germany. Born into an upper-middle class family in Mannheim, Speer studied architecture in Karlsruhe, Munich and Berlin. He joined the NAZI PARTY in January 1931. From 1933 he received a number of architectural commissions from the Nazi leadership, including overall responsibility for the stage-management of the NUREMBERG RALLIES, the design of the new Reich Chancellery in Berlin and of the party headquarters in Munich. Speer gradually developed a close relationship with HITLER, who charged him in 1937 with rebuilding Berlin and other German cities in the neoclassical style which he favoured. On the death of Fritz Todt in February 1942 Speer was appointed Minister of Armaments and Munitions; his authority being widened in September 1943 when he was appointed Minister of Armaments and War Production. Building on the policy initiatives of Todt, Speer sought the fullest mobilization of the industrial economy for war and pressed unsuccessfully for the conscription of women for war work. He also clashed on a number of occasions with the Nazi regional potentates, the GAULEITER, and with the SS (*see* SS), which was building up an economic empire under its sole direction. Under Speer, armaments and munitions production rose dramatically after 1942, reaching a peak in summer 1944. The key to Speer's success was his extension of the involvement of businessmen and experts in the administration of war production, reserving to himself and his ministerial staff only strategic economic decisions and the creation in key areas of production of special working groups, such as the 'fighter staff' established in 1944 to maximize the output of fighter aircraft. His concentration of economic power and his proximity to Hitler made Speer a central figure in the Nazi regime by 1943–4, though his lack of control over manpower allocation and the ability of party potentates to thwart his plans for total economic mobilization set clear limits to that power. From the summer of 1944 Speer's influence waned as GOEBBELS came to dominate preparations in 1944–5 for the regime's last-ditch stand; and by the spring of 1945 he was actively resisting the 'scorched earth' policy ordered by Hitler. Alone amongst the Nazi leaders, Speer acknowledged his guilt during the NUREMBERG TRIALS, and accepted his responsibility for the employment of slave labourers in German industry during the war. He was sentenced to 20 years' imprisonment for crimes against humanity. Released in 1966, he published two volumes of memoirs. He died in 1981. A technocrat rather than an ideological fanatic, Speer claimed in his memoirs to have been ignorant until late in the war of the Nazi mass-murder of the Jews. He was a model of the 'apolitical' functionary whose willingness to submit his expertise to the dictates of Hitler made possible the horrors of the Third Reich. See also SECOND WORLD WAR.

A. S. Milward, *The German Economy at War* (1965)
A. Speer, *Inside the Third Reich* (1970)

*Spiegel* **Affair.** West German political crisis of 1962. When the West German magazine *Der Spiegel* published an article critical of the German army, the Defence Minister, FRANZ-JOSEF STRAUSS had the deputy editor and the writer of the article tried for treason for publishing military secrets. They were acquitted and Strauss was accused of abus-

ing his powers because he had not used the usual legal channels and not informed the Minister of Justice. The affair was seen to cast doubt upon the stability and democratic character of the West German state. It led to the resignation of Strauss. The repercussions of the affair forced the resignation of Chancellor ADENAUER in October of the following year.

**SPÖ.** Sozialistische Partei Österreichs. *See* SOCIAL DEMOCRATIC WORKERS' PARTY, AUSTRIAN.

**SS** (Schutzstaffeln). Literally 'guard detachments', the armed political élite formations of Nazi Germany. Originating in the personal bodyguard established by HITLER in 1922–3, the SS was established in summer 1925 to protect NAZI PARTY leaders and political meetings. Organizationally part of the SA (*see* SA), the expansion of the SS began in earnest only after the appointment of HIMMLER as its leader in January 1929. As the SA increased in size and assumed a more 'proletarian' character, the SS after 1930 took over an élite role within the Nazi party, attracting former officers and nobles. In the summer of 1932 it gained a monopoly over the supply of political intelligence within the Nazi Party. It played an important role in the Nazi seizure of power in 1933, intimidating and arresting opponents of the new regime. With the extension of Himmler's power over political police forces in Germany during 1933–4, the influence of the SS was extended. It played a major role in the 'NIGHT OF THE LONG KNIVES' purge of the SA leadership in June 1934, and was rewarded by Hitler with independent organizational status in July 1934. In succeeding years the SS was to provide the Nazi regime with a very effective apparatus for political repression: eschewing both the crude and disruptive grass-roots violence of the SA and its frequent confrontations with state authority, the SS was to develop a bureaucratic terror machine and to seek to infiltrate the machinery of the state.

With Himmler's appointment as 'Chief of the German Police' in June 1936, the SS was to establish growing control over all aspects of law and order, and to complete its monopoly of control of the concentration camp system, which contained 25,000 inmates by 1939. The period 1937–9 also witnessed the formation of the SS 'Death's Head' units – SS military divisions. With the outbreak of war in 1939 the power of the SS increased dramatically. By the end of the war the concentration camp population had expanded to 800,000 and included prisoners-of-war and hostages from the occupied territories. The SS exploited camp inmates to establish a considerable economic empire by the later stages of the war. From 1943 onwards the SS gained almost total control over law and order within Germany. During the Second World War SS divisions – the WAFFEN-SS (Armed SS) – were to fight alongside the regular German armed forces, and the SS was charged with the implemenation of brutal Nazi occupation policies in Poland and the USSR. In autumn 1939 SS special task forces (*Einsatzgruppen*) carried out a murderous 'purge' of the Polish middle classes in areas of pre-war Poland incorporated into Germany; in the 'General Government' (occupied Poland), the SS was to become virtually a state within the state and participated in the savage suppression of the WARSAW RISING of August–October 1944. SS *Einsatzgruppen* were also deployed in the USSR after the invasion of June 1941, and were charged with the arrest and execution of broad groups deemed to be hostile to the occupying Germans. The initiation of mass shootings of Jews in the USSR in summer 1941 by the *Einsatzgruppen* paved the way for the emergence of the Nazi 'Final Solution' of the 'Jewish Problem' – the HOLOCAUST. The SS controlled the 'extermination camps' established in occupied Poland in which the mass murder of the European Jews was carried out. *See also* EICHEMANN, ADOLF; HEYDRICH, REINHARD.

H. Krausnick *et al.*, *Anatomy of the SS State* (1968)
J. Noakes and G. Pridham (eds.), *Nazism, 1919–1945*, vol. 3: *Foreign Policy, War and Racial Extermination* (1988)

**Stakhanovite.** Term used to describe heroic overfulfilment of production quotas, from Alexei Stakhanov (1906–77), who in 1935 in the Donbass hewed 102 tonnes of coal in a single shift instead of the 7 prescribed. The feat was a publicity stunt achieved by halting all other production and reorganizing the work team to allow Stakhanov to vastly outperform the norm. Stakhanov's 'achievement' and the publicity given to it were part of a campaign to boost industrial production under the second FIVE YEAR PLAN. Similar stunts were orchestrated elsewhere to inculcate an ethic of high production norms in which 'Stakhanovite' workers were awarded higher pay, better conditions and public recognition. The drive to overfulfil targets was part of the almost hysterical atmosphere surrounding the production levels aimed at in the plans; the readiness of STALIN to reward Stakhanovites with higher rewards than the average workers was a significant break with strictly socialist standards of reward, and increasingly typical of the Stalin era.

R. W. Davies, *The Industrialisation of Soviet Russia* (2 vols., 1980)

**Stalin, Josef** (1879–1953). Soviet dictator. His original name was Djugashvili. Born near Gori, Georgia, the son of a cobbler, he was educated in a seminary at Tiflis but was expelled for his political activities in 1899. Twice exiled to Siberia, he also spent some time in London and Vienna. On escaping from Siberia after the February Revolution he became editor of PRAVDA and worked with Lenin in Petrograd. Following the October Revolution he was given special responsibilities as First Commissar for Nationalities. In 1922 he was appointed General-Secretary of the party's Central Committee. Although LENIN expressed misgivings about him, he died before Stalin could be removed. Stalin used his administrative position to build up a powerful place for himself in the power struggles which followed Lenin's death. He enlarged the Central Committee with his supporters and used it as a counterweight to the Politburo; he strengthened the Secretariat, using it to promote his followers and gain control of many local party organizations, who in turn elected delegates to party conferences. Allying first with ZINOVIEV and KAMENEV to defeat TROTSKY, then with BUKHARIN and RYKOV to defeat his former allies, he then attacked them in turn. By 1925 he had already defeated Trotsky's internationalism and had his own interpretation of the course of the revolution, 'SOCIALISM IN ONE COUNTRY', accepted as the party line. Using that as justification he set about the industrialization of the Soviet Union and the collectivization of agriculture (*see* COLLECTIVIZATION, SOVIET) via the First FIVE YEAR PLAN. Although some of the chaos and disruption of collectivization was not entirely Stalin's responsibility, he showed little scruple for the campaign against the KULAKS which accompanied its early stages, and was apparently indifferent to the sufferings of those caught up in the process of transforming the Soviet economy. Having already embarked on a process of discrediting possible rivals and depriving them of political power, he launched a series of PURGES from 1934 which cost millions of lives amongst party members, the armed forces, the professions and the security apparatus. At the same time, Stalin launched a major campaign to 'Sovietize' the country, tightening control on ethnic minorities, suppressing religious expression and curtailing freedom in the arts. He increasingly emphasized his own interpretations of 'Marxist-Leninism-Stalinism', in which his own doctrines were placed in direct succession to those of Lenin. Traces of the influences of other Bolsheviks, such as Trotsky, were removed from the record, and the CULT OF PERSONALITY of Stalin elevated to an almost quasi-religious degree.

In foreign policy Stalin turned the COMINTERN into an instrument of Soviet foreign policy, forcing national parties to conform to the 'Moscow Line'. With the growing threat of fascism, Stalin inaugurated the 'Popular Front' policy from 1933, attempting to achieve broad-based anti-fascist alliances. Stalin sought to encourage a stand against fascism by intervening in the SPANISH CIVIL WAR, concluding an alliance with France in 1935, and offering to support Czechoslovakia over the SUDETENLAND crisis. Finally despairing of Western readiness to confront HITLER, he signed the NAZI–SOVIET PACT in 1939. Following Hitler's invasion of Poland, Stalin operated the secret provisions of the Pact to seize eastern Poland, BESSARABIA and the BALTIC STATES, later incorporating them into the USSR. Stalin, however, almost fatally misread German intentions, and was taken by surprise by the German invasion of June 1941.

Following a succession of crushing defeats, Stalin, as Commissar of Defence, directed the Soviet war effort and rallied the Soviet people by a mixture of coercion and the evocation of traditional Russian resistance to invaders. Some relaxation towards the churches and in the practice of collectivization were accompanied by wholesale deportations of ethnic groups deemed a threat to national security. After the disasters of 1941 and over-hasty counterattacks in 1942 which cost millions of Russian lives, Stalin became an effective generalissimo, directing the campaigns which finally defeated the Nazis on the Eastern Front and took the Russian armies to Berlin in 1945.

In the wartime alliance with Britain and the United States, differences soon developed which were to form the basis of the COLD WAR. Stalin's impatience with delays in opening a second front, his desire to affect the reshaping of the post-war map of Europe in the Soviet Union's favour, and his determination to destroy German power once and for all surfaced in differences at the war-time meetings at the TEHERAN CONFERENCE, the YALTA CONFERENCE and the POTSDAM CONFERENCE. Stalin succeeded in negotiating agreements which after 1945 left much of Poland and the Baltic States in his hands, and set up socialist states in Eastern Europe which, apart from Yugoslavia under TITO, effectively followed Moscow's bidding until the time of his death.

Domestically, Stalin reimposed a rigid orthodoxy on a devastated country after 1945. Wartime concessions in agriculture were reversed, and any signs of potential opposition were ruthlessly crushed by Stalin and his head of security, BERIA. Two months before his death in March 1953, Stalin began what appeared to be a fresh round of purges in the so-called DOCTOR'S PLOT, aimed primarily at Jewish doctors charged with having conspired to murder the head of the Leningrad Party organization.

Stalin was the dominant figure in modern Soviet history, presiding over the country's rise from a weak, post-revolutionary state to a nuclear superpower. KHRUSHCHEV's secret speech to the 20th Party Congress in 1956 began a process of reassessment of Stalin which continues to this day. Responsible through the campaign against the Kulaks, forced collectivization and the purges for the deaths of between 12 and 20 million people, plus those deported and killed from Poland, the Baltic States and parts of the Soviet Union during the war, he stands with Hitler as one of the greatest mass murderers in 20th-century history. Current evidence suggests that it was his very 'greyness' and apparent moderation in inter-party disputes which allowed him to secure a grip on the party in the 1920s against more intelligent and prominent rivals. Once established in a position of power, he used it ruthlessly to impose his own vision of socialist development on the Soviet Union. Stalin skillfully manipulated the authoritarian tendencies within Bolshevism to secure conformity to his views and then turned on the party and other sources of potential opposition to leave him in unchallenged power by 1940. He also brought about an influx of new members into the party, creating his own following, while the Five Year Plans and the modernization of the country evoked much admiration at home and abroad. The purges, especially in the military, did much to disillusion foreign appreciations of Soviet strength as well as genuinely disorganizing the armed forces. Nevertheless, it was only the huge advances in industrial production under the Five Year Plans which enabled the Soviet Union to survive the war. Stalin's later years were noted for their rigid orthodoxy, obsessive suppression of rivals, and almost total subservience to his 'cult of personality'. Modern interpretations note that Stalin combined a highly personal dictatorship with the far-reaching power of an ideology. His rule is understandable only in terms which recognize the ability of Stalin to harness the idealism and commitment of communists at home and abroad while deploying the almost unprecedented power of a modern authoritarian state able to use direct force, bureaucracy, propaganda and ideological monopoly to sustain it. Almost from his death, the Soviet Union has been trying to come to terms with his legacy both for the evolution of communism and for the political, economic and ideological character of the Soviet state. *See also* SECOND WORLD WAR.

R. Payne, *The Rise and Fall of Stalin* (1966)

R. C. Tucker, *Stalinism: Essays in Historical Interpretation* (1977)
G. A. Hosking, *A History of the Soviet Union* (1985)
R. H. McNeal, *Stalin: Man and Ruler* (1988)
R. Medvedev, *Let History Judge: The Origins and Consequences of Stalinism* (2nd edn, 1989)

**Stalingrad, Battle of.** Major battle of the SECOND WORLD WAR on the eastern front, arising from the advance on the southern front in summer 1942 by General von Paulus's German 6th Army. Aiming for the Caucasus in pursuit of HITLER's geo-strategic objective of obtaining oil supplies, the German forces were halted at Stalingrad from September 1942 unable to dislodge its defenders. A Russian counter-offensive in November encircled the German and allied forces. Hitler ordered von Paulus to hold his ground and await relief, but the relieving forces were beaten back leaving von Paulus trapped. Attempts at air supply proved insufficient for the quarter of a million men in the pocket, forcing von Paulus to accept terms for surrender on 2 February 1943. Almost 100,000 surviving Germans went into captivity, the greatest defeat suffered by the German army up to that point of the war. The defeat has variously been blamed on Hitler's over-ambitious plan for the campaign of 1942 and his failure to respond rationally by allowing von Paulus to withdraw, the under-estimation of the Soviet forces' ability to launch a major offensive, and the over-confidence of GOERING that the LUFTWAFFE could supply the encircled army. A defeat which could not be concealed from the German people, Stalingrad marked a decisive turning point in committing the German economy to TOTAL WAR in the face of resurgent Soviet forces.

J. Erickson, *The Road to Stalingrad* (1975)
J. Erickson, *The Road to Berlin* (1983)

**Stalinism.** Term used generally to describe the most rigid and doctrinaire form of MARXIST-LENINISM associated with the name of JOSEF STALIN. It implies absolute obedience to the party line and its hierarchy, and complete conformity to the precepts laid down by the party in all walks of life. Following the policies and practices employed by Stalin it is associated with the use of terror, including 'show trials', PURGES and the extensive use of labour camps to discipline DISSIDENTS and opponents. In practice, following on from Stalin's doctrine of 'SOCIALISM IN ONE COUNTRY', it also implied the subservience of communist movements elsewhere to the requirements of Soviet foreign policy. The term was frequently applied to the most closed and inflexible of the regimes of Eastern Europe established after 1945.

Stalin's own most important theoretical contributions to Marxist-Leninism lay in the increasing abandonment of the concept of world-wide revolution for 'Socialism in one country', his exacerbation of the authoritarian tendencies in Marxist-Leninism to the level of personal dictatorship, and the CULT OF PERSONALITY. Stalin's own role and ideology were expounded systematically in the *Short Course on the History of the Communist Party of the Soviet Union* produced in 1938. This identified Stalin, with Lenin, as the author of the October Revolution in 1917 and vilified the other leading Bolsheviks who had been purged during the succeeding 20 years. The *Short Course* became the compulsory ideological text in schools and higher education under Stalin and his successors. *See also* DE-STALINIZATION.

R. N. Carew Hunt, *The Theory and Practice of Communism* (1963)
R. C. Tucker, *Stalinism: Essays in Historical Interpretation* (1977)

**Stamboliski, Alexander** (1879–1923). Bulgarian politician. Born of prosperous peasant stock in south-western Bulgaria, he was elected to the Bulgarian National Assembly in 1908. The dominant figure in the peasant-based Bulgarian Agrarian National Union, he agitated for an end to the monarchy and the creation of a Balkan Federation. Imprisoned in 1915 for opposition to Bulgaria's entry into the First World War, he was released from prison in September 1918 and his good offices were sought to calm disorder amongst the troops in return for Bulgaria's withdrawal from the war. On visiting insurgent troops at Radomir he found himself declared President of the revolutionary Republic, but the episode was ended when the soldiers were defeated by troops loyal to the crown. Following the abdication of King FERDINAND I in October 1918 and the accession of King BORIS III, Stamboliski entered the government, forming his own

Cabinet in October 1919. He acceded on 19 November 1919 to the TREATY OF NEUILLY, by which Bulgaria was reduced in size and forced to pay reparations, but from 1920 sought to establish a radical agrarian regime which economically favoured the peasantry. His foreign policy of friendship and co-operation with the new Yugoslavian government inflamed right-wing and nationalist sentiment, especially over the suppression of the Macedonian terrorist organization IMRO. A military coup on June 1923 toppled his government; he was captured and killed on 14 June 1923.

G. P. Genov, *Bulgaria and the Treaty of Neuilly* (1935)
J. D. Bell, *Peasants in Power: Alexander Stamboliski and the Bulgarian National Union, 1899–1923* (1977)

**START.** *See* STRATEGIC ARMS REDUCTION TALKS.

**Stavisky Affair.** Scandal in the FRENCH THIRD REPUBLIC concerning the issuing of fraudulent bonds by Serge Stavisky, a French citizen of Russian Jewish origin. Stavisky committed suicide on 3 January 1934. Inquiries revealed that Stavisky had contacts in the highest reaches of the French government. The affair was seen as confirming the corrupt and venal character of the Republic, leading to large-scale protests from the right-wing groups, ACTION FRANÇAISE and the Camelots du Roi. The Premier, Chautemps, was eventually forced to resign, but the attempt to form a new government by DALADIER led to serious rioting by the right-wing LEAGUES and several deaths when police opened fire on 6 February. The seriousness of the challenge on the streets, which was seen as a virtual attempted coup by the Right, brought about Daladier's resignation and the formation of a National Union coalition led by the respected former President, Gaston Doumergue (1863–1937)

S. Bernstein, *Histoire du Parti Radical, 1919–1939* (1980–2)
J. F. Macmillan, *Dreyfus to de Gaulle: Politics and Society in France 1898–1969* (1985)

**Steel, David** (1938–). British politician. He was a Liberal MP from 1965 and was leader of the LIBERAL PARTY, 1976–88. He negotiated the LIB-LAB PACT of 1977–8 to maintain Labour government during the devolution referendum campaigns. He supported the formation of THE ALLIANCE with the SOCIAL DEMOCRATIC PARTY (SDP) after its formation in 1981. With DAVID OWEN he was joint leader of the Alliance campaign in 1987 general election, but immediately afterwards he called for a merger of the Liberal Party and the SDP. He negotiated the merger after protracted talks, forming the Social and Liberal Democrats. He did not stand for the leadership of the new party, becoming instead its foreign affairs spokesman.

C. P. Cook, *A Short History of the Liberal Party, 1900–1988* (3rd edn, 1989)
D. Steel, *Against Goliath* (1989)

**Strasser, Gregor** (1982–1934). A leading German politician of the NAZI PARTY during its rise to power. Joining the Nazi party after service during the First World War and membership of a paramilitary FREI-KORPS unit, Strasser participated in the MUNICH PUTSCH. During the mid- and late 1920s, he played an important role in the establishment of the Nazi party in North Germany, yet he often clashed with HITLER as a consequence of his advocacy of a popu-list and nationalist anti-capitalism. Widely regarded as the leading representative of the 'left wing' of the Nazi Party, Strasser was offered the post of Vice-Chancellor by Chancellor SCHLEICHER in December 1932 in an attempt to split the party. Hitler took negotiations between Schleicher and the party out of Strasser's hands and Strasser resigned all of his party offices. Thereafter he withdrew from active politics and was not offered a post in the Nazi government formed after January 1933. He was mur-dered during the 'NIGHT OF THE LONG KNIVES' in 1934.

P. D. Stachura, *Gregor Strasser and the Rise of Nazism* (1983)

**Strategic Arms Limitation Talks** (SALT). The United States and the Soviet Union embarked upon the Strategic Arms Limi-tations Talks at Helsinki in November 1969 with the object of reducing the level of competition between them in strategic nuclear armaments. An agreement on anti-ballistic missile systems and an interim agreement on strategic offensive arms were concluded in Moscow on 26 May 1972. The SALT I agreement froze the number of land-based Intercontinental Ballistic Miss-iles (ICBMs) and submarine-launched bal-listic missiles (SLBMs) at those in service or under construction on 1 July 1972. This allowed the United States its existing total of 1,054 ICBMs and up to 710 SLBMs, and permitted the Soviet Union up to 1,618 ISBMs and 950 SLBMs.

The second phase of the negotiations, SALT II, opened in Geneva on 21 Novem-ber 1972. In talks between President Ford and Chairman BREZHNEV at Vladivostok in November 1974 an agreement was reached, setting out guidelines for a pact to control the strategic arms race up to 1985. These guidelines would allow each side to build up a total of 2,400 strategic delivery vehicles (ICBMs, SLBMs and long-range bombers), with a sub-ceiling of 1,320 for missiles with multiple warheads. However, a definitive treaty met numerous difficulties, including problems of defining the term 'strategic' and of accommodating the Soviet 'Backfire' bomber and the American CRUISE MISSILE in any agreement. The proposals resulting from Henry Kissinger's visit to Moscow in January 1976 were rejected by the United States in February. But in May 1977 Andrei Gromyko and Cyrus Vance agreed on a new framework for talks. Although the SALT I agreement expired on 3 October 1977, the United States and the Soviet Union agreed to abide by its terms for the time being. Agreement was finally reached on SALT II on 18 June 1979 on missile types and numbers, but the Senate refused ratification following the SOVIET INVASION OF AFGHANISTAN. Resumption of strategic arms talks, the STRATEGIC ARMS REDUCTION TALKS (START), began in Geneva on 1 July 1982, both sides agreeing informally to abide by the SALT II levels while further discussions took place. Under these terms the United States was permitted 1,572 laun-chers and 7,920 warheads (2,151 of them on ICBMs) and the USSR 2,367 launchers with 8,395 warheads (6,170 of them on ICBMs). The talks ranged over several pro-posals, including President Reagan's suggestion that a parity be set at 850 launch-ers with 5,000 warheads. The talks, how-ever, stumbled over difficulties of verifi-cation and the place of CRUISE MISSILES in the discussions. Finally, at the Reykjavik Summit on 11–12 October 1986 an initial agreement on strategic nuclear warhead numbers and the eventual banning of all ballistic missiles failed as a result of Soviet concern about the American Strategic Defence Initiative for a defensive system based in outer space. Renewed discussions, however, have led to the promise of major proposals for the reduction of strategic nuclear forces.

L. Freedman, *The Evolution of Nuclear Strategy* (1981)
J. Newhouse, *The Nuclear Age: A History of the Arms Race from Hiroshima to Star Wars* (1989)

**Strategic Arms Reduction Talks** (START). Talks between the USSR and the USA, begun in Geneva in the summer of 1982. Following the refusal of the US Senate to ratify the agreement reached in SALT II (*see* STRATEGIC ARMS LIMITATION TALKS), the USSR refused to enter further negotiations on arms control. But in July 1980 Chancellor SCHMIDT of West Germany visited Moscow and persuaded the USSR to undertake further bilateral talks with the USA, though with the proviso that no new agreement could be made until SALT II was ratified. With the advent of MIKHAIL GORBACHEV, agreements were reached on Intermediate Nuclear Forces in December 1987, clearing the way for renewed talks on strategic weapons. In 1988–9 a series of summit meetings paved the way for outline agreements on cuts in strategic weapons, although a formal treaty remains to be concluded.

**Strauss, Franz-Josef** (1915–88). West German politician. Born in Bavaria, he served as a CHRISTIAN SOCIAL UNION member of the Bundestag, 1947–78, in alliance with ADENAUER'S CHRISTIAN DEMOCRATIC UNION. He served as Minister of Defence, 1956–1962, in which post he recreated the German army. His behaviour in the SPIEGEL AFFAIR forced his resignation and damaged his career. He served as finance minister, 1966–9, and built up a powerful position in Bavaria. He was the unsuccessful Christian Democrat candidate for Chancellor for the 1980 election, serving as Prime Minister of his native Bavaria, 1978–88. He died in October 1988. He pursued a strong COLD WAR rhetoric in his early years, helping to keep together the right-wing conservative forces of the Adenauer

period. In practice he was a pragmatist towards Eastern Europe, visiting Eastern bloc capitals. He wished Germany to have freedom to operate in international affairs like other states, and has sometimes been described as a German 'Gaullist', determined to pursue German national interests and fearful of 'betrayal' by the United States over such issues as Berlin. With too many opponents for much of his career to reach the top, he was often a behind-the-scenes kingmaker in the Christian Democrats. He was also seen as awaiting an opportunity to champion German nationalism which never came in his lifetime.

W. Paterson and A. Thomas, *Social Democratic Parties in Western Europe* (1977)
F.-J. Strauss, *Die Erinnerungen (The Memoirs)* (1989)

**Stresa Front.** Name for agreements arising from the Stresa conference on 11–14 April 1935 attended by the leaders of Italy, Britain and France (MUSSOLINI, MACDONALD and LAVAL) with their respective foreign ministers. They discussed a common front against Germany following HITLER's declaration of his intention to rearm and his public announcement of the development of an air force (*Luftwaffe*), directly contrary to the TREATY OF VERSAILLES. A condemnation of German rearmament was issued, Austria's independence reaffirmed, and the LOCARNO TREATIES upheld. The 'Stresa Front' was undermined from several directions. Hitler went ahead with rearmament, re-establishing a Ministry of War in May 1935. British sought unilateral negotiations on naval strengths with Germany, leading to the ANGLO-GERMAN NAVAL AGREEMENT in June 1935. France sought her own guarantees, signing a treaty of mutual assistance with Russia in May (*see* FRANCO-SOVIET PACT). Italy's invasion of Ethiopia in October 1935 finally destroyed any realistic hope of a common front against Hitler.

H. Gatzke, *European Diplomacy between the Two World Wars* (1972)

**Stresemann, Gustav** (1878–1929). German politician, Chancellor (1923) and Foreign Minister (1923–9) of the WEIMAR REPUBLIC. Born in Berlin, Stresemann was a legal advisor to the League of Saxon Industrialists from 1902. He entered the REICHSTAG as a Deputy for the National Liberal party in 1907, and was a member, 1907–12 and 1914–18. In 1917 he became the parliamentary leader of the National Liberal party. A member of the Pan-German League and an ardent nationalist, during the First World War Stresemann advocated extensive annexations following a German victory; and played a role in the downfall of the vacillating chancellor BETHMANN-HOLLWEG. He simultaneously pressed for the introduction of a truly parliamentary system of government. With defeat and the outbreak of the GERMAN REVOLUTION of 1918–19, Stresemann founded the German People's Party (*see* DVP), a right-wing liberal party representing industrial interests and committed to revision of the TREATY OF VERSAILLES at the earliest opportunity. In 1919–20 he was a member of the constituent National Assembly; and in 1920–9 of the *Reichstag*.

Stresemann led his party into a coalition government at the height of the hyperinflation crisis in August 1923, and was Chancellor from August to November of that year. Concerned to reconstruct a liberal-capitalist economic order in Germany and to contain the working-class movement, he led his party away from its previously intransigent attitude towards the Republic. From 1923 to 1929 he was a key figure in Weimar parliamentary politics, without whose support Chancellors could do little. As Foreign Minister, he played an important role in securing the international cooperation essential for the stabilization of the German economy; in the negotiation of the LOCARNO TREATIES of 1925, stabilizing Germany's relations with her western neighbours; and in German admission to the League of Nations with a seat on the League Council (1926). In 1926 he was awarded the Nobel Peace Prize jointly with ARISTIDE BRIAND for his work for Franco-German reconciliation. His death in 1929 was regarded by many as a great misfortune, removing from Weimar politics one of its outstanding figures.

During the early 1950s Stresemann was widely regarded by historians in a very favourable light as an advocate of international reconciliation and European integration after the First World War. This picture has been modified somewhat, and the dramatic nature of the break between his early strident nationalism and apparent post-war internationalism has been called into question. A fair degree of consensus now exists concerning his political evolution and the central objectives of his foreign policy during the 1920s. Stresemann remained after the First World War, as before, a calculating nationalist and power-politician, concerned to promote Germany's national interest as he perceived it. The prime objective of his foreign policy was the restoration of German sovereignty and 'great power' status on an equal footing with the other European powers. German economic power and the development of close economic ties with the United States were central to his view of Germany's future role in Europe, as was the settlement of international problems by means of negotiation and agreement – unavoidable, in any case, given Germany's military weakness. To this end, he was concerned to satisfy French concerns for security without bringing about a permanent Anglo-French alliance. Stresemann's revisionism certainly extended to Germany's eastern frontiers, although even here he was concerned to proceed by means of negotiation rather than direct confrontation. Less idealistically motivated perhaps than was widely believed to be the case in the 1950s, his pragmatic nationalist foreign policy may nevertheless be sharply distinguished from the overtly aggressive form of revisionism assumed by German foreign policy in the 1930s.

H. A. Turner, *Stresemann and the Politics of the Weimar Republic* (1963)
M. Lee and W. Michalka, *German Foreign Policy 1917–1933: Continuity or Break?* (1987)
E. Kolb, *The Weimar Republic* (1988)

**Suarez, Adolfo** (1932–). Spanish politician. Educated at Salamanca and Madrid Universities, he rose to prominence under FRANCO, acting as Civil Governor of Segovia from 1969 and then as Director-General of Television and Radio, as well as Vice Secretary-General to the FALANGE until 1975, then Secretary-General, 1975–6. Prime Minister and President of the Council of Ministers from 1976 to 1981, he was leader of the Union of the Democratic Centre (UCD), which emerged as the largest party in parliament following the 1977 elections, the first free parliamentary elections for 41 years.

He supervised the new constitution and negotiations for greater autonomy in the regions, as well as submitting Spain's application to join the EEC. Dependence on minor parties for support led him to call an election in March 1979, but he once again failed to secure an overall majority. Early in 1981, under pressure from the right, he resigned, taking the title Duke of Suarez. In August 1982 he founded and headed a new centre party (*Centro Democratico y Social* – CDS), but secured few seats in the 1982 elections and only 19 seats in 1986. The Party continued to lose ground in 1989, with only 14 seats. The last Francoist Prime Minister, Suarez's attempt to bring Spain into a stable democratic structure was remarkably successful, but his political position was undermined by the rise of the Socialist Party to a majority position from 1982 and the rise of the right-wing Popular Alliance as the second major party.

R. Carr and J. P. Fusi, *Spain: Dictatorship to Democracy* (1979)

D. Gilmour, *The Transformation of Spain* (1985)

**Successor States.** States formed after the First World War from the territory of the former Austro-Hungarian Empire or incorporating parts of it. These included Poland, Czechoslovakia, Yugoslavia, Hungary, Romania and Austria.

Z. A. B. Zeman, *The Break-up of the Habsburg Empire, 1914–18* (1961)

**Sudetenland.** Mountainous area between Bohemia and Silesia of some 11,000 square miles. German-speaking, with over 3 million inhabitants, it had been part of the Austro-Hungarian Empire prior to 1918. At the TREATY OF ST GERMAIN it was transferred from Austrian rule to the new state of Czechoslovakia. The question of the transfer of the Sudeten Germans to German rule became an issue after HITLER's rise to power. A Sudeten-German Party led by KONRAD HENLEIN and financed by the Nazis was set up in 1935 and began to agitate for virtual complete independence from the Czech state. Allegations of ill-treatment and discrimination, combined with the effects of heavy unemployment in the area's industrial concerns, provided Hitler with a pretext for demanding its absorption by Germany in 1938. By threatening war, Hitler was able to obtain the MUNICH AGREEMENT, in which Britain and France agreed to the cession of the Sudetenland to Germany. The transfer was effected from 1 October 1938. Czechoslovakia lost most of her frontier defences as a result of the arrangement, several hundred thousand Czechs came under German rule, and the country lost one-third of its export capacity and one-half of its coal and electricity output. In 1945 Czechoslovakia recovered the territory and expelled most of the German-speaking population, resettling it with people from other parts of Czech Bohemia and Moravia.

J. W. Bruegel, *Czechoslovakia before Munich* (1973)

E. M. Smelser, *The Sudeten Problem, 1933–8* (1975)

**Suez Crisis.** Conflict between the Egyptian government led by General Nasser (1918–70) and the West led to the withdrawal of funding for the Aswan High Dam on 19 July 1956. Nasser retaliated by nationalizing the Suez Canal on 26 July. Protracted negotiations for a diplomatic settlement were abandoned when Britain, France and Israel agreed secretly for Israel to attack Egypt, while Britain and France occupied the canal zone on the pretext of separating the combatants. Israel attacked Egypt on 29 October, followed by an Anglo-French ultimatum to Egypt on the following day. British and French planes began to bomb Egyptian targets, and a full-scale invasion by over 8,500 British and French troops followed on 5–6 November. The attack provoked deep divisions in Britain, Prime Minister EDEN facing a storm of protest from the LABOUR PARTY and outrage from many quarters. The attack was also condemned at the United Nations, and the Soviet Union threatened to intervene. As a result of both domestic and foreign protests, the progress of the invasion was halted on 6 November by a cease-fire. Growing pressure from the United States, especially financial, forced the British and French governments to agree to an unconditional withdrawal from Suez on 29 November.

The Suez débâcle exposed Britain's postwar weakness as an attempt to stand up to Nasser was frustrated by lack of domestic support for 'gunboat diplomacy' and the need to operate with the approval of the

United States. The Suez crisis has remained symbolic of Britain's decline as an independent power in a world of strong nationalist movements, a United Nations representing largely post-imperial nations, and the dominant role of the United States. The Suez crisis destroyed Eden's health, career and reputation; he resigned as Prime Minister in January 1957. The affair had less effect on French domestic politics, although it strained Anglo-French relations because of French reluctance to accede to American and world opinion as readily as Britain.

S. Lloyd, *Suez 1956: A Personal Account* (1978)
D. Carlton, *Anthony Eden: A Biography* (1981)
R. Rhodes James, *Anthony Eden* (1986)
H. Thomas, *The Suez Affair* (2nd edn, 1986)

**Suffragettes.** Supporters of the Women's Social and Political Union, founded in 1903, which agitated for the extension of the franchise to women in Britain, and was responsible for a number of criminal offences prior to 1914. Led by Mrs EMMELINE PANKHURST, her daughters Sylvia and Christabel, Mrs Fawcett, Annie Kenney and others, many of them were imprisoned and subjected to the extreme discomfort and indignity of being forcibly fed during prison hunger-strikes. The role of women during the First World War led to British women aged 30 and over being given the vote in 1918; in 1928 the age limit was reduced to 21, the same as that for men.

Controversy centres on the role of the militant tactics employed by the suffragettes in the years before 1914 in hastening or slowing down the possibility of reform. After 1914 Emmeline Pankhurst threw her energies into a patriotic campaign for women to serve the nation's interest in time of war. The acquisition of the vote has been seen as part of a general enfranchisement of the remaining 40 per cent of men, a concession as much to democracy as to the women's movement. The role of the suffragettes is sometimes contrasted with the so-called 'suffragists' who believed in constitutional methods to obtain women's suffrage and adult suffrage in general.

A. Rosen, *Rise up Women! The Militant Campaign of the Women's Social and Political Union, 1903–14* (1974)
M. D. Pugh, *Electoral Reform in War and Peace, 1906–1918* (1978)
——, *Women's Suffrage in Britain, 1867–1928* (1980)
B. Harrison, 'Women's Suffrage at Westminster', in M.

Bentley and J. Stevenson (eds.), *High and Low Politics in Modern Britain: Ten Studies* (1983)

**Suffragistes.** *See* SUFFRAGETTES.

**Sykes-Picot Agreement.** A secret agreement on behalf of the British and French governments through their representatives, Sir Mark Sykes and Georges Picot, signed on 16 May 1916. It defined respective spheres of interest for Britain and France in the non-Turkish parts of the Turkish Empire in the event of Ottoman defeat. The agreement also extended to the partition of parts of mainland Turkey, with Italy, Russia and France obtaining a large part of Turkey proper. The Turks would have been confined to a minor portion of territory in the north and centre of Turkey around Ankara. Although the Sykes-Picot agreement was not fully implemented, its influence was reflected in the dismemberment of Turkey indicated in the TREATY OF SÈVRES and in the allocation of MANDATES to France and Britain in non-Turkish territory. *See also* LAUSANNE, TREATY OF.

**syndicalism.** From the French word for trade unionism. Syndicalism developed in France in the late 19th century as a means of uniting workers in the industrial sphere. They were to reject political parties and rely upon industrial action to obtain economic and political objectives. In its most theoretical formulations it sought to transform society through the revolutionary general strike which would place all power in the hands of the workers. For some anarchists, as in Spain, syndicalism became the means of obtaining the end of an anarchist transformation of society. Anarcho-syndicalism became an important force in the Spanish, Italian, Russian and French Labour movements by the outbreak of the First World War. Syndicalism in the form of reliance upon industrial action rather than political parties was also prominent in sections of the British labour movement, influencing people such as the miners' leader ARTHUR COOK. Syndicalism tended to be overtaken in countries such as Britain and Sweden where gradualist socialist parties and moderate trade unions were able to make advances in working and social conditions. Elsewhere, as in Spain, it continued to provide an alternative to parliamentary procedures and routine labourism, playing an important part in the largest labour grouping, the CONFEDERACIÓN NACIONAL DEL TRABAJO (CNT), founded in 1911. In the Soviet Union, syndicalist and anarcho-syndicalist elements were strongly represented in the FACTORY COMMITTEES but were gradually eliminated as an effective force by the BOLSHEVIKS, who repressed anarchist movements and independent trade union activists outside Communist Party control. Syndicalism has resurfaced in some aspects of what is loosely called 'Trotskyism' and the movements for greater workers' control in communist regimes such as those in Yugoslavia and the 'PRAGUE SPRING' reforms in Czechoslovakia.

# T

**Tannenberg, Battle of.** *See* FIRST WORLD WAR.

**Tartu, Treaty of** (Treaty of Dorpat). Signed 14 October 1920 between Finland and the Soviet Union, recognizing the independence and sovereignty of Finland. The treaty determined the frontier between the two states; Finland agreed that Eastern Karelia and the two frontier provinces of Repola and Parajärvi should belong to the Soviet Union, with West Karelia assigned to Finland; Russia agreed that the ice-free port of Petsamo on the Barents Sea should belong to Finland; finally, certain Finnish islands in the Gulf of Finland were neutralized. The treaty was reaffirmed in 1932 and 1934 when non-aggression agreements were signed and a Conciliation Commission established for the settlement of disputes. The non-aggression agreements were due to expire in 1945, but were interrupted by the RUSSO-FINNISH WAR of 1939.

M. Jakobsen, *The Diplomacy of the Winter War* (1974)
D. Kirby, *Finland in the Twentiety Century* (1979)

**Teheran Conference.** Wartime meeting in Teheran, Persia (28 November–1 December 1943) between CHURCHILL, President ROOSEVELT and STALIN, with the combined Chiefs of Staff, ANTHONY EDEN and Harry Hopkins attending, to plan military strategy in Europe and the Far East. It was agreed that 'Overlord', the Anglo-American invasion of northern France, would take place on 1 May 1944. Stalin promised that Russia would join in the war against Japan in the Far East after victory over Germany had been achieved. The future of Poland and Germany was discussed and Churchill agreed on the CURZON LINE as a basis for discussion of Russia's western borders with Poland.

H. Feis, *Churchill, Roosevelt, Stalin* (1957)
G. Kolko, *The Politics of War* (1968)

**terrorism, Italian.** Terrorist movements became increasingly active in Italy in the 1970s in the aftermath of the student protests of 1968 and when the Italian economy was disrupted by rising prices for oil, rapid inflation and political stalemate. Political violence of both Right and Left increased dramatically. On 16 March 1978 Red Brigades kidnapped ALDO MORO, a former prime minister, killing five of his bodyguards, apparently hoping to provoke an over-reaction and further weaken Italian democracy. Signor Moro's corpse was found in Rome on 1 May after his party, the Christian Democrats, had refused to negotiate with the terrorists. After a period of political shock and paralysis, the major parties, including the ITALIAN COMMUNIST PARTY (PCI) in fact drew closer together. Political murders by the Red Brigades and right-wing groups steadily increased. On 12 December 1980 Red Brigades kidnapped Giovanni d'Urso, a magistrate, demanding the closure of Asinara top security prison, where several of their members were being held. On 26 December the government met this demand (despite the opposition of the PCI who have always refused to negotiate with the Red Brigades), and in January d'Urso was released. Just after Christmas 1981 Red Brigades kidnapped Brigadier-General James Dozier, a senior American officer, but he was freed by Italian police on 28 January 1982 and five of his kidnappers captured. Within days 30 other suspects had been arrested, and subsequently many members of the Red Brigades were arrested and brought to trial. But 11 political murders were carried out by the Brigades in 1981 and it was calculated that up to 50

394

separate left-wing terrorist groups were operating in Italy by the early 1980s. Neo-fascists groups, such as the Black Order, claimed responsibility for bombing a Rome--Munich train in June 1974, killing 12 people, and carrying out the bombing of Bologna railway station on 2 August 1980, when 84 people were killed. In 1981 the leading masonic lodge, P2 (*see* P2), was implicated in right-wing terrorism and forced to disband. Terrorist attacks continued into the 1980s, but at a lower level than previously, with many of the leading terrorists in prison or awaiting trial. New police powers of arrest and detention in 1978, the fragmentation of the left-wing terrorist movement, and the economic recession after 1979 have been seen as factors leading to its reduction. Italy's experience of terrorism between 1969 and 1982 was the most prolonged of any area of Europe apart from the Basque country and Ulster, claiming over 1,000 victims.

R. C. Meade, *Red Brigades: The Story of Italian Terrorism* (1989)
D. Moss, *The Politics of Left-Wing Violence in Italy, 1969–1985* (1989)
S. Tarrow, *Democracy and Disorder: Protest and Politics in Italy, 1965–1975* (1989)

**Test Ban Treaty.** Treaty prohibiting nuclear tests in the atmosphere, in outer space and under water signed in Moscow on 5 August 1963 by the United States, Britain and the Soviet Union. By 1976 a total of 106 countries had adhered to the treaty; France and China had not signed.

**Thatcher, Margaret** (1925–). British Conservative politician. Mrs Thatcher has been Conservative MP for Finchley since 1959. She was Parliamentary Secretary to the Ministry of Pensions and National Insurance, 1961–4, and Secretary of State for Education and Science, 1970–4. In 1975 she was elected leader of the Conservative Party (*see* CONSERVATIVE AND UNIONIST PARTY, BRITISH). Between 1975 and 1979 she led the party away from the centrist policies of HEATH and adopted a monetarist stance on economic probems (*see* MONETARISM) and a tough line on law and order, defence and immigration. In May 1979 she became Britain's first woman Prime Minister, following her election victory. In spite of considerable unpopularity and very high unem-

ployment, Mrs Thatcher's conduct of the FALKLANDS WAR and Labour's disarray led to a landslide victory at the polls in 1983. Mrs Thatcher's second term was marked by growing emphasis on liberalizing the economy, especially the PRIVATIZATION of public concerns. Although her government was damaged by the WESTLAND AFFAIR, the revival of the economy allowed her to win a record third term of office with a majority of over 100. From 1987 she encouraged further privatization programmes of water, completed in 1989, and of electricity generation, in 1990. In late 1988 she made the Bruges Speech, criticizing the development of a European super-state as foreshadowed in the DELORS PLAN. She faced growing Cabinet opposition to her attitude towards Europe and severe electoral unpopularity over the new system of local government finance, the Poll Tax. The resignation of her Deputy, Geoffrey Howe, over European policy led to a leadership contest in November 1990. Having failed to secure a clear majority she resigned as leader of the Conservative Party and Prime Minister and was succeeded by the former Chancellor of the Exchequer, Mr. JOHN MAJOR.

P. Hennessy and A. Seldon (eds.), *Ruling Performance: British Governments from Attlee to Thatcher* (1987)
K. Minogue and M. Biddiss (eds.), *Thatcherism: Personality and Politics* (1987)
H. Young, *One of Us* (1989)

**Third International.** *See* COMINTERN

**Third Reich.** Term used by HITLER and leading members of the NAZI PARTY, also subsequently by many historians, to describe the Nazi dictatorship established in Germany in 1933. Stressing continuity with the medieval Empire and the German Empire (1871–1918), the term was coined by the nationalist writer Möller van den Bruck in his book *The Third Reich* (1923), which emphasized the cultural uniqueness of the Germans, the special path of German history and Germany's destiny to find a 'third way' between capitalism and socialism based on nationalism, and a revival of the medieval corporate order. Rapidly adopted by the Nazis, the ideology of the 'Third Reich' was to inform many of the quasi-feudal elements of Nazi Party ideology and social practice.

G. L. Mosse, *The Crisis of German Ideology: Intellectual Origins of the Third Reich* (1966)

**Third Republic, French.** The regime established following the Franco-Prussian War of 1870–71 and the fall of the Second Empire. Initially threatened by the restoration of a monarchy or presidential domination, it had matured by 1914 into a well established regime which withstood the disturbances of the Dreyfus Affair and the First World War. The Third Republic kept the constitution of 1875 until it ended in 1940. This provided for two chambers: a Chamber of Deputies and a Senate. The Chamber of 602 members was elected for four years by manhood suffrage on proportional representation. The Senate had 314 members elected for nine years, one-third retiring every three years. The President was a symbolic head of state, theoretically with many powers but in practice not exercising them. He had the right to dissolve the Chamber, but did not use it after 1877; the suspensory veto over acts of parliament was never used. His role in law-making and the determination of policy was controlled by the cabinet. The government's executive power lay with the ministers, who were not necessarily members of either house and were chosen by the President in conjunction with the Prime Minister. Political dissension made for weakness in the executive; the RADICAL PARTY was a major electoral force but was rarely able to support a ministry on its own. It tended to provide Prime Ministers for coalition governments which were rarely able to survive for very long. Ministers seldom felt strong enough to ask for a dissolution and election on the defeat of a measure; they normally resigned, often reappearing in a new coalition. As a result between 1870 and 1934 France had 88 ministries, with an average life of less than nine months. Ministers such as CAILLAUX became semi-permanent members of government serving a variety of premiers.

After 1918 there was growing disillusion with a system which, although it had stood the shock of war, seemed indecisive in the face of the DEPRESSION and the growing threat from fascism. There were 44 governments between 1918 and 1940 under 20 different premiers, leading to the rise of extremism on the right, from the various right-wing LEAGUES, and on the left with the FRENCH COMMUNIST PARTY. Demonstrations in Paris in February 1934 between the factions led to a short-lived 'national' ministry and was followed by the unique electoral collaborations between Communists, Socialists and Radicals which produced the POPULAR FRONT government of 1936–7 led by LÉON BLUM. The Blum government itself fell a prey to economic problems and the challenge posed by the SPANISH CIVIL WAR. Beset by internal weakness France was forced to follow a policy of APPEASEMENT, finding herself reluctantly at war with Germany in September 1939. The Third Republic was finally destroyed, as it had been born, by military defeat with the fall of France in 1940. It was replaced by the VICHY GOVERNMENT led by Marshal PÉTAIN.

Classically described as 'the government which divided Frenchmen least', the Third Republic has been seen as a political system which was in some ways too representative. The suspicions of strong executive power in the Radical Party, a party with most of its great battles behind it, and its desire to maintain conservative economic and social policies, left the Third Republic with little ability or desire to act decisively to meet the growing challenges facing it.

J. P. T. Bury, *France, 1870–1940* (1951)
J. F. McMillan, *Dreyfus to de Gaulle: Politics and Society in France, 1898–1969* (1985)

**Thorez, Maurice** (1900–1964). French Communist leader. He was a member of the Politburo of the FRENCH COMMUNIST PARTY (PCF) from 1926 and later a member of the 'collective secretariat' that was formed in 1929 to replace the General Secretary; he was placed in charge of propaganda and organization. This 'youth group' was dissolved in 1931, but Thorez emerged to co-ordinate the formation of the POPULAR FRONT in 1934–5, proposing the extension of the Communist–Socialist Pact to include the RADICAL PARTY and supporting the FRANCO-SOVIET PACT. Thorez became General Secretary in January 1936, supervising the expansion of PCF membership and its support for the Popular Front. In October 1939 Thorez went to the Soviet Union, escaping the suppression of communist deputies in April–May 1940. Amnestied by

DE GAULLE, Thorez returned to France after liberation and accepted Moscow's advice to dissolve the communist militias and seek power by constitutional means. His attempts to form a united French Labour Party were rebuffed by the socialists in the summer of 1945, but following the PCF success in the October 1945 elections he took office with four other communists as Minister without Portfolio on 21 November 1945. He stood for the presidency of the Council of Ministers in December 1946 but failed to secure a majority. Thorez became Vice-Premier in Ramadier's ministry on 22 January 1947, but was removed on 5 May with the other communist ministers following disputes over strikes and colonial affairs. Thereafter Thorez was excluded from government, and was increasingly critical of France's role in the COLD WAR and in Indo-China. A stroke in October 1950 led to his absence in Moscow, although he continued to issue directives to the party and purged dissident elements. He followed the 'thaw' in Soviet policy after 1953, but sought to limit the effects of DE-STALINIZATION. Under his direction the PCF opposed de Gaulle's FIFTH REPUBLIC, but from 1964 supported aspects of an independent French foreign policy which were favoured by the Soviet Union. Thorez died on 11 July 1964, having given up the post of General Secretary to Waldeck Rochet two years earlier, though retaining the post of President of the Politburo until his death. Thorez, one of the youngest political figures of the Third Republic, played a crucial part in the Popular Front and in the communist successes after the war. The end of TRIPAR-TISM in May 1947 took away the last chance of his dominating the government of post-war France.

R. Tiersky, *The French Communist Party, 1920–1970* (1974)
P. Robrieux, *Maurice Thorez, vie secrète et vie publique* (1975)
E. Mortimer, *The Rise of the French Communist Party, 1920–1947* (1984)

**Three-day Week.** British political crisis which brought about the fall of Prime Minister EDWARD HEATH. In November 1973 the National Union of Mineworkers voted to ban overtime in support of a pay claim in excess of the limit laid down by the government. The fuel situation therefore deteriorated rapidly and was further aggravated by an 'out-of-hours' working ban by electricity workers. It was thus not possible to supply adequate electricity in peak hours, and on 13 November 1973 a state of emergency was declared. Restrictions were placed on the domestic and commercial use of electricity. The government continued to refuse to allow the miners' pay claim and had to introduce stricter controls on the use of fuel. The most important, in force from 1 January 1974, was that electricity would only be supplied to industry on three specified days a week, meaning that many people could only work a three-day week. On 2 February 1974 a general election was called to test support for the government's policy, but Heath lost his overall majority and resigned on 4 March, a Labour government under HAROLD WILSON taking power. On 9 March the restrictions were removed and Britain returned to a normal five-day working week. The failure to win public support for a confrontation with the trade unions greatly increased perceptions of 'union power' in Britain, apparently confirmed in 1978–9 in the 'WINTER OF DISCONTENT' which led to the return of Conservative government under Mrs THATCHER.

R. Taylor, *The Fifth Estate: British Unions in the Modern World* (1978)
P. Hennessy and A. Seldon (eds.), *Ruling Performance: British Governments from Attlee to Thatcher* (1987)

**Tindemans Report.** Commissioned in 1975 by the COUNCIL OF MINISTERS OF THE EUROPEAN COMMUNITY and published in January 1976, the report was prepared by the Belgian Prime Minister, Leo Tindemans, on the means for the achievement of European union. Tindemans advocated the achievement of closer unity between the current nine member states, and suggested that this would require co-ordination of foreign policy, a common economic policy, the development of social and regional policy, and the strengthening of European community institutions. He stressed the importance of the European Council and suggested a clearer definition of its role. He felt that European union would not be achieved without an eventual common defence policy. The plan failed in the short term, primarily because it contained proposals for a joint foreign policy and monetary union which had failed earlier, as well as adding new contentious elements on regional and social policies. These elements, however, soon became accepted in the social and regional policy, greater co-operation and co-ordination in foreign policy, while monetary union returned to the agenda with the DELORS PLAN in the 1980s. The Tindemans Report is now seen as having foreshadowed developments which found growing acceptance a decade later in the drive for European integration. *See also* SINGLE EUROPEAN ACT.

L. Tsoukalis (ed.), *The European Community: Past, Present and Future* (1983)

**Tirpitz, Alfred von** (1849–1930). German Admiral and architect of the High Seas Fleet. He joined the navy as a cadet in 1865; became an early enthusiast for torpedo squadrons and earned the support of WILHELM II for the development of a battle fleet. As State Secretary of the Navy and Prussian Minister of State, 1898–1916, he was responsible for the massive increase in German naval construction through the navy Laws of 1898 and 1900, supplemented by additional bills in 1904, 1906, 1908 and 1912. Initially conceived as a 'risk fleet', sufficiently large to deter attack from any greater naval power, his acceptance of the challenge of the new all big gun ships built by Britain from 1906 precipitated the 'naval race' which did much to sour relations between Britain and Germany before 1914. Supported by the German Navy League, his plans expanded to a fleet which in 1920–21 would consist of 41 battleships, 20 large and 40 light cruisers. Dissatisfied with the outbreak of war before his fleet was ready, he protested when the navy was prevented from taking offensive operations. He urged the adoption of unrestricted submarine warfare and resigned on 17 March 1916 when this was blocked by the Kaiser. He helped in 1917 to create the million-strong right-wing FATHERLAND PARTY which called for major annexations and indemnities. He served as a parliamentary deputy in the Reichstag from 1924 to 1928 for the GERMAN NATIONAL PEOPLE'S PARTY (DVNP) and persuaded HINDENBERG to bid for the Presidency. A major influence in the Anglo-German naval antagonism, he is rightly regarded as the father of the German navy whose influence continued to be felt after his death in HITLER's High Seas Fleet.

J. Steinberg, *Yesterday's Deterrent: Tirpitz and the Birth of the German Battle Fleet* (1966)
H. H. Herwig, *'Luxury Fleet': the Imperial German Navy, 1888–1918* (1980)

**Tito, Josip** (1892–1980). President of YUGOSLAVIA, 1953–80. His real name Broz, he was born at Kumrovec in Croatia. He served in the Austrian army in the First World War and was captured by the Russians in April 1915. He escaped in 1917, participating in the RUSSIAN REVOLUTION and on the side of the 'Red' armies in the RUSSIAN CIVIL WAR. He returned to Croatia in September 1920 and worked in a factory in Zagreb. Active in the illegal YUGOSLAVIAN COMMUNIST PARTY, he was arrested in 1928 and gaoled until 1934. Released, he visited Moscow in 1935, operating under the COMINTERN codename 'Walter'. Following the purge of most of the Moscow-based leadership of the Yugoslavian Communist Party, he was selected by the head of Comintern, GEORGI DIMITROV, as its General Secretary in September 1937. Under the name he now adopted, 'Tito', he rebuilt the party, recruiting younger members and expelling recalcitrant or factious elements. The party loyally followed the changes in Soviet foreign policy during 1939, remaining passive during the Nazi invasion of Yugoslavia in April 1941, although extending its influence via communist cells as the Yugoslavian state was destroyed. The German attack on the Soviet Union in June 1941 transformed the position, Comintern calling on the Yugoslavian Communist Party to undertake PARTISAN warfare and mount a general armed uprising in Yugoslavia to assist the Soviet Union. Tito became military commander of the partisan movements under communist control and led them in a bitter struggle both against the Nazi occupation and rival resistance groups. In November 1943 Tito established at the JAJCE CONGRESS a National Committee of Yugoslavia with himself as President, as a rival to the royal government-in-exile. Viewed increasingly as the strongest and most determined of the anti-Nazi resistance leaders, Tito received Allied aid from 1943 and from the Soviet Union from spring 1944. Receiving the title of 'Marshal of Yugoslavia' in November

1943, Tito captured Belgrade in late 1944 and was able to make himself master of the country. A joint government formed with exiles from London lasted only a few months, from March to August 1945. On 29 November a Federal People's Republic was proclaimed and the monarchy abolished. Opponents were now systematically liquidated, the army and government largely filled with communists, land collectivized, private enterprises nationalized, and a Five Year Plan inaugurated in April 1947 to promote heavy industry.

Tito's independence, as a communist leader who had seized control for himself in a bitter and protracted partisan war, proved increasingly irksome to STALIN. Attempts to force the Yugoslav leader to follow Soviet leadership met Tito's resistance, and on 28 June 1948 Yugoslavia was expelled from COMINFORM in the first major rift in the Eastern bloc. Stalin hesitated to invade, probably fearing a bloody guerrilla war and the likely intervention of the West, already engaged in assisting Greece to resist communism and at this stage the sole possessor of nuclear weapons. Instead, all economic and political support to Yugoslavia was cut off from the Eastern bloc, and purges of 'Titoists' carried out in several communist parties. Free to pursue an independent policy, Tito announced the progressive closing of the border with Greece in July 1949, effectively ending support for the communist side in the GREEK CIVIL WAR. But although he accepted United States aid, he pursued a policy of non-alignment rather than join the Western camp. Domestically, he developed his own form of socialized economy, abandoning 'bureaucratic centralization' in favour of worker-management of enterprises, the devolution of planning and control, and the decollectivization of agriculture. By combining these more flexible policies with a federal state structure and a considerable degree of autonomy for the nationalities within the Yugoslavian state, 'Titoism' had an important part to play in the post-Stalin era of offering an alternative version of socialism to the Soviet model. Tito was elected President on 14 January 1953, then subsequently on five more occasions until a decree in May 1974 made him President for life. In later years he continued to show independence;

in foreign affairs he condemned the suppression of the HUNGARIAN UPRISING in 1956 and the Soviet invasion of Czechoslovakia in 1968 (see 'PRAGUE SPRING'), putting Yugoslavia on a war footing in case of a Soviet assault. Yugoslavia remained the most open of the socialized countries, developing a large tourist industry and a relatively free attitude to the arts.

Tito was genuinely mourned on his death in 1980 as the creator of the modern Yugoslavian state. Succeeded by a collective leadership, the ethnic conflicts which Tito's victory in 1945 and his policies in the immediate post-war years had suppressed began to reappear, particularly between the dominant Serbs and other groupings. The economy, too, began to show signs of weakness by the 1970s, with inefficient industry, foreign debts, high inflation and the emigration of younger workers, leaving a difficult legacy for his successors. Although widely cultivated by the West, Tito's early rise to power had often been brutal and ruthless, accounting for tens of thousands of opponents, and it has been questioned whether the unique political structure he created can survive indefinitely after his departure.

R. H. Bass and E. Marbury (eds.), *The Soviet–Yugoslav Controversy, 1948–58: A Documentary Record* (1959)
P. Auty, *Tito* (1970)
F. Fetjo, *A History of the People's Democracies: Eastern Europe since Stalin* (2nd edn, 1974)

**Togliatti, Palmiro** (1893–1964). Italian communist leader. He attended law school in Turin, where he met GRAMSCI. A founder member of the ITALIAN COMMUNIST PARTY in 1921, he supported Gramsci's positions against Amadeo Bordiga. He was in Russia from 1926, playing an important part in COMINTERN; he became its secretary, supported the Popular Front movement and was involved in the SPANISH CIVIL WAR. He returned to Italy in 1944 and led the ITALIAN COMMUNIST PARTY in support of the existing government, serving as a Minister without Portfolio from 1944 to 1947. During the period of exclusion from government which followed, he developed policies of gradualism and independence for national communist parties. This emphasis on 'polycentrism', together with the emphasis on the humanistic aspects of Gramsci's writings, laid the foundations for EURO-COMMUNISM and for the party's continuing mass appeal.

D. L. M. Blackmer, *Unity in Diversity: Italian Communism and the Communist World* (1968)

**Tomsky, Mikhail** (1880–1936). Russian Bolshevik leader. He started life as a factory worker and became chairman of the Bolshevik Soviet in Tallinin in 1905. He fled abroad in 1906 and returned to participate in the October Revolution in Moscow. He became a member of the Central Committee in 1919 and of the Politburo in 1922. He specialized in trade union matters as one of the few genuine workers in the Bolshevik leadership, chairing the Central Trade Union Council from 1917 to 1929. A member of the 'RIGHT OPPOSITION' with BUKHARIN and RYKOV, he was expelled from his posts in 1929. Publicly implicated in counter-revolutionary activity with ZINOVIEV and KAMENEV, he committed suicide in August 1936. *See also* PURGES.

**Total War.** Phrase used to distinguish wars of mass participation of the 20th century from the 'limited wars' of the past, such as the 18th century, and the effects thereof. The idea was developed by, amongst others, S. Andreski's *Military Organisation and Society* (London, 1954), which proposed that the effects of war on societies depended on the degree of mass support they required, which he called the Military Participation Ratio (MPR); changes in social stratification and social position during or after wars were due to the extension of privileges to groups whose participation in the war effort is required. More recent writing has invoked the degree of mass participation beyond the purely military to the civilian war efforts of the FIRST WORLD WAR and SECOND WORLD WAR. Systematic frameworks for discussion of wars and society have been developed, notably in the work of Arthur Marwick. These include: the destructive and disruptive impact of the war on human and material resources; the dimension arising from the testing of institutions by the strain of the communal enterprise – sometimes called the 'inspection effect' of war; the participatory dimension, highlighted above, involving bargaining with groups whose services are necessary for the efficient prosecution of the war; and, finally, the affective dimension arising from the psychologically wounding experience of war, which leaves a legacy in consciousness and culture. This typology of response has been questioned on individual themes and issues, there being debate about the degree of the effect of war compared with longer-term factors.

S. Andreski, *Military Organisation and Society* (1954)
A. Marwick, *War and Social Change in the Twentieth Century* (1974)

**Trades Union Congress** (TUC). Principal organization of the British trade union movement, founded in Manchester in 1868. Its basic function is to co-ordinate union action by means of annual conferences of union representatives. The conference or congress elects a General Council which has executive functions and seeks to represent the interests of organized labour to the government. Member unions retain autonomy and the TUC has little power, other than expulsion, to control them. The great majority of British trade unions are affiliated to the TUC, which had 6.5 million members in 1919, 7.9 million by 1948, 12.2 million in 1979, and 9.6 million in 1985.

The TUC was responsible for organizing a 'strike truce' at the outbreak of the First World War, but was unable to restrain union militancy in the latter years of the war. In May 1926 it called the GENERAL STRIKE but its climb-down nine days later marked the beginning of a period of attempts to reach accommodation with government and employers. From 1931 the TUC worked closely via the General Council to influence LABOUR PARTY policy, and used its influence to shape the WELFARE STATE and NATIONALIZATION policies which were implemented by the Labour Government under ATTLEE after 1945.

The TUC, with the employers' organization, the CONFEDERATION OF BRITISH INDUSTRY, became part of what was seen as an increasingly corporatist arrangement reflecting the major interest groups in British society. The TUC opposed the introduction of a legal framework for industrial bargaining under both the Labour Government of HAROLD WILSON in 1969 and that of the Conservative EDWARD HEATH in 1971. The TUC was an essential partner in attempts by the minority Labour governments under Wilson and CALLAGHAN in 1974–9 to control wages. The rejection of a 5 per cent wage norm in 1978 by the TUC led to an outbreak of strikes – the 'WINTER OF DISCONTENT' – which contributed to Mrs THATCHER's election victory in May 1979. Since 1979 the TUC has been denied the customary close consultative role enjoyed under the Labour governments. Falling union membership and the decline of strongly unionized heavy industry has contributed to a malaise which has led some unions to accept expulsion from the TUC with equanimity.

The TUC has been a major moderating influence in British politics. Anti-communist between the wars, it has consistently supported the moderate socialism of the LABOUR PARTY, with which it retains close links. Once famously caricatured as a carthorse, it has always found it difficult to act against the wishes of its largest constituent unions.

J. Lovell and B. C. Roberts, *A Short History of the TUC* (1968)

**Transcaucasian Federated Republic.** Following the reconquest in the RUSSIAN CIVIL WAR of the Transcaucasian regions of GEORGIA, AZERBAIJAN and ARMENIA, the Soviet Government set up three Soviet Republics which were federated in 1922 into the Transcaucasian Federated Republic. Subsequently, in 1936, these were formed into separate Union Republics. *See also* NGORNO-KARABAKH; NATIONALITIES QUESTION, SOVIET.

**Transylvania.** A mountainous and wooded region of mixed ethnic composition which, up to 1918, was the most easterly part of the Kingdom of Hungary within the Austro-Hungarian Empire. The urban population and intelligentsia were largely Magyar with a Romanian peasant population. The unification of Transylvania with Romania was one of the principal objectives of Romanian nationalists up to and during the First World War. The offer of Transylvania by the Entente powers was one of the factors used to induce Romanian entry to the war, and by the TREATY OF TRIANON in 1919, Transylvania was transferred to Romania. Containing a sizeable minority of between

1.5 and 2.0 million Magyars, the area was subjected to a process of 'Romanization' between the wars, with the suppression of local autonomy and legislation favouring the Romanian peasantry. Under the terms of the Second VIENNA AWARD on 30 August 1940, dictated by Germany and Italy, Romania was forced to surrender almost half of Transylvania to Hungary. The TREATIES OF PARIS in 1947 re-established the earlier frontier, once again incorporating Transyvlvania into Romania. The Magyar minority received guarantees of linguistic freedom under the Romanian constitution and a Magyar University was established at Cluj in 1952. Under the leadership of GEORGIU-DEJ and CEAUSESCU, however, the autonomous status of Magyar districts was discontinued and there was a greater drive to standardize Romanian life. One of the catalysts for the Romanian uprising of December 1989 which overthrew Ceausescu was the persecution of the Hungarian minority and their clergy in Transylvania, sparking off demonstrations in Timisoara amongst both ethnic Hungarians and the Romanian majority against despotic rule.

C. C. Giurescu, *Transylvania in the History of Romania: An Historical Outline* (1970)
G. Schöpflin, *Hungarians in Romania* (1979)

**Trianon, Treaty of.** The treaty with Hungary signed on 4 June 1920, arising from the PARIS PEACE CONFERENCE. The treaty was delayed by BÉLA KUN's seizure of power. Hungary accepted the breaking up of the Austro-Hungarian empire and surrendered territory to Austria, Romania, Czechoslovakia, Poland and Yugoslavia, including the cession of TRANSYLVANIA to Romania, the loss of SLOVAKIA to Czechoslovakia, and the absorption of CROATIA and BOSNIA-HERZEGOVINA into Yugoslavia. The Hungarian army was reduced to 35,000 men and denied heavy weapons or an air force. Hungary also was called on to pay an unspecified amount of reparations. The Covenant of the LEAGUE OF NATIONS was written into the treaty. Hungary was the most harshly treated of the defeated powers, apart from Turkey, whose initial settlement was revised in the TREATY OF LAUSANNE on a more favourable basis. Hungary was reduced to one-third of her former size and population and lost her access to the sea.

Over 3 million Magyars were made subjects of non-Hungarian governments, half of them in Transylvania. Plebiscites in the Magyar areas of Czechoslovakia, Yugoslavia and Romania were denied. Bitter resentment at the humiliation of the peace and the apparent denial of 'self-determination' to the defeated as well as the victors meant that revision of Trianon became a dominant issue in Hungarian politics, fuelling nationalist and fascist movements.

Z. A. B. Zeman, *The Break-Up of the Austro-Hungarian Empire, 1914–18* (1961)
J. K. Hoensch, *A History of Modern Hungary, 1867–1986* (trans., 1988)

**Tribunites.** A group within the BRITISH LABOUR PARTY, named after the left-wing weekly *Tribune*, founded in 1937. In the years after 1945 the group advocated a programme of further NATIONALIZATION, unilateral nuclear disarmament (*see* UNILATERALISM) and, later, opposition to membership of the EUROPEAN ECONOMIC COMMUNITY. During the early 1950s the Tribune group included ANEURIN BEVAN, HAROLD WILSON, Ian Mikardo and Richard Crossman, and was highly critical of official Labour Party policy, especially on nuclear weapons. The group remains a pressure group within the Labour Party.

**Trident.** *See* POLARIS.

**Trieste.** An Austro-Hungarian port at the head of the Adriatic which was the object of a dispute between Italy and YUGOSLAVIA after the First World War. Italy seized it in 1919 in spite of protests from Yugoslavia. In turn, Yugoslavia seized it in 1945 after the Second World War. Italian protests were backed by the presence of Allied troops under General Freyberg. After a period of tension the issue was referred to international arbitration. The TREATIES OF PARIS in 1947 established Trieste as a Free Port with a British and American military presence in the city itself and Yugoslav troops in the south. After some disturbances, an agreement was reached giving the city and port to Italy and the hinterland to Yugoslavia, with rights of access to the city and port. Residual claims in the area were settled by an Italo-Yugoslav Friendship Treaty in 1975.

**Tripartism.** Name given for the joint governments in post-war France and Italy based on the three principal parties of Christian Democrats, Socialists and Communists. In France tripartism lasted until May 1947 when the communist ministers were dismissed by the socialist premier Ramadier following communist support for strikes. In Italy the Christian Democrat DE GASPERI took advantage of a split in the Socialist Party to attack the extreme left and resign in April 1947, forming a minority Christian Democrat government without communist support. The end of tripartism reflected the break-up of the war-time alliances of resistance partners and the hardening of attitudes towards the Communists in the development of the COLD WAR. *See also* FOURTH REPUBLIC, FRENCH; COMMUNIST PARTY, FRENCH.

P. Williams, *Politics in Post-War France* (1954)
B. D. Graham, *The French Socialists and Tripartism, 1944–1947* (1965)

**Tripartite Pact.** A ten-year military and economic agreement signed in Berlin on 27 September 1940 between Germany, Italy and Japan. Its primary aim was to promote the mutual prosperity and welfare of the states concerned. Formalizing the AXIS and the ANTI-COMINTERN PACT, it fell short of a full-scale military alliance in that the parties were not obliged to declare war on each other's enemies.

**Triple Alliance.** Agreement for mutual support between the three most powerful British unions, the miners, transport workers and railwaymen. Negotiations were opened in 1914 and agreement reached in 1915, but not put into operation until after the First World War. In April 1921 the Triple Alliance broke down when the other two unions failed to call sympathetic strikes in support of a miners' stoppage.

**Trotsky, Leon** (1879–1940). Bolshevik leader and theoretician. He was born of Jewish parents at Ianovka in the Ukraine. His original surname was Bronstein. In 1896 he joined the Social Democratic Party; he was arrested in 1898 and sent to Siberia, but escaped and went abroad, joining LENIN in London late in 1902. He sided with the MENSHEVIKS following the split with the

BOLSHEVIKS in 1903. He participated in the 1905 Revolution, when he became Vice-Chairman of the St Petersburg Soviet. Arrested and exiled again to Siberia, he escaped abroad, spending time in Central Europe, France and the United States. Although he led the internationalist wing of the Mensheviks during the First World War, he attempted to reunite the wings of the party, and on his return to Russia following the Revolution joined the Bolsheviks. As chairman of the Petrograd Soviet and the MILITARY REVOLUTIONARY COMMITTEE he organized the Bolshevik seizure of power in November. As Commissar for Foreign Affairs (1917–18) he conducted the negotiations on behalf of the Soviet government leading to the TREATIES OF BREST-LITOVSK, deploying skilful delaying tactics at the behest of the party in the hope of further revolutionary outbreaks in Central Europe. As Commissar for War (1918–25) he played the leading role in organizing the RED ARMY and crushing the KRONSTADT MUTINY. Trotsky's concentration upon military and foreign affairs, his later conversion to the Bolsheviks, and his somewhat isolated position put him at a disadvantage in the power struggle which began in Lenin's last illness and continued after his death. Moreover, Trotsky was led into increasing conflict by his belief in 'World Revolution' – a reflection of his Menshevik background and more internationalist outlook – in contrast with the doctrine of 'SOCIALISM IN ONE COUNTRY' with which STALIN associated himself. In 1927 he was dismissed from the Politburo and from the party, and in January 1929 expelled from the country. 'TROTSKYITE' was increasingly used as a blanket term for all opponents under Stalin, leading to the trial and execution of several of the most prominent Bolsheviks during the PURGES. Trotsky himself went to Turkey, then to France and eventually to Mexico, maintaining a stream of anti-Stalinist polemics. It was in Mexico that he was assassinated by an agent of Stalin on 20 August 1940. Trotsky's vision of international revolution made him the national focus of opposition to the narrower view held by both Lenin and, later, Stalin. His brilliant, somewhat arrogant stance had earned him criticism even at the time of his greatest triumph in leading the Red Army

to victory in the Civil War. His inability to match Stalin's control of the party administration left him with no base from which to challenge the latter's rise to power and to his eventual political extinction. *See also* RUSSIAN CIVIL WAR.

L. Trotsky, *History of the Russian Revolution* (1932–3)
I. Deutscher, *The Prophet Armed: Trotsky, 1879–1921; The Prophet Unarmed: Trotsky, 1921–29; The Prophet Outcast: Trotsky, 1929–40* (1954–63)

**Trotskyite.** A term used by STALIN to describe his opponents in the PURGES, later adopted by various left-wing groups who wished to distinguish their Marxism from that associated with STALINISM. Trotsky's idea of 'Permanent Revolution', by which he meant the rapid succession of the proletarian revolution upon the bourgeois revolution in the peculiar conditions in which Russia found herself in 1917, was interpreted by left-wing groups as meaning a perpetual revolutionary agitation akin to the Maoist Cultural Revolution of the 1960s. Trotsky also appeared to offer a looser, less centralized form of communism which appealed to the activists of the post-war era. As a result, many of the Marxist groupings in the student upheavals of the 1960s saw themselves as opposed to the rigidities of the existing communist parties. The term is now used very loosely to describe left-wing communists outside the Communist Party.

**Truman, Harry S.** (1884–1972). United States President, 1945–53. A Senator from 1935 to 1944, he was ROOSEVELT's running mate in 1944, Vice President and President (on Roosevelt's death) in 1945. He had to assume immediate responsibility for the conduct of the war, and in 1945 he took the decision to drop the first atomic bomb on Japan. He enunciated the TRUMAN DOCTRINE in March 1947 of providing assistance to states facing internal and external communist threats, first implemented in the GREEK CIVIL WAR and in the BERLIN AIRLIFT. He was an unexpected victor in the 1948 presidential election and took the United States into the NORTH ATLANTIC TREATY ORGANISATION, its first peace-time military alliance. He was President during the Korean War and the crucial origins of the COLD WAR. He retired in 1953. Less influenced by cosmopolitan instincts than Roosevelt had been, he was more suspicious of Russian intentions and played the crucial part in committing America to support Europe both politically and economically in order to resist communism.

H. Feis, *From Trust to Terror: The Onset of the Cold War, 1945–1950* (1970)
D. R. McCloy, *The Presidency of Harry S. Truman* (1986)
H. Jones, *A New Kind of War: America's Global Strategy and the Truman Doctrine in Greece* (1989)

**Truman Doctrine.** A policy enunciated by United States President HARRY S. TRUMAN on 12 March 1947, guaranteeing that the United States would provide financial aid to democratic states facing internal or external aggression. Truman argued that not to do so would endanger the welfare of the United States. A crucial doctrine of the COLD WAR, the Truman Doctrine was prompted by Britain's admission that she could no longer support the effort of combatting communist insurgency in Greece. By offering help to anti-communist forces in Greece, as well as aid to bolster democratic governments in Europe via the MARSHAL PLAN and membership of the NORTH ATLANTIC TREATY ORGANISATION, the United States took decisive steps to resist the threat of communism in Europe. The Truman Doctrine could be invoked world-wide, and increasingly was, to justify American assistance to states that were threatened or appearing to be threatened by communism. As such it played an immense part in the rise of the United States as a global power after 1945. *See also* GREEK CIVIL WAR.

H. S. Truman, *Years of Trial and Hope, 1946–53* (1956)
J. W. Spanier, *American Foreign Policy since the Second World War* (1980)

**Trumbic, Ante** (1864–1938). Slav politician. Born in Split in Dalmatia, he trained as a lawyer. He became leader of Croatian nationalist movement and was elected to the Austrian parliament in 1897. He gradually moved from moderation to support the independence of CROATIA from Austrian rule. At the outbreak of the First World War he fled to Rome. He set up the Yugoslav Committee in London in May 1915. Early difficulties in securing the agreement of the Serbian leader, NIKOLA PASIC, to a South Slav (Yugoslav) state were partly overcome in the Corfu Pact on 20 July 1917. The pact agreed that the South Slav peoples, Serbs, Croats, Slovenes and Montenegrins, should unite to form a single Yugoslav Kingdom under the royal house of Serbia on the basis of equal citizenship. No clear agreement on a form of federation was agreed, however, exposing Trumbic to criticism that the new Yugoslavian state would be dominated by the Serbs. Trumbic also enlisted Italian support for the break-up of the Austro-Hungarian Empire, setting to one side the question of Yugoslavia's future border with Italy until after the conclusion of hostilities. Trumbic was appointed the first Foreign Minister of the new Yugoslav state, and was one of the Yugoslav delegation at the PARIS PEACE CONFERENCE. He negotiated the Treaty of Rapallo with the Italians, signed on 12 November 1920, which arbitrated Italian and Yugoslav claims in the Adriatic. Continuing to serve in the Yugoslav parliament, he played no further major part in government. He remained critical of Serbian dominance in the new state and was bitter at the development of a dictatorial regime after 1929.

I. J. Lederer, *Yugoslavia at the Peace Conference: A Study in Frontier Making* (1963)
H. F. Eterovich and C. Spalatin (eds.), *Croatia: Land, People, Culture*, vol. 2 (1970)

**TUC.** *See* TRADES UNION CONGRESS.

**Tukhachevsky, Mikhail** (1893–1937). Soviet Marshal. Born of poor noble parents, he trained in the Moscow Cadet Corps and Alexandrov Military Academy, joining the Imperial Guard in 1914. He served in the First World War and was taken prisoner in 1915; he escaped and returned to Russia, where he joined the Bolshevik Party. Appointed Military Commissar for the Moscow District, he participated in military campaigns on the eastern and southern fronts in the RUSSIAN CIVIL WAR, and led the drive on Warsaw during the RUSSO-POLISH WAR. He commanded the forces which suppressed the KRONSTADT MUTINY in March 1921 and the ANTONOV UPRISING in Tambov province. He became head of the Military Academy in 1921, and in 1922 was Commander of the Western Military District. Chief of Staff in 1925–8, he became Deputy

Commissar for Military and Naval Affairs and a Marshal of the Soviet Union in 1935. One of the first five Marshals of the Soviet Union at the age of 42 and a hero of the survival of the Bolshevik state, Tukhachevsky was also a proponent of turning the RED ARMY into a modern, mechanized force along the lines being advocated by a new generation of military thinkers. His 'professionalism' appears to have earned STALIN's suspicion, and he was arrested and executed on charges of foreign espionage in 1937, one of the most prominent victims of the PURGES. He was rehabilitated during Khruschev's DE-STALINIZATION in 1958.

E. O'Ballance, *The Red Army* (1964)

N. Davies, *White Eagle, Red Star: The Polish–Soviet War, 1919–20* (1972)

# U

**UCD.** Unión Centro Democrático. *See* UNION OF THE DEMOCRATIC CENTRE, SPANISH.

**UDF.** *See* UNION POUR LA DÉMOCRATIE FRANÇAISE.

**UDI.** Unilateral Declaration of Independence in Southern Rhodesia (Zimbabwe) by the Rhodesian Front Government of Ian Smith on 11 November 1965. The British government rejected the Declaration, which was also condemned by the United Nations because of Smith's opposition to sharing power with the African majority and his rejection of majority rule. Britain imposed trade sanctions and an oil embargo on Rhodesia, but failed to reach an agreement with Ian Smith at talks held between Prime Minister HAROLD WILSON and Smith on HMS *Tiger* in December 1966 and HMS *Fearless* in October 1968. The rebellion came to an end in 1979 following a protracted guerrilla war in Rhodesia which led to a settlement at Lancaster House, London in December 1979. The Lancaster House Agreement provided for a cease-fire and an interim peace-keeping operation by British troops, followed by the holding of elections on the basis of 'one man one vote', with some reserved seats for whites. The elections in March 1980 returned an African majority government led by Robert Mugabe. Britain's failure to end the rebellion by the white settlers added to the malaise of Wilson's Labour Government. The settlement of the long dispute was seen as an early foreign policy success for Mrs THATCHER's Conservative government. *See also* DECOLONIZATION.

M. Loney, *White Racism and Imperial Response* (1974)
R. Blake, *A History of Rhodesia* (1977)
D. Martin and P. Johnson, *The Struggle for Zimbabwe* (1981)

**UGT.** *See* UNIÓN GENERAL DE TRABAJADORES.

**Ukraine.** Area of southern Russia comprising the largest national grouping in the Russian Empire prior to 1917, based around the historic capital of Kiev, latterly a republic of the USSR. Ukrainians comprised almost 18 per cent of the population of pre-revolutionary Russia with an outpost of the Ukrainian 'nation' in Galicia under the Austro-Hungarian Empire. Prior to 1914 the process of RUSSIFICATION largely retarded the development of Ukrainian nationalism, although a Ukrainian literary language had developed and nationalist ideas circulated amongst a small intelligentsia. After the February Revolution (*see* RUSSIAN REVOLUTION) a Ukrainian *Rada* (council) was convened in Kiev under the author Vladimir Vinnychenko and the peasant leader SIMON PETLYURA. In June it proclaimed an autonomous Ukrainian People's Republic under pressure from a Ukrainian Military Congress, representing Ukrainian officers and soldiers from the Imperial Army who had assembled in Kiev, and during the next months a variety of congresses met to formulate and express Ukrainian national identity. Following the October Revolution the *Rada* confirmed the existence of a Ukrainian Republic on 7 November and called a Ukrainian Constituent Assembly. Growing conflict with the Bolsheviks in Petrograd led to the setting up of separate soviets of workers' and soldiers' deputies, some of which were suppressed by troops loyal to the *Rada*. When an all-Ukrainian Congress of Soviets opened in December it contained a non-Bolshevik majority, leading the Bolsheviks to withdraw to Kharkov. In January 1918 Bolshevik forces overran the Ukraine, forcing the *Rada* to evacuate Kiev, but their success was overtaken by the advance of German, Austro-Hungarian and Romanian forces into the Ukraine. A Ukrainian Central Council led by Hetman Skoropadsky were parties to the negotiations towards the TREATIES OF BREST-LITOVSK alongside the Central Powers, signing a separate treaty in March 1918 with the Soviets which recognized an independent Ukraine. The Ukraine became the scene of confused fighting beween White Russian, Bolshevik and Ukrainian forces in the RUSSIAN CIVIL WAR until the victory of the Bolsheviks led to the establishment of the Ukrainian Soviet Socialist Republic in 1919.

The failure to establish an independent Ukraine resulted partly from the divisions into pro- and anti-Bolshevik factions, attacks upon the Jews, and a failure to secure land reform for the peasants. Ukrainian independence left a legacy, however, in the decision to allow the Ukraine considerable autonomy. In 1920 the Ukrainian Soviet government signed a military and economic alliance with the Russian Soviet government, and in 1924 joined the Federation of the Union Republics to form the USSR. As a result of the revision of boundaries following the upheavals of 1917–20 the Soviet Union had jurisdiction over 83 per cent of the Ukrainian population, some 25 million people, with another 5 million belonging to the SUCCESSOR STATES. In order to secure the loyalty of the Ukraine, the Soviet Union initially fostered cultural nationalism, including the return from exile of the historian Mikhail Hrushevsky, 'the Father of Ukrainian Nationalism' and President of the *Rada* in 1918. The development of the SOVIET COLLECTIVIZATION campaign and growing concern about 'national deviationism' led to a clamp-down under STALIN. Hrushevsky was expelled, leading members of the intelligentsia purged, and most of their earlier privileges revoked.

As one of the most prosperous agricultural regions of the USSR the Ukraine prospered under the NEW ECONOMIC POLICY, but bore a disproportionate price in the drive against the KULAKS and collectivization, leading to a disastrous famine in 1932–4 in which several million people died. By 1939 the effects of collectivization and the pro-

motion of the 'new' anti-religious Soviet culture had reversed earlier tendencies towards fostering cultural identity: education was Russianized, Ukrainian churches were closed, village leaders deported and the old system of landholding abolished. Moreover, as fears of German designs grew, memories of Brest-Litovsk led to a renewed purge of 'separatists' in trials of Ukrainian officials in March 1938.

In June 1941 many Ukrainians welcomed the advance of the German armies as offering the prospect of freedom from Soviet rule, a hope which found support in Rosenberg's appointment to run the *Ostministerium*, the German ministery for occupied Soviet territory, and plans to build a pro-German *cordon sanitaire* around 'Muscovy'. Ukrainians formed battalions to fight against the Russians, joined the VLASOV ARMY, and after May 1943 were permitted to join the SS (*see* ss). Ukrainians contributed an estimated 40 divisions to the anti-Soviet forces, many acting as auxiliaries to the 'Final Solution' (*see* HOLOCAUST) as guards, or, like the *Benderovtsy*, acting as anti-partisan forces. But the ruthlessness of the Nazi treatment of the Ukraine under Eric Koch alienated much support, as did the drafting of forced labour (*Ostarbeiter*) into Germany. They not only relentlessly liquidated the Jews, but systematically massacred the Ukrainian intelligentsia, notably at BABI YAR. With Rosenberg's resignation in May 1943, hopes of a constructive policy of fostering a Ukrainian puppet state were ended and were soon followed by the recapture of the Ukraine by the Red Armies.

The scene of much of the bitterest fighting in the Second World War, the Ukraine endured a further devastating famine in 1946, the reimposition of collectivization, a massive purge of suspected 'collaborators', as well as a small-scale anti-Soviet guerrila war carried on into the 1950s by the Organization of Ukrainian Nationalists. Following Stalin's death there was some relaxation and under Peter Shelest, First Secretary of the Ukrainian Communist Party from 1963 to 1972, Ukrainian culture was once again encouraged and its economy fostered. Too strong a revival of Ukrainian culture was met by renewed waves of arrests in 1965 and 1972, and in the latter year Shelest was

replaced by the Brezhnevite V.V. Sticher-
bitsky. The Brezhnev period saw continued
harassment of DISSIDENTS and nationalists;
the Ukrainian Helsinki Watch Group, founded in 1976, had 30 of its 36 members under
arrest by 1981. The coming of the GORBA-
CHEV era released national and cultural
expression on a scale not seen since the
independence period of 1917–20, Ukrainian
representatives making claims for greater
autonomy and even voicing national aspirations through the nationalist Rukh movement. Independence demands were strongest in the former Polish west Ukraine, the
Republic as a whole moving to greater
autonomy under Gorbachev's reforms and
proposed All-Union Treaty. But the hard-
line coup of August 1991 prompted a declaration of independence, followed by hasty
negotiations about its association within a
much looser union.

As the largest Slav minority both under
the Tsars and the Soviets, the Ukraine has
been a test case of the approach to the
SOVIET NATIONALITIES QUESTION. In practice
the Ukrainians have frequently enjoyed
'most favoured nation' status, enjoying considerable autonomy, encouragement for
their cultural identity, and with Russians
proper, making up the higher echelons of
the Communist Party. Only under Stalin
and for a time under Brezhnev has 'Sovietization' been pursued in its full rigour.

R. Pearson, *National Minorities in Eastern Europe,
1848–1945* (1983)
R. S. Sullivant, *Soviet Politics and the Ukraine, 1917–57*
(1962)
J. S. Reshetar, *The Ukrainian Revolution, 1917–20: A
Study in Nationalism* (1952)

**Ulbricht, Walter** (1893–1973). German
communist politician. Born in Leipzig,
Ulbricht joined the SOCIAL DEMOCRATIC
PARTY (SPD) in 1912. Following service in
the army during the First World War, he
joined the GERMAN COMMUNIST PARTY
(KPD) in 1919, shortly after its establishment. Unswervingly loyal to the political
line dictated to the KPD by the COMINTERN,
he rapidly made a career as a full-time party
functionary and sat as a communist deputy
in the REICHSTAG of the WEIMAR REPUBLIC
from 1928 to 1933. With the Nazi seizure
of power in 1933 Ulbricht fled to the Soviet
Union. Surviving the purge of exiled
communists launched by Stalin in the late

1930s, Ulbricht returned to Germany in
April 1945 with the occupying Soviet forces
and played a major role in the establishment of the communist-dominated SED
(*see* SED), of which he became General Secretary in 1946, in the Soviet occupation
zone. With the establishment of the
GERMAN DEMOCRATIC REPUBLIC in October
1949, Ulbricht became one of several deputies to the Minister-President, a modest
position which camouflaged his real political influence. A bland personality, Ulbricht's political mastery was maintained by
his assiduous manipulation of the SED
bureaucracy and the often hesitant support
he received from the Soviet Union. Under
his leadership, the new state pursued
nationalizing and collectivizing economic
policies throughout the 1950s, policies
which contributed to the EAST GERMAN
WORKERS' UPRISING of June 1953 and to the
crisis which led to the construction of the
BERLIN WALL in 1961. In 1960 he became
both Chairman of the National Defence
Council and Chairman of the State Council,
to which the powers of the presidency were
transferred when the office was abolished
following the death of President Pieck.
During the 1960s Ulbricht initiated limited
reform of the centrally planned economy
established during the 1950s whilst maintaining repression of dissident opinion. His
increasing cultivation of managerial technocrats and his concentration of power in the
government State Council, however, gradually aroused the anxiety of some leading
figures in the SED cadre who feared a dim-
inution in the importance of the party.
Alarmed by the *rapprochement* between the
Soviet Union and the Federal Republic
initiated by the government of WILLY
BRANDT, Ulbricht's attempts to sabotage
improved relations between the two states
and secure West German recognition of the
GDR led to the withdrawal of Soviet support for his leadership of the SED. In May
1971 he requested that he be relieved of
leadership of the party. *See also* OSTPOLITIK.

M. McCauley, *The German Democratic Republic since
1945* (1979)
H. A. Turner, *The Two Germanies since 1945* (1987)

**Ulster Conflict.** Although Ulster was
created a self-governing part of the United
Kingdom by the Government of Ireland

Act of 1920, it retained a large Roman Catholic minority, numbering over a one-third of the population, some of whom still favoured the complete unification of Ireland. On several occasions before 1968, the IRISH REPUBLICAN ARMY (IRA) engaged in terrorist operations against the North. A campaign after 1950 led to attacks on customs posts and police barracks before it was finally abandoned in 1962. Fearful of their own security, the Protestant majority had traditionally maintained a policy of discrimination in housing, jobs and political rights. The Royal Ulster Constabulary (RUC) was the only armed police force in the United Kingdom and was supported by the Protestant-dominated paramilitary 'B'-Specials. Regarded by loyalists as a pillar of the Protestant community and a guarantee of the settlement of 1920, the 'B'-Specials were hated by many sections of the Catholic population, who saw them as a symbol of Protestant domination.

From 1963 the Prime Minister of Northern Ireland, Terence O'Neill, began a process of gradual reform in order to give greater equality of political rights to the Roman Catholic community. Encouraged by the election of the Labour government of HAROLD WILSON in October 1964, Campaign for Democracy in Ulster (CDU) was set up. In 1968, at a time of growing world-wide concern with 'civil rights', a moderate but Catholic-dominated organization, the Northern Ireland Civil Rights Association, began to agitate for full equality for the minority community. Serious rioting in Londonderry – a predominantly Roman Catholic city – in October 1968 arose from the questionable behaviour of the RUC. The breaking-up of the People's Democracy civil rights march from Belfast to Londonderry early in January 1969 by the police was widely regarded as a blatant act of discriminatory policing. The resulting government inquiry into the disturbances urged the adoption of a reform programme in Ulster. By the summer of 1969, however, there was widespread violence in the province, including riots against the police and isolated acts of sabotage. In August there were again serious riots in Londonderry following a march by the Protestant Apprentice Boys, and the sectarian rift began to widen alarmingly. The Catholic population

of Londonderry barricaded themselves into the Bogside district and set up 'Free Derry'. Although attacked by the RUC with water-cannons and the incapacitating agent CS gas, the Bogside became effectively a 'no-go' area for the Ulster security forces. On 13 August 1969 the British army was moved into Belfast and Londonderry in order to separate the warring factions and, implicitly, to protect the Roman Catholic population from a now largely discredited Ulster government.

Although welcomed at first by many Catholics, the army soon found itself faced with a deteriorating situation. Serious anti-Catholic rioting in Belfast drove over 500 Catholics from their homes, many of whom sought refuge in the Irish Republic. By the end of the year 13 people had been killed in the conflict. The British army moved into the troubled areas of Belfast and established a 'peace line' between the rival communities, which required 6,000 troops to make it even partially effective. Political reforms were also undertaken: the RUC was disarmed and the 'B'-Specials disbanded in order to replace them with a non-denominational reserve unit, the Ulster Defence Regiment. But the presence of the British army was increasingly resented by the Catholic population, especially those who saw the campaign for civil rights as only the first stage towards the unification of Ireland. As a result, the civil rights movement was increasingly overshadowed by the militant voices of Irish nationalism. During 1969 the PROVISIONAL IRISH REPUBLICAN ARMY split off from the 'Official' movement and set up the Provisional Army Council. Consisting of about 600 activists, the 'Provos' began a campaign of urban terrorism, which included indiscriminate bombings, armed raids, snipings and battles with the army and police. Attempts by the army and police to control the terrorists by searches of Catholic areas and a tougher stance against disorder only increased the antagonism of the Catholic population. The Provisional IRA was able to obtain recruits from the Catholic ghettoes and to use the Irish Republic as a sanctuary area for its attacks on the North. Money and arms came from sympathizers in the south and from the United States, whilst Colonel

Gaddafi of Libya and some Eastern bloc countries provided support.

Even as the violence was worsening, however, the pace of reform was speeded up in an attempt to win over the 'hearts and minds' of the moderate Catholic population. But serious rioting and bombing continued throughout 1970 and at least 25 people were killed in the course of the year. As army and police tactics hardened, in February 1971 the first British soldier was killed in Ulster, and an intensification of street violence led to the introduction of internment without trial. This measure only provoked more violence, so that by the end of the year 173 people had died in bombings and shootings. Car-bombings and sniping attacks became almost routine, and elaborate security checks had to be maintained in the major cities and towns. Considerable disquiet was felt about the policy of internment and the methods being used to extract information from suspects. In the midst of growing concern about Britain's role in propping up the Northern Irish government at Stormont, 13 civilians were killed by the army during a demonstration in Londonderry on 30 January 1972. This incident, which became known as 'Bloody Sunday', snapped the last shreds of support in Britain for the maintenance of the existing Stormont government, and direct rule was imposed in March of the same year. The assumption of power by the British government did not bring an end to the violence; the campaign of terror intensified, reaching a bloody climax on 21 July 1972 when 20 bombs were exploded in Belfast without warning. 11 people were killed outright and 120 wounded, many of them seriously. In reaction, the British government decided to take a strong line against the 'no-go' areas set up by militant Catholics and Protestant organizations such as the Ulster Volunteer Force (UVF). On 31 July 1973 British troops in the province reached 21,000, the largest number this century, and moved into the 'no-go' areas in Operation 'Motorman'. Even so, by the end of the year almost 500 people had been killed in the conflict in Ulster, and the IRA had extended the campaign of bombings to Britain, where seven people were killed.

In 1973 there were renewed attempts to set up a Northern Irish representative body on the basis of proportional representation in talks with the Dublin government at Sunningdale which also agreed to the setting up of a Council of Ireland. In January 1974 a Northern Irish Assembly met with a 'power-sharing executive', but was brought down by a general strike called by the Protestant Ulster Workers' Council in May, forcing the reintroduction of direct rule. Attempts to revive political initiatives failed during the rest of the decade as the situation dragged on into a protracted urban terror campaign by the IRA and splinter organizations such as the IRISH NATIONAL LIBERATION ARMY (INLA). In 1980–81 Republican prisoners went on hunger strike, leading to two deaths in May 1981 and serious rioting in which over 50 people died. In 1982 a new Northern Ireland Assembly was elected but boycotted by the major Catholic Party, the SOCIAL DEMOCRATIC AND LABOUR PARTY and by SINN FEIN. From 1981 meetings of an Ango-Irish Intergovernmental Council had been held and these bore fruit in November 1985 with the ANGLO-IRISH AGREEMENT at Hillsborough, assuring the right of the North to decide its own future, but giving the Irish Government a consultative role in Northern Irish affairs. Denounced by the UNIONISTS as a 'sell-out', leading to mass demonstrations in Belfast and a 24-hour general strike on 3 March 1986, Unionist MPs also boycotted Westminster. The Northern Irish Assembly was finally wound up in June 1986 and direct rule reimposed.

Although the unionist MPs returned to Westminster after the 1987 general election, political progress in the province remained stalemated, while the terrorist activity of the IRA and associated groups continued. On the other side, Protestant paramilitary bodies also stood prepared to conduct reprisals. In 1989 the 20th anniversary of British troops in Northern Ireland was passed without obvious sign of their withdrawal being possible or the end of the terrorist campaign in which more than 2,500 people have died since 1968.

P. Bew and H. Patterson, *The British State and the Ulster Crisis: From Wilson to Thatcher* (1986)

A. Kenny, *The Road to Hillsborough: The Shaping of the Anglo-Irish Agreement* (1986)

P. Buckland, *The Northern Ireland Question, 1886–1986* (1987)

P. Arthur and K. Jeffery, *Northern Ireland since 1968* (1988)

**Ulster Unionist Party** (UUP). The Ulster Unionist Party dominated representation at parliamentary and local level in Northern Ireland from 1921 until the early 1970s as the political expression of the UNIONIST or Protestant majority in Ulster. They took the Conservative whip in the British House of Commons and their dominance was assisted by the first-past-the-post electoral system in the United Kingdom and a degree of electoral malpractice which favoured the Protestant electorate. The Unionist hegemony was broken in the wake of the ULSTER CONFLICT which developed from 1968. The old Unionist Party was split in 1971 with the creation of the DEMOCRATIC UNIONIST PARTY, representing more grass-roots Protestant feeling, demonstrated by their leader, the Rev. Ian Paisley. The introduction of proportional representation in 1973 and a fairer system of local government went some way to mitigating the dominance of the Unionists, but the Ulster Unionists survived as a major representative of Protestant opinion. After a period of rivalry, the UUP have increasingly made common cause with the DUP in opposition to power-sharing in Ulster and the ANGLO-IRISH AGREEMENT.

A. T. Q. Stewart, *The Narrow Ground* (1977)
D. Harkness, *Northern Ireland since 1920* (1983)

**Ultra.** Codename for the information on German movements and intentions obtained in the Second World War by the interception and decoding of German signal traffic encoded on the Enigma coding machine. In 1938 a Polish defector brought news of a new German coding machine. Britain was able to obtain a copy of the machine via the Polish Secret Service and cryptologists based at Bletchley Park were able to break the German coding system to intercept most German military signals. The material provided was of immensely high quality and was used to direct British land and sea operations in the Second World War. So valuable was the decoding secret that it remained under classificaton until 1974.

F. W. Winterbottom, *The Ultra Secret* (1974)
R. V. Jones, *Most Secret War* (1978)

**Umberto II, of Italy** (1904–). King of Italy, 9 May to 2 June 1946. The third child of King VICTOR EMMANUEL III, he served in the army from 1923, reaching the rank of Marshal of Italy in 1942. After the armistice between Italy and the Allies in September 1943 he assumed command of the Italian armies of liberation. A demand for an end to the monarchy began with anti-fascist groups in 1944, when Victor Emmanuel withdrew from active power; Umberto was named 'Lieutenant General of the Realm' and assumed the throne when his father abdicated. Although pro-monarchist groups and the Catholic Church supported him, a referendum on 2 June 1946 decided that Italy should become a Republic. He left Italy on 13 June for exile in Portugal.

R. Katz, *The Fall of the House of Savoy* (1971)
D. Mack Smith, *Italy and her Monarchy* (1989)

**UN.** *See* UNITED NATIONS.

**Unabhängige Sozialdemokratische Partei Deutschlands.** *See* USPD.

**Uniate Church.** Catholics of the Eastern Orthodox rite, primarily concentrated in the Western Ukraine. Historically and constitutionally distinct from the Russian Orthodox Church, the Uniates were forcibly amalgamated with the Russian Orthodox Church in 1946 in an attempt to suppress dissident national feeling in the Ukraine. Since then it has existed as a clandestine church claiming the allegiance of 4.5 to 7.0 million adherents. They have advanced claims for recognition, and following a meeting of Pope JOHN PAUL II with GORBACHEV in December 1989 the Uniates were promised recognition.

**Unilateral Declaration of Independence, Rhodesian.** *See* UDI.

**Unilateralism.** The policy of surrendering use and deployment of nuclear weapons without obtaining similar assurances from other governments, adopted by sections of CAMPAIGN FOR NUCLEAR DISARMAMENT and the LABOUR PARTY from the 1950s. This policy is contrasted with that of multilateralism, which insists on mutual nuclear disarmament as the only basis for peace and security. Unilateralist movements secured majorities in the Labour Party in 1960, provoking bitter divisions, but were overturned in 1961, and again in 1982; but unilateralism was abandoned by leader NEIL KINNOCK in 1989 following Labour's defeat in the 1987 general election and changes in Eastern Europe. Unilateralism has been a major area of conflict within the British Labour Party between Left and Right, often weakening its electoral position. *See also* BEVAN, ANEURIN; GAITSKELL, HUGH.

M. Foot, *Aneurin Bevan, 1945–60* (1973)
P. Williams, *Hugh Gaitskell* (1979)
H. Pelling, *A Short History of the Labour Party* (8th edn, 1985)

**Unión Centro Democrático** (UCD). *See* UNION OF THE DEMOCRATIC CENTRE, SPANISH.

**Unión General de Trabajadores** (UGT; General Union of Workers). The UGT was formed as the industrial arm of the SOCIALIST WORKERS' PARTY, to which it remained closely tied. First organized in 1882, it was largely the creation of the Madrid printers led by Pablo Iglesias, and closely followed his version of evolutionary socialism. Its reformist orientation and virtual rejection of agrarian organization confined its early support to the craft unions of Madrid. To an extent the First World War boom transformed this situation, bringing a wider spectrum of industrial support from miners and railwaymen, and even some rural support in Extremadura and Castile. Even so, numbers remained small, and the UGT could not challenge the predominance of the CONFEDERACIÓN NACIONAL DEL TRABAJO (CNT) in the wider labour movement, with its strongholds in Barcelona and Andalusia. In the post-war crisis the UGT leadership played a contradictory role, temporarily abandoning reformism to attempt a disastrous revolutionary general strike against the RESTORATION REGIME in 1917, then lapsing into quiesence while local unions continued to strike and face repression. With the advent of the PRIMO DE RIVERA regime the UGT leadership – now increasingly dominated by new figures, particularly LARGO CABALLERO, who had made careers as union bureaucrats – chose the path of collaboration offered to it. However, the advantages to be gained from compulsory collective bargaining and preferment over the suppressed CNT proved short-lived. As support waned among miners and rural

labourers suffering from the effects of the DEPRESSION, Caballero chose to break with the dictatorship and throw UGT support behind efforts in the Socialist Party to form an alliance with the Republicans to overthrow the monarchy.

Socialist involvement in the SECOND REPUBLIC provided the conditions to make the UGT a true mass organization for the first time, bringing a flood of new recruits from the countryside, but also faced the organization with growing contradictions between its political and union roles. Hopes that agrarian and industrial reforms would bring material benefits to workers were dashed in the face of employer resistance and Rightist obstruction, bringing into question the continued value of involvement in 'bourgeois' government. Caballero, as Minister of Labour, feared a drift of support to the CNT and consequently began to voice union dissatisfaction with developments, and finally forced the Socialist Party to fight the 1933 elections alone. Radicalism increased after the victory of the Right and the increasingly harsh climate of labour relations that followed. Calls from Caballero's base in the UGT for an increased emphasis on the dangers of fascism and the necessity for a transition to true socialism paved the way for the declaration of a general strike in October 1934 in response to a further rightward move in the government. With the powerful rural sections effectively destroyed after a summer harvest strike, only the miners of Asturias responded to the call, leading to a minor civil war and bloody repression (*see* ASTURIAS RISING). Though further radicalization occurred, putting more unions into the hands of Caballero's supporters, the UGT leadership was prepared to co-operate in the formation of the POPULAR FRONT alliance as a means to remove the Right from power. After victory in February 1936, however, Caballero refused to renew UGT involvement in government on the grounds that the unions had to retain their freedom of action. Strikes and land invasions mounted by UGT supporters determined to achieve real gains followed, complicating the difficulties of the Republican government and contributing to a mounting sense of crisis. At the outbreak of the SPANISH CIVIL WAR, the UGT played an important role in defeating the army rising, organizing a war effort and securing the Republican zone. Some sectors of the UGT, particularly in the countryside, seized the opportunity to collectivize production. However, the move of Caballero into the office of Prime Minister revealed, once again, the ambiguous relationship the federation had with revolutionary methods. Under increasing pressure from the moderate Socialists, Republicans and Communists to resist any equation of the regime with revolution, Caballero refused to give wholehearted support for the creation of a socialist society. Subsequently the UGT lost a lot of its support to the communists before finally succumbing to the emerging Franco regime.

With a leadership in exile in Mexico and France, the UGT played little effective part in the struggle against the dictatorship. Its re-emergence as an effective force was predicated, once again, on support from a Socialist Party that gained influence during the post-Franco era. Although broadly sharing control of the organized labour movement with the Communist Workers' Commissions since the transition to democracy, the UGT has suffered from the generally low levels of union membership that prevail in Spain. The concentration of its membership into the public sector has also brought it increasingly into conflict with its own party, in government since 1982.

G. H. Meaker, *The Revolutionary Left in Spain, 1914–23* (1974)
A. del Rosa, *Historia de la UGT de España, 1901–1931* (1977)
P. Preston, *The Coming of the Spanish Civil War* (1979)
R. Gilespie, *The Spanish Socialist Party: A History of Factionalism* (1989)

**Unionist.** Term used to denote supporter of the union between Ireland and Great Britain dating from the Act of Union in 1801 which united the two countries constitutionally. The term became current in British politics following the introduction of HOME RULE bills in the late 19th century. The Conservative Party (*see* CONSERVATIVE AND UNIONIST PARTY) and a section of the LIBERAL PARTY, the Liberal Unionists, opposed Home Rule. Following the creation of the Irish Free State in 1922 the term lost most of its potency in British politics, but it remains in the official title of the Conservative and Unionist Party. In Ulster, the gov-

erning Protestant party from 1921 to 1972 was the Unionist Party, and the title has been retained by the two current Protestant parties in Northern Ireland, the DEMOCRATIC UNIONIST PARTY and the ULSTER UNIONIST PARTY.

**Union of Soviet Socialist Republics** (USSR). The Union of Soviet Socialist Republics was formally constituted on 6 July 1923, covering the greater part of the old Russian Empire overthrown in 1917, minus the territories which formed Finland, Poland, the Baltic Republics and East Prussia. Following the formation of the PROVISIONAL GOVERNMENT which governed the country from March to early November 1917, the BOLSHEVIKS seized power, vesting authority in the second All-Russian Congress of Soviets, which elected a new government, the Council of People's Commissars. On 10 July 1918 the fifth All-Russian Congress of Soviets adopted the constitution of the Russian Socialist Federal Soviet Republic (RSFSR). In the course of the RUSSIAN CIVIL WAR other Soviet Republics were established in the UKRAINE, BELORUSSIA and Transcaucasia (*see* TRANSCAUSIAN FEDERATED REPUBLIC), which entered into treaty relations with the Russian Soviet Federated Republic and became constituted into the federally organized USSR in 1923. The central executive power was the Council of the Union, together with the Council of Nationalities composed of representatives of the Autonomous and Allied Republics and the Autonomous Regions. Supreme authority was vested in the Central Executive Committee which was elected by the Congress of the Soviets of the Union, the sovereign body and the source of legislation. Between its sessions authority was exercised by the Presidium, a self-electing body virtually identical in membership to the Presidium of the Russian Socialist Federal Soviet Republic. The Presidium became more powerful as it remained in continuous session compared with the Central Executive Committee which met only three times a year by 1926; the Presidium prepared the order of business and executed the resolutions passed. The Central Executive Committee also elected the Council of People's Commissars, originally the cabinet responsible for the departments. Increasingly it was overshadowed by the Presidium, which had power to ratify or stay the execution of the Council's resolutions, to act as a court of appeal against the Council, and to require quarterly reports of all proceedings of the Council.

A new constitution was promulgated on 5 December 1936 and remained in force until 1977. Under it there existed the Council (or 'Soviet') of the Union and the Soviet of Nationalities, forming the two chambers of the Supreme Soviet with equal legislative rights. The Soviet of the Union was elected for a four-year term on the basis of one deputy for every 300,000 inhabitants of the USSR, while the Soviet of Nationalities is elected by citizens of the Union and Autonomous Republics, Autonomous Regions, and National Areas. The Council of Ministers was appointed by the Supreme Soviet and was the highest executive and administrative organ but had no legislative power. The Chairman of the Council was effectively the Prime Minister and there were two First Deputy Chairmen and four Vice-Chairmen. The Council was responsible to the Supreme Soviet or to the Presidium when the Soviet was not in session.

The Presidium, elected by the Supreme Soviet, had 39 members, including a Chairman (the President of the USSR), five Vice-Chairmen and a secretary. The Presidium convenes the sessions of the Supreme Soviet, dissolved it in the event of deadlock, and rescinded orders of the Council of Ministers if not in accordance with the law and constitution. Ministers were appointed and removed by the Presidium. The Presidium had command of the armed forces, the power to declare war, and ratified treaties. The constitution of 1977 defined the separation of powers between the central government and the constituent republics with their Supreme Soviets, Councils of Ministers and Presidiums. GORBACHEV has attempted to reinvigorate the local SOVIETS as a means of permitting a degree of autonomy to Republics. The Republics were also given greater independence through the major reforms to the Soviet constitution approved in 1988. Free elections in March 1989 were the first to allow the expression of movements for autonomy and independence. Under Yeltsin, the Russian Republic sought increased powers, while the Baltic States, Georgia, the Ukraine and Moldavia agitated openly for independence. Gorbachev prepared a new All-Union treaty in 1991 to contain these fissiparous tendencies, but was overtaken by the failed coup attempt of August 1991. Many Republics declared independence and, followed by the dissolution of the Communist Party, effectively destroyed the existing Soviet Union. The Baltic states became independent, as did Georgia. Ten Republics, however, headed by Russia, reformed a loose union with a State Council and executive for common defence and foreign policy. *See also* COMMUNIST PARTY OF THE SOVIET UNION.

L. Shapiro, *The Government and Politics of the Soviet Union* (2nd edn, 1967)
R. Little, *Governing the Soviet Union* (1989)

**Union of the Democratic Centre, Spanish** (Unión Centro Democrático; UCD). Political grouping led by ADOLFO SUAREZ which obtained the largest number of seats, 165 out of 350, in the first post-Franco elections in 1977. It supervised the drawing up of a constitution, grappled with autonomy for the Basque (*see* BASQUES) and Catalan regions, and started negotiations for entry to the EUROPEAN ECONOMIC COMMUNITY. In the 1979 elections, Premier Suarez's bid for an outright majority failed, reaching only 168 seats. In 1981, under pressure from the more conservative elements, Suarez resigned and in the 1982 elections the Socialist Party triumphed over the UDM now led by Calvo Sotelo. The right, formed as the Popular Alliance, won 105 seats, while the UDM obtained only 12 and broke up in February 1983.

**Union pour la Démocratie Française** (UDF). French political group formed in 1978 to unite the non-Gaullist 'majority' candidates. Fighting with the Gaullist successor party, the RPR, it took just over 8 per cent of the total vote in the 1986 elections, compared with 11 per cent for the RPR. It supported Raymond Barre in the 1988 presidential elections, obtaining 16 per cent support on the first-round ballot for the former Prime Minister. Following the success of MITTERRAND in the presidential election the more centrist UDF formed an electoral alliance with the RPR, agreeing to support a joint candidate in each constituency for the forthcoming elections. It denied the Socialists an overall majority in the June 1988 elections, but disarray on the right was compounded by the continued support of the right-wing National Front led by LE PEN. In June 1990 GISCARD D'ESTAING of the UDF and CHIRAC of the RPR agreed to present a single Union pour la France candidate in the 1995 Presidential election, selected by a system of American-style primaries. See also GAULLISM

**United Nations** (UN). International organization founded after the Second World War to replace the LEAGUE OF NATIONS. The term was first used by the Allied powers of themselves in a joint pledge of 1 January 1942 that none of their number would make a separate peace with the AXIS. A conference between China, Britain, the USA and the USSR in October 1943 recognized the need for an international organization, based on the principle of the sovereign equality of all 'peace-loving states', for the maintenance of international peace and security. At Dumbarton Oaks, near Washington, the same powers outlined its structure between August and October 1944; further details were refined at the YALTA CONFERENCE in February 1945 between Britain, the USA and the USSR. These were finalized by 50 nations at war with Germany at the San Francisco Conference between 15 April and 26 June 1945.

Membership is open to any 'peace-loving' state which the UN's general assembly considers able and desirous of fulfilling its obligations under the UN charter. Membership is by a two-thirds vote of the assembly. The main executive organ of the UN is the Security Council, on which Britain, the USA, the USSR and China are permanently represented. 'Nationalist' China (Taiwan) sat from 1949 until 25 October 1971, when it was expelled in favour of the People's Republic of China. Until 1965 their number was ten. The Secretary-General is appointed for five years; past holders of the office have been TRYGVE LIE, DAG HAMMARSKJÖLD, U Thant and KURT WALDHEIM. The present Secretary-General (since 1982) is the Peruvian, Perez de Cuellar (1920-).

The permanent headquarters of the UN is in New York on land paid for by the city and by John D. Rockefeller. The General Assembly, which ultimately takes decisions and hears the Secretary-General's reports, has tended to become an arena for propaganda, but the UN has successfully mediated in numerous international disputes, for example Palestine (1947), Kashmir (1948), Indonesia (1962) and the Middle East cease-fires (1956, 1967 and 1973). It has not been called on to act in European conflicts as much as its predecessor, other than in Cyprus (1964). The UN has proved more effective than the previous League of Nations because of the stronger powers of its Security Council and because member states have to provide armed forces for peacekeeping missions or to resist aggression. The UN's 15 specialized agencies have done much work to improve human conditions and further human rights. The UN's other main organs are the Economic and Social Council, the Trusteeship Council, the International Court of Justice and the Secretariat.

**USPD.** (Unäbhangige Sozialdemokratische Partei Deutschlands; Independent Social Democratic Party of Germany). Left-wing German political party during the late Imperial period and the early stages of the WEIMAR REPUBLIC. Founded in April 1917, the USPD was a minority breakaway party from the GERMAN SOCIAL DEMOCRATIC PARTY (SPD) opposed to its parent party's continuing support for the German war effort during the FIRST WORLD WAR. Initially united only by the internationalist pacifism of its socialist supporters, the USPD gradually emerged as the most radical of the major parties in Germany in the course of 1918. With the GERMAN REVOLUTION of 1918–19, it joined with the SPD in forming a transitional government in November 1918, pending the election of a constituent assembly. It left this coalition in late December 1918, however, believing that the EBERT government was taking insufficient measures to democratize German society. It gained only 7.6 per cent of the vote in the January 1919 elections, yet capitalized on widespread working-class disillusionment with the SPD to secure almost 18 per cent of the vote in the June 1920

REICHSTAG elections. Divided over whether to join the COMINTERN, the USPD split in October 1920, more than half of its 900,000 members joining the GERMAN COMMUNIST PARTY. In September 1922 the 'residual USPD' rejoined the SPD.

A. J. Ryder, *The German Revolution of 1918* (1967)
D. W. Morgan, *The Socialist Left and the German Revolution* (1975)

**USSR.** *See* UNION OF SOVIET SOCIALIST REPUBLICS.

**Ustase.** A Croatian terrorist group founded by the Croatian nationalist Ante Pavelic (1889–1959) to campaign against the Yugoslavian state. It was involved in the murder of King ALEXANDER of Yugoslavia at Marseilles in 1934. During the Second World War the Ustase set up an Independent Croatian State in collaboration with the Germans and Italians. They were accused of many atrocities against Jews, Serbs and communists. Overwhelmed by the forces led by TITO, Pavelic was forced to flee to Spain, and eventually to Argentina. Tito systematically eliminated his rivals, including the Ustase. Croatian terrorist groups have survived to commit terrorist attacks in Sweden, West Germany and Australia. *See also* CROATIA; YUGOSLAVIA.

**UUP.** *See* ULSTER UNIONIST PARTY.

# V

**Vaterlandspartei** (Fatherland Party). German patriotic political party, established in September 1917 to oppose the REICHSTAG PEACE RESOLUTION of July 1917. It advocated extensive annexationist war aims and opposed domestic political reform. It was supported by influential industrialists, conservatives and right-wing liberals as well as (covertly) by the Army High Command under HINDENBURG and LUDENDORFF. By July 1918, it had over 1 million members. It dissolved itself in December 1918.

H. Gatzke, *Germany's Drive to the West* (1950)

**Vatican State.** A small area of Rome under the direct sovereignty of the Pope. The Vatican State was established by the LATERAN PACTS of 1929. It functions as an independent City-State and contains the Basilica of St Peter, the Papal Residence of the Vatican and the Papal Villa of Castel Gandolfo.

**V-bomber force.** *See* NUCLEAR WEAPONS.

**Venizelos, Eleutherios** (1864–1936). Greek statesman and Prime Minister. Born in Crete, he was involved in the Cretan rising against Turkey of 1896. He proclaimed union with Greece in 1905 (ratified 1913). He became President of the Cretan Assembly and the first Prime Minister of an independent Crete in 1908, and was called on to become Prime Minister of Greece in October 1910 following an army coup in 1909. He reorganized the armed forces with French and British help and constructed the Balkan coalition that defeated Turkey in 1912–13 and defeated Bulgaria in 1913, thus gaining most of Macedonia. His attempts to enter the First World War on the side of the Entente ran into conflict with the pro-German stance of the Greek monarch,

CONSTANTINE I, forcing his resignation in March 1915. Having obtained a fresh majority at elections in June he returned to power, obtaining the mobilization of the Greek army and an Anglo-French landing in Salonika. Dismissed by Constantine on 5 October, Venizelos saw Constantine permit the Bulgarian armies to seize Greek border outposts and offer little resistance to advances which threatened the security of the Anglo-French position in Salonika. In September 1916 Venizelos set up a rebel Provisional Government in Crete, which was later moved to Salonika. Following attacks by royalist troops on French and British forces at Athens, the Venizelos government was recognized by the West. In June 1917 Venizelos re-entered Athens and Constantine was forced to abdicate in favour of his son Alexander. Bringing a Greek army into the war on the Macedonian front in early 1918, Venizelos was able to secure Greece a place on the side of the victors at the PARIS PEACE CONFERENCE. Greece gained Western Thrace from Bulgaria, Eastern Thrace and the Aegean islands from Turkey, and by the TREATY OF SÈVRES the city of Izmir (Smyrna) in Asia Minor. Venizelos's advocacy of Greek ambitions in the conference was highly successful, but a disenchanted Greek people, at war for almost eight years, voted him out of office in November 1920. As a result, he escaped the catastrophe which overtook the Greek position in Asia Minor in 1922. Venizelos returned briefly as Prime Minister in January 1924 and again from July 1928 until July 1932, followed by a period from January to March 1933, but was unable to heal the rifts in Greek politics. His supporters staged a rising in March 1935 but he was forced to flee to France, where he died in the following year.

D. Alastos, *Venizelos: Patriot, Statesman, Revolutionary* (1942)

C. Theodoulou, *Greece and the Entente, August 1, 1914–September 25, 1916* (1971)

G. T. Mavrogordatos, *Stillborn Republic: Social conditions and party strategies in Greece, 1922–36* (1983)

**Verdun, Battle of.** Major battle on the WESTERN FRONT in the FIRST WORLD WAR, conducted by the German General VON FALKENHAYN from February to September 1916. Falkenhayn's aim was to force France to defend a crucial sector of France and draw her into an attritional struggle which would 'bleed them white'. The attack was directed on the Verdun salient on 21 February and the loss of forts Douaumont and Vaux was met by French determination to resist. PETAIN was charged with the defence along with NIVELLE and Mangin, feeding fresh divisions into the salient, eventually rotating three-quarters of their infantry battalions in the battle. Successive German offensives in March and April cost the attackers huge casualties, but pressure was eased on the French by the BRUSILOV offensive in the east and the opening of the SOMME offensive in the west. The German offensive closed on 11 July and on the 29 August Falkenhayn was replaced by HINDENBURG and LUDENDORFF who went onto the defensive to meet attacks from Nivelle in the autumn. Losses in dead and wounded reached almost a million on both sides, the French suffering the heavier casualties. By holding their position and recapturing ground lost, the French scored a tactical victory which was the epic French triumph in arms of the war, making the reputation of Petain and Nivelle. The losses, however, deeply affected the French army, revealed in the mutinies of the following year. While Germany's aim to inflict heavy casualties was fulfilled, her own losses of élite troops and NCOs did much to weaken her own forces. *See also*: FALKENHAYN, PETAIN.

A. Horne, *The Price of Glory: Verdun 1916* (1962)

**Versailles, Treaty of.** The settlement signed on 28 June 1919 between Germany and the Western allies as a result of the PARIS PEACE CONFERENCE. By its terms Germany surrendered the following territories: Alsace-Lorraine to France, Eupen-Malmedy to Belgium (following a plebiscite in 1920), Northern Schleswig to Denmark (following a plebiscite in 1920), Pozania and West Prussia to Poland, and Upper Silesia to Poland (following a plebiscite in 1921). The SAAR was put under LEAGUE OF NATIONS control for 15 years and its mining interests placed under French control (returned to Germany following a 1935 plebiscite). DANZIG was put under League of Nations control, as was MEMEL before it was transferred to Lithuania. The German colonies became mandated territories of the League of Nations as follows: German East Africa (to Britain), German South-West Africa (to South Africa), Cameroon and Togoland (to Britain and France), German Samoa (to New Zealand), German New Guinea (to Australia), Marshall Islands and Pacific Islands north of the Equator (to Japan). Germany also lost concessions and trading rights in China, Egypt and the Middle East. Germany was forced to accept the demilitarization of the RHINELAND and of Heligoland, and the internationalization of its major rivers and the Kiel Canal. The German army was limited to 100,000 men, with conscription banned and the General Staff disbanded; heavy weapons were forbidden and Germany was forbidden to build warships over 10,000 tons, possess U-boats, or maintain an airforce. An army of occupation was placed on the West Bank of the Rhine and at the bridgeheads at Cologne, Coblenz and Mainz. Germany was obliged to accept a 'war guilt' clause confirming her responsibility for the war and agreed to pay REPARATIONS to meet all costs incurred in the war. The TREATY OF BREST-LITOVSK was declared void, as was the TREATY OF BUCHAREST, and Germany required to evacuate the BALTIC STATES and other occupied territory. The Covenant of the League of Nations was written into the treaty.

As a result of the settlement, Germany lost 13 per cent of her land area, although some, like the Saar, were not permanently removed. Nonetheless, in the immediate term, Germany's economic losses were considerably heavier, amounting to almost 50 per cent of iron production, 15 per cent of coal production, 10 per cent of total industrial output and 15 per cent of agricultural production. Germany signed the treaty under protest, claiming from the outset that it was a 'diktat' peace, in which no genuine negotiations of the terms took place. The 'war guilt' clause was bitterly resented, Germany claiming that it transgressed the spirit of the armistice signed in November 1918 on the basis of Wilson's FOURTEEN POINTS. The apparently punitive nature of the peace represented an attempt to guarantee French security, the principal objective of the French representative CLEMENCEAU, but served to undermine its moral legitimacy in the eyes of later statesmen concerned with German claims for 'revision' of Versailles. To many in France, however, the peace was not punitive enough; nationalistic French opinion led by Marshall FOCH and POINCARÉ had wanted permanent acquisition of a Rhine frontier or a Rhineland puppet state, and the actual outcome was later rejected as inadequate by Clemenceau. The League of Nations was not considered a sufficient counterweight to a possible German resurgence, especially when the United States both failed to ratify the Versailles Treaty and join the League. Moreover, the treaty could be portrayed as applying a double standard in relation to self-determination, Germans who wanted to join the new German Republic in the Sudetenland and Poland not being allowed the opportunity of voting on the question, while ANSCHLUSS between Germany and Austria was explicitly forbidden. The economic provisions of the peace worked out in the reparations agreements were also a source of criticism. The economist JOHN MAYNARD KEYNES warned in *The Economic Consequences of the Peace* (1919) that the terms were unrealistic and likely to cripple the German economy and hinder a revival of European and world trade. The economic chaos in Germany after 1919 and the onset of the world DEPRESSION was soon to suggest that these criticisms had some validity. Historians have often argued that the Versailles Settlement failed to achieve a clear objective: it was neither a generous settlement on the basis of Wilsonian idealism nor a sufficiently punitive peace to insure against the revival of German power. The political and economic terms of the treaty humiliated Germany while still leaving her the most populous and potentially the strongest economy in Europe; her legitimate grievances undermined a determined response to demands for revision and

played into the hands of nationalist and right-wing sentiment in Germany, notably HITLER and the NAZI PARTY.

H. Nicholson, *Peacemaking, 1919* (1933)
A. J. Mayer, *The Policy and Diplomacy of Peacemaking* (1968)
A. Adamthwaite, *The Lost Peace* (1980)

**VGÖ.** *See* GREEN PARTY, AUSTRIAN.

**Vichy Government.** Government established under Marshal PÉTAIN after the fall of France at the spa town of Vichy in the Auvergne. Following the resignation of Reynaud, Pétain was appointed Prime Minister on 16 June 1940. The Government moved from Paris to Bordeaux the next day and a Franco-German armistice was signed on 22 June which left the northern half of the country occupied by the Germans. The seat of government was moved to Vichy, where LAVAL persuaded the remaining representatives of the THIRD REPUBLIC to invest Pétain with plenary powers as Chief of State, implicitly abolishing the presidency.

Under Pétain's often nominal control, Laval, DARLAN and others attempted to refashion the French state and collaborate with the Germans. Governing by decree, civil liberties were suppressed, political parties banned, trade unions suppressed, and the Chamber and Senate left unconvoked. A wholesale purge of former officials was carried out and trials took place at Riom (*See* RIOM TRIAL) in February 1942 of DALADIER, BLUM and GAMELIN for their part in the French defeat. A major thrust of Vichy policy was the regeneration of France under the slogan of 'Work, Family and Patriotism'. Pétain himself paid particular attention to educational reforms, insisting on physical education, the classics and history as major parts of the curriculum.

Openly authoritarian and supported by many of the former right-wing members of the FRENCH LEAGUES and ACTION FRANÇAISE, the Vichy regime put several thousand of its opponents in prison and concentration camps. Vichy was also profoundly anti-Semitic, reverting to the extreme organic nationalism of the French right. The first anti-Semitic laws were promulgated in October 1940, excluding Jews from public service, the media and the press. Foreign Jews were deprived of French nationality and made liable to internment. In June 1941 Jewish property was Aryanized at minimal compensation. Deportations of French Jews began in 1942, leading to the deaths of 90,000 of the 350,000 French Jews by 1944. The heavy reparations demands of the Germans, combined with charges for occupation and extensive requisitioning, drove French living standards below minimum nutritional requirements for the bulk of the population. From 1942 the Germans also demanded drafts of labour. Laval arranged the *relève* system whereby French labour was supplied in return for the release of prisoners-of-war. A total of 641,000 workers were sent to Germany under the agreements: these, combined with French prisoners of war, voluntary labour, and Frenchmen taken from Alsace-Lorraine, totalled over 1.5 million workers in Germany by 1943.

Pétain governed largely through Laval until 1941, when the latter was replaced by Darlan. Darlan in turn fell foul of Pétain's desire to avoid too close a military collaboration with the Nazis, being demoted in April 1942. Thereafter Laval was in the ascendant, increasing collaboration with the Germans through the forced labour schemes and the deportation of Jews. In so far as Vichy maintained independence, it was through Pétain's influence to at least keep France out of a formal military alliance with Germany. Increasingly, however, many of those who had supported the Marshal recognized that Germany had France at her mercy and independence was a fiction.

Although the majority of the French had supported Pétain's actions in ending the war and most ignored DE GAULLE's call from London on 18 June 1940 to continue resistance, resistance developed rapidly from 1942. Opposition grew from a few inveterate opponents of the Germans to include the communists after the German invasion of the Soviet Union in June 1941, and was swollen by the demands for forced labour and the German occupation of the FREE ZONE in November 1942. The taking of hostages and savage reprisals against the RESISTANCE served to increase opposition which the Vichy regime was unable to coun-

ter. De Gaulle was able to unite the resistance groups in unoccupied France during 1942–3 and at the end of 1942 he was the recognized head of the French forces overseas. In March 1943 resistance groups combined in the Unis de la Résistance which produced the Comité National de la Résistance (CNR). In May this recognized de Gaulle as the national leader of France. As the Vichy regime's authority virtually collapsed from within, quasi-military operations became more common by the winter of 1943–4. At the time of the Normandy landings, the resistance was able to mobilize almost 200,000 armed men who carried out systematic sabotage and obstruction to delay German reinforcements for the front.

Following the surrender of Paris on 24 August 1944, de Gaulle took control of the government, installing his own prefects to supplant the Vichy administrators. Although the Germans carried off the remnants of the Pétain administration to maintain a Vichy government-in-exile, the leaders were brought back to France at the end of the war and tried. Laval and Pétain were both sentenced to death, though Pétain's sentence was commuted.

The central debate about Vichy is the degree to which the eventual liberation masked extensive collaboration with the Germans. There seems little doubt that this was the case in the early years of Vichy, when most of the French accepted defeat and resistance was limited to only a few. Even the communists sought to collaborate until June 1941, although suppressed by the regime. Resistance grew to large-scale proportions only in the last year before liberation, and even then had only lukewarm support from major groups such as the Radicals and the Church. Forced labour, hunger and reprisals were the most effective recruiters against Vichy, which maintained significant support as an orderly, conservative regime stressing traditional values. As a result, Vichy has been seen as a manifestation of the right-wing sentiments in French thought and politics in the inter-war years. Anti-communism, anti-Semitism and authoritarianism were not borrowed from the Nazis, but intrinsic to sections of French society.

R. Aron, *The Vichy Regime, 1940–4* (1958)
R. Paxton, *Vichy France* (1972)

H. R. Kedward, *Resistance in Vichy France* (1978)
G. Hirschfield and P. Marsh (eds.), *Collaboration in France* (1990)

**Victor Emmanuel III, of Italy** (1869–1947). King of Italy, 1900–1946. Born in Naples, the son of Umberto I (1878–1900), he saw military training and ruled as a constitutional monarch, supporting Premiers from the majority parties from 1900. In the First World War he favoured intervention on the side of the Entente and showed strong leadership at the time of the Caporetto defeat, maintaining Italy's place in the war. He gave way to advice from the military and leading industrialists to make Mussolini Prime Minister on 30 October 1922 following the March on Rome. Growing disillusionment with Giolitti and other politicians seem to have influenced him, as did fears for his throne from his pro-fascist cousin, the Duke of Aosta. He refused to dismiss Mussolini at the time of the Matteoti crisis and acquiesced in the virtual destruction of parliamentary democracy by 1929. He supported the war on Ethiopia and accepted the title Emperor of Ethiopia (1936) and later of King of Albania (1939). However, following the Allied invasion of Sicily he began to look for ways of removing Mussolini. Following a vote against Mussolini at the Fascist Grand Council, the King had Mussolini arrested on 25 July, appointing Marshal Badoglio to head the government. After an armistice was concluded on 8 September he fled with Badoglio to Brindisi, and on 13 October agreed to declare war on Germany. Manoeuvres to remove him from the throne and replace him with his son led him to retire to Naples. On 9 May 1946 he abdicated in favour of Umberto II. He went into exile in Egypt.

D. Mack Smith, *Italy and her Monarchy* (1989)

**Vienna Awards.** The Vienna Awards were dictated settlements of Eastern European frontiers under the influence of Germany and Italy. The first Vienna Award (2 November 1938) transferred the Feldvidek region from Czechoslovakia to Hungary. The second Vienna Award (30 August 1940) transferred the greater part of Transylvania from Romania to Hungary.

**Vilna Disputes.** Vilna (also Vilnius, Wilno), the ancient capital of Lithuania, was part of the Russian empire prior to 1917. It became the focus for the new Lithuanian state as the Baltic states asserted their independence after the Bolshevik revolution. It was seized by Polish forces in October 1920 and incorporated into Poland in 1922. Following the German and Soviet invasion of Poland in September 1939, Vilna was returned to Lithuania. It became part of the Soviet Union when the Baltic States were absorbed after 1945. The dispute over Vilna between the wars created antagonism between Lithuania and Poland, inhibiting co-operation in the face of their predatory neighbours.

**Virgin Lands Campaign.** Campaign launched by Khrushchev in 1953 to develop the 'virgin lands' of steppe in Kazakhstan, western Siberia and south-east Russia as grain growing areas. By 1956 90 million acres (36.4 million hectares) had been brought under cultivation, assisted by extensive mechanization and recruitment of thousands of volunteers, some of whom became permanent settlers in the regions. Early good harvests up to 1956 were followed by declining yields and serious land erosion which damaged millions of acres. The unsuitability of the terrain for arable monoculture, a search for quick results and insufficient fertilizers were mainly to blame. Although the scheme added to the Soviet Union's grain output it fell so far short of expectations that it caused serious criticism of Khrushchev's competence as leader. Moreover, antagonisms between national minorities and the settlers and volunteers drafted into the regions led to complaints about Russification, as well as disillusion on their part when the scheme began to prove ill-founded. The campaign formed part of a series of initiatives to raise awareness about the need to improve agricultural production, using the 'virgin lands' to relieve pressure on the Ukraine, which could devote more land to dairy and meat production.

W. Hahn, *The Politics of Soviet Agriculture* (1972)
M. McCauley, *Khrushchev and the Development of Soviet Agriculture: The Virgin Lands Programme, 1953–64* (1976)

**Vlasov Army.** Army of Russian prisoners-of-war formed to fight against the Soviet Union by the Germans. It took its name from General Anrei Vlasov, a Soviet general captured in 1942. Although Vlasov was persuaded to make appeals to Soviet soldiers to desert, German opposition to the setting up of national units of Russian soldiers or a Russian government-in-exile delayed the formation of a Committee for the Liberation of the Peoples of Russia until September 1944. It published a political programme, the Prague Manifesto, in November, proposing a more liberal socialized regime and self-determination for the Russian nationalities. The Vlasov army fought on the Eastern Front in spring 1945, eventually seeking refuge in Czechoslovakia, where it fought against the Germans in the last days of the war. Vlasov, however, was turned over to the Soviet authorities and was shot with his other commanders in 1946. German intransigence, largely on racial lines, prevented them until too late from making much use of Russian ex-soldiers, although formations of COSSACKS and Ukrainians were more numerous. Vlasov, the son of a serf, but also an ex-Communist Party member, offered a left-wing programme not dissimilar to that of the more liberal opponents of Stalin. He and his followers found themselves hopelessly compromised as traitors once the Red Army had defeated the Nazis in the East. *See also* SECOND WORLD WAR.

J. Thorwald, *The Illusion: Soviet Soldiers in Hitler's Armies* (1975)

**V-weapons.** German name for unmanned weapons, from 'V' for *Vergeltungswaffen* or 'revenge weapon'. The Germans began work in 1942 on the V1 or 'flying bomb'. The V1 was an unmanned airframe 27 feet (8 m) in length and with a wing span of almost 18 feet (5.5 m), powered by a pulse-jet. This could carry a warhead of 1,870 lb (849 kg) about 150 miles. The V1 was capable of 390 mph, guided by an autopilot on a fixed trajectory. Over 32,000 V1s were produced, of which 20,000 were fired operationally from June 1944. Over 13,000 were fired against Great Britain, where they killed nearly 6,000 people and wounded another 40,000. The relatively low speed of the V1 meant that it could be shot down by anti-aircraft fire or destroyed by the faster fighter aircraft. The British defences shot down or destroyed 3,957 flying bombs, with fighters and anti-aircraft guns accounting for about equal numbers. Most of the V1 launch sites were overrun or bombed by the end of 1944.

The V2, officially designated as the A4, was a much more advanced weapon, a single-stage liquid-fuelled rocket developed by Wernher von Braun at the research station at Peenemünde. The V2, 47 feet (14 m) long, was fuelled by a mixture of alcohol and oxygen. The first successful test flight took place in October 1942 and the first missiles were launched against Paris and London in September 1944. About 3,000 V2s were fired operationally, nearly 2,000 of them against Great Britain. By the end of the war they had killed 2,724 people in Great Britain and wounded over 6,000. There was no adequate defence against the V2 other than to destroy the launch sites, which the Allies were able to do as they advanced into the Low Countries and Germany. The V-weapons provided some sustenance for German morale in the last months of the war, German propaganda laying great stress on HITLER'S 'secret weapons' as a means of turning the tide. Their evident failure to do so helped to undermine German morale in the last weeks of the war. The V2 was to provide the prototype for the intercontinental and intermediate-range ballistic missiles of the post-war period. Von Braun and many other German rocket experts were soon employed by the United States and the Soviet Union to equip them with a new generation of long-range missiles, soon to be armed with nuclear warheads. *See also* BLITZ, THE; NUCLEAR WEAPONS.

J. Garlinski, *Hitler's Last Weapons* (1978)

**Waffen-SS.** A sub-unit of the SS (*see* ss), expanded into a large independent military force, virtually a separate army, during the Second World War. *Waffen* troops were all supposed to be Aryans, but not necessarily German; they included volunteers from France, Holland, Belgium, Norway, Denmark, Hungary, Spain, Lithuania and Romania. In all there were 40 *Waffen* divisions engaged in the Second World War. The best of them were élite formations given priority in recruits and equipment, but they were also engaged in some of the most controversial operations, such as the suppression of the WARSAW GHETTO RISING in April 1943 and that of 1944.

**Waldheim, Kurt** (1918–). Austrian President, 1986–. Born in St Andräa, Austria, he served a year's military service, 1936–7, and then began law studies at Vienna University. Much controversy surrounds the record of his military and political career during the Nazi occupation of Austria. He is alleged to have joined the National Socialist Student League after the AN-SCHLUSS, but has denied this. He took part in the occupation of the Sudetenland in 1938, with the Fourth Squadron of the 11th Cavalry regiment, but has disputed the claim that he became a member of the SS *Reitersturm* in November of the same year (*see* ss). After serving in France and on the Eastern Front, he was transferred to Belgrade as an interpreter. Following study leave between November 1942 and March 1943 he returned to the Balkans. Waldheim's own statements about his second period of service in the Balkans have been inconsistent and have served to fuel the controversy around his presidency. De-Nazification proceedings were commenced against him after the war, but he was found to be 'less implicated' and, as in many such cases, the proceedings were never concluded.

After serving as Foreign Secretary from 1968 to 1970 Waldheim was elected General Secretary of the United Nations in 1971, supported by the Soviet Union and the United States, but opposed by Britain and China. It has since been argued that both superpowers saw in him a potentially pliable General Secretary. In 1986 Waldheim announced his candidacy for the Austrian presidency, and was supported by the Conservative AUSTRIAN PEOPLE'S PARTY (ÖVP). Allegations of dishonesty about his past, which followed almost immediately, did not succeed in preventing his election, and he narrowly defeated his socialist opponent, Kurt Steiger, in the second round. The controversy surrounding Waldheim's presidency has refused to die down, however, and has served to undermine both the precarious political consensus within Austria and the country's reputation abroad.

R. E. Herzstein, *Waldheim: The Missing Years* (1988)

**Walesa, Lech** (1943–). Polish trade unionist and politician. A Gdansk shipyard electrician, he emerged as leader of the independent SOLIDARITY trade union in summer of 1980, leading a strike at the Lenin shipyard on 14 August. He signed an accord with government on behalf of Solidarity on 31 August 1980, allowing free trade unions and the right to strike. He oversaw the rise of Solidarity to a peak of 9 million members by late 1980 and a growing challenge to the authority of the Communist Party. Detained following the imposition of martial law on 13 December 1981 by General JARU-ZELSKI, Walesa was kept in internment for 11 months and released in November 1983 under virtual house arrest. He was awarded the Nobel Peace Prize during his detention (5 October), but was prevented from attending the prize ceremony in Sweden in December. In March 1985 he called for strikes against price rises but was largely ignored because of the suppression of the Solidarity organization. He helped to organize the boycott of the government referendum on a programme of economic reform in November 1987. In spring 1988 he demanded talks with the government following a renewed wave of strikes. He met the West German Foreign Minister in January 1988 and Mrs THATCHER in November, emphasizing his role as a leading spokesman for the Polish opposition. He persuaded militants to call off strikes so that Solidarity could offer responsible negotiations with the government. Following the acceptance by the government of talks, which were opened in February 1989, Walesa signed an agreement to legalize Solidarity on 5 April, together with terms for participation in free elections and the creation of opposition parties. After Solidarity's sweeping victory in the elections of June 1989 Walesa pressed for the formation of a non-communist government, thus forcing General Kiszczak, appointed on 2 August, to make way for a non-communist. Although Walesa was proposed as Premier on 16 August, he declined the offer of office, allowing Tadeuz Mazowicki, another Solidarity activist, to become head of Poland's first non-communist government for 40 years. Walesa subsequently acted as an unofficial ambassador for the Solidarity-led government, seeking overseas aid for Poland's economic problems. Walesa's remarkable rise from obscurity to become the effective leader and spokesperson for Solidarity owed a great deal to his powerbase in the Lenin shipyard and his ability to offer a possibility of compromise on a programme of economic reform. Although operating under severe restrictions from 1982, he had powerful support and protection from his prestige abroad, including an audience with Pope JOHN PAUL II in 1983, enabling him to re-emerge as the crucial powerbroker with the Communist Party in 1988–9. Walesa also distanced himself from the more intellectual elements in the Solidarity movement, finding himself more comfortable in the search for pragmatic sol-

utions to the problems of the workers he saw himself as representing. With no formal role in the Solidarity Government formed in August 1989, he became travelling spokesman for Poland abroad. In 1990 he declared his intention of running for President and in a bruising campaign against some former supporters the was elected President in December 1990.

N. Ascherson, *The Polish August: The Self-limiting Revolution* (1982)

T. Garton Ash, *The Polish Revolution: Solidarity, 1980–82* (1983)

**War Communism.** Term applied to the Bolshevik government's policies during the RUSSIAN CIVIL WAR. Growing out of Lenin's belief in the need to organize the whole of the national economy on behalf of the proletariat, the Bolshevik Party took control of almost every sector of social and economic life in order to prosecute the war and safeguard the revolution. The policy was characterized by the nationalization of industry and trade, centralized control of the allocation of resources, and the forced requisitioning of agricultural produce. Although War Communism helped to provide the essential supplies which enabled the Bolsheviks to sustain their armies and emerge victorious from the Civil War, it also had the effect of greatly increasing the power of the state and the Bolshevik Party, diminishing the freedoms won in the early phases of the RUSSIAN REVOLUTION. State control of industry antagonized workers seen in the WORKERS' OPPOSITION, requisitioning alienated the peasantry, provoking peasant risings and a collapse in agricultural production, while nationalization of trade and banking produced a large-scale black market and runaway inflation. By 1921, faced with economic collapse and widespread discontent, War Communism was replaced by the NEW ECONOMIC POLICY.

D. Footman, *Civil War in Russia* (1961)

M. McCauley (ed.), *The Russian Revolution and the Soviet State, 1917–21* (1975)

**Warsaw Ghetto Rising.** Jewish rising in the Warsaw ghetto in April 1943. After the concentration of the Polish Jews into the Warsaw ghetto in October 1940 approximately 0.5 million Jews lived in conditions of extreme privation. The removal of Jews for extermination began in July 1942, reducing the number to an estimated 70,000 people in October 1942. On 19 April 1943 the surviving members of the ghetto rose against the German forces, fighting until 10 May with makeshift weapons against 2,000 SS troops (see WAFFEN-SS) backed by tanks and heavy weapons. German forces suffered 200 casualties before the rising was suppressed and the ghetto's inhabitants either killed or captured. Although it is the most famous example of Jewish resistance to the Nazis, the Warsaw Ghetto Rising was not the only example of organized Jewish opposition. There were risings in at least a dozen ghettoes in Poland and Russia, and mass breakouts were attempted at extermination camps such as Sobibor (September 1943) and Auschwitz (1944). Other Jews escaped the ghettoes or round-ups to join partisan groups or live underground. *See also* HOLOCAUST.

Y. Gutman, *The Jews of Warsaw: Ghetto, Underground, Revolt* (1982)

**Warsaw Pact.** The major military-political alliance of Soviet-dominated Eastern bloc since 1955. The Warsaw Pact was signed on 14 May 1955, coming into force on 5 June 1955. The Pact resulted from Soviet concern at the full independence of the FEDERAL REPUBLIC OF GERMANY and her entry into the NORTH ATLANTIC TREATY ORGANISATION (NATO). Signature followed shortly after formal agreements had been signed to this effect in London and Paris at the beginning of May. The Soviet Union also annulled its alliances signed with Britain in May 1942 and France in December 1944. The stated aims of the Pact were: (1) to safeguard the peace and security of members of the pact; (2) to aid with all necessary steps, including armed force, any member of the Pact who is attacked; (3) to establish a joint command, including joint manoeuvres. The original signatories were the German Democratic Republic, Poland, Hungary, Romania, Bulgaria, Czechoslovakia, Albania and the USSR. Albania ceased to participate in 1961 because of its rift with Moscow, and withdrew in 1968. The Pact was extended in 1975 and 1985. The headquarters of the organization is in Moscow. It has a Political Consultative Committee which is intended to meet twice a year with rotating venue and chairmanship, usually meeting in alternate years with delegations led by the First Secretaries of the communist parties of the member states. A Committee of Defence Ministers meets annually and a Committee of Foreign Ministers has met annually from 1976. The Military Council of national chiefs-of-staff meets twice a year. The forces of the Warsaw Pact provide the major military force confronting NATO in Europe, with over 4.5 million men under arms in 1985 drawn from all the Warsaw Pact countries, including over 3.5 million men from the USSR. The Pact was officially stated to be defensive in character, but its offensive capacity, particularly in tanks and tactical and medium-range nuclear weapons, has dictated the military strategy of NATO. To the Soviet Union the adherence of member states to the Pact has been seen as a commitment to the Soviet bloc. Attempts to withdraw from the Pact following the HUNGARIAN UPRISING of 1956 precipitated the Soviet invasion and crushing of the revolt; in 1968 the 'PRAGUE SPRING' prompted an invasion by Warsaw Pact forces. The presence of large bodies of Soviet forces in the Eastern bloc countries was also seen as a potential guarantee of obedience, especially in the German Democratic Republic, where the bulk of the forces are stationed. After a period of increased tension under BREZHNEV, there have been major cuts in Soviet Warsaw Pact forces following the accession of GORBACHEV. In late 1989 the Soviet Union has tolerated, with apparent equanimity, discussion in the non-communist governments of Eastern Europe proposals for withdrawal from the Pact. By the spring of 1990 it was widely perceived in the West that the Warsaw Pact was, effectively, in dissolution, confirmed by a formal declaration that it would cease to exist as a military alliance from June 1991. Representatives of the Pact participated in the negotiations at Vienna from March 1989 under the framework of the CSCE which culminated in the treaty on CONVENTIONAL ARMED FORCES IN EUROPE signed in November 1990, hugely slashing conventional forces held by the Pact west of the Urals.

Z. Brzezinski, *The Soviet Bloc* (1974)

**Warsaw Rising.** The Warsaw Rising was led by General 'Bor' Komorowski

(1895–1956) and the Polish Home Army (AK) in August 1944. The Home Army was a clandestine force, loyal to the Polish government-in-exile in London. Formed from 1939, it was commanded by regular officers and had both ex-soldiers and volunteers in its ranks. It was several hundred thousand strong, largely equipped with small arms and self-made weapons. The Home Army was authorized by the London government to seize Warsaw in advance of the Soviet forces, which had thrown the first bridgeheads across the Vistula. About 20,000 answered a radio appeal on 1 August and attacked the German troops. Although the German forces were driven into pockets they were not eliminated. German forces were able to concentrate on suppressing the revolt as no assistance came from the Soviet armies. After two months of bitter fighting the Home Army surrendered on terms, having lost 10,000 dead and 7,000 wounded. Many civilians died and much of Warsaw was destroyed either in the fighting or in deliberate German destruction afterwards. Poles believed the Soviet lack of assistance was deliberate, STALIN being ready to see potential rivals eliminated. Certainly Stalin was obstructive, delaying permission for Royal Air Force and American planes landing on Soviet-held territory. His land forces, however, were genuinely exhausted, at the end of a headlong advance in which they had lost heavily and were subject to heavy German counter-attacks. A Soviet advance in fact began on 10 September, but met with heavy opposition, although some supplies for Warsaw were dropped by air. Warsaw remained in German hands until 1 January 1945. The Home Army was dissolved by the Soviets when they advanced and several of its leaders were imprisoned or died of ill-treatment. General Bor Komorowski was imprisoned in Colditz and was handed over to the Americans in May 1945.

J. Erickson, *The Road to Berlin* (1983)

**Washington Naval Agreement.** Signed on 6 February 1922 between, principally, Britain, France, the United States, Japan and Italy. The treaty aimed to reduce the number of heavy capital ships by a moratorium on their building for ten years. The United States, Britain and Japan agreed to adjust their fleets to a ratio of 5:5:3 respectively, and France and Italy each agreed to a total just over half that of Japan. A new agreement signed in London on 22 April 1930 by the United States, Britain and Japan covered other warships and submarines, adopting a ratio of 10:10:7.

**Webb, Beatrice** [née Potter] (1858–1943) and **Webb, Sidney** (1859–1947). British pioneers of social and administrative reform and founder members of the FABIAN SOCIETY. They were joint authors of numerous influential works on labour history, including *The History of Trade Unionism* (1894), and *Industrial Democracy* (1897), and were founders of the London School of Economics and of the *New Statesman*. Sidney Webb helped in the reorganization of the University of London and the provision of public education legislation, and held various offices: MP for Seaham, 1922–9; President of the Board of Trade, 1924; Secretary of State for Dominion Affairs, 1929–30; and Secretary of State for Colonies, 1930–31. The Webbs had a powerful influence on the development of the distinctively British form of 'gradualist' socialism, Sidney Webb drawing up the BRITISH LABOUR PARTY constitution of 1918. Their later careers were somewhat blighted by their blinkered admiration for STALIN's Russia.

B. Webb, *My Apprenticeship* (1926)
——, *Our Partnership* (1948)
N. and J. Mackenzie, *The First Fabians* (1977)

**Wee Frees.** 'Independent Liberals' who refused to support LLOYD GEORGE as Prime Minister of a coalition government of Liberals and Unionists after 1918. Very much in the minority in the LIBERAL PARTY, most lost their seats in the House of Commons at the 'Coupon' election of 1918. ASQUITH, their leader, lost his own seat in 1918 and the group was then led by Donald Maclean until he re-entered parliament in 1920. The independents were only truly reconciled to Lloyd George in 1926 when he replaced Asquith as official leader of the Liberal Party.

T. Wilson, *The Downfall of the Liberal Party* (1966)
C. P. Cook, *A Short History of the Liberal Party, 1900–88* (3rd edn, 1989)

**Weimar Republic.** The name by which the German Republic of 1919 to 1933 is generally known, after the Thuringian city of Weimar in which the constituent National Assembly elected in January 1919 set about the task of drafting a constitution for a successor state to the German Empire which had collapsed at the end of the First World War. The National Assembly was dominated by the coalition of the right-wing (Majority) SOCIAL DEMOCRATIC PARTY, the German Democratic Party (see DDP) and the CENTRE PARTY (the so-called 'Weimar coalition') and the new constitution, formally adopted by the National Assembly in late July 1919, was explicitly a democratic one. The head of state was a popularly elected President, whose term of office ran for seven years. The President chose the head of government, the Chancellor, and possessed a range of emergency powers. The position of President was occupied by the Social Democrat FRIEDRICH EBERT from 1919 to 1925; and by the right-wing monarchist Field Marshal VON HINDENBURG from 1925 until the Republic's demise. The Chancellor was formally accountable to the REICHSTAG, elections to which were to be held at least every four years on the basis of a 'party-list' system of proportional representation. The Republic inherited the federal structure of the German Empire in modified form, and the individual states (the largest of which was Prussia) retained powers such as control of education and the police. They were represented at a national level in the upper house, or *Reichsrat*, whose function in the legislative process was essentially an advisory one.

The extreme form of proportional representation embodied in the Republic's constitution combined with the legacy of political culture bequeathed the Republic by the German Empire to ensure that the formation of long-lasting stable coalitions of support for the government in the *Reichstag* would be a difficult task. Although the government was now accountable to the *Reichstag*, the policial parties continued to pursue a form of 'negative politics' in representing the interests of clearly-defined groups within society, making compromise and co-operation between parties difficult during periods of economic or political crisis. The widespread absence of political will to transcend sectional interests at the political level and widespread hostility to the new order doomed the Republic to experience a series of short-lived coalition governments: between 1919 and 1933 the Republic witnessed the formation of 21 cabinet governments with an average life of under eight months. Long-term structural economic problems, exacerbated by the territorial sacrifices and loss of overseas investments arising from the First World War and the TREATY OF VERSAILLES peace settlement, promoted acute class antagonism throughout most of the Republic's history, class antagonism which was particularly apparent in the immediate post-war period, the period of hyper-inflation of 1922–3 and the world economic DEPRESSION of 1929 onwards. At the political level, such antagonism was reflected in hostility to republican order on the part of the parties of the Right, the DNVP and the DVP (see DNVP; DVP) and the extreme Left, the GERMAN COMMUNIST PARTY (KPD).

It is a matter of convention to divide the history of the Republic into three phases. The first, stretching from its inception through to the height of the hyper-inflation crisis (1919 to 1923), was dominated by the attempts of a succession of coalition governments to deal with the problems of concluding the Versailles peace settlement; of seeking to overcome the economic dislocation arising from that peace settlement, the demobilization process and conversion of the economy from a wartime to a peacetime footing; and of warding-off threats to their survival posed by insurrections of both the extreme right and the extreme left. During this period, the right-wing parties refused to participate in government. The crisis of the hyper-inflation of 1922–3 led the more moderate of the right-wing parties, the DVP, to enter government under its leader GUSTAV STRESEMANN.

The second main phase in the Republic's history stretched from the overcoming of the hyper-inflation crisis through to the onset of the world economic DEPRESSION (1924 to 1929). Whilst the economy was to be disrupted by the effects of stabilization of the currency following the hyper-inflation and the impact of a world-wide slump in agricultural prices, this was a period of economic recovery, and by 1928 Germany was once again the world's second largest industrial economy. This period was also, and not coincidentally, one of relative political stability: whilst government continued to rest on a series of fragile centre-right coalitions in the *Reichstag*, this period seemed to witness the emergence of a greater degree of political consensus, illustrated by the participation of the right-wing DNVP in government for the first time. It also saw Germany's reintegration into the international community through the LOCARNO TREATIES and German entry into the LEAGUE OF NATIONS in 1926.

The final phase in the history of the Republic stretches from the onset of the world economic crisis through to the Nazi seizure of power in 1933 following HITLER's appointment as Chancellor. This period was dominated by growing political polarization, to the KPD and to the NAZI PARTY (NSDAP), against the background of deepening economic crisis, together with a clear determination on the part of the élites within East Elbian agriculture, heavy industry, the army leadership, the ministerial bureaucracy and the camarilla around Hindenburg, to exclude the SPD from political power and to restructure the political and social order in a more authoritarian direction. The collapse in March 1930 of the coalition of SPD, DDP, DVP and Centre formed after the May 1928 *Reichstag* elections was to issue in a series of governments by means of presidential decree under BRÜNING, PAPEN and SCHLEICHER, bypassing the *Reichstag*. From the September 1930 elections onwards, it was impossible to form a majority in the *Reichstag* excluding the SPD, the KPD and the NSDAP; and, following the July 1932 elections, in which the NSDAP gained over 37 per cent of the popular vote and became the largest party in the Reichstag, the essential question of German politics was on what terms the NSDAP could be brought to support an authoritarian government. Hitler's appointment as Chancellor in January 1933 in a coalition government with the DNVP, and the subsequent Nazi monopolization of political power, effectively marks the end of the Republic, though its constitution was never formally repealed and, after 1945, the FEDERAL REPUBLIC OF GERMANY was to draw

on its claims to be the successor of the Republic for its political legitimacy.

Scholarly research into the history of the Weimar Republic in the period after 1945 initially concentrated largely on the final phase of the Republic's history, the rise of the Nazi Party and the background to Hitler's appointment as Chancellor. During the 1960s longer-term explanations were sought for the inability of the institutions of the Republic to survive economic crisis and political polarization, through research into the establishment of the Republic and its early history. Simultaneously, detailed examination of the 'middle years' of relative political and economic stability began to be undertaken. Whilst much of the political, social, economic and cultural history of the Weimar Republic has been thoroughly examined, a number of issues continue to provoke disagreement amongst historians. Perhaps three are deserving of special mention, all of which are crucial to any judgement about the long-term viability of Weimar democracy.

The first concerns the nature and extent of the GERMAN REVOLUTION of 1918–19. Did the failure of the Majority Social Democrats to exploit their new-found power and push through a wide-ranging democratization of the institutions the new Republic inherited from the German Empire, socialization of some sections of heavy industry and a thorough reform of the army officer corps, constitute the only reasonable course of action open to them in the economic chaos prevalent in Germany in the winter of 1918–19 and a period of apparently intensifying class conflict? Or did their excessive reliance on co-operation with the élites which survived the revolution ensure the survival of powerful groups which were to play an important role in the elevation of Hitler to the chancellorship in 1933?

The second area of intense historiographical debate centres on the development of the German economy during the 'middle years' of relative economic and political stability. Here the essential question is whether the subsidies and wealth-redistribution policies deployed by Republican governments and the rise in real wages which resulted from stronger trade union power and state compulsory arbitration schemes after 1924 resulted in a dangerous lowering of investment levels, unnecessarily high unemployment even during the 'golden years' of the Weimar economy and a weakening of the international competitiveness of an economy which was heavily dependent on exporting. If this thesis is accepted, one might conclude that the Weimar economy was in a weak state even before the onset of the world economic crisis which exacerbated rather than caused the German depression, and that, given the fragility of the political system even during the mid-1920s, the prospects for German democracy were not encouraging.

The third area centres on the period of rule by Chancellors by means of presidential decree. There is general agreement that the collapse of the 'Grand Coalition' in March 1930 and its replacement by a cabinet dependent on presidential emergency powers constituted a dangerous development in the system of government; but there is as yet no agreement about whether this is best seen as an inevitable consequence of a crisis of the party-political system or the result of a deliberate policy by Hindenburg and élites which surrounded him to seek to transform the political system in an authoritarian direction, creating a government independent of parties and *Reichstag*, and excluding the SPD from any share of political power.

A. J. Nicholls, *Weimar and the Rise of Hitler* (2nd edn, 1979)
R. Bessel and E. J. Feuchtwanger (eds), *Social Change and Political Development in Weimar Germany* (1981)
E. Kolb, *The Weimar Republic* (1988)

**Weizmann, Chaim** (1874–1952). Zionist leader and the first President of Israel. Born in Russian Poland, he studied in Germany before taking up a post as a biochemist at Manchester University in 1906. He became a British subject in 1910, although already an active Zionist (*see* ZIONISM). He worked for the British Government, 1916–19, as Director of the Admiralty Laboratories, and helped to secure the BALFOUR DECLARATION of 1917. He became president of the World Zionist Organisation and of the Jewish Agency in Palestine, 1921–31, 1935–46. He was elected first President of Israel in May 1948, holding office until his death in November 1952. He is regarded as the father of the modern state of Israel.

C. Weizmann, *Trial and Error* (1949)

N. Bethell, *The Palestine Triangle* (1979)
H. W. Sachar, *History of Israel: From the Rise of Zionism to our own Time* (1985)

**Welfare State.** A term used to describe the provision of extensive social welfare by the state, coined in the 1930s to contrast with the 'warfare state' devoting itself to armaments. The phrase has been used to describe the policies of the Swedish governments of the SOCIAL DEMOCRATIC LABOUR PARTY from the mid-1930s who began the introduction of comprehensive social welfare, and in Britain for the social legislation under ASQUITH and LLOYD GEORGE prior to 1914 – the so-called 'Liberal Welfare State'. It is most commonly applied to the introduction of comprehensive social insurance and free health care following on the BEVERIDGE Report of 1942. Most European governments adopted elements of the welfare state after 1945 in the form of extended social provision financed wholly or in part from taxation. The most highly developed welfare states have been in Scandinavia (Sweden and Denmark) and in communist countries where extensive social provision has been often pointed to as a beneficial aspect of their regimes. As early as the 1930s, left-wing sympathizers pointed to the Soviet Union as providing model facilities in such areas as nursery provision and free medical facilities. Though now treated with scepticism, these claims filtered through into socialist and Christian democratic demands for greater planning and comprehensiveness in the provision of social welfare after 1945. Important principles of freedom of access and minimal charges have lately come under attack from more market-orientated critics of social policy, leading many to argue that the welfare state is in crisis and has become overburdensome.

P. Wilding (ed.), *In Defence of the Welfare State* (1986)
J. Clarke, A. Cochrane and C. Smart, *Ideologies of Welfare: From Dreams to Disillusion* (1987)

**Welsh Nationalist Party.** *See* PLAID CYMRU.

**Western European Union** (WEU). The TREATY OF BRUSSELS set up an organization consisting of a Council of Ministers of the five member states and a Permanent Commission consisting of the ambassadors of the Benelux countries and France and an official of the British Foreign Office, who supervised the social and cultural activities under the treaty. In 1954 protocols were signed to the treaty which extended its membership to Germany and Italy and replaced the existing Council of Ministers with a Council of Western European Union, consisting of the members' Foreign Ministers, replaced for most meetings by their ambassadors in London and a Danish Foreign Office official, and set up an Assembly consisting of the representatives of the member states in the Consultative Assembly of the COUNCIL OF EUROPE. Western European Union fulfilled an important initial function in securing the admission of West Germany to NATO (*see* NORTH ATLANTIC TREATY ORGANISATION), and in helping to settle the future of the SAAR, which was incorporated into West Germany. Thereafter its role declined, the social and cultural activities being largely replaced by those of the Council of Europe, and its defence role being fulfilled through NATO. The WEU received a new lease of life in the wake of the COLD WAR as a pan-european organization for discussing security matters and which can mobilise armed forces independent of NATO to police conflicts.

**Western Front.** Battle-zone between Germany and her enemies France and Britain in the First World War, extending from Nieuport on the coast of Belgium through Ypres, Arras, Soissons and Rheims to the area around Verdun. The battle-line remained static through most of the war, until the German spring offensive of 1918. The term is also used as a synonym for the attritional battles of the First World War.
J. Terraine, *The Western Front, 1914–18* (1964)

**West Germany.** *See* GERMANY, FEDERAL REPUBLIC OF.

**Westland Affair.** British political crisis in the winter of 1985–6 over the take-over of Britain's leading independent helicopter manufacturer, the Westland Company. During the winter parliamentary recess a public row developed between the Minister of Defence, Michael Heseltine, and the Trade and Industry Secretary, Leon Brittan, over rival solutions to the company's

problems. Heseltine backed the exploration of a European bid, while Brittan and the Prime Minister, Mrs THATCHER, favoured leaving the decision to the shareholders, who were known to favour a bid from the American Sikorsky Company. Heseltine dramatically resigned from the Cabinet on 9 January 1986, complaining of attempts to shackle his campaign. Intense political controversy was fuelled by allegations of officially inspired leaks of a letter to Heseltine from the Solicitor-General. Brittan came under increasing pressure and was forced to resign on 24 January. The affair was believed to have compromised civil service neutrality and undermined the reputation of the Prime Minister, who was accused of complicity in the leak.

**Wets.** Derisory term applied to members of the British Conservative Party who did not support the more radical policies of their leader and Prime Minister, MARGARET THATCHER. They were generally perceived to be opposed to strict MONETARISM, concerned at the level of unemployment and cautious in foreign policy. The opposite tendency of support for the Thatcher policies was dubbed 'dry'. *See also* PRIVATIZATION.
K. Minogue and M. Biddiss (eds.), *Thatcherism: Personality and Politics* (1987)

**WEU.** *See* WESTERN EUROPEAN UNION.

**Weygand, Maxime** (1867–1965). French general. Born in Brussels, he entered Saint-Cyr in 1886. He served as Chief of Staff to FOCH in the First World War and then as military adviser to PILSUDSKI in the RUSSO-POLISH WAR. He was Commander-in-Chief in the Levant, 1923–4; Director of Military Studies, 1924–9; and Chief of the General Staff, 1930–35. He returned to the Levant in 1939, but was recalled by REYNAUD to replace GAMELIN on 17 May 1940. Weygand soon found the military situation beyond repair and advised PÉTAIN and Reynaud to seek an armistice. He served briefly as Minister of National Defence under the VICHY GOVERNMENT and was appointed Commander-in-Chief of the forces in North Africa, but was relieved of his post for suspected anti-Nazi views. Following the

German occupation of the FREE ZONE he was arrested and imprisoned in Germany until 1945. His reputation as a brilliant staff officer under Foch hid the fact that Weygand had never commanded troops in action. He arrived too late to save France from defeat, although he attempted to counter-attack and prolong resistance. By early June he was firmly committed to an armistice.

J. Williams, *France, Summer 1940* (1969)

**White Russians.** Name given to the anti-Bolshevik forces in the RUSSIAN CIVIL WAR. White Russia is also an alternative name for BELORUSSIA.

**Wilhelm II, of Germany** (1859–1941). King of Prussia and German Emperor, 1888–1918. He was the son of Friedrich III, who reigned for only three months, and of the eldest daughter of Queen Victoria. Wilhelm II became Kaiser in June 1888. Determined to intervene more decisively in government than had his father or grandfather, he was instrumental in bringing about the fall from office of Bismarck in March 1890 and, from 1896–7, set his stamp on government in such a fashion as to lead historians to refer to the late 1890s as the period of the 'personal government' of the Kaiser. An intelligent but unstable man, Wilhelm II had an influence on government in succeeding years that was erratic and sometimes apparently directionless. Determined to uphold the prerogatives of the monarchy, he resisted the evolution of the Imperial German constitutional system in the direction of true parliamentary government. With the outbreak of the FIRST WORLD WAR in 1914, he increasingly withdrew from public life, surrendering real power in the state from 1916–17 to a military quasi-dictatorship led by HINDENBURG and LUDENDORFF. Following the outbreak of the GERMAN REVOLUTION he formally abdicated the throne in late November 1918, having fled to Holland. He spent the rest of his life in retirement on his estate at Doorn.

M. Balfour, *The Kaiser and his Times* (1964)
J. C. G. Röhl, *Germany without Bismarck* (1967)
I. Hull, *The Entourage of Kaiser Wilhelm II* (1982)

**Wilson, Harold** (1916–). British Labour politician. Born of a modest background, Wilson was Director of Economics and Statistics at the Ministry of Fuel and Power, 1943–4. He was Labour MP for Ormskirk, 1945–50, and for Huyton, 1950–83. He served as Parliamentary Secretary to the Ministry of Works, 1945–7; Secretary of Overseas Trade, 1947; and President of the Board of Trade, 1947–51. In 1951 he resigned in protest at the government's decision to impose National Health prescription charges. In 1963 he was elected leader of the LABOUR PARTY. He became Prime Minister in 1964 with a majority of four, inaugurating attempts to devise a National Plan, and promote housing and other reforms. He secured a large election victory in 1966, but his government was increasingly beset by economic problems forcing devaluation in 1967. He proved unable to end UDI in Rhodesia (*see* UDI), and in 1969 was forced to withdraw a proposed bill to curb unofficial strikes. Important social reforms included the expansion of higher education, reforms of the law on abortion, homosexuality and divorce. In 1970 he was defeated but returned in 1974 with a minority government which remained in power after a further election in October of the same year. He renegotiated British terms for entry to the Common Market and conducted a referendum in June 1975 which returned a majority in favour of continuing membership. The Sex Discrimination and the Equal Opportunities Acts were passed in late 1975 but the government was in serious economic difficulties, having to seek a loan of £975 million from the International Monetary Fund. He resigned in March 1976 and was succeeded by JAMES CALLAGHAN.

H. Wilson, *The Labour Government, 1964–70: A Personal Record* (1971)
R. H. S. Crossman, *The Diaries of a Cabinet Minister* (1975–7)
C. Cook and I. Taylor (eds.), *The Labour Party* (1980)
H. Pelling, *A Short History of the Labour Party* (8th edn, 1985)

**Wilson, Thomas Woodrow** (1856–1924). United States President. A lawyer and academic, he became Democratic Governor of New Jersey in 1910 after a period as President of Princeton University (1902–10). He introduced progressive reforms and won the

1912 presidential election. He concentrated on home affairs, pursuing anti-trust and banking reforms. He determined on strict neutrality in the FIRST WORLD WAR, winning the 1916 presidential election on the promise to keep America out of the war. The ZIMMERMANN TELEGRAM following on tension with Mexico and the German declaration of unrestricted submarine warfare forced him to enter the war on 6 April 1917. German calculations that American troops could not arrive in France in time to influence the conflict proved mistaken, sufficiently large forces arriving in spring 1918 to assist in defeating the last German offensives. In January 1918 he announced the FOURTEEN POINTS for reshaping the post-war world on the basis of national self-determination and the creation of an international forum. He participated in the PARIS PEACE CONFERENCE but found many of his proposals overruled, although self-determination played a major part in the final settlement in Eastern and Central Europe. Congress refused to ratify his signing of the TREATY OF VERSAILLES, particularly objecting to participation in the LEAGUE OF NATIONS. He was awarded the Nobel Peace Prize in 1921 but suffered an incapacitating stroke from which he never recovered.

J. A. Garraty, *Woodrow Wilson: A Great Life in Brief* (1956)
R. H. Ferrell, *Woodrow Wilson and World War I, 1917–1921* (1985)

**'Winter of Discontent'.** Period of British industrial unrest in the winter of 1978–9 in opposition to the Labour government's announcement of a 5 per cent pay limit. Strikes by car workers were followed by disruptive strikes by petrol tanker and lorry drivers, water workers, hospital and municipal workers, and railwaymen. The impact of the strikes was made worse by the worst winter weather for 16 years and by the unfortunate remarks by Premier CALLAGHAN on his return from a summit in Guadeloupe, expressing surprise at talk of a crisis. The legacy of strong anti-union feeling arising from the disruption played an important part in Mrs THATCHER's victory in 1979, and remained a theme of anti-Labour propaganda during both the 1983 and 1987 election campaigns.

**Winter War.** *See* RUSSO-FINNISH WAR.

**women's suffrage.** Campaigns for women's suffrage developed before the First World War, but only Norway had given women the vote in 1913, although women were allowed to vote in local and regional elections elsewhere in Europe. Women acquired the vote in two main waves of enfranchisement after the two world wars, often at the same time that the franchise was extended to unenfranchised groups of men. Women in the rest of Europe acquired the vote on the following dates: Denmark, 1915; Russia, 1917; Great Britain, 1918 and 1928; Austria, 1919; Germany, 1919; Holland, 1919; Poland, 1919; Czechoslovakia, 1920; Sweden, 1921; Hungary, 1945; Italy, 1945; Yugoslavia, 1945; France, 1946; Romania, 1946; Switzerland, 1971.

**Workers' Opposition, Russian.** An opposition grouping within the Bolshevik Party which criticized the centralized control of industry by the party and the growing divergence between the party and the workers. It proposed workers' control of industry via the trade unions through its leading spokeswoman, Alexandra Kollontai (1872–1952). The Workers' Opposition was explicitly condemned by Lenin at the tenth Party Congress in 1921 as a 'syndicalist and anarchist deviation', and most of its leaders were expelled from the party.

A. Kollontai, *The Workers' Opposition in Russia* (1923)

**Wrangel, Peter** (1878–1928). White general in the RUSSIAN CIVIL WAR. He served in the Russo-Japanese War and the FIRST WORLD WAR, rising to command a COSSACK division. Joining the southern army of DENIKIN, he captured Tsaritsyn (Stalingrad) in July 1919. In April 1920, after Denikin's retreat in the winter of 1919–20, he was appointed to command the armies based in the Crimea. He mounted a successful offensive against the RED ARMY, holding together his army for several months until finally defeated in November 1920. He was evacuated with almost 2 million White and Cossack forces across the Black Sea to exile. He was head of the émigré movement until his death.

D. Footman, *Civil War in Russia* (1961)

# Y

**Yalta Conference.** The most crucial 'Big Three' meeting of the war held at Yalta in the Crimea (4–11 February 1945). Agreements reached between CHURCHILL, ROOSEVELT and STALIN (with the chiefs of staff, MOLOTOV, Stettinus, ANTHONY EDEN and Harry Hopkins attending) virtually determined the reconstruction of the post-world world. France was admitted as an equal partner of the Allied Control Commission for Germany but the practical details of Allied control were not worked out in Protocols III, IV, V and VI. The future of Poland, one of the most contentious issues of the conference, was referred to in the ambiguously worded Declaration on Poland. Recognition was given to formation of a Polish government containing members of both the LUBLIN COMMITTEE and members of the Polish Government in London, with a promise of free elections. Tacit agreement was given to the ODER–NEISSE LINE as the western boundary of the Polish state and the CURZON LINE for the Polish–Soviet boundary. Agreement was also reached on the inclusion of exiled members of the Yugoslav government in London in Tito's government in Yugoslavia. A 'Declaration on Liberated Europe' expressed the desire for democratic rule in the lands under or formerly under German control. Being anxious to secure a firm Soviet undertaking to join in the war against Japan, Roosevelt acceded to Stalin's condition that Russia should resume her old rights in China, lost as a result of the Russo-Japanese War of 1904–5, and a secret tripartite agreement was signed to this effect on 11 February 1945. Protocol I set out the agreement reached on the creation of a world organization of the UNITED NATIONS and the voting formula for the Security Council. It was agreed to call a conference in San Francisco in April 1945 to draw up a charter for the United Nations. *See also* COLD WAR.

W. H. McNeill, *America, Britain and Russia* (1953)
H. Feis, *Churchill, Roosevelt, Stalin* (1957)
G. Kolko, *The Politics of War* (1968)

**Yeltsin, Boris** (1931–). Soviet politician. Educated at the Ural Polytechnic Institute. Construction worker with various organizations in Sverdlovsk District, 1953–68. A member of the COMMUNIST PARTY OF THE SOVIET UNION from 1961; a Party worker in various capacities from 1968 and First Secretary of the Sverdlovsk District Central Committee from 1976. He was called to Moscow, he became Deputy to Supreme Soviet of the USSR and Secretary of Central Committee of the CPSU, 1985–6. First Secretary of the Moscow City Party Committee, 1985, also becoming a member of the Politburo. Yeltsin was forced to resign as Moscow Party head in November 1987 following his sacking of Moscow Party members and his attacks on Conservatives and the conduct of PERESTROIKA; he was also removed from the Politburo. Elected President of the Russian Republic in May 1990, Yeltsin attracted a large populist following as a supporter of radical reform. His stand against the attempted coup of August 1991 allowed him to dictate the dissolution of the CPSU and a radical restructuring of its Union.

**Yezhov, Nikolai** (1895–1939). Soviet official. He became a member of the Communist Party in March 1917 and was raised by STALIN to the Central Committee in 1927. In 1935 he was one of a group of people, including KHRUSHCHEV and MALENKOV, given key posts, Yezhov becoming a member of the Secretariat and Head of the Party Control Commission. From 1936 to

1938 he was chief of the NKVD (*see* NKVD), directing the most intensive phase of the PURGES, which is sometimes named after him as the *Yezhovshchina*. He was replaced by BERIA in December 1938 and disappeared early in 1939. Known as the 'bloodthirsty dwarf', he was one of Stalin's most brutal henchmen.

R. Conquest, *The Great Terror* (1968)

**Young Plan.** A plan proposed by US businessman Owen D. Young (1874–1962) on 7 June 1929 as a means of settling German REPARATIONS. He suggested that the level of reparations should be reduced by 75 per cent and that remaining payments should be made in the form of annuities paid into an international bank until 1988. Germany accepted the plan in August 1929, but a twelve-month moratorium was granted in July 1931 and payments were never resumed.

**Ypres, Battles of.** *See* FIRST WORLD WAR.

**Yudenich, Nikolai** (1862–1933). White general in the RUSSIAN CIVIL WAR. He served in the Russo-Japanese War and distinguished himself against the Turks in the First World War by capturing the fortress of Erzurum (February 1916). In March 1917 he became supreme commander in the Caucasus but was recalled to Petrograd. He went into hiding following the October Revolution. In November 1918 he fled to Finland to join the anti-Bolshevik forces and commanded the north-western front during the civil war. His assault on Petrograd in October 1919 was beaten off by much superior forces and he went into exile in France in 1920.

D. Footman, *Civil War in Russia* (1961)
W. Rutherford, *The Russian Army in World War I* (1975)

**Yugoslavia.** State created as a result of the break-up of the Austro-Hungarian empire, uniting the Balkan Slavonic peoples in a South Slav State – Yugoslavia. Following the conquest of Serbia by the Central Powers, an agreement known as the Corfu Pact was drawn up on 20 July 1917 between the Serbian government-in-exile on the island of Corfu, led by NIKOLA PASIC, and the leader of the Yugoslav Committee, representing the Slavs in Austria-Hungary, ANTE TRUMBIC. It proclaimed that all the South Slavs, including Serbs, Croats, Slovenes and Montenegrins would unite to form a single Yugoslav kingdom under the royal house of Serbia. The state known initially as The Kingdom of Serbs, Croats and Slovenes was proclaimed on 1 December 1918 with the tacit approval of the victorious powers in the First World War. The Kingdom formally adopted the name Yugoslavia on 3 October 1929. During the Second World War two rival governments emerged, a royalist government-in-exile in London and TITO's self-proclaimed Communist National Committee of Yugoslavia, established in November 1943 at the JAJCE CONGRESS. A joint post-war government was set up on 29 November 1945. According to the constitution passed on 31 January 1946 the Federal Republic was to be composed of six republics: SERBIA, CROATIA, SLOVENIA, BOSNIA-HERZEGOVINA, MACEDONIA and MONTENE-GRO. In April 1963 the country's formal name was altered to the Socialist Federal Republic of Yugoslavia. Serious internal tensions have broken out in Yugoslavia following the death of TITO in 1980. Demands for greater autonomy in Croatia and Slovenia and unrest in the provence of Kosovo have threatened the break-up of the state, compounded by the demand for multi-party elections which have usurped the traditional unifying role of the Yugoslav Communist Party. Non-communist successes in elections in Croatia and Slovenia in April 1990 led to calls for virtual autonomy and even secession. By 1991 increasing tension between Belgrade, Croatia and Slovenia led to a declaration of independence by Slovenia and Croatia, producing fighting between the national militias and the central government. See also PARIS PEACE CONFERENCE.

Z. A. B. Zeman, *The Break-Up of the Habsburg Empire, 1914–1918* (1961)
I. J. Lederer, *Yugoslavia at the Peace Conference: A Study in Frontier-Making* (1963)

# Z

**Zhdanov, Andrei** (1896–1948). Soviet politician. He was First Secretary of the Leningrad Party, 1934–44, and Secretary to the Central Committee. For many years he was the most powerful figure in the Soviet Union after STALIN. Zhdanov supervised the incorporation of Estonia into the Soviet Union in 1940–41 and organized the defence of Leningrad in the SECOND WORLD WAR. After the war he introduced strict ideological control over the arts, strongly emphasizing SOCIALIST REALISM and opposing Western cultural influences in the arts and sciences. Zhdanov was also involved in the founding of COMINFORM in 1947. His sudden death in 1948 prompted a wholesale purge of the Leningrad party organization, possibly because of supposed links with Yugoslavia (recently expelled from COMINFORM) and fears of Leningrad as a rival centre of influence to Moscow.

H. Swayze, *Political Control of Literature in the USSR, 1946–1959* (1962)
R. Conquest, *The Politics of Ideas in the USSR* (1967)
W. Hahn, *Postwar Soviet Politics: The Fall of Zhdanov and the Defeat of Moderation* (1982)

**Zhivkov, Todor** (1911–). Bulgarian head of state. He joined the BULGARIAN COMMUNIST PARTY in 1932, served as a partisan leader in the Second World War and took a leading part in the establishment of the communist regime in Bulgaria. He became General Secretary of the Communist Party in 1954 and consolidated his power with the backing of KHRUSHCHEV, purging rivals to his authority in the party and in the military in 1957, 1962 and 1965. In July 1971 he became Chairman of the Council of State (Presidium), combining it with the post of General-Secretary to give him effective presidential powers. Having maintained Bulgaria as one of the most obedient and loyal of the Soviet Union's allies, a stance he inherited in 1954, Zhivkov was one of the longest serving communist leaders in Eastern Europe when he was dismissed from his posts on 10 November 1989 following a revolt against him in the Communist Party and the spread of unrest from East Germany and Czechoslovakia. Charges of corruption were laid against him, and ten of his supporters were dismissed from the Politburo. He has been succeeded as General Secretary and State Council Chairman by Peter Mladenov (1936–), the former Foreign Minister.

F. Fetjo, *A History of the People's Democracies: Eastern Europe since Stalin* (2nd edn, 1974)

**Zhukov, Georgi** (1896–1974). Soviet Marshal. He was Russia's leading soldier in the SECOND WORLD WAR. He joined the Imperial army in 1916, and served in the cavalry, before joining the RED ARMY in 1918, fighting in the RUSSIAN CIVIL WAR in the First Cavalry Army. He rose to command in the Red Army, leading the counter-offensive against the Japanese in Manchuria in July–August 1939. Appointed Chief of Staff of the RED ARMY in January 1941, he was transferred at the start of the German invasion to assist in the defence of Leningrad and then organized the counter-offensive in December 1941 which halted the German advance on Moscow and saved the city from capture. As First Deputy Commander-in-Chief of Soviet armed forces, he was involved in almost all of Russia's major military operations in 1942–4, including the Battle of Stalingrad (1942), the relief of Leningrad (1943), and the Kursk-Orel battles (1944). In 1944 he returned to a field command at the head of the First Ukrainian and Belorussian fronts, conducting the crossing of the Vistula and the advance on

435

Berlin, where on 8 May 1945 he received the surrender of the German High Command. In 1946 he was removed from his post by STALIN, and after a brief period as Commander-in-Chief of Land Forces and Deputy Minister of the Armed Forces he went into semi-retirement. He was reinstated as First Deputy Minister of Defence upon Stalin's death in 1953, and in 1955 was appointed Minister of Defence. He sided with KHRUSHCHEV in his power struggles and became a full member of the Presidium in 1957. Khrushchev, however, eventually had him expelled from the Presidium and the Central Committee, and he was dismissed as Minister of Defence in late 1957. After the fall of Khrushchev he was partially rehabilitated and awarded the Order of Lenin (1966). Zhukov's military career in the Second World War involved almost all the major operations on the Eastern Front from the defence of Moscow in 1941 to the final Battle of Berlin in 1945. Zhukov earned a reputation for sound strategic judgement, political persuasiveness in his dealings with Stalin, as well as a readiness to obtain his objectives even at the cost of enormous casualties. He has been called 'the complete 20th-century soldier'.

S. Bialer (ed.), *Stalin and his Generals* (1969)
H. E. Salisbury (ed.), *Marshal Xhikov's Greatest Battles* (1969)
G. K. Zhukov, *Memoirs and Reflections* (trans., 1971)
J. Erickson, *The Road to Stalingrad* (1975)
——, *The Road to Berlin* (1983)

**Zimmermann Telegram.** Coded message of 19 January 1917 from the German Foreign Minister, Arthur Zimmermann (1864–1940), to the German minister in Mexico, urging the conclusion of a German–Mexican alliance in the event of a declaration of war on Germany by America when Germany resumed unrestricted submarine warfare against shipping on 1 February. Mexico would be offered the recapture of her 'lost territories' in New Mexico, Arizona and Texas. Intercepted by British Naval Intelligence, the telegram was released to the American press on 1 March, greatly inflaming feeling against Germany, and helping to precipitate the American Declaration of War against Germany on 6 April 1917.

B. Tuchman, *The Zimmerman Telegram* (1958)

**Zinoviev, Grigori** (1883–1936). Russian Bolshevik leader. Born into a Jewish lower-middle class family, he joined the RUSSIAN SOCIAL DEMOCRATIC LABOUR PARTY in 1901, siding with the BOLSHEVIK faction in 1903. He left Russia after the failure of the 1905 revolution and became a close associate of LENIN in exile. He returned with Lenin to Russia but opposed the APRIL THESES and the Bolshevik seizure of power in the October Revolution. He became Chairman of the Petrograd Soviet, joined the Politburo, and was Chairman of the COMINTERN from 1919 to 1926. A member of the triumvirate which conducted Soviet affairs during Lenin's last illness, he emerged as its leading figure after his death. He led the opposition to STALIN and allied himself to TROTSKY, but was expelled from the party and removed from his party posts in 1927. Accused of conspiracy in the assassination of KIROV, he was tried in 1935 and sentenced to ten years' imprisonment, but was retried in August 1936 and executed shortly afterwards. Zinoviev was the leading figure in the great 'show trial' of August 1936 in Moscow, his death eliminating one of Stalin's leading opponents. Zinoviev's name is also remembered in non-Soviet circles for the ZINOVIEV LETTER. *See also* PURGES.

E. H. Carr, *The Russian Revolution: From Lenin to Stalin* (1979)

**Zinoviev Letter.** Letter allegedly sent to British communists by GRIGORI ZINOVIEV, head of COMINTERN, extracts from which were published in British newspapers on 25 October 1924, a few days before the general election. The letter advised communists to foment a revolution. It has been held responsible for the loss of seats by the LABOUR PARTY in the subsequent election. The party had recognized the Soviet Union and was cultivating better trading relations with the communist government, and was therefore vulnerable to 'red scare' tactics. The letter was a forgery, one of many circulating at the time, but taken as genuine by the Conservative press. The incident is often cited as an example of scare tactics used against the Left.

D. Marquand, *Ramsey MacDonald* (1977)
L. Chester, S. Fay and H. Young, *The Zinoviev Letter* (1967)

**Zionism.** Belief in the need to establish an autonomous Jewish homeland in Palestine. It was one of the alternatives developed in the late 19th century by European Jews in the face of increasing ANTI-SEMITISM. Theodore Herzl (1860–1904) was the first to argue that both the problem and the remedy were political. He founded the World Zionist Organisation which called for the establishment of a home for the Jewish people in 1897. The movement quickly attracted many adherents, especially among the beleagured Jews of Eastern Europe. Herzl had been negotiating unsuccessfully with the Ottoman government to obtain a charter for Palestine when in 1903 the British offered Uganda as a homeland. Some Zionists were willing to accept Uganda, but Russian Jews put up such fierce opposition that it was rejected. In 1905 the World Zionist Congress opposed any settlement outside of Palestine, and Jewish immigration to the area continued. Under CHAIM WEIZMANN the Zionists persuaded Britain in 1917 to issue the BALFOUR DECLARATION, a critical document which established British support for a Jewish homeland in Palestine. After the First World War Britain obtained a League of Nations mandate (see MANDATES) for Palestine, and the Zionists concentrated on establishing settlements in the region. However, it was not until the rise of Nazism that Jewish immigration was at all sizeable. The indigenous Arab population opposed Zionism and those who wished to establish a purely Jewish state, leading to Arab revolts in 1936–7. The British, who found it increasingly difficult to maintain order, suggested in the 1937 Peel Commission Report that partition was the solution. Jewish emigration to Palestine greatly increased as a consequence of the HOLOCAUST, with the result that by 1947 almost 400,000 Jews had settled there since the start of the mandate. In spite of Arab hostility, widespread support for the Jewish cause led the United Nations on 29 November 1947 to recommend Partition of Palestine to create a Jewish state, followed shortly afterwards by the creation of the state of Israel.

Between 1948 and 1960 almost 1 million Jewish settlers flooded into Israel, many of them from Europe. Many European Jews continued to look on Israel as an ultimate source of refuge to escape from discriminatory or totalitarian regimes, especially in Eastern Europe. Major political campaigns have been waged by Jewish groups in the Soviet Union and Eastern Europe, seeking the right of emigration to Israel or elsewhere. One of the principal thrusts of Western attacks on the Soviet Union under BREZHNEV was the restrictions placed upon Jewish emigration. Under GORBACHEV these restrictions have been relaxed. Since 1948 the World Zionist Congress has been viewed as a pressure group acting on behalf of the Israeli government. With the Arab–Israeli conflicts in the Middle East in 1967 and 1973 the term 'Zionist' has been overlain by pejorative implications of annexationism and racialism.

N. Bethell, *The Palestine Triangle* (1979)
D. Vital, *The Origins of Zionism* (1980)
——, *Zionism: The Formative Years* (1982)
H. W. Sachar, *History of Israel: From the Rise of Zionism to our own Time* (1985)
D. Vital, *Zionism: The Crucial Phase* (1987)